A ROPE and A PRAYER

ALSO BY DAVID ROHDE

Endgame: The Betrayal and Fall of Srebrenica,
Europe's Worst Massacre since World War II

A ROPE and A PRAYER

A KIDNAPPING FROM TWO SIDES

DAVID ROHDE and KRISTEN MULVIHILL

VIKING

VIKING
Published by the Penguin Group
Penguin Group (USA) Inc., 375 Hudson Street, New York, New York 10014, U.S.A.
Penguin Group (Canada), 90 Eglinton Avenue East, Suite 700, Toronto, Ontario, Canada M4P 2Y3
(a division of Pearson Penguin Canada Inc.)
Penguin Books Ltd, 80 Strand, London WC2R 0RL, England
Penguin Ireland, 25 St. Stephen's Green, Dublin 2, Ireland (a division of Penguin Books Ltd)
Penguin Books Australia Ltd, 250 Camberwell Road, Camberwell, Victoria 3124, Australia
(a division of Pearson Australia Group Pty Ltd)
Penguin Books India Pvt Ltd, 11 Community Centre, Panchsheel Park, New Delhi – 110 017, India
Penguin Group (NZ), 67 Apollo Drive, Rosedale, North Shore 0632, New Zealand
(a division of Pearson New Zealand Ltd)
Penguin Books (South Africa) (Pty) Ltd, 24 Sturdee Avenue,
Rosebank, Johannesburg 2196, South Africa

Penguin Books Ltd, Registered Offices: 80 Strand, London WC2R 0RL, England

First published in 2010 by Viking Penguin, a member of Penguin Group (USA) Inc.

10 9 8 7 6 5 4 3 2 1

Portions of this book appeared in different form in *The New York Times*.

LIBRARY OF CONGRESS CATALOGING-IN-PUBLICATION DATA
Rohde, David.
 A rope and a prayer : a kidnapping from two sides / David Rohde & Kristen Mulvihill.
  p. cm.
 ISBN 978-0-670-02223-6
 1. Rohde, David—Captivity, 2008–2009. 2. Hostages—Afghanistan—Biography.
3. Journalists—United States—Biography. 4. Afghan War, 2001—Personal narratives,
American. 5. Taliban. 6. Mulvihill, Kristen. I. Mulvihill, Kristen. II. Title.
 DS371.43.R64A3 2010
 958.104'7—dc22
 [B]   2010024534

Printed in the United States of America
Designed by Nancy Resnick
Chronology and map by Jeffrey L. Ward

Penguin is committed to publishing works of quality and integrity. In that spirit, we are proud to offer this book to our readers; however, the story, the experiences, and the words are the authors' alone.

To Faith

Every man's hand is against the other, and all against the stranger.

—Winston S. Churchill

The fruit of patience is sweet.

—Pashto saying

ACKNOWLEDGMENTS

For Pashtunwali: Tahir Luddin and Captain Nadeem.

For countless hours: Mary Jane Mulvihill, Lee Rohde, David McCraw.

For never giving up: Arthur Sulzberger, Jr.

For steadfast support and encouragement: Bill Keller, Jill Abramson, John Geddes, William Schmidt, Craig Whitney, Susan Chira, Matt Purdy, Christine Kay, and so many other longtime friends at *The New York Times*.

For friendship, insight, and bravery in Afghanistan: Afghan colleagues and friends, Carlotta Gall, Chris Chivers, Tyler Hicks, Dexter Filkins, Rich Oppel, and many others.

For friendship, insight, and bravery in Pakistan: Ismail Khan, Salman Masood, Beena Sarwar, Pir Zubair Shah, Jane Perlez, and many others.

For pointing Kristen in the right direction: Richard Holbrooke, Karl and Ching Eikenberry, Marin Strmecki, Tim Golden, Kay McGowan, Samantha Power.

For consistency, clarity, eloquence, and humor: Michael Semple.

For working on the case: "John," Mike Taylor, Duane Clarridge, Jack Holly, Dwight, Mark, Chris, Wayne, and all the incarnations of Team Kabul.

Thank you to the government officials who tried to help us, especially Jim, Tom, Joe, John, Cathy, Phil, Leanne, Ken, Tenzen, Mike, Eric.

For help in Washington: Mark Mazzetti, Eric Schmitt, Douglas Frantz, Milt Bearden.

For expertise: Ahmed Rashid, Rina Amiri, Barnett Rubin, James Alvarez, Nancy Dupree, John Dixon, Tom Gregg, Patricia Ferrari, Kelly Moore.

For support and understanding at *Cosmopolitan,* especially: Kate White, Abby Greene, Ann Kwong, John Lanuza, Micah Rubin, Heather Pfaff, Miriam Friedman, Micaela Walker, Maggie Hong, Rebecca Hessel.

For maintaining privacy: Catherine Mathis, Diane McNulty, and Vanessa Palo.

For friendship, empathy, and holidays: Eric and Sylvan Wold.

For support, guidance, confidence: Jonathan and Katie Moore, Chloe Breyer, Marcello Picone.

For happy memories: Vincent Manoriti, Denise Morgan, Julian Borger, Kathleen Reen, Ivan Obregon, Greg Scholl, Lisa Ferrari, Kannan Sundaram, Jay Solomon, Don Nay, Dan Morrison, Paul Haven, Victoria Burnett, Tomas Munita, Bob Nickelsberg, Celia Dugger, Barry Bearak, Shelley Thakral, Anthony Loyd, Gary Bass, Stacy Sullivan, Emma Daly, Laura Pitter, Kit Roane, Katya Jestin, Joel Brand, Mike O'Connor, Tracy Wilkinson, John Pomfret, Roger Cohen, Ben Ward, Mark Dennis, Fred Abrahams, Leigh Cheng, John Bastian, Pete Brandt, Al Erickson, Matt Borger, Rod Peterson, Damon Struyk, Jim Williamson, Bob Perkins, Eric Mabley, Ian Marsh, Steve Cote, Jim Webb, Chris Charters, Peter Boisvert, Jay, Joe, and Doris Brenchick, Rocky and Martha Manoriti, John Atwood, Ed Quinn, and many others in Fryeburg.

For sustenance and support from friends, including: the Moss family, the Chivers family, the Bissell family, Andrea Elliott, Salman Ahmed, Chuck Sudetic, Cindy Searight, Renannah Weinstein, Josh Brown, Claire Mysko, Judson Wright, Madeleine Arthurs, Adivije Sheji, Arthur Belebeau, Juliette Merck, Natalie Hawwa, John Lin, Tamara Schlesinger, Jamal Rayyis, Neal Lesh, Erinn Bucklan, Jim Ledbetter, Erik Swain, Noah Green, Frances Northcutt, Amy Waldman, Megan Re, Sarah Smith, Elliot Thomson, Mariane Pearl, Kati Marton, Nic Robertson, George Packer, Leon Wieseltier, Peter Bergen, Somini Sengupta, Elizabeth Rubin, Jonathan Landay, Faye Bowers, Mary Anne Schwalbe, Sandra Cook, P. J. Anthony, Hari Kumar, Chuni Lal, Pan Singh.

For prayers: Marie Chisholm, Maryann Zocco, Fabienne LeRoux,

Father Renald Labarre, Monika Stedul, Ben Borger, Helen D'Elia, and many others.

For listening: Barbara, Roberta, Jan, Lynne.

For supporting David's research: Aryeh Neier, Patricia L. Rosenfield, and Laura Silber. This book was made possible in part by grants from the Open Society Foundations and the Carnegie Corporation of New York. The statements made and views expressed are solely the responsibility of the authors.

For making this book a reality: Sarah Chalfant, Clare Ferraro, Wendy Wolf, Carolyn Coleburn, Linda Cowen, Sonya Cheuse, Risa Chubinsky, Nancy Resnick, Jeffrey Ward, Emily Votruba, Margaret Riggs, Meredith Burks, Carolyn Freeman, Tracy Breton, Kate Toth.

For courage and bravery: Sultan Munadi, Daniel Pearl, Piotr Stanczak, Asad Mangal, Jere Van Dyk, Sean Langan, Stephen Farrell, John Solecki, Alan Johnston, Roxana Saberi, Maziar Bahari, Amanda Lindhout, Nigel Brennan, Laura Ling, Euna Lee, and all journalists who remain in captivity.

FOR EVERYTHING: our parents Carol, Harvey, Mary Jane, James, Andrea, and George; our siblings Lee, Laura, Erik, Karen, Jason, Joel, Daniel, Christie, Chris, Howard, Christina, and all of our family.

CONTENTS

PRINCIPAL CHARACTERS, ORGANIZATIONS, AND PLACES — AFGHANISTAN AND PAKISTAN

Abu Tayyeb: Taliban commander who invites David to interview and kidnaps him

Akbar: Guard who allows access to newspapers and radio; nephew of Akhundzada

Akhundzada: Taliban commander who serves as Abu Tayyeb's "intelligence chief"

Asad Mangal: Afghan driver kidnapped with David

Badruddin Haqqani: Son of Jalaluddin Haqqani who provides houses and cash during kidnapping

Chunky: Heavyset guard who leads prayers

Jalaluddin Haqqani: Patriarch of the Haqqani family and famed anti-Soviet fighter who is supported by the CIA in the 1980s and who joins the Taliban in the 1990s

Mansoor: Guard who speaks broken English; son of Akhundzada

Mullah Omar: Leader of Taliban movement. Since 2001, he is believed to have been based in the Pakistani city of Quetta. Said to now lead a more moderate Taliban faction known as the Quetta Shura.

Qari: Taliban fighter who carries out kidnapping and later serves as guard

Sharif: Taliban commander whose house serves as a prison

Sirajuddin Haqqani: Son of Jalaluddin Haqqani who succeeded his elderly father as commander of the Haqqani network

Timor Shah: Chief guard, younger brother of Abu Tayyeb

Tahir Luddin: Afghan journalist kidnapped with David

Federally Administered Tribal Areas: Mountainous region in northwestern Pakistan—also known as the tribal areas—that is a Taliban and Al Qaeda stronghold

Helmand: Province in southern Afghanistan—also known as "Little America"—that was the focus of the author's original book project

North and South Waziristan: Regions inside the tribal areas where the author was held captive

Frontier Corps: Pakistani-government–funded tribal militia charged with policing the tribal areas

ISI: Directorate for Inter-Services Intelligence, the Pakistani military's top intelligence agency.

PRINCIPAL CHARACTERS AND ORGANIZATIONS—NEW YORK

David McCraw: Assistant general counsel for *The New York Times*

Mary Jane Mulvihill: Kristen's mother

Lee Rohde: David's older brother

Carol Ruffo: David's mother

Michael Semple: Expert on the region who works on case

AISC: American International Security Corporation. Security consultants hired to work on case

Clayton Consultants: *The New York Times*' crisis management firm

AUTHORS' NOTE

This is not a story of triumph. Throughout our case we made numerous mistakes. We wrote this book in the hope of helping readers learn more about Afghanistan, Pakistan, and the American effort there. This book's central narrative is the seven months when David, Tahir, and Asad were held captive in the tribal areas of Pakistan and Kristen's effort to bring them home. Woven throughout the narrative are sections of history and analysis that are based on David's seven years of reporting in Afghanistan and Pakistan since 2001. We also try to explore militancy, faith, and religion's role as both a positive and negative force.

The second reason we wrote this book is in the hope of helping other kidnap victims and their families avoid the mistakes we made and survive their captivity. Around the world, the number of kidnappings is steadily rising, but governments have failed to develop a coordinated international response. Most hostages survive, but their panicked families frequently empty bank accounts, sell homes, or go into staggering debt to save the lives of their loved ones. We urge governments to develop a more unified approach to kidnapping.

A portion of our earnings from this book will be donated to the FATA Education Foundation, a Pakistani government foundation that provides educational opportunities to the people of Pakistan's tribal areas, and to Kiva.org, a nonprofit organization that allows people to lend money via the Internet to microfinance institutions in developing countries and the United States. We are also working with the Committee to Protect Journalists, a nonprofit press advocacy group, to develop ways to support and assist the families of kidnapped journalists.

For seven months our family negotiated with the kidnappers—directly and through contractors—regarding a potential ransom. No ransom was paid. While David was in captivity, we believed the only way to keep him and his Afghan colleagues alive and encourage the kidnappers to remain in contact was to appear to be willing to pay for their release. In this book, we discuss Kristen's calls with the kidnappers and the negotiations because they bring home the reality and pressures placed on a kidnap victim's family. Yet we are not divulging our negotiation strategy or the amounts of money discussed. We believe such disclosures could encourage or complicate future kidnappings.

What follows is a good-faith effort to reconstruct the period in our lives surrounding David's kidnapping and eventual escape, and its aftermath. David was not able to take notes for the seven months he was in captivity. All descriptions of his experience stem from his memory, supplemented, where possible, by records kept by Kristen, other family members, and colleagues. Direct quotations from his captors are his recollections of what they said and are based on translations from Pashto, the language they spoke. Kristen's descriptions stem from memory and, where possible, journal entries, e-mails, transcripts, and other records. Undoubtedly, our recollections are incomplete, altered by the passage of time and flawed in places. All of the views expressed in this book are solely those of the authors. Any mistakes in the pages that follow are wholly our own. For safety reasons, certain details, information, and names have been withheld.

Chronology

■

1. **Flew from Laskhar Gah, Helmand, to Kabul, Afghanistan:** *November 9, 2008.*

2. **Kidnapped outside Pul-e-Alam, Logar:** *November 10, 2008.*

3. **Held in four different locations in eastern Afghanistan:** *November 10–17, 2008. Moved by car through Logar, Wardak, Ghazni, and Paktika provinces.*

4. **Walked over mountains from Paktika, Afghanistan, into South Waziristan, Pakistan:** *Night of November 17–18, 2008.*

5. **Drove through Wana, South Waziristan, to Miran Shah, North Waziristan:** *November 18, 2008. Held prisoner in five different houses in Miran Shah, North Waziristan: November 18, 2008 to mid-March 2009.*

6. **Moved from Miran Shah, North Waziristan, to Makeen, South Waziristan:** *Mid-March. Held in one house in Makeen until late April 2009.*

7. **Moved from Makeen, South Waziristan, to Dosali, North Waziristan:** *Late April 2009. Held in one house in Dosali until late May 2009.*

8. **Moved from Dosali to Miran Shah, North Waziristan:** *Late May 2009–June 19, 2009. Held in two different houses in Miran Shah from late May 2009–June 19, 2009. Escaped night of June 19–20, 2009.*

9. **Flown by Pakistani army helicopter from Miran Shah, North Waziristan, to Islamabad, Pakistan:** *June 20, 2009.*

10. **Flown by American military plane from Islamabad, Pakistan, to Bagram Air Base, Afghanistan:** *June 20, 2009. Flown by private plane from Bagram to Dubai, U.A.E., June 21, 2009.*

■

CHINA

Area of detail

Kabul

AFGHANISTAN

Kandahar

Islamabad

Lashkar Gah

Lahore

HELMAND

Quetta

INDIA

PAKISTAN

0 Mi.   300

0 Km.   300

IRAN

Arabian Sea

PASHTUN AREAS

KHYBER
PAKHTUNKHAW

NURISTAN

PARWAN

10 Bagram

Parun

KUNAR

LAGHMAN

Asadabad

BAJAUR

Mingora

AFGHANISTAN

Mehtar Lam

MOHMAND

Swat
Valley

1 Kabul

KABUL

Jalalabad

Mardan

WARDAK

NANGARHAR

Landi Khotal

LOGAR

Khyber
Pass

Peshawar

2

Pul-el-Alam

Parachinar

KHYBER

Islamabad 9

PAKTIA

ORAKZAI

Rawalpindi

Gardez

KURRAM

Kohat

Indus River

GHAZNI

KHOST

3

Khost

PUNJAB

Sharan

5 8

PAKTIKA

Miran Shah

Bannu

P A K I S T A N

NORTH
WAZIRISTAN

7 Dosali

FEDERALLY
ADMINISTERED
TRIBAL AREAS
(FATA)

Makeen

6

SOUTH
WAZIRISTAN

Tank

4 Wana

Dera Ismail Khan

PAKISTAN'S

KHYBER
PAKHTUNKHAW
and
FEDERALLY
ADMINISTERED
TRIBAL AREAS

BALUCHISTAN

Indus River

0 Miles   50

0 Kilometers   50

© John Jeffrey L. Ward

A BLOOD MESSAGE TO OBAMA

David, November 9–10, 2008

On a Sunday afternoon, the Kabul Coffee House and Café is an island of Western culture in Afghanistan's capital. American and European contractors, aid workers, and consultants sip four-dollar café lattes and cappuccinos. Young, English-speaking Afghan waiters dressed in Western clothes serve chicken quesadillas, fried-egg sandwiches, and cheeseburgers.

I marvel at—and dread—how much Kabul has changed since I first came to the country to cover the fall of the Taliban seven years earlier. A city I grew to know well has become more and more unfamiliar. Kabul has boomed economically and modernized to an extent I never dreamed when joyous Afghans gouged out the eyes of dead Taliban militants in 2001. At the time, Afghans yearned for a moderate and modern nation and an end to decades of meddling from neighboring countries.

Now, the gulf between the wealthy, westernized pockets of the Afghan capital and the grinding insecurity and endemic corruption that dominate most Afghans' daily lives alarms me. Rivalries between the country's ethnic groups that ebbed after the fall of the Taliban simmer again. Growing mistrust between Afghans and foreigners worries me as well. The American journalists, diplomats, and aid workers who were welcomed here in 2001 are seen by growing numbers of Afghans as war profiteers who do little to aid their country.

I am in the final stretch of conducting research for a book I am writing about the failing American attempt to bring stability to the region since 2001. I hope the book will be the culmination of seven years of reporting in Afghanistan and Pakistan for *The New York Times.* Yet I have become increasingly concerned that I am losing touch with the rapidly deteriorating situation on the ground. After serving as the newspaper's South Asia bureau co-chief and living in the region from 2002 to 2005, I moved back to New York and joined the newspaper's investigations unit. Over the last three years, reporting trips sent me back to Afghanistan and Pakistan roughly every six months, but that is a fraction of the time I spent on the ground when based here. During that period, the Taliban have reasserted control over vast swaths of both Afghanistan and Pakistan.

After privately wrestling with the decision for weeks, I have decided I need to interview a Taliban commander for the book to be as rigorous and thorough as possible. The majority of the population in Helmand—the southern Afghan province that is the focus of my book—appears to now support them. But it's a fraught proposition, one that comes with the kind of extreme risk that I have tried to avoid for years.

Across the table from me at the Kabul Coffee House is Tahir Luddin, an Afghan journalist I met two years ago who works for *The Times* of London. Burly, boisterous, and confident, Tahir has short brown hair, hazel eyes, a round face, and a thin brown beard. He is a proud Afghan and prefers wearing local clothes to Western ones. We had met in 2006 but never worked together before. Recommended to me by two correspondents from *The Times* of London, Tahir is known for having good Taliban contacts and the ability to arrange interviews with them.

Tahir explains that his most trusted contact is a Taliban commander who uses the nom de guerre Abu Tayyeb, or "son of Tayyeb." Abu Tayyeb commands several hundred Taliban fighters in three provinces around Kabul, and has fought against NATO and American troops in Helmand as well. Tahir says he has met him a half dozen times and that Abu Tayyeb has done face-to-face television interviews with two different European journalists without incident. He is aligned with a moderate Taliban faction based in the Pakistani city of Quetta.

"Would you be willing to go to Ghazni?" Tahir asks, referring to a dangerous province that is roughly three hours south of Kabul by car.

Tahir says I could interview Abu Tayyeb there. He could be the final character in the book, I think to myself, a Taliban commander who is the vehicle for describing the hard-line movement's reemergence. I had tried for the last two weeks to set up an interview with a Taliban fighter in Helmand but had failed. I was not willing to leave the heavily guarded center of the provincial capital. No Taliban were willing to meet me there. Dozens of other journalists and I have been doing phone interviews with Taliban spokesmen for years. Yet it was impossible to verify whom, in fact, you were speaking to over the phone or their claims, which were often blatantly false propaganda screeds. I could briefly meet Abu Tayyeb in person, verify that he was, in fact, a Taliban commander, and then do follow-up interviews by phone.

From New York, it seemed as if a growing number of foreign journalists were safely interviewing the Taliban face-to-face. Over the last two months, interviews with Taliban had appeared in my old newspaper, *The Christian Science Monitor,* a French magazine, and one of my colleagues had safely interviewed them for my current newspaper's Sunday magazine. I increasingly worried I was becoming a New York-based journalistic fraud whose book would be superficial and out of date. I felt I had fallen behind reporters based in the region.

At the same time, I knew meeting with the Taliban was perilous. Getting both sides of a story is vital in journalism but hugely dangerous in an armed conflict. In the end, each interview is a judgment call. As we sit in the café, Tahir warns of the danger involved. That spring, an American journalist and a British journalist who ventured into Pakistan's tribal areas to interview militants were kidnapped in separate incidents, Tahir explains. He says the British journalist's family sold their home to pay a ransom for his release. The concept of putting my own family through such an ordeal horrifies me. I had also recently read a story in *Rolling Stone* by an American journalist who was nearly kidnapped by a rival Taliban faction when he drove to Ghazni to interview a Taliban commander.

"Ghazni is too far," I tell Tahir. "I only want to do a Taliban interview in Kabul."

We part ways and Tahir tells me he will contact another Taliban commander who he believes is in Kabul. He promises to call me later that night. I leave with a sense of dread. I have long viewed journalists who interview the Taliban as reckless. Yet I find myself contemplating doing something I have resisted for years.

I was imprisoned for ten days in 1995 while covering the war in Bosnia for *The Christian Science Monitor.* Serb officials arrested me after I discovered the mass graves of Muslim men executed in the Serb-controlled part of Bosnia around the town of Srebrenica. I was freed after my family, friends, and editors put intense pressure on American officials to force the Serbs to release me. War crimes investigators later found that more than 8,000 Muslim men had been executed around the town. My detention in Bosnia was excruciating for my family, and I promised them I would never put them through such an ordeal again. And two months ago, before I left for Afghanistan, I took a momentous step. I married my girlfriend, Kristen Mulvihill.

Kristen is a photo editor at a women's magazine as well as a painter. Her sunny disposition, determination to see the positive side of everything, and fierce love have created a tranquility in my life. My two years with her in New York left me feeling gradually more at peace and at home. At thirty-nine and forty-one, respectively, Kristen and I are eager to focus more on our personal lives and start a family. To the delight of my ever-patient mother, we married in a small wooden chapel in Maine, a state both of us adore and where we each spent time while growing up. I see our marriage and the book as long-delayed positive steps that will take me away from reporting in war zones and allow me to move into a more stable form of journalism and life.

I am also extremely close to my family. My mother is the most iron willed and loving person I know. She successfully raised four children while having a career as a fashion industry executive. She and my father are divorced but he is dogged, successful, and determined as well. He has built an independent insurance practice and a rich life for himself in Maine, where he loves hiking in the woods, running marathons, and exploring spirituality. My stepparents, Andrea and George, have brought joy to my parents and me for more than two decades.

My older brother, Lee, is president of a small aviation consulting firm and the rock of our family who hides his emotions beneath a calm exterior. My younger sister, Laura, has soared in recent years, thriving professionally in the human resources field, marrying, and becoming the mother of two children. And my younger brother, Erik, has happily shifted from being a police officer and paramedic to a business operations manager for a helicopter ambulance company. He has also become one of my closest friends. After driving across the country together three years ago, we talk by phone once or twice a week. My stepbrothers, Joel and Dan, have become dear friends with whom I share an avid love for Boston sports teams. I have a tremendous amount to return to.

My cell phone rings at dusk as I am about to begin an interview. Tahir says the Taliban commander he knows in Kabul despises Americans and refuses to meet me, but Abu Tayyeb is willing to be interviewed tomorrow morning in neighboring Logar Province. We can meet him after a one-hour drive on paved roads in a village near an American military base, he says. Abu Tayyeb needs an immediate answer, he adds. The Taliban have ordered local cell phone companies to shut off service after dark to prevent people from reporting their movements to Afghan and American forces. I ask Tahir if he thinks it is safe. The danger, Tahir says, will be thieves abducting us during the drive itself.

"Nothing is 100 percent," he tells me. "You only die once."

I feel my stomach churn. My mind races. My trips to Afghanistan and Pakistan have become an increasing source of tension with Kristen, who has asked me to be gone no longer than three weeks. A few days ago, I extended the trip to four weeks after landing an interview with Afghanistan's president, Hamid Karzai. I called my father and stepmother and canceled a weekend trip Kristen and I had planned to make with them to his college.

Going to Logar seems safer than Ghazni. If I do the Taliban interview, I can return home with a sense that I have done everything I can to understand the country, get the story, and write the best book possible. The interview is just outside Kabul, I tell myself. I would not be going into the tribal areas of Pakistan, as the kidnapped American and British journalists did. This is safer.

"Yes," I say to Tahir. "Tell him yes."

Tahir tells me he will call me later to set a departure time. As a precaution, I ask him for the number of a European journalist who has already interviewed Abu Tayyeb twice with Tahir. In the fall of 2007, the reporter spent two days filming Abu Tayyeb and his men as they trained. In the summer of 2008, the journalist spent an evening with them and filmed an attack on a police post. I call the reporter and they say we should talk in person. We agree to meet at a restaurant later that night.

Privately, I am still not sure I will go. I am having dinner with two close friends, an experienced journalist and a veteran aid worker who have both worked in Afghanistan for years. I plan to ask them if the interview is a crazy idea. I hurriedly finish the interview and meet the journalist and aid worker at a new Italian restaurant frequented by foreigners. Concrete blast walls separate it from the rest of Kabul. When I describe the opportunity to interview a Taliban commander, the aid worker immediately opposes it.

"You just got married," she says.

"But this is what we do," the reporter interjects.

Then the reporter expresses their own reservations. The journalist says she has never felt the need to interview the Taliban in person and prefers phone conversations. She recommends that Tahir and I hire a driver to serve as a lookout and end the meeting after no more than an hour.

"I know how you drag out interviews," the reporter says, teasing me.

I leave dinner early to meet the European journalist at L'Atmosphère, a well-known French restaurant in Kabul that caters to Westerners. As I enter I notice that it recently installed a reinforced door to stop suicide bombers. The reporter, who I have never met before, says deciding to go to the interview is my responsibility. I agree and say I know the risk. They point out that as an American I am more vulnerable than a European. But they also believe that Abu Tayyeb will not kidnap us, and that his objective is to use the media to get across the Taliban's message.

"I think it is a good chance," they say.

I drive home with an Afghan journalist I regularly work with in Kabul.

I ask him about the interview. He tells me not to make the trip. There are many criminals, he says, on the road to Logar.

Back at the *Times* bureau, the power is out, a daily occurrence in Kabul seven years after the American invasion. I had planned to look up other recent interviews with the Taliban but now have no Internet access. I had also wanted to study maps of Logar. All of my colleagues are asleep.

I go up to my bedroom and wrestle with the decision. I put my video camera, a blank notebook, and my passport on the desk. The European journalist has recommended I bring identification to prove who I am. Otherwise, the Taliban will think I am a spy. They said a passport was best. The Taliban see press accreditations from the American government, U.S. military, or NATO as proof of spying.

I tell myself not to be a coward, that the interview is a risk worth taking. Many other journalists have done the same thing. In 2007, at the last minute I had canceled a drive to Kandahar for safety reasons and been embarrassed by it. If we can make it to Abu Tayyeb, I think, we will be safe.

I text Tahir and tell him to pick me up at 7 A.M. tomorrow morning.

As I lie in bed, I call Kristen, as I do every night. I am convinced that if I tell her about the interview she will demand that I not go and I will silently resent her for curtailing my professional life. I also know that if my new wife asks me to cancel the interview, I will abide by her wishes.

I decide not to mention my plans. I am sparing her worry, I tell myself, and sparing the relationship from conflict. I decide I will tell her about the interview after I return to New York.

I have trouble sleeping. My mind drifts to my captivity in Bosnia. I know this is an enormous risk. If anything goes wrong, the results will be catastrophic.

The next morning, November 10, Tahir arrives fifteen minutes early. The earlier we are on the road, he says, the better our chances of safety. I again tell myself not to be a coward and that other journalists have taken this same risk. I hurriedly put on a pair of boxer shorts my wife gave me on

Valentine's Day followed by running shorts my sister gave me for my birthday. I dress in Afghan clothes so I will not be spotted as a foreigner during the drive. The boxers are emblazoned with dozens of "I love you" logos. I hope they will bring us good luck.

I leave two notes behind. The first is for one of my colleagues in the bureau. It lists Abu Tayyeb's name, describes the location of the meeting, and instructs them to call the American Embassy if we do not return by midafternoon. The other is to Kristen if something goes wrong. The note is rushed but I hope that Kristen will never see it.

I walk outside and meet Tahir and Asad Mangal, a friend who Tahir has hired to work as a driver and lookout for the day. Asad is friendly and appears to be in his late twenties. It is a gray, cloudy morning. As we drive away, Tahir suggests that we pray for a safe journey. We do.

I call Kristen. It is roughly 11 P.M. in New York. I am nervous and she can sense it. When she asks me what I'm doing, I panic and respond that I am going to an interview at a ministry in Kabul. I am saving her from worrying, I again tell myself, and allowing her to sleep. I do, in fact, have an interview at a ministry, but it is scheduled for later that day—after the one-hour Taliban interview. Then I will fly to Islamabad in the late afternoon for a week of reporting there. I tell her I will call her after I arrive in Pakistan.

"I love you," I say.

"I love you too," she replies.

Clad in Afghan clothes and seated in the back of the car, I cover my face with a scarf to prevent thieves from recognizing me as a foreigner. In the car, I get Abu Tayyeb's cell phone number from Tahir and send it to my colleague in the bureau in a text message. I tell them to call him if they do not hear from me by early afternoon. If something goes wrong during the drive, Abu Tayyeb and his men will rescue us. Under Afghan tradition, guests are treated with extraordinary honor. If a guest is threatened, it is the host's duty to shelter and protect him.

During the hour-long drive, I delete all the military, intelligence, and government numbers from my cell phone as a precaution. I worry that the Taliban may check the phone and grow suspicious. I fantasize about the relief I will feel as we drive back to Kabul. After the interview, I will have completed the most dangerous portion of the reporting needed for the book. I will have done everything I could. I will be able to start a new life with Kristen.

We arrive at the meeting point in a town where farmers and donkeys meander down the road. But none of Abu Tayyeb's men are here. Tahir calls Abu Tayyeb, who says an American military operation is going on that morning and he had to change the meeting point. He asks what kind of car we are driving, instructs us to drive down the road another mile, and meet his men there. Asad accelerates down the road. About thirty seconds later, our car swerves to the right and abruptly comes to a halt.

I look up. Two bearded Afghan men carrying Kalashnikov assault rifles run toward us shouting commands in Pashto, the local language. Behind them, a car is blocking the road. The gunmen open the front doors of our car, point their rifles at Tahir and Asad, and order them to get in the backseat with me.

One of the gunmen gets behind the wheel of our car and drives down the road. The other sits in the front passenger seat and trains his rifle on us. Tahir shouts at the men in Pashto. I recognize the words "journalists" and "Abu Tayyeb" and nothing else. The man in the front passenger seat shouts something back and waves his gun menacingly. He is small, with dark hair and a short beard. He seems nervous and belligerent.

I hope there has been some kind of mistake. I hope the gunmen will call Abu Tayyeb. He will vouch for us and quickly order our release, a scenario that played out with the American journalist who ventured to Ghazni.

Instead, our car hurtles down the road, following a yellow station wagon with more armed men in it. The gunman in the passenger seat shouts more commands. Tahir tells me they want our cell phones and other possessions. "If they find we have a hidden phone," Tahir says, "they'll kill us."

"Tell them we're journalists," I say. "Tell them we're here to interview Abu Tayyeb."

Tahir translates what I say, and the driver—a bearish, bearded figure—starts laughing. "Who is Abu Tayyeb? I don't know any Abu Tayyeb," he says. "I am the commander here."

The first hints of panic creep into my mind, but I try to rationalize what is happening. The gunmen could be thieves or members of another Taliban faction. I know that what Americans call the Taliban is really a loose alliance of local commanders who often operate independently of one another. "Taliban"—Pashto for "students" —is a label of convenience that disenfranchised villagers, hardened Islamists, and criminals all use.

In an ominous sign, we turn left off the main asphalt road onto a dirt track. If we somehow overpower the gunmen in our car, the men in the station wagon will shoot us. I don't want to get Asad and Tahir killed. My imprisonment in Bosnia ended safely after ten days. I am hoping our luck is as good here. One of the gunmen says something and Tahir turns to me. "They want to know your nationality," Tahir says. I hesitate and wonder whether I should say I am Canadian. Being an American is disastrous, but lying is worse. If the gunmen search me, they will discover my passport. If I say I'm Canadian and they later find out I'm American, I will instantly be declared a spy.

"Tell them the truth," I say to Tahir. "Tell them I'm American."

Tahir relays my answer and the burly driver beams, raises his fist, and shouts a response in Pashto. Tahir translates it for me: "They say they are going to send a blood message to Obama."

The driver punches the accelerator and we cross into the open desert. The gunman still aims his Kalashnikov at us. No one speaks. I glance at the bleak landscape outside—reddish soil and black boulders as far as the eye can see. I fear we will be dead within minutes. The longer I look at the gunman in the passenger seat, the more nervous I become. His face shows little emotion. His eyes are dark, flat, and lifeless.

I think of my wife and family and am overcome with shame. An interview that seemed crucial hours ago now seems absurd and reckless. I have needlessly risked the lives of Tahir, Asad, and me. We reach a dry riverbed and the station wagon we are following stops. Our car does the same. "They're going to kill us," Tahir whispers. "They're going to kill us."

Tahir and Asad are ordered out of the car. Gunmen from the station wagon beat them with their rifle butts and lead them away. A gunman from our car motions for me to get out of the vehicle and take a few steps up a sand-covered hillside. While one guard points his Kalashnikov at me, the other takes my glasses, notebook, pen, and camera. I am blindfolded, my hands tied behind my back. My heart races. Sweat pours from my skin.

"*Habarnigar*," I say, using the word for journalist in Dari, another local language. "*Salaam*," I say, using an Arabic expression for peace. The few words I know in Pashto, which is spoken by most Taliban, escape me. I wait for the sound of gunfire. I know I might die but remain oddly calm.

A hand pushes me back toward the car. I am forced to lie down on the backseat. Two gunmen get in and slam the doors shut. The car lurches forward. Tahir and Asad are gone and, I think, probably dead.

As we drive away, Taliban prayers blare out from the radio and my captors laugh with glee. They are clearly elated to have an American captive. I try again. "*Habarnigar, salaam.*" In response, the guard sitting in the backseat beside me pats me on the shoulder and says a phrase in Pashto that includes the word for American. I can't tell whether he is gloating over his prize or trying to comfort me.

We drive down what seem dirt roads. Waves of regret, remorse, and humiliation wash over me. I have gotten two Afghans killed in my foolish pursuit of a better book. I have betrayed my wife and family. Even if Tahir and Asad stay alive and we all survive, I will be mocked by my peers as a two-time kidnap victim with a judgment problem.

The car comes to a halt after what seems like a two-hour drive. Guards untie my hands, take off my blindfold, and guide me through the front door of a crude mud-brick home hidden in a ravine. I am put in some type of washroom the size of a closet. After a few minutes, the guards open the door and push Tahir and Asad inside. We stare at one another in relief. About twenty minutes later, a guard opens the door and motions for us to walk into the hallway.

"No shoot," he says, "no shoot."

For the first time, I think our lives might be spared. The guard leads us into a living room decorated with maroon carpets and red pillows. A half dozen men sit along two walls of the room, Kalashnikov rifles at their sides. I sob, bow my head, and try to look like a frightened reporter.

The guard motions for me to sit down across from a heavyset man with a *patu*—a traditional Afghan scarf—wrapped around his face. Sunglasses cover his eyes, and he wears a cheap black knit winter cap. Embroidered across the front of it is the word "Rock" in English.

"I'm a Taliban commander," he announces. "My name is Mullah Atiqullah."

In the months ahead, I will learn that his name means "gift from God."

Seven years earlier, in September 2001, I had arrived in Afghanistan with a consuming desire to cover what I thought would be the defining conflict of my generation. On September 11, I had heard a distant explosion, looked out the window of my Brooklyn apartment, and seen a cloud of smoke rise up the side of the World Trade Center's north tower. After hearing on the radio that both towers had been struck in a terrorist attack, I jumped on the subway to the trade center.

Ten minutes later, I walked out of a deserted subway exit and found myself standing four blocks from the two burning towers. Ten full stories appeared to be ablaze. I scribbled a few words in my notebook: "smoke from something on the ground. Debris all over the ground." I walked closer and ran into Sherry Day, another reporter from the paper, and scribbled more notes: "Debris cascading. People snapping pictures. Smoke rising."

I heard a sharp crack and what sounded, oddly, like a waterfall. Somewhere above us, thousands of panes of glass shattered as the south tower buckled. Looking up, I saw the top half of the skyscraper begin slowly plummeting toward the ground. I grabbed Sherry's hand and we sprinted away from the tower as a roar filled our ears. I felt her hand pull away and turned back to see what had happened. She was gone and a thick cloud of dust—like a giant wall—surged up the street.

I ran around a corner and down a flight of stairs into a subway station, the dust engulfed me and the world turned white. A few feet away, a woman began screaming. After several moments, we took each other's hand, walked upstairs, and emerged into what we thought was the street. We could see nothing in front of us. Finally, a gust of wind revealed a speck of blue in the sky to our right. I told her to walk in that direction and she disappeared.

I tried to find Sherry. White dust covered cars, buildings, and streets. Car alarms wailed. Pieces of office paper cascaded to the ground like oversize snowflakes. Filled with a vague idea of somehow helping survivors, I walked toward the towers. The story—any story—no longer mattered. I simply wanted to help. As I walked, I realized I had no medical or rescue skills to offer. I felt like a vulture with a notebook. A man appeared on the street covered head to toe in dust. I asked him, "Is there anything I can do?" He replied, "There's nothing anybody can do."

Over the next two weeks, the heroism of thousands of volunteers from New York and across the country amazed me. I found Sherry and learned she was unhurt and had run into a store. Still nagged by my sense of helplessness that morning, I considered joining the military or becoming a paramedic. Two weeks after the attack, editors asked me to go to Afghanistan and I leapt at the chance. I had covered religious extremism in the Balkans and thought my stories could investigate, examine, and expose militant Islam. With thousands dead in my home city, I also hoped my journalism might somehow help prevent future attacks.

On September 25, 2001, a rickety, Soviet-built helicopter operated by the Northern Alliance—the ragtag Afghan anti-Taliban group—dropped me and several other journalists in the Panjshir Valley, one of the few areas in the country the alliance controlled.

On the ground, the epic scale of what the United States faced in Afghanistan was humbling. Dozens of burnt-out Soviet tanks lined the valley, a maze of mountains and ravines that seemed to epitomize Afghanistan's reputation as a geographic and cultural fortress. With billions in aid from the United States in the 1980s, the Afghan "mujahideen"—an Arabic term that means "strugglers" or "fighters for justice"—had defeated the Soviets and fulfilled the mountainous country's reputation for repelling foreign armies and humbling empires.

In the 1990s, civil war had erupted with India, Pakistan, and Iran backing the Northern Alliance and Pakistan backing Taliban fighters from the south. When I arrived in 2001, the Taliban and their foreign militant allies controlled roughly 90 percent of the country. The depth of the country's poverty was staggering. Most towns had no paved roads or electricity. Farmers used oxen and wooden plows to till their fields. Twenty years of conflict had shattered government and social structures. Afghanistan was the world's fifth poorest nation. Fifty-five percent of men and 85 percent of women were illiterate. The average life expectancy was forty-three.

When the Taliban front lines collapsed under heavy American bombing in early November, exuberant young Afghans thronged Kabul's streets and hailed the fall of the Taliban. They devoured cellular phones, computers, and any other means of access to the outside world. Girls flocked to school and women relished basic freedoms. After twenty-four years of Soviet occupation, civil war, and brutal Taliban rule, Afghans welcomed stability, moderation, and foreigners. On December 22, 2001, I watched Afghan men weep with joy as Hamid Karzai was sworn in as the country's interim leader. Hope filled the hall and the city. The Taliban appeared vanquished.

Like other foreigners, I was beguiled by Afghans, their bravery and sense of honor. I wanted to follow what unfolded in the country over the long term and answer a central question: how can religious extremism be countered?

I had been intermittently covering religious and ethnic conflict for the past fourteen years. I covered the war in Bosnia for *The Christian Science Monitor* in the mid-1990s and after joining *The New York Times* in 1996 reported on religious conflict in Israel–Palestine, Kosovo, Indonesia, and Nigeria. After covering the fall of the Taliban in 2001, I served as the newspaper's South Asia bureau chief from 2002 to 2005, reporting on sectarian tensions in India, Sri Lanka, and Bangladesh as well. The vast majority of my time, though, was spent reporting in Pakistan and Afghanistan.

I visited Helmand Province in southern Afghanistan for the first time in 2004 while reporting a story on Charles Grader, the last American to head the U.S. Agency for International Development, or USAID, mission in Kabul before the 1979 Soviet invasion. A quarter century later, Grader had returned to Kabul at the age of seventy-two to manage an agricultural development program. We drove into Lashkar Gah, Helmand's provincial capital, and he raved about how the town had changed since the 1970s. Stores brimmed with food, household goods, and televisions.

"Look at that construction!" Grader shouted as we drove down through the city trailed by a half dozen Afghan security guards. "Look at the tractors!"

Lashkar Gah had fascinated me ever since. The town was built by American engineers as part of one of the largest foreign development projects in United States history. For thirty-three years, from 1946 to 1979, a massive American Cold War program tried to wean Afghans from Soviet influence.

In a bleak stretch of Afghan desert that resembled the surface of Mars, several dozen families from states like Montana and Wisconsin lived in suburban tract homes with one-car garages, green lawns and backyard barbecues. The Americans constructed a new provincial capital, two earthen dams, 1,200 miles of gravel roads, and 300 miles of irrigation canals. They promised to make 350,000 acres of desert bloom and create an Afghan version of the Tennessee Valley Authority, the Depression-era hydroelectric system that spans five American states.

In 1960, the British historian Arnold J. Toynbee visited Lashkar Gah and declared it "a piece of America inserted into the Afghan landscape." The American-designed town was an "ultramodern world of workshops and offices," Toynbee wrote in a memoir of his journey. Afghans called it "Little America."

Laid out in a neat square grid, Lashkar Gah during the Cold War was a sweltering, dust-covered settlement of 15,000 residents perched above the swirling brown waters of the Helmand River, according to books and reports from the time. It had a four-lane, pine-tree-lined Main Street, a new hotel with a swimming pool and tennis court, and southern Afghanistan's only coeducational high school. Downtown, a movie theater played the latest Indian films. The province and its massive development project was even a setting of a James Michener novel. After traveling through Afghanistan in the 1950s, Michener wrote *Caravans,* a 1963 novel that described local Afghan disappointment with an expensive foreign aid project that failed to meet their high expectations.

Toynbee, Michener, and other foreign visitors were enthralled by the Pashtuns, a fiercely independent ethnic group of 40 million people that predominate in Helmand, southern Afghanistan, and northwestern Pakistan. Their ancient system of governance is Pashtunwali, a 5,000-year-old tribal code of honor that governs all aspects of a Pashtun's life. Under Pashtunwali, all Pashtuns must display hospitality toward guests, give asylum to anyone in distress, exact revenge on those who injure or insult them, protect the honor of women, and always display unflinching bravery, loyalty, and trust in God.

In rural villages, conservative Pashtun tribal elders tended to be devoutly religious, opposed to central government rule, and suspicious of foreigners. In the large cities and towns, an educated Pashtun elite generally supported modernization of the country.

In "Little America" of the 1960s and 1970s, educated Pashtun moderates dominated. During Christmas and Ramadan in Lashkar Gah, Pashtuns and Americans invited one another to each other's homes to celebrate their respective religious holidays. Americans who worked in Lashkar Gah at the time told me Pashtuns were shockingly poor and isolated, yet dignified, generous, and welcoming.

David Champagne, a Peace Corps volunteer from Chicago, taught English at the high school in Lashkar Gah from 1968 to 1971. He recalled an experimental school where Afghan and American teachers worked together to train a new generation of Afghan leaders and technocrats. Champagne tried to infuse his students—particularly girls—with a sense that they could achieve anything through hard work. The school's goal was to instill an ethos that Afghanistan could develop into a prosperous country through slow, painstaking education and government reform efforts over many years. "There was a certain amount of realism and optimism," Champagne told me. "People thought they could help people with technology. Make the deserts bloom."

The grand American project, though, never achieved the agricultural production promised. It consumed vast amounts of American and Afghan finances and took three times longer to complete than planned. Arriving with Grader in 2004, I found that the American-built suburban tract homes still stood, but their Afghan occupants had built walls around them, a sign of the gulf between American and Afghan notions of privacy.

I learned that "Little America" was one chapter in a century-long effort by the Pashtun elite to modernize the country, all with mixed results. In many ways, Afghan history followed a cycle of Kabul-based, elite-backed reform movements provoking violent opposition from the country's conservative rural tribes.

Yet whenever I began to write off the American Cold War project, other experiences gave me pause. Pashtun farmer after farmer told me "Americans built Helmand." I met scores of Pashtuns who had attended the experimental American-funded high school in Lashkar Gah in the 1960s and 1970s. Thirty years later, they warmly recalled the names of David Champagne and their American teachers, often with tears in their eyes. Dozens had become senior government officials or doctors, engineers, and teachers.

In particular, the sophistication and bravery of one man and one woman from the classes of 1972 and 1974 intrigued me. After the fall of the Taliban, Muhammad Hussein Andiwal became the provincial police chief and Fowzea Olomi became the head of women's affairs in Helmand. They insisted that "Little America" was ripe for another American-backed renaissance.

For my book, I planned to chronicle Fowzea's and Andiwal's efforts to modernize Helmand after 2001. On the day before we drove to our ill-fated Taliban interview, I had met in Kabul with Andiwal, who had been recently fired from his job as Helmand's police chief. Despite the presence of 8,000 British and American troops, the Taliban had gained control of most of the province. Andiwal blamed the British and the British blamed the Afghans. I began to wonder who was telling the truth and if there were any heroes in Helmand.

Twelve hours after interviewing Andiwal, I lay in the back of the car bound and blindfolded. A dynamic that has always existed in journalism had escalated in Iraq and Afghanistan. In an intensifying race to the bottom, the reporter who took the greatest risk often received the highest acclaim. In Bosnia, a desire to expose injustice had primarily driven me, followed by competitiveness and ambition. In Afghanistan, competitiveness and ambition had gotten the best of me. I had lost my way.

As my Taliban captors blared prayers over the car radio and celebrated the capture of their quarry, a new meaning enveloped the sweeping question I had grandly posed to myself in 2001: how can religious extremism be curbed? My life and the lives of Tahir and Asad now hinged on whether we could find a way to placate our captors, gain their sympathy, and stop them from killing us. As I lay powerless in the backseat, the question was simple: how do we survive?

Our kidnapper, Atiqullah, eyes me suspiciously in the living room of the house where Tahir, Asad, and I have been taken. Roughly two hours have passed since we were kidnapped. I still do not know which Taliban faction has abducted us or who Atiqullah is.

A large man with short dark hair protruding from the sides of his cap, Atiqullah appears self-assured. He speaks calmly and confidently, and is in clear command of his men. He offers me back the eyeglasses his gunmen had taken from me and tells me to stop sobbing, a tactic that had eased the suspicions of my captors in Bosnia. Weeping is a great shame, he explains, and it upsets him and his men to see it. Later, I will learn that the Taliban consider crying to be a sign of guilt. If a person is innocent, he does not fear death, because he knows God will save him.

"You will be treated well," he assures me, citing Islam's mandate that prisoners not be harmed. "I understand foreigners get sick. You will be given bottled water. If you need to see a doctor, you will see a doctor."

"Whatever we eat," he adds, "you will eat."

His beliefs appear to be a combination of Pashtunwali and fundamentalist Islam. Gracious treatment of guests is a Pashtun hallmark. Deep suspicion of nonbelievers is an excess of radical Islam. Since the Taliban emerged in the early 1990s, religiously conservative rural Pashtuns have been their base of support.

With Tahir translating, I try to convince him to release us. I tell him that we were invited to Logar Province to interview Abu Tayyeb and hear the Taliban's side of the story. We are journalists, I say, and I served as *The New York Times'* South Asia bureau co-chief from 2002 to 2005. I describe the articles I wrote in Bosnia exposing the mass executions of 8,000 Muslims. I tell him Christians there imprisoned me when they caught me at a mass gravesite and accused me of being pro-Muslim. I tell him I had won the Pulitzer Prize and a half dozen other journalism awards for helping expose the massacres.

I hope I am convincing him that I am an independent journalist. I hope I am convincing him that the United States is not a monolith and some Americans defend Muslims and are rewarded for it. For years, I have thought that if the Taliban ever kidnap me, my work in Bosnia would protect me. I would be investigated online, declared a friend of Islam, and, I hoped, released.

Finally, I take off my wedding ring, show him the engraving of my wife's name on the inner band, and explain that we were married only two months ago. Tears roll down my cheeks again and I beg him to free us. The melodrama is intentional. I have read that a captive's best chance of survival is getting their captor to see them as a human being. I hope my display of emotion will help us.

Atiqullah grows angry, orders me to stop crying, and tells me I will see my wife again. But he denies our requests to call Abu Tayyeb or a Taliban spokesman Tahir knows. He says he controls our fate now.

He hands me back my notebook and pen and orders me to start writing. American soldiers routinely disgrace Afghan women and men, he says. They force women to stand before them without their burqas, the head-to-toe veils that conservative Pashtun villagers believe protect a woman's honor. They search homes without permission and force Afghan men to lie on the ground, placing boots on their heads and pushing their faces into the dirt. He views the United States as a malevolent occupier.

Atiqullah produces one of our cell phones and announces that he wants to call the *Times* bureau in Kabul. I give him the number and he briefly speaks with one of the newspaper's Afghan reporters. He hands me the phone. One of my colleagues from the paper's Kabul bureau is on the line. I say that we have been taken prisoner by the Taliban.

"What can we do?" my colleague asks. "What can we do?"

Atiqullah demands the phone back before I can answer. My colleague—one of the bravest reporters I know—sounds unnerved.

Atiqullah turns off the phone, removes the battery, and announces that we will move that night for security reasons. My heart sinks. I hoped that we would somehow be allowed to contact Abu Tayyeb, the commander we had arranged to interview, and be freed before nightfall. Now, as we wait in the house, I know that my colleague will be calling my family and editors at any minute to inform them that I have been kidnapped.

After praying, our captors serve us a traditional Afghan dinner of rice and flatbread. After sunset, they blindfold us, load us into cars, and drive us into the darkness.

Atiqullah is at the wheel. A man who has been introduced to us as "Akhundzada," Atiqullah's "intelligence chief," sits in the passenger seat with a scarf over his face as well. I am seated in the backseat between Tahir and Asad. Roughly thirty minutes into a jarring drive down dirt roads, Atiqullah allows me to take off my blindfold. We traverse a barren, moonlit desert landscape of dust-covered plains and treeless hills. I recognize nothing. We could be anywhere in Afghanistan.

With Tahir again translating, I ask for permission to speak and offer to answer any questions Atiqullah might have. He assails Israel and accuses the United States of being a greedy colonial power bent on stealing the Muslim world's resources. He is doctrinaire, but we are not being beaten or abused.

After a roughly two-hour drive, we arrive in a remote village where Atiqullah says we will spend the night with his guards. He is leaving and will return the following day. His men lead us into a small, one-room dirt house. A half dozen of us—three guards and three prisoners—lie down on the floor under musty-smelling blankets. I think of my wife and family. By now, they must know.

"FUN FEARLESS FEMALE"

Kristen, November 10–11, 2008

I am sitting atop Times Square. From the thirty-eighth floor, I can see all way to the mouth of the Hudson River. I have just assigned a photographer to shoot a portrait to accompany a first-person magazine account titled "My Bra Saved My Life." We will photograph the once injured hiker who hung her bra out as a beacon to alert passersby. Nothing attracts attention like a bright red sports bra with size D cups, apparently. In a pinch, it's a real lifesaver. I smile to myself. This is a far cry from my husband's line of work.

I am about two weeks into my new job as photography director at *Cosmopolitan* magazine. My train of thought—the combination of humor, absurdity, and mass-market appeal my new job straddles—is interrupted. It's 4:30 P.M. I wonder why I have not yet heard from David, even though I know that power outages are common in Pakistan, as are travel delays. Perhaps he has not yet figured out how to access the Internet from his guesthouse. He's there on assignment and is researching a book on the history of American involvement in Afghanistan and Pakistan since 2001—what went wrong and what should be done to remedy the situation. This is David's final reporting trip to the region. He was scheduled to depart Kabul for Islamabad this morning.

The phone rings. It's my brother-in-law Lee. Not a good sign. "Hello," I say. "Nice to hear your voice, but I am not so sure I want to be hearing from you. What's wrong?"

Lee is the person my husband has designated as a first point of contact for all "worst case scenarios." In the event of a mishap during a reporting trip, the plan is that Lee will be alerted and will in turn contact me. A former member of the Air Force and a pilot, Lee has nerves of steel, but is also a sensitive guy. Three years older than my husband, he has gotten David out of several tight situations. He is the consummate big brother, responsible and protective.

He laughs, understanding my predicament. "Well, it's not good. But it could be worse."

He tells me that David never returned from his last interview in Kabul, a meeting he had arranged with a Taliban commander. This is news to me. David left a note at the bureau with instructions on what to do should he fail to return in three hours. Lee tells me that David wanted him to wait twelve hours before reaching out to me. "Screw that," he says. "I figured you would want to know. And I do not want to deal with this alone."

Right away, my brother-in-law gains a spot near and dear to my heart. He is right. I would have been absolutely livid had he waited to inform me. David's need to "protect" me sometimes infuriates me.

"Christie and I are in Florida on vacation," Lee says, referring to his wife. "Stay calm. Take a moment to take this in." My mind reels as I try to process what he is telling me. Then he continues, "You should jump on the next shuttle to Boston. We'll meet you at Logan." From there, we will drive back to his house in southern New Hampshire for the night. Apparently a meeting has been scheduled with the local FBI bureau there for early tomorrow morning. The FBI agents contacted Lee after David was reported missing to the United States Embassy in Kabul.

Shuttle to Boston? I am new on the job and a little busy at the moment arranging the photo shoot. I am trying to locate a reasonable facsimile of the sports bra worn by the hiker, to run as a still along with her portrait. My rational mind grapples for control. Of course, I quickly realize this is absurd. I need to get to the airport as fast as possible. David is my number one priority. I fight a wave of overwhelming terror, fear, and uncertainty. I am momentarily immobilized, numb, as I glance out the window.

It's a crisp afternoon. The sky is clear, the river calm. Despite the tidiness of my new, modern surroundings, I feel as if my life has plunged into disarray. I thought I was prepared for this kind of call. Before we married, David and I discussed the inherent risks in his work as a foreign correspondent. We talked about several worst case scenarios, including injury and even death. These tragedies are concrete and would follow a prescribed protocol. But I never anticipated what to do in the uncertain face of David going missing. Here it is, I think, my worst fear come true.

I call the managing editor at *Cosmopolitan* and say something vague about a "family health emergency" and that I need to head to New England. She is gracious and does not ask questions. I tell her I will probably be out the next day or so. "Do what you need to do," she says. She knows that my parents live in Maine. I secretly hope the magazine thinks I am running off to comfort an ailing elderly relative. The real explanation is too absurd to believe.

By the time I leave my office and head home to collect my things, I am composed and steady. I have prided myself on being able to stay calm in tense situations. And this is not my first brush with terror. I live a few blocks from Ground Zero. I recall the shock of being displaced for three months following the 9/11 terrorist attacks, the exhaustion, uncertainty. And all my adrenaline-fueled mistakes: forgetting to eat, sleep, and rest. What I learned then protects me now. On my way to Boston, I resolve to take better care of myself this time around, and to call on family and friends for support when necessary.

It's 9:30 P.M. when I arrive at Logan Airport. I wait in the sterile baggage terminal. It's Monday night. A bit deserted. No one else in David's family has been alerted aside from his brother Lee. By chance I hear from my own brother, Jason. He is calling to check in and catch up. All he knows is that I returned from my honeymoon three weeks ago and started a new job. I try to keep my voice calm and upbeat. Jason is exuberant chatting about what a great time he had at our wedding at our family's home in Maine. My sister-in-law chimes in on speakerphone. They are both so happy for us.

When he takes me off speakerphone, I ask if I can tell him a secret. "This is going to sound so far-fetched," I say. "I am sitting at Logan.

David went into an interview and never returned. We think he's alive, but do not know where he is." My brother is a rock. I know he feels terrible for me, but I also know he will not share this information with anyone.

I meet Lee and his wife, Christie. Their two-year-old is asleep in her stroller. We drive to their home in coastal New Hampshire. The last time I was here was five months ago, during a visit with David. It's about eleven o'clock, an exhausting seven hours after I first heard the news. Tonight, none of us will get any sleep.

At eight the next morning, Lee and I go over to the local FBI office, which is nestled discreetly in a bland suburban 1980s-style office park. We are greeted by several agents. This, I will learn, is typical. They travel in packs. They sport clean haircuts and monosyllabic names: Jim, Tom, John, Joe. One would be hard-pressed to pick any of them out of a police lineup. They are nondescript and practically identical in their uniformity.

The FBI is the lead agency in all kidnappings of American citizens, whether at home or abroad. We are a bit baffled, though, as to why we were instructed to meet them in New Hampshire, given that David and I live in New York. It turns out to be agency protocol, which was set in motion when the newspaper's Kabul bureau notified the U.S. Embassy that David did not return from the interview. The case was immediately reported to the FBI, then to David's employer. The newspaper then called Lee, who is still listed as David's emergency contact. I make a note to update this information when David returns. Because Lee's phone number bears a New Hampshire area code, local field agents there were assigned to get in touch with our family. If I was the contact, we'd be having this meeting in New York City.

The local case agent informs us that David was abducted along with his driver and translator as they headed to interview a Taliban commander outside Kabul. I proceed to reel off the name of everyone David has mentioned to me in the past two and a half years who is affiliated with Afghanistan, Pakistan, and the United States government. It's a long list. The interview is largely a one-way flow of information. As we talk about the situation, I begin to feel like I am better versed in the tribal areas of Pakistan and the nuances of Afghan culture than the local agents. This is a little disturbing, since most of what I know is limited to what I have absorbed from David—and from visiting his colleagues, briefly traveling with him to Pakistan, and reading popular books like *Three Cups of Tea* and *The Kite Runner*.

Lee is asked to provide a DNA sample, a cheek swab. This is to help identify David in a worst case scenario, or if any evidence is found in Afghanistan that could indicate the location where he is being held captive.

The agents ask whether David is a friend of the Taliban, and whether the book is about them. I explain that he is writing about the struggling American effort in the region. I edit my words carefully before speaking, fearful of saying anything that could mislead them into thinking that David is somehow in cahoots with the Taliban.

Lee and I leave the interview several hours later with the understanding that another set of agents will be assigned to our case in New York City. We are to update the agents if we receive any new information about David from his colleagues. In turn, the agents will keep us posted on any new developments on their end.

Calls begin to flood in: David's literary agent, the editor of *The New York Times*. The newspaper alerted David's book publisher about the kidnapping. David's agent, in turn, was contacted by his publisher. Despite the fact that Lee and I have made no public announcement of David's predicament, word has traveled like wildfire among the journalism community.

I am relieved to hear from a colleague of David's in Kabul. Upset but calm, this reporter informs me that David left behind a note addressed to me. I ask the reporter to read it over the phone. I sense a hesitation. "He has rather unfortunate handwriting," the reporter jokes between tears. "I will scan and e-mail it to you and send the original in the mail."

A few hours later, the infamous note appears in my BlackBerry inbox. I smile: David's colleague is right about the handwriting. The letter has been scribbled on a page from a notebook. The whole thing feels rushed, like an afterthought. Knowing David, though, he probably agonized over its content.

Kristen—

    I believed I had to do this to make this a credible book. Most people in Helmand support them now and I need to tell that part of the story. I honestly believe this is a calculated risk that will be ok.

Scribbled in the margin is a phrase that makes my heart sink: *This is my passion and I must do what I love.*

The letter continues:

    If I get kidnapped, use money from my book advance. Do not involve money from your family or mine. This is my responsibility.

    I love you so much and am sure this will be ok. Please go and be happy and move forward if things go very wrong.

    I love you so very much and thank you for giving me more joy and love than I've ever known.

    I love you,

    David

Afghanistan has been David's preoccupation for the past seven years, since 9/11. For me, it has been a source of intrigue, sadness, and anxiety—a needy child or mistress that requires his attention, often with the cost of long separations. The events on the ground in Afghanistan have a direct impact on David's moods and motivations. It has been a challenge for me to support such an all-consuming interest.

I was introduced to David by a mutual friend two and a half years ago. We were both in our late thirties at the time and ready to move on to a new phase of life, one that we each hoped would include family and children. Our relationship progressed steadily, despite several month-long periods of separation to accommodate David's overseas reporting trips. These separations were often a strain on my nerves as we both struggled with the tensions inherent in straddling two very different worlds together.

The note does not comfort me. Part of me immediately recognizes that he's thrown us under the bus at month two of marriage. I know that David is writing the book in part to distance himself from his dangerous work as a war correspondent. But pursuing an interview with a Taliban commander was a bachelor's decision. I have just committed the rest of my life to David. I haven't even unpacked from our honeymoon. But if I—we—are going to get through this, I'm going to have to forgive him and set aside my anger. At some point, I am also going to have to deal with the fact that I *am* angry. I realize he took a risk imagining a positive outcome. David does not think that lightning can strike twice. But it has. This is his second detainment. He was jailed in Bosnia for ten days in 1995 while reporting on the mass execution of Muslims in Srebrenica.

I feel like I've been hit by a thunderbolt. I recall our engagement. David proposed to me on a sailboat in the middle of New York Harbor. "Let's lead a big life," he said. I agreed. This is not exactly what I had in mind. I glance at my engagement ring, a pear-shape diamond set on its side. I remember thinking it looked like a teardrop on first viewing. I somehow worried this was a premonition of things to come, but later convinced myself it was a raindrop, which was a more refreshing and fitting thought. Rain is a recurrent theme for us. There was a torrential downpour just before we set sail in New York that day. Hurricane Hannah struck on our wedding day. I often liken the extreme, unpredictable shifts in our circumstances to weather patterns.

Lee offers to drive me to my parents' home in Maine for the night. I will meet up with him tomorrow before I leave for New York. I call my mother from the road. Unaware of what has been going on, she is excited to hear from me. I tell her I have brought a guest along. I know she immediately assumes it's David—perhaps he's come to his senses and returned from Afghanistan early.

I haven't been to the house since we were married in September. David and I decided to marry there, as we each have fond memories of summer childhoods spent in Maine. We wanted to celebrate with our families at a place that had special meaning for us.

The house sits on a sandy tidal beach. The scenery and light shift as the water advances and recedes twice each day. I have always loved the sense of motion, possibility, and renewal these natural changes provoke daily.

I walk into a perfectly preserved moment. The room is still full of an almost palpable sense of love and hope from our celebration. We are greeted by my mother, Mary Jane, a petite, upbeat brunette with a welcoming smile. Despite her five-foot frame, my mother is a powerhouse of strength, tenacity, and positivity. She is a healthy dose of Sally Field, tempered with a shot of Anne Bancroft. She has been drying the wedding flowers. Full bridal bouquets sit in their original places, vibrant, slightly shrunken, preserved. Two months ago we were rolling up the carpets, dancing in the living room, mingling with friends and family. It's odd to be in this space alone, an observer. As I glance out the sliding doors, the ocean is calm, glasslike. I am comforted by memory and surroundings, yet pained to be here without David.

I remember that David looked nervous as we exchanged our vows. To lighten his mood, when I declared "For better or worse," I winked at him on "worse." This definitely qualifies as worse. I now regret my well-intentioned and whimsical act. Perhaps I should not have tempted fate. I promise myself that when David returns, I will restate this promise sans blink.

My mother has prepared a lobster dinner in anticipation of my arrival. I tell her there is no cause for celebration and bring her up to speed while Lee phones his wife from the other room. Mom is quiet, recognizing that this was always within the realm of possibility, given the nature of David's work. When I tell her I am shocked and upset by David's letter— that he was willing to risk everything for the sake of the story, without consulting me—she does not finger point.

"Okay, he made a mistake," she says. "But you need to move forward from there and think positive if you are going to get through this. Don't let your mind be clouded by anger. It's not going to do you any good now. Focus on bringing him home."

"We just took a wedding vow," I say.

"And now it's your chance to live up to it," she responds.

This is a calm but tough pep talk. Confronted by my worst fear, Mom figures the last thing I need is for someone else to stir the pot. She tells me to remain open-minded and offers to accompany me back to New York. I am slightly surprised but thankful for her reaction. Her outward composure keeps me centered. I recognize that while David took a risk in going to the interview, the kidnapping is not his fault. Blaming him for it provides a momentary sense that he has some control over his circumstances. Our reality is much worse—David and the rest of us are helpless in this situation.

I begin to receive calls from friends offering condolences. Each of them has learned about David's situation from a "friend at the *Times*." I have my first brush with what will be an ongoing battle: keeping David's case quiet. Throughout the first days of David's kidnapping, we are able to draw on the camaraderie of the press and the gravitas of *The New York Times* to keep his story out of the public eye. But any bit of information I relay to David's colleagues is quickly common knowledge inside the media bubble. I have to fight repeatedly during these early days to protect our privacy as a couple. I begin my battle at the top, with a heated call to Bill Keller, the paper's executive editor, from my parents' living room. I tell him that his reporters are spreading the word and ask him to put a lid on it. As the wife of a kidnap victim, I have tremendous leeway. Bill is extremely gracious and apologetic. He promises to limit communications within the office.

A call arrives from the FBI on behalf of the Department of Defense. David's brother Lee and I face our first big decision: will we give advance approval for a military raid if it could secure David's release? We are both stunned. "Do you know where he is?" we ask. They cannot say. "How much time do we have to decide?" A few hours.

The Department of Defense ensures us they will not undertake a raid unless they are very confident they will be able to get David and his colleagues out alive. But they give no indication as to how they will assess this risk.

This is the first of many decisions we will agonize over—and revisit during the subsequent months. For now, Lee and I decide against a military raid, unless David or one of his co-captives is severely sick or injured, or if their lives are in immediate danger. We still do not have any information on who is holding him and what it is they are after.

We decide to wait a few days to make a final decision, until we have more information and a sense of David's physical location. We also want to run this by David's parents and other siblings. We do not want to make this decision alone. It is shocking to be confronted with this reality and the grim nature of our choices. We want David to return as quickly as possible. But Lee and I agree that David would never forgive himself if anyone was killed or injured during an attempt to free him by force. Still, we wonder whether our delayed response will work against us, whether this lapse in decision making will mean the difference between his returning home or not.

A short time later, we hear back from the FBI. There is no rush on deciding whether to use military intervention. We are advised that while the kidnappers may move David, there is no imminent threat of harm. In the frustrating days and months to come, we will discover that most of the information and advice we are given is pure speculation.

Night arrives—finally. Unable to sleep in the room I last shared with David at my parents' house, I collapse in my younger brother Jason's vacant room.

My mind races and my body is completely restless, on full alert. I drag my laptop into bed and scan my e-mail for updates from the Kabul bureau and messages from David's family. Lee has told his family the news. I talk to my mother-in-law, Carol, David's sister, Laura, and his younger brother, Erik. Erik and I share our fears. While the situation remains uncertain, we are hopeful. Our collective gut check is that David will return, yet we have no idea how or when. We assume it will be a matter of one to three months, based on what I have learned from the FBI about recent kidnappings in Afghanistan.

I already miss my husband's voice. We routinely speak each night when he is away. Despite the uncertainty of his whereabouts I'm determined to maintain our nightly ritual. I send an e-mail to my husband. I type three simple words into the subject line in the hope that he will one day read them: I love you.

MILLIONS

David, November 11–17, 2008

I awake to the sound of the guards performing a predawn prayer with Tahir and Asad. I sit silently as they press their foreheads to the ground and supplicate to God. We are crammed with three guards in a small, claustrophobic room in a dirt house. Measuring roughly twenty feet by twenty feet, its only furnishings are the carpet on the floor and a dozen blankets.

The gunman with the flat, expressionless eyes who kidnapped us the day before introduces himself as "Qari," an Arabic expression for someone who has been trained to properly recite the Koran. He is shorter and skinnier than he seemed when he glared at me from the front seat of the car the previous day. His mentality proves more disturbing than his appearance. He proudly announces that he is a "fedayeen," an Arabic term the Taliban use for suicide bombers.

Bread arrives for breakfast, and the guards are polite and courteous. No one has beaten us since Tahir and Asad were pummeled with rifle butts during the first minutes of the kidnapping. As the day progresses, though, I grow more worried. Atiqullah has not reappeared. There is no talk of our release.

Confined to the small, crowded room as the morning slowly passes, I find it more and more suffocating. Allowed outside only to go to the bathroom, I am accompanied by an armed guard at all times. As the day crawls by, our guards pray methodically and Qari speaks of his eagerness to die. They act as if I am the first American they have ever seen. They stare at me as if I were a zoo animal, a strange, exotic creature they have long heard about but never beheld.

All this makes me increasingly worried about who is holding us. Thieves might release us if Abu Tayyeb comes to our rescue, or they might settle for a quick deal. Instead, our captors appear to be hard-line Taliban.

Several hours after sunset, we are hustled outside and ordered to get into a small Toyota station wagon.

"We have to move you for security reasons," announces Atiqullah, who is sitting in the driver's seat, his face still concealed behind a scarf. Arab militants and a film crew from Al Jazeera are on their way, he says. "They're going to chop off your heads," he announces. "I've got to get you out of this area."

As we drive away, I ask for permission to speak. Atiqullah agrees. I tell him we are worth more alive than dead. He asks me what I think he can get for us. I hesitate, unsure of what to say. I am desperate to keep us alive.

I have a vague memory of a one-week hazardous environment survival training class that I took in 2002 before being posted abroad. I remember being told by instructors to prolong captivity for as long as possible. The most dangerous period of an abduction is the initial hours. The longer a kidnapping lasts, the higher the chance of survival.

I know that in March 2007, the Afghan government exchanged five Taliban prisoners for an Italian journalist after the Taliban executed his driver. Later, they killed his translator as well. My memory of the exchange was vague, but I thought money was included. In September 2007, the Taliban claimed the South Korean government paid $20 million for the release of twenty-one Korean missionaries after the Taliban killed two members of the group.

"Money and prisoners," I say.

"How much money?" Atiqullah asks.

I hesitate again.

"Millions," I say, immediately thinking I will regret the statement.

Atiqullah and his intelligence chief look at each other. Over the next hour, the conversation continues. Atiqullah repeatedly promises to do his best to protect us. I repeatedly promise him money and prisoners.

As we wind our way through steep mountain passes, an American drone follows us. Remotely piloted propeller-driven airplanes, the drones can easily be heard as they circle overhead for hours. To the naked eye, they are small dots in the sky. But their missiles have a range of several miles. We know we can be immolated without warning. Atiqullah glances warily out the window and tries to locate the drone in the night sky. I silently hope that we miraculously might be found. After a few minutes, the drone disappears.

Atiqullah asks for the names and professions of my father and brothers. I tell him the truth. Given the unusual spelling of my last name, I think he can easily find my relatives online. From past reporting I know that the Taliban are not primitive men who live in caves. They operate in cities across Afghanistan and Pakistan that teem with Internet cafés.

My father, Harvey, is a retired insurance salesman, I say. My two brothers, Lee and Erik, work for an aviation company and an ambulance company. My two stepbrothers, Joel and Dan, work for a bank and a restaurant. I hope being forthright is helping convince him I am a journalist, not a spy. More than ever, I am convinced that being caught in a lie will prove fatal.

In the darkness, I can see little outside the car windows. I don't know if we are passing through clusters of villages or remote areas. After several hours of driving down jarring dirt tracks, we arrive at another small house. Guards cover my face with a scarf and lead us inside in the dark. Atiqullah politely asks me to repeat my earlier statements in the car as a guard records a video of me on his mobile phone. I promise him money and prisoners, recite the names of my male relatives, and list the awards I won for my reporting in Bosnia.

Atiqullah has us answer a series of questions that our families have apparently already relayed to our captors. If our answers are correct, it will prove we are alive. Tahir and Asad are asked to name the first schools they attended. I am asked my wife's name and birth date and what kind of car I have in New York. When I say I do not have a car, Atiqullah is suspicious that I am somehow giving a secret message.

Finally, Atiqullah asks me if I want to convey anything to my wife. "Tell her that the place where I'm staying is better than the farm in India." I'm making a reference to a friend's rustic farm in northern India where we spent a week of our honeymoon. After arriving and discovering it was far hotter than expected, we departed early. I hope the message will prove I am alive, being held in decent conditions, and that it will somehow comfort Kristen.

Then Atiqullah and his intelligence chief disappear. For the next four days, we live in the small house with Qari, the gunman who kidnapped us and hopes to become a suicide bomber. On most days, we hear a motorcycle circle in the distance. More guards have created a perimeter around us.

On the first day, no food or water arrives. For eight hours, we lie on the floor and fitfully try to sleep. My stomach aches. I wonder if the lack of food means they plan to kill us. Qari tells us that an Afghan policeman who secretly supports the Taliban spotted me at a checkpoint. He then warned the Taliban we were coming. I curse myself for not covering my face better.

In brief exchanges, I learn more about Tahir and Asad. In truth, we are strangers. The three of us have never worked together before. Tahir has been working with foreign journalists since 2001 and adores the profession. He brightens when he speaks about other foreign and Afghan journalists we both know. Thirty-four years old, he is a university-educated and religious Afghan who hails from the southern province of Zabul. He has two wives and is the father of seven children, all of whom he moved to Kabul three years ago. He opposed the 2001 invasion of Afghanistan and like many Afghans now views the American and NATO troop presence as a foreign occupation. He is deeply disappointed with the United States' failure to deliver on its promises of stability and reconstruction. A proud Afghan nationalist, he is tired of meddling by foreign countries in his country and wants Afghans to be allowed to decide their own fate.

Asad is twenty-four years old and a scrappy Afghan survivor. He is rail thin, has jet-black hair and beard and dark eyes. Pashtun as well, his family originally hails from Khost province, but Asad was born and raised in Kabul. Married with two young sons, he has worked as a taxi driver in the city and a driver for Tahir and foreign journalists. He and Tahir have become close friends while working together for the past six years.

After dark, someone knocks on the wall of the house and Qari ventures outside. I wonder if our Arab executioners have arrived. Qari and another guard walk in with freshly cooked rice, bread, and meat, as well as bottled water. The guard, whose name is Akbar, profusely apologizes for his lateness. He says Atiqullah has ordered him to see to all our needs. I believe Akbar is the same guard who whispered "no shoot, no shoot" to me on the first day of the kidnapping. The kind treatment surprises and encourages me.

On the second day, Akbar brings us new clothes and warm blankets. I appreciate the good treatment but I am becoming more concerned. There is no word on negotiations. I still hope Abu Tayyeb will hear what has happened and somehow rescue us. Atiqullah is nowhere to be seen and Tahir is barred from calling any of his Taliban contacts.

That afternoon, I decide to pretend I'm sick in the hope it will pressure our captors into resolving our case. After forty-eight hours in one room, Tahir and Asad are increasingly frustrated. I am furious that Kristen and my family are suffering. I go to the bathroom, put my finger in my mouth, and make myself loudly vomit. I return to the room, tell the guards that the food is making me sick, and curl up under a blanket. The guards appear alarmed and I think they call Atiqullah. I make myself vomit once more that evening.

The following day, our third in the house, I make myself vomit several times and spend the day lying on the floor playing sick. The guards appear anxious. After dinner, there is a knock on the exterior wall. I expect a concerned Atiqullah to stride through the door. Instead, a young Taliban doctor does.

To my amazement, he speaks English and carries a fully equipped medical bag, replete with a blood pressure gauge, antibiotics, and an intravenous drip. The doctor takes my blood pressure and gives me an injection that he says will make me feel better. I am afraid the needle is dirty but notice it is wrapped in new plastic. I have no choice but to acquiesce to treatment. I am surprised—and depressed—by the Taliban's infrastructure in Afghanistan. They appear to be well supplied and feel that they are firmly in control of the area where we are being held.

The fourth day, Qari allows us to sit outside in the small walled courtyard. A few hours later, he lets Tahir play a game on his cell phone. I suggest that Tahir try to text "track this phone" or a similar message to the Kabul bureau from Qari's mobile when he is not paying attention. Tahir agrees. When he asks for the phone a second time, Qari is suspicious. He notices that Tahir and I have been talking quietly beforehand. He starts shouting in Pashto. Tahir says he accuses us of trying to send a text message. We deny it. Qari denounces us as liars. Enraged, and irrational, he picks up his Kalashnikov, points it at Tahir's chest, and threatens to shoot him.

Tahir stares back, unmoved. The Pashtun code of honor prevents each man from showing fear or losing face. Asad and I step in front of Tahir. Qari will have to shoot us first before hitting Tahir.

We beg him to put down his gun.

"*Lutfan, lutfan*," I say, using an expression Tahir has told me means "please."

Slowly, Qari lowers his weapon. Then he motions for Tahir to step into an outer room.

I stare at Asad's face to try to gauge what is happening. My limited knowledge of Pashto prevents me from understanding what is being said.

Through the wall, I hear Tahir praying in Arabic. Then I hear a thump and Tahir cry out, "Allah!" A second thump and "Allah!" More thumps follow. Several minutes later, Tahir walks back into the room, crawls under a blanket, and begins moaning. Qari has beaten him with the butt of his rifle. Blow after blow was delivered to his lower back.

Qari unnerves me. In brief and depressing conversations over the last several days, he has earnestly recited hugely inaccurate propaganda about the West's trying to enslave all Muslims. It matches the conspiracy theories I have seen on jihadi Web sites. Qari seems utterly detached from reality. Our other guard, Akbar, jokes that Qari has mental problems.

In my mind, Qari and Atiqullah personify polar ends of the Taliban. Qari represents a paranoid, intractable force. Atiqullah embodies the more reasonable faction: people who could compromise on our release and, perhaps, even on peace in Afghanistan.

I do not know which one represents the majority. I want to believe that Atiqullah does. Yet each day I grow more fearful that Qari is the true Taliban.

Like many other American journalists, I rushed to Afghanistan after the September 2001 attacks with a limited understanding of the Taliban and a cursory knowledge of the country's history. I knew Afghanistan as the "graveyard of empires," a reference to its reputation as a land of indomitable mountain warriors who vanquish invading armies.

Over the next seven years, I gradually developed a more nuanced understanding. Afghanistan was not unconquerable. Foreign armies had taken control of Kabul and other large cities in the strategically located swathe of Central Asia dozens of times. First the Persians, then Alexander the Great, then the Safavids, and finally the Muslim Arabs; Ghengis Khan's Moguls, British, and Soviets did the same.

As a means of self-defense, Afghans deftly cultivated an image of their country as "Yaghestan"—a term used by Persians to describe the lawless areas to their east, a place both chaotic and criminal. In truth, Afghanistan was an impoverished band of high mountains and barren deserts with few natural resources, wholly dependent on outsiders for trade, arms, and wealth. Fractious Afghans also fought among themselves, created divisions outsiders exploited.

Centuries of conquest created a clear pattern. Afghans initially put up little resistance to invading armies and then extracted what lucre they could from their new rulers. Quickly shifting their loyalties, Afghans rebelled when they sensed an end to subsidy, the approach of a wealthier suitor, or flagrant disrespect. Foreigners found that the country was extraordinarily difficult to govern over the long term. The pattern led to a clichéd adage about the country: you can rent an Afghan, but you cannot own one.

Afghanistan did not become an independent nation until 1747, when a tribal council, or "jirga," chose a young Pashtun tribesman from Kandahar, Ahmad Shah Durrani, to serve as its king. For the next 225 years, Durrani's descendants ruled the country.

The new nation was a dizzying ethnic, tribal, and religious mix, "a purely accidental geographic unit," in the words of Lord George N. Curzon, the nineteenth-century British colonialist.

Ethnic Pashtuns spoke Pashto, dominated the south and east, and made up the vast majority of the population. Ethnic Tajiks of Persian descent dominated the north and west, spoke Persian, and were the country's second largest group. Ethnic Hazaras, descendants of the Mongols and minority Shia Muslims, were the country's third largest group. Uzbeks, Turkmen, and other ethnic groups from neighboring countries made up the remainder.

In the mid-1800s, Afghanistan became the coveted prize in the "Great Game," the celebrated British and Russian competition for control of Central Asia. The same pattern of conquest and rebellion emerged. In 1838, a British army seized control of Kabul. Three years later, Afghans revolted, hacking to death two British envoys in Kabul's main bazaar. When the British withdrew from Kabul several months later, Afghan marksmen firing from surrounding hills decimated the column. Out of a force of 15,000, only one man survived, purportedly spared so that he could describe the horrors that awaited future invaders.

In 1878, a larger British force of 40,000 soldiers bent on reasserting the empire's supremacy seized Kabul and other large cities. Three years of relative calm followed, until a rebellion erupted and 1,000 British were killed in the Battle of Maiwand, a few dozen miles from where "Little America" would be built decades later. Two months later, a larger British force decisively defeated the Afghans in Kandahar.

Aware that a long-term British presence would spark another uprising, the British installed an Afghan regent named Abdur Rahman. He agreed to British protection, subsidy, and control of Afghanistan's foreign affairs, moves all designed to block Russian expansionism toward British-controlled India.

In 1893, the British imposed a 1,600 mile border between Afghanistan and British-controlled India that annexed vast parts of Afghanistan and divided the Pashtuns, placing roughly 25 million of them in British-controlled India and 10 million in Afghanistan. The division would rankle Afghan Pashtuns for decades and lead to repeated calls for the establishment of a new nation called Pashtunistan. With the stroke of a British pen, the Afghan Pashtuns lost two-thirds of their population and dropped from being Afghanistan's overwhelming majority to a plurality of its people. Ethnic Tajiks, who dominate Afghanistan's north, had their hand strengthened.

In 1919, a bold young Afghan king named Amanullah Khan attacked the British and tried to retake the Pashtun areas the British had seized. In a three-month war he failed to do so, but regained control of Afghanistan's foreign affairs. For the next decade, American diplomats considered Afghanistan within Britain's "sphere of influence," though, and declined to recognize it as an independent nation.

Leon B. Poullada, an American diplomat who served in Afghanistan in the late 1950s and wrote a history of relations between Washington and Kabul, referred to the American view as the "Afghan blind-spot." Poullada argued that American policy makers dismissed the country as hostile and hapless, and repeatedly failed to see its strategic importance. "This feeling of unreality, of an inability to focus or define American interests in this 'far-off' land will appear as a recurring theme," Poullada wrote, "and will help to explain the many inconsistencies of American diplomacy in Afghanistan."

Poullada blamed the misperceptions on early American writing about Afghanistan. It began in 1838 when Josiah Harlan, a quixotic mercenary from Pennsylvania, became the first American to enter Afghanistan. Over the course of a decade, Harlan carried out an astonishing run of opportunism and skullduggery across South Asia, posing as a surgeon at one point and culminating in his 1838 position as a military adviser to Dost Muhammad, Afghanistan's ruler.

Harlan claimed he led an entire division of Afghan troops—and a heavy artillery train—over the Hindu Kush range, the forbidding mountains that separate northern and southern Afghanistan. Standing astride a 12,500-foot mountain pass, Harlan said he ordered his men to fire a twenty-six-gun salute as he unfurled an American flag. "I unfurled my country's banner to the breeze, under a salute of twenty-six guns, and the star-spangled banner gracefully waved amidst the icy peaks, seemingly sacred to the solitude of an undisturbed eternity," he wrote grandiloquently.

Months later, the British deposed Dost Muhammad and ousted the upstart American, who fancied himself heir to Alexander the Great. Harlan returned to the United States and published a memoir of his exploits, which years later became the basis for Rudyard Kipling's *The Man Who Would Be King.*

Poullada questioned the accuracy of Harlan's memoirs and maintained that Harlan was the first in a long line of American writers who unfairly portrayed Afghans as savages. After driving from British-controlled India to Kabul in 1922, Lowell Thomas, the famed American journalist, wrote a travelogue called *Beyond Khyber Pass: Into Forbidden Afghanistan.* Thomas assailed the Pashtuns, who he said were "more elusive than the robber bands of Albania, more daring than the Moros of Mindanao, more cunning than the Yaquis of Sonora, even more savage than the Mongol bandits of Chinese Tibet."

In truth, Afghanistan's ruling family, which was Pashtun, was desperate for help modernizing the country. Dismissed by British and American officials, Afghanistan's royal family eventually turned to continental Europe for help. In 1929, King Nadir Shah had French and German advisers train a 40,000-soldier army. Palace guards sporting incongruous Prussian-style helmets patrolled Kabul's streets. German-made aircraft supported military expeditions that punished rebellious tribes.

In 1933, Nadir Shah was assassinated and his nineteen-year-old son, Zahir Shah, took the thrown. For the next forty years, he and his uncles would rule Afghanistan. Zahir Shah, who inherited a kingdom with only six miles of railway, all of them in Kabul, and few telegraph and phone lines, redoubled his father's modernization efforts. He recruited Italian, Japanese, and German advisers to develop a new road and communications system. Japanese built Helmand's first canals.

The outbreak of World War II finally ignited serious American interest in Afghanistan. American officials saw that the country offered a land route Allied forces could use to supply Soviet troops. Following the war, the United States vied with the Soviet Union for influence in Afghanistan. While Soviet engineers built roads and factories in the country's north, Americans built a highway linking Kabul and Kandahar, a sprawling new airport in Kandahar, and the massive Helmand project. Professors from the University of Nebraska taught agriculture at Kabul University and Pan American World Airways stewards trained employees of Afghanistan's new national airline.

The massive 1979 Soviet invasion followed the same pattern as past conquests. Soviet forces took control of major cities and faced primarily rural resistance. Thousands of Soviet advisers introduced atheism, a state-controlled economy, and a massive secret police system. Over time, brutal repression by Soviet forces and their Afghan allies—as well as billions in American aid—fueled a broad-based uprising led by religious conservatives.

In 2001, the ease of the American victory should have come as no surprise, given the country's history. A simple lesson should have been apparent to American policymakers: Afghans would welcome Americans, but only temporarily. At most, Washington had three to five years to demonstrate to Afghans that allying with the United States was to their benefit. Otherwise, Washington's newfound allies would desert them.

As our captivity enters its fifth day, Tahir, Asad, and I talk about trying to escape. Asad believes our captors will either kill us or hold us indefinitely. That afternoon, when Qari steps outside and leaves his Kalashnikov rifle behind, Asad grabs the weapon, loads it, and announces he wants to shoot his way out.

We urge Asad to wait. He will kill one or two guards, we tell him, and then be killed by others who hear the gunfire. Asad says he does not care, then reluctantly relents and places the rifle back on the floor.

We agree that Asad should try to escape that night after the guards fall asleep. If he makes it to Kabul, Asad can give the newspaper our location. Tahir and I are happy to stay behind if it allows Asad to return home.

We all know that in post-9/11 Afghanistan and Pakistan all lives are not created equal. If our captors are going to kill one of us, Asad will be the first. Tahir will follow, and I will likely be last, given their view of me as the hostage who can produce the most ransom or publicity.

Our calculus is based on the 2007 kidnapping of Italian journalist Daniele Mastrogiacomo. Two weeks after their abduction in Helmand, the Taliban beheaded the group's driver, Sayed Agha, and threatened to kill Mastrogiacomo and the Afghan journalist working with him, Ajmal Naqshbandi.

After Italian officials pressured Karzai, he released five senior Taliban prisoners in exchange for Mastrogiacomo. The Taliban then demanded another Taliban prisoner in exchange for Naqshbandi. When the Afghan government refused, the Taliban decapitated the soft-spoken twenty-four-year-old Afghan. Tahir and hundreds of Afghans attended Naqshbandi's funeral in Kabul. They bitterly accused the Karzai government of caring more about the life of a foreigner than the life of an Afghan.

While many foreigners are shuttled around Afghanistan in armored cars, Afghan civilians are forced to negotiate Taliban checkpoints largely on their own. The Taliban stop cars, trucks, and buses and arrest or execute Afghans who work with foreigners or the Afghan government. A month before our abduction, the Taliban had killed twenty-seven bus passengers who they believed were Afghan army soldiers in civilian clothes, decapitating six of them. The Afghan government, in fact, does not allow soldiers to travel by civilian bus. The Taliban-executed passengers were innocent men journeying to Iran for work.

That night, Atiqullah arrives with no warning and scuttles Asad's escape plans. "We're going to move you to a place where David can have bottled water," he says. "A place to walk. There will be doctors."

Guards load us into what looks like the same four-door Toyota station wagon. They put blankets in the hatchback and tell me to lie on top of them. Just before we depart, the Taliban doctor returns and gives me a final needle injection for my stomach.

In the car, Atiqullah tells me to cover my face with a scarf whenever we pass through a village or town. Arab militants and hard-line Taliban will try to kidnap and kill me, he says, if they recognize me as an American. He is probably lying, but I feel I have no choice but to obey him.

The four-door Toyota sedan we drove to our ill-fated interview follows behind our station wagon. At times, Asad is ordered to drive it so guards can rest. Qari rides a motorcycle to scout the way ahead. For four to five hours at a time, he rides through billowing dust clouds. He seems inhuman. Altogether we are a small group—two cars and a motorcycle—a modest, seemingly innocuous convoy moving across the Afghan countryside. Tracking us is next to impossible.

For the next three days, we live in the car and endure a bewildering and grueling journey. We traverse mountains and vast stretches of open desert where no roads exist. We cut across paved roads but never drive down them. And we pass through villages where local children bring the Taliban bread and tea. I don't know if they do so out of support or fear. I spend twelve hours a day lying in the back of the station wagon, forbidden from looking out the windows. Meals consist of pieces of flatbread handed to me by guards and sips from bottles of water. Bathroom breaks every few hours occur on deserted stretches where only our captors see me. The entire enterprise is designed to move us while arousing the least possible suspicion.

Throughout the journey, I try to talk with Atiqullah, still blindly hoping he will see us as human beings and quickly agree to a deal. During the first night of the drive, Atiqullah asks us if his guards are treating us well. We lie and say yes, fearing retaliation from Qari if we report his beating of Tahir. Long bouts of silence are interrupted by brief exchanges between Atiqullah and me. Attempting to be cautious, I try not to be cavalier in what I say and offend him.

After journeying all night, the sun rises and we continue driving. Atiqullah and I engage in a seemingly friendly conversation about our families, politics, and religion. We joke, laugh, and discuss life. He tells me the names of his children. I do my best to appease him. When we speak about politics, I say that the United States' dependence on Middle

Eastern oil has warped its foreign policy. When we speak about religion, I try to emphasize the commonalities between Islam and Christianity. I offer to read an English-language Koran if he can find one.

After I describe the book I am writing in an effort to prove I'm a journalist, Atiqullah announces he is taking us to Helmand, where he said we will be released in a few days.

"You will fly home from the British base," he tells me. I do not tell him that I had been on the base three weeks earlier. While researching my book, I had embedded with an American marine unit in northern Helmand Province. The unit arrived for what it thought was a police training mission. Instead, it took far more casualties in Afghanistan than it did in a tour of similar length in Iraq.

As we drive south, I fantasize about seeing the massive American-built hydroelectric dam and irrigation canals of Helmand. I'm getting desperate. I don't want to be the latest in a long line of Americans dating back to Josiah Harlan who experience initial success in Afghanistan, followed by spectacular failure. I tell him I plan to quit journalism if I survive. He encourages me to stay in the profession.

Knowing that Atiqullah is likely to disappear again with little warning, I try to extract promises from him. Under the Pashtunwali code of honor, a promise of protection should be ironclad. I begin by asking him to promise to protect the three of us. Atiqullah responds that he will protect only me.

"I will not kill you," he says. "You will survive."

I insist that he promise to save Tahir and Asad as well. "You will not kill the three of us," I say. "It has to be the three of us."

Atiqullah refuses, and I raise the issue over and over as the drive drags on. At one point, I suggest that he cut off my finger instead of harming Tahir and Asad. He replies that the Taliban are not criminals.

Later that day, he finally promises to protect all three of us. "I give you my promise," he says, as I lie in the back of the station wagon. "I will not kill any of the three of you."

Then he says, "Let's kill Asad first," and laughs. I have no idea what to believe.

On the second night of our drive across rural Afghanistan, we arrive in a darkened village. Its dirt streets are deserted and the cold air suggests we are at high altitude. A spectacular array of stars that is the brightest I have ever seen blazes overhead.

Atiqullah, Tahir, Asad, and the other Taliban get out of the car and go to sleep in a mosque. Under the Taliban's strict interpretation of Islam, I am not allowed in a mosque because I am a *kafir,* or nonbeliever. In the past, moderate Muslims have welcomed me in mosques.

I stay in the car with Akbar, the guard who speaks broken English and brought us food and clothes. Akbar whispers that Atiqullah has told him we will be exchanged within ten to fifteen days. I feel enormous relief. My patience, faith in Atiqullah, and statements about our worth appear to have paid off. Later that night, in another positive sign, I am brought into the mosque. Tahir has convinced the Taliban that it is wrong under Pashtunwali to make a guest sleep in the cold. After spending nearly twenty-four hours straight lying in the back of the car, I am exhausted.

On the third morning of our drive, Tahir's car breaks down. Atiqullah sells it and buys a second station wagon. Tahir is furious but powerless to stop him. During the wait for the new vehicle, Akbar and the guards hold an impromptu machine gun marksmanship competition. Akbar wins.

At dusk, we drive through a barren mountainous area and are met by another Taliban commander. A bone-thin man with a long beard and one arm, he gets into the driver's seat and guides us through barren, rock-strewn territory, steering the car and shifting gears with lightning-quick movements of his one hand.

I will later realize that we are making our way across rural Afghanistan with the help of a network of local Taliban fighters. They escort us from remote district to remote district. As we cross a particularly deserted area with no villages in sight, Atiqullah is so confident of the security vacuum that he allows me to walk outside at dusk. I stretch my legs as he and his men pray. Deserted, dirt-covered mountains surround us in every direction. We have crossed dozens of miles of Afghan government territory. I have not seen any signs of Afghan government or American forces in days.

I knew the vast security vacuum Atiqullah took advantage of was the product of years of American and Afghan government missteps. In 2002 and 2003, early decisions made by officials in Washington severely handicapped the effort to create a strong new Afghan government and national army. And then as Iraq unraveled in 2004 and 2005, Afghanistan was relegated to an afterthought.

A saying I first heard in postwar Bosnia—"Law and order first"—proved true in Afghanistan. Without a basic degree of security, political and economic reforms will all be handicapped. Local corruption as well will stymie reform.

For months in the spring of 2002, Defense Secretary Donald Rumsfeld clashed with Secretary of State Colin Powell over what role American troops should play in Afghanistan. The outcome of the debate was critical. The number of American troops initially deployed—and their marching orders—would set the tone for the international effort for years to come.

In a February 2002 White House meeting, Powell called for American troops to participate in the expansion of a 4,000-soldier international peacekeeping force then patrolling Kabul. In addition to hunting Taliban and Al Qaeda members, the expanded force would patrol Afghanistan's other major cities and enforce the decisions of Karzai's fledgling government.

Powell told me in a 2008 interview that he believed that all other reform efforts would fail in Afghanistan if adequate security was not established. "This would be the number one thing," he said, "You've got to have order in society."

Richard N. Haass, the former director of policy planning at the State Department, told me that informal conversations with European officials led him to believe the United States could recruit a force of 30,000 peacekeepers, half European, half American.

Rumsfeld and his aides were skeptical. Douglas J. Feith, then the Pentagon's undersecretary for policy, told me they feared European countries would not provide enough troops. They also wanted to avoid the

Clinton administration approach of having United Nations officials administer a postconflict country, arguing it would breed passivity and anger in the local population.

"There is a way to do nation building where the UN or someone else takes responsibility out of the hands of the local people and runs the place as a colony," Mr. Feith told me. "We were going against that model."

Feith said Pentagon officials hoped to train Afghan security forces, but not create such a large American troop presence in the country that it stoked what they saw as Afghans' historic resentment of foreigners.

Ali Ahmed Jalali, the country's interior minister from 2002 to 2005, told me in an interview that Afghan resentment of American troops was "a myth." After ten years of internecine civil war fueled by neighboring counties that funneled cash and weapons to each warring faction, he said, Afghans yearned in 2002 for the United States to step in. He said Afghans saw Americans as neutral because they had not strongly backed a side in the bloody civil war as had Pakistan, India, Russia, and Iran.

"They could not help themselves," he argued, referring to Afghans. "They were at war with themselves."

The deadlock dragged on for months.

In the late spring of 2002, Powell's proposal died. "The president, the vice president, the secretary of defense, the national security staff, all of them were skeptical of an ambitious project in Afghanistan," Haass said. "I didn't see support."

Powell said the United States did not make the sweeping commitment needed in Afghanistan. "We never quite bit the bullet that it was going to take all it could," he told me.

President Bush, though, remained skeptical. During the 2000 presidential election, he had said he opposed using U.S. troops for "nation-building." Following the 9/11 attacks and postinvasion chaos in Iraq, his views gradually shifted. He slowly accepted that if the United States toppled a regime it had to help create a new government and security force to fill the ensuing vacuum. By the time the shift in Bush's thinking occurred in Afghanistan, though, it was too late. In the end, the Bush administration deployed 8,000 troops to Afghanistan in 2002, with orders to hunt Taliban and Qaeda members and not to engage in peacekeeping or reconstruction. The 4,000-member international peacekeeping force did not venture beyond Kabul.

As an alternative, the United States and its allies hatched a loosely organized plan for Afghans to secure the country themselves. The United States would train a 70,000-member army. Japan would disarm some 100,000 militia fighters. Britain would mount an antinarcotics program. Italy would carry out reforms in the judiciary. And Germany would train a 62,000-member police force.

But that left no one in overall command. On the ground, holes quickly emerged in the American and European security effort.

The training of a new Afghan army proved difficult. When Robert Finn, the U.S. ambassador, reviewed the first Afghan National Army troops trained by the Americans in the summer of 2002, he was dismayed.

"They were illiterate," Finn told me. "They were at a much lower level than people expected."

American military officials told him that local Afghan commanders sent them their worst conscripts. In 2004, three years after the fall of the Taliban, the new force had only 21,000 soldiers. By comparison the United States had trained five times as many Iraqi soldiers three years after the fall of Baghdad.

The police were even more challenging. Seventy percent of the existing 80,000 officers were illiterate. Eighty percent lacked proper equipment, and corruption was endemic. Afghan police did not patrol. They set up checkpoints and waited for residents to report crimes. Afghans said they had to bribe the police, in fact, simply to report a crime.

Yet Germany, the country responsible for police training, dispatched only forty advisers in 2002 and 2003. They reopened the Kabul police academy and began a program designed to graduate 3,500 senior officers in three years. German officials said developing a core of skilled commanders was the key to reform, frustrating American officials who backed a large, countrywide training effort. Some American and European military units conducted ad hoc, two- to six-week training sessions around the country, but no comprehensive instruction occurred outside Kabul.

James Dobbins, the administration's former special envoy for Afghanistan, said Defense Department hopes that Afghans could quickly take responsibility for their own security proved unrealistic.

"The reason we are there is that these are failed states," said Dobbins, who had also served as special envoy to Haiti, Bosnia, Kosovo, and Somalia. "The thought that this can be quickly remedied has proved unjustified in most cases."

Confusion, infighting, and a failure to grasp the depth of Afghanistan's problems hampered the American reconstruction effort as well. After privately rejecting a large American troop deployment in Afghanistan, Bush publicly announced a vast American reconstruction effort. The move surprised Dobbins, who had lost the fight for more troops. In April 2002, Dobbins received a phone call as he sat in his State Department office. Mr. Bush, he was told, was planning to proclaim America's commitment to rebuild Afghanistan.

"I got a call from the White House speech writers saying they were writing a speech and did I see any reason not to cite the Marshall Plan," Dobbins recalled, referring to the American rebuilding of post–World War II Europe. "I said, 'No, I see no objections,' so they put it in the speech."

On April 17, Bush traveled to the Virginia Military Institute, where General George C. Marshall had trained a century before. In a speech that received scant media attention in the United States but raised hopes in Afghanistan, Bush promised a sweeping reconstruction effort.

"Marshall knew that our military victory against enemies in World War II had to be followed by a moral victory that resulted in better lives for individual human beings," Bush said. He called Marshall's work "a beacon to light the path that we, too, must follow."

Aware that Afghans felt his father's administration had abandoned the country following the 1989 Soviet withdrawal, he vowed to avoid the syndrome of "initial success, followed by long years of floundering and ultimate failure."

"We're not going to repeat that mistake," he said. "We're tough, we're determined, we're relentless. We will stay until the mission is done."

Within hours of Bush's speech, Rumsfeld announced his own approach at a Pentagon news conference. Again, he called for the Afghans to help themselves.

"The last thing you're going to hear from this podium is someone thinking they know how Afghanistan ought to organize itself," Rumsfeld said. "They're going to have to figure it out. They're going to have to grab ahold of that thing and do something. And we're there to help."

At the same time, the American government had nowhere near the personnel needed to carry out such a sweeping reconstruction effort. By 2001, the agency that had spearheaded the Lashkar Gah project decades back had stopped mounting construction projects. USAID officials initially opposed road building and other large infrastructure programs. They said they feared they would consume too much of their agency's limited staff and budget.

The end of the Cold War, complaints from Congress of tax dollars being poured down "foreign rat holes," and the failure of some foreign infrastructure projects prompted massive cuts at USAID. Criticism of failed foreign projects and a drive to privatize aid work by the Reagan and Clinton administrations had shrunk the agency from 3,000 Americans posted abroad in the 1980s to 1,000.

In the fall of 2003, sixteen months after the president's Marshall Plan speech, USAID had seven full-time staffers and thirty-five full-time contract staff members in Afghanistan, most of them Afghans. Sixty-one agency positions were vacant. Slashed in size, USAID had no experts to field.

Overall, from 2001 to 2005, Afghanistan received less assistance per capita than did postconflict Bosnia and Kosovo, or even desperately poor, postcoup Haiti in the 1990s. At the same time, reports began to emerge of endemic corruption in the Karzai government.

The invasion of Iraq only intensified the shortage of troops, civilian experts, and high-level focus. As Washington turned its attention to Baghdad, a massive troop imbalance emerged. In 2003, the United States had 250,000 troops in Iraq and 20,000 in Afghanistan. At the same time, Washington spent half as much money in Afghanistan as it did in Iraq—even though the countries are roughly the same size.

Former CIA officials told me that the agency's best, most experienced officers were shifted from Afghanistan to Iraq in late 2002 and early 2003. That reduced the United States' influence over powerful Afghan warlords who were refusing to turn over to Karzai's weak central gov ernment tens of millions of dollars they had collected in border crossing customs payments. The military's elite special operations units were also diverted to Iraq, along with remotely piloted drones.

"We were economizing in Afghanistan," a former military official, who spoke on condition of anonymity, told one of my colleagues in 2007. "Anyone who tells you differently is blowing smoke."

With a growing insurgency overstretching American forces in Iraq in 2005, Bush further reduced the American commitment in Afghanistan. He asked European officials to have NATO forces take over responsibility for securing southern Afghanistan. Condoleezza Rice, then secretary of state, cut American assistance to Afghanistan by $200 million.

The president and other senior officials saw Afghanistan as a success. They cited improvements in health care, roads, education, and the economy, as well as the quality of life in the cities and the holding of parliamentary elections. President Bush saw President Karzai as a more skilled leader than critics contended and saw no Afghan leader who could replace him. Reports of corruption by Karzai's brother surfaced, but no evidence emerged of Karzai's personal involvement

The then American ambassador in Kabul, Ronald Neumann, bluntly demanded that the $200 million in funding be restored and warned of a Taliban resurgence. In a February 2006 cable to his superiors, he predicted that the cut would handicap U.S. counter-narcotics programs, slow the training of the Afghan army, and make the "Taliban's role easier."

Neumann's warnings fell on deaf ears in Washington. President Bush and his top aides left Afghanistan to European troops and reduced aid levels. Troops from Britain—the historic enemy of the Pashtuns—led the NATO takeover of security in Helmand. Rumors that the West wanted to occupy Afghanistan, not rebuild it, gained credence among Afghans.

In the spring of 2006, the Taliban carried out their largest offensive since 2001. Suicide bombings quintupled to 136, roadside bombings doubled, and Taliban fighters seized control of large parts of southern

Afghanistan. NATO forces—many of whom were barred from engaging in combat by their government—were overmatched. American and NATO casualties rose by 20 percent. For the first time it became nearly as dangerous, statistically, to serve as an American soldier in Afghanistan as in Iraq.

In southern Afghanistan, many rural Pashtuns took up arms against corrupt officials appointed by the Karzai government and joined the Taliban. In eastern Afghanistan, the Taliban mounted cross-border attacks from Pakistan, the United States' purported ally.

As the Taliban confidently ferried us across the Afghan countryside in November 2008, it confirmed what I already knew. The haphazard, eight-year American effort in Afghanistan was a failure.

At sunset, the car stops and Atiqullah announces that we will have to hike through the mountains. A large American base blocks the path in front of us, he says. We protest, but he insists that we must walk. He promises that he will carry me on his back if I am unable to complete the journey.

The Afghan sandals I have been wearing since we were kidnapped will not be strong enough for a trek. The one-armed commander gives me a pair of worn loafers with the words "Made in East Germany" printed on the insole. A guard gives me his jacket.

As we walk, I understand why Western journalists grew enamored of anti-Soviet Afghan resistance fighters in the 1980s. Under a spectacular panorama of stars, we wind our way along a steep mountain pass. Emaciated Taliban fighters carry heavy machine guns with little sign of fatigue. Their grit and resilience seem boundless. I think about making a run for it but have not been able to freely talk with Tahir and Asad. If I run without warning, all three of us could be shot.

As the hike continues, I grow skeptical of Atiqullah's boasts. The man who has promised to carry me if needed proves to be in poor shape. On one of the steepest parts of the ascent, he stops, sits on a rock, and pants for air. Until now, I have only seen him seated on the floor or behind the wheel of a car. As we hike through the mountains, I see that Atiqullah is chubby, fat even, and does not have the same strength as his men.

Nine hours after we set out, the sun rises and the hike drags on. We are walking through low hills covered by orange dirt, an Afghan version of scrub brush, and the occasional tree. The landscape is lifeless. At dawn, we silently pass through a village and our guards ready their weapons for any problems. No one emerges from the houses.

Asad approaches me when the guards lag behind, points at the way ahead and whispers "Miran Shah." Miran Shah is the capital and largest town in North Waziristan, a Taliban and Al Qaeda stronghold in Pakistan's tribal areas. North Waziristan is the home of some of the Taliban's most hard-line members. If we are headed there, we are doomed.

Inside Afghanistan, the American military and Afghan government can carry out raids and put other pressure on our captors. In Pakistan's tribal areas, the Afghan Taliban have free rein. No American combat troops are present, the Pakistani government opposes American raids, and the Pakistani army turns a blind eye to the Afghan Taliban. In Pakistan, our captors can hold us as long as they please.

After eleven hours, our hike finally ends. The guards light a fire, and we warm our hands as we wait for a vehicle to pick us up. For a brief moment, there is camaraderie. We are all bone tired and happily crouch around the warm flames.

I stand up for a moment and walk back and forth to stretch my aching legs. I notice that none of the guards have their Kalashnikov assault rifles at their sides. Instead, one lies on the ground near Asad and another lies near where I am walking. If I move fast enough, I can grab a rifle, signal to Asad to do the same and we can kill Atiqullah and the guards.

As I walk back and forth, I glance at the rifle's safety mechanism but try not to draw attention to myself. I fired rifles while hunting for deer with my father as a teenager and fired them at ranges with my uncle in Colorado as a college student. I am not sure, though, how to disable a Kalashnikov's safety and shoot rounds. The stakes are enormous. Grabbing the weapon could lead to all three of us being immediately shot.

I look at Tahir and Asad and cannot catch their eyes. At the same time, I am not sure I am ready to kill anyone—something I have never done before. I decide to wait. I don't want to risk Tahir and Asad's lives without a clear signal from them.

Roughly fifteen seconds later, Atiqullah notices the situation and angrily orders his men to pick up their rifles. Later, I see that several guards are also standing watch on a nearby hillside. For months, I will think of the moment and wonder what would have happened if I had grabbed the rifle. On many days, I will wish that I had picked up the gun.

The one-handed commander arrives in the same station wagon. Atiqullah tells us that he has pretended to be a civilian and driven past the American base. We climb into the vehicle. Exhausted and anxious, I tell myself that Asad is wrong and Atiqullah is right. I tell myself that we are heading into southern Afghanistan, not Pakistan. I tell myself we will survive.

CRASH COURSE

My mother comes back to New York with me. For the next seven months, we become intermittent roommates, a fact that in turns disturbs and comforts me. I haven't lived with my parents since I was a teenager. Now I'm married, approaching forty, and not eager to revert to an adolescent's existence. But over the months, our relationship grows. In fact, we relate to each other on a more mature level. She becomes, in the end, my hero—and David's, by a strange twist of circumstance.

We are met at Penn Station by two FBI agents. Cathy is tall, blonde, chatty. John is a large, solid man. An unfortunate incident years earlier involving a child captive and a grenade has left him deaf in one ear. Both are middle-aged. Cathy has two children. Dressed in high-heel pumps and stylishly coiffed, she looks like the consummate Manhattan career woman. One would never suspect she is a federal law enforcement agent.

They escort me to *The New York Times* building, an imposing glass skyscraper that fills a solid block on the edges of Times Square, right in the middle of Manhattan. An impromptu meeting has been called by the newspaper's executive editor, Bill Keller. In the bright, modern lobby, hundreds of miniature screens telegraph type from the newspaper's daily stories. Trees are encased in a glass courtyard opposite the reception desk. Security guards wave us through the sleek turnstiles to the elevator bank.

On the eighteenth floor, I am greeted by Arthur Sulzberger, Jr., the paper's publisher, and escorted into a large interior conference room. Senior staff members are assembled, including David's editors in the investigations unit, the foreign editor who occasionally sends him overseas, the newsroom's administrative editor, and its assistant general counsel, David McCraw. McCraw will become a daily fixture in my life for the next seven and a half months and the point person between me, the newspaper, and security experts. David's brother Lee is on speakerphone.

Everyone in the room appears to be seasoned and serious. I feel like I've stepped into a *New Yorker* cartoon but I'm not quite sure of the punch line. David has worked at the paper for twelve years. Most of his colleagues have known him longer than I have. I am overwhelmed by the number of people already involved in his case, and by the visible display of emotion before me. Several of his colleagues have tears in their eyes. Bill Keller calmly tells me that our family has the full support of *The New York Times* staff and that the paper will work with us to secure David's release. They will honor our family's wish to keep David's case out of the press. Lee and I have agreed this is the best course of action at the moment. We think, as the FBI cautioned us, that publicity will only increase David's value as a hostage. And we know that David would not want to be the subject of a news story.

Rejecting my first impulse to crawl under the conference table, I resolve not to be visibly intimidated or upset. There is already enough to handle without the paper having the sense that they need to manage my emotions as well. I want to know as much as possible about my husband's circumstances. So I maintain a tough front. I also feel that if I fall apart, the Taliban will win this crude game of psychological warfare. Falling apart is not an option, philosophically or practically. It is not quite clear how we will work with the newspaper to resolve David's situation or how decisions will be made. I have vague concerns that our agendas could diverge at some point. But for now, I am grateful not to be in this alone.

Cathy and John start preparing me for potential contact with David's captors. Back in my apartment downtown, we begin my first training session.

It is nearly 9 p.m. and I have not been in touch with my office all day. I imagine how *Cosmopolitan* might present this situation, were they to run a dramatic first-person account: "When Danger Calls" or "What's Holding Your Husband Captive?" But this is not a situation one can dress up with a provocative cover line.

In the event that I receive a call, the objective is to keep the captor or captive on the phone as long as possible, in the hope that the call can be traced. If the government can track the call, the military has a chance of going in and rescuing my husband, or so I'm told. That is, if he is still in Afghanistan. There is now some speculation that his captors will move him over the border, into the tribal areas of Pakistan where it is easier for the Taliban to hide and the American military cannot carry out a raid.

I am slightly amused by the "high tech" recording device that is attached to my phone. It looks like the Sony Walkman I jogged with in junior high school.

I learn the key points:

Ask if there is anything the captors or their "guests" require.
Humanize David by stating that you love him, miss him, etc.
Do not make any promises, but let the captors know you will try to
    work to meet their demands.
Avoid setting deadlines, but try to get them to commit to a time to
    talk again, ideally on a regular basis.
Repeat what the captors say to indicate that you are listening and
    also to extend the length of the call.
Be deferential. Do not tell them to bug off or get angry with them.
Ask if the captors can put David on the phone. (It's unlikely they
    would call with him in tow, but it never hurts to ask.)
Keep in mind, the Taliban are religious, "holy warriors."
Mention that you are praying for your husband.
Appeal to their sense of honor.

Cathy assumes the roll of the kidnapper and we rehearse potential phone interactions for about an hour. We work off several scripts, mock conversations. The dialogue has been typed in capital letters and covers many of the talking points we discussed. We spread these out on the floor in front of the sofa. A tall, fair-haired New Yorker, Cathy looks and sounds nothing like a Taliban insurgent, so I hope I will be able to keep as calm when confronted with the real deal.

Cathy forewarns me about the following: "If the captors threaten to chop off a finger or kill David on the spot, don't believe them. Stay strong. Chances are slim that they will actually do this. Remember, their goal is not to kill David, but to extort money from you. They will play on your emotions to do so. Chances are, David is worth more to them alive than dead. Under the traditional tribal honor code of Pashtunwali—and out of sheer greed—they will treat him well and keep him alive."

Over time I will come to realize that kidnapping is a global industry. It is as much a business for the consultants as it is for the kidnappers, due in part to U.S. policy on the kidnapping of American citizens. The U.S. government does not pay ransom, release prisoners, or negotiate with terrorists. Yet many of its officials, off the record, advise private citizens to do so. This creates a demand for services that is often fulfilled by contractors. I have taken my first steps into a large and complicated shadow world of public and private agencies devoted to aiding the families of kidnap victims. It can be an extremely lucrative business; whether it is also an effective one, as far as David is concerned, remains to be seen.

The FBI is the lead agency in kidnappings and proves quite helpful in facilitating my understanding of how the situation and negotiations might unfold. Yet they cannot advise on funds, carry them, directly negotiate, or disclose classified information. They cannot declassify information that has been classified by another government agency. They are not even involved in securing the victim's release. In fact, they are only gathering information in hopes of prosecuting this crime in the future.

Over time our family becomes frustrated with the one-way flow of information. We often feel we're helping the FBI a great deal more than they're helping us, and we need someone dedicated to our goal, on our side. For these reasons, the paper along with Lee and I soon decide to hire an outside security firm to conduct negotiations.

I am suddenly thrust into an atmosphere of intrigue that is both political and personal. This is a sharp contrast to my daily life at the magazine, and to my entire world before November 10. My objective is to do everything possible to keep David alive, to leave no stone unturned in this process, and to stay sane and healthy.

Lee and I meet regularly with U.S. government officials, Pakistani officials, security contractors, and private advisers. I develop love-hate relationships with all of them. I eventually form a solid camaraderie with three people: my brother-in-law, the legal counsel for *The New York Times*, and one other individual, who is operating from overseas—a well-connected Irish national who tries to help via his own network in Pakistan.

As Cathy and John depart and my training comes to an end, I reflect on the long day behind me. I have embarked on a journey through uncertainty, intrigue, and duplicity. It will challenge all my previous understanding of what faith, love, and commitment mean. I think about David. My husband is a strong-willed, patient individual. Slow and steady wins the race is a phrase he often iterates. It is a philosophy of sorts. I am also comforted by the fact that David is most likely the sharpest person in the room, possessing a rare understanding of Afghan culture as well as human nature. And he is a cat with nine lives. I know he will do all he can to keep himself and his fellow captives alive. I know he wants to come home. This is my greatest hope.

Five days have passed since I first heard about the kidnapping, and I've made it through the initial shock. I am now on a steady incline—a steep learning curve. Everything seems beyond my control. I feel the need to gather as much information as possible to have some sense of David's experience and understanding of the region.

David gave me the password to his e-mail account during a recent conversation from Afghanistan before he vanished. He does this periodically, when Internet access is limited, so I can check his account for important e-mails and relay information to him over the phone.

I log in to his e-mail account from my laptop while sitting on the couch.

My sense of boundaries, privacy, and personal space are outweighed by the need to figure out what to do. I hope to find some clue about his situation. I look through the most recent e-mails for anything pertaining to Afghanistan or Logar Province, the site of the fateful interview. I am loosely familiar with some of David's sources. I search for names of people known to be in the region at present and for whom he has expressed trust in the past.

I write to Marin Strmecki, an Afghanistan expert and former adviser to the Bush administration who also has contacts in the Afghan government. I e-mail the Pakistani journalist and Taliban expert Ahmed Rashid, whom I met with David on a trip to Pakistan in March 2008. He has written several books about Afghanistan and Pakistan, including *Taliban* and *Descent into Chaos*. He is moved by our situation and provides his personal assessment of what, perhaps, the motivation of the kidnappers might be. He advises me to keep the case out of the public eye for the moment. He does not think the Taliban will succumb to moral pressure—the argument that holding a journalist is wrong—and he warns that David could become a political pawn or bargaining chip if his case receives media attention.

David's colleagues at the paper are tremendously supportive. Michael Moss, a friend of David's and fellow reporter in the paper's investigations unit, is monitoring David's biography on Wikipedia. He edits out any reference to his recent abduction. He also adds a section about David's coverage of Guantánamo Bay prisoners and stories on injustices in the Muslim world, in the hope that it will prove to the Taliban that David is a fair and impartial journalist, motivated to tell all sides of the story. Much to our dismay, someone in cyberspace keeps trying to reedit the page to inform readers of David's kidnapping.

David's editors and I begin reaching out to international advocacy groups to get their advice on whether to take the case public or keep it quiet. People from the Committee to Protect Journalists, Reporters without Borders, and Human Rights Watch brief us on situations with other journalists who were recently detained around the world. In most cases where the journalist has been held by a government or entity that is concerned with saving face, a public campaign has expedited the process of release. This was true for Alan Johnston, the BBC correspondent who was captured by a small militant group known as the Army of Islam in Gaza in 2007. In his case, Hamas put pressure on the Army of Islam to release him. His family and the BBC waged a global campaign for his release. He was freed four months later. But it appears that in cases where captives are being held by extremists with no direct link to a specific government, remaining private has proven more successful over time. This was true in the recent case of the Canadian journalist Melissa Fung, who was kidnapped in Afghanistan earlier this year. Her employer, CBC, requested a press blackout while negotiations were being conducted for fear that media attention would complicate matters or endanger her life. She was released on November 8—two days before David's abduction—after Afghan intelligence officials detained the kidnapper's mother.

One of David's colleagues, a reporter in Kabul, expresses a strong desire to go public. We speak nightly on Skype. This, the reporter says, is what they would want if they were in David's position. I have tremendous respect for this journalist, who is well versed in the nuances of Afghan culture. The reporter feels making the case public will pressure the Taliban to release David. The reporter tells me that most Afghans trust journalists and that recently Mullah Omar has declared that the Taliban should refrain from kidnapping journalists. The reporter thinks making a public campaign would speed David's release. That said, the FBI and government officials believe it is difficult to gauge if, or how, the Taliban will react to public pressure. Even though we disagree, David's colleague and I remain in close touch over the next few weeks because the bureau remains the point of contact for any initial communication from David's captors.

The day-to-day tasks and sense of responsibility inherent in managing the kidnapping are overwhelming, and despite many opinions offered, isolating as well. I am desperate to find someone who has navigated this emotional terrain. I immediately think of Mariane Pearl, the wife of Daniel Pearl, the *Wall Street Journal* reporter who was abducted and killed by militants in Pakistan after 9/11. No one around me will actually say it, but everyone fears a repeat of the Daniel Pearl murder.

A copy of Mariane's book about her husband, *A Mighty Heart*, stares back at me from a bookshelf in my apartment. After days of resisting, I finally pick up the book and flip through the pages. The very last line is a quote from a story my husband wrote after visiting the site of Daniel Pearl's imprisonment and execution in Pakistan. It is taken from his news account of the July 4, 2003, attack on a Shiite mosque in Quetta, led by the terrorist group Lashkar-e-Jhangvi, in which forty-eight worshippers were killed or mortally wounded. "Saying nothing, looking 'very relaxed' walking 'here and there' in the words of witnesses, the three unidentified gunmen killed and killed and killed here on Friday afternoon."

I take it as a sign to contact Mariane.

We speak over the phone.

Calm and straightforward, Mariane immediately tries to console me. She's heard about David's case through the grapevine and emphasizes that it is very different from Danny's.

"There were never any demands for Danny. We always thought it would be an act of terrorism." At this point, most people assume David's captors will want money or prisoners, because the captors have not gone public.

"Everyone will tell you not to go to Kabul. This is a personal decision." With this and all other decisions to be made, she tells me to follow my gut.

The newspaper provides me with contact information for Jere Van Dyk, an American journalist who was kidnapped in Afghanistan last year and held in the tribal areas for forty-five days. He has been free for six months. I hope to learn something from his experience: how he was treated by his captors; how he stayed alive; how he was released. I want to know as much as possible, regardless of unpleasantness and disturbing details. It is better to know what is within the realm of expectation than to be surprised and horrified later.

Two days after my FBI training session, I meet with Jere at his office on a Saturday afternoon. I am a bit anxious, not knowing who or what to expect. He is waiting in front of the building when I arrive. To my surprise and relief, I recognize him immediately. I had met him at an Afghan charity's fund-raiser several months before with David. Though still shaken from his experience, he is quite lucid in his account of events.

Kind and brave, he sets aside his own discomfort in retelling his experience to help me reach a better understanding of what might be happening to David.

Jere was set up by an Afghan colleague, a friend of twenty years who arranged his interviews and served as a translator. He tells me not to rule out the possibility that one or both of David's fellow captives were complicit in the kidnapping. If they are not involved, he tells me to expect that the captors will threaten to harm or kill them to pressure our family and David. As Afghans working with a foreign journalist, they are viewed as traitors and as such are in greater danger than David. I have never met the two men being held with David. To the best of my knowledge, this is the first time David is working with them.

Jere assures me that David will be treated well. "They won't hurt him physically," he says, invoking Pashtunwali, the honor code under which the Taliban must treat prisoners as guests.

"But," he warns, "the Afghans are master actors and manipulators." He assures me they will seize every opportunity to rile us up in hopes of eliciting an emotional response. He is very forthcoming about his own experience. I ask him not to hold back.

He confides that during his captivity he was psychologically traumatized as he confronted his own mortality daily. He feared he would be beheaded. His captors joked that they would sell his body parts on the black market if his family and colleagues failed to pay for his release. He was also told that upon his release, a suicide bomber would be present to detonate, killing everyone.

"I guarantee David is thinking about you all the time," he tells me. "This will keep him going." He says he invented a wife for himself during his captivity, because the Afghans would find it strange that a middle-aged man was not married.

He tells me that David is also probably thinking about escaping—something he thought about constantly. He advises me not to go public and not to use force to get David out, because it is too dangerous.

He does not know who it was that orchestrated his own release, but tells me there is a man who worked on his case, an Irish national who lives in the region named Michael Semple. Several people involved in his own case, Jere says, have told him that Michael saved his life. I have already heard about Michael Semple from David and his colleagues at the newspaper. He is a former European Union and United Nations official who was banned from Afghanistan by the current Afghan Karzai government for trying to negotiate with the Taliban. He believes there are moderate Afghans and Taliban—and that maintaining communication is essential. Michael has been working in Pakistan and Afghanistan for twenty-five years and is fluent in several local dialects. Irish by birth, he is Muslim and now resides in Pakistan.

Michael is also someone the newspaper has used as an analyst. The Kabul bureau turned to him for advice soon after David's abduction. He has provided his assessment of how our dilemma might play out and has analyzed at great and rather eloquent length the depth of our predicament based on his experience working to resolve other kidnappings. The Kabul bureau has forwarded these written accounts to me.

Jere provides me with Michael's personal e-mail and a suggestion of what to write to make my introduction.

Soon after I write to Michael, I receive his response:

> Dear Kristen,
> Thanks for your note. I hope that you are bearing up in this difficult time. David's experience is both depressingly and reassuringly familiar. I am sure that there was much Jere could share with you.
> Inshallah, it will pass.
> Many friends are bringing all their influence to bear to ensure that David and colleagues get home soon.
> Regards
>
> Michael

While his response is ambiguous, he is prompt in his reply. I decide to try to stay in regular contact with him. I feel his counsel will prove to be beneficial.

On my walk home toward the subway, I receive a call from a colleague at *Cosmo*. There is a celebrity cover shoot tomorrow and she is calling to make sure all the details are in place: catering, lighting equipment, car service. It is quite a shift, but a welcome one, from the conversation of the past few hours. There is always a sense of emergency and importance around these shoots, which are orchestrated with the thought of preventing catastrophe. A celebrity no-show, a controlling publicist, a stubborn hairstylist, insufficient catering—these are the things that instill panic in my other world.

David has been held captive for nearly a week.

An individual who calls himself "Atiqullah" has been contacting the Kabul bureau of *The New York Times*. He claims to be holding David and company. I learn that the two men taken hostage with David are Tahir, an Afghan journalist, and Asad, their driver. Tahir is married with two wives and seven children. Asad is married with two kids.

After spending the weekend with his family, David's brother Lee has returned to New York.

To keep us occupied and optimistic, the Kabul office and the FBI suggest that Lee and I compose a list of proof of life questions (POL), for David. They think another call will be forthcoming and want to ascertain whether the individual on the line does indeed have possession of David, Tahir, and Asad and that they are still alive.

This proves to be an arduous but somewhat amusing task. The gap between our culture and that of the captors comes into focus. Our team suggests that we compose questions that will elicit positive feelings from David without offending his handlers. They suggest "What is the name of your first pet?" Lee points out that their first pet was named Scotch, as in "Scotch and soda." This is not going to work. The Taliban have banned alcohol. The same is true for music, so references to the first song we danced to at our wedding is also discouraged. I am advised against mentioning anything related to our courtship—first kiss, first date—for fear I will seem like a loose woman.

Finally, we settle on "What is the name of your best friend's daughter who was the flower girl at your wedding?" "What is your wife's maiden name?" And "What is your wife's birthday?"

The POL questions are relayed to Chris Chivers, an intrepid reporter and longtime friend of David's who has been answering the regular calls from David's captor Atiqullah. He then sends us written transcripts of each call along with bits of information he and his colleagues discover in their local outreaches. He relays the contents of the latest phone conversation and answers to our POL questions over a conference call with me and Lee.

According to the Taliban, David claims my last name is Lohan—as in "Lindsay Lohan." There is no proper translation of the name Mulvihill, apparently. I do not know if the Taliban are joking around or if David is protecting my anonymity. Perhaps all Irish American names sound the same in Pashto.

The answer to the best friend's daughter question comes back as "David does not have a daughter." True, David does not have a daughter. But his friend does, and they have neglected to provide her name. We make note of this for the next round: names do not translate.

The birth date they provide for me is correct. This is somewhat of a relief, but not enough to assuage my fears as I worry this information could easily be found on the Internet.

Fortunately, David provides a statement that puts me at ease: "Tell my wife that life is better here than when we were on a farm in India."

I am immediately transported back to our honeymoon in Rajasthan, one month ago. The first thing I recall is the birds, their insistent chant. We lived with three pigeons that were in a perpetual state of agitation. They flew through the halls every time we moved between rooms. In the otherwise idyllic desert setting—the rolling hills of Rajasthan, the blooming roses—the wildlife was very aggressive. Atomic geckos jumped from window frames. Bugs worthy of *National Geographic* close-ups emerged at night when we donned our headlamps: walking sticks, damselflies, beetles. Some kind of creature howled—I assumed it was a wolf, but David brushed it off as a stray dog. The housekeeper clarified it for us when we inquired about the strange noise, "Ah, yes. The jackals." We joked that this was the least romantic honeymoon ever.

We neglected to gather a few details prior to our visit, namely that temperatures were unusually high that month. With temperatures soaring above 100 degrees, we relied on a generator to cool the place in the late afternoon and slept outdoors on the roof when it was impossibly hot. It was quite beautiful. We had a makeshift four-poster bed, completely encased in mosquito netting. Mornings we would awake to the sound of singing birds—and the errant pigeons, clearly annoyed by our presence. Their song was quite distinctive. It sounded like they were chanting something . . . a protest. Superstitious, I spent days trying to decode it.

"Listen to the birds," I said over breakfast one morning. "It sounds like they are saying, 'Let's all escape, let's all escape!'"

"Wow, are you that miserable here?" David asked.

"No, but listen to them. They're saying 'Let's all escape'—hear it? They have British accents," I jokingly insisted.

He looked at me like I was slightly crazed—of course, due to the sweltering temperature I could claim heatstroke.

"Maybe they are a reincarnation from the colonial era," I mused, referring to the British occupation during the Raj. He smiled and laughed reluctantly. He had to admit, it did sound that way. I hoped it was not some premonition of trouble ahead.

David and I lived in a large expanse of rooms at the house, while the staff all slept in one room. The farm had an on-site groundskeeper, a cook, a sweeper, and a gardener. All this would cost a fortune elsewhere, but in India it was a matter of a few dollars a day. According to societal norms, we were supposed to ignore them and go about our business. We lacked the ability and desire to do so.

"Life is better than when we were on a farm in India." I think about the intent behind David's statement. The farm did have a generator and an in-house cook. It was quite large, with modern plumbing and a green yard, which was a stark contrast to the rugged desert terrain. I take this to mean David is being fed and taken care of and that, perhaps, he is sitting in a home with electricity. The reference to "better than India" makes me think that he may indeed have been moved to a location beyond Afghanistan—perhaps Pakistan. I think he may be playing on the old rivalry between India and Pakistan. Telling his captors Pakistan is better than India would be a smart move, and I would not put it past David to realize this. Still, I am terrified by the thought that he has been moved into Pakistan.

David took me along for a brief trip to Lahore, Pakistan, in the spring of 2008 just after he had finished reporting on the country's presidential election, after Benazir Bhutto's assassination. It was my first and last visit there. "The cultural center of Pakistan." This is how David referred to Lahore, known for its poets, artisans, and parks.

We drove into the city on a March day to discover that a twin suicide bomb attack had killed four people at Pakistan's Navy War College in the center of the city hours before our arrival. We stayed at the Pearl Continental in a room in the back, away from the parking lot and car entrance as David had requested as a security precaution. We never went anywhere during our three-day stay without our driver close by. And we never lingered anywhere for very long.

The air in Lahore was thick and smoky, burnt. I was never certain of the source: coal, exhaust?

We spent a day with Ahmed Rashid and his wife and later toured a modern, American-style university and the National College of Arts. The students all spoke English and were inquisitive, friendly, and eager to talk to us. On our drive to Badshahi Mosque, a main tourist attraction, women in transit appeared curious and tried to make contact with me. Many of them would lift their veils and smile from the backs of motorbikes. Whole families of five rode on one bike—the babies relegated to the handlebars or their mothers' laps. Occasionally, they would stare quizzically at my Western uniform of jeans, a khaki jacket, and a loosely tied headscarf.

As I try to understand the circumstances around David's kidnapping, I am thankful to have had this experience. For me, it reinforces the reality that there are decent, moderate people in Pakistan and that they, more than anyone, are victims of violence and unrest brought on by a few extreme individuals who seek to limit their freedoms. I am terrified at the thought that David has been transported into the tribal areas of Pakistan. The recent calls to the Kabul bureau have been traced to this area.

I know that unlike Lahore, it is a lawless region, one in which the United States has no jurisdiction or ground presence.

The same day as the proof of life questions are relayed, we receive word from the captors that David has told them he is worth $10 million. Lee raises an eyebrow at this. "Oh, really," he says. They also want ten prisoners released from U.S. custody in Bagram and Guantánamo Bay, Cuba, in exchange for David's freedom and that of Tahir and Asad. They claim that when David was being imprisoned in Bosnia several Serbian military officers were released from custody in the negotiations to free him. This is a complete fabrication, and these are demands we know we can never meet.

We are advised by the FBI that over time and with regular communications, the demands should drop and shift from money and prisoners to a strictly financial transaction.

There is speculation that the group holding David is part of the Haqqani network, a terrorist faction of the Taliban that have been linked to Bin Laden and Al Qaeda. They are able to operate in Afghanistan, Pakistan, and the tribal areas. In recent months, they have taken responsibility for the January 2008 bombing of the Serena Hotel in Kabul. The Kabul bureau has been trying to make contact with Abu Tayyeb, the Taliban commander that David planned to interview. They, along with members of the FBI, now think Atiqullah and Abu Tayyeb are one and the same, as their voices and accents are strikingly similar. And they also believe that David and his colleagues were set up. They think Abu Tayyeb may have handed David over to the Haqqani network, or that he is working on their behalf.

The mention of prisoners reinforces our belief that David's case should remain private. Publicity, we feel, will only increase his political value. We fear more than anything that he will become a public relations pawn or be used by the Taliban as an example of the power they hold in the region.

A day after the Taliban's demands are relayed, Lee and I are contacted by the Department of Defense through the FBI's New York office. Officials there are once again asking whether our family will give approval for a raid if the military is able to locate David, Tahir, and Asad and feels confident it can get them out alive.

At this point, Lee and I are willing to grant them permission. But we do not want to make the decision without talking to David's parents, knowing that the risk involved could be great.

From the seventeenth floor office at the *Times* that has now been assigned to us for our regular visits to the newspaper, we set up a conference call with David's parents, Harvey and Carol. We explain our current understanding of the situation. There is a pause, then Harvey speaks. "I am very confident that you are both doing everything possible to secure David's release and have his best interest at heart," David's father says. "You do not need to ask me for approval going forward. I trust you will do what is best. You have my full support in making whatever decisions you see fit."

David's mother agrees.

For the first time in days, I feel tears well up. As a new wife, having the endorsement of David's parents means a lot. I am thankful for their support and trust. And it is a relief not to bear the burden of this decision alone.

Lee and I tell the FBI and DOD that if a raid is feasible, our family supports it.

THE EMIRATE

David, November 18, 2008

A young Taliban driver with shoulder-length hair gets behind the wheel of the vehicle. Glancing at me suspiciously in the rearview mirror, he starts the engine and begins driving down the left-hand side of the road. It is some sort of prank, I hope, some jihadi version of chicken—the game where two drivers speed toward each other in the same lane until one loses his nerve. If he's not playing a game, which lane he drives down shows what country we are in. If he continues driving on the left, we have crossed into Pakistan. If he drives on the right, we are still in Afghanistan.

A mile down the road, a traffic sign appears in Urdu, the official language of Pakistan.

We're in Pakistan, I think to myself. We're dead.

Instead of taking us to Helmand as he promised, Atiqullah has brought us to Pakistan's tribal areas, an infamous belt of Taliban-controlled territory. In the months ahead, I will learn that the fundamentalist Taliban state the United States purportedly toppled in 2001 is alive and thriving. The loss of thousands of Afghan, Pakistani, and American lives and billions in American aid has merely moved the Islamic emirate a few miles east into Pakistan, not eliminated it.

During the 1980s, the American, Saudi, and Pakistani governments used the tribal areas as a base to train hard-line Islamic guerrillas and launch cross-border raids on Soviet forces in Afghanistan. Thirty years later, the area's roughly 3 million people are isolated, impoverished, and dominated by religious conservatives—and form a perfect base for the Taliban and Al Qaeda.

Through seven years of reporting in the region, I have pitied captives imprisoned here. It is arguably the worst place on earth for an American to be a hostage. The United States government has virtually no influence and is utterly despised. Since 2004, dozens of missiles fired by American drones have killed hundreds of militants and civilians. The Taliban have held Afghan, Pakistani, and foreign hostages in the area for years, seemingly immune to outside pressure.

"We're in Pakistan," I say out loud in the car, venting my anger.

Atiqullah, our kidnapper, laughs, and the driver appears surprised.

"How does he know it's Pakistan?" the driver asks.

"Because you're driving down the left-hand side of the road," I answer.

"How do you know that?" the driver asks, immediately suspicious. "When were you in Pakistan before?"

Atiqullah smiles and appears amused by the conversation. He knows from our conversations and my passport that I have been to Pakistan many times on reporting trips. For years, I have watched the Pakistani government largely stand by as the Taliban murder hundreds of tribal elders and seize control of the area. An abstract foreign policy issue is now deeply personal. When my wife and family learn that I am in the tribal areas, their distress will increase exponentially. They will not expect me to return.

The mountainous area that spans the border represents the gravest single security threat the United States faces. Seven years after being driven from Afghanistan, the Taliban and Al Qaeda have reestablished their training camps in the area. Terrorism experts I have interviewed predict that the next major terrorist attack on the United States will come from the tribal areas of Pakistan.

We arrive in a large town, and I notice a sign that says "Wana" in English. Wana is the capital of South Waziristan, the most radical of the seven administrative districts that make up the tribal areas. Its most powerful Taliban commander is Baitullah Mehsud, a widely feared Pakistani militant blamed for the assassination of Benazir Bhutto and a wave of suicide bombings that killed or wounded an estimated 5,000 Pakistanis over the last year.

We stop in the main bazaar, and I am left alone in the car with the young driver. Desperate rationalizations swirl through my mind. Our captors want a ransom and prisoners. Killing us gets them nothing. The three of us will survive. These are all delusions, of course. Simply getting us this far is an enormous victory for the Taliban. We could be held here for months or killed.

Outside the car, dozens of Pakistani tribesmen and Afghan and foreign militants mill around. Each carries a Kalashnikov assault rifle on his shoulder. Some wear thick black turbans or white prayer caps on their heads. Others wear camouflage jackets. All appear grim faced and menacing. A man with a large turban stops, peers at me in the backseat, and asks the driver a question in Pashto. The driver looks at me and says a sentence that I think includes the word for martyr. I tell myself the driver has said I am on my way to heaven.

Atiqullah gets back into the car and I feel relief for no rational reason. He has kidnapped us, but more and more I desperately view Atiqullah as my protector, the man who will continue to treat us well as other militants call for our heads.

As we drive deeper into the tribal areas, we enter a region that has been battered and neglected by the Pakistani government—and the world—for centuries. A backwater roughly the size of Massachusetts, the tribal areas are dominated by Pashtun tribes known for their independence, criminality, and fighting skills. Afghan, British, and Pakistani forces have all failed to gain firm control of the area. For centuries, bandits, smugglers, and kidnap rings have used it as a base.

The tribes that inhabit the Pakistani side of the Afghanistan-Pakistan border region are the most independent of the Pashtun belt. In Afghanistan, the Pashtun tribes have generally accepted the writ of the national government, in large part because they played a large role in choosing it. For Pashtuns, the term "Afghan" is a synonym for the word "Pashtun." Tajiks and other ethnic groups that inhabit northern and western Afghanistan, in turn, view "Afghan" as a broad term applying to all inhabitants of president-day Afghanistan.

On the Pakistani side of the border, the Pashtuns have long been alienated from the national government and neglected by it. Pashtuns complain that Punjabis, who are the country's largest group and make up 45 percent of the population, dominate Pakistan's national government. Pashtuns are Pakistan's second largest ethnic group and represent 15 percent of Pakistan's people.

The true origins of the Pashtuns are a mystery. They are one of the least studied ethnic groups in the world and follow an oral tradition in which history is passed from generation to generation in folktales and sayings. According to Pashtuns, all tribes trace their lineage back to a single man, Qais Abdur Rashid, who traveled from present-day Afghanistan to seventh-century Arabia, met the prophet Muhammad, and converted to Islam. The names of his descendants are reflected in the names of Pashtun tribes, with "Ahmedzai," for example, meaning "sons of Ahmed" and "Yusufzai" meaning "sons of Yusuf."

Researchers believe that the present-day Pashtun tribal structure goes back thousands of years. For millennia, Pashtun elders ruled tribes. Elders are expected to be well spoken, generous, and brave, and are selected on the basis of family lineage and the individual's ability to help his tribe flourish. If they protect and obtain wealth for a village, their standing soars. If they fail, they lose face. Lengthy jirgas—meetings of tribal elders—settle disputes by consensus and strive to prevent blood feuds. And wealthy tribal elders support impoverished tribesmen by hiring them as field workers. Elders also punish tribesmen who disobey their rulings or commit a crime. In its own way, the tribal system creates order.

The division that foreign visitors noticed in "Little America" between educated urban Pashtuns and conservative rural Pashtuns spans the Pashtun belt and includes those in the tribal areas of Pakistan as well. Pashtuns from a group of tribes known as the Durrani are generally more urbanized and liberal and more accepting of central government rule. Pashtuns from a group of tribes known as the Ghilzai tend to be more disenfranchised, live in rural areas, resist central government rule, and more numerous than the Durrani. Many of the Taliban leaders in Afghanistan and Pakistan are Ghilzai, while many current and past government leaders, including Karzai, are Durrani. While some western scholars highlight the division, the Taliban and many Pashtuns deny that such a rivalry exists.

The creation of the tribal areas dates back to the hated 1848 British demarcation of the 1,600-mile border between Afghanistan and Pakistan, which divided the Pashtuns. The British annexed six Ghilzai-dominated mountain districts along the border with Afghanistan and then declared them "tribal areas" as opposed to "settled areas" under firmer administrative control. Hoping to subdue the area's dozen major tribes, British colonial officials enacted an indirect system of government.

Under the system, British-appointed administrators known as political agents maintained loose control of the tribal area's inhabitants by applying a system of collective punishment. When an individual tribesman committed a crime or defied the government, political agents negotiated only with tribal elders—known as maliks—and demanded that the tribe arrest the wanted person. If that failed, the political agent used the Frontier Corps—a British-paid militia frequently made up of members of rival tribes—to punish a tribe en masse by withdrawing government funds or bulldozing homes. After a carefully calibrated punishment, the status quo resumed.

Twelve years after the creation of the new system of collective punishment, British officials complained that it was failing to stop raids and kidnappings from the tribal areas into Dera Ismail Khan and other nearby towns. "They kidnapped children from the very town of Dera Ismail Khan and demanded exorbitant sums for their release," Brigadier General Chamberlain complained in an 1860 government report. "And if the relations of the captives delayed to ransom them, they cut off their fingers and sent them to their relations to move their tender feeling."

Unbowed, the British launched a series of punitive military campaigns to try to again pacify the tribal areas. Thousands of tribesmen and hundreds of British and Indian soldiers perished in battles that achieved mixed results.

In 1897, an ambitious young British army officer named Winston S. Churchill served as a journalist in an expeditionary force dispatched to punish rebellious tribes. The result was Churchill's first nonfiction book: *The Story of the Malakand Field Force: An Episode of Frontier War*. Littered with openly racist statements, the book catapulted the future British prime minister and World War II leader to fame. It described Pashtuns as barbarians who showed a remarkable ability to embrace modern technology and brutally employ it.

"To the ferocity of the Zulu are added the craft of the Redskin and the marksmanship of the Boer," Churchill wrote. "At a thousand yards the traveler falls wounded by the well-aimed bullet of a breech-loading rifle. His assailant, approaching, hacks him to death with the ferocity of a South-Sea Islander. The weapons of the nineteenth century are in the hands of the savages of the Stone Age."

The book accurately captures a Pashtun tendency toward deeply destructive infighting. In one passage, Churchill describes the fate of a successful tribal leader, referring to him as a "Pathan," the Urdu term for Pashtun.

"His success is now his ruin," Churchill wrote. "A combination is formed against him. The surrounding chiefs and their adherents are assisted by the village populations. The ambitious Pathan, oppressed by numbers, is destroyed. The victors quarrel over the spoil, and the story closes, as it began, in bloodshed and strife."

A Pashto proverb that I had heard conveys the same sentiment: "When the one profits," it states, "the other's house is ruined."

The British struggles continued long after Churchill's departure. In one widely heralded case, a Pashtun from North Waziristan known as the Faqir of Ipi led a tribal rebellion for more than twenty years. From 1937 until his death in 1960, he successfully eluded capture by the British and Pakistani governments. At one point in the 1940s, 40,000 British and Indian troops—backed by squadrons of British airplanes—hunted him.

Despite complaints that the policy kept the area impoverished and isolated, Pakistan retained the system of collective tribal punishment after it won independence from Britain in 1947. Under the country's new constitution, Pakistani laws did not apply in the tribal areas unless specifically decreed by Pakistan's president. Its people were barred from voting in Pakistan's national elections. The 3 million people of the tribal areas had no elected representatives in Pakistan's parliament.

Over the next twenty years, many tribal elders pocketed development funds doled out to them by Pakistani-government-appointed political agents. In order to maintain power, they discouraged education and most contact with the outside world. The result was that an estimated 83 percent of the men and 97 percent of the women in the tribal areas were illiterate—vastly higher rates than in the rest of Pakistan, where roughly half the population could read.

In the 1980s, the United States and Saudi Arabia poured approximately $1 billion a year into weaponry and military aid to mujahideen fighters in the tribal areas. Pakistan's premier military intelligence service, the Directorate of Inter-Services Intelligence, or ISI, oversaw the distribution of guns and cash. Acting as kingmaker, the ISI turned young Afghan and Pakistani fighters into hugely powerful military commanders, slashing the power of Pashtun tribal elders. Pakistani intelligence officials feared that the tribal elders wanted to secede from Pakistan, join their Pashtun brethren in Afghanistan, and create "Pashtunistan."

At the same time, Pakistani intelligence officials introduced a new interpretation of Islam that further undermined the strength of the Pashtun tribal elders. With assistance from Pakistani intelligence officials, Saudi Arabia constructed religious schools that created another source of authority—fundamentalist Wahhabi Islam. When Soviet forces withdrew from Afghanistan in 1989, three sets of power brokers now existed in the tribal areas: young mujahideen commanders, radical clerics, and traditional elders.

In the 1990s, Pakistani intelligence officials used the tribal areas as one of several bases from which they funded, trained, and dispatched militants to fight Indian forces in Kashmir, the disputed region over which Pakistan and India have fought three of their four wars. Hard-line religious schools also spread across other parts of Pakistan. The schools, in turn, supported religious political parties that called for the establishment of Islamic law across Pakistan. They also indoctrinated young Afghan refugees.

In 1994, a group of young Afghans who had been educated in conservative religious schools in Pakistan founded the Taliban movement. First emerging in southern Afghanistan, the name they adopted—"Taliban"—meant "students" in Pashto. They attacked warlords in Kandahar who they accused of rampant criminality and corruption. With the backing of the ISI, the Taliban took Kabul in 1996 and established what Pakistani intelligence officials considered a friendly regime.

The next year, the Pakistani government finally granted the inhabitants of the tribal areas the right to vote in national elections. Civilian political parties, though, were barred from campaigning in the tribal areas. As a result, fundamentalist clerics aligned with Pakistan's religious parties and schools swept elections in 1997 and 2002. The clerics' dominance allowed the ISI to continue to use the tribal area as a training base.

As Atiqullah moves us farther into the tribal areas, I know we are entering an area cut off from the rest of the world where xenophobia and conspiracy theories are rife. One particularly poetic phrase that Churchill penned a century earlier has lingered in my mind for months. Since 2001, I have felt it applies to how effectively terrorist attacks sow fear, division, and mistrust.

"Every man's hand is against the other," he wrote, "and all against the stranger."

Our first home in the tribal areas is in Miran Shah, the capital of North Waziristan. We arrive at night and I see nothing of the town.

Our new quarters consist of two large sleeping rooms that look out onto a small courtyard. One even has a small washroom, separate from the toilet, for showering. Makeshift pipes have been fastened to the walls.

The next morning, I go to the bathroom and make myself vomit in the hope it will somehow pressure our captors. An amiable older man who is a local doctor visits soon after. He speaks basic English and seems puzzled by my presence in Miran Shah. I intentionally tell him I am a journalist with *The New York Times* and hope he might somehow help us. Later, I learn that he did speak with local people about me. As a result, I am banned from seeing other doctors.

All day, a parade of random Pakistani militants stops by the house to stare at us. I again feel like an animal in a zoo. Among them is a local Taliban commander who introduces himself as Badruddin. I will later learn that he is the brother of Sirajuddin Haqqani, the leader of the Haqqani network, one of the most powerful Taliban factions in the region. Miran Shah is its stronghold. Their network of commanders guided us across eastern Afghanistan. They are known for discipline, ruthlessness, and ties to foreign militants.

Badruddin, a tall, talkative man with brown hair, brown eyes, and a short beard, appears to be in his early thirties. He announces that he is preparing to make a video of us to release to the media. He smiles as he shows me a video on his camera of a French aid worker who was kidnapped a week before us as he walked to his office in Kabul. He is in chains and appears to have welts on his face. The aid worker implores his family and friends to save him.

"It's a nightmare," he says. "I really beg you to pay."

I ask if Tahir and I can speak alone with Atiqullah, who I believe is the more moderate commander. I tell Atiqullah we should not make the video. The American and Afghan governments are more likely to agree to a secret prisoner exchange, I say, than a public one. I also know that if the Taliban set a public deadline and it is not met, they will enforce it brutally. Failing to do so would be a public loss of face, something deeply shameful to Pashtuns and all Afghans.

Trying to reduce their expectations, I tell him it would be far easier to get prisoners from the main Afghan-run prison outside Kabul in the town of Pul-i-Charkhi. If the Taliban demand prisoners from the American-run detention centers at Guantánamo Bay and Bagram, they will never succeed. I am not worth that much, I tell him, and he should compromise. I do not say it but I also want to spare my family the pain of seeing me in a hostage video. I know if a video arrives they will fear it shows an execution. To my surprise, Atiqullah agrees.

"I am one of those kinds of people," he says at one point. "I am one of those people who like to meet in the middle."

In the afternoon, he announces that Tahir, Asad, and I will be allowed to call our families tonight to prove we are alive. Atiqullah tells me to emphasize during the call that he wants to reach a deal quickly. He continues to cover his face with a scarf. I hope that means he plans to release us and does not want us to be able to identify him to American or Afghan officials.

Ignoring the countless lies Atiqullah has already told me, I maintain some type of hope. This is my first brush with a dynamic that will unfold multiple times in captivity. My mind's tendency to grasp at straws despite grim evidence to the contrary.

I spend the rest of the day nervously scribbling a list of things I want to say to my wife. I add items and then cross them out. I want to ease my family's fears that I am being tortured, but I also want to do everything possible to free us. I am not sure I will have another chance to speak with Kristen.

THE TALIBAN CALL COLLECT

Kristen, November 19, 2008

The phone rings at 6 A.M. The FBI alerts me that my husband will be calling home. Within a half hour, a group of six agents floods our small apartment in lower Manhattan: a translator, two case agents, the two-person negotiation team, and a victim's counselor. With the exception of Cathy, who led my phone training session over a week ago, all the faces are new to me.

Jim is now the lead agent and investigator on our case. A former Port Authority policeman, he lost several colleagues in the attacks on the World Trade Center on 9/11. When a national Joint Terrorism Task Force was established in the aftermath, he was eager to join the team. The lead FBI negotiation expert, Phil, is a former hostage himself. As a teenager, he and his family were held in their home for a brief but intense period of time. The ordeal ended when Phil distracted the armed hostage taker, a high school student, so his family could escape. Phil was shot in the process, but recovered. I am struck by the fact that each individual on the team has been motivated by personal loss or direct experience of kidnapping. We huddle together around the living room sofa and review the training points.

The FBI learned of the imminent call from the newspaper's Kabul bureau. Atiqullah has alerted Chris Chivers at the Kabul bureau that David will be permitted to phone home. Atiqullah says that when they call, I should look at the number that appears on caller ID and call him back at my own expense, as his phone card is running out of credits. This astounds me. In addition to being ruthless, the Taliban are also cheap! This is absurdly amusing. Finding humor in the most morbid and extreme circumstances actually keeps me from falling apart and gives me some minor sense of control.

At 8:30 A.M., the phone rings. It's David. We have been sitting by the phone for two hours and yet the call still manages to take me by surprise. It's very odd to be sharing this personal moment with a roomful of people I have only just met. I feel like our relationship, all our vulnerabilities, are on display. Oddly, though, this helps me maintain composure. There's nothing like a crowd to ensure a steady performance. As instructed, I don't answer and call David back on the number that appears on caller ID.

It is a relief to hear my husband's voice, to know he is still alive. He sounds shaken, but his voice is strong, his thinking clear. This puts me at ease. I return the favor by maintaining composure for him. I realize this may be the only time we speak and I want to convey a sense that I am holding it together and will not give up, that I can handle this situation.

"Kristen?" David says, "Kristen?"

"David," I say, "It's Kristen, I love you."

"Kristen?" he asks.

"Yes?" I say.

"I love you, too," he says, "Write these things down, okay?"

"Okay," I say.

"Do you have a pen?" David asks.

"I have a pen," I say.

"I'm—we are being treated well," David says.

"Being treated well," I repeat.

"Number one," David says.

"Number one," I repeat.

"Number two," he says. "Deal for all three of us, all three of us, not just me. The driver and the translator also; it has to be a deal for all three of us."

"Deal for all three of us," I repeat. "The driver and the translator as well."

"Okay. Do not use force to try to get us," David says.

"Do not use force," I repeat.

"Four," he says.

"Yes," I say.

"Make a deal now or they will make it public," he says. "They want to put a video out to the media."

I repeat his words back to him.

"It will make it a big political problem," he says. "They want to do it now," David says. "They don't want to make it public. They want—they want to make a deal now."

"Want to make a deal now, okay," I repeat.

"'Cause they don't want, they don't want a big political problem with the leaders on both sides," he says. "They don't want the elders to know."

"Okay, they don't want elders to know," I say, "and they do not want problems on our side, okay."

"Make a deal, just make a deal quickly," David says. "Please make a deal quickly."

He pauses for a moment.

"They said I can't call you again," David says. "They want a deal now and I can't call you again."

"You cannot call me again," I repeat. "I love you. I love you, honey."

"I love you, too," he says. "Tell my family I'm sorry."

"Your family is here," I say. "Lee's here with me."

"I'm sorry," David says. "I'm sorry."

"Lee's here," I say, trying to reassure him.

"I'm sorry about all this," he repeats.

"It's going to be all right," I say. "I love you. I am praying for you every day."

I say I want to make sure I understand what they want. There is a pause and David relays a message from Atiqullah. He says the Kabul bureau should talk to him and negotiate with no one else. David says Atiqullah will call the Kabul bureau after we hang up and provide a list of demands.

"What is the deal? What is the deal?" I ask, trying to extend the call and get specifics. "Is it, what is the exchange? What do you want?"

David again says that Atiqullah will give his demands to the Kabul bureau.

"We are very concerned about you," I say. "And we love you and we're praying for you."

David repeats that Atiqullah will provide his demands to the Kabul bureau.

"Okay, okay," I say, "and how are you?"

There is a beep and the call ends abruptly.

After I catch my breath, our team reviews the conversation. I let them know which parts of the conversation were truly David—namely, the desire to make a deal for all three—and which seemed scripted. They are very optimistic about the call and my performance. I am patted on the back for my composure. It seems I have discovered a new skill set— one that enables me to be calm under pressure. My worst nightmare would be bursting into tears in front of a roomful of people.

At the same time, I feel completely enraged at my husband's captors and utterly confused. If they want to make a deal so quickly, why won't they list their demands? This is all part of a sick psychology on the captors' part: make the family feel totally responsible and utterly without control. Demand they meet demands, but fail to name them. I begin to wonder if the "make a deal quickly" was a signal from David, that perhaps he would be moved or sold up the food chain to a more powerful group of criminals or terrorists. This, I am told, often happens in kidnappings in Afghanistan.

My mind is racing, and I feel trapped. Our one-bedroom apartment is swarming with people. Mismatched dining and living room chairs are scattered all around. There doesn't seem to be enough space or air in our modest living room to accommodate them all. My mother steps in and urges everyone to clear out. She encourages me to go to work to take my mind off the situation—seemingly impossible—or at least to pass the time. I wonder how I can possibly do that.

Our case agents as always advise me to take care of myself. This, they say, is my number one responsibility. I will be better able to help my husband if I am in good physical shape. "Do not forget to eat, try to sleep. A call could arrive at any moment. You need to be prepared. This is the best thing you can do for your husband. David is going to need you to stay strong now and especially for when he returns." I will hear these directives repeatedly over the next few months.

As I walk to the subway, questions reel through my mind: Should I just jump on a plane to Kabul? Is it wrong for me to continue the routines of daily life? Am I being cowardly, or selfish, seeking refuge in my work? Practically speaking, I need to keep working. We have burned through our savings over the past few months between the wedding and honeymoon. And our country is facing the worst economic downturn in decades. Even in the fog of this crisis, I realize I need to keep my job as long as possible. In terms of my own sanity, I know it does me no good to stay in the apartment all day and sit by the phone. The last thing I want to admit to is that I am a victim as well, captive to a call that might or might not come. If I give up on daily activities, his captors will have succeeded in thoroughly disrupting our lives. I do not want them to win. Anger at the creeps holding David and his colleagues propels me forward.

I feel relieved when I ascend the subway steps to 57th Street in Midtown. I give myself a mental pat on the back as I approach the Hearst Publications building, where *Cosmopolitan* is headquartered, and pass through the shiny glass doors, past the security kiosks, and up the escalator. The office building has an air of glamour about it. It's modern, clean, bright. A waterfall serves as a calming backdrop in front of which the escalators ascend. The sound of cascading water soothes my mind. I feel like I have entered a sequestered world, one of well-dressed women and polite security guards. Everything is picture-perfect. Nothing need be explored or examined in too much depth. And you can start over again every month with some new outlook, style, or workout. I am able to skim the surface here and put the vortex of the last few hours behind me, momentarily. I breathe a sigh of relief and feel my energy restored.

An idea meeting has been scheduled for this afternoon. We will be discussing production and casting for our Man Manual shoot. This month it's "Bachelors in Their Boxer Shorts." I wonder if the Taliban wear boxers or briefs.

ALL THREE OF US

David, November 19, 2008

Standing in the remote darkness of Waziristan at the mercy of Taliban militants, I feel at peace. I have spoken to my wife for the first time in nine days. I expected panic or tears, but Kristen sounded collected and confident. Her words "It's going to be all right" will linger in my mind for months. Her composure will sustain me.

Atiqullah and Badruddin had driven us fifteen minutes outside Miran Shah, stopped the car in a dry riverbed, and turned off the engine. Leaving the headlights on, I called Kristen from a small handheld satellite phone Badruddin produced and followed their instructions to tell her we were being held in terrible conditions. I hope the tone of my voice somehow comforted her.

Now Badruddin and Atiqullah tell me to call *The New York Times* bureau in Kabul. Instead of ordering me to make specific demands, they instruct Tahir, Asad, and me to exaggerate our suffering. They also tell me to say that Atiqullah is not with us, even though he is standing beside me.

"We are in terrible conditions, Tahir is very sick," I tell Chris Chivers, a close friend and *Times* reporter who answers the phone.

Tahir then speaks to Chris and asks him to tell his family that he is alive and in good health.

"They keep telling me that if things go wrong they will repeat the story of Helmand," Tahir says, referring to the beheading of the Afghan journalist in 2007. "So I am just afraid they are going to kill me."

Asad then speaks in Pashto with an Afghan reporter in the bureau.

"I am fine, I am okay," he says. "Tell my family that we are in the mountains but we are okay."

The conversation drags on, with Atiqullah continuing to tell me what to say. He orders me to tell Chris that Asad and Tahir will be killed first.

I refuse. "Kill me first," I tell Atiqullah, "Kill me first."

Chris overhears me and interrupts.

"Nobody needs that, David," he says. "Nobody needs to die."

"They are threatening to kill the driver and the translator," I explain to Chris. "I have to tell you, I have to tell you. I don't want to tell you."

"We understand that they are making those threats," Chris says. "But that will not make our job easier."

Chris explains that if the Taliban kill anyone it will make government officials angry and make any deal even more difficult.

"Please don't let them kill the driver and the translator," I say. "Please don't let them kill the driver and translator. I am sorry about this," I add. "I apologize to everyone."

"David, this is not your fault," Chris says. He urges me to tell Atiqullah to keep calling.

I can tell Chris is trying to prolong the call, which drags on for twenty minutes. Growing impatient, Atiqullah and Badruddin order me to end the call.

"Okay, all three of us, Chris," I say. "It's gotta be all three of us. I gotta go."

I hang up the phone and Atiqullah and Badruddin order us back into the car. Worried that the call has been traced and a drone may be approaching, they quickly drive us out of the barren riverbed. Sitting in the back of the car, I am relieved. Kristen sounded calm. Chris said the paper was doing all it could. I feel that I fought for Tahir and Asad.

The car stops. With a scarf placed over my face, I am hustled into a new house. We have returned to Miran Shah.

I awake the following morning and I'm surprised by the quality of our new house. It is the finest of any we have been held in so far. The house has freshly painted white walls and regular electricity. We can wash our-selves with buckets of warm water. I receive a new set of clothes, a tooth-brush, toothpaste, and shampoo. Guards allow us to walk in a large dirt yard, which is roughly fifty feet by thirty feet and has a small patch of grass near the well. The weather is unexpectedly warm. We receive pomegranates and other fresh food. Nestlé Pure Life water bottled in Pakistan is delivered for me to drink. To my amazement, I am even brought English-language Pakistani newspapers. Delivered to a shop in Miran Shah, the newspapers are only a day or two old.

For years, the Pakistani military has portrayed the tribal areas to American officials and journalists as the deeply isolated mountain strong-hold of primitive Pashtun tribes. Instead, I find the tribal areas to be more developed than many parts of neighboring Afghanistan.

After breakfast, Badruddin visits us. He sits me down on the house's front steps and explains to me that the Haqqanis are loyal servants of Taliban leader Mullah Omar. He says that American military reports that the Haqqanis work with foreign militants and operate indepen-dently are false. I don't believe him. His father, Jalaluddin Haqqani, is a legendary Afghan anti-Soviet mujahideen fighter who is believed to shelter Al Qaeda members on the family's territory here in North Waziristan. The Haqqanis are aligned with the Afghan Taliban but they have grown so powerful that they largely operate on their own. They personify how American support for fundamentalist fighters in the 1980s backfired.

During the anti-Soviet jihad, Badruddin's father, Haqqani was on the payroll of the CIA. Twenty year later, he and his sons are allies of the Taliban and operate the most lethal insurgent force the United States faces in Afghanistan. I also know that they are at the center of one of the most hotly contested debates in the American military and intelligence community. Is the Pakistani military—the United States' purported ally—covertly aiding the Haqqanis and other Afghan Taliban as they attack American troops?

———

Twenty-one years before I arrived in Miran Shah as a prisoner, an American congressman named Charlie Wilson met Badruddin's father here in 1987 and declared him "goodness personified." Jalaluddin Haqqani, the family patriarch, was the favorite Afghan mujahideen commander of Wilson, a garrulous, hard-drinking Democrat from the Houston, Texas, area who was famous for womanizing. Eager to exact revenge on the Soviet Union for American deaths in Vietnam, Wilson secretly funneled hundreds of millions of dollars in covert funding to the Afghan mujahideen.

Dressed in Afghan clothes and escorted by Pakistani intelligence officers, Wilson passed through Miran Shah in Pakistan's tribal areas and then secretly crossed the border into Afghanistan. For the next four days, he received a covert tour of mujahideen operations in the Afghan province of Khost from Haqqani and other Afghan commanders. Living in the mountains, Wilson ate dinner in caves with bearded gunmen he saw as the descendants of indomitable mountain warriors who stood their ground against vastly more powerful foreign armies. The Afghans' religious devotion seemed to give them no fear of death, Wilson later recalled. At one point, the congressman even gleefully fired a salvo of rockets at a Soviet base.

On the final night of Wilson's trip, Jalaluddin Haqqani apologized to the American politician for not having a good-bye gift for him. Haqqani demanded that Wilson name the gift he wanted. The congressman half jokingly replied that he wanted helicopter pilots shot down by American-provided Stinger antiaircraft missiles. Roughly thirty minutes later, Haqqani's men produced two terrified-looking Afghan pilots. Wilson expressed his appreciation but said he meant Soviet pilots. Haqqani promised to produce them in two weeks. The following morning, as Wilson prepared to leave, Haqqani had hundreds of mujahideen gather to say good-bye. One of the congressman's guides snapped a photo of a grinning Wilson sitting astride a white horse with four Kalashnikov-wielding Afghans behind him.

"I felt I had entered the ranks of the initiated," Wilson later recalled.

Wilson, like the other American architects of the anti-Soviet jihad, ignored the militant Islam that Haqqani and other mujahideen fighters fervently embraced. In the late 1980s, CIA officers viewed him as one of the most impressive, fearless, and organized Pashtun battlefield commanders. They trusted him with new tactics and weapons, including Stinger antiaircraft missiles, rockets, and even tanks.

Born in the village of Srana in the Garde Serai district of southeastern Afghanistan's Paktia Province, Haqqani was a deeply conservative rural Pashtun cleric. After studying in a local Afghan madrassa as a youth, he completed his religious studies at the hard-line Darul Uloom Haqqania, or "University for Education of Truth," in Pakistan's Northwest Frontier Province. Several other future Taliban leaders would attend the same school as well. The school banned televisions and music, taught young boys to memorize the Koran, and indoctrinated them in conservative Deobandi Islam.

In 1974, Haqqani took up arms against the Afghan government after the country's king was overthrown in a coup Haqqani perceived as left leaning. He left Afghanistan, crossed into Pakistan's tribal areas and based himself in Miran Shah. The town would serve as his headquarters for decades. His presence in Pakistan's tribal areas caught the attention of Pakistani intelligence officials, who began funding him. Later, they introduced him to CIA officials, who did the same. To the delight of his Pakistani and American backers, Haqqani and his men laid siege to Soviet and Afghan forces garrisoned in the Afghan city of Khost in southeastern Afghanistan.

Deft at cultivating support from various sources, Haqqani also spoke fluent Arabic and opened fund-raising offices in the Persian Gulf and Saudi Arabia. Already married to an Afghan woman, he married an Arab woman as well. Between both wives, he fathered nine sons. Haqqani's ability to build coalitions among a dizzyingly diverse array of resistance groups stood out among Afghan commanders.

At some point in the mid-1980s, Haqqani met Osama bin Laden, who had traveled to Pakistan to aid the Afghan resistance. Several months after giving Congressman Wilson his 1987 tour, Haqqani helped Bin Laden achieve his first battlefield victory. The two men and a few dozen of their fighters fought off a weeklong assault by two hundred Soviet paratroopers on a camp Bin Laden had constructed for Afghan and foreign fighters—called the Lion's Den. The following year, Bin Laden founded

Al Qaeda and built training camps in Haqqani-controlled territory in southeastern Afghanistan's Khost Province. Bin Laden would later call Haqqani a "hero mujahed sheikh" and "one of the foremost leaders of the jihad against the Soviets."

When the victorious mujahideen took Kabul in 1992, Haqqani was named justice minister, but fighting over the city quickly erupted between rival mujahideen commanders. Haqqani declined to join any side and returned to Khost, the largest city in his home region. His reputation for piousness and not engaging in the criminality and corruption rampant among other mujahideen commanders gained him standing among local Afghans.

When the Taliban emerged in southern Afghanistan in 1994, Haqqani apparently did not trust them. A year later, he joined the group, possibly after coming under pressure from Pakistani intelligence officials who saw the Taliban as a friendly proxy force against India. During Taliban rule, Haqqani served as the minister of borders and tribal affairs and governor of Paktia, the province in southeastern Afghanistan where he was born. He also commanded members of his Zadran tribe who battled anti-Taliban forces north of Kabul. By joining the Taliban, he greatly strengthened the nascent group whose leaders included many of his fellow graduates of Darul Uloom Haqqania religious school in Pakistan.

That same year, 1995, I visited religious schools in Pakistan while working as a reporter for *The Christian Science Monitor*. On my first visit to the country, I toured three madrassas and two Islamic universities in the city of Peshawar and found burgeoning fundamentalism. An estimated 200,000 Afghan and Pakistani boys studied in 8,000 madrassas, a 50 percent increase from seven years earlier. At one school, young Afghan teachers proudly stated that 400 of the school's students had gone on to join the Taliban. At the same time, Afghan refugees living in a fetid refugee camp accused the United States of mounting an "anti-Muslim" conspiracy to prevent the Taliban from establishing an Islamic government in Afghanistan. They also said the United States had "deceived" Afghans by convincing them to fight the Soviet Union and then abandoning them.

When I spoke with American diplomats, they played down the problem of fundamentalism. Pakistani prime minister Benazir Bhutto was exaggerating the problem, they said, to persuade the United States to lift sanctions it had placed on Pakistan for developing nuclear weapons.

"Pakistan is not a major link in an international terrorist conspiracy," an American diplomat told me in 1995.

A year after I departed, the Taliban took Kabul and began enforcing strict Islamic laws across Afghanistan. Mullah Omar, Jalaluddin Haqqani, and other Taliban leaders welcomed Osama bin Laden back to Afghanistan. With Haqqani's support, Bin Laden refurbished and expanded camps the Saudi jihadist leader originally built in Khost to support the anti-Soviet mujahideen. After Al Qaeda bombed two American embassies in Africa in 1998, the United States fired cruise missiles at the camps in a failed effort to kill Bin Laden. The missiles struck the camp where Congressman Wilson had slept during his tour of Afghanistan eleven years earlier.

A month after the September 2001 terrorist attacks in the United States, the ISI brought Jalaluddin Haqqani to Islamabad for a secret meeting with American and Pakistani officials. The ISI hoped Haqqani would join a new post-Taliban government that did not include officials they viewed as loyal to Pakistan's rival India. The Americans asked Haqqani to defect from the Taliban. Haqqani rejected the offer and complained that the United States had abandoned Afghanistan after the defeat of the Soviets. Soon after, American bombs destroyed three of Haqqani's homes in Afghanistan. He survived and is believed to have played a role in helping Bin Laden—his friend of fifteen years—escape from the battle of Tora Bora in eastern Afghanistan and cross into Pakistan's tribal areas in December 2001.

As they did during the anti-Soviet jihad, Haqqani fighters regrouped in Pakistan and then began launching cross-border attacks from Pakistan into Afghanistan with the support of foreign fighters. Assassinating and intimidating moderate tribal elders, the Haqqanis steadily weakened southeastern Afghanistan's Pashtun tribes. They told the Pashtuns that their primary loyalty should be to Islam, not to their tribe. Gradually gaining strength, they killed moderate clerics and beheaded Afghans working with Americans. Their long-standing ties with Arab militants brought them extensive funding from the Persian Gulf and an acceptance of suicide bombing, a tactic more moderate Taliban still questioned.

Between 2003 and 2007, I embedded with three different American military units that battled the Haqqanis in eastern Afghanistan. The first embed ended with a soldier having his lower leg blown off when our Humvee struck a mine five hundred yards from the Pakistani border. The second involved a unit trying to help a poorly equipped Afghan police chief who feared his own men would kill him because he was from the wrong tribe. And the third involved the Haqqanis beheading a tribal elder who American military officials hoped might work with a team of anthropologists they deployed to better understand Khost's tribal structure.

In 2004, the former NFL player Pat Tillman was killed in a friendly fire incident during an operation to block a cross-border infiltration route used by Haqqani fighters. Two years later, the Haqqanis used a teenage suicide bomber to kill Hakim Taniwal, a former sociology professor who returned from exile in Australia to serve as governor of two southeastern provinces. After killing Taniwal, they dispatched a second suicide bomber to his funeral, killing six more people.

By 2008, the Haqqanis had fielded several thousand fighters and were mounting complex operations in Kabul itself. They carried out a January 2008 assault on the Serena Hotel that killed six, an April 2008 assassination attempt on President Karzai that killed three, and a July 2008 attack on the Indian Embassy that killed fifty-eight people. American intelligence officials reportedly intercepted calls in which Pakistani intelligence officials guided the Haqqani operatives during the Indian Embassy attack. Pakistani officials denied the reports. American officials who were skeptical of the Pakistani military argued that the Haqqanis were still proxies that the ISI continued to use to prevent India from gaining influence in Afghanistan. They argued that the strength of the Haqqanis showed that the Pakistani military was playing a "double game" with the United States. Pakistan arrested Al Qaeda members in the country's cities, but continued to covertly support the Haqqanis and other Afghan Taliban.

After no public statements emerged from Jalaluddin Haqqani for several years, rumors circulated that he had died. His son Sirajuddin was said to have taken over day-to-day operations of the Haqqani network. In the spring of 2008, a frail-looking but ever-wily Jalaluddin Haqqani appeared in a video.

"This is not a battle of haste; this is a battle of patience," he said. "If a strong animal fights with a small and weak animal, the big animal uses all its power, not against the enemy, but against itself."

I had watched the video with a colleague in the newspaper's Kabul bureau after it appeared. I knew the Haqqanis were the Taliban faction with the closest ties to Al Qaeda. Now I am their first American prisoner.

In the day after my call to Kristen, Atiqullah and I discuss religion again. He wants to know how devout I am. I tell him that my parents took me to church when I was young, but I know little about Christianity and am not religious. I don't tell him, but my years of covering religious conflict has made me skeptical of organized religion.

Atiqullah asks me to recite the ten commandments and I struggle to remember them from the Episcopal Sunday school my mother had me attend. My parents were raised Episcopalian but my father became a fiercely independent Unitarian Universalist. In the end, I make up the final three or four commandments. When he asks me if I believe Jesus was the son of God, I say I believe Jesus was one of several prophets, including Muhammad. He tells me that he has sent for an English-language Koran for me to read. My religious beliefs appear to amuse him. I get the sense that he sees me as primitive. The following day, Atiqullah announces that he needs to return to Afghanistan, but that two of his men will stay behind to guard us.

"I will return in seven to ten days," he promises, then disappears.

One of the guards who stays with us is Akbar, the seemingly kind guard who brought us food in Afghanistan. The other is a heavyset young fighter who recites the call to prayer beautifully each day and rarely speaks to me. We nickname him Chunky. I am allowed to exercise in the yard, and I find that any exercise—no matter how small—raises my spirits. I walk back and forth dozens of times in the yard, which is strewn with bits of trash. Pakistani military helicopters occasionally rumble overhead. Airliners do as well. At certain times of day, I think I'm staring at the Dubai-New York flight I have taken home countless times.

One day, the guards buy a board game called Checkah, a Pakistani variation of Parcheesi, to help us pass the time. Instead of beating us, as I expected, our captors are trying to meet at least some of our needs. But as in so much of what will be seven months in captivity, reasons for optimism are overtaken by harsh realities.

At night, a stream of Haqqani commanders overflowing with hatred for the United States, Europe, and Israel visit us, unleashing blistering critiques that will continue throughout our imprisonment. As they enter the room, I stare at the floor as Tahir has advised me. By not looking at their faces, I hope I am being respectful and showing that I will not be able to identify them in the future to American officials.

First, teenage boys bring in large plates of rice, kebab, and spinach for dinner and place them on a plastic sheet on the floor. Our guards, Tahir, Asad, and I scoop up pieces of food with small sections of flatbread and eat it. There are no tables, chairs, or utensils. We sit on thin maroon floor cushions. Cans of Pepsi are brought in for me to drink. Grapes and pomegranates are served for dessert. I decline, fearing the water in the fruit will make me sick.

The commanders harbor many delusions about Westerners. But I also see how some of the consequences of Washington's antiterrorism policies had galvanized the Taliban. One commander demands that I be chained, citing the shackling of prisoners by American forces. Another commander says he was detained for months by Pakistani ISI intelligence agents in a dank underground cell. When American officials arrived to question him, he was brought to a clean, bright room with a bowl of fruit. When the Americans departed, the Pakistanis returned him to his dungeon.

All the commanders fixate on the deaths of Afghan, Iraqi, and Palestinian civilians in American air strikes as well as on the American detention of Muslim prisoners for years without charge. They all know of the physical abuse and sexual humiliation of Iraqi prisoners in Abu Ghraib and are infuriated by it. To Americans, these episodes are aberrations. To my captors, they are proof that the United States is a hypocritical and duplicitous power that flouts international law. America, Europe, and Israel preach democracy, human rights, and impartial justice to the Muslim world, they say, but fail to follow those principles themselves. When I tell them I am an innocent civilian who should be released, they respond that the United States has held Muslims in secret detention centers for years. Why, they ask, should they treat me differently?

Other accusations are paranoid and delusional. Seven years after the September 2001 terrorist attacks, they continue to insist that the attacks were hatched by American and Israeli intelligence agencies to create a pretext for the United States to occupy the Muslim world. They say the United States is forcibly converting vast numbers of Muslims to Christianity. American and NATO soldiers, they believe, are making Afghan women work as prostitutes on military bases. Their hatred for the United States seems boundless.

HUMAN RESOURCES

Kristen, November 20–December 15, 2008

I arrive at *The New York Times* building. The offices are bright and modern. The lively red walls seem a stark contrast to the intense and dour expressions among the employees working there.

David's brother Lee has once again set up camp in an office on the seventeenth floor. David McCraw, the newspaper's lawyer, has been assigned to help us work with the *Times'* crisis management firm, Clayton Consultants, and to coordinate the efforts in New York and Kabul to release David. We speak with him each day at noon for updates on the case, to assess different strategies—for example, whether the media blackout is effective or not—and to figure out our next steps.

Today, David McCraw, Lee, and I will interview a private security firm to work along with the people from Clayton. The head of Clayton is joining us for the meeting. We want his evaluation of the firm as well. We need to send someone to Kabul to represent our family during negotiations and relieve the pressure on the paper's Kabul bureau, which has been fielding the phone calls from David's captors and trying to get information related to the case. Since the FBI's hands are tied in terms of helping get David released, the paper, along with Lee and me, has decided to hire an outside security consultancy to conduct negotiations. The head of Clayton Consultants arrives and greets us. Most of the security contractors I have met so far are former employees of government intelligence agencies. He is no exception.

With sandy brown hair, a handlebar mustache, and a monotone demeanor, Clayton's representative is a walking caricature of an FBI agent—the kind you see on television. He looks vaguely familiar. Later he tells us he has actually portrayed an FBI agent in small parts on television shows.

He also explains that most likely this is a kidnap for ransom case. Our goal, he says, should be to draw out the process, decrease David's value in his captors' eyes, and maintain a dialogue with them. Over time the captors will lower their demands, until a realistic amount is agreed on. Prisoner exchanges are not possible, so he advises that we steer clear of this issue during negotiations with the captors. We expect that any haggling will occur over the phone. He says it is customary for families to think about what they might be willing to pay.

It is surreal to be putting a price tag on David. And trying to figure out what the markup might be when we include his two Afghan colleagues. The whole idea of the captors pricing human life like a perishable commodity is revolting. Yet I do not lose sight of the fact that this is a sad situation all around. I imagine life must be incredibly bleak in Afghanistan for kidnapping to be a viable business. Any potential funds we give them could be used to fuel future terrorist attacks or violence. This greatly disturbs us.

Even more upsetting is that I feel we do not have the luxury to debate this topic. While we hope for a ransom-free solution, we are not idealistic about the situation. There is no question that our family will raise funds in any way possible to protect the lives of David, Tahir, and Asad if it is the only means of seeing them alive again. We've decided to pursue this course in future communications with the captors.

At present, we are not in the same stratosphere: they are now asking for millions of dollars and the release of prisoners from Guantánamo and Bagram. Lee and I resign ourselves to trying to reach an agreement when the captors diminish their demands to a reasonable amount. We have no idea how long this will take, and at this point we also know that it is nearly impossible to apply logic and reason to an irrational situation.

Lee, McCraw, Clayton's representative, and I are seated around a conference table in a corner meeting room, tucked away behind the stairwell and removed from the flow of office traffic. The interview begins. We hear from the leader of the private security consulting firm American International Security Corporation, or AISC, which has been recommended to us by a former special operations soldier.

Mike Taylor, the head of the firm and a special forces veteran as well, explains that he has experience "in the field, on the ground." He is very fit and seems to be in his forties. He never cracks a smile and at first appears put off by our questions. Quiet but hyperalert, he seems to be taking in the details of our surroundings as he seats himself a few feet away from the table.

He proclaims that his agency has never paid ransom for a hostage. "We've never exchanged funds," he says. Awkward silence. Lee and I glance at each other.

We are all a bit baffled by this statement. We thought the private security team would be providing a negotiator. We ask what exactly he means. Mike replies that his team has contacts on the ground, through a local network of informants in Afghanistan, and the region. They have the ability to move money and evacuate hostages. They are not opposed to paying ransom, he says, but have never needed to do so in previous kidnapping cases.

Uncomfortable pause.

I ask bluntly how it is possible to get someone out if no money is paid.

"Snatch and grab," he says, referring to a rescue. "Or an exchange of another sort," he says, adding that we may be able to barter with other goods—medical supplies, vehicles.

Lee and I step out for a moment to share our impressions while the Clayton and AISC representatives talk privately.

I'm a little hesitant because it seems to me that AISC might take a bit of a bold approach. Lee has the same concern but asks me, "If you knew this could be solved quicker, would you be opposed to a more aggressive approach?" We both feel we are in a race against time. I worry that each moment that ticks by is taking a chunk of David's sanity along with it.

When we return, the head of Clayton is very confident that AISC is a good choice. "They bring a different set of assets and skills to the table," he says archly. "We've checked out their bona fides," he adds. "They are the real deal. We feel comfortable working with them."

On the basis of this recommendation, we set aside our fears and decide to hire AISC. They will send a negotiator to Kabul to represent our family and to work alongside a kidnap expert from Clayton. We will come to refer to this duo as Team Kabul. We will be in regular contact with them, along with McCraw, on a daily noon conference call.

Both teams advise us to keep "the bureau," or the FBI, out of it. They are useful for some things, but cannot deliver funds, release prisoners, or provide direct negotiations when discussions involve ransom. They are strictly an information-gathering agency.

I've confided in several of David's closest friends at this point. Each of them offers unwavering emotional support. A few also provide invaluable practical advice. One longtime friend, Samantha Power, suggests that I reach out to Richard Holbrooke, a former official in the Clinton administration who knows my husband and is aware of our situation. Rumor is he will be assuming a diplomatic position in the incoming Obama administration, with a focus on Afghanistan and Pakistan. While our friend admits that Holbrooke is often referred to as the diplomatic equivalent of a "bull in a china shop," he is also smart, passionate about causes, well respected, and personally moved by our situation.

As fate would have it, David had introduced me to Holbrooke and his wife, Kati Marton, several months ago at Samantha's wedding. We sat next to each other at the church service. David respects him, but is a bit embarrassed in his presence because of their history.

Thirteen years ago, Holbrooke played a key role in negotiating for David's release from Serbian authorities. During the Dayton peace talks in 1995, which Holbrooke had convened to help end the bitter civil war in Bosnia, ten members of David's family showed up and threatened to protest on the street outside if the Clinton administration did not pressure the Serbs to free David.

I call Holbrooke in the evening to ask his advice about what more I can be doing to get assistance from the United States government and to hear his thoughts on our decision to keep David's case out of the public eye. He responds with a reference to the wedding.

He reminds me that he orchestrated David's release in Bosnia. "I put our peace talks on hold for three days to work for the release of your husband, simply because it was the right thing to do," he says. "What were my parting words to David this past summer—do you remember?" Holbrooke reminds me that when he learned David would be going back to Afghanistan soon after our own wedding, he half jokingly told him, "Don't get captured again."

Holbrooke ruminates as he speaks. You can hear the wheels turning. His speech is deliberate, thoughtful, and slightly muffled. I have to strain to hear him. As a result, he has my undivided attention. He tells me he has been turning this over for quite some time—especially the thought of whether to go public or remain quiet. "Given that we are not dealing with a legitimate government, I think you are right to keep this private. You are dealing with a set of unpredictable, ruthless individuals.

"I am sure you have Googled the Haqqani family, and if you've done your research, you know of the connection to the ISI. So, you might want to think about reaching out to them. Rumor is I may be working with the new administration, but I won't assume my post until January. I promise to work on this, to make this a priority when I assume my post. Until then, I suggest you stay in close contact with Condi Rice. Have you contacted her? It would be good to check in with the State Department on a regular basis in case anything can be done, any pressure applied on the diplomatic front to keep this on the radar of the Pakistanis."

Before we say good-bye, Holbrooke emphasizes that it is a good sign that David has survived the first few weeks. He reassures me David will come home.

Atiqullah continues to call the Kabul bureau of *The New York Times* regularly, reiterating his possession of "our three," as we have come to refer to them. Since the beginning of the case, the FBI has been sending negotiations experts to the Kabul bureau to assist in communications and record these phone calls.

On November 21, Atiqullah calls with a grim message for Chris Chivers, the reporter who has been fielding the calls: If the demands are not met, they will go public with the case and set a three-day deadline. They will kill Asad first and then Tahir. We know there is no way we can meet their demands but we must keep them talking. Coached by the FBI, Chris pleads with Atiqullah to keep our three alive until we can reach an agreement. We realize that if the kidnappers publicly announce a deadline, they will have to carry it out. In Afghanistan, never losing face is paramount. We anxiously await the next phone call.

On Thanksgiving eve there has been no word from David's captors in five days. Heightened security in the wake of a car bomb prevents the FBI from getting to the Kabul bureau in time to take a call from Atiqullah. The FBI experts advise Chris to delay speaking with Atiqullah until they are present. In truth, Chris is poised by the phone.

By the end of the day, Atiqullah has not called back the Kabul bureau. Apparently the delay has upset him and made him skittish. We have no new information about our three. This reaffirms our decision to hire a private security firm.

I am completely exhausted, on edge, and angry at the FBI agents in Kabul for scuttling our communications with David's kidnappers. I pace back and forth in our small galley kitchen, then collapse on the living room sofa. I turn on the television, hoping to take my mind off our situation.

CNN presents an emergency newscast of an unfolding tragedy. I watch in horror as our honeymoon spots from a weekend in Mumbai—the Taj Hotel, the Oberoi, the harbor—are in chaos and smoke. Mumbai is burning. It is sad to see our recent history in flames and disturbing to see that India has been hit by terrorists.

Lee and I immediately personalize this horrifying event: How will it affect David? Does the recent silence in his case relate to the bombing? Once again, we question whether to make the kidnapping public. I check in with our various advisers. The FBI votes yes, but cannot provide specifics as to why they take this stance. I disagree. Our private security team advises us to keep it private. Bill Keller, the *Times'* executive editor, sends me an e-mail suggesting that we revisit the situation.

This is the first of many long periods of silence.

It is also our first holiday as a married couple, and we will spend it apart. My family has rallied to my side in New York. I am thankful for their presence but feel a mix of emotions. I was single for thirty-nine years, and now, confronted with my first married Thanksgiving, I am disappointed that I am still the odd girl out—the only one without a date.

I have been restless of late. The stress of the situation is starting to have a physical impact. My arms are often numb. It's disturbing not to be able to reach out to David and help him in a tangible, immediate way. I have gained weight around my middle, which I attribute to the buildup of the stress hormone cortisol, a natural by-product of sustained tension. My chest is wound up. I liken my mental experience to the moment when a jetliner touches down and the engines are at full force but the brakes are engaged. Everything has come to a screeching halt momentarily. Suspended animation. Fear. No sense of what will come next. Not knowing whether we will move forward or spontaneously combust. My entire mode of being is stuck in the moment of not knowing, waiting, having no control over the next moment. Life is simultaneously in intense overdrive and stalled. The only thing to do is to surrender and trust that some greater benevolent force is at work. Many people have told me that this journey will be a marathon, not a sprint.

My mother, Mary Jane, is still living with me and brings some levity to the situation. One of her volunteer projects in her community back home in Maine is to make "dishware gardens" for shut-ins—patients, the elderly, and the disabled. As I look around the room, I see she has applied this practice in my own apartment. I notice that several of our spider plants have new companions. She has been cooking up a storm of late and placing the seeds and pits remaining from our meals in planters around the apartment. I am somewhat amused to find an avocado pit beginning to sprout among the leaves of a spider plant. I point this out to her.

"I thought it would be a positive way to mark time," she tells me. "It's good to bring new life into the situation. Let's see if he's home before it bears new fruit."

"Thanks," I tell her, and then admit to myself: I officially feel like a shut-in, albeit an emotional one. Thank you very much. Still, I have to smile.

This is one of the reasons I love my mother—she always maintains a positive outlook and an offbeat sense of humor, and she never lets anything go to waste. Once when I was home from college, after a breakup with a serious boyfriend, I found her on the back step with a carton of expired eggs. "They are wonderful for the soil," she said, launching one at nearby tree. "It's good exercise. And, it's very satisfying when you are feeling frustrated and want to channel your energy in a positive way."

She was right—hurling a few eggs through space at a nearby target was incredibly satisfying, especially when faced with the reality that romance had gone rotten.

There is always a certain wisdom hidden in her somewhat quirky behavior. I have no doubt there is a koan or parable embedded in these actions somehow. She can nurture anything, including my now improving mood. On the windowsill above the would-be avocado plant, she has created a miniature "zen garden" that consists of a glass vase, pebbles, and a plant. It sounds completely tacky, but it is actually quite beautiful to behold. Several friends inquire about it during their visits. They think it is exquisite. I derive great joy in revealing the punch line to these Manhattan sophisticates: That beautiful piece of zen art is the remains of a sweet potato.

I receive a call from Secretary of State Condoleezza Rice. As Holbrooke suggested, I have been trying to reach out to her in an attempt to have regular contact with the State Department. She is aware of David's case and has agreed to speak with me. I've spent most of the morning preparing a list of questions. She is warm and forthcoming. I ask if the captors or anyone else connected with David's case is making political demands that perhaps we are not aware of. She denies this. No demands have been made to our government, she says. She advises us to keep the situation quiet. She reiterates what others have said: that we are not dealing with a legitimate government, and that the group holding David is immune to moral pressure.

I pray that David, Tahir, and Asad will have the strength to endure this uncertain period and find peace of mind. I make the same request for me and all our families. I was raised Catholic, so my go-to device for all situations beyond my control is prayer. I try to view this through a larger lens: Why is this happening? What am I meant to learn from this situation? Patience. Surrender. These things spring to mind. Patience is my least favorite virtue, but I am certain this is the lesson I am meant to master through this harrowing test. And I am torn between feeling completely responsible for our three and realizing I may ultimately have no control over the outcome of this situation. I pray for the strength to not give up and, simultaneously, the ability to surrender. My prayer does not take a traditional or eloquent form of incantation. I do not have the strength for this. I merely express the words, "Help me, help us." These seem the most fitting and easiest to access.

Yet at the same time, I am having great difficulty acknowledging my own vulnerability. It must be a trick of the mind, a survival tactic. My thoughts wander to David. Is he being held with other people, or are they keeping him in a hole somewhere, underground? Does he know what day it is, how much time has passed? Has he found his own way to cope? I know it is futile to try to imagine his circumstances. Speculation only leads to a downward spiral. I am confident he will know what to say and do to keep himself and the others alive as long as possible. I worry more about his peace of mind. What is he doing to ease his own boredom and lack of control?

David's religion is the pursuit of the truth. An agnostic with a Unitarian-Episcopalian upbringing, he does not hold to one religious ideal or path. His reporting experience covering atrocities related to religious bigotry have made him skeptical of organized religion. With this in mind, I hope he is able to find some sort of comfort during this time— some personal expression of faith and a belief that some higher force will look out for him.

SPEAK GOOD WORDS TO AN ENEMY

David, Late November–Late December 2008

Atiqullah promised to return in seven to ten days. Yet ten days pass and he does not appear. Instead, in a worrying sign, Badruddin Haqqani now seems to be in charge. A dozen members of his family have been killed by American drone strikes. He himself is a primary American target.

Badruddin moves us to a far smaller, dirtier house five minutes away by car. Transported at night, again with a scarf placed over my face, I have no idea where our new home lies in Miran Shah. We are confined to two small rooms in the back of a large traditional Pashtun family compound with mud-brick walls. An old man and a young boy bring us meals three times a day, often with meat that appears several days old. We sleep on dust-covered mattresses.

One room has posters on the walls. One shows a Swiss chalet in the snow-covered Alps, a setting often used in Indian movies. Another features a majestic Ottoman mosque in Istanbul, a city I have visited with Kristen. The other room holds sleeping bags and camping equipment apparently used by Taliban fighters when they enter Afghanistan. A large radio antenna perched on a nearby rooftop is part of a seemingly sophisticated Taliban communications system in Miran Shah.

We are allowed to walk in a small courtyard that is the width of a city sidewalk. Direct sunlight reaches it for a few hours each morning.

Throughout the day, we hear children playing and laughing on the other side of the walls but never see them.

Akbar—the seemingly kind guard—departs. Qari—the unstable guard who nearly shot Tahir—arrives with a new Taliban fighter in his early twenties named Mansoor, who speaks broken English.

During our first night here, the Taliban commander who owns the house introduces himself to us. At first, he is polite and respectful. He promises to update us every three days on negotiations for our release. As the conversation continues, though, my optimism fades.

He proclaims that he was held in American detention and I am receiving vastly better treatment than he endured. Then he complains that the Taliban released the group of Korean missionaries they kidnapped in 2007 far too quickly. I had covered that kidnapping. The Taliban first demanded that the Afghan government free twenty-three Taliban prisoners in exchange for twenty-three Koreans. President Karzai flatly refused, citing the blistering domestic criticism he came under for releasing five Taliban prisoners for the Italian journalist four months earlier. In response, the Taliban executed two male Korean missionaries.

The Korean government then carried out direct negotiations with the kidnappers, who released the remaining twenty-one hostages after six weeks in captivity. The Taliban triumphantly announced they had been paid a ransom of roughly $20 million. Afghan officials said the actual number was closer to $1 million. American and NATO special forces units later hunted down and killed the Taliban leaders involved in the kidnapping. The commander tells me the Taliban mishandled the case. If they had held the Koreans longer, he believes, the Taliban could have forced the world to accept them as Afghanistan's legitimate government.

"The elders should have listened to me," he says. "I could have gotten the Emirate recognized."

I think to myself that we are in a giant insane asylum. Next, he asks me if I support the American government. I respond that I am an independent journalist and try to explain that American government and military officials frequently do not like journalists and are often angered by our stories.

"Who did you vote for in the presidential election?" he asks.

Sensing a trap, I tell him that I did not vote in the American election because I was in Afghanistan at the time. In truth, I voted by absentee ballot. He says that if I had voted in the election it would mean that I am personally responsible for the actions of the American government, including drone strikes carried out in the tribal areas. He promises to give us an update on the negotiations in three days and leaves. We will not see the commander again for months.

In our first days in the new house, I try to engage Mansoor in more in-depth conversations. Mansoor is short—roughly five foot six inches tall—but stocky and strong. He has dark hair, a thin beard, and a boyish face. He and Qari occasionally wrestle each other to pass the time. Mansoor wins every time.

Our talks do not go well. During one, Mansoor complains that when he got married in Afghanistan, American warplanes circled over the large crowd that formed in his village in a pro-Taliban part of Afghanistan. His family was terrified that the group would be seen as Taliban fighters and bombed. During another, Mansoor agrees with me that he will teach me Pashto and I will teach him English. He buys me a notebook in one of his trips to the local market. For a few days, we give each other brief lessons. Then we both lose interest. Mansoor and I fail to connect on a fundamental level. What interests me—the outside world and my wife and family—does not interest him. What interests Mansoor—religion and jihad—does not interest me.

Qari increasingly unnerves me. He spends hours each day memorizing verses in an electronic Koran. Seated on his knees, he holds the small device—which looks like a digital camera—in his hands. As a computerized voice repeats verses in Arabic, he rhythmically recites them. Rocking back and forth, he seems to be in a trance. After each session, he gently kisses the electronic device, recites a blessing, and wraps it in a small cloth. He then carefully places it on a shelf to ensure it does not make contact with the ground. Qari is polite to me but we rarely speak. I fear provoking him and have no interest in trying to understand him. He has no interest in trying to understand me.

When we hear over the radio of the November 26 terrorist attacks on luxury hotels in Mumbai, our guards are elated. Mansoor cheers as the carnage drags on for three days and 173 people are killed. I ask him why he is celebrating. Mansoor declares that the luxury hotels are dens of prostitution, alcohol consumption, and debauchery. The guests deserve to die because they are sinners.

Another week passes and it becomes clearer that Tahir and Asad will be separated from their families for Id al-Adha—a major Muslim holiday on December 8 that marks Abraham's willingness to sacrifice his son and show his devotion to God. They are more and more frustrated.

Tension is also growing between me, Tahir, and Asad. They are angry with me for my promises to Atiqullah on the second night of the kidnappings that he would get prisoners and millions of dollars for us. I tell them I was trying to save our lives. They say I have vastly raised our captors' expectations.

My attempts to play sick are going nowhere. I have made myself vomit in the new house but the guards do not appear worried. Qari says that I am intentionally making myself sick. December 10, the one-month anniversary of our kidnapping, is approaching. There are no signs of a deal. After taking Tahir to a local doctor several times for stomach and skin problems, the guards stop taking him to the doctor without explanation.

Becoming more desperate, Tahir and I talk over what we can do to create pressure for our release. We settle on a hunger strike, an option we have both been considering for weeks. We have no idea if it will work, but are running out of options. That night before dinner, Tahir announces that he is going to stop eating food. I decide to stop eating food and drinking water, hoping it will make the guards think I will die quickly. Asad does not join us.

The following day, I lie on the mattress where I sleep, staring at the ceiling for hours at a time. I think of the hunger strikes I have read about over the years but cannot remember how long a person can survive without water. I experience less pain than expected and I am pleased by the initial results. At the end of the first day, our guards panic and beg us to eat dinner. We refuse. Relatives of the commander who owns the house beg us to eat as well. It is an enormous shame to them, they say, to have guests who refuse to eat. We decline.

As the second day comes to a close, my stomach begins to ache, my throat is dry, and I have cottonmouth. Pressuring our captors, though, elates me. I am finally doing something concrete to relieve the suffering of my wife and family. That night, the guards announce that Atiqullah has called and said a deal for our release is imminent. It only needs the approval of Karzai, who is on a foreign trip. The French aid worker whose video I was shown when we first arrived in Miran Shah has been released, they say. We are next.

Tahir says we should continue the strike. As a Pashtun, he does not want to show weakness by stopping without achieving our goal. Asad urges us to begin eating again. He says we are angering our captors, not pressuring them. I am torn. A recent radio news broadcast confirmed that Karzai is, in fact, at a meeting abroad. I worry that our continued defiance will cause our captors to refuse to compromise and scuttle a final deal that could be days away. Recent kidnap cases in Afghanistan have ended in four to eight weeks. I hope our month-old case will end in that range as well.

I tell Tahir that we should end the strike. He has kidney problems, is in intense pain, and I worry about his health. The guards have promised to begin taking Tahir to the doctor again if we begin eating. At first, Tahir refuses. We receive a second call from Atiqullah, who swears our release is days away. Tahir relents and we eat for the first time in forty-eight hours.

Instead of releasing us, Badruddin moves us to a nicer house. It is larger than the previous one but feels more like a prison. Twenty-foot-high brick walls covered in peeling white paint surround a thirty- by thirty-foot concrete courtyard. We have a freshly painted blue bedroom to ourselves and the guards sleep next door in a room of their own. Three times a day, a boy from the family who brought us food in the previous house arrives with our meals. When the electricity goes out and the house's water pump has no power, another boy brings us barrels of water for washing.

After several days, the guards announce that we must begin cooking our own meals. The family that has been preparing our food will no longer do so. With cash from Badruddin, the guards buy food from the local market and order Asad to cook it. I try to wash the dishes, but the guards initially urge me to stop, saying it is shameful to have an elder clean for them. We agree that I will wash only the breakfast dishes. At dusk each day, Asad sautés onions over a small propane burner before adding rice. There is a momentary sense of good cheer among us. The food, at least, is fresher, cleaner, and better tasting. But cooking for ourselves gives a worrying sense of permanence to our imprisonment.

Our lives settle into a monotonous routine of meals, washing our clothes, and Checkah board games. While washing the dishes one morning, my wedding ring falls off my finger. I frantically chase it across the courtyard, grab it, and put it back on. Later, it falls off as I take a bucket shower in the bathroom. I am losing weight, but I wonder if this is a sign that something is wrong with Kristen. Worried I will lose the ring, I take it off before I wash in the bathroom, kiss it, and carefully place it in the pocket of my baggy local pants for safekeeping. The narrow gold band with KRISTEN engraved on its interior is the only physical connection I have to the outside world.

Boredom and claustrophobia begin to take a toll on the guards. Qari tears the Checkah board to shreds after he loses several games. Then Tahir and Asad rip up two Checkah boards out of frustration when they lose as well. I worry that Qari will shoot Tahir if he loses another game.

Each day, I spend hours walking in circles in the walled courtyard alone. In my mind, I relive happy memories of my times with my family, friends, and wife. I play out trips I took with Kristen to Europe and South Asia, our wedding, and our honeymoon. I remember the small, everyday beauties of life with her, such as having coffee together each morning. I pretend I am walking beside her down the Hudson River bank at dusk as we do in New York.

As time passes, I realize I must control my thoughts to fight off depression. Certain actions immediately raise my spirits, such as walking, talking with Tahir, and reliving moments with Kristen. Other actions leave me discouraged, such as conversations with the guards. Strictly managing my day and my thoughts becomes a survival tool.

For the first time in my life, I begin praying several times a day. I struggle to remember the Lord's Prayer and don't know if I'm reciting it correctly. Resorting to prayer heightens my sense of desperation, but it also gives me something to do each day, a task the guards cannot stop me from silently completing. In the months ahead, I will realize that prayer is something they can never take from me.

One day I pray in front of Mansoor and Qari, trying to demonstrate that I, too, have faith. They seem unmoved by it. I shift to silently praying as I walk in the yard. I don't know if some higher being is hearing my prayers, reaching down and comforting me, or if prayer is simply a psychological trick that gives humans a false sense of control. I decide it does not matter. Whatever is happening, prayer centers and strengthens me.

Badruddin visits us intermittently at night and promises that negotiations are continuing. He is generally polite and respectful. During one visit, he gives me a woolen Afghan blanket to stay warm. During another, he gives us a Chinese-made shortwave radio with a hand crank to generate electricity when the batteries run out. It is familiar to me. The American military has distributed thousands of these radios to Afghan villagers in the hope of winning their support.

To my amazement, Badruddin arrives with a laptop computer one evening, opens it, and plays *Taxi to the Dark Side*, an American documentary film that won a 2007 Academy Award. The film recounts how two of my colleagues from *The New York Times* exposed that American soldiers had beaten to death a young Afghan taxi driver in the main American detention center in Bagram, Afghanistan. I am elated. The film is a perfect opportunity to explain American journalism to Badruddin.

As Badruddin and the guards watch, the documentary recounts how the American military initially stated that Dilawar, a twenty-two-year-old Afghan taxi driver, died of natural causes in 2002. One of my colleagues then visited his family in Khost Province and discovered an American military death certificate that declared the driver's death a "homicide." His brother could not read the document, which was in English.

"My friend!" I shout, as my colleague describes confronting the commanding American general in Afghanistan. "My friend!"

A still photo of two men arrested with Dilawar in his taxi that day flashes across the screen.

"I found those two men in Khost," I say, explaining that I helped write a follow-up story. "I interviewed them and took that picture."

The next segment describes how another colleague obtained a 2,000-page American military report that confirmed Dilawar was innocent and had been beaten to death. A final segment recounts how the same American military police unit was transferred to Iraq's Abu Ghraib prison where similar abuses occurred. Photographs then flash across the screen of a female American soldier, Lynndie England, smiling as a naked Iraqi prisoner masturbates in front of her. Other images show naked Iraqis stacked in pyramids and England's boyfriend, Specialist Charles Graner, giving a "thumbs up" over the body of a dead Iraqi prisoner.

Badruddin and the guards grow visibly angry. The images reinforce their view of Americans as malevolent hypocrites who preach human rights but torture privately. I try in vain to explain that American journalists, in fact, exposed the Abu Ghraib abuses. My explanations do not matter. My captors pick the information that fits their worldview and ignore the rest. I realize that Badruddin does not fit the Western caricature of a Taliban fighter—a cave dweller who rejects modern technology. Instead, he and other young Taliban embrace technology and use it to strengthen and spread their worldview. Globalization impacts their lives and exposes them to vast amounts of new information, but does not moderate them.

At the end of the film, autopsy photos of dead prisoners appear. Each prisoner is naked. I am sure the film's director included the images to force American viewers to face the reality of the abuses. To an Afghan audience the images further insult the dead. For Afghans, public nudity is deeply humiliating.

After the film ends, the guards complain that none of the American prison guards were seriously punished for the abuses. I have no answer for them.

We reach mid-December and I find myself hanging on to each word uttered by Badruddin. We have not heard from Atiqullah for weeks. Badruddin is increasingly unpredictable. During one visit, he declares the Taliban will not kill me.

"You are the golden hen," he says, expecting me to lay a golden egg.

I ask him to promise not to kill Tahir and Asad. Speaking directly to me in broken English, he says the Taliban have decided to kill Asad if their demands are not met in a week. Then he leaves the house. I panic. Our worst case scenario is unfolding.

When we tell Asad about the deadline, he is fatalistic. Escape from our current house—with its twenty-foot walls—is impossible.

"The Afghan always gets fucked," Asad says.

Over the next two days, I frantically try to think of ways to save our young driver. Since we were abducted, I have spent hours talking politics, religion, and survival with Tahir, but I can barely communicate with Asad. I speak little Pashto, he speaks little English. I try to help him with chores, searching the rice for stones each day before it is cooked. When an English-language newspaper arrives, I show him photos and try to explain what they are about. He laughs, but I feel like a monster. Asad is an impoverished, hardworking father of two—and I am going to get him killed.

On the third day after Badruddin's visit, I tell Mansoor that I am willing to make a video—or do anything they want—to save Asad. Mansoor says he will check with Badruddin. The following day, Mansoor announces that it has all been a misunderstanding. There is no deadline to kill Asad. I feel enormous relief but do not know what to believe. The lies from our captors are constant and, it seems, intentional. While researching my book, I had heard a Pashto saying that described lying as a tactic of war.

"Speak good words to an enemy very softly," the proverb says, "then gradually destroy him root and branch."

Several days later, Badruddin arrives to make the video. He tells Asad that he had recently watched the video of the beheading of Sayed Agha, the Afghan driver kidnapped with the Italian journalist in 2007.

"I've decided that I don't want to do that to you," Badruddin says with a smile.

He promises us that the video will go only to our families, but what he instructs us to say makes me think it will be released publicly. As we sit in the room where we normally sleep, Mansoor and Qari put scarves over their faces and point assault rifles at our heads. Badruddin aims a handheld camera at me. Following Badruddin's orders, I call for President Bush and President-Elect Obama to meet the Taliban's demands.

"If you don't meet their demands," I say, "they will kill all of us."

Tahir and Asad then make similar statements in Pashto. Badruddin departs, and I tell myself that our families will at least know we are alive.

Several days before Christmas, Atiqullah and Akhundzada appear. Atiqullah has spectacular news.

"We are here to free you," he declares, wearing no scarf over his face for the first time. "We have come here to release you."

Atiqullah is bald and his face is pudgy. He is not the dashing Afghan warrior that Americans idealized during the anti-Soviet jihad. Delivering the news of our release, though, his round face looks sincere to me. I am euphoric. My confidence in Atiqullah is not misplaced. He is a moderate and reasonable Taliban leader who will release us.

Two of Atiqullah's younger brothers accompany him as well. They also make him seem more moderate. One is a respectful young man in his late twenties named Timor Shah. The other is in his early twenties and says he is a fan of American wrestling. He lifts weights and says his favorite wrestler is John Cena.

After dinner, my conversation with Atiqullah turns menacing. Before we are released, he says, we must answer his questions.

"We've investigated you," he declares. "We know every interview you did. We've analyzed every stamp in your passport."

I tell him I have nothing to hide and to ask any questions he wants. Atiqullah announces that on the morning we were kidnapped the American military had mounted an operation to arrest Abu Tayyeb, the Taliban commander who had invited us to the interview. Stunned, I tell Atiqullah I know nothing about a military operation.

He accuses me of sending text messages from my cell phone to Saudi Arabia before the interview, to tip off the American military about Abu Tayyeb's location. I tell him I have no idea what he is talking about.

Finally, he declares that I am a spy, along with other employees of *The New York Times* in Afghanistan. His men have prepared a suicide attack on the paper's Kabul bureau, he says, which he could set off with a single phone call. His men nearly kidnapped another one of our reporters, but they left an interview just before the Taliban arrived, he says. I know he is probably lying on both counts, but I fear he is telling the truth.

Finally, Atiqullah begins asking me a series of questions about the time I lived in New Delhi and served as the newspaper's South Asia bureau co-chief. He demands to know exactly how many times I met the American ambassador there. I answer truthfully, saying that I spent the vast majority of my time in Afghanistan and Pakistan and met the American ambassador in New Delhi once at a group interview and once at a holiday dinner. Atiqullah scoffs at my reply.

Our imprisonment, I think, has reached a low point. Our captor believes I am a spy and my colleagues in Kabul are now in danger as well. Atiqullah's talk earlier in the day of our imminent release seems farcical. The following morning, Atiqullah insists that there is, in fact, a deal. At one point, he says we will be exchanged within "days." He toys with me, asking which flights I will take back to the United States and how many television cameras will be at the airport. He asks me what I will say to Kristen when I see her.

By this point, I have begun to doubt everything he says. Then I learn that he has lied to us from the beginning.

In separate conversations when our guards leave the room, Tahir and

Asad each whisper to me that Atiqullah is, in fact, Abu Tayyeb. They have known since the day we were kidnapped, they say, but dared not tell me. They ask me to stay silent as well. Abu Tayyeb has vowed to behead them if they reveal his identity.

Abu Tayyeb invited us to an interview, betrayed us, and then pretended he was a commander named Atiqullah.

I am despondent and left with only one certainty: We have no savior among the Taliban.

VIDEO GAMES

Kristen, December 22, 2008–Early January 2009

Around noon I receive a call at my office at *Cosmopolitan* from Jim, the Joint Terrorism Task Force FBI agent assigned to our case. The kidnappers have made a video of David. Jim cannot say how the FBI obtained the video, but offers to bring it to me for a private screening. The FBI is honoring our family's request to see the footage first, before the newspaper and security team, in a discreet setting. Everyone involved in the case has been jockeying for my trust of late. This is clearly a gesture on their part. Jim and his fellow agents tell me to look for the blue car parked outside Starbucks on West 57th Street, not far from my office in Midtown Manhattan. I find this slightly amusing as I recall a similar scene from a *Sopranos* episode.

I am so thankful my office has a door. This is not typical at women's magazines. A glass wall separates me from the rest of the photo department—very convenient when planning a clandestine meeting with federal agents. From the exterior cubicles, I can be seen but not heard. This is a great advantage in terms of keeping my situation secret, although the isolation the secrecy fosters leaves me feeling like a lone fish in an aquarium at times.

I'm only a month into my new job, but I regularly fail to arrive at the office before 10 A.M., delayed by phone calls and updates, and then I usually need to leave well before 7 P.M. My associates must be thinking the new girl is a real prima donna. While I have informed the top editors at the magazine of my predicament, the rest of the staff is unaware of my unusual situation. As a newlywed, I am often asked about my husband: Do I have a photo from the wedding I can show? When will I be bringing him to the office for a visit? Has he returned from his reporting trip? I find new and inventive ways to respond to or, in effect, not answer these questions.

I meet Jim, Cathy, and another agent for a private screening in their four-door sedan. This gives new meaning to the phrase "drive-in movie," I think. Jim produces a silver laptop. I assume the video has been intercepted somehow, but do not know from where. The video is poor quality black-and-white footage. David sits between two men Jim tells me are Tahir and Asad. Immediately I notice David is wearing his glasses. This is a huge relief. I was worried they had been confiscated. He is nearly blind without them, and I have spent nights tossing and turning over this fact.

Two Taliban gunmen frame the image, each with a Kalashnikov. One of them has a scarf over his face. The other is cropped out from the neck upward.

David speaks first.

"I am David Rohde, a journalist for *The New York Times*," he says. "I was detained on November 10 and have been held captive for thirty-four days. It's very cold, very difficult. They are moving us around the mountains of Afghanistan and we are not allowed to make calls."

"I ask my office, President Bush, and President-Elect Barack Obama to meet their demands," he says. "If you do not meet their demands, they will kill all three of us. Please meet their demands. Please meet their demands. Please meet their demands."

Tahir and Asad repeat similar speeches in Pashto and plead to Afghan president Hamid Karzai in addition to the American government. All three look remarkably calm, which surprises us. The guns remain pointed at David throughout.

It's the first time I have seen my husband in a month and a half. He seems like a foreign object to me. His expression is a little vacant and glassy-eyed. He is well groomed, cleaner than I expected. He wears a salwar kameez, the baggy pants and shirt that are the local dress. A woolen blanket covers his shoulders. I try to discern information, signals from his eye movements. His hands, concealed by the blanket, are behind his back. I have no idea if they are bound or free. I am struck by the fact that his beard is neat. I was expecting unkempt hair akin to John Walker Lindh, the American who was captured fighting for the Taliban in 2001.

The world within the video feels so removed from my own—distant, foreign, staged. It is not every day one sees one's husband videotaped by terrorists. I find it difficult to absorb this fact. I am at once enraged and relieved. It incenses me to see David used as a mouthpiece. Yet it is comforting to see that he has not been physically mishandled. And, odd as it seems, I am simply relieved to have contact with him. No one has heard a word from him or his captors in over a month. I interpret any form of communication, after this long a silence, as a sign of hope.

And yet there are no specific demands being made in the video. I worry that the Taliban are directing their vague message to the United States government. In addition to being a disturbing situation, it is also bad timing. We are between administrations—in political limbo. The old guard is on its way out; the new is not yet able to step up to the plate.

I watch the video over and over. I can't stop looking at it. One of the drawbacks to clandestine meetings in cars on 57th Street in the middle of Manhattan is traffic. Someone bumps the fender. A traffic cop arrives and threatens to issue a ticket. Jim has to produce his credentials—apparently even the FBI is not exempt from traffic laws. The irony and humor of the situation is not lost on Jim. Months later, when we review the list of communications received from David's captors, he will refer to this one as "the car bump video."

I head back to my office to complete the day, a difficult proposition given that I am now thoroughly distracted. Composing shoot budgets, editing film, and sketching storyboards provide me with a momentary, tangible sense of control, order, and escape. But my solace is fleeting as my mind wanders back to the dubious messages in the video. A few days before Christmas, this was not the holiday greeting I was hoping for.

Back at home, from our apartment window I can see the Christmas trees lined up on the corner for sale, a singular ritual of city life. Cheerful white lights illuminate an overpriced selection of firs and pine trees from

Vermont, Maine, and upstate New York. An enormous plastic snowman flashes a red candy cane and green top hat.

I've been trying to come up with positive ways to reinforce my connection with David during his absence. I decide to go ahead and buy our first Christmas tree as a married couple. A close friend comes over and we drown our holiday sorrows in cheese fondue. Just what the doctor ordered. Then we proceed to the tree stand on the corner. I ask the vendor what I can buy for $40. He produces a sparse sapling, barely a foot high.

"That's one sad-looking Charlie Brown tree," I say.

"Not even!" he admits.

I point to another tree that is a few feet taller, fuller, and more hopeful. Then he tries to sell me a nine-foot tree. "Just sold one of these to Mrs. Gandolfini," he says proudly, referring to the wife of the Sopranos star. It's $300. We settle on the smaller but hopeful-looking tree and some stringy tinsel.

At home, we set it up in David's office alcove. We add lights and miniature ornaments, including one David and I bought on a recent trip to Paris. I also pull out every religious relic I can find. There is the "longevity" charm we picked up at the Takstang Monastery in Bhutan, a scared heart from Sacré-Coeur in Paris, and a Buddhist prayer bracelet from Varanasi in India.

Along the window ledge of the living room, I set up all the cards we've received from relatives still unaware of our situation, wishing us a happy first Christmas together. I want to inject as much positive energy into this space as possible in hopes that it will somehow reach David. For the first time in weeks I feel more connected to my husband and hopeful that he will return. I notice a sense of peace I have not felt in quite some time.

Ruhullah, David's former translator in Afghanistan, who is now a college student in the United States, stops by for a visit. After years of working together in tense situations, David and Ruhullah are very close. David treats him like a younger brother. He helped bring Ruhullah to the United States after the work he was doing for David and *The New York Times* bureau made him a target of the Taliban. Ruhullah is headed back to Kabul for the holidays and has offered to remain there to work on David's case.

I tell him David would be very upset if he knew Ruhullah was missing school because of him. Maybe he can think of something more I should be doing, or some type of message I should be trying to send as David's wife. What would a Pashtun woman do?

Ruhullah begins to write a plea for me in Pashto to send to David's captors. "It is a popular saying in my culture: My husband is my veil. Please return him to me." Ruhullah underscores the significance of this phrase: "It means my husband is my honor and you are denying me my honor by keeping him away from me. It is shameful for Afghans to do such a thing. I think this will help."

I scan and e-mail the note to our consultants who are in the process of setting up a base in Kabul, suggesting that they keep it on file for a time when it is possible to send it.

On New Year's Eve I get a call from Jill Abramson, Bill Schmidt, and Craig Whitney—senior employees at the *Times*—all of whom are working late. They have been following David's case and are calling to wish me a happier New Year. While their New Year's Eve has been less than stellar, they all agree mine is probably worse.

We have assembled our consultants in Kabul: Team Kabul.

The team consists of two patient individuals who are tasked with fielding phone calls from the captors, a job that is mostly a waiting game. One of them is a Clayton kidnap expert; the other is an AISC consultant. After much deliberation, the newspaper, Lee, and I have decided to move the operation out of the *Times*' bureau there. The newspaper does not want to endanger its staffers. We also want to shift the kidnappers' perception that *The New York Times* is handling this case. The security team also feels the bureau is not a secure location. They prefer to work from an anonymous compound.

We want to encourage direct contact with our family. And because some people at the Kabul bureau are opposed to the payment of ransom, we do not want them to be the ones to negotiate on David, Tahir, and

Asad's behalf. We also do not want the FBI to oversee our negotiations, because the terms they could discuss are very limited, but we do update them periodically on the status of our communications. We have stuck with David's request to negotiate for all three together. We want the kidnappers to realize that our family, Lee and me, is the correct point of contact for negotiations. We hope the change in venue will achieve this. The phone number the captors have been calling is forwarded to this location.

The downside of moving the call center is that the personnel from AISC and Clayton who will man it rotate out every month. The other disadvantage is that once we move, we won't have nearly the same access to David's colleagues at the Kabul bureau and their enormous expertise in the culture and politics of this region. They have completely dedicated themselves to working for the release of our three, desperately trying to gain on-the-ground intelligence from their local network of sources. They have contacted local tribal elders, the Quetta Shura, and Afghan officials in hope of coming to a resolution that will not involve ransom. One of David's colleagues e-mails daily updates on their progress. This journalist has also researched Abu Tayyeb's background in hopes of gaining insight into his motives, and provides updates to the families of Tahir and Asad. David's colleagues are hesitant to move the call center, but are under pressure from superiors. And they are exhausted, having also to continue to provide daily news coverage of events in the region for the *Times*.

The security team is skeptical of the Kabul bureau's actions. They want to limit outreach done on David's behalf, as they feel it creates confusion about who is running the negotiations and raises his value as a hostage.

Chris Chivers, another reporter in the Kabul bureau and a friend of David's, has returned to the States. He has graciously brought me the laptop and notebook David left behind at the bureau when he set out for the interview on November 10. It is chilling to flip through David's notes. Written on the last page of a small Moleskine are the words *Abu Tayyeb*. This was the Taliban commander David was due to meet that fateful day. The computer, too, is unaltered since David last used it. The Novem-

ber 9 front page of *The New York Times* Web site pops up, an eerie reminder of all the time that has passed while our life together remains on
hold.

I have one new friend and confidant, the enigmatic Irishman Michael
Semple. He and I have developed a rapport over Skype. He is gracious
enough to provide his assessment of how the case is going from time
to time on an informal basis. I trust Michael. He knows an enormous
amount about what is happening on the ground in Afghanistan and
Pakistan and has been brought up to speed on our case by a reporter in
the Kabul bureau. He is fluent in several local dialects and understands
the complexities of the tribal structures in the region. And he is familiar
with members of the Haqqani network, which most people involved in
our case now think is responsible for David's kidnapping.

Michael has worked on other kidnapping cases on an unofficial basis,
so I hope he has some sense of how this might play out. I value his insight
and appreciate his eloquence, which is always tempered with a healthy
dose of Irish humor.

I have forwarded the scan of the plea to the captors that Ruhullah
wrote in Pashto. Michael promises to pass it along to a mullah who is
known to have contact with the Haqqani family. Michael feels that even
though the man who has been identifying himself as Atiqullah has been
the point person on the phone, it is unlikely he has much authority in striking a deal for the release of David, Tahir, and Asad. Michael, along with
our security team, think that Sirajuddin Haqqani is the person ultimately
in charge of David's fate.

I have heard of Siraj—the elusive second son of Jalaluddin Haqqani,
the mujahideen warrior who helped the United States drive the Soviets
out of Afghanistan but then later aligned with the Taliban after 9/11.
Siraj rarely grants interviews, eschews photography, and is often referred
to as bipolar or schizophrenic. I do not know if this is a clinical term or
merely hyperbole. At any rate, he is viewed as erratic and unpredictable.
I Google him and learn that he is "so elusive that only a sketch exists of
him." The FBI has informed us that one of the captors' voices on the
phone—perhaps Atiqullah himself—is Badruddin Haqqani, Siraj's
younger brother. Badruddin is believed to be in charge of orchestrating

kidnappings for the Haqqani network. We now think "Atiqullah" is the alias that both Abu Tayyeb and Badruddin use when they call us. They are working in tandem.

Every day at noon, we conduct a conference call during which we receive updates on David's case from Team Kabul and discuss the way forward. My day is scheduled to allow for this. As I duck into my office at *Cosmopolitan* and shut the door, I secretly hope my assistant thinks I am talking to my husband or negotiating photography contracts. I phone into an assigned number on a private call box.

A beep precedes the announcement of each participant. We have a lot of cooks in the kitchen. Our noon calls include me, Lee, McCraw, Team Kabul, and an AISC employee in the United States. Michael continues to advise me privately, but does not participate in the daily group calls. Lately, personalities have begun to clash. A kind of turf war, perhaps inevitable, is starting to break out. The security consultants feel all other inquiries and activities, namely the Kabul bureau's outreach to local government officials and elders, should stop. I am hesitant about this, but Lee, McCraw, and I support the suggestion because we feel it will give the new team a chance to establish one clear, direct channel to our family.

Team Kabul has received word, via rumor, that the Taliban want $25 million and ten prisoners in exchange for David. We also hear that David is not well. He is sick from the food and other conditions of captivity. Michael Semple assures me not to be alarmed. "Every hostage is, quote, 'gravely ill' or 'suicidal.' This is merely a way to assert pressure on you." In the meantime, a reporter in the Kabul bureau has gotten in touch with the International Committee of the Red Cross to see if they can make contact with the people holding David in order to send medicine or assistance. The Red Cross informs us that it may be able to act as an intermediary if we want to write letters to our three. Everyone agrees this is a good idea.

At home, I once again Skype with Michael. He assures me that many of his contacts are continuing to inquire about David and are working for his release. Ever the poetic Irishman, he tries to buoy me up. The Afghans have a saying, he tells me: "The fruit of patience is sweet." He encourages me to keep this in mind. Then adds, "Think of yourself as Helen of Troy. Many ships have been launched for your cause." This is rather intriguing, and sustains me for a moment. But when I log off, my mood drops. All illusions aside, my hope is stranded: Afghanistan is a landlocked country.

FUTILITY

David, Late December 2008–Mid-January 2009

The day after Christmas, Abu Tayyeb announces that his negotiator in Kabul—a man they call the engineer—has reached an agreement to exchange us for female prisoners from the Afghan national prison in Pul-i-Charkhi.

"Don't you think it's wrong to hold women prisoner?" he asks me.

"Yes," I say, playing along.

I pace in the yard, telling myself not to believe him. He has lied to us from the beginning, inviting us to an interview, kidnapping us, and then masquerading as someone named "Atiqullah." Yet he continues to treat us well physically, and I find myself unable to stop daydreaming about our release. Again, my mind seems to be instinctively drawn to a narrative of survival, not death.

Our living conditions have improved again. On Christmas night, Abu Tayyeb moved us to a larger, more modern house in Miran Shah. The next morning I was allowed to lie on a cot outside and soak up direct sunlight. The owner of the house, a tall Afghan Taliban commander named Sharif, is friendly and encourages me to walk in the yard. The house's eight-foot walls allow the courtyard to be flooded with sunlight. It is the most modern house we have inhabited since being abducted. It is a one-story, five-room structure built in 2005, according to a date scrawled in one corner of the concrete floor. It has metal doors and window frames, two bathrooms, and an electric pump that fills a rooftop water tank on the intermittent days when Miran Shah has electricity.

Bedspreads manufactured by a Pakistani textile company for export to the United States cover the floor of the room where we sleep. They are emblazoned with characters from the American television shows *Hannah Montana* and *Littlest Pet Shop,* and the movies *Spider-Man* and *Cars.* My blanket is a pink Barbie comforter. Our guards have never heard of any of the characters. Each night, all of us curl up beneath icons of American pop culture.

Abu Tayyeb spends a few days with us in the new house. He says I am confined for my own safety. If word spreads that an American is being held prisoner in Miran Shah, he says, Arab or Pakistani militants could demand that I be executed in revenge for a drone strike. One night, he returns home and announces that there is an agreement to release us in exchange for seven male prisoners from the Afghan national prison. The exchange will happen in "days," he says.

The following morning, Abu Tayyeb vanishes again. Timor Shah, his younger brother, is now our chief guard. He seems amiable and respectful. To my relief, Qari departs and Mansoor stays. Sharif and one of his gunmen live with us as well.

The next night, Badruddin arrives and shatters my hopes of release. No agreement has been reached for the exchange of seven prisoners from the Afghan national prison, Badruddin says. And the Taliban are continuing to demand a $15 million ransom in addition to prisoners. His description of how our captors are conducting negotiations, though, demoralizes me most of all.

Their negotiator in Kabul—"the engineer" mentioned by Abu Tayyeb—is an Afghan man whom the Haqqanis kidnapped along with his son several months ago, according to Badruddin. At some point, the Haqqanis decided to keep the engineer's son in captivity, release the engineer, and tell him that if he obtained the desired prisoners and ransom in our case, his son would be released. If not, the engineer's son would remain in captivity.

I tell Badruddin their demands will never be met and that blackmailing a man into serving as a negotiator will never succeed. Badruddin says he has no choice. The Afghan government arrested the negotiator the Haqqanis used in their last kidnapping. Badruddin departs and I am livid. I am desperate to speak with Tahir about what to do, but the guards insist we go to bed. Unable to sleep, I grow increasingly angry. I want to punish Badruddin for his obstinacy. I want to show our captors that we will not wait forever for an agreement.

I decide to fake a suicide attempt the following morning. Before dawn, I hear Sharif and one of his gunmen walking around outside. They are performing ablutions before waking the others for predawn prayers. I get up, grab the Afghan scarf my captors gave me to cover my face, and walk out of the room where we sleep with our guards. The gunman greets me and I motion to him that I am waiting for the bathroom, which Sharif occupies. The gunman walks into the yard to perform ablutions at a spigot around the corner.

I push the cot the gunman sleeps on up against a wall, step onto it, and tie one end of the scarf to a metal bar I have seen during the day. I tie the other end of the scarf around my neck. When I hear the gunman walking back toward the house from the yard, I step off the cot, hang in the air, and start kicking my feet.

"Sharif!" the guard shouts. "Sharif!"

Seconds later, someone places me in a bear hug and lifts me up. The scarf is loosened from around my neck. Tahir rushes out of the bedroom and starts shouting.

"David! David!" he thunders. "Can you hear me? What are you doing?"

His voice is filled with anger, not sympathy. All the guards rush out of the bedroom and glare at me. Tahir leads me back into the bedroom, tells me to lie down, and asks me why I did this.

"I have no hope because of Badruddin," I say, and break into false tears. I do my best to look depressed and desperate to Sharif and the guards. Tahir and the guards speak in Pashto. I am left alone for several minutes with Asad and one of the guards watching me. Asad walks over to me, tugs my beard, and embraces me. I tell him that I'm sorry.

Tahir returns to the room and is irate. "Are you a child?" he shouts. "Why did you not speak to me before doing this?"

He explains that attempting to commit suicide confirms that I am guilty in the eyes of our captors. The Taliban believe that if a human being is truly innocent, they will patiently wait for God to save them. If they try to kill themselves, they are guilty. My head spins. Another rash decision by me has endangered us. I ask Tahir to forgive me. He says he no longer trusts me.

Badruddin arrives an hour later. As he walks through the door, I stare down at the floor. He slaps me on the shoulder and shouts, "Sit up straight!" Incensed, he turns to Tahir and accuses him of telling me to attempt suicide. Tahir denies it but Badruddin does not believe him. Everything I do is blamed on Tahir. I apologize to Badruddin, tell him I have made a terrible mistake, and promise not to do it again. Seething with anger, he leaves.

Timor Shah takes away my scarf and issues new orders. I am not allowed to leave the bedroom at night without the permission of the guards. I must ask them before walking from room to room and going to the bathroom. And when I am in the bathroom, I must leave the door open at all times so the guards can watch for a suicide attempt.

Abu Tayyeb arrives several days later. He tells me that if I do this again my life will end.

"If you want to die," he says, "this is a very easy place to die."

I apologize to him and again promise nothing will happen. Abu Tayyeb says we will now be guarded by three of his men at all times. Chunky will be joining us as well. The following morning, he departs again.

Tahir tells me the attempt has exponentially increased our captors' suspicions of me. Sharif does not think it was real. If I was serious, I would have tried in the middle of the night when no one would find me. Tahir's disappointment devastates me. I have let him down in a way I never intended.

Trying to regain the trust of the guards, as well as Tahir's and Asad's, I comply with all the new rules and sheepishly ask for permission to do the smallest of acts. I do more chores to show my loyalty. Along with washing the breakfast dishes, I sweep the floors, and look for stones in the rice before Asad cooks it.

Trying to stay patient, I multiply the amount of praying I do. Three times a day, I silently pray for Kristen, my family, Asad, and Tahir, confess my sins, and ask for forgiveness and for our freedom. I repeat each one-line prayer forty-one times, the number of years I have lived. I count the prayers on my fingertips while I'm walking in the yard, varying the order depending on what seems most dire that day. If I have made a mistake with the guards, I pray for forgiveness first. If there is a recent threat of Asad's or Tahir's being executed, I pray for them first. If it is a holiday or family birthday, I begin with Kristen and family. I sense that I am becoming compulsive about praying, but it continues to give me a sense of control when I have none.

I know the guards would find it blasphemous that I dare formulate my own prayers. The hard-line Wahhabi Islam they follow focuses on exacting ritual. Sharif and the guards wear their hair, beards, and clothes precisely as they have been told the prophet did. Mustaches are neatly trimmed to prevent food from gathering in facial hair. Beards are not allowed to grow longer than the width of a man's fist. Pants hang three to four inches above the ankle. As the prophet did, they brush their teeth with a miswak, a twig from an arak, or peelu, tree that contains natural disinfectants.

The guards' five daily prayers themselves are soothing. As they rhythmically confess sins and appeal for mercy in Arabic, they press their foreheads to the ground and supplicate to God. The tremendous discipline they show is impressive, but the rigidity of their interpretation of Islam rings false to me. If there is a higher being, I believe it will hear a sincere and humble prayer no matter how it is delivered.

In early January, Asad tells Tahir that he is going to try to escape on his own. I am elated by the news. By dutifully cooking our meals and essentially serving as slave labor, Asad has gradually gained the trust of the guards.

Tahir, by comparison, is defiant. He refuses to do any chores. His attitude toward the guards is a lesson in Pashtunwali. He refuses to show weakness.

"They can't touch me," he says.

Tahir's powerful tribe—the Luddin—will take revenge on anyone who harms him, he believes. The man who kills him will die along with ten members of his family. I admire his bravery. I know Afghanistan's tribal structure has weakened over the years. The Taliban do not fear Afghanistan's tribes as they once did.

Asad believes that Tahir is being reckless and his escape plan is simple. The guards have started taking Asad with them on regular trips to Miran Shah's busy central market to buy food. On a recent trip, Asad slipped away and met a taxi driver who said he would drive Asad to the Afghan border. Asad returned to the guards and apologized for getting separated. He now plans to slip away again from the guards on his next trip to the market, jump in the taxi, and head for the Afghan border. Tahir, who brought several hundred dollars in cash to our ill-fated interview, gives Asad extra money to pay the driver.

The following morning, Asad departs with the guards. The thought of his being reunited with his wife and two sons is thrilling to me. I pray he will succeed. Several hours later, there is a knock on our compound door. Asad enters ashen faced. The guards are nowhere to be seen. Asad whispers to Tahir that he evaded the guards in the crowded market and reached the taxi. But when the driver tried to leave Miran Shah, Taliban fighters stopped the taxi at a checkpoint. When the Taliban grew suspicious, Asad had the taxi return him to Miran Shah and walked back to our house.

The guards return from the local market and berate Asad for getting separated from them. Asad tells them he got lost. We return to our bleak daily routine. All of our attempts to fight back have proven futile

MULTITASKING

Kristen, Early to Mid-January 2009

"Nothing to report" has become the standard daily update from Team Kabul as we endure the quiet winter months.

Today's noon call is a surprising exception. Team Kabul informs us that they have been contacted by Atiqullah and that they have made an offer to counter his demands for $25 million and ten prisoners. We are all a bit stunned, because our family has not preapproved any amount. "What did you offer?" we ask. They tell us.

You can hear a pin drop. While it is nowhere in the range of what the kidnappers are demanding, it is much more than we ever intended to offer up front. We have been told to offer low, in hopes of lowering expectations. For weeks we have been debating with Team Kabul what this might mean. We were forewarned about offering too little—we need enough on the table to keep David and his colleagues alive. But this number seems way too high.

We have no intention of paying any amount, at this time, but we hope the offer will keep the conversation going. It does not.

Word comes back from the kidnappers that our offer is offensively low. They turn their phones off. We do not hear from them for several weeks. The Clayton consultant who made the offer did so with the best intentions. He valued all three lives equally. We think he was going for a slam-dunk. But, clearly, this has backfired. He rotates out of Kabul and does not return for a second rotation.

It's been several weeks since we've heard from David's captors. Despite the fact that phone communication has come to a halt, the two-man Team Kabul remains in place. Each day they try the mobile phone numbers that Atiqullah had previously given to us. No answer.

One day, a person who identifies himself as "the engineer" shows up at Team Kabul's compound with a bold claim. The Haqqanis have sent him to negotiate a deal for the release of our three, he says. The engineer is a former Afghan military official who once worked with Americans. He himself was kidnapped several months ago by the Haqqanis. He was released in exchange for his son, who is now in captivity. He announces that the Haqqanis want prisoners and money in exchange for David, Tahir, and Asad—as well as several prisoners to gain his son's release.

We are skeptical as to why he would help us. Does he have a side agenda? Can we trust him? Team Kabul meets with him on numerous occasions and reports that the engineer appears to be well educated and genuine. He does not ask for money for any of his efforts.

Team Kabul decides to take him up on his offer. He begins to contact representatives for the Haqqanis and relays messages back that our family is working to resolve this issue, but will never have the amount of money they are asking for.

Back in New York, our noon updates continue with *The New York Times*, Team Kabul, and AISC, the private security contractors. Weekends are no exception. This particular weekend I am checking in on a *Cosmo* cover shoot a few blocks from my home. We are photographing one of the *Gossip Girls* at a loft studio in Tribeca. Everything—the floor, the ceiling, the furniture—is stark white. The space is a mix of modern and vintage architectural details. We have also put up a backdrop of colorful seamless paper.

All morning the actress has been getting *Cosmo*-ready: full hair, makeup. Racks of designer dresses and platform shoes line the dressing area. Pop music blares in the background. Push-up bras, pins, and cleavage enhancers are on hand.

I'm hoping we will start shooting before my noon call so I can duck out to listen to the latest update from Kabul. No such luck. Instead, I phone in to our call box from the set and look for a quiet corner.

The update is horrific. A messenger was sent in to obtain recent proof of life from David's captors. He has not resurfaced. We receive news that he never returned and might have been shot en route. It is not clear whether the incident was due to his attempt to help us or random fire. The border area is a war zone, after all. We are not quite sure which route he took or his intended final destination, only that he claimed to be able to make contact with people in proximity to David. A death might have occurred as a result of our case. I feel nauseated.

The call continues. Mike, the head of AISC, weighs in on the latest speculation on David's whereabouts. Another individual who AISC brought onto the case has recently begun to frequent our noon calls. Until now he has been working behind the scenes. We hear from him next. A gruff voice proceeds to tell us what he has learned from an American government official with contacts in the region. I have not met the owner of the voice on the other end of the line, so I have yet to match a face with the speaker. But his voice is distinct and he seems to be quite the mastermind, able to think of long-term connections and associations of the Haqqanis. The gravelly older voice on the end of the line, with a hint of a New England accent, is Dewey Clarridge. Over the course of the next few months, his colorful personality emerges. We quickly learn that Dewey has two modes: grumpy and "grandfatherly." He shifts between the two periodically, occasionally offering me heartfelt encouragement: "We're gonna win this thing, kiddo!" And at other times, he is disgruntled and tells me to take up needlepoint. He often punctuates his point by hanging up on the noon calls or telling us all to shut up. McCraw refers to the softer side of Dewey as "Grandpa Dewey."

Dewey seems to be a sharp strategist and savvy operator. I consider his opinions, though I do not always appreciate the delivery. Today he informs us as to how he thinks David's case might play out. If David or his captors are still in Afghanistan, the winter storms will be kicking in, followed by the spring offensive—this is a period of time during which the Taliban fighters regroup and redouble their efforts—typically in April.

On the basis of this pattern, he estimates David will not be released before May.

May! I am outraged—inconveniently so, as the photo shoot is beginning to take shape in the background. The actress is finished with hair and makeup and is getting ready for her close-up.

"May is thoroughly unacceptable," I respond, my imperious fashion editor voice creeping in. "How can you tell me this? David has been gone for two months. Every day he sits there takes a toll on his sanity."

I realize this is a business on both sides and wonder what the incentive is to get him out quickly if our security team is paid by the day. I say as much, which thoroughly offends and pisses off half the team. The rest of the group is silent, understanding it's my prerogative as the hostage's wife to lose my cool now and then. I am disgusted at the prospect of facing more months of uncertainty. I am also tired of dealing with a virtual roomful of men. Not the eager-to-please pinups we exhibit in *Cosmo*, but the macho former-intel and military types who comprise our team. As Dewey interrupts to tell me to calm down—and shut up—I hang up. I do not want to incur more damage. And my tolerance for speculation coupled with chauvinism is exhausted.

The shoot gets under way and seems on track, so I head home. It has begun to snow. The cool air is a calming relief. No sooner do I round the corner than I get a call from someone at the shoot. Lunch has arrived. Shrimp. And the publicist has neglected to tell us that the actress is allergic to shellfish. What should the crew do? I suggest ordering extra sandwiches. They inform me the water for tea is cold. *You've got to be kidding me,* I think. Yet it's my job to manage every detail of a shoot, large and small, from budgeting and location down to gastronomic minutiae. The big picture and the smallest detail. But given the fact that I have been told that someone surrounding David's case may have been shot and that I should expect to face the cold winter months without my husband, I find it impossible to care.

Trudging back to the apartment I hit an all-time low. I am exhausted to the point of tears. I don't see how I can juggle my work life and the demands of the kidnapping. Pleasing a celebrity and chewing out a security team are incongruous and perhaps irreconcilable activities.

At home, my mother encourages me to get some rest, but my mind is on overload. I find no peace in sitting still. I glance at the avocado plant my mother has been growing in the apartment since Thanksgiving. It is now a hearty sapling and has sprouted several leaves.

"I should leave work," I say. She encourages me to hang on. Work, she says, while stressful, provides a sense of stability and routine. And, oddly, a respite from being completely consumed by crisis. I am frustrated because I am unable to give 100 percent to work. I have to resign myself to the fact that my energy is finite. If working at half speed is all I can do right now, I need to accept it. The magazine has recently offered to let me hire a freelancer to fill in for me a few days a week. My mother encourages me to take advantage of this and rest when I can.

My mother and I have made very different choices in life. She married young and had three children. Motherhood was a priority for her in her twenties and thirties.

I am nearly forty and have just gotten married. I hope to have a family, but other things were more important to me until now. I regret to admit that the clock is now ticking full force. In fact, the alarm bell rings every hour. One subtext to all this uncertainty and waiting is that I wonder if David and I will miss the opportunity to have a family together.

My mother and I are quite different, yet I know no one feels my pain more than her. It's tough for her to see me in distress. She has been a real trouper, doing her best to conceal her own sadness and fear. This alone is a huge service. I often feel I have no room for anyone else's emotion. I am constantly barraged with well-meaning but often tearful inquiries about David. Calls from friends and family once a comfort now feel like an added responsibility. I do not know what to tell them. I have hit full saturation. It's all I can do to keep myself composed, let alone comfort someone else.

At this point, David's colleagues, other news organizations, the United States government and close relatives are aware of the situation. Yet most of my colleagues, with the exception of the top editors at *Cosmopolitan* and a few close friends, are still in the dark.

My mother tells me on occasion that she does not quite know what to do to help me. I reassure her that just her presence is enough—the fact that she has kept the apartment in order, reminded me to eat and rest. These things, while so basic, are so easily forgotten in the midst of crisis. She is also quite handy, I have learned, and regularly assigns herself home improvement projects, executing them flawlessly. They involve everything from putting a closet door back on track to repairing floor tiles and managing the plumber when the faucet leaks. As I look around, the apartment seems brighter. She confesses that she has painted the hallway. "When?" I ask, astonished. "While you were at work one day, just some minor touch ups," she replies. I am exhausted by the thought of her seamless productivity around the home. Exhausted and thankful.

If nothing else, I have a newfound respect for my mother; not just her efficiency, but her strength and her complete willingness to be my silent hero. I appreciate the power her presence has to make everything seem like it will be all right. My father, too, has been a strong support, shuttling my mother between New York and Maine and visiting on the weekends. He has been a selfless advocate, willing to accommodate my mother's long absences as he knows her presence has been an essential part of my ability to cope with the daily challenges of the kidnapping.

I never wanted to be the spouse stuck at home, waiting for someone to return. For years, I chose a career that would enable me to be the one off having adventures, often at the expense of my personal life. In David, I chose a partner who had taken a similar path. Our desire to reform our solitary lives and build a home life seemed to converge. I recall our first meeting in New York, or the first meeting I remember. I had met David briefly in college, at Brown where we were both students. He had bright red carrot-top hair, was always dressed in khakis and an oxford shirt, and never said a word to me. He swears we met in New York five years or so after graduation when he stopped by my apartment with a mutual friend. I have no memory of it. The same friend suggested we meet in June 2006.

We exchanged e-mails and met at a restaurant in my neighborhood. At any rate, the David of 2006 breezed into the restaurant, only a few minutes late.

I didn't consider our dinner to be a date, but merely two people with a mutual friend, meeting for a casual meal. He had just finished a day of reporting. I'd just come from a still-life shoot for *Self* magazine, where I was working as a photo editor.

I was pleasantly surprised. For starters, David was taller than I remembered. I was in heels and he still had a few inches on me. He was also friendlier, more talkative. And he was a good listener—probably a side benefit of his job, or perhaps the reason he was so good at it. We spoke freely. He told me he had recently returned to the States from a reporting posting in Delhi. He was looking to slow down a bit, maybe settle down. He asked how I felt about my life now. I said I had spent a lot of time thinking only of me. I was ready to share my life with someone else. This was risky for a first nondate, but I was tired of game playing: I was ready to think about someone else for a change. I wanted to start a family. We also shared a mutual connection to Maine. By coincidence, his father lives twenty minutes from my parents. We each treasured our fond memories of spending time there.

At the end of the night, I kissed David on the cheek. He told me he was headed off to Afghanistan, but would call from there. The very notion of calling me from a war zone seemed a bit improbable, impractical. To my surprise, that is exactly what he did, on a regular basis during his monthlong assignment.

I remember saying good-bye to David that night and rushing home to call my mother. "I met the most interesting man," I told her.

THE TALIBAN TRUST
THE RED CROSS

David, Mid-January 2009

B adruddin arrives for another visit. He walks into the room and I greet him respectfully, shake his hand, and sit on top of my pink Barbie bedspread. He formally greets everyone else in Pashto. As he makes small talk, I am on my best behavior and trying to regain the trust of the guards. I brace myself for the bad news that seems to come with each of Badruddin's visits.

After several minutes, he pulls papers from his pocket that bear the seal of the International Committee of the Red Cross. "Red Cross Message" is printed just below the seal, followed by a blank form where prisoners or refugees give their name, date, and place of birth as well as other details that prove their identity. I'm going to be allowed to write a letter to my wife. My fake suicide attempt may, in fact, have placed some pressure on our captors.

For weeks, I've been practicing what I would say to my family if given the chance. I want to communicate far more than I did in the first video. Someone produces a pen and I stare at the form. Badruddin and the guards stare at me.

The form asks the prisoner to list the full names of their mother, father, and grandfathers. I hesitate, fearing that listing names could endanger my family. At the same time, I know that if I refuse to name them or give false names it will raise my captors' suspicions.

I write down their names, hoping my family will understand the ratio-
nale that has gradually solidified in my mind. Crying on videos, begging
my family for money, and obeying my captors' commands is justifiable if
it saves the lives of Asad and Tahir. My wife, family, and friends are strong,
I tell myself, and they will able to bear this burden.

I begin writing the letter. To make it seem like I have nothing to hide,
I describe each sentence to Badruddin before writing it on the form in
clear capital letters.

"Thank you for our wonderful wedding on September 6, 2008," I
write in clear capital letters that I hope will be easy to read. I try to include innocuous details that will both prove I am, in fact, the author of
the letter and bolster my wife's spirits. "Memories of that wonderful day
and our beautiful time together keep me strong here."

I tell Kristen I love her "so very, very, very much" and thank her, my
family, and my friends for all they are doing to help us. Then I try to ease
any guilt they may feel. I know I might not have another chance to communicate with them and I want to give them closure if our case ends badly.

"Simply do the best you can," I write. "That's all I ask.

"I accept the consequences of my actions and thank you all for all of
the joy you've given me," I write. "I thank you and love you all so much."

Badruddin declares that the next portion of the letter should focus on
the Taliban's demands. We briefly argue over what those should be. I
insist they are vastly too high. He says he is already compromising.

"The Taliban started out asking for 10 prisoners and have reduced their
demand to 5 prisoners from Pul-e-Chargi prison," I write, using the spelling for the government prison that Tahir gives me. "They have reduced the
money from $25 million to $15 million."

The figures deeply depress me. They refuse to reduce them further.

Badruddin will not allow Tahir and Asad to write letters to their families. In mine, I insist that their release must be part of any agreement.
"Any deal must be for all three of us," I write. "Again, any must be for all
three of us."

"Please tell the International Red Cross to tell Asad and Tahir's family they are alive + well," I write, using a "+" to save space. "Tell Asad +

Tahir's family to please send messages to them through the International Red Cross. They love their families very much."

I urge my family to negotiate through the Red Cross. I want to somehow shift Badruddin's and Abu Tayyeb's attention away from the *Times'* Kabul bureau, which I worry is still the focus of their paranoia. I am also desperate to find a middleman who they believe will not steal any ransom.

"The Taliban do not trust and are very angry + suspicious of the office," I write, referring to the bureau. "You should negotiate through the Red Cross only. All negotiations and transactions of any kind should be through the Red Cross. The Taliban trust the Red Cross."

Hoping to increase the pressure on my family, Badruddin orders me once again to falsely state that we are in the mountains of Afghanistan. Hoping to tip off my family that I'm being ordered to lie, I write: "They are telling me to tell you that we are in a mountain area in Afghanistan with cold weather, snow and Afghan food + water that make me sick." Badruddin then dictates more lines. "They say that if their demands are not met they will kill the three of us," I write. "They are telling me to tell you to hurry up + meet their demands."

There are only a half dozen blank lines left on the small form. I try to communicate the argument I've been making to our captors. "I've said I'm a journalist who has spent my career writing to help Muslims but they say you must meet their demands," I write.

Three lines remain on the page. I scribble my final words.

"Please, please, please help us," I say. "I'm so sorry. I'll pay back anyone who helps us for the rest of my life."

"I'm so, so sorry," I repeat. "I apologize to you, my family and friends." I scrawl "I love you!!!" in large letters and sign my name.

Badruddin takes the letter and has Tahir slowly translate each passage to him. When he hears the phrase "they are telling me to tell you," he grows suspicious. I immediately offer to blot those words out with the pen. He agrees and then departs. For hours afterward, I berate myself for how I constructed the sentence. I need to be humble and patient and think small. Haste had gotten us into this disaster. Being impatient will only make things worse.

Roughly two weeks pass and we hear nothing from Badruddin. Then he arrives without warning and tells us we are going on a picnic. At first, I think he is joking. The guards tell me to cover my face with a scarf, follow Badruddin outside, and get into his pickup truck. After a five- to ten-minute drive, I am allowed to take the scarf off and look around.

Dust-covered hillsides surround us as we wind our way up a valley somewhere outside Miran Shah. There are no trees or discernible landmarks. We could be anywhere in the tribal areas. As we drive, I ask Badruddin if he has any response to my letter. He says the International Red Cross will not act as an intermediary for negotiations. My hopes fade. Badruddin stops the truck and we walk up a barren hill. I ask him how the negotiations are proceeding. He says he has nothing new to report. What has he been doing all this time? I ask. He says the problem is on my side. He scoffs at the amount of money they are offering for our release.

Badruddin asks me if I want to fire one of the guard's Kalashnikovs. I decline. If I look like I know how to fire the rifle, I will appear to be a soldier. And if I take the rifle and try to shoot Badruddin and the four guards who are with us, I'm unlikely to kill all of them before they shoot me. Asad walks to a nearby hillside and fires a Kalashnikov with one of the guards. Badruddin has the most advanced Kalashnikov, which has a grenade launcher mounted on the end of it. For entertainment, he fires a grenade at a nearby hillside and it detonates loudly, and he and his men watch to see if it frightens me. I try to show no reaction.

Badruddin, the guards, Tahir, and Asad then spread scarves on the ground and perform afternoon prayers. After they finish, Badruddin invites me to sit down. I oblige him. Unsure when I will see him next, I again tell him he will never get five prisoners and $15 million for us. He vows that he will and tells me the United States freed seven Serbian military officers in exchange for my 1995 release in Bosnia. Amazed by his statement, I tell him that is absolutely false. He responds that I told him that when we first arrived in Miran Shah.

"You said I was slow," he says, smiling. "You said seven prisoners were released for you after only ten days."

He is lying, apparently for the fun of it. No Serbian prisoners were released for me in 1995. The Haqqanis have turned my arrest for helping to expose the massacre of 8,000 Muslims into a liability in my case, not an asset. We sit in silence for several minutes.

"I could shoot you here and end this now," Badruddin offers with a smile.

I do not respond.

He again ridicules the ransom being offered for us. "I will sell your bones to your family" for that amount, he says.

Again, I do not respond.

We drive back to the house in silence. The following day, I learn that the guards are angry with me. They say Badruddin took me on a picnic and I was rude to him.

As January progresses, events in the outside world become a growing source of tension. The Israeli attack on the Gaza Strip infuriates the Taliban. Along with monitoring Western news broadcasts on Afghanistan, our guards closely watch world events as well. As the number of Palestinians killed spirals to 1,400—as compared with 14 Israelis—the Taliban seethe. Our guards see the campaign as the latest example of Muslims being slaughtered by an arrogant, hypocritical West. I wonder if we will be killed on videotape in retaliation. A second date also hovers: January 20, the inauguration of Barack Obama. I worry that the "blood message to Obama" that our kidnappers promised on the day we were abducted will finally be delivered.

The Israeli assault on Gaza ends on January 18 and Obama's inauguration passes without incident two days later. I read about it in one of the Pakistani English-language newspapers the guards bring me once or twice a week. The newspapers continue to be a godsend. I have begun reading each newspaper cover to cover to pass the time. I find myself drawn to stories that I glanced at in the past. Reading them transports me to another place.

Editorials condemning the Taliban remind me that most Pakistanis oppose the group. A book review on a study that examines the history of religion states that human beings create gods when confronted by forces greater than themselves. Science section stories bolster my belief that human civilization is progressing. A paid advertisement printed on the day of Obama's inauguration shows me another side of the Pashtuns.

It is a historical piece about a nonviolent Pashtun political leader known as the Frontier Gandhi. The political party he founded purchased ad space to print a biography of his life on January 20, the eleventh anniversary of his death. The party's version of his life is glowing and I know from things I have previously read that much of it is true. The existence of a pacifist Pashtun seems improbable. Their fighting skills are what has made the region so forbidding.

Born in 1889, Khan Abdul Ghaffar Khan was a devout Muslim and lifetime follower of Mahatma Gandhi's philosophy of nonviolent resistance. A towering figure who was six and a half feet tall and had a hawk nose, Ghaffar Khan founded a 100,000-strong movement called the Servants of God, or Red Shirts, in the 1920s. Its members were famous for their willingness to stage nonviolent strikes to protest British colonial rule—and die by the hundreds in the process.

A friend and compatriot of Gandhi's, Khan had the goal to free South Asia from British colonial rule and establish one independent, secular state where Muslims, Hindus, and people of all faiths could live peacefully. Later in life, he also campaigned for the reunification of the Pashtuns divided by the despised British-dictated border between Afghanistan and Pakistan.

Before dying at the age of ninety-eight, Ghaffar Khan achieved one of those goals but failed at the two others. Colonial India won independence from Britain in 1947 but was divided into two countries—a predominantly Muslim Pakistan and a predominantly Hindu India. Pashtuns in Afghanistan and Pakistan also failed to be reunited. The partition of British controlled India into two nations sparked one of the greatest and bloodiest mass migrations in human history. Over the course of several months in 1947, 14 million Hindus and Muslims crossed the newly created borders in the hope of finding a safer life in the country where they would be in the religious majority.

To the dismay of Ghaffar Khan and Gandhi, cataclysmic religious clashes erupted. As many as one million Muslims and Hindus perished on both sides of the new border. Two months after independence, war broke out after the Hindu ruler of the majority Muslim state of Kashmir said it would join India, not Pakistan. It was the first of four wars that India and Pakistan waged between 1947 and 1999.

Since arriving in the region in 2001, I had seen how the rivalry between the two countries fueled instability in Afghanistan and the wider region. For sixty years, partition colored nearly every move by India and Pakistan. Since 2001, India had backed the Karzai government with vast aid programs and record numbers of Indians living in Kabul. Threatened by what it saw as India encroaching on its flank, Pakistan's military quietly maintained its longtime support for the Afghan Taliban. Over time, I came to see the fighting in Afghanistan on one level as a proxy war between India and Pakistan, with American soldiers caught in the middle.

As I finish reading the story, Ghaffar Khan emerges as a tragic figure. In some ways, he reminds me of the educated Pashtun moderates I have followed in "Little America" since 2004. Their efforts to promote reform were hampered by religious conservatism and regional rivalries as well.

Instead of being hailed as a hero after Pakistan achieved independence in 1947, Ghaffar Khan was repeatedly placed under house arrest or jailed by the military-dominated Pakistani government. His fealty to Gandhi was seen as loyalty to India, not to the principle of nonviolence. All told, he spent more than twenty years in Pakistani and British detention. Ghaffar Khan died in Peshawar in 1988 and retained some popular support among Pashtuns for his campaign for Pashtun reunification. He asked to be buried in Afghanistan to show his continued devotion to the goal of unifying the Pashtuns.

His pro-Gandhi and pro-socialist stance, though, took a toll on his popular support on both sides of the border. Pakistani nationalists marginalized him by declaring him pro-India. Afghan's mujahideen accused him of supporting the Soviet Union, the country's atheist occupier. In the decade after his death, the Taliban in Afghanistan and hard-line religious parties in Pakistan proclaimed themselves the true leaders of the Pashtuns. A moderate Pashtun nationalist political party founded by Ghaffar Khan's son gained only limited electoral support from Pashtuns.

In February 2008, I covered elections in Pakistan's Pashtun-dominated northwest that pitted the secular Pashtun nationalist party of Ghaffar Khan's descendants—the Awami National Party—against Pakistan's hard-line religious parties. In 2002, conservative parties had won control of the provincial government for the first time, but subsequently failed to deliver economic growth, clean government, and security. In the 2008 elections, the moderate party of Ghaffar Khan triumphed. Now led by his grandson, Asfandyar Wali Khan, the moderate Pashtuns defeated hard-line religious parties and won control of the provincial government. The question I posed in 2001 about how best to counter religious extremism seemed to have an answer: electoral politics.

Yet after taking office the moderate Pashtuns struggled to effectively govern. Stepped-up Taliban suicide attacks and kidnappings ravaged Peshawar, the largest Pashtun-dominated city in northwestern Pakistan. In the newspapers I received from our guards, story after story described public disappointment with the moderate Pashtuns' inability to stop suicide bombings and abductions. Rumors of corruption hovered over the government as well. The pattern was similar to what I had seen in Afghanistan.

After decades of neglect, moderate Pashtuns were weak and poorly organized. Trying to reverse decades of shortsighted American, Saudi, and Pakistani support for hard-line Pashtuns was enormously difficult, slow moving, and bloody. Yet it was vital. To me, finding ways to more effectively support Pashtun moderates was the key to stabilizing Afghanistan and Pakistan.

LOVE LETTERS

Kristen, Late January 2009

David McCraw has become a stable, regular character in my life. His calm and wholesome midwestern manner is paired with a savvy wit and deep intelligence.

He, David's brother Lee, and I talk all the time about everything from conflicting reports and information to media strategies and personal frustrations. McCraw is also thoughtful enough to contact me in advance of the noon call on days when updates may be unpleasant. A few weeks ago, McCraw forewarned me that in response to our request for proof of life, the captors responded: "We'll give you a finger." (My mother was present while I took this call. She was quick to point out, "A finger is not proof of life.")

Today, McCraw is calling with the latest rumblings from the Afghan rumor mill. A tribal elder who knows the Haqqanis has relayed a message to the paper's Kabul bureau. Rumor is that David is on a "ransom farm" in Afghanistan with as many as sixty other hostages, including the engineer's son. The elder claims that David has his own room, but keeps Asad and Tahir with him at all times. He is free to move about the compound and chat with other captives. It sounds like he is at the Club Med of hostage camps. It seems too rosy to be true. We have heard stories of other people currently being held hostage, among them a Polish hostage, and several aid workers from the World Food Program. It is difficult to know if this information is accurate or merely a fabrication, though the messenger did not request money.

A few days later, on January 24, the International Committee of the Red Cross delivers a letter to the Kabul bureau. We have no idea what route it has traversed or how many hands it has passed through. It bears no date. One of David's colleagues scans it and forwards it to my e-mail.

I know instantly the letter was written by him.

"Thank you for our wonderful wedding on September 6, 2008. Memories of that wonderful day and our beautiful times together keep me strong here. I love you so very, very, very much and thank you for all the joy you have given me. Thank you for all you and my friends and family are doing to help us. Simply do the best you can. That's all I ask."

It's incredibly moving just to see his handwriting.

The demands have dropped from $25 million to $15 million. And from ten prisoners from Guantánamo and Bagram to five from Pul-i-Charkhi, a less-secure prison in Afghanistan. But David's captors are still in a different stratosphere from us.

Pul-i-Charkhi. This is interesting, as the newspaper's Kabul bureau has found out that Atiqullah's real name is Najibullah Naeem and he also goes by Abu Tayyeb. Abu Tayyeb has twice been a prisoner at Pul-i-Charkhi, but was able to bribe his way out. He lived for years in Zabul Province, the same as Tahir. We are now certain that the Taliban commander David went to interview is also his captor. To add to the intrigue, the FBI has "declassified" the identity of Atiqullah. They claim Atiqullah is an alias for not one, but two individuals working in tandem: Abu Tayyeb and Badruddin Haqqani. They think Abu Tayyeb originally abducted David and perhaps sold or handed him over to Badruddin Haqqani.

David insists that this be a deal for all three. The letter also states: "The Taliban do not trust and are very angry and suspicious of the office and the head of the office in Kabul. You should negotiate through the

Red Cross only. All negotiations and transactions of any kind should be through the Red Cross. The Taliban trust the Red Cross."

Something has been obliterated and is unintelligible, followed by: "We are in a mountain area of Afghanistan with cold weather, snow and Afghan food and water that make me sick. The conditions are very difficult. They say that if their demands are not met they will kill the three of us. They are telling me to tell you to hurry up and meet their demands. I've said I'm a journalist who has spent my career writing to help Muslims but they say you must meet their demands. Please, please, please help us. I'm so sorry. I'll pay back anyone who helps us for the rest of my life. I'm so, so sorry. I apologize to you, my family and friends. I LOVE YOU!!!"

I spend the next few days in my apartment writing a response, and then rewriting it. I show drafts to Lee, McCraw, our security team, and the FBI for feedback. Their responses are typically contradictory: I do not feel there is one channel giving Lee and me clear and authoritative advice. Our team members are sometimes at odds because of their background, agenda, and viewpoint. I spend days fine-tuning the letter. I want to include enough personal information to put David at ease, without revealing any additional information to his captors. This means omitting the names of family and friends—and referring to them simply by relationship. As a team, we debate content, word choice, as well as etiquette. The competing strategies are becoming clear. Some feel we should play on the captors' sense of honor by thanking them for treating David well. Other members feel they have no honor and should not be praised for their behavior. I'm trying to strike a balance between cultural sensitivity and authenticity.

Our team debates the merits of including a counteroffer within my letter, even though we have already been told by the head of the International Red Cross in Kabul that the organization will not participate in or facilitate negotiations. They will not carry a letter containing negotiation points. This is very frustrating. Why would the Haqqanis select the Red Cross as an intermediary when they are not permitted to act in this manner? We compose two letters—one that is personal and a second that also contains a counteroffer. We are mentioning it to keep the conversation going, until we are in striking distance of their demands. Or, no matter how improbable, until the FBI can get a fix on David's location and facilitate a rescue attempt. We also send a backup message through the engineer.

We also debate the meaning of David's reference to "the office in Kabul." The security contractors claim this is the paper's Kabul bureau. The *Times* thinks it refers to the security contractors. A jousting match ensues. McCraw steps in to referee.

One of the Clayton kidnap experts on Team Kabul has worked on many cases in Colombia. While the negotiation strategies do not always translate across cultures, his knowledge of what will help sustain a hostage does. He advises me to put something in the letter that lets David know we will never give up and asks him to promise to do the same. He advises me to tell David that I am well and that he must promise me that he will do his best to keep himself in good spirits. In my letter I say, "You must promise me you will not give up. You must be strong, because I am strong." I carefully write the entire letter out in longhand, and I sign it "Love always." I underscore the always.

In the letter, I refer to our respective families—the Mulvihills, the Rohdes—as one unit: our family. One of the side effects of the last two months is that I've gotten to know my in-laws—and my brother-in-law Lee in particular—quite well. Mary Jane and Lee have been my intermittent roommates. Lee makes frequent trips to the city. I marvel at the irony that I have spent more time at home with Lee than I have with my husband. While Lee has taken on the role of updating David's siblings and parents with daily text messages, I also speak regularly with Erik and Laura. Both families have rallied to support me, emotionally and at times geographically. I feel we are one family now. I think this is something David would be proud to hear.

On January 24, I scan and e-mail the letters back to the International Red Cross in Kabul and copy all our team members and our FBI case agent, Jim. Copies are translated and read to the families of Tahir and Asad and they are encouraged to write their own replies.

The letter containing negotiation points is rejected by the Red Cross director in Kabul. The first, more personal letter is passed along. We have no idea how or when it will reach David.

———

While we wait for a response to our letter, McCraw receives another confounding message from an Afghan source. A person who identifies himself as a relative of Afghan president Karzai claims that the Haqqanis want to use him as a middleman to secure a deal for our three. He says the Haqqanis have not been satisfied with the engineer—they feel he is too sympathetic to our family. This person, who also says he is a former mujahid, asserts that five parties have a stake in our three. Each expects to be compensated—$5 million apiece—in the event of a negotiated release. The five parties include the original kidnapper, the Haqqanis, Baitullah Mehsud, a tribal shura, and a Pakistani government agency. In addition, Siraj Haqqani is demanding the release of Taliban prisoners.

Even though this explains the astronomical nature of the initial demands, it does not bring us any closer to securing a clear communication channel. When McCraw tries to follow up with this source, he is told that while the Haqqanis would like the mujahid to work on their behalf, he will not be able to do so. According to him, the five parties have not been able to reach an agreement on what they are willing to settle for. Once again, we feel we are just chasing shadows.

In the meantime, Team Kabul begins to draw up an exit strategy in the event David is released. Given that we've still had no phone contact with the captors for over a month, this seems premature. But it keeps our spirits up. We appreciate their foresight. We all know that if or when a release happens, there will be a mad rush to get David home and reunite Tahir and Asad with their families. Team Kabul and the other consultants in the United States advise us to make private arrangements for David's transport home. We should not count on the United States government to get him home. With two wars going on, extracting David from the region may not be their top priority. Also, they tell us not to rely on the FBI because they cannot guarantee assets, such as helicopters, when needed. They add that they might want to keep David at the embassy in Kabul or Pakistan for questioning, as it is their duty to gather information in hopes of prosecuting this crime in the future.

Lee and I are beginning to wonder if we should leverage the U.S. government to do more to help us during David's captivity. We're still optimistic about their influence. Later on, we will become all too aware of the limits of their power in that part of the world. One of the many useful contacts in David's e-mail is Zalmay Khalilzad. He is the former United States ambassador to the United Nations and also an Afghan. I decide to set up a meeting.

Khalilzad is a large man, with a Cheshire cat grin and a mastery of the sideways glance. He is also very astute. "What you need is a high-level advocate, someone to represent your family, someone in the U.S. government, who can assign tasks to members of foreign governments and also keep abreast of what U.S. agencies are doing." He suggests someone well respected, with a bit of gravitas and experience in the region. Hillary Clinton and Richard Holbrooke are his suggestions.

With this in mind, Lee and I decide to take a day trip to Washington to meet with officials at the State Department as well as Senators John Kerry and Joe Lieberman, both of whom have expressed an interest in helping in David's case. We want to put a face to our issue. Our hope is to find an advocate within our government to keep our issue at the forefront and possibly to coordinate information coming in from various agencies: FBI, CIA, State Department. We hope this advocate will be Clinton or Holbrooke.

We arrive in D.C. on a snowy morning and walk from Union Station to the Senate offices in the Russell Building. The place is in transition. Office furniture is stacked in the hallways: camelback sofas, Chippendale chairs, dark wooden desks. It looks like an Ethan Allen showroom exploded.

Our first meeting is with Senator Kerry and his chief investigator for the Senate Foreign Relations Committee, Douglas Frantz. Doug is a former investigative reporter who worked at *The New York Times* and knows David. Doug is the one actively keeping our case on the senator's radar.

My mother has given me a recent photo of David and me that was taken at my brother's wedding last year. We look very happy and relaxed.

She has put the photo in a paper frame and suggests I show it to everyone I meet with from now on as a way to humanize our issue. Most people are moved by the fact that we are newlyweds. Our apparent happiness in the photograph underscores the sadness of our current situation.

Senator Kerry is a tall, imposing man. He looks exactly like he does on television. "Your husband certainly likes to push the envelope," he says, referring to David's decision to interview the Taliban commander. He then asks us for an update on the situation, apologizing for not knowing more about the case. He agrees that it is best for us to keep David's case out of the media.

He'll be in touch with Pakistani officials about the case, he says, and will get back to us. Senator Lieberman's aide suggests that he and his colleague compose a letter to Hillary Clinton, telling her they feel this is a matter that deserves her attention as secretary of state. It is surreal but reassuring to have former presidential and vice presidential candidates in our corner. Over the next few months Lee and I remain in touch with Doug Frantz, who informs me that the letter drafted by the senators was received by Secretary Clinton. Senator Kerry continues to follow our case and informs us soon after our meeting that he has raised the issue with Pakistani officials and will continue to do so.

From the Senate office building, Lee and I rush off to meet with Richard Holbrooke, now the special representative to Afghanistan and Pakistan, for lunch. We had assumed this meeting would be top secret. Holbrooke has selected the venue: the Four Seasons restaurant in George-town. Lee and I arrive early and request to be seated at a quiet table in the lounge. Holbrooke arrives soon after. A large man with piercing blue eyes, he breezes in, complete with State Department badge and binder. He gives me a bear hug, then requests we move tables, to the middle of the restaurant, where we can order a meal.

He asks us where things stand. We give him a brief update, including that we now think David is in Miran Shah, Pakistan, the stronghold of the Haqqani Taliban network. The FBI has traced earlier calls and video communications to this region. Holbrooke promises to check with the FBI and CIA. He will be traveling to the region soon and says he will raise David's case with Pakistani officials. We think this is the most efficient use of his energy, as we believe the Pakistani intelligence agencies may be able to get word to the Haqqanis and pressure them to release our three or prompt a resolution to negotiations.

The Pakistani intelligence agency, the ISI, has been linked with the Haqqanis. There is an assumption that Siraj Haqqani, the head of the faction, is considered to be an ISI asset. If he is indeed financed by the agency, they may be able to apply pressure on him to release David. Holbrooke also suggests I get in touch with the United States ambassador to Pakistan, Anne Patterson, who is also following David's case. He promises to raise our case with her on his upcoming trip as well.

When I'm back in New York, the following day, Michael Semple, my chief confidant, writes to me that he's learned from Pakistan contacts that a mullah with links to the Haqqani family is moved by my personal plea. He is referring to the Pashto note that David's friend Ruhullah had composed for me to give to the captors: "My husband is my veil, my honor. Please return him to me."

Michael suggests a brazen move: that I come to Pakistan and visit the mullah's mosque in Swabi, just outside of Peshawar. Atiqullah and Badruddin are the ones holding David, but Michael feels the real authority to release our three lies with Siraj Haqqani. He feels the mullah can make contact with Siraj Haqqani or a close family elder and create one clear negotiation channel.

Peshawar. David visited the city several times, always with the utmost caution. Despite my desire to see David home soon, I have no wish to don a headscarf and travel to Pakistan alone. Everything in my being feels opposed to this. I tell myself I am just being a wimp—maybe fear is clouding my judgment. Still, I cannot ignore the sinking feeling in my gut. I turn to others for a reality check.

Lee is immediately opposed. I do not ask him to consider joining me. He has a two-year-old daughter. I mention it casually to my sister, which leads to a flood of calls and e-mails from her begging me not to go. "It is enough that David is in harm's way. You do not need to make the same mistake," she says.

McCraw, at the *Times*, is also skeptical, but tells me the paper will help facilitate my transportation within Pakistan if I decide to go. He advises, though, that it might be best to hold off on a trip until we have reestablished contact with the captors or are somehow close to a release of our three. He suggests I consult Jane Perlez, another correspondent and colleague of David's who is based in Islamabad. Jane tells me to stay put. She says there is a lot of anti-American sentiment in Pakistan at the moment and adds that all the local news people are aware of David's case. The minute I arrive, the story of David's kidnapping will most certainly become public. This is the most persuasive argument against visiting Pakistan.

Nevertheless, I contact Ambassador Anne Patterson at the embassy in Islamabad. She reluctantly agrees to put me up at the embassy if I decide to take the trip, but advises me that I will not be able to come and go freely. Basically, I would be under "house arrest." She cannot guarantee my safety. She informs me that a member of her staff was nearly abducted recently. The woman was only able to avoid capture because her driver had recently taken an evasive driving course.

I am concerned it may look suspicious if I am a guest of the United States Embassy. Many Taliban think that all American journalists are spies. A jaunt to the embassy on my part could be misconstrued to mean that either David or I work for the government. If word got out that I was a guest at the embassy, the captors might think David is indeed a spy. I also know that airfare to Pakistan is not cheap. I do not want to send a message that we have money to spare.

Even though I have more than a dozen sane excuses for not traveling overseas, I secure a visa and purchase a ticket to Islamabad for the first week in February, less than a week away. Flights are scarce and fill up quickly. I will see what transpires in the next forty-eight hours, then I'll make my decision to stay put or head east.

WORDS AND PICTURES

David, Late January 2009

Tahir and Asad ask me to make our case public as the end of January approaches. The American and Afghan governments have forgotten us, they believe, and public pressure is the only way to get them to act. I believe going public could result in the Taliban's setting a deadline and first Asad, then Tahir, and finally me being killed. Tahir and Asad say they are ready to die. I defer to their wishes and tell Timor Shah that I want to make a video for the news media.

For the next several days, we receive contradictory reports on when and how the video will be made. At one point, our guard Akbar suggests that a local prisoner be brought to the house. With cameras rolling, the prisoner would be executed in front of us. Hoping to prevent an execution, I offer to weep on camera instead. Over the next few days, I silently prepare for the video, memorizing sentences I plan to say to Kristen and my family. I sit in the sun for long stretches, hoping sunburn will make me look healthy.

Badruddin arrives several days later with a video camera and, to my relief, no prisoner for execution. Instead, white sheets inscribed with the seal of the Islamic Emirate of Afghanistan and a verse from the Koran are taped onto the wall of the room where we sleep. Our Barbie and Hannah Montana comforters, my stack of English-language Pakistani newspapers, and my bottles of Nestlé Pure Life bottled water are moved out of the shot.

Tahir, Asad, and I sit side by side on the room's red-checkered carpet. We wear salwar kameezes, jackets to make us look cold, and prayer caps to make us look devout. Two guards with scarves over their faces stand on either side of us pointing machine guns at our heads. Badruddin turns on the camera and motions with his hand for me to speak. Tahir stares straight ahead. Asad looks at the floor. I say my name, identify myself as an American journalist, and give the date of our kidnapping. Then I recite the words that Badruddin specifically demanded.

"Our lives are in great danger," I say. "I ask President Barack Obama, I ask Secretary of State Hillary Clinton, and I ask special envoy Richard Holbrooke to please meet the Taliban demands."

I try to convey a message to our families and tears well up in my eyes. I'm more emotional than I expected. On one level, it's a relief. I worried I would be unable to cry on cue. As he holds the camera, Badruddin nods. He is happy with my performance.

"I want to apologize from the bottom of my heart to the families of Asad and Tahir," I say, beginning the message. "I'm so sorry that they are going through this.

"And I apologize from the deepest part of my soul to my wife Kristen," I say. "And to my parents, and to my siblings, and to all my family and all my friends.

"I love you all very, very much and I thank you for all the joy you've given me throughout my life," I add. "I've lived a very blessed life because of you.

"I'm so sorry that you have to see this video and I'm so sorry that you're going through this again," I say. "If we are released I promise to spend the rest of my life doing absolutely everything I can to pay you back. And to do absolutely everything I can to somehow make this up to you. I apologize to you all."

Badruddin continues filming. I am thrilled that I have been able to express a message that I hope will console Kristen and my family if we die. I then repeat my call for Obama, Clinton, and Holbrooke to meet the Taliban demands.

"I beg you, I'm so, so sorry, I beg you, please, please meet their demands," I say, hoping this will satisfy Badruddin. "Please save the three of us. Please save the three of us. Please save the three of us."

I bow my head and Tahir introduces himself. He speaks in Pashto and appeals to Afghan president Hamid Karzai to please help us. Asad does the same. After the video, the guards quietly snicker at me for weeping on camera. I don't care and feel relieved. I hope my words will comfort Kristen and my family.

Badruddin says he will be back in two days. He returns a week later. After several minutes of small talk, he casually pulls a white envelope from his pocket, places it on the floor, and announces he has Red Cross letters for all three of us. The envelope is like a talisman. Tahir, Asad, and I stare at it eagerly. It holds words from our families.

Badruddin hands me the envelope. I give Tahir and Asad their letters and suddenly find myself staring at Kristen's unmistakable handwriting. Her words flood my mind. "It was wonderful to hear from you," she writes. "I am warmed by memories of our marriage and time together with our family."

She apologizes to our captors and asks them not to be angry with her. "I am also frustrated with this process," she writes. "Trust and a clear channel of communication are both important to all of us."

She encourages me. "There is hope. No matter how long it takes, we will not give up and we will not forget about you. Not a moment goes by without us trying to bring you, Tahir, and Asad home."

She talks about the effort to free us. "Our family is doing all we can, as quickly as possible, but some things are beyond our control. We will keep trying."

I am not sure, but believe she is referring to prisoners.

"But, you must promise me, that you are going to do your best to survive this ordeal," she writes. "You must be strong because I am strong."

Kristen says she will meet soon with my mother and siblings to continue working for our release. She says my brother and father have been strong. I am touched. She knows news of my family will buoy me.

"Your father is grateful to the men holding you because they are keeping you safe," she says. "He asks for their patience."

I am impressed. She is clearly trying to navigate Pashtun culture. She is making requests herself but also having my father—the patriarch of my family—pose them as well.

Her next line is an attempt to comfort Tahir and Asad. It touches me that she shows respect for them, their lives and families. "I will relay your message to the dear families of Tahir and Asad," she states. "Please tell them *salaam alaikum* and they should not lose hope."

She concludes the letter with her trademark positivity. "I know God is watching over all three of you. I hope your spirits will be strengthened by this," she says, her words echoing her cheery voice. "Thank you for writing to us! Love always, Kristen."

I am disappointed by the seeming lack of progress in negotiations, but heartened by the letter's eloquence. Tears come to my eyes. Her words will strengthen me for months.

Tahir translates the letter to Badruddin, who is disappointed that it contains no offer of high-level prisoners and millions in cash. I again tell Badruddin that it is impossible for my family to produce five prisoners and $15 million. He pays no attention.

Badruddin inspects Tahir's and Asad's letters as well. Tahir's eldest daughter has written that she and her siblings deeply miss their father. Asad's father has written that Asad's two sons miss him but are well. At the end of the note, Asad's father makes a seemingly casual comment. "People say you're in Miran Shah."

Badruddin explodes in anger. He is furious that our location is known and quickly departs. The momentary bliss generated by our letters evaporates.

Later, the guards tell us Badruddin has decided not to send our video to the news media. Instead, we will shoot a new scene that will prove we are being held in Afghanistan, not Pakistan.

I spend my days doing chores and saying my prayers. I place Kristen's letter in the left-hand pocket of a vest I wear every day, close to my heart. A week later, the guards ask for all three of our letters and say Badruddin wants to copy them. The letters are never returned.

In late January, Badruddin arrives and announces he is going to drive us to a remote, snow-covered hillside to shoot the final scene of our video. Roughly ninety minutes after we leave the house, Badruddin sees a group of trucks stopped on the opposite side of the road and quickly pulls over. A nervous-looking Pakistani soldier points a rocket-propelled grenade at our pickup truck. Mansoor, the guard sitting beside me and Tahir in the backseat, loads his Kalashnikov and orders me to put a scarf over my face. A group of Pakistani civilians standing nearby moves out of the way, anticipating a firefight.

The soldier is in the lead vehicle of a Pakistani army supply convoy in North Waziristan. After surveying the road, the soldier gets back in his truck, and the convoy rumbles forward.

Running into a Pakistani army resupply convoy at first appears to be an enormous stroke of luck. As I watch the convoy drive toward us, I hope that the Pakistanis might somehow rescue us.

I wonder if we should make a run for it, but quickly realize Tahir and Asad will never make it. I am seated in the left rear passenger seat and can open my door and jump out of the truck. Tahir is in the middle of the seat and will be shot by Mansoor if he moves. Asad is riding in a car behind us and I have no way to signal him.

Frustrated, I watch in dismay as Badruddin gets out of the truck and calmly stands on the side of the road. As trucks full of heavily armed government soldiers roll by, he smiles and waves at them.

After the convoy disappears, Badruddin seems amused.

"Do you know who that was?" he asks me.

"No," I say, playing dumb.

"That was the Pakistani army," he responds.

Badruddin explains that under a cease-fire agreement between the Taliban and the Pakistani army, all civilians are required to get out of their cars when an army convoy approaches. For Taliban vehicles, though, only the driver has to get out. The practice, I realize, allows the Taliban to hide kidnapping victims and foreign militants from army convoys.

As we continue our journey, we pass a half dozen government checkpoints that have been abandoned by the Frontier Corps, a tribal militia that is supposed to police the tribal areas. Badruddin says that under the cease-fire agreement, only unarmed militia members can stand at the checkpoints. He is correct. As we drive, I occasionally see members of the militia standing on the side of the road without guns. Some casually chat with local tribesmen.

The trip confirms suspicions I have long harbored as a reporter. The Haqqanis oversee a sprawling Taliban ministate in North Waziristan with the acquiescence of the Pakistani military. A 2006 truce the Pakistani army signed with militants has given them complete control of North Waziristan. Repeated Pakistani army claims to the contrary are false. The Haqqanis are so confident of their control of the area that they take me—a person they consider to be an extraordinarily valuable hostage—on a three-hour drive in broad daylight to shoot a location scene for an outdoor video.

For years, dozens of Pakistani, Afghan, foreign journalists, and I have written about the systematic takeover of the tribal areas by foreign militants and the Afghan and Pakistani Taliban. After being driven from Afghanistan by the 2001 American invasion, Uzbek and Arab militants began slowly reorganizing themselves. The foreigners rented compounds from local tribesmen who fought alongside them in Afghanistan, sympathized with their cause, or were in search of money and security. The foreign fighters paid two to three times the normal rate for rent in the impoverished area. The Haqqanis—my kidnappers—welcomed Arabs and Uzbeks.

Surrounded by high mud-brick walls, the Pashtun family compounds are oases of privacy and protection for conservative tribesmen. The high walls prevent strangers from seeing—and dishonoring—Pashtun women and shelter families from attacks from rival clans. They also hide the inhabitants' identity.

In some ways, the Arabs and Uzbeks are returning home. Many of them used the tribal areas as a base during the anti-Soviet jihad of the 1980s. Dozens of Arabs and Uzbeks married local women.

In the spring of 2002, CIA officials began reporting to Pakistani army commanders that large numbers of foreign fighters appeared to be hiding in South Waziristan. Pakistani military officials were skeptical. In an interview nine months before I was kidnapped, a former Pakistani military official who served in the tribal areas told me that he did not believe large numbers of foreign militants had settled there. "There were conflicting figures about the number who crossed the border," he told me. "Nobody was sure. It was all guesswork."

General Ali Muhammad Jan Aurakzai, a tall, commanding Pashtun whose family hailed from the tribal areas, was Pakistani president Musharraf's main adviser on the issue. After serving as the military commander of the region from 2001 to 2004, he served as its civilian governor from 2006 to 2008. For years, he argued that American officials exaggerated the threat in the tribal areas and that the Pakistani army should avoid sparking a tribal rebellion at all cost.

The former senior Pakistani military official defended the army's record to me, contending that the Pakistani military had doubled the number of troops in South and North Waziristan from roughly 2,000 to 4,000 in September 2002. He said Pakistani soldiers also pushed into dozens of square miles of "no-go" areas that Pakistani or British forces had never before entered but "found nothing."

American officials said that Pakistani army sweeps, though, were slow moving and easily circumvented by militants. A former CIA official who served in Islamabad told me that Pakistani generals were "dismissive" of the reports because they feared sparking a tribal rebellion.

"Aurakzai and others didn't want to believe it because it would have been an inconvenient fact," the former official recalled. "Going out there, rooting around, trying to root out foreigners was going to cause real problems for them."

Another American official was blunt. He derided Aurakzai as a "snake oil salesman" and "the Neville Chamberlain of Pakistan," a reference to the pre-World War II British leader who downplayed the threat from Nazi Germany.

Throughout 2002, officials in Washington largely ignored a chorus of warnings from American officials in Afghanistan that the Pakistani tribal areas were becoming the Afghan Taliban's new base of operations. Instead, they downplayed the group's importance and praised the Pakistani government for arresting Al Qaeda members in Pakistan's major cities.

A conversation with one American diplomat in Islamabad illustrated the mentality. He told me that the Afghan Taliban no longer represented a national security threat to the United States while Al Qaeda remained one. When I contended that the Taliban and Al Qaeda worked closely together, he dismissed my argument.

In December 2002, I visited Miran Shah on a reporting trip. At that time, it was still under Pakistani government control. Escorted by members of the Frontier Corps, the government-paid tribal militia, I found the tribal areas simmering with anger at the United States. On the roads leading to Miran Shah, men carried Kalashnikovs. On the roofs of houses, flags of Pakistan's hard-line religious parties fluttered. And in front of religious schools, fierce-looking young students strung ropes across the road, stopped cars, and demanded donations.

"Mosques, mosques, mosques," I scribbled in my notebook. "This is a completely different world."

We first stopped at a border crossing between Pakistan and Afghanistan fifteen miles outside Miran Shah. Members of the Frontier Corps went through the motions of checking cars as they rolled across the border. An officer told me it was impossible to control the border because smuggling routes blanketed the surrounding hills.

In Miran Shah itself, I met the Pakistani government–appointed political agent charged with governing North Waziristan. He said anger was simmering in the town because of a recent joint Pakistani-FBI raid on the sprawling Manba Uloom madrassa the Haqqani family had built north of the city in the 1980s. No foreign militants—and no Haqqani family members—had been found.

Rumors abounded that the FBI agents wore boots into madrassas and mosques, an insult and desecration to Pashtuns. Furious local tribesmen fired rockets at an abandoned technical school where the Americans were believed to be staying. Six local tribal elders gathered by the North

Waziristan political agent fumed. They denied that any Afghan Taliban or foreign militants were in North Waziristan.

"The Americans have fifteen to twenty times disgraced our soil and our sacred mosques," one tribal elder told me, vastly exaggerating the number of raids. "They cannot produce a single man from the fourteen or fifteen attempts."

The elders believed that the American bombing of Afghanistan in 2001 had killed 50,000 Afghan women and children. They said the United States had invaded Afghanistan to control the oil and gas riches of the Middle East and Central Asia. Asked about the 9/11 attacks, they said there was no proof who had carried them out.

"People have actually started believing Osama never existed," one elder told me. "They think it is a conspiracy against us."

I later learned that Americans—most likely CIA operatives—had, in fact, raided the Haqqani madrassa and found nothing. Before the raid, the Americans intercepted communications in which a local Pakistani official called the madrassa and warned the occupants that the Americans were on their way.

My trip was part of a sophisticated campaign by Musharraf's government to show that the Afghan Taliban were not using Pakistan as a base. The Pakistani military ferried American journalists, diplomats, and intelligence officials to the tribal areas and told them the area was ungovernable. In many ways, the trips mirrored the tours the Pakistani military conducted in the 1980s for Congressman Wilson and other American government officials. The only difference was the message. Now, the Pakistani military said it could not control the tribal areas.

Evidence that the Afghan Taliban were, in fact, reorganizing inside Pakistan abounded. In September 2003, I interviewed two Afghan Taliban members in the southwestern city of Quetta, which lies several hundred miles south of the tribal areas. Afghan officials had long charged that Taliban leader Mullah Omar was based in the city.

Hajji Abdul Majid denied that the Afghan Taliban were receiving support from Pakistan. A wizened Afghan Taliban commander who had lost his right leg fighting Soviet troops, he appeared completely at ease in Pakistan. He and the other former Taliban commander met me in the basement of the office of a local radio reporter. He predicted the United States would eventually fail in Afghanistan. He said Afghans initially supported the Russians to "take their money" and then turned against them.

"The same case will be the Americans," the Taliban commander told me confidently. "For two or three years, they will support the Americans for their money but after that they will leave them."

Hostility toward Westerners simmered in Quetta as well. The same false stories of American bombs killing tens of thousands of civilians swirled. During a subsequent reporting trip to Quetta, a young Pashtun spit in my face as our car drove past a religious school. My translator, who was also a Pashtun, profusely apologized. He was ashamed that a Pashtun would do such a thing.

Complaints that Pakistan was failing to crack down on the Afghan Taliban reached the White House in October 2003. In a principals meeting, American military and diplomatic officials based in Afghanistan said that Pakistan had become a major safe haven for the Afghan Taliban. They presented their argument that Musharraf was playing a "double game," periodically arresting Al Qaeda members but allowing the Afghan Taliban to regroup on Pakistani territory.

Bush, Secretary of State Colin Powell, and Deputy Secretary of State Richard Armitage believed the allegations that Musharraf was playing a double game were false. In meetings with senior American officials and interviews with me and other journalists, Musharraf vehemently denied the charges.

Armitage insisted that Musharraf did, in fact, break the ISI's ties with the Taliban from 2001 to 2005. "There was little contact between the ISI and the Taliban other than liaison," Armitage told me when I interviewed him for my book.

Armitage said that during those years the administration focused its efforts on persuading Musharraf to end the ISI's support to two Pakistani militant groups targeting India: Lashkar-e-Taiba and Jaish-e-Muhammad. The two groups had carried out a December 2001 attack on India's parliament that nearly sparked a war between nuclear-armed India and Pakistan.

Armitage, who left the Bush administration with Powell in early 2005, said that he believes the ISI reestablished its ties with the Taliban later that year when the ISI saw the Taliban successfully reorganizing and the American-led military effort flagging. "My personal view is that the ISI began increasing support for the Afghan Taliban when they started to see the Talibs regrouping," Armitage said. "ISI was coming of the view that the coalition might not prevail."

In 2005, the Haqqani network and other Taliban did gain strength, doubling American deaths in Afghanistan from fifty-two in 2004 to ninety-nine in 2005. American military officials requested permission to carry out commando raids into Pakistan's tribal areas. Military officials argued that as long as the Taliban safe havens existed in Pakistan, American troops could not stabilize Afghanistan.

American troops carried out two cross-border raids into the tribal areas in 2006 and 2008, but they sparked an immediate outcry from the Pakistani army. Bush opposed further operations inside Pakistan. He worried that unrest could topple Musharraf or derail his personal efforts to persuade the Pakistani leader to take off his military uniform, become a civilian president, and reinstate democracy in Pakistan. As part of his commitment to spreading democracy abroad, Bush had privately and repeatedly lobbied Musharraf—who was both Pakistan's president and army chief—to resign from his army post and become simply president.

CIA officials based in Pakistan argued that it was far better to have Pakistani troops carry out such operations. The arrival of American troops in the tribal areas would confirm Islamist conspiracy theories that the United States planned to occupy Pakistan, the world's only predominantly Muslim country with nuclear weapons.

In an attempt to get the Pakistani army to be more aggressive in the tribal areas, the Bush administration backed a loosely monitored billion-dollar-a-year reimbursement program where the United States paid fuel, ammunition, and other costs incurred by Pakistani forces in the tribal areas. The massive program was by far the largest source of American funding to Pakistan.

American military officials detected that the Pakistani military was inflating their claims under the program and receiving tens of millions of dollars in fraudulent reimbursements. They also warned of a more dangerous problem: The Pakistani army was so weak, they warned, that it could not defeat the Taliban and Al Qaeda if it confronted them.

For the next three years, that appeared to be true. The Pakistani military fought brief operations against militants in the tribal areas and then struck two peace agreements. Each cease-fire further emboldened the militants, who killed more than 200 tribal elders they saw as potential rivals in 2005 and 2006. The army signed a third and final cease-fire agreement—known as the Waziristan accord—in Miran Shah in September 2006. In exchange for militants promising to halt attacks in Pakistan and Afghanistan, the Pakistani army agreed to withdraw its forces from all checkpoints in North Waziristan. The Taliban ministate that I later inhabited was born.

Militants in other parts of Pakistan were emboldened. Students in the Red Mosque, a hard-line mosque and madrassa in the center of Islamabad, demanded that local stores stop selling DVDs they considered indecent. Then they took a local woman hostage in July 2007 and accused her of operating a brothel. Security forces surrounded the mosque and after an initial gun battle stormed it, killing roughly 100 people. Pakistani militants claimed that 1,000 students—many of them women— were killed in the attack.

Enraged, they declared war on the Pakistani government. In the tribal areas, the Haqqanis played a central role in brokering the creation of a powerful and unprecedented alliance of Pakistani militant groups—the Tehrik-i-Taliban Pakistan, or Taliban Movement of Pakistan. Founded in December 2007, the alliance of previously disparate groups fielded an estimated 5,000 fighters. They unleashed attacks that killed former prime minister Benazir Bhutto in 2007 and killed or wounded 5,000 Pakistanis in 2008.

As I received newspapers from my captors in January 2009, more Pakistanis were dying in terror attacks than Afghans or Iraqis. The Pakistani Taliban had seized control of all seven agencies that made up the tribal areas and a famed tourist area sixty miles from Islamabad known as the Swat Valley. Declaring a complete ban on girls' education, the Pakistani Taliban destroyed or damaged 175 girls' schools in Swat.

I recalled a meeting I had with a retired senior official from the ISI four months after the storming of the Red Mosque. Asking that he not be named, he was the first senior ISI official to admit to me that some ISI officials had been playing a "double game."

He said that while he and other ISI officials arrested Al Qaeda operatives and impressed American officials, other ISI officials turned a blind eye to the Afghan Taliban and Pakistani militants they thought could be useful proxies against India. With suicide bombings besetting Pakistan's largest cities, the former ISI official admitted that his agency had lost control of the militants it had nurtured for the last thirty years.

"We indoctrinated them and told them, 'You will go to heaven,'" he told me. "You cannot turn it around so suddenly."

After a two-hour drive in Badruddin's truck, we arrive in a snow-covered valley with towering pine trees. The hills and snow, he hopes, will convince the world we are being held in Afghanistan, not in a bustling town in Pakistan.

The drive has been a delight for me. After nearly three months of living in walled compounds, I relished looking out the window as we drove through towns, villages, and open spaces of North Waziristan. Much of the landscape is dry, desolate, and reminiscent of the American Southwest. Other areas have the rolling hills and soaring trees of the Rocky Mountains.

Badruddin orders Tahir, Asad, and me to put on new black Chinese-made high-top basketball sneakers he has purchased. I fold my pants into the tops of the sneakers and wrap the blanket Badruddin gave me months ago around my neck as a scarf. I hope both steps will make the video look more ridiculous than frightening. Badruddin tells his men to set up a tent he has purchased as a prop on the hillside. His men can't figure out how to assemble it. I think about helping them but decide not to.

As a backup plan, Badruddin instructs us to walk up a snow-covered hillside with a half dozen guards. Scarves cover their faces and each carries a machine gun or Kalashnikov. Timor Shah leads the way. He peers through a tiny pair of binoculars Badruddin has given him. We follow him up the hill, and I exaggerate my movements to try to make the video appear staged.

We are led into a small cave where one of Badruddin's men has lit a fire. Badruddin orders us to say we are sick and in the mountains of Afghanistan. I do so but try to show little emotion. As I speak, I place my left hand over my right, hoping my wife will see that I am flashing my wedding ring at her.

Outside the cave, we sit on the hillside and Badruddin orders me to again call for President Obama to meet the Taliban's demands. I do so but add a new line. At Tahir and Asad's request, I explicitly ask journalists to publicize our case.

"We ask journalists to please help us," I say. "Please write stories about us. Please don't let us be forgotten."

I fail to cry. After the last video, I am less willing to placate our captors. Badruddin does not seem to care. After a few more minutes, he stops filming. Our location shoot has taken roughly thirty minutes.

As we walk down the hill, the guards get into a snowball fight with Tahir and Asad.

A FRENCH STREET GANG

Kristen, Early to Mid-February 2009

A rumor has spread that an unidentified person has a video of our three and is shopping it around Kabul to American and foreign news organizations. The BBC and several others refuse to purchase it. Al Jazeera Arabic allegedly buys it for an undisclosed amount.

Michael Semple and I are now in daily contact. He tells me not to panic—this is most likely what he refers to as "a midterm fund-raising effort." Most likely the captors have raised a few thousand dollars from the sale of the video footage, he says. Kidnapping is a group endeavor and the individuals guarding and feeding David, Tahir, and Asad need to be compensated for their time and effort. Michael has been the one consistent presence in this experience—in advice and in manner. For this reason, I have come to trust his opinion above the others.

A colleague of David's in Kabul, Dexter Filkins, tracks down an Al Jazeera representative and asks to see a copy of the video. While he isn't permitted to copy it, he and his translator are allowed a viewing and type up notes.

His transcript serves as a preview for Lee and me. We are struck by a few observations he makes, namely that David looks old and "his shoes are not his own." This seems odd. How would Dexter know this? Soon enough, we understand.

Al Jazeera Arabic airs a snippet of the video a few days later. It is a twelve-second segment in which David, Tahir, and Asad appear outside, against a snowy backdrop. This is the promotional teaser to a full-length broadcast scheduled for that day.

The New York Times comes to our rescue. Bill Keller, the executive editor, calls the head of Al Jazeera's station in Doha and requests that it refrain from showing the video in its entirety because of our safety concerns. Al Jazeera agrees to pull it off the air. We are terrified the video will be leaked and end up on the Internet. Our main concern is that a public airing will give the captors the attention and acclaim they seek in holding an American.

We do not want David's value to become that of a political spectacle. We do not want him to be used to test or challenge the new Obama administration.

With the video taking up my attention, I cancel my flight to Pakistan. I will stay put.

Keller's office alerts me to expect a call from Secretary Clinton. She has heard about the Al Jazeera segment. I am told she wants to console me and provide reassurance.

I am at home when she calls. I am struck by her appealing combination of warmth and composure. Helpful and efficient, she assures me that David's case is being worked on "at the highest level."

"My heart goes out to you," she adds. "I can only imagine—actually, I cannot imagine what you must be going through."

I ask her if David's captors have made additional demands—political demands—that perhaps we as a family are not aware of. She reassures me that no one in our government has received communication from the group holding David. Holbrooke will be making a trip to the region soon, she says, and I should stay in touch with him.

"I am a longtime admirer and supporter of yours," I say, thanking her. "I feel very confident knowing you are at the helm and aware of this issue." I can't resist adding, "And, frankly, I am so thrilled and relieved to have another woman in the mix!"

She bursts into laughter. "Oh, dear," she says, "I know *exactly* what you mean!"

The next day, February 7, I receive a call from a journalist in New York who has obtained a copy of the video. The sound is still spotty but the visuals are clear. The journalist offers to meet me at the United Nations building.

I have spent the last few days agonizing over my decision not to travel to Pakistan. Tonight I am thankful that my gut check was right: I am relieved to be in New York to view the only communication from my husband in six weeks.

Lee flies in to join me. He is able to do so on a moment's notice because he runs a corporate aviation consulting company. He's constantly flying somewhere for work and often makes last-minute pit stops in New York. This also serves as his cover with business associates and some family members who are not yet aware of David's situation. Our immediate family knows, but the extended family—cousins, uncles, nieces—do not.

It is 5 P.M. on a snowy, cold Saturday. The journalist meets me at the security gate and assures me that while I cannot obtain a copy of the video, I can make arrangements for our security advisers to view it.

Apparently, our security advisers don't want to wait that long. AISC has overnighted to me a pen that doubles as a camera. They suggest I use it to take covert footage of the video. I was expecting something worthy of James Bond—perhaps a chic, ultra slim version of a Bic pen. Instead, a large heavy fountain pen, the size of a small telescope—or an engorged Mont Blanc—arrived this morning. It looks like a sight gag from a Peter Sellers film.

It has a hole toward the top and a small blue light the size of a pinhead that lights up when it's filming. I call the security team and tell them that while I appreciate their efforts, I do not feel comfortable with their plan. I do not want to be busted by UN security for packing a suspicious fountain pen.

I breeze through security. They do not X-ray me. I could have gotten the pen in no problem, I say to myself. Lee, however, is asked to submit to a full security screening. At six feet tall, with a buzz cut and military training, he looks like a contractor or government agent.

The journalist ushers us into an elevator, then through increasingly narrow corridors to a small, carpeted room at the end of a neglected, dimly lit hallway. The windows of the room overlook the East River. The three of us cram into the tiny room and gather around a small monitor.

The video is rather surprising, and long—twelve minutes in total. It begins with David. "I want to apologize, from the bottom of my soul, to my wife Kristen," he says. I am moved by this genuine expression. Soon after, it is followed by an obligatory plea and what look clearly like fake tears. David makes it obvious he is reading from a script. He is dressed in a salwar kameez, prayer hat, and jacket. His hands are unbound. He is still wearing his wedding ring. A banner hanging behind his head bears the emblem of the Islamic Emirate of Afghanistan and an Arabic slogan that says "There is no God but Allah and Muhammad is his prophet."

We note that Tahir is wearing a large gold watch. Dexter had made reference to "handcuffs" in his account of the video. It turns out he mistook the watch for a shackle. We are relieved and slightly perplexed. It is surprising that the money-grubbing Taliban would not confiscate valuable personal items like the wedding ring and watch.

Once again, gunmen flank the edges of the video frame, but they appear at ease. Tahir speaks next in Pashto. Asad makes a brief statement as well.

The video then cuts to a strange clip of our three walking up a hill in what looks like suburban Westchester County in New York. The incline is not steep, but the camera is tilted at an angle to make it appear more precipitous. They are surrounded by ten men in turbans, pajama-type pants, and camouflage jackets. Everyone sports oversize black basketball high-tops with thick white soles—Chinese knockoffs of Reebok. David has tucked his pants into his sneakers and the result is a somewhat comical fashion statement. They look more like a French street gang than a bunch of terrorists. The camera cuts to David and he explains that they are in the mountains of Afghanistan, where it is cold and difficult. In a matter-of-fact way, he adds that the food and water are making him sick.

"I thought he might convert to Islam, but I never dreamed he'd go hip-hop," I tell Lee. He smiles and adds: "Clearly they are feeding him. There's no way he has diarrhea." David appears to have gained weight. Maybe it's the full beard. He looks like a burly mountain man. Grizzly Adams springs to mind. His beard, although thick, is well groomed. His face is tan. We are relieved to see this, and our relief takes the form of humor. We actually have a laughing fit over the footwear and general attire, which is incongruous with David's traditional New England style: khakis and an oxford cloth shirt.

In the next segment of the video Tahir laments, "It's so cold, so cold." Yet they all have their jackets unzipped and the tree branches are bare—the snow is clearly melting. One of the Taliban fighters sports opera glasses and pauses occasionally to survey the area.

In the final portion David appeals to "President Obama, Secretary of State Hillary Clinton, and special envoy Richard Holbrooke to meet the Taliban demands." He also asks that journalists write stories about them so that they will not be forgotten. I do not think this is coming from David as he is clearly reading from a script and staring blankly ahead as he relays this sentence. "Please meet the Taliban demands. Please save the three of us, please save the three of us, please save the three of us." He adds the word "again" before restating this plea, as if repeating the cameraman's directions to him.

We watch the video several times, obsessing over details. We are not quite sure who its producers consider to be the target audience: our family, the government, or the public. We ponder this as we head back to the apartment in lower Manhattan.

It's been quite a day and we decompress in the living room over diner food. We call Lee's wife, Christie. Lee says Christie insisted that he join me in New York so I would not have to watch the video alone. She has been a source of strength and calm throughout this ordeal, willing to accommodate Lee's last-minute trips to New York and Washington in support of David and me. We tell her about the video and admit that we are baffled by its somewhat comical staging, which seems at odds with its disturbing message.

We discuss our impressions of the footage, briefly laughing as we recall the more absurd moments—the release is crucial, given the confusing reality of the situation. The captors have not made explicit demands in the video. We have no idea what, if anything, they plan to do next.

We worry the video will surface on the Web and make our case public. Due to its political undercurrent—the mention of Obama, Clinton, Holbrooke—we feel more strongly than ever that we should keep the case quiet. While our government and the journalism community are well aware of the case by now, the public at large is not. I alert Holbrooke to the contents of the video and forward him my notes and a written transcript.

Two days later, the FBI alerts me that a video execution of a Polish hostage is on the Internet. I'm haunted by the idea that we may one day receive similar footage of David.

The New York Times agrees that we should remain silent, but wants us to have a plan in place in the event that another news organization or blogger is less amenable than Al Jazeera in respecting our choice.

As part of the preparation, the newspaper's public relations office arranges for Lee and me to receive media training. Defensiveness training is actually a more accurate description. The goal is to learn how to deflect questions. Neither one of us has any desire to appear on television. We decide Lee will be the family spokesman should the story ever break. He assumed this role before on behalf of David when he was imprisoned in Bosnia. He is the perfect choice. My mother often refers to Lee as "the epitome of an officer and a gentleman." He has quite a fan club among our media experts and FBI agents because he projects both strength and calm. Cordial and soft-spoken, he could easily disarm reporters.

We arrange for two separate sessions. I meet the training crew at a glass office building in Midtown after I finish work. A chair, video camera, and monitor have been set up in the corner of a conference room. In the mock interview, I feel like a deer in the headlights. A tired looking deer at that. I glance at myself in the monitor. I've aged several years in the last few months, I think. I am wearing a gray button-front crocheted sweater. I look like a tired old lady, a gray presence with circles under my eyes. My interviewer comes to my rescue and suggests the cameraman back up a few feet—"Give her a break," she says.

The public relations team has compiled a notebook of talking points and suggested answers. We role-play through them.

Who is working on David's case?

Answer: Many people and agencies are involved in working toward his release.

Have you spoken to David?

Answer: Yes, but I am not going to discuss additional details.

Do you have any indication of what the abductors want?

Answer: We are not going to discuss details.

Why has the *Times* not reported on this?

Answer: We were told by his abductor that the safety of David and his colleagues would be in jeopardy if we discussed this publicly.

Then the interviewer asks me a series of more personal questions:

What is your husband like? How are you getting through each day, how are you not falling apart? Is there something you'd like to say to David or to his captors?

This is no one's business, I think. My voice gets notably more formal as the questions get more personal. It's impossible to define my husband and our relationship with a sound bite. It throws me off kilter to talk about David in this format. I have expended so much energy trying to stay positive and strong. Once again, I feel the desperation of our situation.

I have no desire to sit across from Matt Lauer. Ever. I do not wish to be comforted by Ann Curry. I keep this in mind as I practice thwarting direct questions about ransom, government agencies, communication with captors.

While I am no screen goddess, I am a quick study at deflecting questions and, after several takes and critiques, I am given permission to call it a day.

I talk to Lee on the phone afterward to compare training stories. It's past 11 P.M. and I have just polished off some leftover pizza. He has flown home and is back in New Hampshire.

He informs me he was caught off guard during the training session. Normally cool and composed, he choked up when confronted with questions about David. Neither one of us has had a chance to stop and reflect. He confides that this is the first time he has really felt the depth of his sadness over his missing brother.

ARE YOU THERE?

David, Early to Mid-February 2009

In the first week of February, our hopes plummet. An American who works for the United Nations is kidnapped on February 2 in the Pakistani province of Baluchistan. Gunmen open fire on the car of the worker, John Solecki, kill his driver, and abduct him. Solecki, a career humanitarian aid worker, leads the United Nations refugee office there. Over the next several days, I learn about the details of his case from radio and newspaper reports.

A previously unknown group calling for Baluchistan to become an independent country—the Baluchistan Liberated United Front—claims responsibility. Secular nationalists, they have no relationship with Pakistan's Islamic militants but their demands are just as astronomical. They threaten to kill Solecki if 141 women they say are being held captive by the Pakistani government are not released. The Pakistani government responds that it does not have 141 women in custody. In the perverse world of ransom demands, their call for the release of 141 female prisoners—who may not even exist—makes my captors seem reasonable.

Five days after the kidnapping of the American UN worker, a Pakistani Taliban group beheads a Polish hostage. Piotr Stanczak is killed after the Pakistani government refuses to release twenty-six Taliban prisoners. He is the first foreign captive to be executed in Pakistan since the murder of the *Wall Street Journal* reporter Daniel Pearl seven years ago. I never met Stanczak but immediately grieve for him and his family. I assume Stanczak, like me, spent months pacing in a small yard, dreaming of release and trying to reason with his captors. In the end, none of it mattered.

His abduction and execution are a symbol of the growing reach of the Pakistani Taliban. They kidnapped Stanczak, a geologist who was surveying oil and gas fields, an hour's drive outside the country's capital in September 2008, two months before our abduction. They shot his driver, guard, and translator and took him into the tribal areas.

Stanczak's killing calls into question the logic of the one instruction I remember from my hostile environment training course: prolong a kidnapping. A kidnapper is hypothetically less likely to kill a hostage after investing funds, manpower, and time into their care, according to experts. They want to recoup their investment, in a sense, after spending time and resources on the prisoners. In Stanczak's case, his captors held him for five months and then killed him. They received no money or prisoners in return for their effort. As I read about it, his case presents a different logic.

The Pakistani Taliban seemingly want to defy the Pakistani government, show its weakness, and generate widespread press coverage of their brutality. While a criminal is in search of ransom, militants may be simply interested in generating publicity. I don't know which path our captors will follow.

Evan after Stanczak's death, the Pakistani Taliban find a depraved way to still make money off his case. Echoing Badruddin's threat to sell my bones to my family, Stanczak's executioners vow to hold the Polish geologist's body until the Pakistani government pays a ransom for it.

His execution leaves me grasping at straws. In an earlier conversation, Badruddin told me that the Haqqanis had decided to never set a deadline in our case. I don't believe him. As an American, I don't know if they see me as worth more alive or dead. Stanczak was Polish and hailed from a small country with several hundred soldiers in Afghanistan. I am American and hail from the nation the Taliban view as their central enemy. My captors' demand for five prisoners is small in comparison with the demand of Stanczak's captors for twenty-six prisoners.

Other cases in Pakistan involving foreigners set no clear precedent. Over the last several years, the Pakistani Taliban had kidnapped four Chinese engineers in an effort to embarrass the Pakistani government and deter foreigners from coming to the country. Two were released, one was still in custody, and one had escaped. None of the Chinese had been executed within days like Daniel Pearl.

Throughout my captivity, I often thought of Pearl. I never met him but had many colleagues who passionately liked and respected him. I had become close friends with the *Wall Street Journal* correspondent who succeeded Pearl as the newspaper's South Asia bureau chief. Pearl was tricked into going to an interview as well. A British-born militant of Pakistani descent, Ahmed Omar Sheikh, first held a friendly meeting with Pearl in the northern city of Rawalpindi in January 2002 and won his trust. Then he promised Pearl an interview with a senior militant accused of involvement in the case of Richard Reid, the British "shoe bomber" who tried to blow up a U.S.-bound passenger jet in December 2001.

I wrote about Pearl's case. I visited the site of his captivity and execution—a small tree nursery several hundred yards from a conservative religious school in Karachi. I saw the perimeter wall Pearl tried to scale when he attempted to escape. Five years later, I know that the only thing that separates me from Pearl is luck.

In mid-February, Timor Shah, our chief guard, informs us that Badruddin has sent the video to Afghan and foreign media outlets but that only Al Jazeera has broadcast it. The news frustrates Tahir and Asad, who had hoped that the video would be widely broadcast and stimulate negotiations. I am not surprised and assume my colleagues believe that my request to publicize our case was coerced. Incensed, Badruddin washes his hands of us. Timor Shah says that Badruddin has declared me "worthless" and will no longer pay for our food.

Desperate to spark negotiations, we ask Timor Shah to call Abu Tayyeb and beg him to help us. To our relief, Abu Tayyeb says he will return to

Miran Shah in a few days. He promises to take charge of the negotiations and finally secure our release. After so many lies, I doubt he will actually do it.

Several days later, on February 14, two missiles fired by an American drone kill thirty people in South Waziristan, the area to our south. Most of them are Uzbek militants, a development that infuriates our guards and others around us. The guards say the Uzbeks were teaching the Afghan Taliban how to make roadside bombs.

Four weeks into the Obama administration, it is clear that the United States is not decreasing drone attacks. In fact, it is increasing them. Several times a week, drones circle over Miran Shah. Tiny specks in the sky, the whir of their propellers announces their arrival. They sound like single-engine Piper Cubs circling overhead for hours at a time. Seemingly surprised by the escalation, the Taliban bitterly criticize President Obama, who is the focus of more hatred from the Taliban than President George W. Bush.

I am not sure of the exact number, but it seems like roughly a half dozen drone strikes have been carried out in the three months since we arrived in Miran Shah. Based on the reaction of the guards, the attacks appear to primarily kill militants. Yet the Taliban exaggerate the number of civilian casualties killed and use the strikes to attract more recruits. A stalemate has emerged between the United States and the Taliban. The Americans kill top leaders and inhibit their movements with drone strikes, but the Taliban slowly generate new leadership. Neither side is able to win a decisive victory. To me, the deadlock will continue until the Pakistani army ends its cease-fire and moves into the tribal areas in force.

The drones also represent an entirely new form of warfare. The United States is able to carry out assassinations thousands of miles away without deploying American troops. No declaration of war is required. The American public hears little about the attacks. And no American lives are lost. The military itself is not necessarily involved. Some drones are operated entirely by the CIA. An agency employee sitting in an office in northern Virginia can guide the drones remotely and fire its missiles.

Our guards believe I am a target of the drones. United States officials want to kill me, they say, because my death will eliminate the enormous leverage and credibility the Haqqanis believe a single American prisoner gives them. Whenever a drone appears, I am ordered to stay inside the house. The guards believe that its surveillance cameras can recognize my face from thousands of feet above.

A week after he promised to return to Miran Shah, Abu Tayyeb, to my surprise, actually arrives and says he will allow me to call Kristen. The engineer, who is still acting as a liaison between the captors and my family, has brokered a deal to exchange us for five male prisoners from the Afghan national prison, Abu Tayyeb says. A lingering disagreement is over money, but he promises to lower the Haqqanis' demand from $15 million to $7 million. The figures are still astronomical, but I cannot keep from yet again seeing him as a potential savior. He is bound to settle for far less in direct talks with Kristen.

Later that night, Abu Tayyeb toys with me again. He and Akhundzada, his intelligence chief, announce that I am good friends with Obama's new envoy to Afghanistan and Pakistan. They ask me his name. I play dumb. They have apparently Googled my reporting in Bosnia and seen that Richard Holbrooke was the American diplomat who pressured the Serbs to release me in 1995. Fearing this moment, I have not mentioned Holbrooke's name since we were kidnapped. In January, he was named the Obama administration's special representative for Afghanistan and Pakistan. In my captors' eyes, this proves yet again that I am a "big fish." In truth, I felt that Holbrooke has been mildly irritated with me ever since I complicated his Bosnia negotiations. Each time I have seen him since then he has reminded me not to get myself kidnapped again. I have repeatedly promised him it would not happen.

The disappointments continue the following day. Instead of leaving early in the morning to call Kristen, we are delayed because no phone is available. Finally, several hours late, we depart with Abu Tayyeb for a spot near the Afghan border where we will make the call. On the way Abu Tayyeb tells me what to say. I make a detailed list in the battered reporter's notebook that I brought to what I thought would be a Taliban interview. I also have a plan. With Tahir's encouragement, I have compiled a list of the first names of friends I believe can help Kristen raise money. The vast majority of them are reporters with limited resources, but thoughts of my family selling their homes haunt me. By giving her the names I will ease the burden on Kristen.

We arrive at a remote location near the Afghan border. Badruddin is already there in a separate car. Apparently, they hope to get close enough to the border that a cell phone tower in Afghanistan will handle the call and disguise our location inside Pakistan. Badruddin gets in our car and hands me a cell phone. The phone's display shows that it's on an Afghan cellular network. I think it might be midnight in New York. Abu Tayyeb orders me to give Kristen their cell phone number and have her call us back. They are demanding $7 million in ransom but are too cheap to pay for the phone call.

I dial my home number and the answering machine picks up. I hear Kristen's joyful voice ask callers to leave us a message.

"Kristen, it's David," I say into the machine. "Kristen, are you there?"

No one picks up.

"Kristen, can you hear me? Kristen, Kristen, can you hear me?" I repeat, thinking she might be asleep. "I'm calling, I'm with the Taliban. We're calling to try to negotiate."

"Kristen, are you there?" I say, increasingly worried we will miss this opportunity. "Kristen? Kristen?"

Abu Tayyeb orders me to end the call. Fearing I won't be able to call again, I blurt out "I love you" and hang up. We sit in the car for roughly fifteen minutes. Abu Tayyeb and Badruddin are nervous that the calls are being traced. They fear our car will be targeted in a drone strike. I ask them to let me try one more time. I dial our home number. Again, the answering machine picks up.

"Kristen, Kristen, it's David, can you hear me?" I say. "Kristen, Kristen, Kristen, are you there? Kristen, are you there? Please wake up."

"Kristen, it's David," I say. "Please wake up, Kristen."

MY FUNNY VALENTINE

Kristen, February 15, 2009

I hear a man's voice calling my name as I stand outside the front door. "Kristen, Kristen, are you there?" For a brief moment, I think some strange guy has broken into my apartment and is now pleading to be let out. Then I realize it's David!

My mom has gone back to Maine for the week, and my brother and his wife are here for the long Presidents' Day weekend and Valentine's Day. On Sunday we go out to dinner and a movie, something I have not done in a long time. It's more apparent to me that I have become a captive as well. This experience is shifting from a crisis to a lifestyle.

I rush to get the key in the door, stumble over to the answering machine and pick up just in time. "David, David!" I say breathlessly. "Can you hear me?"

"Yes," he replies.

"I love you, honey," I add.

"Can you get a pen and paper. I am going to give you a number to call me back on," he says tensely, adding, "do not trace the call. Do not let anyone trace the call. Do not let the government trace it."

GOLDEN CHANCE

David, February 16, 2009

T he phone rings. Kristen is calling back. I am elated: there will be negotiations. I answer and immediately begin dictating from my notes. "Write this down," I say. "I cannot talk for very long. You cannot try to call me back."

"Okay," Kristen says, "I will write this down."

I look over the list of things Abu Tayyeb has ordered me to tell her.

"Okay," Kristen says again. "Hello?"

"Okay, this is the last call," I say. "This is my last chance."

Kristen repeats what I say.

"She's writing it down," I tell Badruddin and Abu Tayyeb.

"Okay, do not trace call. Don't use force to try to find us," I say, as Kristen repeats after me. "It puts us in great danger. We are in the mountains of Afghanistan."

"Uh-huh," Kristen says.

"It's very cold," I say.

"Yep," Kristen responds, sounding unimpressed.

"There's snow and I am very sick," I say.

"Yeah, okay," Kristen responds again.

"It's very difficult for us," I say. "And the video is on Al Jazeera."

"Al Jazeera overseas?" Kristen asks.

"I don't know," I reply.

"Okay, I do," Kristen says. "Okay."

"It was shown once," I say.

"Yes it was," Kristen replies.

"We called Atiqullah, the commander that arrested us," I explain.

I continue to call our captor by his false name, even though I know Atiqullah is Abu Tayyeb. Tahir and Asad still fear that Abu Tayyeb will decapitate them if he learns they revealed his true identity to me.

"Yes," Kristen says.

"He has come back to help us. He is a very big commander," I say, trying to play to his ego. "He took many, many risks, he came very far through many, many checkpoints so he could come and he is going to leave now."

"Okay," Kristen says.

"And I asked him to let me call you," I say, my voice cracking.

"Thank you," Kristen says.

"Because I thought it was the best thing to do," I say.

"Yes, it is," Kristen says, reassuring me.

"Okay, Atiqullah will negotiate with the family about money," I say. "And then the office in Kabul should negotiate with a man called Engineer." I explain to her that the engineer is their representative for negotiating prisoners.

"I know who he is," she says.

Kristen then asks me if Atiqullah is aware of the ransom offer. I say yes and then ask Kristen if she knows anything about an agreement for five prisoners.

"I am not aware of that," she says. "I am not aware of that."

"Have you heard—do you think that's not true or you don't know?" I ask, devastated by her response.

"Uh, I don't think it's true," Kristen says.

My chest tightens. We have been lied to yet again. There is no agreement for prisoners.

Kristen tries to set a time for the next phone call.

"We're running out of time," I say, repeating what they're telling me. "Atiqullah is willing to make a deal now for $7 million. Instead of for $15 million, he will drop to $7 million. And that's their last offer—and five prisoners."

I explain that the Taliban say the current ransom offer is "a joke." They claim that $38 million was paid for the French aid worker whose video I saw. They also believe that the Italian journalist was exchanged in 2007 for prisoners and $15 million in cash.

Kristen says that the U.S. government will not exchange prisoners or pay ransom. "Our government does not do that," she says.

Abu Tayyeb interrupts us and tells her to speak with the engineer about prisoners. He says any ransom payment must be done through the International Red Cross. Kristen thanks him for trying to work with our family but says that is not possible.

"I just want him to know the ICRC will not help us negotiate," she says. "I don't think they will carry funds. So I just want to make sure he knows that."

Abu Tayyeb says he will call her.

"Don't let this opportunity end," I say, repeating one of the points Abu Tayyeb dictated to me. "It's only a short time. He would like to finish everything within a week. If not, he will leave. He'll take his guards away from us and we'll be left with these other people who will kill us."

I start giving Kristen the names of the people who I think could raise ransom money. Abu Tayyeb says he will call again in four days, but will not name a time.

"She can't have a translator sitting in her house twenty-four hours a day," I say. He promises to call on Thursday.

The phone starts beeping. I know some Afghan mobile phone companies charge for receiving international calls. Even though Kristen called us, our phone will soon run out of minutes.

I quickly tell Kristen the remainder of the names.

"Honey," Kristen says, "we're doing everything we can."

The line goes dead. The phone has run out of credits.

MIDNIGHT

Kristen, February 16, 2009

I 've just gotten off the phone with my husband. I am surprised that the Taliban let him stay on the phone that long. Then again, I am footing the bill.

I feel a mix of elation and desperation. From what I could gather, David knows nothing of the ongoing negotiations. While I tried to assure him we would not give up, I also had to alert him to the fact that the Red Cross cannot assist in any negotiations. And that a prisoner exchange is not possible.

David's voice sounded strong. He was also very lucid in his thinking. This is the upside. And I have a promise that his captors will call back in a few days. We even have an assigned time.

"Midnight," I say triumphantly. Midnight on Thursday.

Midnight? Now I realize that this is the worst choice possible. Does it mean midnight on Wednesday, the very beginning of Thursday? Or the end of Thursday? I exhale an expletive.

GIFT FROM GOD

David, February 16–20, 2009

As we drive back to Miran Shah, I am shattered. There is no deal for prisoners, the Red Cross will not handle a ransom payment, and Abu Tayyeb is refusing to budge from $7 million and five prisoners. Worst of all, I have placed my wife in a horrific position—she is now directly negotiating with our captors. She will feel that she holds our lives in her hands.

Abu Tayyeb asks how I'm doing. "We're fucked," I say. Before the call, I had let myself believe that his false name, Atiqullah, "gift from God," might be a sign he would still somehow save us. Yet again, I am wrong.

We return to the house and the guards stare at me as I walk through the front gate. My face is ashen and my clothes are covered in sweat from lying under a blanket in the back of the car. I sit down next to Asad and tell him in broken Pashto that the call went badly. He pats me on the back and urges me to wash. I take a bucket shower in the bathroom, change clothes, walk in the yard, and try to gather my thoughts.

The call was a disaster. If Abu Tayyeb abandons us and Badruddin sets a deadline, we will be killed one by one.

That afternoon, I watch Asad as he prepares dinner for us. He had no idea how to cook when we were abducted three months ago but has proven to be a fast learner. As a means of survival, he is making himself useful to our captors. He and I still struggle to communicate but connect in small ways. Asad jokes with me when we are alone in the kitchen.

Tahir has become my only companion and my only attachment to reality. We have become close friends, encouraging each other in our lowest moments. He continues to fight like a lion, haranguing our kidnappers for hours at a time and threatening vengeance from his tribe.

In recent weeks, I have started encouraging Tahir and Asad to escape on their own. As Pashtuns, they have a chance of making it to the Afghan border if they can somehow slip out of our compound. Tahir adamantly refuses to leave without me. Under Pashtunwali, I am his guest and abandoning me would shame him for life. As soon as he departs without me, Tahir says, the protection of his tribe will be lifted and the Taliban will kill me.

When the guards leave us alone, Tahir whispers to me about how much he misses his seven children. He is determined to educate his daughters and is unabashedly proud of his eldest girl, who is an excellent student. Asad's two boys are younger but his face brightens each time he speaks of them. I think of how Tahir and Asad's nine children will fare without them. As adult males, they are their families' main providers. If they die, their families will be destitute.

My own death is a growing possibility as well. As the months pass, though, that prospect is gradually becoming less frightening. I tell myself that I will simply go to sleep. On a few days, I accept my death, relish the life I've had, and silently relish the idea that our greedy captors will get nothing for me. On most days, I am heartbroken at the thought of never seeing Kristen, my family, and my friends again.

What haunts me most is picturing Kristen as a widow at forty. She is dressed in black, a color she rarely wears, and her sunny countenance is dark. Her glow—the radiant smile that drew me to her at our first dinner together—is gone. I promised her a new life and a family. Instead, I have given her this.

Abu Tayyeb joins us that night for dinner. I ask him to promise that he will stay in Miran Shah until there is a resolution to our case. He does. For the next four days, we wait for him to call Kristen back. Our conversations leave me doubtful that he will ever compromise in a case involving an American.

He weeps at a radio news broadcast about civilian deaths in Afghanistan. A guard explains to me that Abu Tayyeb reviles the United States because of the civilian deaths he believes it causes. Abu Tayyeb says that Americans fixate on wealth, comfort, and fame and ignore the crimes the American government commits abroad. My captors see me—and seemingly all Westerners—as selfish, morally corrupt, and focused on pursuing the pleasures of this world. They believe Westerners will pay staggering sums to keep a kidnapped family member from being executed. They believe that Westerners' fear of death is their fatal weakness. They are convinced the Taliban will prevail because they do not fear death.

Abu Tayyeb and our guards see the American-led reconstruction effort as a giant fraud scheme designed to enrich Westerners and shortchange average Afghans. They say the American-backed Karzai government is enormously corrupt. And Akbar, our friendliest guard, says he has heard stories that American companies intentionally build low-quality bridges in Afghanistan so they can be awarded lucrative repair contracts in the future. He says Americans came to Afghanistan to enrich themselves, not to help average Afghans.

For years, I have reported on the shortcomings and waste of the American-led reconstruction effort, but I also knew the Taliban caricature of the endeavor is exaggerated. Yes, Afghan expectations of a sweeping reconstruction of the entire country were raised and then not met. And yes, corruption in the Afghan government is a staggering problem.

Evidence of how flawed the American effort even lies on the floor of our bedroom every day. One of the machine guns our guards have was apparently given to the Afghan army or police force and then sold to the Taliban or captured by them. The gun has a tag on it with handwritten instructions in American English that tell users which settings to use when firing the weapon. Our guards ask me to translate the words for them.

At the same time, Abu Tayyeb and his men ignore the fact that the United States has built hundreds of miles of paved roads in Afghanistan and more than a thousand schools and health clinics. They deny widespread news reports that the Taliban have burned down scores of newly built schools to prevent girls from getting an education. And they ignore the Taliban's killing and kidnapping of dozens of Afghan and foreign engineers and road workers.

He complains that foreigners have not kept their promise to rebuild the country. But the Taliban, in fact, have done more to thwart the reconstruction effort than any other group. In conversations with him, I argue that the United States is not the menacing, predatory caricature that he believes it to be. I also try to counter his belief that all Americans are astonishingly rich hedonists. Nothing I say, though, seems to change his view. He sees himself as the noble defender of a culture and faith that are under assault.

PEACE BE UPON YOU

Kristen, Late February–Early March 2009

G etting a Pashto translator is not as daunting a task as it might seem, at least not in New York. With the help of David's colleagues at the newspaper, I am able to track down a translator who lives in Brooklyn and will come over to my apartment on Wednesday and Thursday night, when I'll be waiting for the next phone call from the captors. By this point we have opted to conduct negotiations privately, but we continue to send tapes of phone calls to the FBI in case they are able to pinpoint a call location or provide voice recognition.

I recorded my phone call with David three nights ago. I play it back for Lee, David McCraw, Team Kabul, and our AISC consultants. I send a recording to Michael, in Pakistan, who instructs me to forward the upcoming call to the man he works with in the tribal areas, who asked to be identified in this book as John. John has worked with Michael on prior kidnappings. We will direct all calls with the Taliban to him. At Michael's request, John has traveled to the region as our family's representative to meet with a mullah at Swabi who has connections to the Haqqanis. Now he will serve as our primary negotiator. The security consultants agree. I should not be pressured with the responsibility of negotiating directly with the Taliban on my husband's behalf. This is typical protocol—it's far too easy for captors take advantage of direct contact with family to frighten or threaten them and thus extort even more money.

Lee comes back to the city to join me in waiting for the impending call, which we plan to relay to John in hopes of making him the primary negotiator. "I thought my days of sitting and waiting by the phone for a man to call would end with marriage," I joke as I greet Lee.

Our translator arrives at 5 p.m. on Wednesday. He is a Pashtun from southern Afghanistan who has lived in the United States for several years. I serve an eclectic feast of tea, pizza, salad, and snacks—a far cry from the well-balanced cuisine Lee and I have become accustomed to during my mother's visits. "When does Mary Jane return?" Lee asks with a hint of humor.

To pass time as we all wait, I turn on the television. A *Top Chef* marathon is on. Our translator is transfixed by the host, Padma Lakshmi. "Excuse me," he asks. "Who is she? What show is this?" Then a revelation: "This is cable," he says happily. "I have cable. I could watch this at home, too?" Lee looks up at me from his computer and rolls his eyes. "Yes," I say, "in the privacy of your own home."

We share our recent histories. Our translator is from Kandahar. "This is a very interesting case for me. I left Afghanistan because my family wanted me to join the kidnapping business," he tells me. I don't know if this is true, but it doesn't seem far fetched, given how dire the situation is abroad. He also explains that in Pakistan and Afghanistan, people with relatives in the United States are often kidnapping targets, as it is believed anyone lucky enough to be living in America has money or access to it.

We talk about photography, and he asks me about the famous photograph of the Afghan girl that appeared two decades ago, on the cover of *National Geographic*. The one with the terrorized, intense green eyes. "What was so compelling about it?" he asks. "She looks like every other Afghan girl."

I tell him my husband has been held since November 10, just over three months. He says I am a brave woman and is amazed I am not a puddle of tears. I think brave is overstating it—I have no other option, I respond. And thanks to a hefty share of defense mechanisms—denial, distancing, humor—I'm still able to function.

For some reason—most likely stress—I am incredibly exhausted. I take a nap. One would think it would be difficult to sleep under the circumstances, but I have learned to sleep when I can. Rest is an essential part of staying sharp. I have been on an adrenaline rush since David's call and am now experiencing the downswing. The hours tick by: 1 A.M., 2 A.M., then 3 A.M. We have well surpassed our midnight deadline. At 3:30 A.M. we tell the translator he can leave and that we will see him again tomorrow evening.

Lee settles in on the couch and I retire to the bedroom. At 4:30 A.M. the phone rings. I jolt out of bed and run into the living room. Lee is in his running shorts and a T-shirt, looking equally startled and disheveled. I pick up the phone. Lee reads and records the phone number off the caller ID. The area code indicates a Pakistani number. He texts it to the FBI.

"Hello, *salaam alaikum*," I say. This is a Muslim greeting which means "Peace be upon you." It never hurts to be polite.

"Alaikum asalaam," or "The same to you," the caller responds. What a gentleman, I think.

"Call me back, this number," the voice says before the line goes silent.

Several rings later, a small eternity, our call resumes.

"This is Kristen, can you understand?" I ask. I hope.

"No speak Eng-leeesh," he exaggerates. "Only Pashto."

Oh no. I am concerned they think I slacked off on finding a proper translator. Screw it, I say to myself, and proceed to speak in English, without making any apologies. They will either understand me or they won't. I tell them to call John's number in Afghanistan and that he will be representing the family in negotiations. This is Michael's contact. The captors have long stopped calling the security experts that make up Team Kabul for fear that they are government agents. They have also shunned *The New York Times* bureau, because we have convinced them that this is a family matter.

Michael suggested I use specific wording in conveying information to the captors. I recite the phrases I have memorized: "My representative, my friend, John, is in Afghanistan and he is authorized to help you. He is the only one you should speak to."

For the next five minutes, a somewhat comical exchange ensues as I relay numbers to Atiqullah and he repeats them back to me. He is oddly polite and somewhat cheeky. I laugh triumphantly when he gets all the digits correct and in proper sequence. Lee looks somewhat quizzical as he witnesses this exchange. Lee calls Michael on the other line to alert him that his contact should expect a call.

Luckily, Atiqullah knows his English numbers. Within minutes, Michael calls to alert us that Atiqullah has already made contact with John. I hope passing Atiqullah on to this negotiator is the right decision.

It's now early March and my mother has returned to New York with my father, Jim, for a visit. My parents have been happily married for over forty-five years. Seeing them together gives me a sense of comfort, but also makes David's absence more palpable.

Two weeks have passed since my call with Atiqullah. Our noon updates continue. Atiqullah had at first made repeated calls to our contact, John, then stopped abruptly. John informs me and Lee over Skype that during the initial calls, Atiqullah said he would kill David on the spot, a threat John found ludicrous. "I knew there was no way David was with him," John tells us. "It would be too risky." When John remained unfazed, the kidnapper's tone once again shifted to "Let's make a deal." John says they have come down from $7 million to $5 million and that they are trying to arrange to meet face-to-face in a few days. To my knowledge, this never transpires.

A few days later, on a Sunday morning, my phone rings at 7:30 A.M. Unfortunately, I've left the cordless handset in the living room, where my parents are sleeping.

I wish this was not happening in front of them. My father has not yet been subjected to a call from the captors. I know he would do anything to protect me. Proactive and sensitive, seeing me go through this ordeal and feeling he cannot remedy the situation is a strain on him as well. I motion for them to leave the room to avoid distraction. I hit the record button attached to my answering machine.

"Hello, *salaam alaikum*," I say.

"*Alaikum asalaam*," he responds.

"This is Kristen. Who is this?" I ask, trying to buy some time to catch my breath.

"This is the translator for Atiqullah. So what is the progress?" he asks.

My heart is racing but I try to sound as calm and casual as possible and stick to the talking points outlined by our security team. I continue: "I gave Atiqullah the phone number of John, our representative in country. We are still working on raising money. It has been difficult to raise money because it is illegal to do so, so people have been, you know, a little hesitant." I chastise myself for the stupidity of this statement, then add, "I have a friend in country now who could arrange to get it to David's hosts." The line goes dead.

I phone Michael to alert him that I have just received another call. I ask him why they are contacting me when John is still in Afghanistan. He tells me to stonewall them if they call again. "Keep referring them back to John," he advises. "Also, tell them you are shocked they are speaking with you directly. You are a woman and it is dishonorable for them to be speaking to you. It goes against all they preach."

I wait several minutes for Atiqullah's translator to call me back, then take matters into my own hands, realizing once again they are going to stiff me for the cost of the phone call. I dial the number from caller ID. "Hello," I say. "This is Kristen."

"Hello, hi," he says, seemingly surprised to hear from me. "Yes, go on. So you continue." he adds casually.

I am struck by the conversational way the translator speaks English. I realize he's fluent in "American."

"My representative in country. Atiqullah has talked to him before," I say. "He can tell you more specifically what we can do. Do you need his phone number?" I ask.

"Listen, listen. Master John is not good man, he is creating problems," the translator responds.

I take this to mean John has stood firm and not agreed to give them $5 million. Lee and I have decided to stand firm on our offer. AISC has advised us to stand fast, too. Increasing the amount while our captors remain at an unmatchable level on both money and prisoners is futile, and they claim it will only further extend our ordeal. They are of the "give them an inch and they'll ask for a mile" school of thought. Anyway, we don't have this kind of money and have no intention of trying to raise it.

"And your husband has said that you speak directly to my wife," the translator claims.

I try to thwart this idea. "I am very concerned, but I am a woman. I am surprised you are calling me direct," I say.

"Well," he says a bit sheepishly, "we are interested to hear from you, what progress you have made. So far your husband is in good condition but over time anything can happen."

"The newspaper will not help me and our government will not pay. Our government is very different from the Italian government or the Korean government," I inform him, knowing that those countries had recently paid ransom in Taliban kidnappings. "So we will keep trying. Five million is a lot. We will never have it. We have a certain amount now and we can get it to you very quickly," I add, as I have been instructed to do by John and Michael.

"Yes. You know our circumstances," he explains. "Everybody is putting nose in. We should not talk all the time because it is dangerous. So try to keep it limited."

I agree with him and add, "That is why our representative is in the country. He can talk to you and the government cannot trace the call."

"Atiqullah says to you he is the only authentic representative for this issue," he adds.

"Okay, for the money issue?" I ask.

"Yeah, yeah," he confirms.

I am relieved he has not made any mention of prisoners.

"Okay," I repeat. "John is my only rep in country. Can we have him and Atiqullah talk again? He knows my father. He is a family friend. He also knows Afghanistan. That is the connection between us." I know invoking one's father is a form of credibility in Pashtun culture. I also don't want to let on that we think David and his captors are in Pakistan.

"Listen, you just try to prepare to arrange the money, then we will talk to you. You try to prepare the money as quietly as possibly," he states.

"Okay, we will keep trying," I say, to let them know more funds may be available if we keep talking. "We have an update about funding in the country, if you want to contact John he should know about it. He has access to the money and can get it to you."

"Yeah, we are going for praying," he says, wanting to get off the phone, in just one of the absurdities of the situation. He may be a criminal and a kidnapper, but he's observant. "After two days we will have another conversation, *inshallah*," he adds. God willing.

"Okay, Tahir and Asad—they are okay?" I ask. I know their families are worried sick. And I want to reinforce the idea that they must be part of the deal.

"Yeah, yeah, completely well. There is no problem," he says. "Is okay— one hundred percent."

"Okay," I add, "and tell David I love him and I pray for you all. I pray for you *all* every day." I hope in some bizarre way this will play on their sympathies, if only momentarily. There is a muffled pause, a fumbling in the background.

"God bless you," he responds.

Michael alerts me he will be traveling to Washington in a few days, and I plan to meet him there. We exchange text messages and set a meeting point: the bookshop at Union Station, just in front of Au Bon Pain. At this point, we have only seen each other in miniature during our telephonic computer exchanges on Skype. I tell him I will be wearing a red scarf.

I have no idea what to expect beyond the sandy brown hair, prophet-length beard, and broad smile I have seen on my computer screen. I have heard rumors about Michael. Mystery precedes him. A Google search reveals he was expelled from Afghanistan by President Hamid Karzai in 2007 for trying to negotiate with the Taliban. He has worked in the region for the United Nations and the European Union as a diplomat. Some speculate that he is a member of British intelligence. This is most likely wild rumor fueled by the fact that he has worked in Afghanistan and Pakistan for the last twenty-five years and is fluent in several local dialects and well versed in the nuances of tribal structures and custom. He is an expert on Taliban leadership. Two former hostages I met claim he was their lifesaver. The Kabul bureau trusts him and uses him as an analyst. David viewed Michael as a well-respected expert on Afghanistan and Pakistan. I have found him to be an insightful and articulate Skype correspondent.

He arrives on time. I'm relieved to see he is somewhat older than I expected and slightly professorial in his demeanor. A tall man with a warm smile, he greets me with three kisses, alternating cheeks. There is an awkward charm about him and something fatherly that puts me at ease. He is quite sensible, respectful, decent—and every bit as eloquent in person as on a computer screen. He's married and has a normal family life outside the business of kidnapping. He informs me he has just been offered a fellowship at Harvard and seems genuinely surprised by the honor. Michael says he is in Washington on business. He occupies quite a niche: a person who has talked to the Taliban. He jests that Karzai has done wonders for his brand.

"I should tell you, your husband was due to interview me before this unfortunate incident. Did you know this?" he asks as we settle into the lobby coffee shop of a nearby hotel.

Of course I do. I've scoured David's e-mail account for references to Michael and found out he was indeed going to meet with him in Pakistan, the day after his fateful interview with Abu Tayyeb. "David would be slightly upset knowing I have now scooped him on several interviews, including you," I joke, recalling my brief chats with Condoleezza Rice and Hillary Clinton.

Michael says he still believes that Atiqullah is not the ultimate decision maker in the kidnapping and that he does not have the authority to release our three. Michael is pushing for John to meet with a relative of Siraj face-to-face to try and strike a deal. Upon parting he praises my patience. I think this is a dubious honor. I have been beating myself up for days with the thought that if I were truly doing a good job, David would be free by now. Michael counters that the United States government cannot find Siraj Haqqani. Why should it be any easier locating David and securing a deal for his release? He adds that Siraj cultivates a self-image of being moral, but in reality heads a criminal conspiracy. "When you're dealing with one of the world's most formidable characters," Michael tells me, "things take time."

AN ALTERNATE UNIVERSE

David, Late February 2009

A bu Tayyeb calls Kristen to negotiate and informs me that she told him to speak with someone in Kabul. Then he disappears again. I am relieved in a way. At least Kristen is not negotiating herself. Over the next several weeks, we receive contradictory reports from our guards about the negotiations. On one day, they say an agreement is close. On another, they say there is no progress.

Our existence reverts to its old pattern. Each day consists of the same tedium: prayers, meals, naps, and depression. Tahir and Asad grow more and more pessimistic. I tell them to be patient. They shake their heads at me.

My mind-set is gradually shifting. For the first three months of captivity, I tried to find ways that I could somehow help engineer our release. Now, as we begin our fourth month, I tell myself it is my job to wait as long as it takes for our release. I am sure that Kristen and my family are doing all they can to free us. My part of the bargain is to be patient and strong and do nothing rash. We are being treated well compared to other hostages, many of whom spent far longer in captivity. I think of Terry Anderson, the American journalist held for seven years in Lebanon. I try to look at my time in captivity as a jail sentence that I must serve until release. At the age of forty-one, I have twenty to thirty years of life ahead of me. A few more months of imprisonment in exchange for decades of happiness are worth it.

The question I posed about who represented the true Taliban in the first days of our kidnapping now seems silly. In my mind, Qari, the unstable guard who nearly shot Tahir and our kidnapper who uses multiple false names are one and the same. As I come to know the alternate universe the Haqqanis have created in Miran Shah, I grow more and more dejected. Our captors are unwavering in their belief that the United States is waging a war against Islam.

It is a universe filled with hypocrisy. My captors bitterly denounce missionaries, but they press me to convert to their faith. They complain about innocent Muslims being imprisoned by the United States, even as they continue to hold us captive and try to extort money from my family. They rail against American, Israeli, and European mistreatment of Muslims, but they celebrate suicide attacks on mosques that kill dozens of Muslim worshippers as they supplicate to God. Those living under Afghanistan's and Pakistan's apostate governments, they say, deserve it.

Yet in our day-to-day existence, when commanders are absent, some of our guards show glimpses of humanity. These moments give me hope that we may somehow be able to talk or reason our way to freedom. I do not know if they are simply humoring me so I will remain an obedient and patient captive. I do not know which side of our contradictory captors is real.

Over the last three months, I have gradually gained a clearer sense of our guards and their backgrounds. They are mostly Afghan men in their late twenties and early thirties. Some have grown up as refugees in Pakistan. All have the equivalent of elementary or junior high educations from government or religious schools. None have seen the world beyond Afghanistan and Pakistan.

Waging jihad seems to give them discipline, self-respect, and a sense of belonging to a greater cause. They see the United States military as the latest foreign force trying to subjugate Afghanistan and Islam. Akbar believes he must have many children because they will be needed to fight Afghanistan's next foreign invader: China.

I talk the most with Akbar, who seems to illustrate how the United

States lost the initial popular support in Afghanistan in 2001. In the first years after the fall of the Taliban, Akbar worked as a painter on some type of construction project. Over time, he turned against the United States as American forces arrested local leaders, searched houses, and, in his mind, humiliated Pashtuns. He also embraces wild conspiracy theories about the United States. He is convinced the American military uses some type of weapon that sterilizes Muslim men. Several of his Afghan friends, he tells me, are unable to have children.

He praises the Taliban for cracking down on warlords, combating corruption, and delivering law and order. He despises the Pakistani army. In Miran Shah, he spends many afternoons using a Taliban radio scanner to discover the frequency used by nearby Pakistani forces. Speaking in Urdu, he lures soldiers into a conversation and then curses them in Pashto and English. He seethes with hatred toward what he sees as an apostate army that oppresses their fellow Muslims in exchange for Western cash.

He and the other guards speak of the foreign militants in the tribal areas with reverence. In conversations, they refer to Osama bin Laden with the honorific "Sheikh Osama." For several weeks, they take turns attending bomb-making classes from Uzbek militants in Miran Shah. They set off enormous explosions but Pakistani forces never come off their base to investigate. The only signs of a Pakistani military presence are planes and helicopters taking off from an airstrip somewhere to our east.

Timor Shah—our chief guard—is particularly proud when he comes home one day from bomb-making class with skinned knees. He set an explosive but did not give it a long enough fuse. As he ran away from the bomb, he dove to the ground as the blast erupted behind him. In some ways, the guards remind me of young soldiers anywhere. They enjoy playing with guns and testing their own strength. Chunky enjoys taking apart and cleaning his machine gun over and over. When I tell the guards my pen is my weapon, they laugh.

Day and night, they monitor American-funded Voice of America Pashto-language service radio and celebrate reports of the deaths of Afghan and American soldiers. Whenever a guard hears a news bulletin describing a major Taliban suicide bombing, he excitedly calls for the other guards to come listen. Hunched around the shortwave radio, they shout "God is great!" in unison after the number of dead is announced.

I try to get to know one of Sharif's fighters, a young Pakistani Pashtun named Hamid who is training to be a suicide bomber. In his twenties, he has a slim build, brown hair, and brown eyes. He graduated from a high school in Pakistan and at one point hoped to become an engineer. He never attended college but is relatively well educated compared with the other fighters.

Conversations with him help me understand how hard-line Islam's focus on the next world eases the training of suicide bombers. Taught that their relationship with God is all that matters, young recruits are slowly distanced from their families. When I ask Hamid why he wants to die, he replies that living in this world is a burden for any true Muslim. Heaven is his goal, he says. Earthly relationships with his parents and siblings do not matter. Music, laughter, and idle chatter are seen as distractions from worship. Life is a flat, colorless existence that is something to be endured, not enjoyed. Days are spent studying the Koran, praying, and fearing judgment day. If he successfully carries out a suicide bombing, he believes he will die as a martyr and ensure he goes to heaven, not hell.

Hamid speaks a smattering of English, and my own beliefs seem to interest and amaze him. During our six weeks together, he asks me a series of questions. Is it true, he asks, that a necktie is a secret symbol of Christianity? Is it true that Christians want to live a thousand years? Is it true that American soldiers hunt wild pigs—animals that Muslims consider unclean—and feed them to their commanding officers?

Sharif, a tall, burly, and imposing figure, tells me that the Taliban have been unfairly portrayed by the Western media. He says that the Taliban would have allowed girls to attend school when they governed Afghanistan, but security problems prevented them from doing so. Once security improved, he insists, girls would have been allowed to enroll in classes. He expresses dismay at the United States, a country he considered an ally against the Soviets. The 2001 American invasion was unjustified, he says. The Taliban should have been allowed to try Osama bin Laden on its own and determine if he was guilty of the 9/11 attacks.

When I ask him about my captivity, he tells me that each day the Taliban hold me they deliver "massive political blows" to the American government. When I tell him that my case is not public and Americans don't know I'm a prisoner, he insists that my case is still consuming American government time and resources.

When we discuss journalism, he declares that he is an enemy of *The New York Times* because it supports secularism. He says that secularism is the Taliban's adversary and religion must govern all aspects of life. He flatly rejects my compromise suggestion that strict Islamic law be enacted in Afghanistan's conservative rural south, while milder forms of Islam be followed in the comparatively liberal north.

Citing the Taliban's interpretation of Islam, Sharif says it is every Muslim's duty to try to stop others from sinning. If one person in a village commits a sin, God will also punish those who witness it and do not stop him. The concept of God judging us as individuals does not seem to exist for him. To ensure that he goes to heaven, Sharif believes he must persuade others to become strict Muslims as well.

One day, I receive a Pakistani English-language newspaper with a photograph of Barack and Michelle Obama dancing at an inaugural ball. For weeks, Sharif has looked through the newspaper and used a pen to scribble out women's faces from photographs. Any portrayal of the human form is an affront to Islam, according to the Taliban's interpretation of the faith. Hamid burns newspapers after I have read them, seemingly convinced that their removal cleanses the house. On the day I receive the newspaper with the photo of the Obamas dancing, Sharif flips through the paper and stops at the picture of the Obamas. He stares at it briefly and then spits on it.

One morning, two of our guards leave for bomb-making class and Mansoor leaves for the market. As one guard naps in Sharif's bedroom, Hamid announces he is going to pick up bread for our lunch from a nearby madrassa. He departs and I realize we have a chance to escape. I find Tahir and tell him that we can close the door to the room where the guard is sleeping, slide the bolt on the door's exterior, and lock him inside. If we act quickly, we can take his rifle and radio and walk out of the compound.

Tahir rushes to Asad and the two speak feverishly in Pashto for several seconds. Asad picks up a machine gun that is lying on the floor and I don't understand what is happening. We do not need the machine gun. It will make us more conspicuous and slow us down. We need the Kalashnikov. The Taliban and local tribesmen consider any man walking through Miran Shah without one suspicious.

"He is acting strangely," Tahir says, referring to Asad.

The two speak again in Pashto. If we do not act now, Hamid or Mansoor will soon return. Tahir walks outside to see if anyone is nearby. He walks back inside the compound and again talks with Asad. Finally, Tahir announces that Asad thinks it is too dangerous for us to simply walk out of the compound. Tahir agrees with him. The area is filled with Taliban, he explains. We will quickly be shot or arrested. We decide to wait.

Their judgment proves wise. A few minutes after our conversation ends, Mansoor walks through the front door. He says he was walking home from the market and saw Tahir step out of the compound. He demands to know what happened. Tahir says he stepped outside to get water from a nearby stream to wash clothes. Mansoor remains suspicious.

Later, Tahir tells me that he is worried about Asad. Our driver is having, long secretive conversations with the guards. When Tahir asks him what they are speaking about, Asad does not give clear answers. I do not worry and assume that Asad is pretending to befriend the guards in order to keep himself alive.

As February comes to an end, the guards demand I stop washing the group's dishes because they do not want to catch my diseases. They believe the intermittent diarrhea I suffer stems from being an inherently unclean non-Muslim, not from unhygienic food.

Sharif begins repeatedly pressing me to convert. In excruciatingly long conversations, he tries to get me to agree with him that there is only one

God. He asks me to repeat after him in Arabic "There is no God but Allah and Muhammad is his prophet"—the words uttered by someone converting to Islam. He orders me to read a passage of the Koran each day and discuss it with him at night. He dismisses my arguments that a forced conversion is not legitimate. He and the guards politely say they feel sorry for me. If I fail to convert, I will suffer agonizing pain in the fires of hell.

Whether or not I read the English-language Koran that Atiqullah gave me has become a source of tension. Some guards argue that I should not be allowed to touch a Koran because I am an unclean non-Muslim. Barring nonbelievers from reading the Koran baffles me. I do not understand how a non-Muslim is supposed to learn about Islam if they are not allowed to read its holy book.

Sharif believes it is permissible for me to touch the Koran Abu Tayyeb gave me because it includes Arabic, Urdu, and English script. An actual Koran, he says, is written only in Arabic. In a compromise, he tells me to not touch the part of the pages of the Arabic, Urdu, and English Koran that contain Arabic script. That part of the pages, he says, is sacred.

Each time I touch the book I fear I will accidentally drop it. Each time I turn the paper I fear I will tear it. Either act will be seized upon by my guards as blasphemous. In an effort to show respect, I place a scarf over my hands to prevent my flesh from making direct contact with their holy book. Before I pick up the Koran, I whisper "In the name of Allah, the most merciful and beneficent" in Arabic as they do. After Mansoor accuses me of insulting Islam by pointing my feet—which Muslims consider unclean—toward Mecca while reading, I sit cross-legged. Eventually, I copy passages into a notebook so I can read them in peace.

The English-language Koran I have been given has a brief biography of the prophet Muhammad as its introduction. It describes Islam's founder as a great social reformer of his time. He called for equality, justice, and an end to the tribal feuds and greed that beset the Arabian peninsula in the seventh century A.D. Most of all he calls for honesty, piousness, and justice.

"O ye who believe! Be steadfast witnesses for Allah in equity, and let not hatred of any people seduce you that ye deal not justly," reads one verse. "Deal justly, that is nearer to your duty. Observe your duty to Allah. Lo! Allah is informed of what ye do."

To me, Muhammad's calls for honesty, humility, charity, compassion, and confession of sins echo the tenets of all the world's faiths. Instead of making me want to join their cause, reading the Koran makes me believe our captors are not following his core teaching. The dishonesty, injustice, and greed they show in my case are the opposite of what I am reading.

Since arriving in the region in 2001, I have come to see the West and the Taliban as competitors in a race to put in place a government system that can produce noncorrupt leaders who provide security and jobs for their people. The Taliban argue that implementing their strict version of Islamic law—replete with beheadings—is the best way to do so. The United States and its allies argue that free-market democracy is the answer.

My time living in India has shown me that steadily implemented, indigenous versions of free-market democracy can work. India is a place of hope for me. While not perfect, I see it as a relative success story that may offer lessons for Afghanistan and Pakistan.

Based on my reporting there, I feel that religious extremism is a problem among all faiths in India, but the country's messy and chaotic democracy generally tends to slowly mollify it. When allowed to vote freely, impoverished, illiterate Indians show remarkable savvy in choosing leaders. Minority groups often feel they receive some airing of and response to their grievances. Elections are generally considered credible in India due to the vital role played by a handful of strong, independent institutions: a national supreme court, an independent election commission, and a free news media, among others. Corruption and poverty remain crippling across India, but the country's free-market economy and educational institutions are steadily growing.

Pakistan, on the other hand, remains hugely fraught with ethnic and political divisions and handicapped by inconsistent economic growth. The country's powerful army continues to quietly manipulate politics, and the three institutions that play a central stabilizing role in India—the supreme court, the election commission, and the free press—remain only partly independent in Pakistan. Coups and manipulations by the military have resulted in no democratically elected government serving its full term since Pakistan won independence from Great Britain in 1947. In the army's defense, the country's civilian political class has also performed poorly. Unlike in India, no comprehensive land reform has been carried out in Pakistan to break the lock on civilian power enjoyed by the country's landed oligarchs. Pakistan's current president, Asif Ali Zardari, is ineffective, surrounded by cronies, and widely viewed as corrupt, according to Pakistani newspaper editorials I receive.

Afghanistan is in an even more dire state politically. After thirty years of war, the country's institutions have been shattered. Deep suspicion divides its ethnic groups. Its most basic form of government, its tribal structure, has been severely weakened. And President Karzai is seen as increasingly mercurial, opportunistic, and unwilling to control corruption.

A question that has hovered over many other developing countries I have covered lingers over Pakistan and Afghanistan: Is a messy, unstable democracy better than a stable one-party or military-led government? Judging by my reporting in India, I still agree with moderate Pakistanis and Afghans who see an imperfect, locally created representative democratic system and education reform as the best hope of creating long-term stability in their countries. It may take decades to achieve in Pakistan and Afghanistan—as it has in India—but it can work.

Living in the tribal areas has made me even more convinced. Compared with the dynamism of New Delhi, Islamabad, and Kabul, Miran Shah seems frozen in time. An incessant focus on the next world has led to intolerance, zealotry, and stagnation in this one.

On some days, the virulence I see among the Haqqani foot soldiers eases. Amid the monotony and tension are moments of kindness and levity.

When no commanders are present, Mansoor allows me to walk in a small walkway between the house and perimeter wall. If I follow the narrow path, I can walk in large circles around the house. For a few moments during each loop, I am momentarily alone. Since my fake suicide attempt in late December, I have been constantly under the watchful eye of a guard. Moments of solitude are blissful.

Taking advantage of the privacy of walks around the house, I sometimes touch a spot on the wall where I imagine Kristen's face is. On others, I run back and forth in the small alleyway, eager for endorphins that will raise my spirits.

To my relief, on one afternoon, the guard we have nicknamed Chunky leads me through the jihadi-version of calisthenics. He and I perform deep knee bends in the yard as Tahir, Asad, and the other guards guffaw. I look like a white-bearded, geriatric militant, but the exercise—and laughter—are a godsend.

With the guards' approval, Asad buys a volleyball in the local market one afternoon. For several weeks, the guards, Tahir, and Asad play volleyball in the small, dirt-covered yard. During the games, they spike the ball at one another's head as powerfully as they can. They invite me to join them but I decline. Eventually, they hit the ball so hard it careens into a neighboring compound and is never seen again.

For several weeks, Tahir is allowed to play in a local pickup soccer game held near our house and Asad is allowed to hunt birds in our yard. He and Akbar construct a crude cage out of slats of wood and chicken wire, stand it on its side, and spread bird food on the ground. When birds come to feed, they pull the cage down with a string. Each day, they spend hours waiting for birds to be lured into their trap. They eat the handful of birds they manage to catch. Tahir and I oppose the hunting. We argue it is wrong to kill anything simply for sport. I have an irrational fear that God will punish us for Asad's bird hunting and prolong our imprisonment.

On one Saturday night, Akbar helps me find an Indian music station that plays Western music. In broken Pashto and English, I try to explain the meaning of the INXS song "Beautiful Girl" and the Lenny Kravitz song "Fly Away."

One young Talib even tells us that his commander has ordered him to kidnap a foreigner working in Afghanistan, but he refuses to do so. If a foreigner has come to help the people of Afghanistan, he says, they should be treated well. He suggests I read a passage from the Koran each day for comfort.

"Allah tasketh not a soul beyond its scope," it says. "For it is only that which it hath earned, and against it only that which it hath deserved. Our Lord! Impose not on us that which we have not the strength to bear! Pardon us, absolve us, and have mercy on us, Thou, our Protector, and give us victory over the disbelieving folk."

At night, Sharif and the guards search for ways to break the monotony. If it weren't for us, they say, they would return to Afghanistan and help prepare spring offensives. After dinner, Sharif often tells long jokes. He tells one joke involving a man who stutters in Pashto so convincingly that I find myself laughing while not understanding a word he says. On many nights, he seems to sincerely want to cheer us up.

Still trying to gain their sympathy, I reenact my wedding for Sharif and the guards one night. I have Akbar stand beside me and play the part of Kristen. They seem fascinated as I describe how Kristen's father walked her down the aisle and gave me her hand. They listen intently as I explain how Kristen and I placed rings on each other's fingers and recited our wedding vows. When I take Akbar's hand and pretend I'm sliding a wedding ring on his finger, they howl with laughter.

During the wedding reenactment, I decline to mention other details that will paint me as a hedonistic nonbeliever. I do not say that the service took place in a church and ended with the bride and groom publicly kissing, a scandalous act for Pashtuns. I know it is odd to share my wedding with my captors, but I am still trying to humanize myself in their eyes.

The activity Sharif and the guards love most, though, is singing Pashto songs after dinner. My voice and Pashto pronunciation are terrible, but our guards urge me to sing along. The ballads vary. On some evenings, I find myself reluctantly singing Taliban songs that declare, "You have atomic bombs, but we have suicide bombers."

On other nights, at Sharif's urging, I switch to American tunes. In a halting, off-key voice, I sing Frank Sinatra's version of "New York, New York" and describe it as the story of a villager who tries to succeed in the city and support his family. I sing Bruce Springsteen's "Born to Run" and describe it as a portrayal of the struggles of average Americans. When

I sing John Lennon's "Imagine," Sharif shows little interest in the lyrics and asks for something livelier.

I realize that my guards, too, need a break from our grim existence. But I feel like a performing monkey when they tell me to sing in Pashto for visiting commanders. I know they are simply laughing at me.

I intentionally avoid American love songs, trying to dispel their belief that all Americans are hedonists. Despite my efforts, romantic songs—whatever their language—are the guards' favorites.

The Beatles song "She Loves You," which popped into my head soon after I received my wife's letter from the Red Cross, is the most popular. For reasons that baffle me, the guards relish singing it with me. I begin by singing its first verse. Timor Shah, Akbar, and Chunky, along with Tahir and Asad, then join me in the chorus.

"She loves you—yeah, yeah, yeah," we sing, with Kalashnikovs lying on the floor around us.

A GOAT WILL NEVER BE A COW

Kristen, Early to Mid-March 2009

I receive a text on my BlackBerry from an American who works with local journalists in Afghanistan and Pakistan. He has heard of our alleged communications with Siraj Haqqani. "Siraj is hopeful," he claims. How he knows this, I am not quite sure. He asserts that a local journalist has just interviewed Siraj and inquired about David.

I relay this to the team in our noon call. Our team has been on a cultural sensitivity kick of late, perhaps influenced by information from John and Michael. After four months of this nightmare, we want to deliver the message to Siraj that enough is enough, urging him to accept what has been offered, an amount well below what the Taliban are asking.

The gruff voice of Dewey Clarridge chimes in and tells us we need to be mindful of the local culture. "We need to say it in the Afghan, Pashtun way: 'What you have is a goat and a goat will never be a cow.' This is the Pashtun way of saying things," he states plainly.

Frustrated with the lack of progress, I simply cannot resist, and chime in, "Then tell those jackasses to let my husband go." Dewey is clearly amused. "That's pretty good," he admits. Dewey and I have had a love-hate relationship over the phone. This is one of our lovelier moments. I think back to the very beginning of this ordeal. The captors referred to David as a "golden hen." Tahir's father sent me a moving letter in which he thanked our family for continuing to work on behalf of our three, adding that without our help he would be like "a blind rooster." I also recall a recent interview with Siraj that was e-mailed to me by a local Afghan journalist. In it Siraj notes the similarities between the Obama and Bush administrations by stating, "They are two ears of the same donkey." It seems the only common and consistent thread in our communications—and cultural exchanges—has been the repeated reference to barnyard animals. A mildly amusing but sad comment on our state of affairs.

The divided agendas in our team are starting to turn into a full-fledged schism. Consultants from Clayton, the security team on contract for *The New York Times*, disagree with AISC, the private security team we have hired, and vice versa. One of the contractors calls me and claims that McCraw is giving Dewey a hard time because of his role in the Iran-contra affair. Lee, David McCraw, and I are constantly having to weigh contradictory opinions. Clayton has years of kidnapping negotiating experience, but very little of it has been in Afghanistan or Pakistan. The private security team has contacts within the region and within the governments there. AISC is often skittish about sharing information with Clayton. The lack of transparency, maintained with the intention of protecting sources, has at times led to division and mistrust among our team members. At times we have considered jettisoning some or all the consultants. But we feel that starting from scratch would only confuse the kidnappers and prolong David's captivity. The one player who seems to get along with everyone is Michael. He is also the only one who actually lives in the region. He does not try to divide and conquer. I don't know what his larger agenda might be, but at least it doesn't get in the way here.

We are told by Michael that contact from the captors will be imminent. Someone who identifies himself as Atiqullah has started calling John again. Back in January, the FBI told us that Atiqullah was an alias used by both Badruddin Haqqani and Abu Tayyeb. They also told us that as the head of the Haqqani network, Siraj is ultimately the one in charge.

Michael maintains that Atiqullah is just a middleman. He is uncertain as to whether it is Abu Tayyeb, Badruddin, or some third party trying to take a cut of the money for himself. Michael believes the real point of contact needs to be Siraj Haqqani or a family elder close to him. He continues to push to have our guy on the ground meet face-to-face with them. But each time a meeting is set to take place, there is a delay. The weather turns foul, or it's suddenly time for a hajj to Mecca, or an elder simply fails to show up.

I have learned through months of dashed hopes, bizarre video communications, and misinformation to embrace the old adage, "Believe half of what you see and none of what you hear." Privately, Lee and I speak with the other members of our team one by one and get their recommendations. Should we increase our offer, and if so, when?

John insists it should be at a face-to-face meeting and that the captors need to come down and name a price we can match. The Clayton team advises us to raise our offer preemptively. We are told by John that it seems we are close to reaching an agreement.

My fortieth birthday is March 9, also the four-month anniversary of David's abduction. It's a dreaded milestone—not so much in terms of my age, but because it has been a time the family looked forward to, thinking surely David would be home by then. I now fear I will be a widow at forty, after only six months of marriage.

To boost my spirits, I decide to pack a suitcase. If David is indeed released, I am to meet him in Dubai. Lee will come along to fend off the press. We have had the "evacuation strategy" in place for months. The situation has been so unpredictable, I haven't been getting my hopes up, but I also cannot let myself wallow in sadness.

I recall my conversation with Alan Johnston, a BBC journalist who was held hostage in Gaza for nearly four months, in 2007. I remember thinking four months was an unfathomable amount of time.

Alan reached out to me a few weeks ago and his words of wisdom linger. "This situation is going to run its course. You will not have control over the outcome," he says. "It will have the same outcome whether you spend fifteen hours a day worrying about it—or whether you try to make the space and time to relax and find some joy in your life." He encouraged me to find and embrace the moments that sustain me—time with friends, family—and not to feel bad for continuing to find those moments of happiness in my life. He told me that during his own captivity, he learned a lot about how his mind worked. He quickly realized which thoughts would boost him, and which ones would lead him down a negative spiral. He trained himself, over time, to extend the positive thoughts. He encouraged me to do the same. He added that he was certain, judging from his own experience, that David would want me to do this. He also reminded me that in some ways, the situation is worse for the family.

"David knows his circumstance. He will adapt. And he can imagine what your life is like back home," Alan said, pointing out that for me and other family members, everything about David's experience is an unknown.

BIRTHDAY WISHES

David, Early to Mid-March 2009

In early March, Badruddin arrives for a visit. We have not seen him for weeks. At this point, I'm entirely dubious of him. He is either making impossible demands or telling outrageous lies, both of which I find infuriating.

He sits down and we exchange pleasantries. Each meeting is more formulaic than the last. I pretend to be meek and respectful; he pretends he is seriously negotiating for our release. He tells me that the engineer's son has been released. I am delighted for the engineer's family, but see this as another setback. The engineer is out of the picture. Another negotiation channel has failed.

Tensions continue to simmer between Tahir and Asad. One day, they come to blows and none of us is sure why. Asad said that Tahir insulted him. Tahir accuses Asad of the same.

March 9—a day I have dreaded for months—arrives. It is Kristen's fortieth birthday, and I have visions of her alone in New York. I spend the morning praying for her and then, to my surprise, Timor Shah takes Tahir and me on a rare drive outside the walled compound. In reality, it's not simply a magnanimous gesture. A drone has been circling over Miran Shah all day. Fearing a missile attack, Timor Shah hustles me into the back of the station wagon and speeds away from the house. Once we are outside town, I am allowed to sit up, remove the scarf from my face, and look out the car's back windows.

My first trip outside in weeks instantly raises my spirits. I watch the Waziristan countryside roll by and relish its arid beauty. Farmers tend fields of wheat and rice surrounded by networks of irrigation canals amid rock-strewn hillsides. While thirty years of conflict have devastated Afghanistan's infrastructure, Pakistan's infrastructure appears comparatively intact. The canals were one of the products of limited Pakistani, American, and British development programs designed to pacify the tribal areas.

I had recently found out that our house-turned-prison was as well. To my surprise, Tahir informed me that our house was built by the Pakistani government in 2005 to serve as a health clinic. When I looked at our bedroom, I saw it was a waiting room. The two adjoining bedrooms were examination rooms. The construction of the clinic was likely part of a government campaign to win the support of the local population. After the Taliban seized control of Miran Shah in 2006, Sharif took over the clinic and made it his house.

As we drive past more of the irrigation canals, they appear similar to ones I have seen in Helmand Province, the part of southern Afghanistan that was the focus of my book and site where the United States built "Little America." I have fond memories of the province, which fascinated me. As I completed my research, I had come to see Helmand as a case study of how the American and Afghan governments had grown vastly weaker between the Cold War and the war on terror. The post-2001 effort in Helmand was a shadow of the endeavor there in the 1960s and 1970s.

After the fall of the Taliban, the only foreign troops to deploy to Helmand, a province twice the size of Maryland with a population of one million, were several dozen American Special Forces soldiers. They built a base in the center of the province in 2002, hired several hundred Afghan gunmen to protect them, and focused solely on hunting Taliban and Qaeda remnants.

Helmand Province's voluble young governor, Sher Muhammad Akhundzada, was largely left to do as he pleased. The son of a famed local commander who fought the Soviets, Akhundzada entered Taliban-controlled Afghanistan in 2001 at Karzai's request and won control of

Helmand with the help of American Special Forces. Rumors abounded about the boyish governor. In interviews with journalists, Akhundzada said he was in his early thirties and a high school graduate. Afghan aid workers said he was in his late twenties and illiterate.

Whatever he may have lacked in administrative skills, he made up for in muscle. As the head of Helmand's largest and most influential Pashtun tribe, the Alizai, he commanded several thousand gunmen. As time passed, other Pashtun tribes grew frustrated with Akhundzada. First, tribes accused him of falsely declaring his potential rivals Taliban and having American troops arrest them. Then they accused him of funneling land, reconstruction projects, and cash to his own tribe. Finally, reports began to reach the American officials in 2003 that Akhundzada himself was promoting the growth of opium poppy, the raw form of heroin.

After the fall of the Taliban, poppy growth had exploded in eastern and southern Afghanistan, fed by poverty and weak law enforcement. An epic five-year drought made poppy—a lucrative cash crop that required little water—a talisman to farmers in Helmand. Partly in response, American officials expanded their development effort in Afghanistan in 2003, increasing American assistance from $962 million to $2.4 billion. In Helmand, a field commander in the new development effort was Charles Grader, the contractor who first brought me to Helmand in 2004. Twenty-five years after running USAID's Afghanistan office, he was back at the age of seventy-two, managing a $130 million U.S. government contract to revitalize agriculture and slow the growth of poppy.

Grader's career was a marker of how the American approach to development had changed since the 1970s. No longer a government worker, he was now a private contractor paid $130,000 a year by Chemonics International, a for-profit consulting firm based in Washington. Short on personnel, USAID hired the company to implement and manage its agricultural development program across Afghanistan.

In 2004, I was with Grader when he toured a USAID-funded demonstration farm bursting with cotton, pomegranates, and other crops designed to show farmers they could make a legal living. Grader asked the Afghans who ran the farm what would persuade others to stop growing poppy. Their responses had little to do with agriculture. They said the biggest problem was poverty and corruption. Farmers, they said, no longer believed the government would punish them for growing poppy.

"There is an inverse relationship between security and poppy growing," said a local engineer trained in Lashkar Gah by the Americans in the 1970s.

A local farmer was more blunt. "We don't have law. This is a warlord kingdom."

Grader discussed creating public works projects that would repair the province's irrigation system and employ large numbers of farmers. But four months later, he resigned after clashing with USAID officials over the direction of the program. He was not alone. High turnover rates among aid agency officials, contractors, and the military were common. Americans generally arrived in Helmand on twelve- to eighteen-month tours. Determined to make a mark, they announced new projects or revamped existing ones. The result was a constantly shifting array of Americans and projects that to Afghans produced few tangible results.

Some American projects did get under way in Helmand. And an alternative-livelihoods program put 37,000 Afghans to work cleaning hundreds of irrigation canals. By 2006, a dozen new or refurbished health clinics were opened, more than a hundred wells dug or deepened, and ninety miles of highway paved. Overall, USAID spent about $180 million in Helmand between 2001 and 2006.

Over time, though, the American-funded development projects did not provide enough jobs for Helmand's 100,000 farmers to counter the lure of growing opium or joining the Taliban. In addition, a popular perception took hold that after foreign contractors and subcontractors took their cut of aid money, little cash was left for average Afghans. Locals grew suspicious of the foreigners who lived in heavily guarded compounds with electric generators and satellite televisions while local people lacked regular running water and electricity. Afghan government officials were seen as corrupt as well.

One Afghan working on an American agricultural development program declared both Americans and Afghans corrupt. Americans made their money through high overhead and expense rates, he said. Afghans made their money through old-fashioned kickbacks and bribes.

"For you, it's white-collar crime," he told me. "For us, it's blue-collar crime."

Along with the stepped-up reconstruction effort, the United States deployed one of eight new military units known as Provincial Reconstruction Teams in Helmand in 2004. The units tried to integrate efforts to provide security, mount small reconstruction projects, and help Afghan government offices deliver schools, health clinics, and jobs. The units were recognition that the various efforts were interconnected. Over the next two years, the team spent $9.5 million to build, refurbish, or equip twenty-eight schools, two police stations, two orphanages, a prison, a hospital ward, and twenty miles of roads.

A few hundred yards from the Provincial Reconstruction Team base on the edge of town, the United States built a women's job-training center for Fowzea Olomi, the Afghan woman educated by American teachers in the 1970s who was one of the people I was following for my book. The Americans provided dozens of computers and sewing machines and even set up a mock beauty salon so women could learn marketable skills.

In May 2006, Taliban gunmen on a motorcycle shot dead Fowzea's driver as he drove through Lashkar Gah. False rumors had been spread that the center's female students were being taken to the nearby American military base and forced to have sex with soldiers. The center was closed for security reasons. The attack was one of several by the Taliban that shut down American projects across the province, including the canal-cleaning project that employed 37,000 men—perhaps the Americans' most successful undertaking in Helmand to date.

Security quickly emerged as the single most important factor in developing Helmand, but the country's nascent army and police force were unable to deliver it. The first units from the new, American-trained Afghan National Army arrived in Helmand in 2005, but they comprised only several hundred soldiers and carried out few operations. A new provincial antinarcotics force was created that year, but it consisted of just thirty officers.

Police training also lagged. Police from Helmand attended a two- to four-week training course in Kandahar run by contractors from DynCorp International, an Irving, Texas, company, hired by the State Department.

European officials derided the classes as "conveyor-belt courses." In 2006, two retired American sheriff's deputies arrived in Lashkar Gah to serve as advisers to roughly 2,000 police in Helmand. One was from Santa Cruz, California, and had trained police in Bosnia, Indonesia, and the Philippines. The other was from a small town in Wyoming and before arriving in Helmand had never been east of Wisconsin. Security was so bad that the two advisers could not leave Lashkar Gah to visit any of the province's thirteen districts.

The Bush administration, meanwhile, declared success in Afghanistan and handed over responsibility for security and development in Helmand to the British. One of the foreign occupiers most hated by Pashtuns, the British were still despised for dividing the Pashtuns between Afghanistan and Pakistan. Their arrival appeared to boost Taliban recruitment.

More than 3,600 British troops arrived in Helmand in 2006, ten times the number the United States had deployed there, and set up bases across the province. In response, the Taliban launched their largest offensive since 2001, killing twenty-nine British and dozens of Afghan police. Scores of schools and courts were also shuttered.

As a condition of their arrival, the British demanded that Sher Muhammad Akhundzada, the province's young governor, and the local police chief, Abdul Rahman Jan, be removed from power. Both were reported to have links with the narcotics trade. Karzai agreed to the move but it added to growing suspicions he held that the British—and later the Americans—planned to weaken the Afghan leader and remove him.

Muhammad Hussein Andiwal, the other moderate Afghan from "Little America" who I was following for my book, became Helmand's new police chief in 2007. Educated by American teachers in Lashkar Gah High School in the early 1970s, he represented the kind of moderate, educated Afghan that Western officials hoped could do an effective job running the province. At first, he did. Lashkar Gah residents lauded Andiwal—whose name means "friend" in Pashto—for arresting a 13-member kidnap gang that had been abducting local children. He and his men intercepted 11 suicide bombers before they carried out their attacks. Most important, he arrested 117 police on corruption charges, displaying the rule of law that Afghans craved.

British advisers hailed Andiwal as well, but they said he was "in command but not in control" of Helmand's roughly 2,000 police. Outside Lashkar Gah, police were loyal to their local tribe. Worst of all, the former governor and police chief tried to win back their jobs by sowing chaos and undermining their successors.

In September 2008, the Taliban took two strategic districts outside Lashkar Gah—Marja and Nad Ali—and panic spread among Afghans that Lashkar Gah itself would fall. Police who were members of the former police chief's tribal militia reportedly handed over the districts without firing a shot. Officials in Kabul blamed Andiwal for the loss of the two districts and fired him after fourteen months on the job. An ally of the former police chief replaced him.

On the night before going to my Taliban interview, I met with a frustrated Andiwal in Kabul. He said officials in Kabul were not interested in fighting corruption and the British were not aggressively confronting the Taliban in Helmand. Disgusted by the level of Afghan government corruption and angered by British and American raids that killed civilians, most of the people in Helmand were beginning to support the Taliban.

"They are completely dissatisfied with the government," Andiwal said. "In my lifetime, I have never seen such a corrupted government."

The Taliban, meanwhile, stopped some of their harshest practices from the past and promised to create law and order. In the two districts they seized outside Lashkar Gah, residents reported that the Taliban were not enforcing unpopular, pre-2001 edicts against television, radio, kite flying, shaving beards, or growing poppy. They also reported a major improvement in security under strict Taliban rule.

In October 2008, in my last interview with her before the kidnapping Fowzea told me she feared that the Taliban would take "Little America" itself. Two years after her driver was shot, the American-built women's center remained closed due to poor security. Eight years after the fall of the Taliban, Lashkar Gah still lacked regular power.

"The situation that I see now, it's not 'Little America,' it's a village," Fowzea lamented. "'Little America' had schools and roads and electricity."

Americans, meanwhile, expressed frustration with corruption among Afghans. One American aid worker who had served in Iraq and several other countries told me that the corruption in Afghanistan was the worst he had ever seen. Police and government officials demanded bribes for the most basic of services.

"It just seems to be endemic in the whole society," he said. "They just don't seem to have any compunction about it."

Four years after I first visited it, "Little America" highlighted the worst of Afghanistan and the United States. After thirty years of chaos, Afghans took whatever they could whenever they could for their families. With no strong institutions and a weakened Pashtun tribal structure, they had no guarantee how long they would hold their posts or that merit would be rewarded.

Helmand acted as a mirror for the United States as well. It showed how the American government's ability to devise and carry out complex political and development projects had atrophied. Since the cold war USAID had shrunk and the American public's desire for quick solutions had grown.

With the Taliban on the doorstep of "Little America," the United States deployed 2,200 marines to the province in 2008 to aid the British. I embedded with an American marine company dispatched to the town of Naw Zad in northern Helmand to train police. Instead, the marines found themselves engaged in heavy combat, short on helicopters, and suffering heavier casualties than they did in Iraq.

While most of the Taliban they fought were local Afghans, they heard militants they battled in one corner of Naw Zad speak a foreign language. It was Urdu, the national language of Pakistan. The marines nicknamed the area "Pakistani alley." Like American soldiers I had occasionally embedded with since 2001, they expressed frustration at the Taliban safe havens in Pakistan.

The final blow to the troubled American and British effort in Helmand was the ability of the Taliban to carry out a ruthless insurgent campaign.

More than anything else, relentless Taliban attacks derailed the American effort to re-create "Little America." With their safe havens in Pakistan, the Taliban could not be stopped.

Our afternoon drive in Pakistan's tribal areas continues. At one point, I see furtive figures clad in burqas crossing a distant field. It is the first time I have seen a woman since arriving in Waziristan four months earlier. Women are virtually invisible in public.

Like so much else, they are surrounded by contradictions. According to the introduction to my English-language Koran, Muhammad expanded the rights of women. He urged his followers in seventh-century Arabia to stop the widespread practice of burying baby girls at birth. He increased women's inheritance rights.

Yet the Taliban are accused of reducing women's freedoms. In our conversations Abu Tayyeb argued that the Taliban protect women from dishonor, sexual exploitation, and other harm. Women in the United States are forced to wear revealing clothes, he said, and define themselves solely as sex objects. To him, the Taliban treat women better than Americans do. I realize that I do not fully understand his views, but this core difference between us seems irreconcilable.

On the ride home, I see groups of teenage boys and young men playing cricket and volleyball. They appear to meet at dusk and celebrate the end of the day with a game at a local park. In some small ways, life inside the emirate is no different than life outside it.

We stop and watch a local soccer game. Several dozen men sit around a dirt field with virtually no grass. Young male soccer players battle furiously on the field for the ball, like young men in any corner of the globe. Pakistani and Afghan jihadists dot the crowd of spectators. They have long hair and beards, wear camouflage jackets, and relax as they watch the game.

For me, the drive cements my belief that the Haqqanis run a Taliban ministate in North Waziristan. Taliban policemen patrol the streets, Taliban road crews carry out construction projects, and Taliban religious teachers indoctrinate young boys in local schools. Haqqani commanders and foreign militants stroll the streets, comfortable and confident in their sanctuary.

We return to the house at dusk and are greeted with horrible news. Sharif announces that the negotiations have failed. Tahir, Asad, and I will be moved to South Waziristan, he says, the stronghold of the Pakistani Taliban that lies roughly fifty miles south of Miran Shah.

South Waziristan is a worst case scenario. We will be under the control of Baitullah Mehsud, the leader of the Pakistani Taliban, the man blamed for the assassination of Benazir Bhutto, and the mastermind of suicide attacks that have killed hundreds of civilians. For months, Tahir has heard rumors of an underground prison there where other hostages are being held in caves. Now we will join them.

Our departure from Miran Shah is deeply depressing, the clearest sign yet that the negotiations for our release have failed. Our captors, I assume, refuse to lower their demands. I walk in the yard and let my mind yet again come up with rationales for why the situation is not, in fact, hopeless. I have none. I think of Kristen, who is likely just now rising in New York, where it is her birthday morning. Our chances of surviving will be much lower in South Waziristan.

That night to our delight, Sharif tells us that our move to South Waziristan has been canceled. Overjoyed, we tell ourselves that this may finally be the breakthrough in negotiations that we've been waiting for. I again somehow think Kristen has managed to give me a gift on her birthday.

A week passes. Sharif announces that we will definitely be moving to South Waziristan. Again, nothing is as it seems. The following morning, we silently load our sleeping bags, clothes, and pots and pans into the back of an Afghan police pickup truck that has been captured by the Taliban. A green Ford Ranger with an Afghan flag painted on the door, the truck is one of hundreds of American-made pickups the United States has provided to the Afghan police as part of the American police training effort.

I lie down in the back of our station wagon, on top of blankets that our guards have placed there for me. The guards—Timor Shah and Akbar—insist they will continue living with us and we will not be handed over to the Pakistani Taliban. As we drive away, I feel an emotion I never expected: I long for Miran Shah.

For the next several hours, we drive south down a modern, two-lane asphalt road in broad daylight. I stare out the window at the green tree-covered hills. The landscape again reminds me of the Rocky Mountains.

We cross into South Waziristan and enter the territory of Baitullah Mehsud. At dusk, our car pulls into the parking lot of a large government building or school. Sharif says good-bye. "We're bringing you here because you're going to cross back into Afghanistan," he says. "Ten days, ten days."

A Pakistani Taliban commander politely ushers all of us into a room at the rear of the compound. I am told again that no one must know that I have arrived in the area. If local Arabs find out an American hostage is present, they will kill me. We are given fresh tea, rice, and bread for dinner. As we eat, the Pakistani Taliban commander stares intently at me. I'm sure I am the first American he has ever seen up close. The zoo animal phenomenon is happening again but I don't care. As the months pass, the experience has become normal. After sharing a cup of tea with him, we drive in the darkness to a house that will serve as our new prison.

Over the next several days, it becomes apparent that the Afghan Taliban have not handed us over to their Pakistani counterparts. Instead, the two groups work seamlessly together. The Pakistani Taliban are giving the Haqqanis a remote house where we can be imprisoned. In military terms, they are providing logistical support for their Afghan allies.

Our new house has a half dozen rooms and is the largest we have been imprisoned in. It is also the most primitive. All the floors are dirt. There is no running water. Within days, fleabites begin appearing on my skin.

I feel for the family that normally lives here. A cowshed with heaps of drying manure is located inside the compound. Pots, pans, and other utensils in the mud-floored kitchen appear to be poorly washed, apparently due to the lack of water. Piles of ash show where they cooked food over an open fire. The people of the tribal areas are destitute.

GREETING CARDS FOR
THE MUJAHIDEEN

Kristen, Late March–Early April 2009

My suitcase has been packed for nearly three weeks, but there has been no word from the captors.

Silence is torturous. Our imaginations run rampant when things are quiet. This leads to all kinds of impossible schemes. The latest: AISC, the private security team, wants to bribe David's guards. They also want to enlist the help of the United States military to retrieve David. By official policy, our government will not interfere in Pakistan.

The FBI continues to maintain that David is in the tribal areas of Pakistan, specifically an area called Miran Shah, known to be a Haqqani stronghold. But the private security team says David continues to be moved between Miran Shah and surrounding border areas of Afghanistan. We spend hours on noon calls and follow-up calls debating these issues. It passes the time, but gets us nowhere.

There are three tracks our team is simultaneously pursuing: the moral track, which consists of pressuring the mullah in Swabi to continue to plead for the release of our three on humanitarian grounds; the monetary or negotiation track, which at the moment has come to a standstill; and the bribery track, which seems highly unlikely since none of us know for sure exactly where David is.

Word comes back to us from John that Siraj and the kidnappers are now demanding $5 million and prisoners. They are sure that we actually have the $5 million. They will not settle for less. This is a far cry from the report a few weeks ago from an Afghan journalist that they were "hopeful" about a deal. Someone has apparently told the kidnappers we have $5 million. Something has happened to stop communications.

Soon after, we find out that the State Department has recently raised the bounty on Siraj Haqqani's head from $200,000 to $5 million. This is a stunning example of the lack of communication between government entities. How hard would it be for one agency to touch base with another? We have kept the State Department and FBI aware of our progress and of the captor's slow decline in demands. The State Department and the FBI clearly have no plan to keep each other updated on current cases. We know the captors are Internet savvy, despite their archaic beliefs. It's quite possible they set up a Google alert and found out about the increase in bounty that way.

The private security team blames the FBI. The FBI claims another agency has set the government's bounty and that they are not responsible. I fire off an e-mail to Richard Holbrooke, asking what the State Department was thinking—is this a tactic or negligence? He says he had no idea they'd raised the bounty. He calls me soon after to tell me in no uncertain terms that any other course of action beyond family negotiations is futile at this time. He feels the contractors are grossly misleading us and "playing a dangerous game" with David's life in considering alternative options. A rescue operation is out of the question because our government believes David is in Pakistan. And the diplomatic approach, meaning pressuring the Pakistanis, has yet to yield a tangible result. Holbrooke advises me to ignore the advice of AISC. "You are the only person in this situation who has David's interest purely at heart. Everyone else has to worry about setting precedents."

I appreciate his candor, but I am frustrated by our exchange. I feel caught between a rock and a hard place. Even if we do raise some substantial money, what good is it going to do if we can't communicate with the kidnappers?

At this point, I am going to work three to four days a week and dedicating the rest of my time to David's case. I feel like I am living a double life, experiencing global terrorism at the most personal level. There is a constant influx of information and misinformation. Sifting through it proves to be exhausting, maddening. Each entity involved in David's case—the newspaper, the government, the security team—has its own bias and agenda, despite their good intentions. I do not fully trust any of them. My own agenda is simply to secure my husband's release. I listen to all opinions, but trust no one. It is not unusual for me to spend entire days on the phone or computer, contacting government officials, sharing concerns with Lee and McCraw, and following up with Michael Semple. Days have lost their significance. I am stuck in a seamlessly never-ending season of waiting. I feel I am in the middle of a complex game in which time and silence are my opponent's greatest weapons. I have no control over the situation. Despite the collective efforts made on David's behalf, only the captors have the power to release him. I am increasingly convinced that our fate lies in their hands.

On March 22 we receive a message from Team Kabul concerning the engineer, the go-between whom the Haqqanis dispatched in David's case. The plan was that the engineer would work on a negotiated resolution for our three as he made his own attempts to free his son, who was also being held by the Haqqanis.

The message from Team Kabul is that the engineer's son has been released. Their report reads: "Approximately two weeks ago the engineer was finally successful in resolving his son's situation. He was able to convince the Haqqanis that he had no power to enable prisoner release and that the governments were not going to help. In addition to whatever had been paid on his release, he was able to negotiate a payment of $60,000 for his son (down from $100,000)." The update continues: "The engineer continued to make efforts to call Atiqullah on behalf of Team Kabul/David. He states that Atiqullah has not taken his calls for approximately sixteen days. He states he will continue to try."

Not a good development. And local negotiations through John have produced no better results. The kidnappers have turned off or dumped their cell phones. Michael still tries to create a channel directly to Siraj, the older brother of Badruddin whom the FBI has identified as one of

David's kidnappers and who he believes has the authority to strike a deal for our three.

I have spent most of my work day securing a location for an upcoming celebrity cover shoot. I have successfully negotiated a 20 percent discount on the day rate for a Malibu beach house and booked an on-set chef to cater a vegan meal. I have also learned that in addition to being an avid vegetarian, the young actress is very concerned about our environment and requests that she be chauffeured to the shoot in an environmentally conscious vehicle—a Prius or similar.

Meanwhile I worry David is stuck in a cave somewhere, eating nothing but rice, or that he is being shuttled through a war zone. It is amazing to think our two disparate worlds coexist. And that my life is now in a constant state of tug-of-war between the two.

At home, bills mark the passage of time: another maintenance check, an outstanding invoice, a payment to a trauma therapist. March is nearly behind me. In an attempt to spark communication once again, Michael asks that I compose several letters: greeting cards for the mujahideen.

I have accumulated a strange arsenal of pen pals. "Pals" is a misnomer; it implies a two-way communication. I send letters out into the great void, hoping they will have some impact on David's release.

The men Michael has suggested I write to are Haqqani elders in Afghanistan and Pakistan, including the mullah who may have direct contact with Siraj. The others are to Siraj's uncle and to an aspiring politician who was once an underling to Siraj's father, Jalaluddin. I have no idea if these messages will reach the intended targets. If they do, most likely the recipients will reject them, for fear they are sprinkled in a magic dust that doubles as a tracking device. I am told by American officials and security consultants that the Taliban believe such things, including that beacons are placed on objects like letters to guide drone attacks. These beacons, they think, can take many forms: liquid, solid, particles.

I have mixed emotions about this task. On the one hand, it is hugely time-consuming and a bit unorthodox. Yet it makes sense to try to estab-

lish a point of contact and seems no less plausible than other channels we
have tried. Now that the engineer seems to be out of the equation and no
one is contacting Team Kabul, I feel I have nothing to lose. I wonder if
this is merely a way to keep me occupied and optimistic—if so, this is
perhaps one of the kinder agendas I am tasked with in these long months.

It is impossible to apply logic to any considerations at this point, given
how irrational the whole situation has become. The strangest of my
"greeting cards" is to Siraj himself. Michael has advised me to "just briefly
make the moral case."

"You should use a slightly anonymous form of address instead of his
name so that our contact does not feel vulnerable carrying it," Michael
writes to me in an e-mail. "I suggest something like 'Dear Brother in
God'—Charm him! We use the letter to establish direct connection and
a lever that our contact can work on. In other words, you do not have to
agonize too much about the wording—it's our contact's job to advocate."

I have no idea if this is an exercise in futility, but I compose the following and ask David's young friend Ruhullah to translate it into Pashto
for me. It may read like a second-rate soliloquy, but it is certifiably cultur-
ally sensitive:

> *Dear Brother Mujahid,*
>
> *I am the wife of David Rohde. As a woman whose protector
> has unjustly been taken, I implore you to use your influence to
> return him to me. We believe in the same God and have faith that
> he rewards such acts of righteousness.*
>
> *David is a decent man and an honest journalist who has ded-
> icated most of his career and life to writing good things about
> Muslims. By your act of goodness you will free him to continue
> to use his pen to defend the rights of others who have suffered
> injustice, so many of whom are Muslims.*
>
> *Thank you for your kind consideration.*
>
> *May God bless and protect all who struggle in his name,*
>
> *Kristen*

I cannot help thinking what the Hallmark equivalent might be, imagining a category for "Captives and Their Handlers" somewhere between Birthday and Sympathy cards. This strikes me as precisely the kind of art project that would garner a rave review in the New York edition of *Time Out* magazine.

Michael also suggests that I write a letter to David, in case one of the elders has the ability to pass it on. I will also e-mail a duplicate to the International Red Cross, even though they have been unable to confirm the status of my previous letters. In it, I refer to a conversation David and I had the day after our wedding along a rocky coastal park in southern Maine. Following the torrential arrival of Hurricane Hannah at our reception, the day after the wedding was calm, sunny, and clear.

Dear David,

I write this with no other agenda than to simply tell you I love you. Please promise me you will stay strong and have hope.

Remember our wedding vows: "One day at a time."

I have not forgotten this promise. And, I continue to look forward to our shared calm after this storm.

Our family and friends love you and send prayers and support. This has been an endurance test—but, hopefully one that leads us all to find our better angels.

I pray you find strength, peace, and your way home. Thank you for the joy you have given me, my dear.

Love Always,

Kristen

In addition to pursuing a negotiated release, AISC, through the use of their local Afghan network, is also trying to infiltrate the guards. A few days later, a report comes in from AISC. Their local sources claim that David is being guarded by as many as ten people. They rotate in and out and include several foreign militants. Our security team's informants on the ground claim they have succeeded in bribing David's guards to walk him out when the time is right. They also claim that David has been separated from Tahir and Asad and is being held at a village named Kharcin along the Afghanistan-Pakistan border.

Their report is rather detailed. They add that some of David's guards are so young that they are devoid of facial hair. The specificity of this report temporarily gives us hope in its veracity; they even send us coordinates of the village and a Google Earth map to match. Still, I decide not to hold my breath on this one. Misinformation and false reports from local Afghans has been rampant. While we have received information of a potential location, we have not received proof of life. The FBI still maintains that our three remain in Miran Shah in the tribal areas of Pakistan—far from the border—and that they have been there since my first phone call with David in November. They say there is no benefit for the kidnappers in moving David over the border and into Afghanistan, where they would be vulnerable to surveillance, rumors, and military intervention.

A week later, we hear from our team's Afghan network that David has been moved and is once again being held with Tahir and Asad. They are now in a village called Shinkay. The number of guards has increased from ten to twelve. One of the bribed guards has agreed to bring in a beacon to show their exact location. Once again we are reminded that he is standing by to walk our three out.

At the beginning of April, a third update comes in from the local network. Our three have been moved to a house in Miran Shah. Their guards have changed and now include young men from Chechnya and the Pakistani province of Punjab. Later we will learn that most of the reports from the Afghan network are wrong.

It has been five months since David was abducted. We have spoken only twice. I make a list in my journal of all the things he's missed, from holidays to disasters and personal milestones: Thanksgiving, the Mumbai attacks, Christmas, Gaza, New Year's, the inauguration of Barack Obama, the miraculous landing of a plane on the Hudson River, Valentine's Day, my fortieth birthday. We are nearing Easter. More important, we are nearing the six-month mark. I feel this as an ominous shift: from months to a half a year. I fear this will drag on indefinitely.

The security consultants have told us to sit tight and wait. But Lee and I feel we need to expand our outreach once again to the United States government. If David is indeed in Pakistan, they can continue to pressure the Pakistanis to find him and pressure for a release, assuming they can get word to the kidnappers. It is tough to accept that the American government can do so little to effect change.

A STONE WILL NOT BECOME SOFT

David, Late March–Late April 2009

Two deafening explosions shake the walls of the compound in South Waziristan. My guards and I dive to the floor as chunks of dirt hurtle through the window.

"Dawood?" one guard shouts, saying my name in Arabic. "Dawood?"

"I'm okay," I reply in Pashto. "I'm okay."

The plastic sheeting covering the window hangs in tatters. Debris covers the floor. Somewhere outside, a woman wails. I wonder if Tahir and Asad are alive. Chunky grabs his rifle and orders me to follow him outside.

"Go!" he shouts, his voice shaking with fury. "Go!"

Our nightmare has come to pass. Missiles fired by an American drone have obliterated their target a few hundred yards from our house in Makeen, a remote village in South Waziristan. Dozens of people are probably dead. Militants will call for our heads in revenge.

Outside, shredded tree leaves litter the yard, but the house and its exterior walls remain intact. Tahir and Asad look worried. No one is hurt, but I know the three of us may not survive for long. It is March 25, and for months the drones have been a terrifying presence that has un-nerved and angered the guards.

In the courtyard after the missile strike, the guards clutch their weapons and anxiously watch the sky. Fearing a direct attack on our house, Timor Shah orders me to cover my face with a scarf and follow them outside the compound. I know that enraged Arab militants or local Waziri tribesmen can identify me once I am outside, but I have no choice.

They hustle me down a hillside to where our station wagon is parked between rows of trees. Opening the rear door, they order me to lie inside and keep the scarf on so passersby cannot see my face. Then they disappear.

I lie in the back of the car and silently recite the Lord's Prayer. In the distance, I hear men shouting angrily as they collect their dead. For months, I have promised myself that if they tape our execution I will remain calm for my family and declare our innocence until the end.

After about fifteen minutes, Timor Shah returns to the car and leads me back to the house. The missiles have struck two cars, killing seven Arab militants and local Taliban fighters. I feel a small measure of relief that no civilians have been killed. But I know we are still in grave danger.

For the next two hours, I do my best to placate the guards. I do not walk in the yard. I do not speak unless spoken to. I praise God for saving us. Later, I learn that one guard was so enraged that he called for me to be taken to the site of the attack and ritually beheaded as a video camera captured the moment. Timor Shah rejected his suggestion after Tahir argued furiously with him and again threatened retribution from his tribe if I was harmed.

Several days later, we hear that foreign militants have arrested a local man. After the militants disemboweled the local man and chopped off his leg he purportedly "confessed" to being a spy. Then the militants decapitated him and hung his body in the town bazaar as a warning to the local population.

In the days after the drone strike, my focus begins to slowly shift. Instead of thinking I need to be patient, stay calm, and serve out my time as a captive, my goal becomes simply to survive.

Nestled in the mountains, Makeen is colder than Miran Shah, and frequent rain and frigid temperatures create miserable conditions. Hailstorms are common and viewed as punishment from God by our guards.

Timor Shah gives me additional chores. Along with sorting stones from our rice before it is cooked and the Sisyphean task of sweeping dirt floors, I fill the barrel in the bathroom with water twice a day so that we can clean waste from the toilet, a porcelain hole in the floor. Using a tube the guards placed in a nearby stream, I fill two fifty-gallon plastic drums with water once or twice a day. As we quickly use up water for ablutions, cooking, and cleaning, I see it more and more as a magic elixir that I took for granted when it surged out of a pipe in New York at the twist of a knob.

The chores are demeaning, since elders are normally treated with reverence in Pashtun culture, but I do not care. The tasks help me pass the time and appear to give the guards the sense that I am loyal.

Rarely allowed outside the house, I see my world shrink to a few dozen square feet. Training my mind to stay optimistic becomes more difficult. Walking back and forth in the yard is complicated by the drones. Tahir struggles as well, telling me at times that he can no longer remember the faces of his seven children. "This is not life," he says. "I want to die."

I urge him to be patient. He prays more and memorizes larger portions of the Koran. He prepares for salvation no matter what happens to us. His faith seems to give him peace and strength. To me, it is an example of religion as a positive force. Tahir has no fear of death because he is absolutely certain he will go to heaven.

Two weeks go by and Sharif's promise we would be crossing into Afghanistan proves to be another lie. With each passing month, we feel increasingly forgotten by Abu Tayyeb and Badruddin Haqqani. Abu Tayyeb talks with our guards by phone but refuses to speak with us. One day, Timor Shah speaks with Abu Tayyeb by phone and tells us there is an agreement for our release. We are elated. The next day, Timor Shah says there is no agreement.

We are now at the mercy of the young guards who control our daily existence. Soon after we arrive in Makeen, Timor Shah begins pocketing some of the money given to him by Badruddin to buy our food and supplies. He dares us to try to escape so he could end our captivity with "one bullet." He complains that "great mujahideen" are dying in the drone strikes yet enormous attention is being wasted on one American prisoner.

When I show Timor Shah several dozen fleabites on my stomach and arms, he buys a farm pesticide and suggests that I put it on my sleeping bag. Fearing it will make me sick, I decline. When the bites continue, I show Mansoor, our other guard. His response is to show me his own stomach, which has no bites on it.

"I never get sick while I'm on jihad," he says.

The guards begin blaming me for things I did not do. Someone places a piece of toilet paper in a bucket the guards use for ablutions and I am accused of putting it there. Mansoor announces one day that I was about to pick up the machine gun when he walked into our bedroom. In truth, I had been sweeping the floor and was startled by his arrival. Another Pashto expression I researched as a possible book title refers to Pashtuns' reputation for tenaciously fighting their enemies. "A stone will not become soft," it says, "nor an enemy a friend."

For hygienic reasons, I decide in Makeen to cut my hair for the first time in four and a half months. I had refused to do so because I felt cutting my hair was an acknowledgment that we were still many weeks from being released. Asad cuts the hair on my head but we do not trim my beard. The guards urge me to grow the beard until it is the length of my fist, the way the prophet wore it. My beard is gray, like my father's and grandfather's before me. I look like an elderly man but relish it. I want the guards to feel ashamed for kidnapping an old man.

Several hourlong conversations between Tahir and me have prompted the guards to accuse us of planning an escape. As a result, we speak less and less. Some days, we talk only for five to ten minutes. At the same time, the guards are furious that I have not converted to Islam despite reading the Koran for several months. I stop reading it in an effort to decrease tensions. As these sources of stimulation disappear, I become lost in my own thoughts, and memories of the world I had known begin to fade.

Trying to stay connected, I begin listening to the BBC's shortwave radio broadcasts for hours at a time. I hear my colleague from the newspaper, Jane Perlez, interviewed by the BBC in Islamabad. I know she is roughly a hundred miles away, but I feel physically farther and farther away from the world I knew.

News stories about New York make my heart leap and I instantly think of Kristen. I relish an arts program called *The Strand*, a celebration of human creativity. I follow English soccer teams, something I have never done in my life.

I listen to an interview with a Baghdad-based mediator who tries to resolve kidnapping cases. He says that cases involving foreigners can drag on for years. I do not tell Tahir what I have heard.

On weekends, I try to catch a show called *The Forum*, in which British hosts discuss contemporary thought and life. In one program, a guest declares that humanity has finally reached an age where people expect to work at jobs that fulfill them. Human existence has moved beyond simply subsistence toiling to feed one's family, they say. The comment—and my surroundings—make me realize how truly disconnected some Americans and Europeans are from the rest of the world.

On another BBC program, a writer describes how there are two narratives in life. There is the narrative that we actually experience each day and the narrative we create in our minds of how it occurred. I wonder what narrative I will construct of our captivity if we survive.

The BBC broadcasts raise my spirits each day, but they also give me the sensation of being in a coma. I can hear how the world is progressing but cannot communicate with anyone in it.

The video image is grainy but I immediately recognize the Polish hostage.

"Hello, Peter," an off-camera questioner asks. "How are you?"

"Fine," answers Piotr Stanczak, the Polish geologist who was kidnapped by the Taliban six weeks before us.

"Fine?" the questioner asks.

"Fine," Stanczak answers, nodding. Two masked militants holding Kalashnikov assault rifles stand on either side of him. A black sheet with jihad slogans in Arabic is tacked to a mud-brick wall behind him.

I read about Stanczak's execution in a Pakistani newspaper a month ago. Our guards have somehow gotten a copy of one of the videotapes made of him while he was in captivity. They are playing it for me, Asad, and Tahir on a small DVD player that Mansoor has bought.

"You feel good?" the questioner asks.

"Yes," Stanczak answers, again nodding. He is soft-spoken and appears to be in his forties.

"Okay," the questioner answers. "And what is your message for your people, for the people of Poland?"

"I would say to my people, to people from Poland, to make pressurize for my government," Stanczak replies in broken English. "Because government send too much army, too much soldier to Afghanistan, and to Muslim country. And I want stop this fight."

Seated on a plastic mat, Stanczak appears calm. He holds his hands in his lap and occasionally glances to his right as he speaks. He is dressed in tan local clothing. He wears a dark brown winter jacket as well. His clothes are more or less identical to mine.

"Okay," the questioner answers. "And what is your message for the government of Poland?"

"My message to my government of Poland is don't send more army for Muslim country," Stanczak replies, clearly trying to play along with his captors. "Because Muslim people they fight with, with another army."

"And now, what you want to give a message to your country?" the questioner asks. "What will they make their relationship with Pakistan country?"

Stanczak stares at the camera. "I would say to government of Poland break, break relation with Pakistan because, because government of Pakistan nothing do for me," Stanczak replies. "I am here four months and nothing do for me.

"Nothing contact with me," Stanczak adds, as the camera slowly zooms in on his face. "I am self here. Not, not security. This country is not safety for me."

"And what do you think about the people of Pakistan, who kidnapped you, the surrounding people?" the questioner asks, apparently referring to the men with Kalashnikovs.

"About people, yes, of Pakistan?" Stanczak replies.

"Yes," the questioner says.

I realize this is the second tape made of Stanczak, not the first. The tape will end in his beheading.

I immediately stand up and begin walking out of the room. I do not want to see it—or give Mansoor the satisfaction of watching me see it.

"I would say people of Pakistan is very good, people is very good," Stanczak says as I walk out the door and into the yard.

Each time we think our captivity has reached its low point it somehow gets worse. The videos are the latest example. They are impossible to avoid at night, when I am confined to the room where we sleep alongside the guards. Instead of singing after dinner, we watch jihadi videos that are little more than grimly repetitive snuff films.

The Taliban execute local men who they have declared pro-American. Taliban roadside bombs blow up Afghan government trucks and American Humvees. Taliban plunder the limp bodies of dead Afghan policemen. The moment of a sniper firing a shot or a roadside bomb exploding—the moment of death—is shown over and over in slow motion. As I silently watch, Mansoor repeatedly asks me what I think of seeing American soldiers killed on the screen in front of us.

"All killing is wrong," I say.

The high-quality sound tracks include prayers, religious chants, and computer-generated gunshots. To aid foreign viewers, English subtitles and computer-generated graphics have been inserted. An arrow indicates which Humvee is about to be incinerated. A circle shows how a roadside bomb tosses a human torso in the air like a rag doll. Snipers gun down American soldiers and veiled women donate their jewelry to aid insurgents in Iraq. In other videos, unidentified young boys miraculously recite vast portions of the Koran. Men compete in Koran recitation competitions and Taliban prisoners in Afghan government jails recite the Koran together. One video features dozens of images of the word "Allah" miraculously appearing on clouds, mountainsides, rocks, flowers, gourds, and other objects.

On some nights, we watch American movies and television shows apparently downloaded from the Internet. In a movie called *Windtalkers*, Nicolas Cage battles Japanese soldiers in World War II. In an HBO series, *Band of Brothers*, American and German soldiers fight the Battle of the Bulge.

We are also shown a popular—and heavily edited—YouTube video of George W. Bush stuttering as he tries to make a statement at the White House. To an American, the video makes fun of President Bush's halting oratory. To the Taliban, it is proof that God is on Islam's side.

"He is trying to insult Islam," Mansoor says. "But Allah is stopping him."

The longest videos—and the most popular among our guards—document the final days of suicide bombers. Most are young men in their twenties. The videos follow the same formula. In the first scenes, the bomber happily receives military training, jokes with friends, and explains why he is eager to die. Then he builds the bomb that will kill him. Finally, he bids his friends good-bye, hugs them, and climbs behind the wheel of the vehicle and drives into the distance. His car or truck is shown speeding toward its target. The vehicle detonates and the cameraman shouts "God is great!" as an enormous plume of smoke rises in the air. As they watch the explosion, my guards utter the same phrase. Finally, a computer-generated graphic lists the number of American or Afghan soldiers killed in the attack.

Other videos show dead American soldiers in Afghanistan and Iraq, wreckage from downed American helicopters and drones, and frenzied Taliban fighters pounding a captured Humvee into small pieces with hammers. My guards rejoice at each image of American impotence. The videos—and their reactions—are evidence of how desperately the Taliban want to exact revenge on Americans—and how valuable a prize I am in their eyes. A constant theme is that the United States and NATO underreport the number of their soldiers who are dying in Afghanistan. Overall, the videos create a false, pro-Taliban narrative of the war in Afghanistan. My guards denounce journalists for reporting American military "lies."

"How can only one or two people have died?" Mansoor scoffs, as we watch a dust cloud from a roadside bomb engulf an American Humvee. "The vehicle was completely destroyed."

The videos are not limited to the conflict in Afghanistan and Pakistan. Images of dead Palestinian, Kashmiri, and Iraqi civilians deliver the message that vast numbers of Muslims are being slaughtered across the globe. A series of flags flashes on the screen—American, Israeli, Indian, British, French, German, and United Nations—representing the international Judeo-Christian conspiracy against Islam that they believe exists. Finally, bearded men dressed as seventh-century Muslim warriors are shown galloping across the desert on horseback wearing conical helmets and carrying scimitars. Young Taliban are taught that they are Muslim warriors battling crusader Christian armies that have again invaded the Middle East.

The tapes strike me as jihadi versions of Western music videos. Militant groups compete with one another to produce the most sophisticated and gruesome scenes. Our guards cannot get enough of them. For the few hours each day that electricity is available in our house, they watch the videos over and over. The constant images of violence seem to numb our guards to the idea of death. Over and over again, human beings are killed on the small screen in front of us. To me, the videos are cynical efforts by Taliban commanders to brainwash their foot soldiers. While death is ignored in the West, it is embraced in the videos. Death, the message goes, is not a distant fate. Instead, it is a friendly companion and a goal.

Our guards share a book that glorifies martyrdom. Several hundred pages long, it makes saccharine promises of fruit juices, sumptuous food, and seventy virgins in heaven. One of the guards reads haltingly, pronouncing each word out loud as if he were an elementary school student.

Most worrying of all, I fear that the videos are brainwashing Asad as well. After we move to Makeen, he seems friendlier toward the guards and begins carrying a Kalashnikov rifle they have given him. He also stops smoking, which the guards say is forbidden under Islam. According to Tahir, Asad has told the guards that Tahir encouraged him to make his failed escape attempt in January. He also told the guards how we nearly walked out of our compound when our guard fell asleep in February. Asad has also told the guards that I am playing with Islam and not serious about studying the Koran.

In mid-April, Abu Tayyeb strides into our compound just before dinner in an expensive white tunic. We haven't seen him in the eight weeks since he had me call Kristen. Akhundzada accompanies him. In Makeen, I have learned that our guards are related to either Abu Tayyeb or Akhundzada. Mansoor is Akhundzada's son and Akbar is Akhundzada's nephew. And Timor Shah is Abu Tayyeb's younger brother. The disclosure makes me realize that a small group—many of whom are related to each other—has kidnapped us. We are being guarded by Abu Tayyeb's closest relatives. They seem to function like an organized crime group. Abu Tayyeb is a young leader—or capo—who tries to impress his Taliban commanders with his schemes. My case is one of them.

Abu Tayyeb sit downs in the room where we sleep with the guards and immediately begins toying with me, raising our hopes that negotiations are progressing.

"Dawood," he asks, "what would you say if I told you that you could start your journey back to New York tomorrow?"

"That would make me incredibly happy," I say, trying to be polite.

He tells me to get a notebook and pen and orders everyone else to leave the room except for his intelligence chief and Tahir.

"Your family has been very slow," he says. "Write this down."

"This is my proof-of-life video," he dictates. "Maybe another video will come that will be very bad."

He pauses and tries to think of his next line.

"If this message does not help," he says. "I cannot say what will happen to me."

I realize he is not here to complete a deal. He is here to make another video to pressure my family. When we called Kristen in February he demanded $7 million and five prisoners. I have no idea what his demands are now.

Calmly sitting across the room from me, he dictates more lines.

"If you don't help me, I will die," he says. "Now the key is in your hand."

He pauses for a moment.

"Please save me, I want to go home," he adds. "Don't you want me to stay alive with you? Hurry up. Hurry up."

Then he tells me I must cry. I look at Tahir. I can barely contain my contempt for Abu Tayyeb and what he is doing to my wife and family. At the same time, if I refuse to make the tape, the Taliban might kill Tahir or Asad to drive up a potential ransom payment. Tahir is the father of seven children. Asad is the father of two. I agree to make the video.

Akhundzada, a man who appears to be in his fifties, places a scarf over his face and picks up the guards' .50-caliber machine gun. He points it at my head, and one of the guards turns on a camera.

During the filming, I try to convey that I am reading a prepared statement by intentionally looking down at the pad of paper. I sob intermittently but no tears flow from my eyes.

I read the message word for word and Abu Tayyeb announces that I haven't cried enough. He orders me to read the message a second time. Standing behind the guard holding the camera, Abu Tayyeb waves his hands in the air, as if he were a film director. He wants me to sob louder. I try to cry in such an exaggerated fashion that my family will recognize that none of it is real.

Later that night, Abu Tayyeb announces that the Afghan government had agreed to free twenty prisoners in exchange for our release. The problem, he says, is that my family will not agree to pay a $5 million ransom.

"My family does not have $5 million," I tell him angrily, making the same point I did after we called Kristen eight weeks earlier. "Why do you think we have been here for so long? Do you think they're sitting on $5 million and just playing a game? If they had the money, they would offer it."

Abu Tayyeb ignores me. He smiles and tells me I am a "big fish." He says my brother is the president of a company that manufactures jumbo jets. If my brother would sell one plane, he explains, my family could pay the ransom.

He has clearly looked up my family on the Internet. My brother is, in fact, the president of a small aviation consulting company, but it consists of four full-time employees and manufactures nothing.

Abu Tayyeb goes on and appears completely convinced that he is right. He claims that the American government paid $10 million for the release of John Solecki, a United Nations worker kidnapped in Pakistan in February. As I have for months, I tell him that the American government does not pay ransom.

Ignoring me, he says that the head of the FBI's office in New York has traveled to Afghanistan to secure my release. He vows to force the United States government to pay the $5 million.

"You know where the money will come from," he says. "And I know where the money will come from."

I tell him that he is delusional and that he should just kill me. Tahir refuses to translate my words. "Don't provoke him," he whispers.

I tell Abu Tayyeb we will "be here forever" if he does not reduce his demands.

"You are a spy," Abu Tayyeb declares. "You know that you are a spy."

I respond that he is absolutely wrong and that I am a journalist. Then I try to shame him in front of his men.

"God knows the truth," I say. "And God will judge us all."

THE GIRL WITH THE SAD STORY

Kristen, April–Early May 2009

Walking to the subway one night after work, I notice a news flash on the JumboTron in Times Square: US DRONE ATTACKS TARGET BAITULLAH MEHSUD. The news feed feels like an oversize text message intended just for me. I now have a new fear: David and his colleagues will be killed by friendly fire.

Pakistan seems to be rapidly deteriorating. The Taliban are closing girls' schools by force in Swat Valley. I have read that drone strikes are targeting the Haqqani network in North and South Waziristan. The rumor from ground intelligence is that our three may have been moved to this area. We fear they may have been handed over to Baitullah Mehsud, the Taliban commander responsible for the murders of Benazir Bhutto and, most recently, the killing of the Polish hostage Piotr Stanczak. The latest strike occurred in a place called Makeen. I have been checking David's e-mail each day and reading the automatic updates he still gets from the American military spokesmen in Afghanistan that detail targets and casualties—a far cry from *Women's Wear Daily*.

I've acquired some unusual new habits and routines. The most out of character: I've taken to watching C-SPAN religiously from my couch in the evenings. I actually find it enjoyable, as I now recognize many of the players related to Afghanistan and Pakistan. I marvel at how familiar it's all become to me: Pakistan's Federally Administered Tribal Areas, or

FATA, the area where the Taliban took David after kidnapping him in Afghanistan; Miran Shah, the capital of the North Waziristan tribal area and the town where David is most likely being held hostage; and the ISI, which has done so little to help our three. This is a sharp contrast to the tabloid reports I'm required to follow for my day job: the latest celebrity hookups, the newest reality show starlets, and recent fashion dos and don'ts from Hollywood awards ceremonies. I'm being pulled into a deeper direction, a broader world.

The confirmation hearing of the new American ambassador to Afghanistan, General Karl Eikenberry, is televised. My mother, Mary Jane, and I spend several late evenings watching the proceedings. "He looks and sounds more like a college professor than a general," Mom observes. Eikenberry seems to be an interesting man—with degrees from Harvard and Stanford and the ability to speak fluent Mandarin. The general was to have been a character in David's book. David interviewed him several times before the kidnapping. I wrote to the general's wife, Ching, when I first learned of David's abduction, knowing she would recognize my name from David's recent visit to their home. After seeing the confirmation hearing, I e-mail Eikenberry directly and explain the current situation.

> *Ambassador Eikenberry,*
>
> *Congratulations on your new post. I am certain the region will benefit under your guidance.*
>
> *David Rohde is my husband. We were engaged and married soon after his visit with you in Brussels. He spoke fondly of you and your wife Ching and was excited about including you in his forthcoming book. And, he enjoyed your visit to Waterloo immensely.*
>
> *As you know, David was abducted in Logar Province on November 10. We have since been working to get him released, but it has been a slow process.*
>
> *I spoke with David several weeks ago. He has called home twice. His captors have contacted me on numerous occasions. I*

have a representative in the region who has also spoken with the Haqqani representatives.

Please let me know if you have any suggestions or insights into what more I could be doing to secure my husband's release. This has proven to be quite an endurance test akin to a marathon for myself, my family, and most of all for David. I appreciate any advice or information you might be able to offer.

All the best to you and your family,

Kristen Mulvihill Rohde

He responds immediately, e-mailing to ask for my phone number and then calling to invite me to two upcoming events: his retirement from NATO and his swearing in as the new ambassador to Afghanistan. I receive his call while I'm at Whole Foods. It is distinctly strange to be talking to a soon-to-be-retired general, soon-to-be ambassador in the middle of the whole grain cereals and gluten-free desserts aisle. I am slightly embarrassed and amused by the background music—"Waiting for You" by Seal is playing. How appropriate.

Eikenberry informs me that he originally planned to invite David to these events, but requests that I attend in his place. He promises me, "Rest assured, not a day goes by without my thinking about your husband."

I appreciate his reaching out to me in this personal way. Of all the government institutions we have consulted, the military seems to be the most understanding about what it means to be separated from a loved one who is in harm's way. I accept his offers, thinking this will be a good chance to bump into other government officials, namely Secretary Clinton, and refocus their attention on David's case. My hope is that they will apply pressure to Pakistan's intelligence agencies as well as our own.

Eikenberry's aide follows up with a call to explain protocol for a Pentagon event, and to forward information about the general's swearing-in as ambassador, which will take place at the State Department. I have not completely lost touch with my once fashion-conscious self. What does one wear to a military service? I muse. This is quite an unusual fashion dilemma, and it provides a momentary escape to be able to focus on solving a mundane problem. I settle on a gray skirt suit, black pointy-toed pumps and a simple blouse with a slight ruffle—conservative business attire, softened by a touch of "damsel in distress" detailing.

Throughout this ordeal, I have been conscious of the fact that people look to me, to my moods, tone of voice, and even appearance, to gauge the status of our situation. If I appear pulled together, this gives other people confidence that I am hopeful and that David will return. This proves essential when catching up with friends and David's colleagues. His mother, Carol, informs me that she also looks for cues in the sound of my voice when we speak by phone.

I am taking a week off from work. It's becoming increasingly difficult to straddle both worlds. I go into the office often on weekends—only to end up taking calls on my cell phone from security consultants and others in the case. The kidnapping has invaded every space I inhabit. It has become an unwanted occupation. On my computer desktop are photographic files of the latest fashion trends: denim biker chic, minidresses. A click away are several files of letters to the kidnappers and others translated in Pashto, as well as Google Map images of David's rumored locations.

I find myself jumping every time the phone rings past 9 P.M. or before 9 A.M., thinking it will be a call from Atiqullah. I've learned to recognize the numbers of various government agencies on my office and home caller ID: 646 is FBI, a lot of zeros usually indicates State Department, and a consecutive series of ones is the unmistakable calling card of *The New York Times* office. My mind has to shift between the kidnap strategies: pursuing a humanitarian release; negotiating a ransom; or bribing David's guards. The security consultants' claim that their local network bribed the guards and that David would be released "within days" is beginning to look false. I have no doubt they are well intentioned. But I have become skeptical of their sources on the ground. Interspersed among these moral dilemmas are the issues of how to illustrate the stories sitting in my desk inbox: "What a Guy's Butt Says About Him." "How to Be a Lucky Bitch." And "The One-Hour Orgasm." Haggling over the beach house location for the upcoming cover shoot in Los Angeles while contemplating the value of my husband's life has proved to be quite jarring.

Exhaustion has set in. Sadness has become a permanent resident and has morphed into physical pain: backaches, sore arms, and the occasional migraine. The stress also weighs heavily on my mother, who has thrown her back out and returned to Maine to recuperate for a while.

At work, the circle of people who know about my situation has expanded. I am often asked about David. I feel stigmatized. In my own mind, I am rapidly becoming the girl with the sad story. I find it hard to relate to normal conversations: exchanges about weekends, home life, celebrity gossip—normal office banter. It all feels like a remote foreign language—one I studied as an adolescent but have now forgotten. My situation has also taken a toll on my co-workers' schedules. I have missed two trips for our spring and summer issues, the first to Miami in February, the second to Los Angeles in early April. David's release would be imminent, I was told. A generous art director filled in for me. Time, too, has lost its meaning. Months and events all blend into one endless season of uncertainty, waiting, and loneliness.

I miss the everyday moments most couples share: coffee in the morning, grocery shopping, sleeping intertwined. Occasionally, I hear couples arguing on street corners—this is a common occurrence in New York City, where much of one's private life is lived in public. Sometimes I think, *What a waste of time.* In other moments I wish I had the luxury of being able to argue with David over some small detail. I try to escape by going to the movies, attending a yoga class. But I am averse to fabricated violence or intrigue and have no patience for a well-intentioned, three-part breath.

On April 27, I pack my carefully chosen outfit and catch a train to Washington for General Eikenberry's swearing-in ceremony. On the way, I call my sister, Karen, for advice on my job. I do not think I can keep working, but I am hesitant to make David's abduction my full-time occupation. I have briefly discussed the option of taking a leave of absence with the magazine's managing editor. I was relieved and surprised that they were willing to accommodate a leave and would later welcome me back. Karen encourages me to take them up on the offer.

I meet up with my brother, Jason. His apartment will become home base for my numerous visits to Washington over the next four weeks. I will only be in town for two days on this trip, but will return with David's brother Lee in another week to meet with Pakistani officials.

The next morning is overcast. I take the metro to the Pentagon stop for General Eikenberry's reception. I am nervous as I ascend on the escalator and proceed to the security line, where I am to be met by a military escort. I chat with other attendees, many of whom have known Eikenberry for decades. I am vague when asked about my connection. I say that my husband is a journalist who is friendly with Karl and Ching and that he is currently overseas, so I am attending in his place.

We walk upstairs to a reception hall with blue carpeting, a small platform, and fold-up chairs. Seating is assigned by name tags. I have been given a prime view, an aisle seat in the third row. Eikenberry nods and smiles at me as he proceeds down the aisle to the stage. A military band plays "The Army Song." Admiral Mullen, chairman of the Joint Chiefs of Staff, presides over the ceremony. There is a formality and sense of tradition to it all. Eikenberry is given a retirement plaque.

After the ceremony, we convene as a group in a small, modest reception room. Coffee, tea, cookies, and Middle Eastern appetizers are served buffet style. I thank Eikenberry for the invitation. He informs me that David e-mailed him just prior to his fateful interview. Eikenberry tells me David's e-mail remains in his inbox and that he will not let David be forgotten. I chat with his wife, Ching. She asks a family member to take our photo. She will be joining her husband in Kabul. "This is in case I see David first," she says, optimistically. "I will show him this photo." I appreciate her kindness and hopefulness. I know she truly understands what it means to have a spouse in a high-risk job that demands time in dangerous places.

In the evening, I join a friend of David's for dinner. Kay McGowan worked for the State Department in Afghanistan for several years. Two years ago, her fiancé, a microfinance expert working with the World Bank, was murdered at gunpoint in Kabul in an attempted kidnapping. She was eight months pregnant at the time and has since rebuilt her life.

I admire her courage and appreciate her kindness. She has helped me make contact with government officials on numerous occasions.

Tonight, we meet at an outdoor café in downtown Washington, and she introduces me to her friends. Among them is a young man named Philippe Reines, a senior adviser and spokesman for Hillary Clinton. Philippe is well aware of our case, as are most government officials here. Washington, after all, is very much a rumor mill. Any bit of information spreads like wildfire in this one-industry town. In many ways, it has come to remind me of Los Angeles—a city I have spent a good deal of time in over the last few years on photography shoots. Philippe will be at Eikenberry's swearing in tomorrow. He tells me to look for him when I arrive. He will do his best to give me the opportunity to speak with Clinton in person to update her on the progress, or lack of, on David's case.

The next morning, I get up early, anxious about the upcoming ceremony. I arrive at the State Department. The midcentury-modern lobby gleams. Through the courtyard window I see the *Man and the Expanding Universe* fountain. A mythical figure sits astride the universe. I am ushered to the Benjamin Franklin reception room on an upper floor. Its colonial moldings and furnishings are in sharp contrast to the modern lobby below. The crowd is composed of foreign and American dignitaries, journalists, and friends of Eikenberry's. A colleague of David's from the newspaper recognizes me and keeps me company before the ceremony begins.

The Pakistani ambassador to the United States approaches me. "I am so sorry about David. We will do everything we can to help get him released. But you know, David is in Afghanistan," he says, kissing me on each cheek before rushing off. I feel violated by this outpouring of superficial concern and casual dishonesty. We have known for the last five months that our three are in Pakistan. David's colleague is speechless.

The swearing-in ceremony proceeds. Clinton is dressed in a bright red suit. A receiving line forms and Philippe, her senior adviser, waves to me from across the room. He brings the secretary over to say hello after the line disperses. Clinton is petite but charismatic. I am struck by her warmth. She immediately takes me by both hands and asks for an update. I inform her that David has been in captivity for six months. We have had no word from his captors in six weeks. "We need to get them to call you again," she says, cutting to the heart of the matter. I tell her, with all due respect, that the move by the State Department to increase the bounty on Siraj Haqqani may have interfered with our ability to make a deal. She looks aghast and pulls me into a conversation between General Petraeus and Richard Holbrooke, the State Department representative. Tough and articulate, she does not mince words. "This has gone on long enough," she says, seemingly feeling my frustration. "Her husband has been gone for six months. This needs to be a priority. I mean it." She all but adds "boys" to the end of her remark. I am thankful to have her as an advocate. She is so focused and determined.

I am told Holbrooke will once again be traveling to the region and will continue to raise David's case. Later, he informs me that several Pakistani officials will be in D.C. in early May for the Afghanistan-Pakistan summit. He suggests that I make a return trip to Washington to meet with these officials on David's behalf and offers to facilitate these introductions. This has been the best opportunity I've had so far to spotlight David's case. I spot Eikenberry across the room and thank him for inviting me. He smiles knowingly.

Back in New York a few days later, we deal with the threat of publicity once again in what normally would have been a jubilant occasion. David and several of his colleagues have won a team Pulitzer Prize for their reporting in Afghanistan and Pakistan. David's stories focused on the failure of Pakistan to confront militancy inside its own borders.

The newspaper has alerted us that another news organization may decide to write a story. The *Times*' preference is to maintain silence. The paper will only issue a statement if prompted by another news organization. David McCraw, the paper's lawyer, proposes that the public relations department at the *Times* prepare a low-key statement confirming the kidnapping and stating that we kept the matter quiet because of concerns for our three's safety. Lee and I agree.

I receive a copy of the press release, which contains the following statements:

David Rohde, forty-one, a correspondent for *The New York Times* who is on leave to write a book about Afghanistan, was abducted south of Kabul on November 10, along with a local reporter, Tahir Luddin, and their driver, Asadullah Mangal. Rohde had been invited to an interview with a Taliban commander in Logar Province and never returned. Information indicates that Rohde and his Afghan colleagues are being held by the Taliban. The families of the three men are doing everything they can to secure their release and we are working closely with them.

From the early days of this ordeal, the prevailing view among David's family, experts in kidnapping cases, officials of several governments and others we consulted was that going public could increase the danger to David and the other hostages. The kidnappers said as much. We decided to respect that advice, as we have in other kidnapping cases, and a number of other news organizations that learned of David's plight have done the same. But now that other news organizations have chosen to report on the case, we have little choice.

The statement goes on to include a brief section on David and Tahir's professional bios. It ends: "The families, wives and children, friends and colleagues of all the men await their safe return." To our amazement and relief, no other news organization reports on David's being part of the Pulitzer Prize–winning team. Once again, we are able to keep David's case off the public radar.

April is coming to a close, and this is my final photo shoot. *Cosmopolitan* has been quite gracious. They have agreed to let me take a three-month leave of absence, basically a maternity leave minus the baby. I spend my last few days tying up loose ends on an upcoming issue, which features stories entitled "Stalking Danger," "How Yoga Can Help Your Sex Life," and "Confronting Your Gyno Fears."

Our crew consists of a hairstylist, a makeup artist, their two assistants, a fashion stylist, a photographer, two photo assistants, a prop stylist, and five models. We base ourselves out of a photo studio in Tribeca. We shoot the dramatic stalking scene "cinema verite" style on the surrounding streets. We dress the models—a hunky male model and a svelte brunette—in black, white, and shades of gray. This is what we refer to stylistically as "colorless color."

For the yoga piece, the prop stylist arranges a mattress, pillows, and mosquito net in the center of the studio—everything in shades of purple. We photograph a couple in this setup using only available light to evoke the sense of twilight. The entire crew contributes suggestions for sexy and slightly suggestive yoga poses, though, looking around the room, it's safe to estimate half of us have not been to the gym in quite some time, me included. The female model has never done yoga. Our male model saves the day, as he is über-fit and able to hold poses for a long time.

The gyno setup is the most elaborate. We assemble a medical exam table and props in the corner of the all-white studio, using a modern paneled wall partition as a backdrop. It all looks rather convincing. The prop stylist stands in as the doctor, complete with lab coat and stethoscope. We dress our model in a pink exam robe and pull her long blonde hair into a loose ponytail. Her nails have been painted a tasteful buff. Her skin glows, thanks to a healthy application of shimmer lotion. She is the chicest gynecological patient I have ever seen. I am relieved she does not leave the room in a panic or call her agent to complain about the content of our story. We assure her we will crop out part of her face to protect her anonymity.

Most of today's crew does not know anything about my personal life. It has been difficult to live with this burden, but I've learned to artfully dodge questions about my new husband.

By day's end we have achieved our goal of capturing convincing moments in a digital frame. The work provides me with a sense of control, even if it is only for a brief moment. I am sad to be leaving this job, but know there is no other option. I have to ration my energy. I can no longer accept the fact that my husband is not yet home—not that I have ever accepted this. Next week will be six months since the abduction.

My first week of full-time devotion to David's case begins today with another trip to Washington. This time I am accompanied by Lee and a new addition to our small lobbying unit. We hope to meet with senior Pakistani and Afghan officials who are in town for a summit and who may be able to influence David's case.

I am nervous about this visit. I will be out of my element. Then again, after years of working at fashion magazines, I am used to smoke and mirrors and discerning illusion from reality. I reassure myself that this skill will serve me well. Lee and I are exhausted. I convince him we need extra support on this trip. We are both so good at staying calm—Lee in particular. I think we need someone who can make a fuss, create a scene, and be emotional without consequence. We need backup. We need Carol.

David's mother has been ready to spring into action since day one. She is smart, spirited, and attractive. She is also a social creature and very good at managing people. Lee, Carol, and I meet up at 8 A.M. on May 4 at the Monaco Hotel in downtown Washington. Our morning begins with a visit from two *New York Times* reporters who are colleagues of David's. Coffee is interrupted by an urgent e-mail from Nic Robertson, a senior international correspondent for CNN.

We have exchanged e-mails a few times over the last few months. I contacted Nic after I found an e-mail from him in David's inbox. It was simple and heartfelt. He repeated the words "you are not forgotten" several dozen times. He and his wife have offered their emotional and professional support. Nic agrees that it is wise to keep David's case out of the public eye. He has been discreet in his inquiries, but keeps David in mind when meeting with sources in Pakistan and Afghanistan.

Today Nic informs me that he has just interviewed a Taliban spokesman in Afghanistan who seems to know quite a bit about David's case. I am skeptical, as many Afghans have come forward with information regarding David in the past, very little of which has proved accurate. The Taliban claim that David is a "friend of Obama's," Nic informs me, and that they are demanding prisoners for his release. If true, this is a massive setback. Our security consultants and the FBI have been saying for months that the case could only end with ransom, not a prisoner exchange.

I e-mail back to Nic and tell him I think his source may not be reliable. I cannot believe I am criticizing Nic Robertson's source. He is a seasoned journalist, but the demands don't match our current understanding. I am suspicious that this is merely a false channel and also don't want to believe that the demand for prisoners is real.

Soon after, the FBI calls my cell phone. They have received a new video of David, along with a written list of prisoners that the Taliban demands be released in exchange for his freedom. The local FBI agents offer to show us the video in their Washington headquarters in the Hoover Building.

When we arrive we are ushered through the lobby security checkpoints and into the counterterrorism office. The agents warn us that some of the content is disturbing, but they assure us this is not an execution video.

The video was dropped off by a source in Kabul, someone who claimed to have access to David. It was delivered to the FBI at the American Embassy there, along with a request for $8 million and four of eleven prisoners named on an attached list. The FBI cannot reveal their source, but tell us they are willing to send a message back through the channel to the kidnappers. They do not produce the list of prisoners. Despite our repeated inquiries about it, we are never permitted to view it.

We watch what we will come to refer to as "the crying video." Shot in black and white, with harsh lighting, and from a slightly elevated angle, the video's content is in fact disturbing. David appears to have lost weight, his face is ghastly white, perhaps enhanced by the blown-out lighting, but the effect is upsetting nonetheless. He is clean, but gaunt. The language is inflated, like a bad snuff film.

"It's April 20, this is my proof of life video," David says. "Maybe another video will come that will be very bad. If this message does not help, I cannot say what will happen to me."

He is sobbing as he speaks. An unseen gunman points a machine gun at his head. Tahir and Asad are nowhere to be seen. We fear they have been killed and that is why David is so upset. For a moment, I think David has gone insane.

"If you don't help me, I will die," he says. "Now the key is in your hand.

Do you want to kill me or do you want to save me?" he says. "If you do not meet their demands you will be responsible for my killing, not the Taliban." He urges us to hurry up, says this is his last video, and pleads for us to help him.

"I am so, so sorry," he says. "Please help me, please help me. I love you all very, very, very much."

The video enrages me—the ridiculous language, the sense that David is at fault. I also think my husband has crossed a threshold. He appears completely distraught and broken in the footage. Carol feels the same. Lee stands by, speechless.

"Sorry to say this in front of you, Carol," I inform everyone, "but my husband has definitely crossed a line. He looks like crap—that is a man that has not seen daylight in quite some time."

I am also angered that David's appearance does not match the description our security consultants provided recently through intelligence from Afghan and Pakistani local sources: that he was being treated well and allowed outside while being held in a small village on the border between Afghanistan and Pakistan. I feel completely duped. The insistence from the consultants—and the FBI—that the case could be solved with only money now seems utterly false. The situation feels hopeless. Securing $8 million and the release of four prisoners will be impossible.

Carol is in tears. Until now, we have shielded her from the harshest portions of the other videos and communications. I pound my fists on the desk in the office and demand that everyone see the video—President Obama, the head of the FBI, Holbrooke, Secretary Clinton—in the hopes of sparking an urgent response. I feel staying calm has gotten us nowhere. Time to try a different approach. Lee remains silent. I worry that he has been caught off guard by the extreme display of emotion in the video and in Carol's and my reactions.

The lead FBI counterterrorism agent chimes in. "I notice there are no tears in David's eyes," he says. "When he cries, does he typically produce tears?"

Carol and I both shoot him looks that say, "How dare you."

The agency promises to accommodate our request to send copies of the footage to high-ranking American officials. They suggest we take a few days to craft the message they will send back through their channel to the kidnappers. They emphasize that the FBI will not get involved in the negotiations; they are simply relaying the video and our response. The family must conduct negotiations privately.

We press them about their source and whether he is close to the Haqqanis. An agent will tell us only that the source is someone who has access to the Haqqanis and to David. This is assuming that David is indeed still under the control of the Haqqanis, the agent adds. I take this to mean that perhaps they think David has been moved or sold to a different group. I ask them if this is the case. They cannot say.

We make arrangements for local agents to show the video to David's father in Maine and to his sister, Laura, and younger brother, Erik, in their home states. I talk to Laura and Erik to forewarn them that the content is disturbing and that unlike previous footage, David does not look well. I send them the transcript as a preview but discourage them from actually viewing the footage, admitting that images from the video will haunt me indefinitely.

Our private security team is furious to learn of our meeting with the FBI. When we call to inform them of the latest video communication, they chastise us, claiming that our outreach to government officials has "put the stamp of USG on the case." This will set us back, they claim. It's difficult to know whether it was merely a coincidence that the video emerged during our visit to Washington. Dewey adds that my generation as a whole is impatient and all about immediate gratification. Then he suggests I consider "taking up needlepoint." I fire off an e-mail telling him I can stomach any offense he throws at me—except needlepoint. Later we will learn that David made the video on April 20—a week before either of my trips to D.C. Still our outreaches appear to be another lesson in futility.

I relay the contents of the video to Michael. He considers it a setback, but recommends that we move forward with our plan to meet the Afghan and Pakistani officials and continue to push for contact with Siraj Haqqani.

"Up until now the kidnappers have been relatively sedate in their communications," Michael says. "I am sorry you have to deal with this now—no one should ever have to go through this."

Exhausted and upset, I go over to Jason's apartment for the evening, but I can't sleep. Around 1 A.M. he finds me sprawled out on the couch in the living room. We talk about the video and my growing sense of hopelessness. "I'm embarrassed that I have not been able to bring David home," I tell him. "I feel like I have failed him." Jason assures me I am doing everything possible in the face of an impossible situation. Then we sit in silence for the next half hour.

The next morning, at 8:30, I meet Lee and Carol at the Willard Hotel, the site of the Afghanistan-Pakistan summit. It is a grand old hotel, with a touch of European flair. We set up camp in one of the seating areas along the wide carpeted corridor that connects the lobby to several conference rooms. The walls are mirrored and the hallway is punctuated by love seats, coffee tables, and upholstered chairs. It's a rainy day and the air-conditioners are on full force, adding to the already uncomfortable atmosphere.

We wait for several hours before finally meeting with a senior Pakistani intelligence official. As we ascend the elevator to the top floor and follow the circuitous security detail, I try to catch my breath. Holbrooke told me that this man has a soft spot and that I should not hold back from showing emotion. Several Pakistani security guards and aides line the hall. I recognize one of the aides from Eikenberry's confirmation.

We join the intelligence officer in a large suite. He is affable and courteous. "Up until now, we have thought that David was in Afghanistan," he says, a hint of surprise in his voice. "My American friends informed me today that he is in Pakistan."

We all keep quiet, having heard this excuse before. It's all I can do not to blurt out, "No kidding." He adds that David is being held by "the most despicable people," not referring to the Haqqanis or the Taliban by name. He adds that Pakistan's ISI does not talk to these people directly, but can reach them through intermediaries. He says he sent a message regarding David a while back, but that the captors responded that one order of business needed to be cleared up before they could move onto David.

"They wanted us to pay for the dead body of the Polish hostage," he states plainly, referring to Piotr Stanczak, who was executed on video two months ago. It is believed Piotr was under the control of Baitullah Mehsud, a Taliban commander affiliated with the Haqqani network.

My heart sinks. I feel sick to my stomach. Tears well up in my eyes as I realize how gruesome and twisted this situation is. The Pakistani official notices and stops for a moment, realizing the impact of his words. He asks his aide to bring me a glass of water. He looks a bit teary-eyed himself and seems choked up by my sadness.

"Do you have children?" Carol asks.

"Yes," he replies.

"Well then you know how horrible this is," she says.

This is Carol's go-to comment, part of her emotional arsenal. She asks this of all officials and it always allows room for a thoughtful pause and then an empathic response.

Shortly after, the Pakistani official resumes, adding that his agency will do what it can. We should not lose hope. At the end of the conversation, he turns to Carol and says, "Don't worry, ma'am. You will have your son back." Then he adds, "And when he gets back, I personally think you should spank him."

This odd comment takes us all by surprise. After showing sympathy, he jokingly admonishes David for the situation and the grief he has caused his mother. It is the latest example of the contradictions and unpredictability we have grappled with for months.

After we depart and convene in the elevator, I say, "Carol, I think if you offered to spank David in front of that guy, he'd be out tomorrow!" We all have a laugh.

At the end of the evening, we meet with another Pakistani government official, a man who has been personally touched by terrorism. He offers little hope, beyond encouraging the three of us to "draw upon the power of the universe." Think positive. This is a surreal comment, coming from a senior official of a conflict-torn country. And yet it is perhaps the most sound advice I have received to date. It is the only thing over which we have any sense of agency—our own ability to maintain hope. To possess blind faith that there will be a positive outcome. This by far is a more appealing endeavor than merely flying blind.

The following day, we drive to a hotel near the Pentagon for a meeting with another high-ranking American military official. I have exchanged e-mails with him over the last few months, but this is our first meeting. Lee, Carol, and I are greeted by his assistant and ushered into a conference room off the lobby. The officer arrives with several aides and analysts in tow. As promised, the FBI has given him a copy of the latest video of David, the "crying video." He offers his sympathy and shares what he knows.

Thoughtful and straightforward, he proceeds to tell us that this is a very complex situation. He believes David is in the tribal areas of Pakistan. "We believe he is on the Haqqani compound in Miran Shah, but do not have a fix on a specific location. Anyone that tells you they know exactly where your husband is is lying."

While I appreciate this honest admission, I am crushed. I had hoped the lack of information from government officials was due to secrecy. I hoped there was some greater knowledge of David's case or plan in the works to secure his release. In the movies, our government's intelligence and military institutions always have a card hidden up their sleeves. This, sadly, is not reality. I have been hearing about the Haqqani compound for weeks. "Exactly how big is this compound?" I ask.

"About twenty square miles," he says, referring to the Miran Shah area. He goes on to tell us what he knows about the Taliban group holding David, stating that the different groups function much in the way syndicated crime families do. There are different factions, including the Haqqani network, Baitullah Mehsud, Lashkar-e-Taiba, and Hizbi-i-Islami. "They compete with each other, but they also help each other out—guarding each other's prisoners, etc." He reiterates that the United States military cannot intervene if David is in the tribal areas. Once again, we are confronted with the reality that our only means of getting David out will be through private family negotiations.

Back at the hotel over dinner, Carol concedes: "You two have done everything possible. I feel at peace knowing that all avenues have been pursued. Our government can't do anything. They don't even know where David is." I agree. I am increasingly convinced that my energy should be expended elsewhere, namely in maintaining my sanity. If negotiating doesn't get us anywhere, all I have to fall back on are faith and prayer.

LIES

David, Late April–Early June 2009

On April 24, we are told that we are moving back to North Waziristan. Elated, we depart Makeen on my brother Lee's birthday. As we leave the house in the darkness, I pray that this is somehow the beginning of our journey home.

After driving for several hours, we arrive in an area roughly twenty miles south of Miran Shah. Later, I will learn that we are in Dosali district. Our new prison is a school that was built by the Pakistani government to teach local women how to make textile weaving and other skills to support themselves. It has been taken over by the local commander who is overseeing our imprisonment. The school has concrete floors and is a vast improvement over our house in Makeen, but the basic circumstances of our captivity are not changing. We continue to be lied to constantly and have no idea what negotiations, if any, are taking place.

Over the next four weeks, we receive contradictory reports. First, our guards repeat Abu Tayyeb's story that an agreement has been reached to exchange us for twenty Taliban prisoners. Then they say my family is not offering enough money along with the prisoners. Finally, they tell us that only sixteen of the twenty prisoners have been agreed on.

I am horrified that the Taliban may receive sixteen prisoners for us. The deal would set a terrible new precedent that will encourage future kidnappings.

I ask Tahir if there is any way we can escape from the house at night. A set of power lines runs nearby that we could potentially follow. Tahir laughs at me and says it is too remote and too far from the Afghan border. I decide to wait.

Tahir and Asad are barely on speaking terms, and I increasingly distrust Asad. He continues to carry a gun and according to Tahir is bad-mouthing me to the guards. He tells them that I am the dirtiest foreigner he has ever worked with, according to Tahir. He also brags that he stole money from the foreign journalists he worked with in the past.

My hopes of ever leaving the tribal areas are slowly fading. From the yard of the house, the remains of a nineteenth-century British army post can be seen on a hillside. According to villagers, 1,000 British soldiers were killed in a battle there. I assume the figures are exaggerated, but the story is one more episode in the history of fierce Pashtun resistance to foreign occupation.

During one of the trips I made with Kristen to India, we visited St. Paul's Cathedral in Calcutta. Built by British merchants during the height of the British raj, the walls of the Anglican, Gothic revival church are lined with marble plaques praising the heroism of British soldiers who died in Afghanistan and the tribal areas. A century later, the plaques are largely forgotten.

On another nearby hillside, a newly constructed health clinic appears to sit unused. I had read that many doctors and nurses fear working in the tribal areas. Even before the rise of the Taliban, rumors circulated that medical vaccines for children are secret efforts to sterilize Muslims.

News broadcasts continue to serve as Rorschach tests for our odd group. In early April, our guards cheer an attack on an immigration center in upstate New York that kills thirteen people, firing their Kalashnikovs in the air in celebration. The Pakistani Taliban leader Baitullah Mehsud claims a Muslim he recruited carried out the attack in revenge for American drone strikes in the tribal areas.

When subsequent news reports say the gunman is a disgruntled Vietnamese immigrant who has no links to terrorist groups, our guards are puzzled. Having little knowledge of the world beyond Afghanistan and Pakistan, they ask me if Vietnamese people are Muslims.

When swine flu begins spreading across the globe later in April, our guards see it as God's punishment to people who eat pork, a practice forbidden by Islam. On May 4, they excitedly cheer a news report that says masked men gunned down forty-four people at a wedding in southeastern Turkey and assume it is a terrorist attack that shows the steady spread of jihad. Later reports say the attack was the result of a blood feud between two local families.

The guards continue to assail the Pakistani army. Akbar and Chunky say they were nearly killed by a Pakistani army resupply convoy that opened fire on a group of civilian vehicles. They curse the army and say it fires wildly and needlessly endangers civilians.

Anecdotal evidence of Afghan and Pakistani Taliban using the tribal areas as a safe haven and embracing a jihad that spans the Muslim world continues to unfold before me. We are told that Mullah Dadullah, a widely feared Taliban commander whose men beheaded the Afghan journalist Ajmal Naqshbandi and driver Sayed Agha in the 2007 kidnapping, used a nearby house as a base. While in the tribal areas of Pakistan, Dadullah organized the Afghan Taliban's first group of suicide bombers.

On another night, I meet Mullah Sangeen, a Haqqani network commander who oversees their operations in Afghanistan's Paktika Province. He accuses the United States of launching an unprovoked war on Islam and sees the conflict as a global struggle between faiths. He tells me our release is close and departs. I know he is probably lying, but cannot stop myself from feeling hopeful for the next forty-eight hours.

Young Taliban fighters visit and express the same support for a jihad that spans the Muslim world. They discuss a prophecy that an army carrying black flags will someday emerge from Khorasan—the ancient name of Afghanistan—and liberate the holy cities of Mecca and Medina from foreign occupation. One of them said if it was up to him he would take me outside and give me one last chance to convert to Islam. If I refused, he would shoot me.

The only bright spot is a local man who visits the house and is compassionate toward us. He seems to embody the positive side of Islam and Pashtunwali that I remember. While our guards see me as dirty and refuse to share a plate of food with me, the local man scoffs at their bigotry. He announces that he would happily reach into my mouth and eat a morsel of food I had started chewing.

"He is God's creation," he says.

In late May, we move back to Miran Shah, and Sharif, the tall Taliban commander, informs us of a final deal. All that is needed, he says, is for the two sides to agree on where the prisoner exchange will take place. The next day, Sharif announces that there is no agreement.

We see Badruddin for the first time in three months and he is utterly contemptuous of us. He claims he has no idea what is happening with the negotiations and then leaves. Everyone is sick of us. Yet no one will free us.

We are visited by two teenage boys, one of whom is a computer wiz who apparently edits jihadi videos for the Taliban. Using his laptop, he shows us a PBS documentary called *Return of the Taliban*, which documents the group's resurgence in the border area. The teenage boys cheer each time one of their commanders appears on the video. The film presents detailed evidence that the Pakistani military continues to support the Afghan Taliban. It features experts who say the Haqqanis—the group that is holding us—have been an asset of the Pakistani intelligence since the 1980s. I know that no Pakistani rescue mission will be arriving to save us.

The dirt room where we are being held is the most cramped of our captivity. We inhabit one fifteen-foot-by-ten-foot room and are not allowed to leave it. Throughout the day, children come to the well in our yard to fill up buckets of water. They are covered in dirt and fleabites. Human waste flows down a drainage ditch that runs through the center of the yard. We chat with children to pass the time.

One afternoon, a student who appears to be roughly ten years old arrives from one of the local hard-line religious schools. When I ask him what he wants to be when he grows up, he says he wants to be a suicide bomber. When I ask him his second choice, he says he wants to be a mujahideen or "freedom fighter." When I asked him his third choice, he says he wants to be a Muslim.

On June 4, Abu Tayyeb reappears without warning. He announces that the American government is now offering to trade the seven remaining Afghan prisoners at Guantánamo Bay, Cuba, for us. I tell him that is ridiculous. For months, Abu Tayyeb has been vastly exaggerating my value. I am furious that he will not stop. He insists that I am best friends with Richard Holbrooke.

"Then why am I still sitting here after seven months?" I ask him.

He smiles. If I make one more video, he says, I will be released. Ashamed of my previous video and convinced that Abu Tayyeb is lying yet again, I refuse.

"This is all about you," I say, raising my voice. "You are demanding millions of dollars so you can make yourself look good to the other commanders. You are the problem."

He declares that he is doing everything "for the jihad." Visibly angry, he again tells me to make the video and leaves the room. Thirty minutes later, he returns and says that making the video is not a choice but an order. The half dozen guards in the room stare at me. Once again, Abu Tayyeb repeats his order, and I say no. I know it's reckless, but standing up to him feels enormously liberating after months of acquiescing.

Sensing that Abu Tayyeb and his men are about to beat me, Tahir and Asad step in. "Just do it," Tahir says. I relent, but I am determined to turn it into an opportunity to console our families, not worry them. Abu Tayyeb has no guards pointing guns at my head. I refuse to cry.

"My name is David Rohde. Today is Thursday, June 4, 2009," I say calmly. "Myself, Tahir, and Asad are alive and well. Please tell our families that we are alive and we miss them very, very much and we are so sorry for the pain they are feeling.

"I want to say to my wife Kristen that what you said in your January Red Cross letter still helps me. I am strong because you are strong," I continue. "Your love helps me so much during this time. And the love of Asad and Tahir's family has helped us during this time."

"However this ends, Kristen and all my family and friends should live in peace with yourselves," I say. "I know you have all done absolutely everything you can to help us.

"I am responsible for this situation," I add. "And I apologize to you all from the bottom of my heart and thank you for all you have done for us."

I finish with several lines Abu Tayyeb asks me to include. Without them, I fear he may not actually send the video. "Please do all you can to release us as soon as possible," I say. "We are in a very difficult situation. Please help us, please help us now. Please help us as quickly as possible. Please free us soon. Please."

Abu Tayyeb departs and I feel at peace for the first time in months.

HOME MOVIES

Kristen, Early May–Mid-June 2009

W e spend days crafting and redrafting a message to the kidnappers that the FBI says it will channel through the source who provided the "crying video." Despite the fact that the letter will be arriving via the FBI, we are advised by them to remove any references to the United States government. We are also advised by our private security consultants not to respond with a specific offer of money. A low offer could endanger the lives of our three; a high offer could extend captivity by increasing the expectation that more money could be raised the longer this drags out. We are told merely to ask for proof of life and state that we are ready to settle this matter through communication. We include Tahir and Asad in the letter.

> *This is a message from David's family:*
> *We want to bring David home. Please allow us to come to an agreement that returns David to his wife and family. David is a journalist and a good man. We are very concerned about David, Tahir and Asad. Please let David phone home so we know this is the authentic way to get him released. We are available and ready to communicate. We respectfully await your reply.*

We list the local contact numbers for John and for Team Kabul. Lee sends a copy of the statement to the rest of our family via text message. The letter is dispatched on May 9, a few days before Mother's Day. Then we wait.

I spend the rest of May in our New York apartment, feeling no further along than when I left for our meetings in Washington. At times, I glance at our wedding photo, which sits on a console in the hallway. It's an exuberant photo—my mouth permanently shaped into a wide-open smile. David, too, is beaming. The background is marsh grass and fog—the fog gives the image the feeling of a dreamscape. I stare at my expression and think how easily this open-mouth laugh could be reinterpreted as a scream, should our situation end in tragedy. The fog, too, takes on an eerie quality. It's difficult to know which world or reality will prove true. The idyllic marsh or the eerie fog. I recall Munch's painting, *The Scream*, and cringe thinking that this will forever be my association with this photo should things end badly.

I try to think of a way to maintain a positive connection to David. I remember our wedding service. One of the songs we chose was based on the prayer of St. Francis, entitled "Make Me a Channel of Your Peace." I have a prayer card of it, at the back of my nightstand drawer. I pull it out and tuck it into the photo frame.

It reads:

> Lord, make me an instrument of Your peace.
> Where there is hatred, let me sow love;
> Where there is injury, pardon,
> Where there is doubt, faith,
> Where there is despair, hope,
> Where there is darkness, light,
> And where there is sadness, joy.
> Divine Master, grant that I may not so much seek to be
>   consoled, as to console;
> To be understood, as to understand;
> To be loved, as to love with all my soul;

For it is in giving that we receive—
It is in pardoning that we are pardoned;
And it is in dying that we are born to eternal life.

I decide to say this prayer each night for me and for David as a way to stay connected and centered until he returns. I can no longer find this positivity within myself. I rely on this prayer and hope its recitation brings us both some peace, strength, and acceptance. Faith is an old resource of mine. Having gone through decades of exploring, questioning, and rediscovering my religion, I am still a practicing Catholic. And these are the words that feel most genuine as I surrender to a need for something beyond me. Prayer and positive intention offer me the ability to let go without feeling like I am giving up. Reciting prayers I knew from childhood provides me with a sense of continuity.

More than ever, I realize the need to take care of myself. That means reaching out for help, and then embracing the help that is offered to me. I have been obsessed with David's well-being for the last few months. Yet the only thing I have the ability to maintain is my own sense of wellness.

In late May, one of our Clayton team members in Kabul puts me in touch with Dr. James R. Alvarez, a hostage negotiations specialist and psychologist whose writing appears in the book *Trauma Psychology: Issues in Violence, Disaster, Health and Illness*. Alvarez's chapter, "Psychological Impact of Kidnap," addresses the stress and emotional issues experienced by kidnap victims and their families. While it is not an uplifting read, it is a life preserver of sorts. Reading it, I feel less isolated. It gives voice and perspective to our situation and to my own conflicted feelings, which Alvarez claims are "normal reactions to an abnormal situation." I e-mail a digital scan of the chapter to Lee and the rest of our family.

Throughout the case, I've heard periodically from the FBI's victim specialists. Their job is to provide support to family members as well as prepare them for the return of their loved one—and introduce the idea that there may be aftereffects from captivity, namely posttraumatic stress.

While I don't take this idea lightly, I do marvel at the fact that David was kidnapped in a country that has been at war—civil and otherwise—for the past three decades. Afghanistan and the neighboring tribal areas are home to millions of PTSD sufferers and survivors—almost none of whom, in all likelihood, are in therapy. It seems a Western notion to deal with a disorder before one has even been affected by it.

Physical numbness and pain have proved to be chronic side effects of dealing with the emotional pressures and uncertainties of the past few months. However skeptically, I decide to see a somatic therapist to ease my own growing physical discomfort. Needless to say, finding a therapist in Manhattan is even easier than locating a Pashtun translator. Despite my skepticism, the treatment technique called somatic experiencing proves to be a welcome release and a way to feel grounded in my own body again. The method, developed by the psychophysiological theorist Peter Levine, is based on the concept that the body stores memories and that we respond to trauma with fight, flight, and fright response—much like predatory animals. The idea is that traumatic events can leave you immobilized. The body needs to release this blocked energy to prevent chronic ailments and to find a new vocabulary that emphasizes support and groundedness.

During our first meeting, the therapist asks me about my situation, and interrupts as she notices physical tensions and movements that may indicate that my body's natural defensive systems have been activated. She tells me to identify the parts of my body that feel most supported and at ease. Then apparently because I have acknowledged places of safety and solidity, when I'm guided again to notice where I'm tense, subtle releases take place. She also asks me to do some visualization. This proves to be quite satisfying; I'm comfortable working with images. These practices will turn out to be invaluable tools that enable me to manage my stress and carry on over the next few months.

Several days later from the other side of the globe Michael e-mails to say he has spoken to the mullah, the religious figure in the Swabi district in Pakistan that claims to have contact with the Haqqanis. Michael complained to him that the kidnappers do not know how to negotiate and settle this. Our letters were ignored because the Taliban thought they were spoofs. According to Michael, the mullah advises that I make a video to prove the communication is indeed from our family. The mullah has said that the kidnappers have provided us with videos and it would be fitting to respond in kind.

Michael asks that I film the footage as soon as possible and e-mail it to him. He will have it translated into Pashto and give it to the mullah to deliver to the "Waziristan brothers," a.k.a. the kidnappers Siraj and Badruddin Haqqani. Michael jests that he had considered sparing me this activity by wrapping himself in a headscarf and making the recording himself, but thinks it best that I do it.

"It will be helpful to David because we'll use it to establish clarity in our communication, demonstrate the family is ready to settle, and point to the channel they must use to settle," Michael says. "We are herding them towards the final deal."

I am skeptical, but I defer to Michael's judgment and agree to make a video. My friend Josh comes over to my apartment the next day. It's a sunny afternoon in late May. I have known Josh for more than twenty years. We were classmates at Brown and sat next to each other in film class. We moved to New York around the same time, following graduation. He is now an independent filmmaker who also produces and edits for TV shows. His latest project is editing the reality show *The Real Housewives of Atlanta*.

We set up a makeshift studio in the living room, removing paintings from the wall to create a neutral backdrop, one that provides no clue as to my whereabouts or circumstances. I prop myself up on the back of the sofa, against the wall. Josh frames my face, cropping the image at my shoulders. My wardrobe is a maroon pashmina that David purchased for me during a trip to Islamabad. I wrap it around my head loosely. Michael has advised me to emulate Benazir Bhutto when it comes to styling a headscarf. I am to gently cover the top of my hair and let the fabric drape around my neck. I overthink this process every step of the way. Maroon, a relatively sedate color, now seems a bit brazen in this context.

"Is this too racy?" I ask Josh.

Josh assures me my wardrobe will not offend anyone. "You look like a Connecticut housewife in a headscarf."

I laugh at the accuracy of his description. I never could have imagined that I would consider this a reassuring statement or affirmation of my styling abilities. Nonetheless, we decide to convert the footage to black and white, just to be on the safe side. Despite the humor, I can tell Josh feels bad for me.

"This is the latest act of desperation," I say.

It's true. It all seems so futile, but I am willing to try anything. I have written the script in consultation with Michael and now recite my lines as Josh signals that the camera, a portable Flip video recorder, is rolling:

"*Salaam alaikum*. My name is Kristen. I am the wife of David Rohde. Our family wants to settle this situation. We have been ready to settle this for quite some time and are concerned that you have not contacted our representative in country, John. To settle this immediately, please contact John. His phone number is on this CD. Please contact him so that the long wait may be over for all of us. Thank you."

Looking at the footage later, Lee remarks that as a newlywed couple, David and I have compiled quite a unique DVD collection over the past six months.

Carol and I remain in close touch. She has invited me to visit her at home on the Connecticut coast. Up until now I have been too busy or exhausted to accept. I have also had reservations about staying in her home. The last time I did so was with David, en route to our wedding in Maine. While I have only happy memories of that visit, I do not know how I will react to staying in the guest bedroom alone.

It's a sunny Saturday, and I take the local train to New London. Carol greets me. I am glad to see her. She and her husband, George, make dinner, and we reminisce about happier times and talk about how we plan to move forward when David returns. David's captivity has been a strain on all of us, but it has also brought us closer. Of all the support Carol has provided, I am most grateful for the fact that she has respected my position as David's wife. She has been willing to step aside and let me and Lee take the lead, while also remaining at the ready to jump in and offer support on a moment's notice. This is something I imagine must be difficult for a new mother-in-law to do, and it is a testament to her strength.

I retire early and am surprised to find that it is comforting to be in the familiar wicker bed that I last shared with David. I fall asleep quickly and awake feeling closer to my husband. In the late morning, Carol and I visit St. Edmund's Church on Enders Island, an idyllic waterfront retreat and chapel located a few minutes from her home. Carol is not a Catholic, but she takes time each week to go to mass at this church, light candles, and say prayers for David, Tahir, Asad, and our families. She says it gives her a sense of peace.

I've visited Enders Island before with Carol and David, and once on my own as a teenager, when I attended a mandatory retreat before making my Confirmation. In addition to a traditional church, the island also has an outdoor chapel that abuts the water. It consists of three modest stone walls. The front of the chapel is open and faces the ocean. The floor consists of natural stone that gradually descends into the water. Its modesty is reassuring and calming. The chapel contains a small altar cluttered with prayers, stones, charms—memorabilia of loved ones, written requests left by former visitors. Carol and I decide to say a prayer for David and leave symbolic personal items to help him find his way home.

Carol has been concerned about David's eyesight throughout his captivity. With this in mind, she leaves a bottle of Visine on the altar as a symbol of protection, to help him see clearly—as well as to ease any tears.

Before David departed New York for Kabul back in October, I gave him a sacred-heart charm I had purchased on our honeymoon in Paris from Sacré-Coeur in Montmartre. I wear an identical charm around my neck. I recall that David looked at me quizzically when I gave it to him, because he is neither Catholic nor religious. But being somewhat of a reticent romantic, he took it with him. I was shocked at my own insistence that he do so, because I had never before given him anything to carry as a memento or good luck charm. Still, I wanted him to keep it in his pocket or duffel as a reminder of our recent time together and as reassurance that there would be cheerful times ahead.

I now remove the matching charm from the chain around my neck and fasten it to one of the branches of the twig cross that is centered on the altar. I hope that David and I will one day return to retrieve it together.

Back in New York, on June 8, I am surprised by a Google alert about David. It links to the *Huffington Post,* which has put up a story titled "U.S. Journalists Arrested, Kidnapped Abroad." It's a roundup of American journalists detained in the past and present and includes a short bio and photograph of each: Daniel Pearl, kidnapped and murdered in Pakistan in 2002; Jill Carroll, kidnapped and eventually freed in Iraq in 2006; Roxana Saberi, charged with espionage in Iran and recently freed on appeal; Euna Lee and Laura Ling, detained in North Korea in March and recently sentenced to twelve years in a work camp for "hostile acts." I am mortified to see that David is included as "still missing." A photo accompanies his bio. I am shocked that the Web site did not consult our family before posting this. While it is not the best-kept secret in town, it's also common knowledge among the journalism community that David's case has been kept out of the news as a safety precaution.

Lee and Ling have been in jail for three months. Recently, their families have gone public, making a plea to the North Korean government on *Larry King Live* and holding a candlelight vigil in Rockefeller Center. My heart goes out to their families. The decision to go public seems to be helping in their case because they are able to appeal to an established, albeit unreasonable, government. Recent press coverage of their case has sparked renewed interest in the issue of journalists' safety and the role of diplomacy. It has also begun to draw attention to David's plight.

I contact Lee and David McCraw at the *Times* and alert the paper's vice president of communications, Catherine Mathis. Catherine has done an expert job of tracking media activity and requesting the removal of any content that may endanger David. I tell her I have no qualms about contacting Arianna Huffington and holding her accountable should anything happen to David because of the publication of this piece. But there is no need to do so. The *Huffington Post* honors Catherine's request and immediately removes David's name and portrait.

The main side effect of being on leave from work is that I now have twenty-four hours a day to devote to obsessing about David's case. This is a blessing and a curse. My mother, Mary Jane, returns in mid-June after a six-week absence. She is in good spirits, but still limits her movements and activities because of the healing slipped disc in her back.

I have no idea if the family's message sent through the FBI or my video has made it to any of our intended targets. But we receive word that another video of David has emerged through the FBI's unnamed contact, the same one who provided the crying video. The FBI, along with a member of our private security team, plan to meet with the source of the video, who will travel to Dubai in the next few days.

As always, I am reassured by the agency before I watch that this is not an execution video and that David appears to be in good condition. They add that this video is not as menacing as the last. My mother and I huddle together on the sofa and watch it on my laptop. The sound and image do not sync up. I have to periodically stop and resume by hitting the play/pause button. The audio is clear, and David's voice is strong, but the video is stilted and appears as a series of stills. David seems at peace as he sits on a cushion with a full white beard, wire-frame glasses, and a white salwar kameez. He looks like John Lennon. He seems to have come to some inner resolution. He is clean and calm. His words are personal.

"My name is David Rohde. Today is Thursday, June 4, 2009. Myself, Tahir, and Asad are alive and well. Please tell our families that we are alive and we miss them very, very much and we are so sorry for the pain they are feeling."

He addresses some short comments to me and the family and then concludes by asking us to help them. "Please help us as quickly as possible," he says. "Please free us soon. Please."

It is a relief to know he has received my Red Cross letter—and that he knows he has not been forgotten.

I find the video reassuring: David's message is largely personal. I take this as a good sign, as it seems his captors have permitted him to speak freely. I am comforted to hear him repeat the words in my letter. He has not given up. It is a relief, too, that he realizes the futility of our situation on the outside and trusts that we are doing everything possible to bring him home. He is composed, a striking contrast to the seemingly broken subject in the "crying video" we saw in Washington. So much for the previous video being "his last."

I begin to realize there is a pattern to the captors' communication. Six to eight weeks of silence, followed by some form of contact. It seems that communications will resume again. Although it is tough to think in terms of eight-week cycles of waiting, it is somehow reassuring to know the captors may actually be following some kind of thought-out strategy. My greatest fear now is not that they will harm or kill David, but that they will hold him indefinitely.

A few days later, I receive an e-mail from a friend and colleague of David's in Pakistan, Beena Sarwar. She has been in touch with me several times over the last few months to check on David.

It seems I am not the only one who is looking for an alternative, positive outlet. Beena and some of David's colleagues have come up with a meaningful way for people to reach out to David. Beena's e-mail explains:

> *Dear Kris,*
>
> *Just want to let you know that David has many friends here and elsewhere who are all thinking of him. I was online with a reporter just now and she wanted me to let you know that the mood in Pakistan is changing, too, and things will come right. That is what I believe, too.*
>
> *So here's a bizarre notion I'll share with you which sounds very silly—but the idea is basically for all those who know and care about him to spend ten minutes, all at the same time on the same day, all over the world, thinking of him and sending good vibes, goodwill, reiki, whatever, all at the same time. It can't hurt. And it may comfort friends and family members if nothing else.*

We were thinking a good time would be when it's morning in the U.S. and evening here—say this Sunday (June 14) 10 a.m. EST, 8 p.m. in Pakistan.

We don't need to go public on it if you don't want but just let everyone who already knows to spend ten minutes at that time, like a kind of a worldwide mental vigil.

Let me know what you think.

With very best wishes and hopes that you and the rest of the family remain strong and positive.

Beena

This is a lovely sentiment, and I write back to her to thank her and tell her I support her efforts.

A few days later, I hear from Michael Semple. John has made contact with the uncle of Siraj and Badruddin Haqqani and claims that they are willing to settle for much less money than what they have been demanding. Lee, McCraw, and I are skeptical, because the FBI's point person, the one who has provided the last two proof-of-life videos, is still asking for $8 million and four prisoners.

The FBI and Team Kabul meet with the FBI source in Dubai twice over the next two days. On day one, he claims he can get David released and would be willing to carry funds should the family be able to raise them. He adds that the kidnappers are willing to be "flexible" and settle the deal for reasonable money. Day two, he changes his story, stating that he will not be able to facilitate an exchange and that the Taliban still want prisoners in addition to money. The family must work through a third party.

Similarly, we have recently heard from Karzai's government in Afghanistan, which says the Taliban are asking them for three Taliban prisoners in exchange for David. Michael has forewarned me about these pleas. He tells me to ignore them because both channels are false. He believes John's contact has the ability to cut a deal, even though this channel has produced no proof-of-life videos. We are told that if John's source is correct, we should expect to hear back for instructions on how this will proceed.

Still on leave from *Cosmo*, I keep myself busy at home and sort through a clutter of papers in an attempt to restore some semblance of order to my life. My dining table overflows with notes pertaining to David's case, updates or "sit-reps," from our security team, and thoughtful letters from extended relatives—all of whom are now aware of our situation. Amid the random pile is a prayer card from Mother Teresa's mission in Calcutta, a place David and I visited together during my first trip to India a year ago. Mother Teresa's calling had always intrigued me, and we had flown in specifically to see her orphanage and home for the destitute. For me, growing up Catholic, there seemed to be only two cool contemporary female role models: Madonna and Mother Teresa. Together their various behaviors seemed to define what was possible within the realm of my faith.

I am a big believer in the power of intention, and in writing things down. With this in mind, I compose a written prayer to Mother Teresa, who died in 1997 and is on the road to sainthood, having been beatified by the Church. In doing so, I feel I am recruiting a higher entity to share in the responsibility for David's release. Over the past few months I have written to my husband, government officials, CNN reporters, former CIA officials, newspaper editors, Taliban elders, religious extremists, and Siraj Haqqani. By now, writing to a Catholic icon on her way to sainthood doesn't seem far-fetched in comparison. And it doesn't seem any less likely to produce a response. It's a surrender of sorts. A last-ditch effort.

I ask for the safe return of David, Tahir, and Asad, by whatever means possible. I believe in and would welcome a miracle.

In the days ahead, I make an effort to fill my time with activities that will boost my spirits—catching up with friends, talking with family, walking along the Hudson River—which is particularly meaningful because David and I did this weekly. I recall David's romantic marriage proposal, and how nearly a year has passed since then. My only comfort is the realization that nothing is permanent. Things are inherently ephemeral. At some point, this situation will change—it will end. I desperately hope it resolves with David's release and our reunion, but if it ends otherwise, there is some small relief in knowing that this suffering will cease. We have been in limbo for far too long.

PASHTUNWALI

David, June 19–20, 2009

I lie awake in the darkness and wonder if the guards have fallen asleep. Their breathing is heavy and regular but I cannot see them. I blink over and over in the darkness but see no difference when my eyes are open or closed. I turn around and look at the orange light on the swamp cooler—an antiquated version of an air-conditioner—to make sure I can still see.

It is roughly 1 A.M. on Saturday, June 20. After seven months and ten days in captivity, Tahir and I have decided to try to escape. I fear that the guards will wake up and catch us. I fear even more that our captivity will drag on for years.

The confidence I felt while walking around Sharif's house—the belief that we would be released if we were patient—has faded. The determination to survive in Makeen, the willingness to wait as long as it took, has been replaced by a searing rage at our captors. As my abject hatred for Abu Tayyeb, Timor Shah, and Badruddin has grown, my judgment has weakened and my patience has wavered. As I lie in the darkness, I wonder if trying to escape is another rash decision that will have disastrous consequences.

I try to calm myself by praying. In February, Sharif told me that if I said "Forgive me, God" a thousand times each day, our captivity might end. I have done as he suggested for the last four months with no results. But I do not care. As it has for months, prayer soothes and centers me.

Each day, I stare at the ceiling and say, "Forgive me, God" a thousand times while the guards take naps. Counting on my fingers, it takes me roughly sixty minutes to reach one thousand. Tonight, as I wait to make sure the guards are sound asleep, I ask God to forgive me two thousand times.

That day, Tahir and I were told yet another lie regarding the negotiations for our release. Timor Shah said that an Afghan government negotiator had failed to show up at a scheduled meeting in the Pakistani city of Quetta. Instead, he had departed on a religious pilgrimage to Saudi Arabia. The negotiator was supposed to be finalizing the deal that Abu Tayyeb had told us about on June 4: the exchange of all remaining Afghan prisoners in Guantánamo Bay for the three of us. Tahir and I knew Timor Shah's claim was absurd.

Since we returned to Miran Shah, we have been talking about trying to escape, but disagreed on exactly how to do it. Infuriated by Timor Shah's lies that day, we finalize our plan. I will get up first, go to the bathroom without asking the guards for permission, and wake Tahir as I leave. If the guards remain asleep, Tahir will follow.

Following our plan, I slowly stand up and creep across the room. I pass Timor Shah on my left and then crouch down and tug Tahir's foot. Tahir groans and I fear the guards will wake up. But their heavy breathing continues.

To my right, Akbar is sleeping with his head a few feet from the door's hinge. I worry that opening the door will wake him, but I have no choice. I'm desperate to proceed with our plan. If Akbar wakes, I will tell him I was simply going to the bathroom. I open the door and the roar of the swamp cooler and ceiling fan seems to drown out the noise. I slowly step outside and gently close the door behind me.

I slip on my sandals, walk to the bathroom, and wait for Tahir to emerge. My heart pounds. Twenty feet away, on a shelf outside the kitchen, is a car towrope we plan to use to lower ourselves down the ten- to fifteen-foot wall ringing the compound. I had found it two weeks earlier on a shelf beside motor oil and car wrenches. Compulsively cleaning as I had in every house, I placed some old clothes on top of the rope to prevent the guards from seeing it. The discovery, I thought, was the first stroke of good luck in our seven months in captivity.

Several minutes pass, though, and Tahir does not come out of the room. I stare intently at the door—roughly fifteen feet away and directly across the courtyard—still Tahir does not emerge. When I pulled his foot to rouse him, he had groaned and I assumed he was awake. As the minutes pass, I'm unsure what to do. I stand in the darkened bathroom and wonder if Tahir has changed his mind. If the guards catch us, they might kill me, but they will definitely kill Tahir. Part of me thinks it was wrong even to have asked him to do this. I wonder if we are still capable of making rational decisions.

Even if we make it over the wall, we will have to walk for fifteen minutes through Miran Shah to reach a nearby Pakistani base. The town is full of Afghan, Pakistani, and foreign militants. Whoever catches us might be far less merciful than our current guards. And we are not necessarily safe once we get to the base. We could fall into the hands of members of the ISI who are sympathetic to the Taliban. They could simply hand us back to the Haqqanis. Months ago, our guards had told us that the Pakistani tribal militia had handed back one escaped prisoner to the Haqqanis and they had executed him. A week ago, another worrying sign of cooperation had emerged. The Afghan Taliban in Miran Shah had apparently received orders from Haqqani commanders to not fight the Pakistani army if it tried to regain control of Miran Shah. Instead, the Pakistani Taliban would fight them.

But I desperately want to see Kristen and my family again. And I want our captors to get nothing in exchange for me. The last video I filmed with Abu Tayyeb was enormously liberating for me. I felt I had signaled to them that if I died they should feel no guilt and move on. I alone was responsible for the situation.

In the three weeks since taping the video, I've felt more and more willing to take risks and plan an escape. I started performing tests in the last house we inhabited. In the middle of the night, I got up and walked to the bathroom without asking for permission from the guards. To my surprise, they stayed asleep. Then I walked to the compound door, pulled on the handle, and found it locked. When I told Tahir about my test run the next morning, he said I was crazy to try such things. Along with finding the rope in our current house, I found a set of padlock keys and tried to see if they opened the padlock on our compound's exterior doors. None of them worked.

Now, standing in the bathroom, I try to decide what to do. I could walk back in the room and go to sleep, or I could follow a seemingly foolhardy backup plan that Tahir and I had devised to make sure he woke up. Telling myself that we may never have another chance to escape, I push ahead.

In the darkness, I step out of the bathroom and pick up a five-foot-long bamboo pole that's leaning against the adjacent wall. I walk to the living room window and peer inside to make sure the guards are still asleep. I slowly open the window beside the cooler, point the pole at Tahir's side, and poke him. I quickly close the window, walk back to the bathroom, and lean the pole against the wall. I step inside the bathroom and wait again. Still Tahir does not appear. I am convinced that he has changed his mind. It isn't fair of me, I think, to expect a man with seven children to risk his life.

Then like an apparition, Tahir's leg emerges from the window. His upper body and head follow and, finally, his second leg. As he stands up, I rush out of the bathroom to meet him and accidentally kick a small plastic jug used for ablutions. It skids across the ground, and I motion to Tahir to freeze.

Tahir and I stare at each other in the darkness. The cooler roars. No guards emerge from the room. Taking a few steps forward, I whisper in Tahir's ear. "We don't have to go," I say. "We can wait."

"Go get the rope," he says.

Inside the room, Asad is sound asleep with the guards. This afternoon, Tahir and I made the gut-wrenching decision to leave without him, fearing he would inform the guards of our escape plans—as he had repeatedly in the past.

Two weeks ago, after Abu Tayyeb had me make the last video, Tahir had whispered to Asad "Let's escape" at night while the guards slept. Asad did not reply, according to Tahir. Instead, a guard told Tahir that he had heard Tahir was talking about trying to escape. Finally, Asad had seen me trying the keys in different padlocks in our current house and told the guards, according to Tahir.

Our rupture with Asad has become the darkest aspect of our captivity. Over the months, the solidarity the three of us shared immediately after the kidnapping frayed under the threat of execution and indefinite imprisonment. Yet Tahir and I also know that Asad is under enormous pressure. He may be cooperating with the guards in order to save his life. In the end, though, we decide we cannot trust him. If Asad tells the guards, we will squander an opportunity for freedom we might never have again. We know that this house is closer to Miran Shah's Pakistani military base than any we have been held in.

Since we arrived in the house two week ago, we have been trying to think of ways to flee. When the guards let me sit on the roof with them as they prayed at dusk, I noticed that a five-foot-high parapet surrounded it. If we could hoist ourselves over the wall, I thought, we could use the car towrope I had found to lower ourselves the ten to fifteen feet to the street.

At the same time, Tahir had surveyed the area around the house when the guards took him outside to buy food and watch cricket games. He plotted a route to the Pakistani military base. Finally, a few hours after Timor Shah lied to us about the negotiations, electricity returned to Miran Shah for the first time since fighting cut power lines six days earlier. We knew electricity meant the swamp cooler and ceiling fan would help conceal any noise we made when we fled. Unsure when we would have power again, we decided to make our attempt that night. We also added one last touch. We agreed Tahir would try to keep the guards up late playing Checkah. If they were tired, they would sleep more soundly.

Our plans for how to get over the wall were in place. Unfortunately, we disagreed about what to do next. Tahir believes the militiamen who guard the military base will shoot us if we approach them at night or

hand us back to the Haqqanis. He says we should hike the roughly fifteen miles to the Afghan border. I do not think we could ever make it
that far without being caught. Going to the Pakistani base is a risk we
have to take. If we surrender to an army officer, I told Tahir, he will
protect us.

One of our guards then walked into the room and Tahir and I stopped
speaking. For the rest of the evening, we were not alone again. Our plan
still had no ending.

After Tahir and I meet in the courtyard, I retrieve the rope and we slowly
walk up a flight of stairs leading to the roof. Threading the rope through
a drainage hole in the bottom of the five-foot parapet, we tie the rope to
the wall and throw the long end toward the street below. Placing his toe
between two bricks, Tahir climbs to the top and peers at the street below.
He steps down. "The rope is too short," he whispers.

I shift the knot on the rope to give it more length, pull myself up on
the wall, and look down. The rope does not reach the ground, but it appears close. I glance back at the stairs, fearing the guards will emerge at
any moment. "We don't have to go," I repeat to Tahir. "It's up to you."

He signals that he wants to try again. I get down on my hands and
knees. Tahir steps on my back and lifts himself over the wall. I hear his
clothes scrape against the bricks, look up and realize he is gone. I grab his
sandals, which he left behind, and stuff them down my pants. I climb
over and momentarily snag a power line with my foot as I slide down the
wall faster than expected. I land in a small sewage ditch. I look up and
see Tahir striding down the street in his bare feet. I run after him.

For the first time in seven months, I walk freely down a street. Glancing over my shoulder, I don't see any of our guards coming out of the
house, which looks even smaller than it felt like inside. We head down a
narrow dirt lane with primitive mud-brick walls on either side of us.
Makeshift electrical wires snake overhead in what looks like a densely
populated neighborhood. I have no idea where we are or where to go.

I follow Tahir and we walk into a dry riverbed and turn right. I keep slipping on the large sand-covered stones and feel punch-drunk. I catch up to Tahir and hand him his sandals. "My ankle is very painful," Tahir whispers as he slips them on and continues walking. "I can't walk far."

A large dark stain covers his lower left pant leg. I worry that he has ripped open his calf on his way down the wall. At the same time, my left hand stings. I notice that the rope has made a large cut across two of my fingers.

"Where are we going?" I whisper to Tahir as we quickly make our way down the riverbed, afraid someone will see or hear us.

"There is a militia base over there," Tahir says, gesturing to his left. "I don't trust them."

Neither do I. Earlier, Tahir had told me the Pakistani government tribal militia maintained a small checkpoint near the house. Turning ourselves in there would be a gamble. I still believe that our best chance is to surrender to a military officer on the main Pakistani military base in Miran Shah. I do not know where the base is, though. I am completely dependent on Tahir's knowledge of the town's layout.

"We have to go to the main base," I say.

"Impossible," Tahir says, continuing down the riverbed. "The guards said that Arabs and Chechens watch the main gate twenty-four hours a day."

I start to panic. We have made it over the wall but do not know where we are going. Despite his ankle, Tahir seems determined to hike fifteen miles to the Afghan border. As we walk, we argue over which way to go.

"We have to go to the Pakistani base," I tell Tahir.

Striding ahead, he doesn't respond. Dogs begin barking from one of the walled compounds to our right. "We can't make it to the border," I say. "We have to go to the base."

Tahir continues walking, but after a few minutes he complains about his ankle. "There is too much pain," he says.

We stop and I pull up his pant leg. His calf has not been cut. The dark stain on his pants is from the sewage ditch we both landed in outside our house. "There is another gate," Tahir says, changing his mind. "Come."

As we continue walking, I expect Taliban fighters to rush out of the darkness, but none do. Tahir tells me to put the scarf I am carrying over my head. "If anyone stops us, your name is Akbar and my name is Timor Shah," he says. "Act like a Muslim."

My sense of time is distorted, but it seems as though we have been walking in the darkness for five to ten minutes. I do not feel free. If anything, I am more frightened. I worry that a more brutal militant group will capture us.

We leave the riverbed and walk down an alleyway between two compounds for about fifty yards. We arrive at a two-lane paved street.

"This is the main road in Miran Shah," Tahir whispers. We turn right and begin walking down the street. To our left is a vacant stretch. To our right stands a gas station with four pumps and several shops. Dim lightbulbs outside the shops illuminate the area. As we walk down the street, I silently question why Tahir is leading us down the center of a paved road where we can be easily spotted. I have no idea if he knows where we are going.

Suddenly, shouts erupt to our left and I hear the sound of a Kalashnikov being loaded. Tahir raises his hands and says something in Pashto. A man shouts commands back in Pashto. I raise my hands as my heart sinks. The Taliban have recaptured us.

In the faint light, I see a figure with a rifle standing on the roof of a dilapidated one-story building. Beside the building is a mosque with freshly painted white walls. The building and mosque have concertina wire and earthen berms in front of them.

"If you move," Tahir says, "they will shoot us." Then he says words I can scarcely believe. "This is the base."

We have made it to the Pakistanis. Tahir has guided us brilliantly.

I hold my hands high in the air and dare not move an inch. With my long beard, scarf, and salwar kameez I look like an Uzbek suicide bomber, not an American journalist. Another voice comes from inside the building. It sounds as if the guard is waking up his comrades. One or two more figures appear on the roof and aim more gun barrels at us.

The Pakistani guard on the roof intermittently speaks in Pashto with Tahir. I hear Tahir say the words for "journalist," "Afghan," and "American." I struggle to slow my breathing. My arms begin to burn, I desperately try not to move my hands. "Tell them we will take off our shirts," I tell Tahir, thinking that will show we are not suicide bombers wearing explosive vests.

Tahir says something in Pashto, and the man responds

"Lift up your shirt," Tahir says. I immediately oblige.

The guard speaks again. "He is asking if you are American," Tahir says.

"I am an American journalist," I say in English, surprised at the sound of my own voice in the open air. "Please help us. Please help us."

I keep speaking English, hoping they will recognize that I am a native speaker. "We were kidnapped by the Taliban seven months ago," I say, in the darkness. "We were kidnapped outside Kabul and brought here."

"Do you speak English?" I say, hoping one of the Pakistani guards on the roof understands. "Do you speak English?"

The guard says something to Tahir in Pashto. "They are radioing their commander," Tahir says. "They are asking for permission to bring us inside."

Tahir has asked the guards—who are also Pashtuns—to protect us under the tenet of Pashtunwali that requires a Pashtun to shelter a stranger in need, even at the cost of the host's fortune and life. He urges them to take us inside the base before the Taliban come looking for us. About two or three minutes pass. The Pakistani guards stand behind sandbags on the roof. Above us, stars glitter in a sparkling, crystal clear sky.

For the first time that night, it occurs to me that we might actually succeed. Escape—an ending I never conceived of—might be our salvation.

I hold my hands still and wait. Several more minutes pass, and Tahir and I grow nervous. "Please allow us in the mosque," Tahir says. "Please let us inside."

The Pakistani guard on the roof says they are waiting for a senior officer to arrive. Tahir asks what we should do if the Taliban drive down the road. The guard says that we should dive behind the dirt embankment, and that they will open fire on anyone who approaches. But they still will not let us inside. Tahir complains to me about the pain in his arms as he holds them in the air. His ankle hurts as well.

"Please wait, Tahir," I say, encouraging him. "Please wait. We're so close."

Tahir asks for permission to sit on the ground. The Pakistani guard grants it. Tahir groans and seems exhausted. I sense less nervousness from the guards. Soon after, the Pakistani guard says we can take a few steps toward the mosque. With our hands in the air, we walk over the surrounding earthen berm unsteadily. As the loose soil gives way, we both nearly lose our balance. I worry that we will be shot if we slip and fall.

"Lie down on the ground," Tahir says. "If you move, they will shoot us." I do so and stare at the stars above us.

Several minutes later, a Pakistani officer arrives, and Tahir tells me to stand up. The officer stands a few feet from us on the other side of the concertina wire. He speaks with Tahir in what sounds like a reassuring tone. "He is a very polite person," Tahir says. "We are under their protection. We are safe."

The frustration I have felt for months begins to fade. We are achingly close to going home. I thank the officer in Pashto, Urdu, and English, desperate to win his trust. Then in one moment, the humiliating narrative of our captivity reverses itself.

"How are you?" the senior officer says in English.

"How are you?" I reply loudly in English, trying again to demonstrate that I am a foreign journalist, not a suicide bomber.

At this point, Tahir and I have been standing outside the base for fifteen or twenty minutes. We still need to get inside. We again offer to take off our shirts, and the officer tells us to do so. Then we are officially instructed to come inside.

I watch Tahir step unsteadily over the concertina wire and into the base. "Come," Tahir says. "Come."

I follow Tahir inside, and the senior officer and several Pakistani guards shake my hand. "Thank you," I say to them in English, over and over. "Thank you."

The politeness of the Pakistani guards amazes me. I know we could still be handed over to the Taliban, but I savor the compassion we are receiving from strangers. For the first time in months, I do not feel hostility.

We are blindfolded and walked farther into the base. The officer politely apologizes and says this is temporary. He is following their standard protocol. A pickup truck arrives and they let us put our shirts on. We climb into the back of the truck and it drives us toward the center of the base. I stare at Tahir and slap him on the back. We are both in shock.

"Thank you," I say to Tahir. "Thank you."

I ask Tahir to tell the officer that I want to call Kristen. I need to somehow communicate to the outside world where we are—on a Pakistani base in North Waziristan. If we can get word to American officials, it will be extraordinarily difficult for the Pakistanis to hand us back to the Haqqanis. Tahir tells me to be patient and wait. I stop talking. Since we were kidnapped, Tahir has skillfully kept us alive and given me sound advice. He has never shown fear and navigated a cultural and religious labyrinth I do not understand. He has not abandoned me and remained true to his ideals, beliefs, and traditions. I know I will be eternally grateful to him for this night.

We arrive in the center of the base, and I get out of the back of the truck. A row of well-lighted, white one-story, colonial era offices sits fifty feet away on the other side of a neatly manicured lawn. It is the first green grass I have seen in seven months. I walk across it and relish the smell, sense of openness, and safety. The Pakistani officer brings us to a clean, modern office with a large desk and couches along the walls.

After several minutes, a young Pakistani captain who speaks perfect English introduces himself as Captain Nadeem, the duty officer. He looks as if he had just gotten out of bed. He says he had no idea that any American and Afghanistan hostages were being held in Miran Shah. No one had informed him of our case.

After explaining our kidnapping, I ask him if I can please call my wife. He hesitates at first and then says he will try to find a phone card to make a long distance call. As we wait, Tahir speaks in Pashto to the various militia members in the office. A doctor cleans and bandages cuts on Tahir's foot and on my hand. Tahir laughs and his face beams as he speaks. I have never seen him so happy. But after several minutes, his face darkens.

"David, I feel terrible about Asad," Tahir says of our driver. "What have we done?"

I look out the window in the direction of Miran Shah and wonder whether our former guards have awakened yet. When they do, they will be furious. "We had no choice," I say, trying to rationalize abandoning Asad. I know our escape could prompt our captors to kill him. I pray that they will spare him.

My stomach churns and I make small talk with Captain Nadeem. I remain eager to call Kristen. After what seems like an hour, a soldier arrives with a phone card, and I write my home number on a white slip of paper. The captain dials the phone on his desk and hands me the receiver. The phone in our apartment back in New York rings repeatedly. No one answers.

Finally, the answering machine picks up and I listen to Kristen's cheerful voice ask callers to leave us a message. Our escape still seems like a fantasy. The machine beeps, and I speak in an unsteady voice.

"Kristen, it's David," I say. "It's David. Please pick up."

I repeat the words several times. Fearing that the tape on the answering machine will run out, I finally blurt out, "We've escaped."

Moments later, someone picks up the receiver in New York.

"David," a woman's voice says. "It's Mary Jane."

My mother-in-law has answered.

"We've escaped and are on a Pakistani military base," I tell her.

I ask her to call the *Times* immediately and tell them to evacuate Tahir's and Asad's families from their homes in Kabul, as well as the people in the newspaper's bureau there. I remember Abu Tayyeb's threat in December that he could trigger a suicide attack on the bureau at any time.

I spend the next several minutes describing our exact location. I give my mother-in-law the names of the tribal area, town, base, and commanding officer. I tell her she needs to contact American officials and ask them to help evacuate us. I want Captain Nadeem to hear that the American government will soon know we are on his base. At the end of the conversation, I apologize to her for all the pain and worry I have caused.

"Just come home safe," she says.

ANSWERED PRAYERS

Kristen, June 19, 2009

It's a warm summer Friday evening. I am sitting at an outdoor café along the Hudson River in Battery Park. I have tried to fill my spare time in the hopes that it will make waiting easier. I am catching up with an old friend from college who has been working abroad in Africa on a public health project. It's a calm, still evening, and the sun begins to set. There is the faint churning of river ferries and sailboat masts in the distance. Just as dinner arrives, my cell phone rings. It's my mother.

"Hello," I say. She is frantic.

"Kristen—come home right away. David called. He's with Tahir. They escaped. They need help getting out of there. Asad chose not to join them. He joined the Taliban.

"He asked me to call *The New York Times*," she adds breathlessly, "and tell them to evacuate the Kabul bureau and inform them that the families of Tahir and Asad should evacuate their homes. He's on the scout base in Miran Shah. But he needs help getting out of there."

My first reaction is one of terror. Then disbelief. It's one thing to escape captivity, quite another to get out of Miran Shah. I know they are in danger of being picked up by another militant group, shot by the Taliban, handed back to the Haqqanis, or detained by the Pakistani military for questioning. All these are harrowing options, and they're overshadowing the exciting fact of David's escape. I hurriedly say good-bye to my friend and head home. I glance at my cell phone. It is 7:15 P.M. The date is June 19. It must be early morning Saturday in Pakistan.

As I rush home I call David McCraw, our invaluable ally throughout. He will meet my mother and me at the apartment, along with the paper's foreign editor, Susan Chira, who has contacts in the region.

Part of me wonders if the escape is part of a deal—a planned release. Michael has been optimistic about a settlement of late. Yet when I call to alert him of David's status, he is shocked as well. He assures me that no money has changed hands.

I return to a sunny apartment with papers scattered everywhere. My mother has called *The New York Times*. They, in turn, relay information to the office in Kabul and on to the families of Tahir and Asad.

My mother looks frazzled but maintains her composure. She has written the details of her conversation with David on a Post-it pad. We sort through all the stickies. Miran Shah. Tochi Scouts base. Captain Nadeem. We spend the next hour calling government officials—our travels to Washington come in handy after all. David McCraw and Susan Chira arrive. Among the four of us, we are able to contact Richard Holbrooke, Hillary Clinton's office, and Ambassador Anne Patterson in Pakistan. This proves vital. The government officials alert their counterparts in Pakistan that we know David is on a scout base in Pakistan—and that we expect him and Tahir to be safely exited. Everyone is tense.

We fear the ISI will detain David for questioning. But Holbrooke's involvement serves as a safety net. He has repeatedly raised David's case with high-ranking officials in the ISI and pressured them to make the Haqqanis release him. As a result, the ISI insists on helping to facilitate David's transport out of Miran Shah.

I have waited months for this moment. I never thought it would end quite this way, but I am thrilled. I realize that David is not completely safe yet, but my prayers truly have been answered. John, our contact and negotiator on the ground, calls after hearing the news from Michael. He is overjoyed and amused at the outcome. "What can I say," John says. "Your husband saw an opportunity and he took it. He is a brave man." Michael tells me that he knows one of the officials on the scout base and calls to alert them that David is a decent fellow and to not let anything happen to him.

Agent Jim from the FBI stops by briefly. He is delighted. He has devoted the past seven months to our case and feels a huge sense of relief as well. He tells me he will be in touch with Lee and me regarding arrangements to travel to Dubai to meet David.

THE GLORIOUS ISLAM

David, June 20, 2009

A half hour passes, and Captain Nadeem again agrees to let me try to call my wife. With each minute, I begin to believe that we may finally return home. The phone rings. This time, Kristen picks up.

"David?" she says, breathlessly. "David?"

"Kristen," I say, savoring the chance to utter the words I have dreamed of saying to her for months.

"Kristen," I say, "please let me spend the rest of my life making this up to you."

"Yes," she says. "Yes."

My wife sounds exactly the same—calm, iron-willed, and utterly committed to me. I struggle to express all the regrets, thoughts, and emotion that have swirled through my mind and body for the past seven months. I also know that we are not completely safe and repeatedly ask her to help get us out of Miran Shah. I repeatedly praise Captain Nadeem and his men for allowing us on the base. I say we never could have escaped without their help. As he listens to my end of the conversation, I hope I am persuading him not to hand us back to the Taliban.

When I try to explain to Kristen what happened with Asad, I hear the confusion in her voice. I know part of me will never be proud of this night. Captain Nadeem urges me to finish the call and I tell Kristen good-bye. The conversation is rushed but blissful.

I ask the captain to let Tahir call his family. He reaches them and is ecstatic. Tahir—my sole friend and companion of seven months—looks as if he has been physically transformed. In captivity, a shroud seemed to hang over his features. His face now has a glow to it that I vaguely remember from our meeting at the Kabul Coffee House.

The captain's phone rings and he begins speaking with someone in English. "Yes," he says, "this is Captain Nadeem." Someone speaks on the other end of the line and the captain states that I am, indeed, on his base. The conversation continues for roughly thirty seconds and Captain Nadeem hands me the phone.

"David?" a man with an American accent asks. "Is this David Rohde?"

"Yes," I reply.

"This is Keith from the American Embassy," he says. "I'm a security person here."

He apologizes and says he must ask two questions to prove that I am, in fact, David Rohde. I name the university I attended and the town where Kristen and I married. As I speak with him, I feel my confidence rising. If the embassy knows we are here, the Pakistani military will have more difficulty turning us over to the Haqqanis. Covertly supporting the Taliban is one thing. Openly handing a kidnapped American back to a militant group, I hope, is another.

"Please do everything you can to get us out of here," I tell Keith. "Please, we need your help."

He says the embassy has contacted the Pakistani government and made it clear that our evacuation is vital. He promises to call back again with more details. I take down his phone numbers and say good-bye.

We move into Captain Nadeem's regular office. Outside, the sun is rising over Miran Shah. His office is identical to Pakistani military offices I have visited countless times for interviews. Heavy wooden furniture gives the office a British colonial feel. Plaques on the wall list the previous commanders of his unit, the Tochi Scouts. The first names on the plaque are British and date back to their founding in the late 1800s.

The young captain is a Pashtun himself but attended Pakistan's military academy—the equivalent of West Point. I will later learn that being posted in the area is extraordinarily dangerous for young officers. Pro-Taliban members of the tribal militia have killed or "fragged" young officers in the past.

With each passing hour, I am more impressed by his bravery and kindness. From the moment I met him, I have had the sense that Captain Nadeem will protect us. As we continue talking, I feel myself come back to life.

Keith calls back from the embassy and again asks if I feel safe in our current location. "Yes, yes, I do feel safe," I say, looking at Captain Nadeem and smiling. "Captain Nadeem and the brave men on this base have been wonderful to us." Privately, I hope that I'm adding to enormous pressure being placed on the Pakistani military. I repeat that we are eager to get out of Miran Shah. Keith says arrangements are being made to fly us out of the town. I thank him again for all his help and hang up.

More sandwiches and tea arrive. Giddy, I tell Captain Nadeem that he and his men, in fact, are the true Muslims, not our kidnappers. I tell him about reading the Koran and seeing the difference between the ideals the prophet preached and how our captors acted.

To my delight, Captain Nadeem agrees. He gives me a book entitled *The Glorious Islam* by a Pakistani writer. He says that the Islam followed by the Taliban is a distortion of his faith. As he speaks, my heart races in my chest. The world—and the Pakistan—I remember is still here.

I make him add an inscription in the book. In neat blue ink, he writes:

From Capt. Nadeem
To David Rohde
20th June 2009
Tochi Scouts Miran Shah
North Waziristan Agency

I will cherish this book for the rest of my life. He reminds me of all my other Pashtun friends—most of them fearless journalists who work on both sides of the border. Churchill was wrong. All Pashtuns are not inherently violent. They are deeply disenfranchised. The biggest difference between the Pashtuns who kidnapped me and the Pashtuns who saved my life is education.

Captain Nadeem tells us his men are reporting activity by the Taliban in Miran Shah. They are searching for us, but Captain Nadeem reassures Tahir and me that we are safe. Again I think of Asad. A Pakistani helicopter is on its way, Captain Nadeem says. We will be flown out of Waziristan in a few hours.

GRATITUDE

Kristen, June 19–20, 2009

I begin to feel that after seven months of working together as a team that my interests are suddenly at odds with those of the newspaper. Susan Chira, the foreign editor, is extremely helpful in assisting us to make calls to officials. Yet it becomes increasingly obvious that she is also under pressure to deliver a story about David's kidnapping and escape. Periodically she turns to me and says, "At some point, we need to start thinking about what we are going to write, what the story will say."

I tell her there is no need for a story now. In fact, I think it would put David in harm's way to write about his escape before he has safely left the region. She presses the point all night. I feel the wall I've built around myself over recent months begin to collapse with the realization that our struggle is nearing an end. Unfortunately, this wall does not crumble quietly. Frazzled, I finally tell her to stop mentioning the story and demand that she leave.

I just want to take this in and focus on getting David out of Miran Shah. The last thing I want is publicity. Lee and I are on the phone all night. He gets us two seats on a flight to Dubai for this evening—it's now early Saturday morning—from John F. Kennedy International Airport in New York. It was sorted out long ago that if David was freed, we would meet him in Dubai. I recall my conversation with Sean Langan, the British journalist and former Taliban hostage who contacted me several months ago. Sean urged me not to rush off to Kabul or Pakistan upon David's release. He suggested I give David a moment to collect himself. "He may need the time to make himself presentable and get his bearings.

"Meeting in Kabul would be tense," he cautioned me, adding, "most likely it would consist of the two of you in the backseat of an armored vehicle, covered or with a third party urging you to keep your heads down for security reasons."

Sean told me that his own debriefing was tiresome after the Taliban freed him, but it also made him feel like a journalist again, giving him a chance to tell his story and in the process resume his professional bearing. He advised me to keep the return as low key as possible. His own return was rather public and proved challenging when he was immediately confronted with cameras on the tarmac in London.

When David McCraw leaves the apartment, at 3 A.M, we are still awaiting confirmation that David and Tahir have been helicoptered out of the scout base in Miran Shah. My mother retires to the couch. I head to the bedroom to pack for tonight's journey. I am overjoyed at the thought of seeing David again, and slightly overwhelmed that this time tomorrow I will be on a flight to Dubai. It is impossible to sleep.

I've said countless prayers over the last seven months. They have taken various forms—from spontaneous pleas to personal rituals and traditional recitations. For me, prayer is a conversation of sorts. A give-and-take. A question seeks to be met with an answer or to elicit greater understanding. Occasionally the response is unexpected and unpredictable, yet makes complete sense at a deeper level.

I've always believed David would return—even though I could never pinpoint when. My internal clock never had a sense that it would be anytime soon. The conversation seemed to be lagging as I felt my questions were always met with an unsettling reply: *Wait.*

Tonight my lesson in patience is approaching an end. My prayers—and those of friends and family—have been met with a surprising response.

As I lie awake, I utter two simple words: *Thank you.*

INTELLIGENCE

David, June 20, 2009

At roughly 9 A.M., Captain Nadeem brings Tahir and me to his personal quarters. We have now been on his base for roughly five or six hours. A television plays a Pakistani news station. Captain Nadeem changes the station to CNN International and I stare at the television transfixed. The studio and stage lighting have changed slightly since the last time I saw it seven months ago. Images of protests in Iran flash across the screen. We are back in the universe I have inhabited all my life. I am amazed that I have been so physically close to civilization but felt so far removed from it.

Captain Nadeem lets me take a shower. When I return to his room, a Pakistani military officer is present. He welcomes us, takes photos of us, and asks us a few questions. All of them focus on Baitullah Mehsud, the leader of the Pakistani Taliban who is considered an enemy of the state by the Pakistani military. He shows little interest in hearing about the Haqqanis, Abu Tayyeb, or the Afghan Taliban. He leaves after half an hour.

Tahir and I are taken to an ornate bedroom for VIP guests. We are given more food. Sitting alone for the first time, we recount our escape. Tahir worries that something could still go wrong. I tell him what I have repeated for months: I'm confident my family is doing everything they can to help us.

There is a knock on the door, and two beardless Pakistani men with neatly trimmed mustaches, crisply ironed salwar kameezes, and sunglasses greet us. They announce that they are from the ISI, Pakistan's premier military intelligence agency said to still tacitly support the Haqqani and Afghan Taliban. This is the moment we have feared.

At first, they are friendly. "We have been looking for you," one of them says as he opens a thin green file. Inside is a white sheet of paper that looks like a news story about me. A photo printed out from the Internet is on top of it. I ask him why they were unable to find us, given that we were so close to the base. They insist again that they have been looking for us. As the conversation continues, it becomes clear they, too, are more interested in getting information about Baitullah Mehsud than about the Haqqanis.

One of them pulls out a video camera and begins filming us without asking. I don't trust them and demand that they stop. The ISI operative continues filming. I stop answering questions and demand to see Captain Nadeem. The two men disappear and Captain Nadeem arrives and apologizes. He insists that a helicopter is on its way to evacuate us. It should arrive in two hours.

Tahir and I remain alone in the room. Two hours pass. No helicopter arrives. Captain Nadeem says the flight has been delayed by the weather. The two ISI officials sit outside in the courtyard. I am concerned about what is happening. There is still a chance we could be handed back. I ask Captain Nadeem if I can call Islamabad or New York. He says he has no more phone cards left.

At around 1 P.M., we hear two helicopters land, and the head of the ISI office in Peshawar walks into our room ten minutes later. He is urbane, educated, and intelligent. He orders tea and in five minutes of polite conversation gets more information out of me than the low-level ISI officers. After roughly twenty minutes, we are driven to the helipad, where two Vietnam-era Huey helicopters await us.

We get into one of the helicopters with the ISI chief, and the military pilot informs us that we are in the wrong helicopter. This one is loaded down with cargo. He asks us if we can switch to the other helicopter.

The ISI chief stares icily at the pilot.

"Move the gear," he says, refusing to budge. I have long heard of the arrogance of some ISI officers. Now I see it.

While we wait, I ask the ISI chief to help other hostages in the area. He is polite but sounds disdainful of them. He explains that he has just spent several months bargaining with the Taliban to buy back the body of Piotr Stanczak, the executed Polish geologist. He is courteous but clearly sees me and other foreign hostages as reckless people who are a burden to him. I know that in some respects he is right.

The helicopter starts its engine and I try to grab Tahir's hand but can't reach it. Instead, I place my hand on his shoulder. For months, we have heard airplanes and helicopters take off from an airstrip somewhere in Miran Shah. We have stood in yards and watched Pakistani helicopters lumber across the sky. Now we are finally in one of them.

As we take off, I wait for a rocket to be fired at the helicopter. Instead, we levitate smoothly through the air. I look down at Miran Shah and see a sprawling, dusty town like so many I have visited across Afghanistan and Pakistan. I look for the house where we were held captive but have no idea of its precise location. I think of Asad and pray he is alive.

We gain altitude and fly toward a nearby mountain ridge. Once we pass over it, we will be out of Taliban rocket range. As we approach the crest, I stare intently at the hilltops and scour them for gunmen. They are deserted. I squeeze Tahir's shoulder as we clear the ridge.

We are free.

FEED THE BEAST

Kristen, June 20–21, 2009

At 6 A.M. New York time, David McCraw calls to confirm that a helicopter is en route to Islamabad, the capital of Pakistan. From there, David and Tahir will be escorted to a plane for transport to the American military base at Bagram and then on to Dubai.

It is now Saturday morning. I continue to prepare for my trip as I await further word from David that he is safe. Bill Keller phones to tell me matter-of-factly that the paper will run a short piece on David.

The *Times* has kept David's case quiet until now, but it is a news institution, and this is big news. They will need to report it. Calm and straightforward, he asks if I will give them a quote. I tell him I am grateful for all that he and the newspaper have done, but do not want to give any information until David is safely out of Pakistan and has left the region.

"I don't think I should talk to you now," I caution, knowing my emotions are a little raw. "You'll get a really sassy quote. Let's wait until David is safe." I do say that I am comfortable conveying my gratitude to government officials, the newspaper, and David's colleagues, but that is all I can provide at this time.

He understands, but says he wants to talk to David when I hear from him again. After keeping this story silent for so long, they'd like to "feed the beast."

While I respect Bill—and do not want to pick a fight with my husband's boss—I feel an intense need to hold my ground and protect David's privacy.

"Bill, I think David would ask that you starve the beast and let it die," I respond. (I'm going to be amazed if my husband still has a job when he returns home, given that I have spoken so bluntly. But I do not care.)

"Okay, but do you have any updates?" he asks casually.

"I don't know, Bill," I say exasperated. "They just walked over the wall of the compound."

The sass comes back to bite me. In a story about David's escape on the paper's Web site that afternoon, a quote appears from me: "They just walked over the wall of the compound."

Moments later, someone from a local news outlet shows up at the front desk of my apartment building. I alert the doorman to say that I am out. I also answer one or two calls on my home phone from reporters. I pretend to be a relative.

"Kristen? I'm sorry, she's out of town. Can I take a message or be of assistance? She does not plan to grant any personal interviews."

Being married to a reporter, I shouldn't be surprised at how aggressive and persistent television reporters are in their requests. Word has spread rapidly in the news community. A certain morning talk show calls the apartment three times, then moves on to contacting Lee, then my parents, David's mom, and even David's teenage nephew. The evening news has a story about David's escape. They use old photos because we have refused to provide current images of David, knowing that he would not want to be the story. It's somewhat comical to see him looking thirteen years younger, holding the four-year-old nephew who is now a young man.

Another quote from me in the *Times* is used as an innocuous sound bite on television news. "'We've been married nine months,' his wife said, 'and David's been in captivity for seven of them.'"

RETURN

David, June 20–21, 2009

At first, the sensation of hurtling through the air in a Pakistani military helicopter is delightful. I stare at the controls of this refurbished American-built Huey helicopter. For years, Pakistani military officials have seen this kind of secondhand matériel as a slight by the U.S. government. After my seven months in Waziristan, to me the helicopter is an astounding feat of engineering.

As the flight drags on, I find myself growing nervous for no logical reason. We are headed to the Pakistani capital of Islamabad, according to the ISI official, but the flight continues for more than thirty minutes. As I study the landscape outside, my thoughts are irrational. Part of me fears the helicopter will crash.

The terrain flattens beneath us and I realize we are moving from the mountains of northwestern Pakistan toward the plains of central Pakistan. The flight drags on for forty-five minutes. Finally, the four towering white minarets of the Faisal Mosque—an enormous house of worship funded by King Faisal of Saudi Arabia in the 1980s—emerge in the distance. It is one of Islamabad's landmarks. With a purported capacity of 100,000 worshipers, it was constructed in the 1980s when Saudi Arabia and the United States spread hard-line Wahhabi Islam to Pakistan. Today, it is a beacon of hope to me.

We fly over the city and approach Islamabad International Airport. As passenger jets land, I long for us to do the same. We circle for a few more minutes. Finally, our two helicopters fly low over the runway and touch down near the main passenger terminal. Our helicopter's landing gear gently touches the ground and relief washes over me. The surreal twelve-hour period that began when I first got up and crept to the bathroom as our guards slept is ending.

I step out of the helicopter, get down on my knees, and kiss the tarmac.

Brought inside a VIP lounge by the ISI officials, we are told to wait as the Pakistanis coordinate our handover to American officials. I speak with Tahir and urge him to remain in Islamabad and travel with me directly to the United States. If he returns to his house in Kabul, I believe Abu Tayyeb's men will kill him.

For months, Abu Tayyeb and the guards have repeatedly told Tahir and Asad that I would abandon them and leave them at the mercy of American, Afghan, or Pakistani intelligence officials when our captivity ended. As we wait, I am absolutely determined to protect Tahir and prove Abu Tayyeb wrong.

I ask the ISI station chief from Peshawar to allow Tahir to call his family, and he agrees. Tahir's father tells him to travel where he pleases. After fifteen more minutes, we are driven to the military side of the airfield by the ISI in brand new sport utility vehicles. I have visited the area before. In 2005, I boarded helicopters here that ferried supplies to victims of a massive earthquake in northern Pakistan.

We enter the main terminal and several minutes later, the ISI walks us out onto the tarmac. I see a group of Americans staring at us. Anne Patterson, the American ambassador to Pakistan, steps forward and shakes my hand.

"I'm sorry for the problems I've caused you," I shout over the din of nearby aircraft engines.

"Welcome," she says.

Patterson is polite but icy. I realize that many people are probably furious with me for foolishly pursuing a Taliban interview. I turn and thank the ISI officials again for flying us to safety. I worry they will suddenly try to detain Tahir. Instead, they wave good-bye and quickly walk away.

Patterson motions for us to walk farther onto the tarmac and I grow confused. I assumed we would be driven to the U.S. Embassy, where I planned to profusely thank Keith, the security officer who had spoken with me by phone from the Pakistani base in Miran Shah.

Instead, we walk toward a C-130 military cargo plane with its engines running. As we approach the aircraft, I see that the plane's crewmen are Americans. After seven months in Waziristan, the clean-shaven Americans with their buglike flight helmets look like alien creatures. I shake Patterson's hand and she quickly says good-bye. Tahir and I follow an American woman onto the back of the plane. She tells me that we are flying to the U.S. military base in Bagram, Afghanistan, just north of Kabul. This flight, like the last, seems to drag on. Over the din of the engines, I shout to Tahir that he should not go to Kabul to see his family. He agrees that it is too dangerous. I make small talk with the woman escorting us but we can barely hear each other. I want the flight to end.

Our landing is flawless. I thank the crew and we step onto Bagram Air Base. In 2001, I visited the base when it was the front line between Taliban and Northern Alliance forces. Today, it hums with American attack helicopters, transport planes, and troops.

We are brought to the base hospital and examined by American military doctors. Band-Aids are placed on the cuts on my hands from the rope. An X-ray shows that Tahir's ankle is sprained but not broken. Still wearing a six-inch-long beard and my baggy local clothes, I notice that the soldiers are staring at me.

Karl Eikenberry, the American ambassador to Afghanistan, and his wife, Ching, greet me warmly. Three months before the kidnapping I spent a weekend at their home in Brussels interviewing Eikenberry for my book. They hug me excitedly and tell me they met Kristen before arriving in Afghanistan. They rave about her strength and composure. I feel enormous pride.

Tahir calls his family and they now demand to see him. Saying they don't believe he is free, his family tells him to come to Kabul immediately. The sun is beginning to set and there is no easy way to transport him there. I beg him to wait and at least spend the night on the base.

An embassy official tells me that Kristen is trying to reach me and hands me a mobile phone. I step outside the hospital and speak to her alone for the first time in seven months. I tell her I love her, apologize again, and begin saying things I have thought about for months. "Your god saved me," I say, and explain how praying each day helped me.

She laughs and says she hoped that I might find some type of spiritual connection during captivity. As she describes her efforts, I am more and more touched. She has been hurled into a chaotic morass and handled it skillfully. She urges me to fly out of Afghanistan immediately. The sun is setting and a flight the newspaper has arranged must depart during daylight under military rules.

Determined not to abandon Tahir as Abu Tayyeb predicted, I tell her that I want to spend the night in Bagram. I want to try to convince Tahir to leave with me for Dubai. Showing immense patience, she agrees.

I walk back into the hospital and I'm told that Richard Holbrooke wants to speak with me. A sense of shame washes over me as I dial his number. "I apologize" are the first words I say to him.

Holbrooke is gracious. "God, it is so good to hear your voice," he says. He too praises Kristen and tells me I am an extraordinarily lucky man. I agree wholeheartedly.

Tahir agrees to stay on the base that night and we are given adjoining bedrooms in a prefabricated living container. We turn on the desktop computer that is for guests and Tahir checks his e-mail. I check for a story about our escape that Kristen said is on the *Times* site. We have returned to the outside world with astonishing speed.

"Times Reporter Escapes Taliban After Seven Months" reads the headline. At first, I find it hard to believe that the story is referring to me, both in terms of the captivity and the escape. As I read the piece, I am alarmed to see it states that Asad is still in captivity. It also mistakenly says that Tahir and I climbed over the wall and ran into a Pakistani militia member who led us to the base. My exaggerated praise of Captain Nadeem and his men during my first phone calls to New York was misunderstood.

Fearing that too much publicity will endanger Asad, I e-mail the foreign editor, Susan Chira, and ask her to withhold his name. I also ask her to cut the incorrect reference to a militia member guiding us to the base. After welcoming me home, she happily agrees.

Tahir goes to sleep, and I venture outside to call members of my family. I tell my mother how sorry I am to have put her through this. She cries, tells me how elated she is to hear my voice, and says she is revoking my passport. My father is calm and tells me to look forward in life. I thank my stepparents, Andrea and George, for helping my parents survive this.

When I thank my brother Lee and his wife, Christie, for his seven months of effort, he says he knew I would do the same thing for him. My sister, Laura, and brother-in-law, Chris, had their children pray for me while I was in captivity. They say they are simply overjoyed that I am safe. My brother Erik says he missed our daily calls and friendship. He remains calm and supportive of me, as always.

I apologize in each conversation and promise that my days as a war correspondent are over. I describe how much I've missed them and tell them I want to spend more time with them. I try to explain how eager I am to come home. After the phone calls, I am astonished by everything Kristen, Lee, my family, my editors, and friends have done to help us. I am also deeply touched by what my parents, Laura, and Erik have endured. All of them stepped back and allowed Kristen and Lee to make major decisions. While I was in captivity, they had the strength to let go. In some ways, that is more arduous and courageous than insisting on being involved.

Exhausted after being awake for twenty-four hours, I try to go to sleep. The black duffel bag I left in the Kabul bureau on the day we left for the interview has been brought to Bagram for me. For the first time in seven months, I put on a T-shirt.

I climb into bed and I fear closing my eyes. I'm afraid I will wake up in Miran Shah and this all will have been a fantasy. As I try to go to sleep, an alarm sounds outside and a voice on a loudspeaker announces that all personnel should go to bomb shelters. A Taliban rocket attack is under way. I make my way outside but Tahir remains inside.

I crouch inside a concrete bomb shelter with a handful of American soldiers and embassy personnel. The soldiers wear reflective vests that are designed to prevent them from being hit by vehicles when they walk around the base at night. The shelter and vests seem odd to me. They embody a focus on safety and preventing death—that did not exist in Waziristan.

The all-clear sounds over the loudspeaker. I return to my bed and lie down. Again I fear closing my eyes and waking up beside Timor Shah and our other guards. I awake early the next morning and feel euphoric. We have, in fact, escaped.

I plug in my BlackBerry and charge the battery. I turn on the phone and Kristen's face stares at me from the small screen. It is the first time I have seen her image in seven months. She is beautiful.

Three hours later, I say good-bye to Tahir. He insists on going to Kabul to see his family. They continue to not believe that he is actually free. Embassy officials have promised me he will not be detained. We hug good-bye, and for the first time in months, we are not in the same house together. I am delighted he will finally see his family, but miss him.

My plane takes off for Dubai and I stare out the window. For months, I looked up at the planes flying overhead as I paced back and forth in Waziristan and dreamed of being on one of them. As I fly over southern Afghanistan, I look down and wonder if "Little America" is somewhere in the desert below. I know I will probably never be able to return there.

I look to the east, think of Asad, and break into tears. He is dead or remains in captivity.

REUNION

Kristen, June 21, 2009

round noon, I speak to my husband again briefly. The Pakistani military has flown David and Tahir to Islamabad, where they were picked up by an American military plane and taken to the sprawling base in Bagram, just north of Kabul. He refuses to leave Bagram until Tahir is safely reunited with his family. He does not want to leave Tahir in the lurch. He feels that the Haqqanis will target Tahir if he returns to his unguarded home in Kabul.

I am slightly hurt by his overwhelming desire to stay put until the situation is resolved, but I understand his concern. I know David will do everything possible to ensure that Tahir, who injured his foot during their escape, receives good care and is treated well. I also realize this is a confusing time and that perhaps David needs a moment to adjust.

The last few months have taught me to be patient. And I know no one suffered more from David's decision to go to the interview than David himself. If there is a reason to his surviving misfortune—lessons learned, wisdom gained—he has been given the chance to express it.

A few hours later, David calls back and says something unexpected. "Your God helped me through this experience," David says. I think it is somewhat funny that he would frame God in this way, as belonging to someone else—or anyone for that matter. But I assume he means that prayer and belief in a beneficent higher force has helped him survive this ordeal. I am relieved. My one wish was that David would find some sort of inner peace during captivity, a personal expression of faith. Clearly he has.

I tell him to take the time he needs—but not too long! I will be on the next flight to Dubai, which gives him about twenty-four hours to leave Bagram. Arrangements have been made to transport him to Dubai and he promises to be at the airport to greet me.

In the early evening, David McCraw stops by with a bottle of champagne. The label has an image of a windmill. "So you can stop chasing windmills," McCraw says, referring to Don Quixote. I save the bottle, vowing to share it with McCraw, Lee, and David when the four of us are together.

On the way to the airport, Lee and I listen to our voice mail, now overflowing with messages of relief and happiness from family, friends, and co-workers. Arthur Sulzberger Jr., the paper's publisher, left a message expressing the paper's joy at David's freedom. Throughout our ordeal, he's been kind and supportive—often inviting me into his office for coffee and pep talks during my frequent visits to the *Times* building. Christine Kay, David's editor, calls and says, "You made all the right decisions. He is alive. You kept him alive." Tearful, elated words pour in.

I also speak to David's sister, Laura, who is ecstatic about this unexpected turn of events. "I am so happy to think of him back home in your arms where he belongs," she says. She, too, has spoken with David and gotten more details of his escape, which she relays to me. From David and Tahir's bold, impromptu decision to flee and their physical discrepancies—David is thin, Tahir is stocky—we both agree that the whole thing is amazing and, at this safe distance, amusing—Butch Cassidy and the Sundance Kid meet Abbott and Costello.

The flight to Dubai is long—thirteen hours. Lee and I spend a good deal of it watching movies. I am too anxious to sleep. We are both rendered speechless by our long ordeal finally having reached a happy and unexpected ending.

Toward the end of the flight, I duck into the ladies room to change. This is my second trip to Dubai. The first was with David more than a year ago. I was careful to keep my neck and legs covered at all times, so as not to stand out as a foreigner. Despite its modern trappings, Dubai is still conservative. But this time around, I think it would be tragic to greet my husband after seven months of captivity wearing sweatpants and a baggy sweater. I change into a modest but flattering dress and heels.

As we descend into Dubai, I glance out the window. Dubai is eight hours ahead of New York. We have lost a day in transit, as if propelled forward in time chronologically and emotionally. The desert below begins to glow in the last vestiges of sunlight. I think about what I want to do when David and I are reunited. We traveled a lot throughout our courtship, and spent our honeymoon in France and India. Friends have assumed that we will now want to run off somewhere together. The truth is, the last thing I want to do now is jet to an exotic location. I simply want us to be at home together, enjoying the daily things—drinking coffee in the morning, grocery shopping, going to the dry cleaner, riding the subway—that give life continuity, consistency. I realize I have made many mistakes over the last few months. We probably both have. But, ultimately, we have each survived. David is alive. That is all that matters. We must have done something right.

The Dubai airport is massive and modern with touches of Middle Eastern detailing. Female customs agents greet us at passport control in full headscarves, their eyeliner exquisitely applied in a striking contrast to the modesty of their dress. Large, modern white columns flank the sides of the baggage terminal. I am slightly tipsy from exhaustion and apprehension as we proceed to the exit.

I spot David waiting with several men and carrying flowers. My first thought is that he looks unchanged. He is the David I remember, only slightly thinner and paler. His hair is well groomed, trimmed. His face is clean-shaven. He is wearing the same gray V-neck sweater and brown khakis he wore on our honeymoon and on the day he departed New York for Kabul in late October.

He runs toward me.

EPILOGUE

David

F ive weeks after our escape, Asad crossed from Pakistan into Afghanistan, called his family, and said he was free. Ten days later, I spoke with him by phone.

Asad said the guards had slept until predawn prayers on the night Tahir and I escaped. At first, they thought we were in the bathroom. Then they realized we were gone.

Asad said Timor Shah ordered the other guards to hunt for us. "If you find Tahir," he said, "shoot him." When Badruddin Haqqani learned we had escaped, Asad said, he "lost consciousness."

All three of our guards were jailed and questioned about our escape, according to Asad. The guards called Abu Tayyeb for help but he said he would face problems in Miran Shah and declined to return. Two of the guards were released but Timor Shah was taken to a Taliban jail in South Waziristan for punishment.

Asad said Taliban commanders accused him of knowing about our escape plan. They chained and held him underground for seventeen days. For three of those days, he was beaten, he said. Removed from the underground jail, Asad was then used as a forced laborer on construction projects.

In mid-July, Asad's family, with the support of *The New York Times,* sent a tribal delegation to press his captors to release him. On July 27, Asad was building a wall and the guard watching him said he was going to make some tea. Left alone, Asad fled, found a taxi, and took it to the Afghan border.

In our phone call, Asad denied cooperating with the guards during our captivity and said he had carried a gun because the Taliban had ordered him to do so. In the end, I believe that Asad played along with the Taliban to survive.

After returning home, I learned of the wide array of people who had worked for our release. Among them were Afghans and Pakistanis who offered to try to obtain information about our whereabouts or to gain our release. Some of them volunteered; others asked for money. Two of the Afghan men died in ambushes. A man carrying a message to our captors was killed in Pakistan in January, and an Afghan died in an ambush in Afghanistan in April.

Whether those attacks were definitely related to work on our case remains unclear. Determining the truth of events in the border areas of Afghanistan and Pakistan is notoriously difficult. Killings are rarely investigated. I believe the only responsible thing to do, though, is to assume that the two deaths were related to our case. I will always deeply regret going to the interview. I will always be deeply grateful to everyone who tried to help us.

After our escape, rumors surfaced that a ransom had been paid. Neither my family nor *The New York Times*, nor any contractors who worked on our case paid a ransom. American government officials maintained their long-standing policy of not negotiating with kidnappers, freeing no prisoners and paying no ransom. Pakistani and Afghan officials said they also released no captives and provided no money.

Reports also circulated that our guards had been bribed. Security consultants who worked on our case said paid Afghan informants reported giving cash to Taliban members who said they knew our whereabouts. The paid Afghan informants provided the detailed reports on our location that Kristen received from March through June, including the names of guards they said were bribed.

None of the available information supports claims from the Afghan informants that they successfully bribed our guards. The locations where they reported us being held were wrong during three of the four months when they purportedly tracked us. In June, they correctly reported we were in Miran Shah but said we were being frequently moved around the town in a black Suzuki jeep, which was false.

The names the Afghan informants gave for our guards were wrong and no guards helped us before or during our escape. On the night of our escape, the contractors expressed absolute surprise that we had gotten away and did not suggest to my family or newspaper that their informants had any involvement. After I returned home, American government officials said their sources were never able to pinpoint the exact house where we were being held or identify our guards. They backed the statement a senior American military official made to Kristen in April that "anyone who tells you they know exactly where your husband is is lying."

Tahir and I do not believe our guards were successfully bribed. We believe the local informants hired by the private contractors did what people who inhabit the Afghanistan-Pakistan border area have done for centuries: When being paid for information, they told the foreigners what they wanted to hear.

Nine months after our escape, two of my colleagues at *The New York Times* reported that two of the contractors who worked on our case participated in a secret Defense Department project. Under the program, Pentagon officials reportedly hired private contractors to help track and kill militants. It is generally considered illegal for the military to hire contractors to act as covert spies. As a result, Defense Department officials launched an investigation.

Michael Taylor of AISC and Dewey Clarridge were subcontractors in the program, which was run by a civilian air force official named Michael D. Furlong. In the story, Taylor denied any wrongdoing and said they gathered information about possible threats to American forces but were not specifically hired to provide information to kill insurgents.

After the story appeared, Taylor and Clarridge told me they worked for Furlong from November 2009 until the contract expired in May 2010. They said they did not work for the program while I was in captivity.

My family and newspaper had no contact with Furlong and were unaware of Taylor and Clarridge's work for him until my two colleagues learned of it. Furlong played no role in our case. When this book went to press in September 2010, military officials were still investigating the program.

My suspicions regarding the Pakistani military's relationship with the Haqqanis proved to be true. Some American officials told colleagues at the *Times* that the ISI provides money, supplies, and strategic planning to the Haqqanis. Other administration officials were more conservative and said there was no definitive proof of direct Pakistani military assistance to the Haqqanis.

But nearly every American official interviewed agreed that the ISI at the least turns a blind eye to the Haqqanis' activities in North Waziristan. Pakistani officials told my colleagues and me that the contacts were part of the Pakistani military's long-standing strategy to maintain influence in Afghanistan to prevent India from gaining a foothold.

After our escape, the Pakistani army mounted major offensives in South Waziristan. To their credit, the town of Makeen—where the American drone strike occurred on March 25, 2009, just outside our house—was retaken by the Pakistani army. But Pakistani officials rebuffed a request from United States Defense Secretary Robert Gates in January 2010 that Pakistan launch a military offensive in North Waziristan, the stronghold of the Haqqanis. Pakistani officials said they did not have enough troops to carry out the operation, even though they later carried out a military exercise involving 50,000 Pakistani troops posted on the border with India.

When this book went to press, the Haqqanis continued to use North Waziristan to train suicide bombers and explosives makers who kill Afghan and American forces. From its base in the tribal areas, the Haqqani network has carried out a series of high-profile attacks in Kabul, including one in February that killed nine Indian development workers. To me, the attack appears to be an effort by the Haqqanis to please the Pakistani military. At the same time, Pakistani Taliban are using North Waziristan to carry out attacks in Pakistan and the United

States. Faisal Shahzad, the failed May 2010 Times Square bomber, was trained in North Waziristan.

Pakistani military officials refuse to confront the Afghan Taliban inside their borders. They continue to differentiate between Afghan and Pakistani Taliban groups and insist Afghan Taliban are proxies they can use to counter Indian influence in Afghanistan. My own experience in captivity shows that the Pakistani differentiation between the two Talibans is false. The Afghan and Pakistani Taliban clearly work together, strengthening and supporting each other in myriad ways.

The Haqqanis and other hard-line Afghan Taliban will not agree to a negotiated peace settlement unless the surge of 30,000 additional American troops in Afghanistan coincides with a serious Pakistani military drive to pressure the Haqqanis on the Pakistani side of the border. The Haqqanis, as they have done for decades, will continue to curry support from multiple sides, playing along with both Al Qaeda and the Pakistani army. They may tell the Pakistani military they are willing to break with Al Qaeda and the Pakistani Taliban, but use the time that buys them to build up all three groups' strength in North Waziristan. They may even agree to expel Al Qaeda and claim they have done so but continue to harbor them in their territory as they have for decades.

Pakistan's relations with the Haqqanis is the focus of debate in the Pakistani government, according to a senior Pakistani official. Some Pakistani civilian officials argue that they should be confronted militarily. While many army officials and Pakistani nationalists argue they can be moderated and relied upon.

"It's an internal Pakistani policy debate," said a Pakistani official who supports confronting the Haqqanis. "There are people in Pakistan who think that the Haqqanis are not reliable. We think that when the chips are down the Haqqanis will side with Al Qaeda."

What happens next with the Haqqanis and other Afghan Taliban groups will be telling. If the Pakistani military can convince them to reconcile with Karzai's government, it will give the lie to years of Pakistani military protestations and prove that the Pakistani army does control the Afghan Taliban. It will show that since 2001 Pakistan's military—even as it received $1 billion a year in American aid—backed the Afghan Taliban as they killed 1,200 American soldiers.

If they show that they do, in fact, control the Haqqanis and the Afghan Taliban, the Pakistani military will have cynically won the war in Afghanistan. They will have persuaded Washington to give them billions in aid while the ISI quietly supported militants the United States was trying to eradicate. The Pakistani military will have used those funds to bolster their own strength in Pakistan, frustrating the growth of civilian institutions there and thwarting Indian attempts to gain influence in Afghanistan.

Another more frightening possibility is that the Haqqani sons and other young Afghan Taliban will prove immune to Pakistani influence. The Afghan Taliban will rebel against the Pakistani military, as the Pakistani Taliban have already done. Pakistan's generals will find that they do not have the control over the Haqqanis and other Afghan Taliban that they believe. A new generation of Afghan Taliban could emerge, one unwaveringly committed to the jihad being waged with their Arab, Uzbek, and Pakistani allies.

As in the past, India and Russia will back northern militias, Pakistan will back the Taliban, and regional rivalries will beset Afghanistan again. A civil war far bloodier than the one of the 1990s will emerge in Afghanistan. A hasty withdrawal by defeated American forces and the chaos that ensues will be a triumph for Al Qaeda, the Afghan and Pakistani Taliban, and jihadists worldwide.

The Taliban continue to abduct journalists. Three months after our escape, on September 6, 2009, fighters in the Afghan province of Kunduz kidnapped a *New York Times* correspondent, Stephen Farrell, and the Afghan journalist working with him, Sultan Munadi, as they reported on a NATO bombing that had killed dozens of civilians. Four days later, a raid by British commandos freed Stephen, but Sultan was killed, along with a British soldier and an Afghan woman. Sultan was the father of two and home on a break from studying public policy in Germany. After receiving his degree, he planned to return to Afghanistan and work to stabilize his country. He was also a wonderful colleague and friend.

British officials defended the military raid that killed Sultan. They said they had received intelligence that the Taliban planned to move Steve and Sultan to Pakistan's tribal areas. Afghan journalists dismissed the British claim and accused *The New York Times* of approving the raid instead of taking more time to negotiate. In truth, the British government carried out the raid without asking Farrell's family or *The New York Times* for permission. While the American military seeks family approval to intervene in such cases, the British military does not.

The discrepancy reflects the far broader problem of the lack of a coordinated international response to kidnapping by Islamic militants. The American and British governments refuse to pay ransoms, but the French, Italian, Dutch, and Korean governments reportedly pay them.

Around the world, Islamic militants are increasingly using kidnapping as a weapon of war. In Iraq, an estimated two hundred foreigners and thousands of Iraqis have been kidnapped since the American-led invasion of 2003. Some of the kidnappers were insurgents. Some were criminals. Many were kept quiet. At least forty hostages are believed to have been killed.

Islamic militants in Somalia, the Philippines, Yemen, and North Africa have adopted the tactic as well. Three weeks before our escape, a North African military group that calls itself Al Qaeda in the Islamic Maghreb executed Edwin Dyer, a British tourist it kidnapped in Mali. The group released other foreign hostages it had abducted after their governments reportedly paid ransoms or members of the group were released from local prisons. Dyer was executed after British officials refused to release Abu Qatada, a hard-line preacher with close ties to Al Qaeda imprisoned in the U.K. In July 2010, the group killed a seventy-eight-year-old French hostage, Michel Germaneau, after a rescue attempt by the French military failed.

Today, dozens of people remain captives in the tribal areas of Pakistan, most of them wealthy Pakistanis. Tahir and I were extraordinarily fortunate to have escaped. Countless others in the tribal areas have not been—and will not be—so lucky.

American officials say a unified international approach will not stop Islamist militants from kidnapping, but could make it less lucrative and appealing over time. So far, attempts to broker an agreement among industrialized nations have failed. The lack of a coordinated approach to kidnapping makes it easier for families to be thrust into the murky world that we inhabited. Governments will say they are working closely with local officials to free hostages, but often be unable to do so. Contractors will continue to make promises that may be beyond their reach. And militants will continue to trade lives for ransom and executions for publicity.

Six years after I first journeyed to "Little America," southern Afghanistan is the epicenter of what is now called "Obama's war." Over 20,000 American troops and 10,000 British soldiers battle the Taliban in Helmand, where twice as many American, British, and NATO troops have died as in any other Afghan province. As has occurred throughout the war, American troops are able to drive the Taliban out of districts but Afghan government troops and police are too weak to hold the areas on their own.

In phone conversations in July 2010, Fowzea and Andiwal—the two moderate Afghans I had followed in Helmand—apologized to me for the kidnapping. They also called on the Obama administration to not hurriedly withdraw American soldiers from Afghanistan when the eighteen-month deadline Obama set for his troop surge arrives in July 2011.

With the arrival of more foreign troops, security in Lashkar Gah improved in 2010, according to Fowzea. She reopened the women's center she shuttered after the killing of her driver in 2006 and expanded programs for women. The amount of poppy produced in Helmand dropped by one-third in 2009, fueled both by a flooded market and a crackdown on growers. And the number of Americans assigned to training the Afghan army and police is beginning to finally reach the levels American commanders have requested for years. Some Taliban commanders in southern Afghanistan have reportedly expressed interest in a political settlement of the conflict. Both the Afghan government and the Pakistani military are now trying to broker peace agreements with the Afghan Taliban.

Enormous challenges remain. Fowzea's department and the provincial government in Helmand are wholly dependent on American funding. In February 2010, more than 5,000 American marines and soldiers retook Marja—the district that Andiwal lost his job over—but the Taliban contine to mount ambushes and few Afghans are willing to join the area's new police force. Eight years after the fall of the Taliban, the Afghan central government remains a shell. Fairly or unfairly, it is widely viewed as ineffective and corrupt. At the same time, distrust of the United States is increasing among Afghans. Tahir says the United States was initially welcomed by Afghans in 2001 but did too little in the early years and has now lost the trust of the population. He believes all foreign troops should withdraw from Afghanistan and Afghans should be allowed to choose their own future without foreign meddling.

Clearly, a long-term American troop presence in Afghanistan is not sustainable. As Afghan history shows, foreign armies easily win control of the country's cities. Over time, though, the population rebels against the foreign military. In the years ahead, the number of Afghans who see the United States as an occupier is only likely to grow. At the same time, simply walking away from Afghanistan and Pakistan and hoping for the best is not an option in an increasingly interconnected world. The Times Square bombing case showed that. Based on my experience in the tribal areas, a sweeping Taliban victory in Afghanistan would embolden hard-line militants who hope to forcibly impose sharia law across the Islamic world. Their belief that they can defeat Westerners who fear death and are unwilling to endure sacrifice will be reaffirmed. It will also send a signal to moderate Muslims that the United States will not stand by them. No clear answer has emerged to the question I posed in 2001: how can religious extremism be countered? But that does not mean the effort should be abandoned or the danger of what I saw in the tribal areas should be downplayed. It took decades to create the vexing problems there, and it will likely take decades to resolve them.

American, Afghan, and Pakistani analysts say the United States should pursue a political solution to the conflict in Afghanistan while placing as much pressure on the Pakistani military and the Taliban as possible. If the Pakistani army fails to aggressively attack the Afghan Taliban—or deliver a reasonable peace settlement with them—the United States should cut its military aid to Pakistan, they contend. As long as the Taliban continue to enjoy a safe haven in Pakistan, there is no chance of defeating them in Afghanistan.

The American troop surge should be allowed to play out for its full eighteen months, analysts argue. American troop levels should then be gradually reduced and the primary American military mission shifted to training Afghan security forces. At the same time, Karzai, the Pakistani military, and other third parties should be allowed to carry out talks with the Afghan Taliban.

Public opinion polls in both Afghanistan and Pakistan show negative views of the United States but they also show that the vast majority of Afghans and Pakistanis disapprove of the Taliban. For years, Afghans and Pakistanis have told me they want a third way—an effective, stable, and noncorrupt government that is not dictated to them by Western secularists or Arab militants. Security remains the single most important issue to Afghans and Pakistanis, followed by corruption. The competition for which system can deliver stability, jobs, and an accountable government continues. The United States should focus on helping train a strong, multiethnic national army in Afghanistan, according to analysts. It should try to aid the creation of strong political parties in Pakistan. The long-term solution in Afghanistan and Pakistan is strong, balanced national institutions, not a long-term foreign troop presence.

In the end, American success or failure will hinge on the Pashtuns. The Pashtuns dominate the area from southern Afghanistan to northwestern Pakistan that is the focus of Obama's surge. After thirty years of conflict, the Pashtuns are arguably more disenfranchised, fragmented, and religiously conservative than ever in their history. Pashtun tribal networks remain influential but any young Pashtun with weapons, cash, or a false claim of religious authority can seize control of a tribe from weakened traditional elders. Halting the Pakistani military's backing of radical Pashtuns in the tribal areas, brokering political agreements with Pashtun insurgents in southern Afghanistan, and improving education in both countries will gradually strengthen Pashtun moderates. Pakistan must regain control of the tribal areas and enact long-promised reforms that introduce an independent court system, reduce the power of unelected political agents, and allow political parties to campaign there.

Pashtuns say they want stability, security, and an end to corruption, but on their own terms. Outsiders—whether they are American soldiers, Pakistani intelligence operatives, or foreign militants—will never be able to impose stability on the Pashtun belt. Only the Pashtuns can. I remain convinced that Captain Nadeem is the true Pashtun, not our Taliban captors. And in the wake of this experience, I believe more than ever that patiently engaging, empowering, and revitalizing moderates is the way forward in an age of extremism.

I am still in touch with Captain Nadeem. When I spoke with him once by phone, in the spring of 2010, I asked him why he was so kind to me that night. His answer was immediate.

"It's only natural," he said. "One man can see another man's suffering."

One of the most vivid memories I have of our time in captivity was seeing religion at its best and at its worst. On one level, religion was a nefarious force that gave our captors their rationales for abducting us, terrorizing our families, and trying to extort staggering amounts of money from them. I also saw religious faith as a positive force that gave Tahir the strength to survive and Captain Nadeem the compassion to see us as human beings. Personally, praying proved invaluable in keeping me centered, hopeful, and rational.

I do not believe that religion itself is inherently divisive or destructive. For me, religion in moderation brings out our better angels. If I follow a faith at this point, it is the Unitarian Universalism that my father introduced me to as an adult. Religion in extremes, though, frequently brings out our worst. It plays upon what is perhaps our gravest flaws as humans: our ability to lose our compassion, to be dogmatic, to think our ideological beliefs are right and others' are wrong, to turn members of different groups into a dangerous other.

I have reported on or heard of members of every major faith committing tremendous acts of kindness as well as horrible atrocities. In general while covering religious conflicts, I find that people who did unspeakable things to their fellow man were not sadists who knew they were doing wrong and perversely enjoyed it. Instead, they were people who believed they were acting in self-defense and saving their faith, group, and culture from attack. They believed they were acting righteously, just as my captors did.

My feelings toward my captors are fluid. Most of the time, I rarely think of them. At times, I despise them again for what they did to our families and us. I, of course, am guilty of the sins of selfishness, recklessness, and ambition. Tahir and I spent hours in captivity talking about how we had wronged our families by going to the interview and been punished for it. During my flight back to the United States, I wrote down three things as Kristen sat next to me. "This world is fleeting," "I had my chance," and "Now everyone else first." Since I have returned home I try harder to live by those principles. Sometimes I succeed. Often, I do not.

For me, what I witnessed in Miran Shah is still vastly worse than the many mistakes of the American effort in Afghanistan and Pakistan since 2001. There, an unrelenting ideology made nonbelievers subhuman. It brainwashed young men into carrying out depraved acts of brutality. It disparaged human life instead of cherishing it. I believe that no God would support such hatred. Many Afghans and Pakistanis agree with me. They say the ideology that exists in the tribal areas must be challenged militarily, politically, economically, and religiously. I agree. I believe that type of bigotry is something we all must fight.

In the wake of this experience, I have an even deeper respect for people who are religious, but also believe that they have more in common with other faiths than they realize. And I passionately believe that if you are skeptical of organized religion—as I remain—you can still have ideals.

Professionally, my days as a war correspondent are over. I intend to make my calling the continued pursuit of truth through journalism, public service, and teaching. Personally, I recommit myself to supporting my wife and family. My family, friends, and editors never gave up on me.

Most of all, Kristen never gave up on me. For that, I owe her the world.

Kristen

During the weeks after David's return, we compared notes. Few of the reports we received and few of the rumors we heard from local sources matched his actual experience. David maintains that if he had not escaped, he would probably still be in Miran Shah. We may have made some mistakes on our end—trusting some reports, overlooking others, perhaps inadvertently raising David's value by reaching out to American and foreign officials. But neither David nor I felt the kidnappers were ready to negotiate. I think it's likely that their demands would have continued to shift and that they would hold David indefinitely. This is not to belittle the efforts of our security teams, government officials, and advisers. Many of the people who worked on our case devoted long hours and expertise, often with personal sacrifices, to help bring some semblance of clarity or conclusion to our case. We appreciate their efforts. And thank them for never giving up.

Over time I came to learn that kidnapping is a global phenomenon with entrepreneurs on all sides. Its aim is to terrorize people and to exploit suffering for profit. The effect is to make family members feel responsible and hopeless simultaneously. It is maddening to be singled out in this way. But it is also empowering to have survived the experience.

I also realized the limits of our own government in dealing with the issue of kidnapping. I've learned firsthand about our government's limitations in dealing with the Taliban as well. It is not only a matter of political or strategic disagreement; it's a much deeper cultural divide. We inhabit two incongruous worlds—or, as one of our good friends put it: They are playing Parcheesi and we are playing Monopoly. Our ordeal was an ongoing process of sifting through information and misinformation as well as dealing with a cast of ever-changing characters. I listened to all opinions, but trusted no one completely. At times it felt like the different agencies and consultants involved in trying to secure David's release were at odds with one another. Each held vehemently to their own beliefs based on their allegiances and experience. As a result, we often received well-intentioned but conflicting advice. In the end, I realized I had no control over the situation. Despite our collective efforts back home, it seemed only the captors had the power to release my husband and his colleagues. We thought our fate was in their hands.

I am most grateful to former hostages and their family members who reached out to me, shared their experiences, and in the process demystified a strange emotional terrain. I will always appreciate their emotional honesty and bravery in revisiting their awful memories in order to help me.

Our family, friends, and colleagues provided support and sustenance. As a result, existing relationships were strengthened and many new friendships were forged. For this, I am grateful.

My mother used to joke that for a couple to live happily ever after, they'd have to both expire after saying their vows. I often thought of that statement during the seven months David was gone. I took our vows to heart, but never thought that "worse" would come so soon. While happily ever after is a false claim, sometimes adversity can transform circumstances into something better and propel you forward. This experience has tested my own level of commitment and endurance. It has given me faith in my own resiliency and an appreciation for the fact that while things can go horribly wrong, they can also improve unexpectedly.

My mother went back to Maine, but we talk all the time—more than before. I have a greater appreciation for my mother and for motherhood in general—I now realize that this relationship, while so basic, is vast and dynamic. Lee has become a big brother to me as well. He and his wife, Christie, have been great confidants and supporters to David and me both.

The only journey of which I am certain is the inner one. The spiritual insights that I held tightly during the kidnapping still resonate. This experience ultimately taught me how to let go without giving up, and that sometimes there is strength in patiently waiting. And I learned a few things about myself along the way. When the depths of my own sense of loyalty and commitment—an extreme interpretation of wedding vows— were tested, I did not waver. This was something I could not have predicted in the early days after David disappeared, when I was overwhelmed with fear, anxiety, and loss.

I kept faith throughout. I knew my husband would do everything he could to survive. I knew his patience, tenacity, intelligence, and reserve would serve us well. I also knew David would be able to be low key and appear meek as a cover. In reality, there is nothing meek about my husband. I am so thankful he had the courage to seize the opportunity to escape and the patience and endurance to wait for the right moment to do it.

I would have preferred that David had consulted me on his decision to go to interview the Taliban commander. But I cannot say I would have stopped him. I knew I'd married a war correspondent. I am simply grateful that in going through this experience, we have safely fulfilled our purpose and have another chance to move forward in life together.

NOTES

Wherever possible, we have consulted news stories, e-mails, and other sources to verify our recollections of what occurred and ensure the accuracy of the dates given in the book. The following notes are designed to give additional background and describe suggested readings on various topics.

A BLOOD MESSAGE TO OBAMA

6   **A European journalist:** The journalist asked not to be identified.

6   **An experienced journalist:** The journalist asked not to be identified.

10   **The driver punches the accelerator:** Rohde wrote a five-part series on his time in captivity for *The New York Times*. See David Rohde, "Held by the Taliban," *New York Times*, October 17–21, 2009. For the full series, videos, maps, graphics, and reader comments, see: www.nytimes.com/2009/10/18/world/asia/18hostage .html.

15   **wean Afghans from Soviet influence:** See Cynthia Clapp-Wincek, "The Helmand Valley Project in Afghanistan," United States Agency for International Development (1983), 1–3. The full report is a detailed history and assessment of the Helmand project.

15   **"Little America":** For elegant descriptions of Cold War Lashkar Gah see Arnold Toynbee, *Between Oxus and Jumma* (1961) and Nancy Dupree, *An Historical Guide to Afghanistan* (1977). For an exhaustive collection of the USAID-commissioned studies of the projects during the Cold War see Richard Scott, "Scott's Helmand Valley Archives" at www.scottshelmandvalleyarchives.org.

16   **a 5,000-year-old tribal code of honor:** See Louis Dupree, *Afghanistan* (1970), 104, 126–27.

16   **The grand American project:** Dupree is very critical of the project, particularly in its early phases. See Dupree, *Afghanistan*, 482–85, 497, 499–507, 634–35. Nick Cullather also criticizes the project; see Nick Cullather, "Damming Afghanistan: Modernization in a Buffer State," *Journal of American History* 89, September 2002, 2: 512–37. For USAID descriptions of the project see Lloyd Baron, "Sector Analysis: Helmand-Arghandab Valley Region" (1973), 2, 7–9, and

Mildred Caudill, *Helmand-Arghandab Valley, Yesterday, Today and Tomorrow* (1969), 31. Residents of Helmand and former USAID officials generally praised the project in interviews conducted in Afghanistan and the United States between 2004 and 2010.

17   **a cycle of Kabul-based, elite-backed:** One famous example is the 1929 uprising by conservatives that deposed King Amanulllah Khan. After he returned from a seven-month trip to Egypt, Italy, France, Germany, Britain, Russia, Turkey, and Iran in 1928, he convened a grand council and announced sweeping reforms. A new national parliament elected by male voters would be created. All young men would be conscripted for the army and all boys and girls would receive education. In the most shocking move, he declared that all visitors to Kabul should wear Western dress and all women should no longer wear veils. An uprising by conservative Afghans forced him from power the following year. See Willem Vogelsgang, *The Afghans,* Blackwell Publishing (2002), 281.

MILLIONS

32   **the Afghan government exchanged:** Figures stem from Sami Yusufzai, "For the Taliban, a Crime That Pays," *Newsweek,* September 6, 2008, and "Taliban Say S. Korea Paid over $20 Million Ransom," Reuters, September 1, 2008.

37   **Foreign armies:** Leon Poullada describes the phenomenon in his book. See Leon B. and Leila D. J. Poullada, *The Kingdom of Afghanistan and the United States: 1828–1973* (1995), 1. Poullada quotes from Arnold Fletcher, *Afghanistan: Highway of Conquest* (1965).

37   **Afghans deftly cultivated an image:** This argument comes primarily from Sarah Chayes, whose survey of Afghan history is incisive, exhaustive, and thoughtful. See Sarah Chayes, *The Punishment of Virtue: Inside Afghanistan After the Taliban* (2006), 68, 101, 202, 247.

38   **"a purely accidental geographic unit":** Cullather, 6. Cullather states that the Curzon quote is from Cuthbert Collin Davies, *The Problem of the North-West Frontier, 1890–1908,* Cambridge University Press (1932), 153.

39   **The division would rankle:** Poullada, *The Kingdom of Afghanistan and the United States*, 83.

39   **declined to recognize it:** Ibid., 37–40.

39   **the "Afghan blind-spot":** Ibid., 40–41.

39   **early American writing about Afghanistan:** Ibid., 9–17. Ben Macintyre, *The Man Who Would Be King: The First American in Afghanistan,* Farrar, Straus and Giroux (2004), xiv. Macintyre's book describes Harlan's many adventures and claims.

40   **Afghanistan's ruling family:** Poullada describes how the royal family began sending young Afghans to be educated in the United States and Europe in the 1930s. Several dozen young Afghan men studied at Cornell, Columbia, and other elite American universities. At the same time, Afghan officials invited young German, French, and American teachers to instruct in Afghanistan. See Poullada, *The Kingdom of Afghanistan and the United States*, 28.

41   **World War II finally ignited:** Ibid., 70.

46   **years of American and Afghan government missteps:** Much of the narrative
describing the post-2001 American effort stems from interviews with senior Bush
administration officials from 2006 to 2010 as well as David Rohde and David E.
Sanger, "How a Good War Went Bad in Afghanistan," *New York Times,* August
12, 2007; www.nytimes.com/2007/08/12/world/asia/12afghan.html.

51   **he predicted that the cut:** Ronald E. Neumann, *The Other War: Winning and
Losing in Afghanistan,* Potomac Books (2009), 50.

CRASH COURSE

61   **One of David's colleagues:** The reporter asked not to be identified.

62   **Jere Van Dyk:** Author of *Captive: My Time as a Prisoner of the Taliban* (2010) and
In Afghanistan: An American Odyssey (1983).

63   **Michael Semple:** Semple is head of Talk for Peace International (TFPI). "TFPI
is a network of concerned idealists who want to make a tangible contribution to
achieving peace. We promote the use of dialogue and political engagement,
backed up by practical interventions to improve people's lives, as a way of trans-
forming conflict." For more information about this organization go to www
.talkforpeace.org.

68   **American-style university:** We visited Lahore University of Management
Sciences.

THE EMIRATE

72   **the Taliban and Al Qaeda have reestablished:** See Mark Mazzetti and David
Rohde, "Amid U.S. Policy Disputes, Qaeda Grows in Pakistan," *New York
Times,* June 30, 2008; www.nytimes.com/2008/06/30/washington/30tribal.html.

75   **"They kidnapped children":** See *Report on Waziristan and Its Tribes* (1901), 21.

77   **83 percent of the men and 97 percent of the women:** See Zulfiqar Ali, "Under
standing Tribal Areas," *Dawn,* April 2, 2010; www.dawn.com/wps/wcm/connect/
dawn-content-library/dawn/the-newspaper/local/peshawar/understanding-tribal-
areas-240.

78   **"Every man's hand is against the other":** Winston S. Churchill, *The Story of the
Malakand Field Force: An Episode of Frontier War* (2005), 15–16. The book's first
chapter, "The Theatre of War," is an extraordinarily vivid piece of writing, but
deeply flawed and bigoted.

ALL THREE OF US

89   **"goodness personified":** Much of the Wilson narrative stems from George Crile,
Charlie Wilson's War, Grove Press (2003), 470–74.

89   **The congressman half jokingly replied:** The prisoner anecdote is from a lecture
Wilson delivered in Washington, D.C., in October 2008, one month before the
author was kidnapped by Haqqani's sons.

90   **Born in the village of Srana:** In southeastern Afghanistan, his tribe—the
Zadran—formed his main power base, in particular his subtribe, the Sultankhel.

90   **conservative Deobandi Islam:** This is the interpretation of Islam followed by
many Taliban members. It emerged from the town of Deoband in northern
India in response to British colonial rule in the late 1800s.

90   **He left Afghanistan:** Haqqani built the sprawling Manba Uloom madrassa in
      the 1980s just north of Miran Shah in the town of Danda Darpa Khel. The
      school's students served as his fighters in the 1980s and after 2001. The author
      was imprisoned in houses near the madrassa for most of his time in Miran Shah.

90   **garrisoned in the Afghan city of Khost:** The Soviets responded by building a
      sprawling airfield and flying in supplies. A massive 1988 Soviet offensive broke
      Haqqani's siege. It was the last Soviet victory of the war.

90   **Deft at cultivating support:** Throughout the 1980s, the ISI played Haqqani
      against Gulbuddin Hekmatyar, another mujahideen commander who competed
      with Haqqani for Pakistani and American support. For years, Haqqani would
      resent the ISI for not promoting him as the sole Pashtun leader of the Afghan
      resistance. See Ahmed Rashid, *Taliban: Militant Islam, Oil and Fundamentalism
      in Central Asia* (2000). During a fund-raising tour of Persian Gulf countries,
      Haqqani so impressed a young Egyptian journalist that the budding reporter
      traveled to Afghanistan and fought alongside Haqqani and his men. The writ-
      ing of the journalist, who later became a senior member of Al Qaeda, turned
      Haqqani into a folk hero among the "Arab volunteers" who came to fight the
      Soviets. One of those volunteers was Osama bin Laden.

90   **The two men and a few dozen of their fighters:** The battle was in the village of
      Jaji in Paktia Province. Whether Haqqani was present is disputed by some re-
      searchers. Most describe him being there.

91   **"hero mujahed sheikh":** The descriptions of Haqqani's relationship with the
      CIA and Bin Laden stem from Steve Coll, *The Bin Ladens: An Arabian Family
      in the American Century* (2008), 294. For a detailed and insightful description of
      Haqqani's receipt of American funding, closeness to Bin Laden, and support for
      the Taliban see Steve Coll, *Ghost Wars: The Secret History of the CIA, Afghanistan,
      and Bin Laden, from the Soviet Invasion to September 10, 2001* (2004), 131, 157, 167,
      202, 227, 231, 293, 521.

91   **When the victorious mujahideen:** The capital of Khost, the province Wilson
      toured, was the first major city to fall to the mujahideen. In April 1991, Haqqani
      and his men entered the city, but they continued to heavily rely on the support of
      the ISI. Pakistani army artillery and tanks reportedly fired shells from Pakistan
      to support Haqqani's assault. Khost was the first major city to fall to the muja-
      hideen, but problems quickly emerged. After local mullahs told their followers
      that foreign aid workers were telling Afghan women to have free sex, an enraged
      mob burned a health clinic and threatened Afghan nurses and teachers. One was
      kidnapped and murdered. The American ambassador to Pakistan called for the
      CIA's covert support to the mujahideen to stop, and the administration of Presi-
      dent George H. W. Bush requested no funding for fiscal year 1992. Yet Wilson
      continued to finance them, using his position on the House Intelligence Com-
      mittee to maneuver $200 million in secret monies through Congress. Crile, *Char-
      lie Wilson's War*, 515–19.

91   **He also commanded:** At the time, Haqqani funded the operations with dona-
      tions from Arab countries and complained to journalists that the Taliban were
      unable to organize themselves.

92   **missiles struck the camp:** Crile, *Charlie Wilson's War,* 522.

92   **American bombs destroyed:** Haqqani became the third highest target on the

U.S. bombing list, ibid., 521. In a 2010 interview, a former American intelligence official confirmed the meetings with Haqqani in the fall of 2001.

92 **an acceptance of suicide bombing:** As many as 80 percent of suicide bombers dispatched to Afghanistan between 2001 and 2007 are believed to have passed through North Waziristan, according to a September 2007 United Nations study For detailed accounts of the resurgence of the Haqqani network see Thomas Ruttig, "The Haqqani Network as an Autonomous Entity," in *Decoding the New Taliban: Insights from the Afghan Field* (2010), 57–88 and Anand Gopal, Mansur Khan Mahsud, and Brian Fishman, "Inside the Haqqani Network, The AfPak Channel, June 3, 2010, at afpak.foreignpolicy.com/posts/2010/06/03/inside_the_haqqani_network_0.

HUMAN RESOURCES

97 **The head of Clayton:** The subject has asked not to be identified.
100 **Samantha Power:** Senior director for Multilateral Affairs, National Security Council.

SPEAK GOOD WORDS TO AN ENEMY

112 **One of my colleagues:** The colleague asked not to be identified.

MULTITASKING

133 **They tell us:** We have not mentioned offer amounts to protect future captives. We do not want to set a precedent for future kidnappings.

THE TALIBAN TRUST THE RED CROSS

145 **I know from things I have previously read:** For a detailed description of Ghaffar Khan see Rajmohan Gandhi, *Ghaffar Khan: Nonviolent Badshah of the Pashtuns*, Viking (2004) and *Frontier Gandhi: Badshah Khan, a Torch for Peace*, a 2008 documentary written and produced by T. C. McLuhan.

WORDS AND PICTURES

162 **welcomed Arabs and Uzbeks:** Much of the background narrative in this section comes from Mazzetti and Rohde, "Amid U.S. Policy Disputes, Qaeda Grows in Pakistan." It was also supplemented with interviews in the United States and Pakistan from 2008 to 2010.
167 **tens of millions of dollars:** See David Rohde, Carlotta Gall, Eric Schmitt, and David E. Sanger, "U.S. Officials See Waste in Billions Sent to Pakistan," *New York Times*, December 24, 2007; http://www.nytimes.com/2007/12/24/world/asia/24military.html.
168 **The Pakistani military fought:** See Carlotta Gall and Mohammad Khan, "Pakistan's Push in Border Areas Is Said to Falter," *New York Times*, January 22, 2006. For a detailed history of missteps by Musharraf and American officials see Ahmed Rashid, *Descent into Chaos;* www.nytimes.com/2006/01/22/international/asia/22pakistan.html.
168 **killed or wounded:** See Associated Press, "Civilian Deaths Spike in Afghanistan, Pakistan," April 28, 2010; www.cbsnews.com/stories/2010/04/28/world/main6439690.shtml.
169 **a retired senior official from the ISI:** See Carlotta Gall and David Rohde, "Mil-

itants Escape Control of Pakistan, Officials Say," *New York Times*, January 15 2008; www.nytimes.com/2008/01/15/world/asia/15isi.html.

ARE YOU THERE?

179   **threaten to kill Solecki:** See Associated Press, "Kidnappers Threaten to Kill U.N. Worker," story on Solecki kidnapping, February 13, 2009; www.msnbc .msn.com/id/29183644/.

179   **Piotr Stanczak:** Pakistani journalists reported that Stanczak was killed because Pakistani Taliban commanders were fighting over him. See Mazhar Tufail, "TTP Infighting Led to Beheading of Polish Engineer," *The News*, February 12, 2009; www.thenews.com.pk/print1.asp?id=162048.

GOLDEN CHANCE

186   **The phone rings:** Parts of the conversation in which the authors discussed how much was offered at the time have not been included in the chapter. We are not disclosing the amount of the offer because we believe it could encourage or complicate future kidnappings.

GIFT FROM GOD

192   **weeps at a radio news broadcast:** It is not clear what civilian casualty report Abu Tayyeb heard that day. It may have been a UN report that said civilian casualties had increased in Afghanistan by 40 percent in 2008; www.nytimes.com/2009/02/18/ world/asia/18afghan.html.

PEACE BE UPON YOU

195   **Afghan girl that appeared:** Photograph by Steve McCurry.

AN ALTERNATE UNIVERSE

205   **uses some type of weapon:** Akbar may have been referring to depleted uranium. American military officials say they have used no depleted uranium in Afghanistan, but some experts question their claim; www.news.bbc.co.uk/2/hi/science/ nature/3050317.stm.

205   **they take turns attending bomb-making classes:** See David Rohde and C. J. Chivers, "Qaeda's Grocery Lists and Manuals of Killing," *New York Times*, March 17, 2002, http://www.nytimes.com/2002/03/17/world/a-nation-challenged-qaeda-s-grocery-lists-and-manuals-of-killing.html.

227   **my English-language Koran:** The English-language Koran I read was Marmaduke Pickthall, The Holy Quran with English and Urdu Translation, Kitab Bhavan (2001).

BIRTHDAY WISHES

220   **A shadow of the endeavor:** Much of the Helmand narrative stems from David Rohde, "An Afghan Symbol of Change, Then Failure," *New York Times*, September 5, 2006; www.nytimes.com/2006/09/05/world/asia/05afghan.html.

224   **"conveyor-belt courses":** The European official who derided the DynCorp police training was Michael Semple, who later advised Kristen on David's kidnapping.

225   **handed over the districts:** Tom Coghlan, "Weak Government Allows Taleban to Prosper in Afghanistan," *The Times* (of London), September 29, 2008; www .timesonline.co.uk/tol/news/world/asia/article4842499.ece.

225   **she feared that the Taliban:** While she expressed disappointment with the British, Fowzea reflected the shortcomings of the Afghan effort herself. Since 2001, Fowzea had not once traveled to Kabul to lobby for funds from the Ministry of Women's Affairs, even after USAID established direct, regular flights for Afghans. She could not tell me the size of her annual budget and appeared poorly organized.

226   **"Pakistani alley":** For an excellent piece on the company's deployment see Kristin Henderson, "A Change in Mission," *Washington Post*, June 12, 2009; www .washingtonpost.com/wp-dyn/content/article/2009/06/12/AR2009.

A STONE WILL NOT BECOME SOFT

244   **The videos are the latest example:** Rohde and *The New York Times* compiled a six-part video series that appeared on the newspaper's Web site with a five-part series he wrote on his captivity.

      To go to the beginning of the five videos: projects.nytimes.com/held-by-the-taliban/#intro.

      To go to the video that includes some of the films we watched: www./Proj ects.nytimes.com/held-by-the-taliban/#part-4.

LIES

270   **Vietnamese people are Muslims:** For more detail on the shooting in upstate New York see Robert D. McFadden, "Thirteen Shot Dead at Class on Citizenship," *New York Times*, April 4, 2009; www.nytimes.com/2009/04/04/nyregion/04hostage .html.

270   **an unprovoked war on Islam:** For additional information about Mullah Sangeen and his views see Bill Roggio, "An Interview with Mullah Sangeen," *Long War Journal*, September 17, 2009; www.longwarjournal.org/threat-matrix/ archives/2009/09/an_interview_with_mullah_sange.php.

270   **the Taliban's first group of suicide bombers:** For more information about Mullah Dadullah, who was killed by American Special Forces soldiers in May 2007, see his final two interviews at www.counterterrorismblog.org/2007/05/ video_the_last_words_of_mullah_1.php.

270   **black flags:** Various postings appear online discussing the prophecy, which supporters say is a Hadith. One example can be found at www.freerepublic.com/ focus/religion/771345/posts.

HOME MOVIES

277   **somatic experiencing (SE):** www.traumahealing.com.
277   **Peter Levine:** Author of *Waking the Tiger*.

PASHTUNWALI

287   **I lie awake in the darkness:** To see detailed graphics that show the layout of the house and how we escaped, see a video that *The New York Times* produced along

with the written series on our captivity in October 2009. The video can be seen at http://projects.nytimes.com/held-by-the-taliban/#part-5.

295   **to protect us under the tenet of Pashtunwali:** The specific element of Pashtunwali that Tahir requested asylum under is *nanawatai*.

THE GLORIOUS ISLAM

305   **He gives me a book:** A full description of the book is Muhammad Asghar Qureshi, *The Glorious Islam*, Lahore: Sajjad Asghar Qureshi (1997).

EPILOGUE

325   **secret program . . . to help track and kill militants:** See Dexter Filkins and Mark Mazzetti, "Contractors Tied to Effort to Track and Kill Militants," *New York Times*, March 14, 2010, http://www.nytimes.com/2010/03/15/world/asia/15contractors.html.

BIBLIOGRAPHY

Numerous books and studies are available for readers interested in learning more about Afghanistan, Pakistan, the Taliban, and kidnapping. The list below includes books we have read fully, read partially, or consulted. Numerous newspaper articles were consulted as well. Only the most central to our book are listed here.

ARTICLES

Ali, Zulfiqar, "Understanding Tribal Areas," *Dawn*, April 2, 2010, www.dawn.com /wps/wcm/connect/dawn-content-library/dawn/the-newspaper/local/peshawar /understanding-tribal-areas-240.

Associated Press, "Civilian Deaths Spike in Afghanistan, Pakistan," April 28, 2010, www.cbsnews.com/stories/2010/04/28/world/main6439690.shtml.

———, "Kidnappers Threaten to Kill U.N. Worker," February 13, 2009, www.msnbc .msn.com/id/29183644/.

Al Balagh Media Center, Interview with Sirajuddin Haqqani, April 10, 2010, http://www.globalterroralert.com/images/documents/pdf/0410/flashpoint _haqqani041210.pdf.s.

CBS News Investigative Unit, Interview with Taliban Commander Sirajuddin Haqqani, August 20, 2008, http://www.cbsnews.com/8301-502683_162-4366029 -502683.html.

Coghlan, Tom, "Weak Government Allows Taleban to Prosper in Afghanistan," *The Times* (of London), September 29, 2008, www.timesonline.co.uk/tol/news/world /asia/article4842499.ece.

Coll, Steve, "The Case for Humility in Afghanistan," *Foreign Policy*, October 16, 2009, http://www.foreignpolicy.com/articles/2009/10/16/the_case_for_humility_in _afghanistan?page=full.

———, "Letter from Afghanistan: War by Other Means," *The New Yorker*, May 24, 2010.

———, "Think Tank," *The New Yorker*, http://www.newyorker.com/online/blogs /stevecoll/.

Cullather, Nick, "Damming Afghanistan: Modernization in a Buffer State," *Journal of American History* 89, September 2002, 2: 512–37, http://www.indiana.edu/~hist web/faculty/Display.php?Faculty_ID=52.

Filkins, Dexter, "Afghan Civilian Deaths Rose 40 Percent in 2008," *The New York Times*, February 17, 2009, http://www.nytimes.com/2009/02/18/world/asia/18afghan. html.

————, and Mark Mazzetti, "Contractors Tied to Effort to Track and Kill Militants," *The New York Times*, March 14, 2010, http://www.nytimes.com/2010/03/15/ world/asia/15contractors.html.

Gall, Carlotta, and David Rohde, "Militants Escape Control of Pakistan, Officials Say," *The New York Times*, January 15, 2008, www.nytimes.com/2008/01/15/world /asia/15isi.html.

————, and Mohammad Khan, "Pakistan's Push in Border Areas Is Said to Falter, *The New York Times*, January 22, 2006, www.nytimes.com/2006/01/22/international /asia/22pakistan.html.

Gopal, Anand, Mansur Khan Mahsud, and Brian Fishman, "Inside the Haqqani Network," The AfPak Channel, June 3, 2010, afpak.foreignpolicy.com/posts/2010/06/03 /inside_the_haqqani_network_0.

Gregg, Tom, "Caught in the Crossfire: The Pashtun Tribes of Southeast Afghanistan" (policy brief), The Lowy Institute for International Policy, October 2009, http://www.lowyinstitute.org/Publication.asp?pid=1157.

Gul, Pazir, "Waziristan Accord Signed," *Dawn*, September 6, 2006, www.dawn .com/2006/09/06/top2.htm.

Haider, Zeeshan, "Pakistani Taliban Force Girls Schools to Close," Reuters, January 17, 2009, www.reuters.com/article/idUSISL282445.

Henderson, Kristin, "A Change in Mission," *The Washington Post*, June 12, 2009, http://www.washingtonpost.com/wp-dyn/content/article/2009/06/12 /AR2009061202123.html.

Kirby, Alex, "Afghans' Uranium Levels Spark Alert," BBC News, May 22, 2003, http://news.bbc.co.uk/2/hi/science/nature/3050317.stm.

McFadden, Robert D., "Thirteen Shot Dead at Class on Citizenship," *The New York Times*, April 4, 2009, www.nytimes.com/2009/04/04/nyregion/04hostage.html.

Mazzetti, Mark, and David Rohde, "Amid U.S. Policy Disputes, Qaeda Grows in Pakistan, *The New York Times*, June 30, 2008, www.nytimes.com/2008/06/30 /washington/30tribal.html.

————, and Eric Schmitt, "Afghan Strikes by Taliban Get Pakistan Help, U.S. Aides Say," *The New York Times*, March 25, 2009, http://www.nytimes.com/2009/03/26/ world/asia/26tribal.html.

Moore, Jonathan, "Morality and Foreign Policy," speech given in Hanover, NH, The Dickey Center, 2007.

Rashid, Ahmed, "The Afghanistan Impasse," *The New York Review of Books*, October 8, 2009.

Reuters, "Taliban Say S. Korea Paid over $20 Million in Ransom," September 1, 2007, http://in.reuters.com/article/idlNIndia-29278920070901.

Roggio, Bill, "An Interview with Mullah Sangeen," *The Long War Journal*, September 17, 2009, www.longwarjournal.org/threat-matrix/archives/2009/09/an_inter view_with_mullah_sange.php.

Rohde, David, "An Afghan Symbol for Change, Then Failure," *The New York Times*, September 5, 2006, www.nytimes.com/2006/09/05/world/asia/05afghan.html.

———, "Held by the Taliban," *The New York Times*, October 17–21, 2009, www .nytimes.com/2009/10/18/world/asia/18hostage.html.

———, "Army Enlists Anthropology in War Zones," *The New York Times*. October 5, 2007, http://www.nytimes.com/2007/10/05/world/asia/05afghan.html.

———, "GIs in Afghanistan on Hunt, but Now for Hearts and Minds," *The New York Times*. March 30, 2004, http://www.nytimes.com/2004/03/30/world/gi-s-in-afghanistan-on-hunt-but-now-for-hearts-and-minds.html.

———, "The Other Conflict Continues to Take a G.I. Toll," *The New York Times*, November 24, 2003, http://www.nytimes.com/2003/11/24/world/the-other-conflict-continues-to-take-a-gi-toll.html.

———, "Pakistan's Terrorist Factory: Fact or Figment," *The Christian Science Monitor*, April 14, 1995.

———, "Left Alone, Refugees Decry U.S. Indifference," *The Christian Science Monitor*, April 19, 1995.

———, and C. J. Chivers, "Qaeda's Grocery Lists and Manuals of Killing," *The New York Times*, March 17, 2002, http://www.nytimes.com/2002/03/17/world/a-nation-challenged-qaeda-s-grocery-lists-and-manuals-of-killing.html.

———, David E. Sanger, "How a Good War Went Bad in Afghanistan," *The New York Times,* August 12, 2007, www.nytimes.com/2007/08/12/world/asia /12afghan.html.

———, Carlotta Gall, Eric Schmitt, and David E. Sanger, "U.S. Officials See Waste in Billions Sent to Pakistan," *The New York Times*, December 24, 2007, http://www.nytimes.com/2007/12/24/world/asia/24military.html.

Ruttig, Thomas, "The Haqqani Network as an Autonomous Entity," in *Decoding the New Taliban: Insights from the Afghan Field* (New York: Columbia University Press, 2010), 57–88.

Shah, Pir Zubair, "U.S. Airstrike Kills 30 in Pakistan," *The New York Times*, February 14, 2009, www.nytimes.com/2009/02/15/world/asia/15pstan.html?_r=1.

Tufail, Mazhar, "TTP Infighting Led to Beheading of Polish Engineer," *The News International,* February 12, 2009, www.thenews.com.pk/print1.asp?id=162048.

Yusufzai, Sami, "For the Taliban, a Crime That Pays," *Newsweek*, September 6, 2008, http://www.newsweek.com/2008/09/05/for-the-taliban-a-crime-that-pays.html.

BOOKS

Adair, Liz, et al. *Lucy Shook's Letters from Afghanistan*. Ferndale, WA: GAL Editing & Publishing, 2002.

Alvi, Sohail Masood. *FATA: Beginning of a New Era*. Lahore, Pakistan: Printhouse, 2006.

Anderson, Terry. *Den of Lions: Memoirs of Seven Years*. New York: Crown, 1993.

Bissell, William Nanda. *Making India Work*. New Delhi: Penguin Viking, 2009.

Caroe, Olaf. *The Pathans 550 B.C.–A.D. 1957*. Oxford: Oxford University Press, 1958.

Carothers, Thomas. *Aiding Democracy Abroad: The Learning Curve*. Washington, D.C.: The Carnegie Endowment for International Peace, 1999.

Chatterjee, Pratap. *Iraq, Inc.: A Profitable Occupation*. New York: Seven Stories Press, 2004.

Chayes, Sarah. *The Punishment of Virtue: Inside Afghanistan After the Taliban*. New York: The Penguin Press, 2006.

Gul, Imtiaz. *The Most Dangerous Place: Pakistani's Lawless Frontier*. New York: Viking, 2010.

Churchill, Winston S. *The Story of the Malakand Field Force: An Episode of Frontier War*. Rockville, MD: Wildside Press, 1898, 2005.

Coll, Steve. *The Bin Ladens: An Arabian Family in the American Century*. New York: The Penguin Press, 2008.

————. *Ghost Wars: The Secret History of the CIA, Afghanistan and bin Laden from the Soviet Invasion to September 10, 2001*. New York: The Penguin Press, 2004.

Crile, George. *Charlie Wilson's War: The Extraordinary Story of How the Wildest Man in Congress and a Rogue CIA Agent Changed the History of Our Times*. New York: Grove Press, 2003.

Dupree, Louis. *Afghanistan*. Princeton, NJ: Princeton University Press, 1973.

Dupree, Nancy. *An Historical Guide to Afghanistan*. Kabul, Afghanistan: Afghan Tourist Organization, 1977.

Fergusson, James. *A Million Bullets: The Real Story of the British Army in Afghanistan*. London: Bantam Press, 2008.

Gandhi, Rajmohan. *Ghaffar Khan: Nonviolent Badhshah of the Pakhtuns*. New Delhi: Penguin Viking, 2004.

Ghani, Ashraf, and Clare Lockhart. *Fixing Failed States: A Framework for Rebuilding a Fractured World*. Oxford: Oxford University Press, 2008.

Giustozzi, Antonio, ed. *Decoding the New Taliban: Insights from the Afghan Field*. New York: Columbia University Press, 2009.

Gul, Imtiaz. *The Most Dangerous Place: Pakistani's Lawless Frontier*. New York: Viking, 2010.

Jones, Owen Bennett. *Pakistan: Eye of the Storm*. New Haven, CT: Yale University Press, 2002.

Jones, Seth G. *In the Graveyard of Empires: America's War in Afghanistan*. New York: Norton, 2009.

Keenan, Brian. *An Evil Cradling*. London: Hutchinson, 1992.

Kiviat, Katherine, and Scott Heidler. *Women of Courage: Intimate Stories from Afghanistan*. Layton, UT: Gibbs Smith, Publisher, 2007.

Leeson, Frank. *Frontier Legion: With the Khassadars of North Waziristan*. West Sussex, England: The Leeson Archive, 2003.

Loyn, David. *Butcher & Bolt*. London: Hutchinson, 2008.

Macintyre, Ben. *The Man Who Would Be King: The First American in Afghanistan*. New York: Farrar, Straus & Giroux, 2004, xiii–xiv, 209–29.

Mohsin, Hamid. *The Reluctant Fundamentalist*. New York: Houghton Mifflin Harcourt, 2007.

Neumann, Ronald E. *The Other War: Winning and Losing in Afghanistan*. Washington, D.C.: Potomac Books, 2009.

Olivetti, Vincenzo. *Terror's Source: The Ideology of Wahhabi-Salafism and Its Consequences*. Birmingham, AL: Amadeus Books, 2001.

Pearl, Mariane, with Sarah Crichton. *A Mighty Heart: The Brave Life and Death of My Husband, Danny Pearl*. New York: Scribner, 2003.

Peters, Gretchen. *Seeds of Terror: How Heroin Is Bankrolling the Taliban and Al Qaeda.* New York: Thomas Dunne Books, 2009.

Pickthall, Marmaduke, trans. *The Holy Quran with English and Urdu Translation*, New Delhi: Kitab Bhavan, 2001.

Poullada, Leon B., and Leila D. J. Poullada. *The Kingdom of Afghanistan and the United States: 1828–1973.* Omaha and Lincoln, NB: The Center for Afghanistan Studies at the University of Nebraska at Omaha and Dageforde Publishing, 1995.

Punjab Government, *Report on Waziristan and Its Tribes*, Lahore, Pakistan: Sang-e-Meel Publications, 1901, 2005.

Rashid, Ahmed. *Taliban: Militant Islam, Oil and Fundamentalism in Central Asia.* New Haven, CT: Yale University Press, 2000.

———. *Descent into Chaos: The United States and the Failure of Nation Building in Pakistan, Afghanistan and Central Asia.* New York: Viking, 2008.

Rushdie, Salman. *Midnight's Children.* New York: Random House, 1995.

Sanger, David E. *The Inheritance: The World Obama Confronts and the Challenges to American Power.* New York: Crown, 2009.

Toynbee, Arnold. *Between Oxus and Jumma.* Oxford: Oxford University Press, 1961.

Van Dyk, Jere. *Captive: My Time as a Prisoner of the Taliban.* New York: Times Books, 2010.

———. *In Afghanistan: An American Odyssey.* New York: Coward-McCann, 1983.

Vogelsang, Willem. *The Afghans.* Oxford: Blackwell Publishers, 2002.

Woodward, Bob. *Bush at War.* New York: Simon & Schuster, 2002.

———. *Plan of Attack.* New York: Simon & Schuster, 2004.

———. *State of Denial. Bush at War, Part III.* New York: Simon & Schuster, 2006.

———. *The War Within, a Secret White House History 2006–2008.* New York: Simon & Schuster, 2008.

Zaeef, Abdul Zalam, with Alex Strick van Linschoten and Felix Kuehn, eds. *My Life with the Taliban.* London: Hurst & Company, 2010.

DOCUMENTS AND REPORTS

Aziz, Khalid. *Causes of Rebellion in Waziristan.* Peshawar, Pakistan: Regional Institute of Policy Research & Training, 2005.

Baron, Lloyd. *Sector Analysis: Helmand-Arghandab Valley Region,* Kabul, Afghanistan: Agency for International Development, 1973.

Caudill, Mildred. *Helmand-Arghandab Valley: Yesterday, Today and Tomorrow.* Lashkar Gah, Afghanistan: Agency for International Development, 1969.

Dobbins, James, et al. *America's Role in Nation-Building: From Germany to Iraq.* Santa Monica, CA: RAND, 2003.

International Crisis Group. *A Force in Fragments: Reconstituting the Afghan National Army.* Brussels, Belgium, 2010.

Jones, Seth G. *Counterinsurgency in Afghanistan.* Santa Monica, CA: RAND, 2008.

———, et al. *Establishing Law and Order After Conflict.* Santa Monica, CA: RAND, 2005.

Jordan, Leonard B. *Report on Development of Helmand Valley, Afghanistan.* Washington, D.C.: Tudor Engineering, 1956.

Neumann, Ronald. *Reconstruction Strategy in Post-Bonn Afghanistan—Setting Priorities to Galvanize International Donors, the Short Cable*. Washington, D.C.: U.S. State Department, October 18, 2005.

Singer, P.W. *Corporate Warriors: The Rise of the Privatized Military Industry*. Ithaca, NY: Cornell University Press, 2003.

Williams, Maurice. *Retrospective Review of U.S. Assistance to Afghanistan, 1950–1979*. Washington, D.C.: Bethesda, MD: Devres, Inc., 1988.

Wincek, Cynthia. *The Helmand Valley Project in Afghanistan*. Washington, D.C.: U.S. Agency for International Development, 1973.

RESOURCES FOR KIDNAP VICTIMS AND THEIR FAMILIES

Alvarez, James, "The Psychological Impact of Kidnap," in Elizabeth K. Carll, ed., *Trauma Psychology: Issues in Violence, Disaster, Health and Illness, Volume 1: Violence and Disaster*, Westport, CT: Praeger Perspectives, 2007.

Anderson, Terry. *Den of Lions: Memoirs of Seven Years*. New York: Crown, 1993.

Committee to Protect Journalists, 330 Seventh Avenue, 11th floor, New York, NY 10001, 212-465-1004, info@cpj. com, http://www.cpj.org/.

Johnston, Alan, "My Kidnap Ordeal," *From Our Own Correspondent*, BBC News, October 25, 2007, http://news.bbc.co.uk/2/hi/programmes/from_our_own_correspondent/7048652.stm.

Keenan, Brian. *An Evil Cradling*. London: Hutchinson, 1992.

Van Dyk, Jere. *Captive: My Time as a Prisoner of the Taliban*. New York: Times Books, 2010.

INDEX

mc

12/10

RACHEL
GIBSON
Is Back in Town!

"Are you here to start things up again? Continue right where we left off?"

"Don't, Jack." She raised her hand between them and pressed her fingers against his lips. "Don't say any more."

Her touch took him off guard. He caught the scent of perfume, but underneath that, he smelled her. Daisy.

Sometimes he'd have to search hard for the scent, but he'd always found it. Usually in the crook of her neck. He grabbed her wrist and took a step back. "What do you want from me?"

"I told you. I want to be friends."

"We could never be friends."

"I'm trying to be nice about this, but you really don't have a choice. You're going to listen to me; and if you get ugly, I'll become your worst dang nightmare."

Damn, but she was the old Daisy. All hot temper and feisty belligerence wrapped up in such a soft girly package. He almost smiled. Almost.

"Too late, buttercup," he said as he turned to go. "You became my worst nightmare years ago."

RACHEL GIBSON

DAISY'S BACK in Town

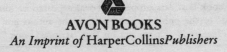

AVON BOOKS
An Imprint of HarperCollinsPublishers

This is a work of fiction. Names, characters, places, and incidents are products of the author's imagination or are used fictitiously and are not to be construed as real. Any resemblance to actual events, locales, organizations, or persons, living or dead, is entirely coincidental.

AVON BOOKS
An Imprint of HarperCollins*Publishers*
10 East 53rd Street
New York, New York 10022-5299

Copyright © 2004 by Rachel Gibson
The Thing About Men copyright © 2004 by Elizabeth Bevarly; *Daisy's Back in Town* copyright © 2004 by Rachel Gibson; *A Wild Pursuit* copyright © 2004 by Eloisa James; *Your Wicked Ways* copyright © 2004 by Eloisa James
ISBN: 0-06-000925-X
www.avonromance.com

First Avon Books paperback printing: February 2004

Avon Trademark Reg. U.S. Pat. Off. and in Other Countries, Marca Registrada, Hecho en U.S.A.
HarperCollins® is a registered trademark of HarperCollins Publishers Inc.

Printed in the U.S.A.

10 9 8 7 6

*This book is dedicated to
the original tyrannosaurus Tex,
Mary Reed,
who is my inspiration for all things Texas.*

Acknowledgments

I would like to express my appreciation and gratitude to those who helped in the writing of this book. Craig Clark of C. C. Photography and Graphic Design, for sharing with me his experience and knowledge of photography and for making me look good. Jamie G, for his engine expertise, for drawing diagrams and patiently explaining the difference between a V8 and a straight 6, a camshaft and an intake valve. Fellow author Rachelle Morgan and her husband, Deputy David Nelson of the Morris County Sheriff's Dept., Morris County, Texas. Your time was invaluable.

Chapter 1

*H*eat waves drifted across the concrete as the '63 Thunderbird slid from the shadow of the garage. Her big V8 and Holley two-barrels purred like a satisfied woman, all warm and sexy and throaty. The hot Texas sun made a hundred little bursts of light within her wire wheels, slid along the chrome fins, and poured over the glistening black paint. The owner watched as she rolled toward him, and he smiled in appreciation. Several months ago, the Sports Roadster had been little more than a home for mice. Now fully restored to her former glory, she was dazzling—a reminder of a time when Detroit had been more interested in cracking sixty in eight seconds than miles per gallon, safety features, or where to put the cup holder.

Jackson Lamott Parrish sat within the red leather interior of the big T-Bird, one wrist hanging over the red steering wheel. The light caught in his thick brown hair, and fine lines creased the corners of his green eyes as he lowered his lids against the blinding sun. He revved the big engine one last time, took his hand from the steering wheel, and shoved her into park. He swung the door open, and the sole of his cowboy boot hit the pavement. In one smooth motion, he stood and the owner of the restored Roadster stepped forward and handed him a check. Jack glanced at it, noted that all the zeros were in the right places, then folded it in half. He slipped it into the breast pocket of his white dress shirt.

"Enjoy," he said, then turned and walked into the shop. He moved passed a nineteen-seventy 'Cuda 440–6, its huge Hemi engine suspended from a cherry picker. Over the sounds of air compressors and power tools, Jack's younger brother, Billy, called out to a mechanic beneath a '59 Dodge Custom Royal Lancer.

The space just vacated by the T-bird would be filled the next day with a nineteen-fifty-four Corvette. The sports classic had been found in a dilapidated garage in Southern California, and Jack had flown out three days ago to take a look at it. When he discovered it had only forty thousand original miles and all the numbers matched, he bought it for eight grand on the spot. Once fully restored, the 'Vette would bring ten times that. When it came to restoring vintage cars, Parrish American Classics was the best. Everyone knew it.

Ground-pounding, ear-assaulting muscle cars were in the Parrish boys' blood. Since they'd taken their first steps, Jack and Billy had worked in their daddy's garage. They'd yanked their first engine before either of them had grown their short and curlies. They could tell a 260 V8 from a 289 with their eyes closed and could rebuild fuel injectors in their sleep. Proud native sons of Lovett, Texas, population nineteen thousand three, the Parrish boys had grown up loving football, cold beer, and tearing up asphalt on the flat open roads—usually while some big-haired, loose-moraled female repaired her lipstick in the rearview mirror.

The boys had been raised in a small three-bedroom house behind the garage. The original shop was gone now. Torn down and replaced by a bigger, more modern space with eight bays. The yard behind the garage had been cleaned up. The old cars and junked parts had been towed away long ago.

The house was the same, though. Same roses their mama had planted, same patches of dirt and grass beneath the towering elm. Same concrete porch and the same screen door that needed a good dose of WD40. The house had just been given a fresh coat of paint, inside and out. The same white color as before. The only real difference was that Jack now lived there alone.

Seven years ago, Billy had married Rhonda Valencia and had happily given up his wild ways for domestic bliss. As far as anyone in town could recall, Jack had never been tempted to give up his wild ways. As far as they knew, he'd never met a woman who'd made him want a one-on-one. A forever.

But they didn't know everything.

Jack made his way to his office at the rear of the garage and closed the door. He stuck the check in a desk drawer and pulled out his chair. Before he'd purchased the '54 Corvette, he'd searched out her history then flown to California to inspect her to make sure there wasn't any serious damage to the structural integrity of the car. Searching the history of a vehicle, finding replacement parts, and restoring it, compelled him and kept at him until the vehicle was once again perfect. Fixed. Better. Whole.

Penny Kribs, Jack's secretary, walked into his office and handed him the day's mail. "I'm leaving to get my hair done," she reminded him.

Jack looked up at the wispy black pile on top of Penny's head. He'd gone through all twelve years of school with Penny, and he'd played on the football team with her husband, Leon.

He rose and set the mail on his desk. "You goin' to get yourself beautiful for me?"

She had rings on just about every finger and long pink nails that curled like claws. He'd often wondered how she typed without hitting extra keys or managed to put on all that mascara without poking out an eye. He didn't even want to think about her wrapping her hand around Leon's johnson. The thought sent a shiver down his backside.

"Of course," she said through a smile. "You know you've always been my first love."

Yeah, he knew. In the third grade, Penny'd told him she loved him then she'd kicked him in the shin with her black patent leather shoes. He'd always figured he didn't need that kind of loving. "Don't tell Leon."

"Oh, he knows." She waved a hand and moved to the door, leaving a trail of perfume in her wake. "He also knows that I would never get involved with you."

Jack folded his arms across his chest and leaned his butt against the edge of his desk. "Why's that?"

"Because you treat women like an anorexic treats a Whitman Sampler. You nibble here and nibble there. Maybe you take a few bites, but you never eat one whole."

Jack laughed. "I think there are a few women who could set you straight on that."

Penny wasn't amused. "You know what I mean," she said over her shoulder as she walked out the door.

Yeah, he knew what she meant. Like most women, Penny thought he should be married, raising children, and driving an SUV. But as far as Jack was concerned, he figured his younger brother had taken care of that task for both of them. Billy had three daughters ranging in age from six months to five years. They lived on a quiet cul-de-sac with a swing set in the backyard, and Rhonda drove a Tahoe, the alternative choice of soccer moms everywhere. With all those nieces, Jack felt no pressure to bring another Parrish into the world. He was "Uncle Jack," and that suited him just fine.

He returned to his chair and unbuttoned his cuffs. He rolled his sleeves up his forearms, and got back to it. It was Friday and he had a mountain of work to clear off his desk before he could start his weekend. At five, Billy opened the door to tell him he was leaving. Jack glanced at the Buick Riviera clock sitting next to his computer monitor. He'd been at it for three hours and fifteen minutes.

"I'm headed for Amy Lynn's T-ball game," Billy said, referring to his five-year-old daughter. "You gonna make it by the park?"

Amy Lynn was Billy's oldest and Jack tried to make it to her games when he could. "Not tonight," he answered and tossed his pen on the desk. "Jimmy Calhoun's bachelor party is tonight over at The Road Kill," he said. Until recently, Jimmy had been a real carouser. Now he was giving up his freedom for a pair of matching gold rings. "I told him I'd stop by for a few."

Billy smiled. "Is there gonna be strippers?"

"I imagine."

"Don't tell me you'd rather watch naked women than a game of T-ball?"

Jack's grin matched his brother's. "Yeah, it was a tough choice to make. Watch women take their clothes off or five-year-olds run around bases with their helmets on backward."

Billy laughed, in that special way he always had of tipping his head back and letting loose with a few heh-heh-hehs. It sounded so much like their father, Ray, Jack figured it had to be genetic. "Lucky bastard," Billy said, but without much heart. They both knew that Billy would rather watch Amy Lynn run around with her helmet on backward. "If you need someone to drive you home from The Road Kill," Billy added on his way to the door, "call me."

"Of course." A drunk driver had taken their parent's lives when Jack had been all of eighteen. The brothers made it a point to never drive drunk.

Jack worked for another hour before he turned off his computer and headed out of the garage through

the bays. Everyone else had already left for the day,
and his bootheels echoed in the silence. He locked
the door and set the alarm, then he jumped into his
Shelby Mustang. It started to rain as he drove toward the outskirts of Lovett. A light sprinkle of
drops mixed with the dust and wind, and turned the
car's shiny black paint a dull gray.

The Road Kill was a lot like other bars strewn
throughout the Texas panhandle. Country music
poured from the juke while the patrons drained the
beer spigots of Lone Star. A big red-white-and-blue
DON'T MESS WITH TEXAS sign hung on the mirror behind the bar, while old road signs, stuffed armadil-
los and rattlers decorated the walls. The owner of
the bar was also a taxidermist, and if a patron was so
inclined, or was drunk enough, he or she could purchase a rattler belt or an ultra-attractive armadillo
handbag at cut-rate prices.

When Jack walked into the bar, he pushed up the
brim of his Stetson and paused in the doorway long
enough to allow his eyes to adjust before he made
his way to the bar. He exchanged a few heys with
some of the regulars. Over Clint Black on the jukebox,
he could hear the sound of Jimmy's bachelor party
going full tilt in the back room.

"Bottle of Lone Star," he ordered. A bottle appeared on the bar and he handed over a five. He felt
a soft hand on his arm and looked across his shoulder into the face of Gina Brown.

"Hey there, Jack."

"Hey, Gina." Gina was the same age as Jack and
twice divorced. She was a tall, lean cowgirl who
liked riding the mechanical bull at Slim Clem's over

off Highway Seventy. She wore her Wranglers tight, her Justins stacked, and her hair dyed red. Jack knew she dyed her hair because she liked riding him too. But lately she'd hinted that she had him in mind for husband number three. He'd had to cool things down so she would get that idea right out of her head.

"You here for the bachelor party in the back?" She gazed up at him out of the corners of her blue eyes. He would have to be blind to miss the invitation curving her lips.

"Yep." Jack raised the bottle to his mouth and took a long drink. He had no interest in heating things back up. He liked Gina, but he wasn't husband material. He grabbed his change from the bar and shoved it in the front pocket of his jeans. "See ya around," he said and turned to walk away.

Gina's next question stopped him in his tracks. "Have you seen Daisy Lee yet?"

Jack lowered the bottle and suddenly had trouble swallowing the beer in his mouth. He turned back to face Gina.

"I saw her this morning at the Texaco. Pumping gas into her momma's Cadillac." Gina shook her head. "I think it's been what, about ten or twelve years since she was last in town?"

It had been fifteen.

"I recognized her right away. Daisy Lee Brooks hasn't changed that much."

Except that Daisy Brooks was now Daisy Monroe and had been for the past fifteen years. And that had changed everything.

Gina took a step closer and played with a button

on the front of his shirt. "I was sorry to hear about Steven. I know he was your friend."

He and Steven Monroe had been almost insepara-ble since the age of five when they'd sat next to each other at the Lovett Baptist Church, belting out "Yes, Jesus Loves Me." But that had changed too. The last time he'd seen Steven was the night the two of them had beat each other bloody, while Daisy looked on horrified. It was the last time he'd seen Daisy too.

As if she didn't notice that Jack wasn't keeping up his end of the conversation, Gina rattled on, "I can't imagine dying at our age. It's just horrible."

"Excuse me, Gina," he said and walked away. An old anger, one he'd thought he'd buried, threatened to pull him into the past. He pushed against it, tapped it down tight, and shut it out.

Then he felt nothing at all.

With his beer in his hand, he wove his way through the rapidly filling bar and moved to the crowded room in the back. He leaned a shoulder into the doorframe and turned his full attention to Jimmy Calhoun. The man of honor sat in a chair in the middle of the room, surrounded by a dozen or so men, all watching two women dressed like rodeo queens bumping and grinding against each other while the Dixie Chicks sang about a sin wagon. Al-ready stripped down to sparkly G-strings on the bottom, the girls popped the snaps to their silky blouses. In unison their shirts slid down their toned shoulders and perfect bodies, exposing big breasts crammed into tiny sequined bikini tops. Jack low-ered his gaze from their full breasts to their G-strings tied at their hips.

Marvin Ferrell paused in the doorway beside him to watch the show. "Do you think those breasts are real?" he asked.

Jack shrugged a shoulder and raised the beer to his mouth. Obviously Marvin had been married too long because he was starting to sound like a woman. "Who cares?"

"True." Marvin laughed. "Did you hear Daisy Brooks is back?"

He looked down the bottle at Marvin then lowered it. "Yeah, I heard." Again he felt the old anger, and again he tapped it down until he felt nothing. He returned his attention to the strippers and watched them sandwich Jimmy between their half-naked bodies while they kissed each other above his head. The wet, open-mouthed tongue-thrusting kisses had the guys hollering for more. Jack tipped his head to one side and smiled. This was getting good.

"I saw Daisy at the Minute Mart," Marvin continued. "Damn, she's still hot as she was in high school."

Jack's smile flat-lined as an unbidden memory of big brown eyes and soft pink lips threatened to drag him into the black hole of his past.

"Remember what she looked like in that little cheerleader outfit of hers?"

Jack pushed away from the door and moved farther into the room, but he couldn't escape. It seemed everyone wanted a trip down memory lane. Everyone but him.

While the strippers took off each other's tiny bikini tops, the topic of conversation was Daisy. Between whistles and catcalls, Cal Turner, Lester Crandall and Eddy Dean Jones all asked if he'd seen her yet.

Disgusted, Jack left the room and made his way back to the bar. It was a hell of a deal when a man wasn't allowed to enjoy two mostly naked women making out with each other six feet in front of him. He didn't know how long Daisy would be in town, but he hoped like hell it was a short trip. Then maybe people would have something better to talk about. Mostly he hoped she had the good sense to stay the hell out of his way.

He set his bottle on the bar and made his way back out of The Road Kill, leaving behind talk and speculation of Daisy Monroe. Rain pelted the top of his hat and wet his shoulders as he made his way across the parking lot. But with each step he took, the memories followed close behind. Memories of looking into a pair of beautiful brown eyes as he kissed soft lips. His hand sliding up the back of her smooth thigh, slipping beneath her blue and gold cheerleader skirt. Of Daisy Lee wearing a pair of red cowboy boots with white hearts on the sides, and nothing else.

"Leaving the party so soon?" Gina asked as she walked toward him.

He looked over at her. "Boring party."

"We could make a party of our own." Typical of Gina, she didn't wait for him to make the first move. Usually that bothered him. Not tonight. She raised her mouth to his, and she tasted of warm beer and need. Jack kissed her back. With her firm breasts crushed against his chest, the first tug of desire stirred low in his gut. He pulled Gina into him and heated things up until all he felt was lust and the rain soaking his skin through his shirt. He replaced all thoughts of brown eyes and cheerleader skirts with the woman pressing herself against his button fly.

Daisy Monroe raised her hand to the screen door then lowered it again. Her heart pounded in her chest and her stomach twisted into one big knot. Rain beat against the porch all around her, and water ran from the downspout and into the flower beds. The garage behind her was lit up, illuminating every nook and cranny surrounding Parrish American Classics. But where she stood was pitch black, as if the light didn't dare creep any farther into the yard.

The garage was new, rebuilt since she'd seen it before. The yard surrounding the garage had been cleaned up. The old cars towed away. From what she could see the house was exactly the same, though, bringing a memory of a nice summer breeze lifting her hair and carrying the scent of roses. Of the many nights she'd sat on the porch where she now stood, wedged between Steven and Jack, laughing at their stupid jokes.

Thunder and lightning boomed and lit up the night sky, shattering the memory. An omen that she should leave and come back again some other time.

She wasn't good at confrontation. She wasn't one of those people who liked to face problems head on. She was better at it than she used to be, but . . . maybe she should have called first. It wasn't polite to just show up on someone's doorstep at ten o'clock at night, and she probably looked like a drowned cat.

Before she'd left her mother's house, she'd made sure her hair was brushed smooth and flipped under just below her shoulders. Her makeup looked perfect and her white blouse and khaki pants pressed. Now she was sure her hair had frizzed, mascara had run, and her pants were splattered with mud from the puddle she'd accidently dashed through. She turned to go, then forced herself to turn back. Her appearance wasn't really important, and there was never going to be a good time for what she had to do. She'd been in town three days already. She had to talk to Jack. Tonight. She'd put it off long enough. She had to tell him what she'd been keeping from him for fifteen years.

She raised her hand once more and nearly jumped out of her skin when the wooden door swung open before she could knock. Through the screen and dark interior, she could make out the outline of a man. His shirt was missing, and a light from deep within the house cast a warm golden glow from behind, pouring over his arms and shoulders and halfway down his naked chest. She definitely should have called first.

"Hello," she began before she could give into her trepidation. "I'm looking for Jackson Parrish."

"My-my," his voice drawled in the darkness, "if it isn't Daisy Lee Brooks."

It had been fifteen years and his voice had changed. It was deeper than the boy she'd known, but she would have recognized that nasty tone anywhere. No one could pack as much derision into his voice as Jack. She'd understood it once. Known what lay behind it. She didn't kid herself that she knew him anymore.

"Hello, Jack."

"What do you want, Daisy?"

She stared at him through the screen and shadows, at the outline of the man she'd once known so well. The knot in her stomach pulled tighter. "I wanted to . . . I need to talk to you. And I-I thought . . ." She took a deep breath and forced herself to stop stammering. She was thirty-three. So was he. "I wanted to tell you that I was in town before you heard it from someone else."

"Too late." The rain pounded the rooftop and the silence stretched between them. She could feel his gaze on her. It touched her face and the front of her yellow rain slicker; and just when she thought he wasn't going to speak again, he said, "If that's what you came to tell me, you can go now."

There was more. A lot more. She'd promised Steven that she'd give Jack a letter he'd written a few months before his death. The letter was in her coat pocket, now she had to tell Jack the truth about what had happened fifteen years ago, then hand over the letter. "It's important that I talk to you. Please."

He looked at her for several long moments, then he turned and disappeared into the depths of his house. He didn't open the screen for her, but he hadn't slammed the wood door in her face either. He'd made it clear that he was going to be as difficult as possible. But then, when had he ever made things easy?

Just as it always had, the screen door squeaked

when she opened it. She followed him through the living room toward the kitchen. His tall outline disappeared around the corner, but she knew the way.

The inside of the house smelled of new paint. She got an impression of dark furniture and a big-screen television, saw the outline of Mrs. Parrish's piano pushed against one wall—and she wondered briefly how much had changed since she'd last walked through the house. The light flipped on as she moved into the kitchen, and it was like stepping into a time warp. She half expected to see Mrs. Parrish standing in front by the almond-colored stove, baking bread or Daisy's favorite snicker-doodle cookies. The green linoleum had the same worn patch in front of the sink and the counter tops were the same speckled blue and turquoise.

Jack was in front of the refrigerator, the top half of him hidden behind the open door. His tan fingers were curled around the chrome handle, and all she could really see of him was the curve of his behind and his long legs. One pocket of his snug Levi's had a three-corner tear, and the seams looked like they were just about worn through.

Adrenaline rushed through her veins, and she balled her hands into fists to keep them from shaking. Then he rose to his full height, and everything seemed to slow, like someone flipped a switch on a movie projector. He turned as he shut the refrigerator door, and he held a quart of milk in his hand by his thigh. Her attention got momentarily stuck on the thin line of dark hair rising from the waistband of his Levi's and circling his navel. She lifted her gaze up past the hair on his flat belly and the defined muscles of his chest. If she'd had any lingering doubts, seeing him like this removed them. This was not the boy she'd once known. This was definitely a man.

She forced herself to look up at his strong chin, the etched bow of his tan lips, and into his eyes. She felt the back of her throat go dry. Jack Parrish had always been a good-looking boy, now he was lethal. One lock of his thick hair hung over his forehead and touched his brow. Those light green eyes that she remembered, that had once looked at her so full of passion and possession, looked back at her as if he were no more interested in seeing her than a stray dog.

"Did you come here to stare?"

She moved farther into the kitchen and shoved her hands into the pockets of her raincoat. "No, I came to tell you that I'm in town visiting my mother and sister."

He raised the milk and drank from the carton, waiting for her to elaborate.

"I thought you should know."

His gaze met hers over the carton, then he lowered it. Some things hadn't changed after all. Jack Parrish, bad boy and all around hell-raiser, had always been a milk drinker. "What makes you think I give a shit?" he asked and wiped the back of his hand across his mouth.

"I didn't know if you would. I mean, I did wonder what you'd think, but I wasn't sure." This was so much harder than she'd envisioned. And what she'd envisioned had been pretty dang hard.

"Now you don't have to wonder." He pointed

with his milk carton toward the other room. "If that's all, there's the door."

"No, that's not all." She looked down at the toes of her boots, the black leather spotted by the rain. "Steven wanted me to tell you something. He wanted me to tell you that he's sorry about . . . everything." She shook her head and corrected herself. "No, . . . was sorry, I mean. He's been gone seven months and it's still hard for me to remember him in the past tense. It seems wrong somehow. Like if I do, he never existed." She looked back at Jack. His expression hadn't changed. "The flowers you sent were really nice."

He shrugged and set the milk on the counter. "Penny sent them."

"Penny?"

"Penny Colten. Married Leon Kribs. She works for me now."

"Thank Penny for me." But Penny hadn't sent them and signed *his* name without *his* knowledge.

"Don't make it a big deal."

She knew how much Steven had once meant to him. "Don't pretend you don't care that he's gone."

He raised a dark brow. "You forget I tried to kill him."

"You wouldn't have killed him, Jack."

"No, you're right. I guess you just weren't worth it."

The conversation was headed in the wrong direction and she had to turn it around. "Don't be ugly."

"You call this ugly?" He laughed, but not with pleasure. "This is nothing, buttercup. Stick around and I'll show you how ugly I can get."

She already knew how ugly Jack could get, but while she might be a coward, she was also as stubborn as ragweed. Just as Jack was not the same boy she'd once known, she was not the same girl he'd once known either. She'd come to tell him the truth. Finally. Before she could get on with the rest of her life, she had to tell him about Nathan. It had taken her fifteen years to get to this point, and he could get ugly all he wanted, but he was going to listen to her.

A flash of white caught the corner of Daisy's eye a second before a woman entered the kitchen wearing a man's white dress shirt.

"Hey, y'all," the woman said as she moved to stand by Jack.

He looked down at her. "I told you to stay in bed."

"I got bored without you."

Heat crept up Daisy's neck to her cheeks, but she seemed to be the only embarrassed person in the room. Jack had a girlfriend. Of course he did. He'd always had a girlfriend or two. There had been a time when that would have hurt.

"Hello, Daisy. I don't know if you remember me. I'm Gina Brown."

It didn't hurt any longer, and Daisy was a bit ashamed to admit to herself that what she mostly felt was an overwhelming relief. She'd come all the way from Seattle to tell him about Nathan, and now all she felt was relief. Like an axe had been lifted from her throat. She guessed she was more of a coward than she thought. Daisy smiled and moved across the kitchen to offer Gina her hand. "Of course I remember you. We were in American Government together our senior year."

"Mr. Simmons."

"That's right."

"Remember when he tripped over an eraser on the floor?" Gina asked as if she weren't standing there wearing Jack's shirt and, Daisy would bet, nothing else.

"That was so funny. I just about—"

"What the hell is this?" Jack interrupted. "A damn high school reunion?"

Both women looked up at him and Gina said, "I was just being polite to your guest."

"She isn't my guest and she's leaving." He pinned his gaze on Daisy, just as cold and unyielding as when she'd first walked in the door.

"It was nice to see you, Gina," she said.

"Same."

"Good night, Jack."

He shoved his hip into the counter and crossed his arms over his chest.

"See you two around." She walked back through the dark house and out the door. The rain had stopped and she dodged puddles on her way to her mother's Caddie, parked on the side of the garage. Next time, she would definitely call first.

Just as she reached for the car door, she felt a hand on her arm whipping her around. She looked up into Jack's face. Security lights shined down on him and shadowed the angry set of his jaw. His eyes stared into hers—no longer cold, they were filled with a burning rage.

"I don't know what you came here looking for, absolution or forgiveness," he said, his drawl more pronounced than before. "But you won't find it."

He dropped her arm as if he couldn't stand the touch of her.

"Yes, I know."

"Good. You stay away from me, Daisy Lee," he said, drawing out the vowels in her name. "You stay away or I'll make your life a misery."

She looked up into his dark face, at the passion and anger that had not abated in fifteen years.

"Just stay away," he said one last time before he turned on his bare heels and disappeared into the shadows.

She knew she would be wise to heed his warning. Too bad she didn't have that option.

Although he didn't know it yet, neither did he.

Chapter 2

*D*aisy blew into the mug of hot coffee as she raised it to her lips. The sun had yet to rise, and her mother was still asleep in her bedroom down the hall. Besides updated appliances, little had changed in her mother's kitchen. The counter tops and floor tiles were the same matching blue, and the same Texas bluebells were painted on the white cabinets.

As quiet as possible Daisy slipped into her raincoat, hung by the back door the night before. She threaded one arm then the other through the slicker until it covered her short pajamas. She crammed her feet into her mother's garden clogs, then she slipped outside into the deep shadows of early morning. Cool air touched her face and bare legs, and a slight breeze pulled several strands of hair from the claw at the back of her head. The Texas air filled her lungs and brought a smile to her lips. She didn't know why, or how to explain it, but the air was different here. It just seemed to settle in her chest and radiate outward. It whispered across her skin and answered a hidden longing she hadn't even known rested deep in her soul.

She was home. If only for a short time.

For fifteen years she'd lived in the Seattle, Washington, area. She'd grown to love it there. She loved the rich green landscape, the mountains, the bay. Snow skiing. Water skiing. The Mariners. So many things.

But Daisy Lee was a Texan. In her heart and in her blood. In her DNA, like her blond hair. Like her birthmark in the shape of a little love bite on the top of her left breast. And like her love bite, Lovett hadn't changed in the past fifteen years. The population had grown by several hundred; there were a few new businesses and one new grade school. The town had recently added an eighteen-hole golf course and a country club to its landscape, but unlike the rest of the country, and more urban Texas, Lovett still moved at its own laid-back pace.

Daisy gazed into the shadows of her mother's backyard. The outline of the five-foot windmill, an Annie Oakley statue, and a dozen or so flamingos were etched in black. Growing up, her mother's taste in exterior decor had been a constant source of embarrassment for her and her younger sister, Lily. Now the parade of flamingos brought a smile to her lips.

She took a drink of coffee, then she sat on the top concrete step next to a stone armadillo with several babies stacked on its back. Daisy hadn't slept well the night before. Her eyes felt puffy and her mind sluggish. She shivered and set the mug on her knee. Before she'd seen Jack last night, her plan had been so clear. She'd come to Lovett, intending to visit with her mother and sister for a few days, then talk to Jack and tell him about Nathan. All within twelve days. Which, until last night, she'd figured would be plenty of time.

She'd known it would be difficult, but clear-cut. She and Steven had talked about it before he'd passed. In her pocket, she still had the letter Steven had written before he'd lost the ability to read and write. When he'd accepted that he would die, that there would be no cure for him, no more experimental drugs to take, no more radical surgeries to try, he'd wanted to make things right with the people he'd felt he'd wronged in his life. One of those people was Jack. At first he'd thought to send the letter, but the more the two of them talked about it, the more they'd concluded that it should be delivered in person. By her. Because ultimately, she was the one who had to deal with Jack Parrish, and she was the one who'd wronged him most.

They'd never really meant to keep Nathan a secret from him. Her mother knew. So did her sister. Nathan knew too. He'd always known that he had a biological father named Jackson who lived in Lovett, Texas. They'd told him as soon as he'd been capable of understanding, but he'd never expressed any interest in meeting Jack. Steven had always been enough father for him.

It was time. Perhaps past time that she told Jack he had a son. A moan escaped her lips and she took a sip of coffee. A fifteen-year-old son with a pickle green Mohawk, a pierced lip, and so many dog chains hanging off him he looked liked he'd broken into the animal shelter.

Nathan had had such a hard time these past two and a half years. When Steven was diagnosed, he'd been given five months to live. He'd lasted almost two years, but it hadn't been an easy two years. Watching Steven fight to live had been hard on her, but it had been hell on Nathan. And she hated to admit it, but there had been times when she hadn't been at all attentive to her son. Some nights, she hadn't even known he was gone until he'd returned. He'd walk in the door and she'd scold him for not telling her where he'd gone. He'd look at her through those clear blue eyes of his and say, "I told you I was going to Pete's. You said I could." And she'd have to admit to herself that it was entirely possible that he'd told her, but she'd been focused on Steven's medication or his next surgery—or perhaps that had been the day when Steven lost his ability to use a calculator, drive a car, or tie his shoes. Watching her husband struggle to maintain his dignity while trying to recall a simple task he'd been performing since he was four or five had been heartbreaking. There were times when she'd simply forgotten whole blocks of conversations with Nathan.

The day Nathan had walked in the house with that Mohawk had been a real wake-up call for her. Suddenly, he was no longer the little boy who played soccer, loved football, and watched "Nickelodeon" curled up on the couch with his special blanket. It hadn't been the color of his hair that had alarmed her most. It had been the lost look in his eyes. His empty, lost gaze had shocked her out of the depression and grief she hadn't even known she'd fallen into for almost seven months following Steven's passing.

Steven was gone. She and Nathan would always feel his loss, like a missing part of their souls. He'd been her best friend and a good man. He'd been a buffer, a comfort, someone who made her life better. Easier. He'd been a loving husband and father.

She and Nathan would never forget him, but she could not continue to live in the past. She had to live in the present and begin to look toward the future. For Nathan, and for herself. But in order for her to move forward, she had to take care of her past. She had to quit hiding from it.

Fingers of morning sun crept into the backyard and sparkled in the dew-covered lawn. The early sun cast long patterns in the wet grass, crept up the windmill, and shot sparks off the tip of Annie Oakley's silver rifle. Daisy wished she had her Nikon and wide-angle lens on her. It was up in her room, and she knew if she ran up to get it, she'd miss the shot and the rising sun. Within seconds, dawn broke over Daisy's feet, legs and face; she closed her eyes and soaked it all in.

Living in the Northwest, Daisy had lost most of her accent, but she'd never lost her love of wide-open spaces and the huge blue sky stretching across the horizon in unbroken lines. She opened her eyes and wished Steven were here to see it. He would have loved it as much as she did.

Daisy looked down at the rubber garden clogs on her feet. She wished for a lot of things. Like more time before she had to confront Jack again. She was in no hurry to see the anger in his face. She'd known that he would not welcome her back with open arms, but she was surprised that after all of these years, he clearly hated her as much as he had the last time she'd seen him.

You call this ugly? he'd said. *This is nothing, buttercup. Stick around and I'll show you how ugly I can get.*

She wondered if Jack had realized he'd called her buttercup. His old name for her. The name he'd first called her on her first day at Lovett Elementary.

She remembered being nervous and scared on that day, so long ago. She'd been afraid no one would like her, and she'd suspected that the big red bow clipped to the top of her head looked stupid. Her mother had pulled it off the handle of a Welcome Wagon basket filled with coupons, a recipe book, and Wick Fowler's chili kit. Daisy hadn't wanted to wear the bow, but her mother had insisted that it looked good and matched her dress.

All that first morning, no one had spoken to her. By lunch, she'd become so upset, she was unable to eat her cheese yum-yum sandwich. Finally, during recess, Steven and Jack walked up to where she stood with her back against the chain link fence.

"What's your name?" Jack had asked.

She'd looked into those green eyes of his, surrounded by long black lashes, and she'd smiled. Finally someone was talking to her, and her little heart leapt with joy. "Daisy Lee Brooks."

He'd rocked back on the heels of his boots as he looked her up and down. "Well, buttercup, that's the stupidest hair bow I ever did see," he'd drawled, then he and Steven howled with laughter.

Hearing that the bow was stupid confirmed her worst fears, and the backs of her eyes started to sting. "Yeah, well y'all are so stupid you have to take off your shoes to count," she'd responded, proud that she stood up for herself. Then she'd ruined everything by bursting into tears.

The memory of that day brought a sad smile to her face. She'd vowed to hate those two boys as long as she lived. It lasted until Jack had asked her to play on their softball team, three weeks later. It was Steven who showed her how to play second base without getting hit in the face with the ball.

At first, Jack had called her buttercup to tease her, but years later, he'd whispered it as he kissed the side of her throat. His voice would go all dark while he discovered whole new ways to tease her. There had been a time when just the memory of his kiss had sent a warm shudder through her chest, but she hadn't felt anything warm and tingly for him in years.

She thought of how he'd looked last night, half naked and fully ticked off. His lids lowered over his sexy green eyes, and that sardonic curl of his lips. He'd grown even more handsome than the last time she'd seen him, but Daisy was older and wiser and no longer tempted by good looks and bad attitudes.

Nathan didn't resemble Jack much. Except maybe the attitude part. He was staying with Steven's sister in Seattle while Daisy was in Lovett, but he knew the reason behind her trip. She'd learned her lesson about lies, no matter how well intentioned, and she never lied to Nathan. But she had purposely chosen his last week of ninth grade to make the trip so he couldn't come along. She didn't know what Jack's reaction would be once she told him about Nathan. She didn't think he would be cruel, not to Nathan anyway, but she wasn't certain. She didn't want Nathan here if Jack got truly ugly. Nathan had had enough pain in his life.

From inside the house, she heard her mother moving around. She stood and walked back inside.

"Good morning," she said as she hung up her coat. The warm scent of her mother's kitchen filled her nose. The smell of baked bread and home-cooked comfort food surrounded her like a familiar blanket. "I watched the sun come up, and it was absolutely gorgeous." She kicked off the garden clogs and looked over at her mother, who was stirring cream into her coffee. Louella Brooks wore a blue nylon nightgown, and her blond hair was piled on top of her head like cotton candy.

"How was your party last night?" Daisy asked. Every second Friday, the Lovett single's club held a dance, and Louella Brooks hadn't missed one since she'd joined in nineteen ninety-two. She paid fifty dollars a year to belong to the club, and she believed in getting her money's worth.

"Verna Pearse was there, and I swear she looks a good ten years older than her real age." Louella placed her spoon in the sink and raised her mug to her lips. Her brown eyes looked back at Daisy over her coffee. "She was surely saggin', baggin' and draggin'."

Daisy smiled and filled her own mug. Verna had once worked at the Wild Coyote Diner with Louella. The two had been friends at one time. During Daisy's junior and senior years of high school, she'd worked at the diner too, but she couldn't recall what had happened to break up the friendship. "What happened between you and Verna?" she asked.

Louella put her mug on the counter and grabbed a loaf of bread from the pantry. "Verna Pearse is as loose as a slipknot," she said. "For a year she told me she got paid ten cents more an hour than me because she was a better waitress. She bragged and held it over my head, but come to find out, she was earning it in other ways."

"How?"

"With Big Bob Jenkins."

Daisy remembered the owner of the diner, and he hadn't been called Big Bob for nothing. "She was having sex with Big Bob?"

Louella shook her head and pursed her lips. "Oral gratification in the storeroom."

"Really? That's criminal."

"Yes. It's a form of prostitution."

"I was thinking it was more like slave labor. Verna blew Big Bob for what turns out to be like—eighty cents a day? That's not right."

"Daisy," her mother scolded as she got out the toaster. "Don't talk filth."

"You brought it up!" She'd never understand her mother. "Oral gratification" was okay, but somehow "blew" wasn't.

"You've been in the North too long."

Maybe she had, because she just didn't get the difference. Although there had been a time when she never would have uttered the word in that context.

Louella opened the loaf of bread. "Do you want toast?"

"I don't eat in the morning." She took a drink of coffee and moved to the corner breakfast nook. The bright morning sun poured in through the sheers and lit up the yellow table.

"Did you go out last night?" her mother asked as she toasted one slice of bread.

Meaning, did she work up her nerve to drive to Jack's. "Yes. I went to his house last night."

"Did you tell him?"

Daisy sat on one of the bench seats and looked down at her hands wrapped around her mug. She had a chip in her red fingernail polish. "No. He wasn't alone. His girlfriend was there, so it wasn't a good time."

"Maybe that was a sign you should leave it alone."

Growing up, her mother had always liked Steven more than Jack. Although, Louella liked Jack too. When the three of them got into trouble, Jack was often blamed. And while it was true that he'd usually come up with the offense that landed them in hot water, Daisy and Steven would gladly go along with him. "I can't do that," Daisy said, "I have to tell him."

"I still don't understand why." Louella's toast popped up and she set it on a little plate.

"I told you why." Daisy didn't feel like discussing her reasons again. She opened the bottle of fingernail polish she'd left on the table yesterday and set about repairing the chip.

"Well, if you're determined to do this, you shouldn't go over there at night." Louella lifted the lid off the butter dish and buttered her toast. "People talk about widows. They say you're desperate."

Daisy's father had died when she was five, but she'd never heard any gossip about her mother being desperate. "I don't care." She covered her index fingernail with red polish, then screwed the lid back on the bottle.

"You should." Louella grabbed her plate and coffee and sat across the table from Daisy. "You don't want people to think you're going over there for relations."

Daisy blew on her wet fingernail to keep from laughing. It had been over two years since she'd had *relations*, and she wasn't sure she knew how to do it anymore. After Steven's diagnosis and first surgery, they'd tried to have a normal, healthy married life, but after a few months, it just got too difficult. At first she'd really missed sex with her husband. Then the more she'd gone without, the less she'd missed it. Now, she really didn't think about it all that much.

"Tell me about all those flamingos in your backyard," Daisy said to change the subject.

"I think they're pretty," her mother said. Growing up, her mother had been into Disney. Their yard had been overrun with Snow White, the Seven Dwarfs, and several characters from *Alice in Wonderland*. "I got the big flamingo with the little pocket book in its beak from Kitty Fae Young. Her granddaughter

Amanda makes 'em up special order. You remember Amanda, don't you?"

Just like she was a kid again, Daisy felt her eyes glaze over. Her mother had always had a tendency to ramble on forever about people Daisy didn't know, had never met, and didn't give a rat's about. Growing up, she and Lily had been involuntary victims, trapped into listening to the hottest gossip going around the diner, which usually wasn't all that hot. It didn't matter how often they hinted that they didn't care about so-and-so's new Buick, arthritis or yummy homemade cookies, Louella was like a needle stuck in a record groove and absolutely couldn't stop until she came to the end.

She shook her head and said a weak, "No."

"Sure you do," her mother said. "She had those really bad buck teeth. Looked just like a little beaver."

"Oh yeah," she said although she didn't have the foggiest. There were quite a few kids in west Texas with buck teeth.

Daisy slid from behind the table and stood. While her mother talked about Amanda and her yard art, Daisy walked to the sink and rinsed her mug. She glanced up at the purple and green stained-glass frame making patterns on the sill. She'd taken the photo in the picture frame. It was Steven and Nathan on Nathan's fourth birthday, and she'd used a wide-angle lens to distort the closeup shot. Both wore party hats and were grinning like lunatics fresh from the asylum, their eyes huge. She'd taken it when she first started photography classes and was experimenting. They'd all been so happy then.

A frown creased her brow and she looked away.

She didn't want to think about the past today. She didn't want to get sucked into the emotional morass of it. She put the mug in the dishwasher and her gaze fell on a grocery list clipped in a clothespin recipe holder.

". . . but of course you didn't live here then," her mother was saying. "That was the year a twister took out Red Cooley's trailer."

"Are you going to the store?" she interrupted.

"I need a few things," her mother answered as she rose from the table and put the bread away. "After church tomorrow, Lily Belle and Pippen are coming over for Sunday dinner, and I thought we'd have a nice ham."

Lily was three years younger than Daisy, and Pippen was her two-year-old son. Lily's husband had run off with a cowgirl, and they were in the process of a messy divorce. She was having a difficult time, and as a result, men in general were on Lily's hit list. "I'll go to Albertsons for you," she offered. That way she could choose something beside ham. She'd never been a big pork fan, and after Steven's funeral, a lot of well-meaning people had dropped off baked hams. Some of them were still in her freezer in Seattle.

She took a shower then dressed in a pair of jeans and a blue T-shirt. She dried her hair and put on a little makeup. With the list in her back pocket, she jumped in her mother's Cadillac. The car had several dents up and down each side due to her mother being nearsighted. A flamingo air freshener hung from the rearview mirror, and the Caddie whined when she turned corners.

Inside Albertsons, the Muzak of choice was Barry Manilow's "Mandy," an abomination in any state, but especially Texas. She tossed a box of tea bags and a can of coffee into her cart, then she headed for the meat section. She was in the mood for steak and grabbed a package of three rib-eyes.

"Well hey, Daisy. I heard you were back in town."

Daisy glanced up from her steaks. The woman in front of her looked slightly familiar. Her hair was pinned up in big pink rollers, and she held a big can of Super Hold Aqua Net in one hand and a pack of bobby pins in the other.

It took Daisy a few seconds to place a name with the face. "You're Shay Brewton, Sylvia's little sister." Daisy and Sylvia had been on the same cheerleader squad at Lovett High. They'd been good friends but had lost touch when Daisy and Steven had moved away. "How's Sylvia?"

"She's good. She lives in Houston now with her husband and kids."

"Houston?" She set the steaks back in the case and placed her foot on the bottom rung of the cart. "Shoot. I'm sorry she moved away. I'd hoped to look her up before I left."

"She's in town this weekend for my wedding."

Daisy smiled. "You're getting married? When? To whom?"

"I'm marrying Jimmy Calhoun over at Whiley Baptist Church. Tonight at six."

"Jimmy Calhoun?" She'd gone all through school with Jimmy. He'd had flaming red hair and a silver tooth. There were six Calhoun boys; all of them trouble. If she'd had to lay odds, she would have bet the lot of them were living in Huntsville with prison tattoos by now.

Shay laughed. "Don't look at me like I've come off my spool."

Daisy hadn't realized her mouth was hanging open and she snapped it shut. "Congratulations, I'm sure you'll be very happy," she said.

"Come to my reception afterwards over at the country club. It starts at eight."

"Crash your wedding?"

"It's going to be a big party. Lots of food and liquor, and we hired Jed and the Rippers to play music for us. Sylvia will be there, and I know she'd just love to see you. Mom and Daddy, too."

Mrs. Brewton had been an adviser for the squad. Mr. Brewton had made his own liquor in the back shed. Daisy knew from experience that it could eat a hole in your esophagus. "Maybe I will."

Shay nodded. "Good, I'll tell her I ran into you and that you're coming to the reception. She'll be tickled."

Daisy hadn't brought anything to wear to a wedding reception. The only dress she'd brought was a white tank, and it really wasn't appropriate. Maybe she'd just send a gift. "Are you registered anywhere?"

"Oh, don't worry about that." She smiled. "But yes, I am. Donna's Gifts on Fifth."

Of course. Everyone registered at Donna's.

"See ya tonight," Shay said as she moved away.

Daisy watched her disappear around a corner and she smiled again. Little Shay Brewton was marrying wild Jimmy Calhoun. Growing up, there really hadn't been any boys more insane than Jimmy and his brothers.

Except maybe Jack.

Jack had always been wrapped crazy. It had never been enough for him to race his bike as fast as it would go; he had to lift his hands from the handle bars, or stand on the seat. It wasn't enough to chase dust devils; he had to play outside when the weather service predicted an F1 tornado. He thought he was invincible, like superman.

Steven had been more daredevil than Daisy, but even he hadn't attempted half the stuff Jack had. He'd never jumped from his roof into a pile of leaves and broken his leg. Or put a motorcycle engine on a homemade go-cart and driven around town as if he were at Talladega.

Jack had done that. He'd done it even though he knew his dad would whoop his butt. And Ray Parrish had, but it'd been worth it to Jack.

Steven Monroe had always been the safe one— dependable—while Jack had raced through life full throttle as if his hair was on fire.

Hanging around with the craziest boy in school had been a lot of fun. Getting romantically involved with him had been a huge mistake.

One in which she and Steven and Jack had all paid a high price.

Chapter 3

The Lovett Country Club sat on the edge of an eighteen-hole golf course. Elm trees lined the drive from the gates to the entrance of the building. Visitors had to walk across a bridge to get to the front doors. A stream ran beneath the bridge and emptied into a pond filled with koi, their red and white bodies swaying in the slow current.

At half past eight, Daisy pulled into a parking spot next to a Mercedes. This was the first time she'd gone out by herself since Steven's passing, and it did feel strange. Like she'd forgotten something at home. The sort of panicky feeling she'd usually get when she was in line at the airport before a trip, like she'd left the tickets on the dining room table even though she knew they were in her purse. She wondered how much longer until the panicky feeling went away? Until she was used to going out alone.

And dating. Forget it. She didn't think she'd ever be ready for that.

Daisy entered the glass double doors and caught a glimpse of her smeared reflection in the polished brass railing as she walked past the restaurant and down a long hall toward the banquet room. She wore a red sleeveless cocktail dress she'd borrowed from Lily. Daisy was a few inches taller than her five-foot-two-inch sister, a little bigger in the chest too. Red might not be the most appropriate color to wear to a wedding reception, but it was the only dress Lily owned that wasn't too short or too tight across Daisy's breasts.

Covered silk buttons ran up the right side from the hem to her armpit, and her mother's small red purse hung from a long gold chain on her shoulder.

She set the gift she'd bought earlier on a table beside the door, and she moved just inside the banquet room. The bridal party stood before teal-and-gold swags in a traditional line while a male photographer snapped pictures with a digital camera.

About two hundred people toasted the happy couple with flutes of champagne. Teal and gold festooned everything and colored candles flickered atop round tables covered in white cloths. To Daisy's left, rows of chafing dishes served what looked like barbeque chicken, roast beef, vegetables, and chili. Most of the guests were already seated while others milled around.

The photographer wasn't using a video light to capture the glow of the room, which Daisy thought was too bad. If she'd been hired for the shoot, she would have packed a number of cameras and numerous lenses in her gearbox. In this particular room, she would have used 1600 color film with on-camera flash and a video light to enhance ambient light in the background. Every photographer worked a little differently, though. This guy's photographs would probably turn out all right.

". . . to Jimmy and Shay Calhoun," someone toasted. Daisy grabbed a flute of champagne and turned her attention from the photographer to the bridal party. As her gaze scanned the line, she raised the glass to her mouth, careful not to smudge her red lipstick. Behind her flute, Daisy smiled as her eyes took in her friend from high school. Sylvia was decked out in some sort of teal gauze and gold satin harem-girl outfit. She was as big as a house. Not fat. Very pregnant. She looked tired, but as cute as ever, and was as short as Daisy remembered; and she still wore the same lacquered bangs and big hair as in school.

Shay looked beautiful with her Texas-sized curls bouncing at her shoulder and soft veil floating like a cloud around her. Jimmy Calhoun was better looking than he'd been when Daisy had lived here before. Or maybe he just cleaned up nice in his tux. She wasn't sure, but his red hair was a shade or two darker and all his freckles had faded.

"Excuse me, ma'am," a voice she instantly recognized spoke directly behind her. She scooted sideways out of the doorway and glanced over her shoulder, looking past the defined line of Jack Parrish's mouth and up into his beautiful eyes.

His gaze locked with hers as he passed, and the sleeve of his charcoal blazer brushed her bare arm.

Surprise halted his footsteps for about half a heart-beat, and within that fraction of a second, something hot and alive flashed behind his eyes. Just as quickly it was gone, and Daisy wasn't sure if it had been a trick of the two chandeliers overhead or of the flick-ering candlelight. He moved past, and she watched his broad shoulders and the back of his head as he wove his way through the crowd toward the bride and groom. His dark hair brushed the back of his collar and looked finger-combed, as if he'd just taken off his hat, tossed it on the seat of his car, and fixed his hair. In his suit, he looked liked he'd just stepped out of a fashion magazine. And as always, he moved with an easy, laid-back stride that made it clear he was in no great hurry to get anywhere.

A little flutter that had nothing to do with his looks, and everything to do with who he was to her and her son, stirred in her stomach.

"Daisy Lee Brooks!" Sylvia hollered and Daisy turned her gaze to her friend. "You get over here." Sylvia's voice had always been bigger than the rest of her. It had made her an excellent cheerleader.

Daisy laughed and walked to the front. She moved to stand beside Jack, who was speaking with the groom. She hugged her friend and Mr. and Mrs. Brewton. Sylvia introduced her to her husband, Chris, then said, "You remember Jimmy Calhoun."

"Hello, Daisy." Jimmy grinned, his silver tooth gone, replaced by porcelain. "You look great."

"Thank you." She glanced up at Jack who was do-ing a good job of pretending she wasn't alive. Her gaze lowered to his shoulders and the blue dress shirt between the lapels of his suit jacket. He wasn't wearing a tie. She returned her attention to the groom. "You look good yourself, Jimmy. I can't believe you married little Shay Brewton. I remember when Sylvia and I tried to teach her to ride a bike and she ran into a tree."

Shay laughed and Jimmy said, "I bet you thought I'd be in prison by now."

In the seventh grade, Jimmy and his Calhoun brothers had piled into their daddy's Monte Carlo, pressed their naked behinds to the windows, and mooned the middle school. In the tenth, Jimmy had called in a bomb threat because he wanted to get out of school a few hours early. He got caught because he used the pay phone outside the principal's office. "The thought never entered my head."

Sylvia laughed because she knew better. Daisy felt herself relax. The flutter in her stomach calmed. Now wasn't the time nor place to tell Jack about Nathan. She didn't have to think about it. She could relax. Have fun with old friends. It had been a long time since she'd had a little fun.

"Jack, do you remember the time you and Steven and I got arrested for racing out on the old highway?" Jimmy asked.

"Sure." He pulled back his cuff and looked at his watch.

"Were you there that night, Daisy?"

"No." She once again glanced up at the man by her side. "I never liked it when Steven and Jack raced cars. I was always afraid someone would get hurt."

"I was always in control." Jack dropped his hand to his side and his fingers brushed her dress. He lowered his gaze to her, and his eyes were without expression when he said, "I was always safe."

No, being with him had rarely been safe.

"I was real sorry to hear about Steven," Jimmy said and she returned her gaze to him. "He was a good guy."

Daisy never knew what to say to that, so she raised her glass to her lips.

"Shay told me he died of brain cancer."

"Yes." It had a name, glioblastoma. And it was horrible and always fatal.

"I've been fixin' to get a hold of your momma to ask how you're doing," Sylvia told her.

"I'm okay." Which was the truth. She was okay. "Goodness, when's this baby due?" she asked Sylvia, purposely changing the subject.

"Next month." She rubbed her big belly. "And I am more than ready. Do you have children?"

"Yes." She was very aware of Jack, of the sleeve of his jacket so close to her arm that if she moved just a fraction, she would feel the texture of it against her bare skin. "My son, Nathan," she said and purposely didn't reveal his age. "He's in Seattle with Steven's sister Junie and her husband Oliver." She glanced up at Jack and gone was his carefully blank expression. Surprise filled his green eyes and lifted a brow. "You remember Junie don't you?"

"Of course," he said and looked away.

"I remember her," Sylvia elaborated. "She was a lot older than us. I remember Steven's parents were pretty old too."

Steven had been a real surprise when his parents were in their mid forties. They were both sixty-three when he graduated high school. His mother was gone now, and his father lived in a retirement community in Arizona.

"Shay and I are gonna get to work on making a baby tonight." Jimmy laughed. "Don't want to wait too late in life to have a baby."

Jack reached inside his jacket and pulled a cigar from the breast pocket of his dress shirt. "Congratulations," he said and handed it to Jimmy.

Jimmy pulled the cigar through his fingers. "My favorite. Thanks."

"Don't I get one?" Shay protested with a smile.

"I didn't know you smoked cigars," Jack said as he reached for her hand. He took it from the folds of her dress and brought it to his mouth. "Congratulations, Shay. Jimmy is a very lucky man." He kissed her knuckles and drawled just above a whisper, "If he doesn't treat you right, you let me know."

Shay smiled and touched her curls with her free hand. "Are you going to open a can of whoop ass on my behalf?"

"For you, I'll open two." He dropped her hand, then he excused himself.

Daisy's gaze fell to his broad shoulders as he made his way to the bar set up in one corner.

"He could always charm the pants off anyone," Sylvia sighed. "Even in the fifth grade."

She turned her attention to Sylvia as the others around them talked about football. While they debated whether the Cowboys needed stronger defense or offense, Daisy leaned her head closer to Sylvia.

"What happened with you and Jack in the fifth grade?" she asked her friend.

A wistful smile curved Sylvia's lips, and the two of them turned to watch Jack order a beer at the bar.

"Come on," Daisy wheedled.

"He talked me into showing him my bottom."

In the fifth grade? She and Jack and Steven had been playing NASCAR in the fifth grade. Not doctor. "How?"

"He told me he'd show me his if I showed him mine."

"That's all it took?"

"I don't have brothers, and he doesn't have sisters. We were curious and checked out each other's bottoms. Nothing bad happened. He was real sweet about it."

She'd never known that while he was boring her with Richard Petty stats, he was running around checking out other girl's bottoms. She wondered what else she didn't know.

"Don't tell me you were friends with Jack Parrish all those years and never showed him yours."

"Not in the fifth grade."

"Honey, sooner or later, everyone showed Jack their bottom." She ran her hand over her big belly. "It was just a matter of time."

Daisy was seventeen and practically had to beg him to look at her bottom. If she remembered correctly, his words had been, "Stop, Daisy. I don't mess around with virgins." But he had, and they'd begun a wild sexual relationship that they'd kept secret from everyone. Even Steven. Especially Steven. It had been crazy and thrilling and intense. A roller coaster ride of love and jealousy and sex. And it had ended very badly.

Long forgotten memories rushed at Daisy, as if suddenly set free. One here, another there. A tangled mess of memory and chaotic emotion, as if they'd been smashed together, thrown in a box, and hurriedly taped shut. Waiting all these years for someone to rip the tape off and throw open the tabs.

She recalled her own wedding. She and Steven at the courthouse. Her mother and his parents standing with them. Steven squeezing her hand to keep it from shaking. She'd loved Steven Monroe for years before she married him. Maybe not a hot burning kind of love. Maybe she didn't crave him like a drug, but that kind of love didn't last. It burned out. The love she'd felt for Steven had always been warm and comfortable, like coming home cold and tired, curling up in front of a fire. That kind of love lasted, and it would last long after Steven's passing.

She remembered riding with Steven in his car, on their way to tell Jack about their marriage. Her pregnancy had made her sick to her stomach. What they were about to do made her chest tight. She'd started to cry even before they pulled onto Jack's street. Again, Steven had held her hand.

She and Steven had been through a lot together, and everything they'd faced had brought them closer. Their first few years of marriage while he was attending school had been rough financially. Then when Nathan turned four, Steven got a good job and they decided to add another child to their family only to find out that Steven had a low sperm count. They'd tried everything to conceive, but nothing worked. After five years, they decided to give up and were happy with their lives.

The room suddenly went dark and Daisy was jarred from the past. A spotlight shined on the center of the dance floor, and she tried to push all thoughts of the past from her head. Jed and the Rippers picked up their instruments and Jimmy and Shay danced their first dance as husband and wife.

When Daisy had decided to come home and tell Jack about Nathan, she hadn't counted on the memories. She hadn't even known they were there, locked away, waiting for her.

Daisy moved away from the dance floor and placed her empty glass on a table. She headed to the bathroom in the bar down the hall, and while she washed her hands, she looked at her reflection. She was no longer a scared, heartbroken girl. She was a lot tougher than she'd been growing up. While she wasn't here to relive memories, she wouldn't hide from them either. She was here to tell Jack about Nathan. She would tell him that she was sorry and hope he'd understand. Although she was fairly certain he wouldn't understand and would make things difficult, she still had to do the right thing. No more putting it off. No more hiding.

She reapplied her red lipstick and dropped it into her purse. Let Jack do his worst. She might even deserve some of it, but she'd survive. She'd lived with just about the worst that life could deal her, and nothing Jack could do would be as bad as that.

Daisy stopped in the bar and bought a glass of wine, then made her way back toward the banquet room.

Jack stood in the long hall with one shoulder shoved against the wall. He held a cell phone in one hand, the other was in the front pocket of his pants. He glanced up and watched her as she moved toward him.

"That'd be fine," he said into the phone. "I'll see y'all first thing Monday."

Her first impulse was to hurry past, but she stopped in front of him instead. "Hey, Jack."

He disconnected and put the phone in his pocket. "What do you want, Daisy?"

"Nothing. Just being friendly."

"I don't want to be 'friendly' with you." He straightened away from the wall and took his hand from his pocket. "I thought I made myself clear last night."

"Oh, you did." She took a drink of her wine, then asked, "How's Billy?" All she remembered of Jack's brother was a pair of shiny blue eyes and sandy blond hair. Other than that, she couldn't recall much about him.

He looked over her head and said, "Billy's good."

She waited for him to elaborate. He didn't. "Married? Kids?"

"Yep."

"Where's Gina?" His gaze met hers and, in that suit, his eyes appeared more gray than green.

"At Slim Clem's, I imagine."

"She's not here?"

"I don't see her."

She took another sip of her wine. She was going to be pleasant if it killed her. Or him. "You didn't bring her with you?"

"Why would I?"

"Isn't she your girlfriend?"

"Whatever gave you that idea?"

They both knew what had given her that idea. "Oh, maybe because she was wearing your shirt last night, and nothing else."

"You're wrong about that. She was wearin' a black lace thong." One corner of his mouth slid up, purposely provoking her—*the jerk.* "And a satisfied smile. You remember that smile, don't you, Daisy?"

She would *not* lose her temper and give him what he wanted. "Don't flatter yourself, Jack Parrish. You weren't that memorable."

"What? I was talking about Gina's smile last night." The other corner of his mouth slid up and laugh lines appeared in the corners of his eyes. "What were *you* talking about, buttercup?"

They both knew he hadn't been talking about *Gina's* smile. "You haven't changed since high school." She gave him a withering glance and walked away before she lost her temper and said something she might regret. Like that he should grow up.

Jack watched her go. His smile flat-lined, and his gaze slid from her blond hair, all slick and smooth, down the back of her red dress to her behind and the backs of her thighs. Who the hell was she to judge him? She'd screwed around with him, said she'd love him forever; then married his best friend the same week he buried both his parents. In his book, that made her a hardcore bitch.

She disappeared into the banquet room, and Jack waited a few moments before he followed. At thirty-three, Daisy was even more beautiful than she'd been at eighteen. He'd seen it last night. In his kitchen, and he saw it now. So much about her was different, yet the same. Her hair was still the same shiny blond, but it wasn't big and curly and sprayed stiff. Now it was smooth and sexy as hell. She'd grown an inch maybe two, to what he figured was about five-foot-five, but she carried herself like she was still queen of the Lovett Rose Festival. Her large eyes were still the color of rich mahogany, but they'd lost the innocence and passion that he'd once found so fascinating.

He walked down the hall and entered the dark banquet room. Marvin stopped him to talk about the '67 Ford Fairlane he'd just bought.

"It has its original 427," he said while Jed and the Rippers sang a Tim McGraw song about a girl in a miniskirt.

Like a magnet, Jack's gaze found Daisy. She stood at the edge of the lighted floor across the room, chatting with J. P. Clark and his wife, Loretta. Daisy's red dress hugged the curves of her body without looking too tight. She clearly hadn't gone too fat. Didn't have thick ankles or a droopy butt. Which was too bad, as far as Jack was concerned.

For years he'd forgotten about her and Steven. He'd buried them in the past and got on with his life. Now here she was, dredging it all back up again.

Cal Turner approached her and she followed him to the middle of the dance floor. Everyone knew Cal was a horny bastard and would naturally take all those buttons on the side of that dress as an invitation to let his fingers do the walking. Maybe that's what she wanted. To get something going with Cal.

Didn't matter, though. It was none of Jack's business.

"The vinyl roof needs to be replaced," Marvin said, then rambled on about the interior.

Cal wrapped an arm around Daisy's waist and she smiled up at him. Light from the crystal ball slid along her cheek and got caught in her hair. Her red lips parted and she laughed. Daisy Lee Brooks, the fantasy of every horny guy at Lovett High, was back in town, turning heads and leading guys on with a smile.

Some things never changed.

Only she wasn't Daisy Lee Brooks. She was Daisy Monroe and she had a kid. A son. A baby with Steven. He didn't know why that surprised him. It shouldn't. Of course they'd had a kid. When he thought about it, it was more surprising that they'd just had the one.

Unexpected and unwanted, the memory of her flat stomach flashed across his brain. His mouth tasting her bare skin just above her navel as he gazed up into her face. At the hot drowsy passion in her eyes as he worked his way down. Her lips moist and abraded from his kiss.

"Excuse me," he said just as Marvin was getting all hot about the Ford's dual carbs. He walked toward the exit sign and out the doors. He moved down the hall and out the front doors of the country club. The warm June night touched his face and throat. The sound of insects was thick in the air. There was some sort of pond to Jack's right and lightning bugs blinked like white Christmas lights on the golf course beyond. A memory of catching lightning bugs with Steven and Daisy flashed across his brain. That had been back before insecticides reduced their numbers, and they were still easy to catch in Mason jars. He, Steven and Daisy would smear the bugs on their arms, making fluorescent streaks that lasted a good ten minutes.

He pulled a cigar from his breast pocket and walked to a stone bench just beyond the lights of the club. He sat and slid off the cigar band. He stuck it in the corner of his mouth and patted his pockets, searching for the box of matches he'd picked up in the tobacco store. He didn't smoke that often, but he did occasionally enjoy an expensive cigar.

His pockets came up empty and he stuck the cigar back in his breast pocket. A bank of windows from the restaurant threw watery light on the pond. He ran his fingers through his hair, leaned his head back against the building, and stared out at the night. His life was good. He had more business than he could handle and was making more money than he needed. He'd taken Parrish American Classics and made it bigger and better than his father had ever dreamed. He owned his home and his business. He drove a Mustang worth seventy grand and a new Dodge Ram truck to pull his twenty-one-foot boat.

He was content, so why did Daisy have to show up now and dredge up old memories that were better left long buried? Memories of him and her. Of him and Steven. Of the three of them.

From almost the first day in grade school, he and Steven had both been a little in love with Daisy Brooks. It'd started out innocent enough. Two boys looking across the playground and seeing a little girl with gold hair and big brown eyes. A girl who could play baseball, swing on the monkey bars, and outrun them. The attraction had been pure and naive.

In the third grade, when Daisy had worried about who she'd marry when she grew up, they'd all three decided that she would marry the both of them. They'd all live in the tree house they planned to build, and Jack would get rich and famous driving NASCAR. Steven would become a lawyer like his dad, and Daisy a beauty queen. They'd never heard of polygamy, and neither he nor Steven had thought of Daisy in a sexual way. Not that he and Steven hadn't talked about sex. They just hadn't thought about it in relation to Daisy.

But all that changed the summer going into the eighth grade. Daisy had gone away to work on her aunt's ranch in El Paso, and by the time she'd come back, she'd popped out a pair of perfect breasts. She'd left looking like the girl they'd always known, skinny and flat-chested, but she came back changed. Her legs longer. Her breasts bigger than his hands. Her hips fuller. Even her hair had seemed shinier.

Back then, his body had never needed a reason to get an erection. It was just something that happened to all pubescent boys for no reason at all and was embarrassing as hell. Sometimes it'd just happened when he was doing nothing more exciting than geometry or mowing the lawn.

But that summer, he'd taken one look at Daisy, and his body had reacted to the two very distinct reasons pressed against her T-shirt. His thoughts had dropped right to his crotch, and he'd gotten so hard he'd about passed out from lack of blood to his brain. She'd come over to tell him about her aunt's ranch, and while she was sitting there beside him on his front porch, talking and laughing and filling him in on the horses she'd ridden, he was trying not to stare at her tits. *Yee-freakin'-ha!*

That summer, he and Steven had known without exchanging words that each felt an attraction for her that was no longer innocent. It was there between them. For the first time in their friendship, they had a real big problem. One that wasn't going to be solved with an apology or an extra slug to equal things out.

Later they'd talked about it, about how they felt about Daisy. They decided that neither could have her. In order to remain friends, they promised to keep their hands to themselves. Daisy was off limits. Jack had broken that promise, but Steven had ended up with her.

The front door of the club swung open, and as if his thoughts had conjured her, Daisy stepped outside. She settled the little gold chain of her purse on her shoulder and glanced around as if she couldn't quite recall where she'd parked her car. Her gaze locked with his, and she stared at him across the distance. The light from the front of the club lit half her face and left the rest in variegated shadow.

"Shay's going to throw her bouquet in a minute," she said as if he'd asked. "And I don't want to pretend to catch it."

"You don't want to get married next?"

She shook her head and her hair brushed her shoulders.

He didn't ask why. He didn't want to give a shit. His gaze moved to her full breasts pressing against the red material of her dress and down all those buttons on the side.

"This morning I was thinking about my first day at Lovett Elementary," she said and took a step toward him. "Do you remember that?"

He stood and looked back up into her face. "No."

Her red lips turned up at the corners. "You told me my hair bow was stupid."

And she'd burst into tears.

"My mama made me wear that dumb thing."

He looked down into her face, with her smooth perfect skin, straight nose, and full red lips. She was as beautiful as she'd always been, maybe more so, and he was doing a really good job of feeling nothing. No anger. No desire. Nothing. "What are you doing here?"

She took a step closer. If he reached out, he could touch her. Daisy's big eyes stared into his and she said, "Shay invited me to her reception this morning when I saw her buying a can of Aqua Net at Albertsons."

That wasn't want he'd meant. "Why are you in Lovett? Dredging up the past?"

She lowered her gaze to his chest but didn't answer.

"What do you want, Daisy?"

"I want to be friends."

"No."

"Why, Jack?" She looked back up, her gaze searching his face. "We were friends once."

He laughed. "Were we?"

She nodded. "Yes."

"I think we were more."

"I know, but I mean friends like in before all that."

"Before all that sex?"

He wasn't sure, but he thought she blushed. "Yes."

"And before you had sex with my best friend?" He folded his arms across his chest. Maybe he did feel something. Maybe he was a little more pissed off than he'd thought, because he said, "Are you here to start things up again? Continue right where we left off?"

She looked away. "No."

"I know I'm not supposed to flatter myself, but are you sure you don't want to tear one off in the back of my car?" She shook her head, but he didn't stop. "For old time's sake?"

Her gaze returned to his. "Don't, Jack." She raised her hand between them and pressed her fingers against his lips. "Don't say any more."

The touch of her fingers took him off guard. He caught the scent of perfume, but underneath that, he smelled her. Daisy. She might cover it with perfume and move away for fifteen years, but it hadn't changed. Even at the age of seventeen, when she'd worked at The Wild Coyote Diner; even beneath the scent of fried chicken and barbeque, she'd always smelled like a warm summer breeze.

With her fingers pressed to his mouth, he stared at her for several long heartbeats. Sometimes he'd had to search hard for the scent of her beneath the smell of all that grease, but he'd always found it. Usually in the crook of her neck. He grabbed her wrist and took a step back. "What do you want from me?"

"I told you. I want to be friends."

There had to be more. "We can never be friends."

"Why?"

He let go of her wrist. "You married my best friend."

"You broke up with me."

No, he'd told her he needed time to think. "So, to get back at me, you married Steven." It wasn't a question. Rather a statement of fact.

She shook her head. "You don't understand. It wasn't like that."

It was exactly like that. "You and I were lovers. We were doing it every which way to Sunday. Then you up and married my best friend the same week I buried my parents. What part did I get wrong?" Through the darkness he watched a crease draw her brows together.

"The timing was real bad."

Bitter laughter clogged his chest. "Yeah."

"I'm sorry Jack." She looked sorry, too.

He didn't care. "Don't be. It all worked out for the best."

"I came back because I have to talk to you."

There was absolutely nothing she had to say that he wanted to hear. "Save your breath, Daisy," he said as he walked past her toward the bridge separating the entrance from the parking lot.

"It's the reason I'm here," she called after him.

"Then you've wasted your time."

"Don't make me chase you."

That stopped him and he looked back at her. Her hands were on her hips, and although he couldn't see her features clearly, he could feel her gaze on him, staring him down. It was like looking at the old Daisy.

"I'm trying to be nice about this, but you really

don't have a choice. You're going to listen to me; and if you get ugly like you said, I'll become your worst dang nightmare."

Damn, but she was the old Daisy. All hot temper and feisty belligerence wrapped up in such a soft girly package. He almost smiled. Almost.

"Too late, buttercup," he said as he turned to go. "You became my worst nightmare years ago."

Chapter 4

*D*aisy hung her dress in the closet, pulled the red slip over her head, and put on her short nightgown. Then she washed her face. It was a little after ten, and her mother was already asleep.

She sat on the edge of her bed and dialed her son in Seattle. It was only eight in Washington; she was sure that Nathan was still up.

She was right. "Hey, sugar muffin," she said after Nathan picked up on the fourth ring.

"Mom."

Well, it wasn't a great beginning to their conversation, but it was great to hear his voice. "How are things?"

"Gay."

"I miss you."

"Then come home."

"I will a week from Sunday."

"Mom, I do *not* want to stay here for a week."

She'd had this same conversation with him before she'd even left. Junie and Oliver were not his favorite relatives. They weren't horrible, just boring. Especially to a fifteen-year-old boy. "It can't be that bad."

"How do you know? Have you ever lived with Aunt Junie and Uncle Know-it-Olly."

"Nathan, they'll hear you!" Unfortunately Oliver was one of those men who liked to impress people with his limited knowledge on every subject known to man. Steven had started calling him Know-it-Olly years ago.

"No, they won't. They're not even here. They left me to baby-sit Michael Ann and Richie."

Daisy wedged the phone between her jaw and shoulder. "Michael Ann is only a year younger than you."

"I know. And she's a pain in the butt. She follows me around asking me if I get food stuck in my lip ring."

Daisy had asked him that too and thought it was a fair question. "I think she has a crush on you."

"Oh my *God*! That is so gross, Mom," he said, his voice cracking with indignation. "How can you say that? She's my cousin."

"Haven't you ever heard of kissing cousins?" Daisy teased him.

"Yuck. She still picks her nose!"

Daisy laughed and the conversation turned to school. There was only five more days left, than he would be out for the summer. He'd just turned fifteen in December, and since about first grade, he'd been counting the days until he could take driver's education. He had one more year to go, but he already had his car picked out. For this week anyway.

"I'm gonna get a Nova Super Sport. A four-on-four, too. None of that wussy three-speed crap. Why bother if you can't burn 'em off? It'll be fat." She didn't even pretend to know what he was talking about. He'd been born car crazy. No way around it. She figured it was in his DNA. Plus, chances were good that he'd been conceived in the back of a Chevy. Nathan had been doomed to be a gear head.

"What color?" she asked, not in the least concerned that he would ever actually drive a Nova SS and burn 'em off. Nathan didn't have a job.

"Yellow with a black top."

"Like a bumblebee?"

There was a long pause before he said, "White with a black top."

They talked for a few more minutes about the weather and where he might want to go on vacation when she got back. He'd just seen a teen skin-flick and thought Fort Lauderdale would be good. Or Hawaii.

By the time she hung up the telephone, they'd pretty much decided on Disney World, although with Nathan that could change by the next time she talked to him. She squirted almond-scented lotion into her hands and rubbed it up her arms. A thin white strip of skin barely marked her left finger where her wedding ring had been for fifteen years. She'd slipped the two-carat solitaire into the inside breast pocket of Steven's burial suit. She thought it appropriate that it should rest above his heart.

As she rubbed the lotion into her hands, she

glanced about the room where she was staying. It was her old bedroom, but nothing remained except the bed itself. Framed posters of windmills, the Alamo, and the River Walk in San Antonio hung on the walls, replacing her certificates from local photography contests she'd entered, her cheerleading plaques, and a poster of Rob Lowe she'd pinned up during his *St. Elmo's Fire* days.

She stood and moved to the closet and opened the door. The closet was empty except for a few old prom dresses, a pair of her old red cowboy boots with white heart inserts, and a big box with her name written across it in black. She scooted the box across the floor to the bed, then sat looking at it for several long moments. She knew what she would find in there. Bits and pieces of her life, the memories she'd long ago shoved in a box and taped shut. Earlier at the reception, she'd pushed the memories from her head, now here she sat staring at them. Did she really want to look into her past?

No, not really.

She tore off the tape and opened the box.

A dried wrist corsage, her graduation tassel, and a few name tags that said HI MY NAME IS DAISY, sat on top. She couldn't recall why she'd kept the name tags, but she recognized the corsage. She touched the dry rosebuds that had once been pink and white but were now a faded yellow. She brought the dried corsage to her nose and breathed deep. It smelled of dust and of old memories. She set it next to her on her bed, then pulled out her baby blanket and christening gown. A heart-shaped box with the necklace her grandfather on her daddy's side had given her was next, followed by her school annuals. She reached for her tenth-grade yearbook and opened it. She flipped through the pages and paused on a group photograph of the teaching staff standing in front of the school. She'd taken the photo her first year of photography class, before she'd learned much about composition and lighting.

She turned to the pictures of her and Sylvia and the rest of the cheerleading squad. The picture had been taken of them in their gold-and-blue uniforms doing Herkie, toe-touch jumps, and handsprings. That was the year she'd cut her hair short like Princess Diana. While Diana had looked great, Daisy had looked like a boy in a short pleated skirt.

She flipped to her class picture and cringed. Her big smile was filled with braces, and she had raccoon eyes from all the makeup she'd spooned on her face.

She turned a few pages and her finger moved along the row of photos and stopped on Steven. She touched the smooth paper and smiled. He'd always been such a handsome all-American boy, with his wavy blond hair, smiling brown eyes, and a Texas grin as if he hadn't a care in the world. He'd played football and basketball and been involved in student government, going on to be class president his senior year.

Daisy thumbed a few more pages and looked at Jack's yearbook photo. Unlike Steven, Jack never grinned and smiled as if he didn't have a care in the world. It wasn't that he was more serious than Steven, it was just that he didn't waste energy laughing and smiling when he didn't feel like it.

During that school year, he'd turned sixteen, a year older than Nathan was now. The two had the same dark coloring in hair and skin tone, and perhaps their noses were similar. She looked for other resemblances and found none.

That was also the year Jack had quit football because his father needed him after school in the garage. Up until his sophomore year, Jack had always been the first string quarterback. When he quit, Steven took over the position. As far as she recalled, he'd never had any hard feelings toward Steven, only a sadness that he could no longer play ball.

That was also the year she'd started to fall in love with him. Oh, she'd always loved Jack in the same way she'd loved Steven, but it seemed that one moment she'd been looking at him as she always had, and in the next everything changed.

On that particular day, he'd been waiting for Steven to finish football practice, sitting on the tailgate of his daddy's old truck. She'd stayed after school to make posters for the homecoming dance and later saw him in the parking lot, sitting and watching instead of playing.

Perhaps it had been a trick of the light, an early fall sunset casting him in gold. She didn't know, but she'd noticed more than his usual good looks. More than his lashes that were longer than hers. More than the slight stubble on his jaw. More than his arms folded across his chest and the defined balls of his biceps and the hard cord of muscle of his forearms. Jack did not lift weights. He lifted car engines.

"Hey there," he said, and patted the tailgate next to him.

"What are you doing?" she asked as she sat. She placed her school books in her lap and looked out over the field as the Lovett Mustangs broke practice and the players jogged toward the locker room.

"Waiting for Steven."

"Do you miss playing, Jack?"

"Nah, but I miss the pretty girls." It was of course true that the football players did get the prettiest girls. But it wasn't true that just because he no longer played, he didn't get his share.

"Now you have to settle for the ugly ones," she teased and looked at him out of the corner of her eye.

"Daisy, don't you know there aren't any truly ugly girls in Texas?"

He was so full of it. "Where'd you hear that?"

He shrugged. "It's just a fact. Like the Alamo and the Rio Grande, is all." He took her hand and brushed his thumb over her knuckles as he studied her fingers. "You'll still be seen with me, though, won't you?"

She turned her head and gazed more fully at him, all prepared with a flip answer, but he glanced up and something in his green eyes stopped her. For about half a second, she saw something, something in the way he looked back at her, something that made her think the answer was important to him. As if he wasn't sure. She got a surprising glimpse inside of Jack that she'd never seen before. Maybe things didn't bounce off him like he was superman. Maybe he felt things like everybody else. Maybe more.

Then he flashed her a smile and it was gone.

"Of course, Jack," she said. "I'll always be seen with you."

"I knew I could count on you, buttercup." For the first time, his voice slid inside her chest and warmed her up with hot tingles. It was all so incredible and fantastic and left her stunned. And it absolutely could not happen. She couldn't fall in love with Jack. He was a friend, and she didn't want to lose him. But even if he wasn't her friend, she'd be an idiot to let it happen.

He squeezed her hand and stood. "Do you need a ride home?"

She looked up at him, standing in front of her with his hands shoved in the front pockets of his Levi's, and nodded. Jack Parrish had many wonderful qualities. Being faithful to one girl wasn't one of them. He'd shatter her heart like glass. If that happened, they couldn't be friends anymore. And she'd miss him terribly.

By the time Steven walked out of the boy's locker with his wet hair slicked back, she'd convinced herself that she wasn't falling in love with Jack. He'd made her momentarily confused. Like when they'd been kids and would ride the merry-go-round too long. Jack used to spin it so fast that for a while after she couldn't think or see straight.

But she was over it now. Thinking straight once again. Thank God. "Are y'all going somewhere?" she asked.

"We're driving over to Chandler," Jack answered, referring to a town the size of Lovett and about fifty miles to the west.

"Why?"

"There's a '69 Camaro Z-28 I want to look at."

"A '69?" She'd never understood Jack's fascination with old cars. Or as he called them, "classics." She preferred new cars with upholstery that didn't snag her nylons. With Jack, it was more than just a case of not having money for a new car. Although he certainly didn't. In that respect, she and Jack had a lot more in common than either did with Steven. Steven's father was a lawyer and his family had money. His biggest responsibility was to maintain his grades. By contrast, her mother was a waitress who depended on survivor benefits from the government, and Jack's family had a garage that never seemed to bring in a lot of money. She and Lily were responsible for keeping the house clean and starting supper, while Jack helped out in the family business. "Does the car run?" she asked.

"Not yet."

Exactly.

"Hey, Daisy," Steven said as he approached. "What are you doing at school so late?"

"Making homecoming posters. Are you going to the homecoming dance?"

"Yeah, I'm thinking about asking Marilee Donahue. Do you think she'll go with me?" Steven smiled and there wasn't a doubt that Marilee would say yes.

She shrugged. "Are you going, Jack?" she asked, although she was fairly sure she knew the answer.

"Nope. You know I only put on a suit when my mom forces me to for Sunday School and funerals." He shut the tailgate and walked to the driver's side. "And I hate to dance."

Daisy suspected that it wasn't so much that Jack hated to dance as much as he just didn't know how to dance. And he'd always been the kind of person that if he didn't do something well, he didn't do it at all. "You could just wear a nice shirt and tie," she told him, but for some reason, the fact that Jack wasn't taking a girl to the school dance warmed her heart more than it should have, given that she was over her earlier confusion.

"Not a chance." The three of them got into the old truck and Jack fired it up.

"Have you been asked yet?" Jack asked her as he drove from the parking lot with her sitting between them like always.

"Yes." They were so weird about who she dated she didn't want to say.

"Who?" Steven asked.

She looked straight ahead at the dashboard and the road beyond.

Steven hit her with his elbow. "Come on, Daisy Lee. Who asked you?"

"Matt Flegel."

"You're going with Bug?"

"He doesn't like to be called that anymore."

Jack looked at Steven over the top of her head.

"What's wrong with Bug . . . I mean Matt?" She held up a hand before either could answer. "Forget I asked. I don't care what y'all think. I like Matt."

"He gets around a lot."

"He's the wrong kind of boy for you," Jack added.

She folded her arms and was silent the rest of the way home. The pair of them were serial daters, and that was putting it nicely. She wasn't about to listen to their opinion, and if there ever was a "wrong kind of boy" for her or any girl, it was Jack. Which made her doubly glad she wasn't really falling in love with him.

She spent the rest of her sophomore year dating boys that neither Steven nor Jack approved of, but she didn't care. Like most girls her age, she learned how to make out and drive boys crazy. And more important, she learned where to stop before things went too far. As a result, she developed a reputation for being a tease. Which she didn't think was fair at all. Boys kissed her. She kissed them back. As far as she could tell, a girl was either a prude, which meant she didn't kiss at all. A tease, meaning she kissed and perhaps a bit more, or was a slut. And everyone knew what that meant.

That summer, she'd let Erik Marks touch her breast on the outside of her T-shirt. Jack and Steven heard about it and made a special trip over to her house to talk to her. She'd gotten mad and slammed the front door in their faces.

The hypocrites.

She made varsity cheerleader her junior year. Her hair had grown out to her shoulders and she got a spiral perm. Steven was still in football and basketball, and of course, student government. Jack was racing his Camaro on the flat Texas roads, and she was still telling herself that she wasn't attracted to him. She told herself that she loved him but she wasn't in love with him, and that her heart didn't pinch when he drove by with his arm around some girl. He was her friend, just as he'd always been. Nothing more. And she wouldn't allow herself to feel anything more either.

All that changed a few weeks before Christmas her senior year when she got asked to the Christmas prom by J. T. Sanders. J. T. was gorgeous and drove a new Jeep Wrangler. Black. Daisy worked nights at the Wild Coyote Diner, and she'd managed to save enough money to buy the prefect dress. White satin. Sleeveless with tiny rhinestones on the tight fitting bodice and tulle skirt. It was the most beautiful thing she'd ever owned. The night before the dance, she picked up J. T.'s boutonniere on her dinner break. When she got home, he called and canceled. He said his grandmother died and that he had to go to her funeral in Amarillo. Everyone knew that he'd actually started dating another girl the week before. Daisy had been dumped. Flat.

And everyone knew it.

The Saturday of the prom, Daisy worked the lunch shift at the Wild Coyote. She kept it together and acted like she wasn't humiliated. She pretended she wasn't sad or hurt. She joked with her co-workers about J. T. being a loser anyway.

No one bought it. Getting dumped the night before the prom with some lame-o excuse was the worst thing that could ever happen to any girl.

And everyone knew it.

After her shift, she went home and locked herself in her room. With her dress hanging on her closet door, she threw herself on her bed and had a nice long cry. At four, her mother stuck her head in the room and asked if she wanted some mint chocolate chip ice cream. She didn't. Lily made her a cowboy pie sandwich, but she couldn't eat it.

At five-thirty Jack knocked on her bedroom door, but she wouldn't let him in. Her face was splotchy and her eyes puffy, and she didn't want him to see her that way.

"Daisy Lee," he called through the door. "Come out of there."

She sat up on her bed and pulled a Kleenex from the box. "Go away, Jack."

"Open up."

"No." She blew her nose.

"I have something for you."

She stared at the door. "What?"

"I can't tell you. I have to show you."

"I look really bad."

"I don't care."

Well she did. She slipped from the bed and opened the door a crack. She stuck her hand out. "What is it?" He didn't answer and she was forced to peer out the crack. Jack stood in the hall, the light from her sister's bedroom shining on him like a dark angel or at the very least a choirboy. He wore his navy blue Sunday suit, and a cream-colored shirt. A red tie hung loose around his neck. "What's going on, Jack? Did you go to a funeral?"

He laughed and brought his hand out from behind his back. He laid a wrist corsage of white and pink roses in her palm. "Will you go to the prom with me?"

"You hate school dances," she said through the crack.

"I know."

She brought the corsage to her nose and breathed deep. Her nose was clogged so it wasn't that deep. She bit her bottom lip to keep it from trembling. And as she looked at him, standing in the hall of her house, wearing a suit he hated and asking her to a dance he loathed, she fell helplessly in love with Jack Parrish. It expanded her heart and flooded her chest and scared her to death. All those years of fighting it faded away to nothing.

She'd fallen in love with Jack and there hadn't been anything she could do about it.

That night Jack kissed her for the first time. Or rather, she'd kissed him. During the dance, while she'd been falling in love for the first time in her life, he treated her as he always had, as a friend. While he made her whole body feel hot and alive, he'd stayed cool. It had all been wonderful and awful, and after the prom, when he walked her to her front door, she wrapped her arms around his neck and kissed him.

At first he stood with his hands to his side. Then he grasped her shoulders through her coat and pushed her away, angry.

"What are you doing?"

"Kiss me, Jack." If he rejected her, she was sure she'd just die right there. On the porch.

His grip tightened and he brought her forward and pressed his warm lips to her forehead.

"No, don't treat me like a friend." She swallowed hard past the ache in her chest. "Please," she whispered as she looked up at him. "I want you to kiss me like you do other girls. I want you to touch me like you do other girls, too."

He pulled back and his green gaze slid to her mouth. "Don't tease me, Daisy. I don't like it."

"I'm not teasing you." She ran her hand across the shoulder of his jacket to the side of his neck. "Please, Jack."

Then as if he didn't want to kiss her, but he couldn't fight it any longer, he slowly lowered his mouth to her. This time the touch of his lips stole her breath. She tilted her head back and sank into his chest. Until that moment, she'd thought she knew what it was like to kiss a boy. Jack showed her she hadn't a clue. The kiss was hot and wet and filled with so much hunger that it changed her forever.

Even now, after all these years, Daisy remembered standing on her mother's porch as Jack turned her world inside out. She'd clung to him as he'd fed her those liquid kisses that had made her breasts ache and her body tremble. His hands had never moved from her shoulders, but he'd made her crave his touch. She'd wanted him to touch her all over. Instead he'd walked away, leaving her stunned and wanting more.

Chapter 5

*T*he next day, Daisy called Jack but he didn't pick up. The longer she put off telling him about Nathan, the harder it was going to get. She knew that, having already put it off for fifteen years. But what she hadn't realized before she'd arrived was that the longer she put it off, the more memories of her life in this town would drag her back into the past. Before she'd arrived, the plan had been to tell Jack, give him Steven's letter, and deal with the fallout: if not easy, at least straightforward. Now, it didn't seem real straightforward either. But it had to be done. She was leaving in seven days.

Before noon, she tried Jack's number two more times, but he didn't answer. She figured he was probably not answering on purpose. She went to church with her mother, and afterward, they had an early dinner with Lily and Pippen. Phillip "Pippen" Darlington was two and had a blond mullet because his mother couldn't bear to cut the curls at the nape of his neck. He had huge blue eyes like Lily, and he loved Thomas the Tank Engine. He also loved wearing his faux coonskin cap and shouting NO! loud enough to be heard into the next county. He hated food with texture, spiders, and his Velcro Barney sneakers.

Daisy looked at him sitting in his high chair at her mother's dinner table and tried not to frown as he poured grape Kool-Aid from his Tommy Tippy cup into his baked potato. Daisy's mother and Lily sat across the table from her and didn't seem to mind that Pippen was making a disgusting mess.

"He's a rat bastard!" Lily was telling her, referring, of course, to her soon to be ex-husband, The Rat Bastard Ronald Darlington. "A few months before he ran off with his jailbait girlfriend, he took all the money out of our accounts and put it somewhere."

Louella nodded her head sadly. "Probably in Mexico." Growing up, if either had uttered the word "bastard" at the dinner table, they'd have been sent from the room.

"What is your attorney doing about that?" Daisy asked

"There isn't a lot he can do. We can prove the money was in the account, but not where it went. The judge can order him to give me half, but that doesn't mean he will. And for years, Ronnie was paid under the table in order to avoid paying the IRS, so it looks like he only makes twenty thousand a year instead of seventy-five." Lily sliced a piece of meat with a vengeance. Even though they were sisters and had grown up together, they weren't very close. Growing up, they'd mostly fought or ignored each other. Lily had been in middle school when Daisy had moved away, and they'd never really maintained a relationship after that. Losing Steven had made her realize how important her family was to her. She needed to work on her relationship with her sister.

"He said that if I tell the IRS about it," Lily continued, "he'll fight for custody of Pippen. What can I do?"

When both her mother and Lily stared at her, Daisy realized it wasn't a rhetorical question. There were dark circles under Lily's eyes as if she hadn't had a good night's sleep in a long time. Her blond hair was cut short and framed her pretty face with soft curls, but at the moment, she looked anything but soft. No, she looked scared as hell. "You're asking me? How should I know?"

"Darren Monroe is a lawyer," her mother provided.

"Steven's father is retired and living in Arizona. And besides, he was a criminal defense attorney; Steven designed computer software programs. I know nothing about the family courts." She recognized the fear in Lily's blue eyes. It was the fear of being suddenly alone with the responsibility of raising a child. But unlike Daisy, Lily wasn't financially secure, nor did she have a career to fall back on. Not that Daisy's career had ever provided a huge income, but she was a good photographer and had connections. If she had to support herself and Nathan on her income alone, she could. Lily had been a stay-home wife and a mom, which was admirable but weren't marketable skills. She was terrified. "I'll try to think up something," Daisy said, although she had troubles of her own and was only here for a week now.

Lily smiled, "Thanks, Daisy."

"I ran into Darma Joe Henderson, the other day," her mother said as she dug into her okra, Lily's worries apparently solved for the moment. "You girls remember Darma Joe. She used to work at the Trusty Hardware across from the Wild Coyote. Her son Buck had that car accident a few years back, and they had to amputate his leg below the knee. Well, he has a daughter who sings with the church choir. You girls might have noticed her today." Louella paused to take a bite before launching into, "She kinda looks like Buck, bless her heart, but she has such a nice voice and a kind personality. She was dating the boy . . . oh, what was his name? I think it started with a G. George or Geoff or something like that. Anyway . . ."

Daisy slid her gaze from her mother to her sister. Lily's eyes were starting to glaze over and her head was drifting back. Things really hadn't changed very much since she'd been gone. She knew it would be useless to ask her mother to get to the point, because she already knew there wasn't a point and there never was going to be one.

Daisy started to laugh. Lily's eyes refocused and she looked at Daisy. She laughed too. Pippen threw his coonskin cap on the floor and broke in giggles as if he knew the joke. He was only two, but he'd been around his grandmother enough that perhaps he did.

Louella looked up from her plate. "What are you girls laughing about?"

"That Darma Joe's granddaughter looks like Buck," Lily lied through a grin. "Bless her heart."

"It's unfortunate." Louella frowned. They continued to laugh and she shook her head. "Well, y'all have come off your spools and taken poor Pippen with you."

After dinner, Daisy got up her nerve for the fourth time that day and called Jack; he didn't pick up, but she left him a message this time: "It's Daisy. I'm not going anywhere until you talk to me."

He didn't return the call, of course, so she phoned him the next day at work. She and Penny Kribs chatted about old times and she thanked her for sending flowers to Steven's funeral. Then she asked for Jack. "Don't tell him it's me on the line," she said. "I want to surprise him."

"He could use a good surprise," Penny said. "He's in a nasty mood."

Great. Daisy was put on hold and after listening to about half of "The Night the Lights Went Out in Georgia," Jack came on the line.

"This is Jack Parrish," he said.

"Hi, Jack." He didn't respond, but he didn't slam the phone down either. "Surprise, it's me, Daisy."

"Don't hassle me at work, Daisy Lee," he finally responded, dragging out those vowels for all they were worth. Yep, definitely in a nasty mood.

"Don't make me. Meet me later."

"Can't. I'm flying out for Tallahassee this afternoon."

"When will you be back?"

He didn't answer and she was forced to blackmail him. "If you don't tell me, I'll just call back every day. All day." That didn't prompt a response either. "And night."

"That's harassment."

"True, but filing charges is such a pain." She didn't believe for a minute that he'd actually have her charged for harassment. "Let's meet the day you get back."

"Can't. It's Lacy Dawn's birthday."

"Lacy Dawn? Stripper or hooker?"

"Neither."

"It sounds like a stage name."

"Probably a girl named Daisy Brooks shouldn't cast stones."

He had a point. "Meet me after the party."

"No can do. Those dancing bears take it out of me."

"Jack—"

"Goodbye."

The dial tone filled Daisy's ear as she thought about what to do next. *Dancing bears?* What was Jack into these days? "Hey, Ma," she called from the kitchen into the living room. And over the sound of sirens coming from the television she asked, "Is there some place in town that has dancing bears?"

"Dancing bears?" The sirens quieted, then her mother stuck her head into the kitchen. "The only place I know is Showtime."

"Is that a strip club?"

"No it's a pizza place, but it also does little kids' birthday parties. Lily had Pippen's party there last year. He wasn't quite old enough to understand that those big scary bears weren't going to hurt him. He screamed the paint off the walls. Juanita Sanchez was there with her grandson, Hermie. You remember Juanita, don't you? She lived down the road in that pink stucco, bless her heart. One day . . ."

Daisy didn't ask why living in a pink stucco deserved a "bless her heart," but she wasn't about to ask. She called information and came up with a plan. She got the number for Showtime, and dialed it. After getting transferred around by teenagers who didn't know anything, she finally got put through to the party planner. "Hello," Daisy began, "I've lost my invitation to the birthday party of a little girl named Lacy Dawn. I'm not sure of her last name, but if we miss that party, my daughter will be so upset. Could you please tell me what time it starts?"

The party planner sounded older than the teens working there, and it took her about thirty seconds to get back with the answer. "I don't have a Lacy Dawn, but I do have a Lacy Parrish."

"That's it."

"Her mother booked a front table from six to seven-thirty."

"On Saturday?"

"No. Wednesday."

"Oh my gosh. I'm so glad I called. Thank you." So, Lacy Dawn was Lacy Parrish. Obviously Jack's niece, and he'd be back in town Wednesday.

She dialed Lily and didn't feel the least guilty for what she planned to do next. She'd warned Jack that she'd become his worst nightmare. At the time she'd been mostly bluffing. She wasn't bluffing now, and she wasn't going away. She didn't plan to tell him about Nathan at his niece's birthday party, but he needed to know that he wasn't going to get any peace until he agreed to meet with her.

When Lily picked up, she asked if she and Pippen would go with her to Showtime Wednesday night. Her sister wanted to know why, and she explained the situation.

"This will be good," Lily said. "Not only will Pippen be your cover, but I went to school with Billy and Rhonda. Rhonda's sister, Patty Valencia, was your age."

"Was she a real pretty Hispanic girl with long black hair?"

"Yeah, they're both real pretty. Although, I hear Rhonda and Billy have been cranking out the kids, so she may look a little crazy these days."

"Probably." Daisy glanced at her mother's calendar of Texas landscapes. "Are you sure you want to do this with me? Mom told me Pippen screamed the paint from the walls last time."

"He doesn't do that anymore." She turned her mouth from the phone and said, "Pippen, you're a big boy now. Aren't you Momma's sweet baby?"

"No!"

Great. Daisy hung up and spent the rest of the afternoon helping her mother pull weeds in her flower gardens. She brought out her Nikon and knelt amid the pink flamingos, resting her elbow on her knee to steady the camera. She positioned herself toward Louella's shadow so that the sunlight hit one side of her face. She wished she'd loaded the camera with black-and-white film so that the vibrant pink of the flamingos wouldn't take on more importance than her mother. Or if she'd brought her Fuji digital, she could have loaded it on her computer once she got back home and made the image real high-impact.

She moved to her stomach and rested the weight of the camera equally on both elbows. She shot up at her mother, catching Annie Oakley in the background.

"Daisy Lee," her mother said through a frown, "don't take a picture up my nose."

She sighed and sat up. It had been a while since she'd felt the urge to bring out her cameras and get back into something she used to love. She'd had to quit working for Ryan Kent, an artistic photographer in Seattle, in order to take care of Steven.

She'd gotten into photography in high school, and when Nathan had turned four, she'd signed up for classes at the University of Washington. After four years, she'd received her B.A. and began interning with top photographers in the area. Her photographs hung in some studios and galleries around town. And a photograph she'd taken of a man standing on top of a crushed vehicle after the earthquake in two-thousand and one, had been featured in a local magazine.

She'd thought that once things settled, she'd go back to work for Ryan, but lately she'd been thinking of opening her own studio. One of the most successful photographers she'd ever worked for had once told her that the key to success was finding a visible location and staying there for at least five years. Talent was important, but visibility was most important when starting out.

The more she thought about it, the more she thought that's exactly what she'd do. Once she put the past behind her, she'd be free to start over completely. Maybe she'd sell her house. Upon Steven's death, the home owner's insurance had paid off the mortgage. Maybe she'd sell it, and she and Nathan could move into a loft in Belltown.

She shrugged and focused her lens on an orange-and-yellow rose. "I'm thinking of selling my house once I get back," she told her mother as she snapped the picture.

"Don't get ahead of yourself," her mother warned. "Colleen Forbus sold her house soon after her husband, Wyatt, took his journey to heaven, and she's been sorry ever since."

Maybe she could wait a few more months just to be sure. She'd find out how Nathan felt about it first, of course. But lately she'd started to feel as if too much of her past was tied to that house. She didn't have to decide today. It was something to think about. Something to put at the bottom of her mental to-do list.

She placed her elbow on her knees and adjusted the aperture to bring the roses and flamingos behind

Louella's head into focus, giving the photograph a nice rich texture and depth of field. She snapped the photo and thought how nice it would be if everything in her life could be made clear by the turn of a focus ring.

Chapter 6

$\mathcal{J}$ack was late. He'd waited until that morning to call Rhonda and ask what to get Lacy for her birthday. Rhonda told him she wanted something called a Kitty Magic. She told him to make sure it was a *Kitty Magic* and not a *Fur Real Friends*. According to Rhonda the latter didn't nurse her babies. Then she wished him luck finding it.

He'd called around to the few stores in Lovett that carried toys, and ended up driving into Amarillo. He'd spent the afternoon looking for the damned thing, and finally found it in one of the last stores he'd walked into.

He'd stood in the aisle, reading the back of the box, making sure he had the right one, and feeling the back of his skull tighten. The pink Mommy Kitty had long fur and two fluffy kittens. The three of them had toys and matching bows for their heads and god-awful heart-shaped sunglasses.

He'd kept reading and uttered, "For the love of Christ." According to the box the mother cat purred and said, "I love you" and made nursing sounds when one of the kittens was stuck to her side.

What the hell was a nursing sound? he'd wondered.

Jack had the present wrapped in bright pink paper with fairies on it. A big iridescent pink bow about the size of his head was taped on top. The bow was beyond frilly, but Billy's girls loved that kind of crap.

The kind of girl stuff that had been completely foreign to him and his brother growing up. They'd played with cars and BB guns and had set their army men on fire. They'd been hell on wheels, but as soon as Billy's first girl had been born, Billy had taken to baby dolls, Barbie sneakers, and pink tutus like a duck to water. He made it all look easy and natural while Jack was left watching and wondering where Billy's paternal instincts had come from. Jack didn't have any. At least he didn't think he did. Although he was learning fast, he didn't know very much about little girls. Maybe because until Amy Lynn, he'd never been around little girls. Except Daisy, and if she'd played with dolls, and dressed up like a fairy princess as Billy's girls did, she'd done it with her friends that were girls. Not with him and Steven.

He pulled open the door to Showtime and stepped inside. He hadn't seen Daisy for four days. Hopefully she'd given up on her plan to pin him down and make him relive the past. Hopefully she'd left town.

The inside of Showtime was a collision of bright color and sound—of flashing arcade games directly at eye level, and those big plastic tubes that kids climbed through overhead. Of bells and sirens and screaming children. Jack had been here once before, on Amy Lynn's birthday, and he wondered how anyone worked here without going insane.

He moved to the dining room and discovered that it was relatively quiet—for now. He knew that would all change once the show started. He found his brother and Rhonda and the girls sitting at a round table near the stage.

And Daisy.

About ten feet from the table, he stopped in his tracks. Daisy Monroe had managed to get herself invited to his niece's party.

She'd tracked him down. She'd told him she'd become his worst nightmare. It hadn't been an idle threat. His anger rose but he pushed it back. Controlled it for now. She didn't belong here. With his family.

His gaze moved to the woman sitting next to Daisy. He recognized Lily, and he supposed the kid with the mullet belonged to one of them. The boy had some sort of pudding on his face like someone had been feeding him with a slingshot. He wondered if the kid belonged to Daisy and Steven.

"Uncle Jack!" five-year-old Amy Lynn yelled. She jumped up from her chair and ran toward him. The birthday girl, three-year-old Lacy ran toward him too. Lacy tended to watch her feet while she ran, and he picked her up with his free arm to keep her from head-butting him in the nuts. "Hey there," he said. "Someone feels like she's three years old today."

"Me," she said and held up three fingers.

"I'm still five," Amy Lynn told him and wrapped her arms around his leg.

As he approached the table with Amy Lynn on his leg and Lacy in one arm, Billy glanced up from the dark-haired baby on his knee and smiled. "Hey, Jack, look who's in town."

Daisy looked at him, her brown eyes sparkling. She'd pulled her smooth hair back in a ponytail and her full lips were a soft shiny pink. She wore a tight green tank top with the name Ralph Lauren in black across her breasts.

"You didn't tell Billy I was back in town," she scolded, as a smile curved that mouth of hers.

Jack stood Lacy in her chair. His brother didn't know his history with Daisy. Billy'd been too young, and it wasn't something that Jack had ever wanted to talk about. Not even with his brother. Billy probably remembered her, though. Growing up, she'd been over at their house a lot. He probably thought they were still friends. Probably thought Jack'd be slaphappy to see her. "It must have escaped my mind," he said as Amy Lynn let go of him and took her seat.

Daisy laughed, very amused with herself, and that bumped up his anger a notch. "You remember my sister Lily?" she asked.

"Of course. How are you?"

Lily came out from behind the table and gave him a big hug as he set the present on the table. "I've been better." She looked a lot like Daisy, only with blue eyes. A lot like she had growing up, only for some reason she looked terminally pissed off now.

"How're you, Jack?"

He looked over her head at Daisy. "I've been better."

"This is Lily's son Pippen."

So, the kid belonged to Lily. For some reason, he was relieved that the boy with the mullet wasn't Daisy and Steven's. But he couldn't begin to understand why he should care.

Lily stepped back and shook her head. "You look as good as you always did."

"Thanks, Lily. You do too," he said, and meant it. "Hey, Rhonda"—his sister-in-law had *I haven't had sleep in five years* smudges under her dark brown eyes—"You okay, girl? Billy tells me you had a hard night."

"I was up most of it with Tanya. She has an earache, but we got a bottle of the pink medicine today, so she's feeling better."

Billy pulled the baby's sock up her pudgy leg. "We yanked the 'Vette engine while you were gone today."

He pulled out a chair between Lacy and Rhonda and across from Daisy and Lily. "Did you get a look at the clutch?"

"You were right," Billy said. "It needs to be completely replaced."

"I found one in Reno," he told his brother.

"How was Tallahassee?" Daisy asked him.

"When were you in Tallahassee?" Billy wanted to know.

"Last year."

Daisy's eyes rounded and her mouth fell open. "You lied to me."

He smiled as he leaned forward and poured himself a Dr. Pepper from a pitcher. She gave him that *grow up* glare like she had the other night, then she turned to his brother.

"Do you mind if I hold Tanya?"

"Not at all." Billy handed her over the baby, and Daisy stood Tanya in her lap. Jack half expected the six-month-old to start screaming, instead she laughed and pinched Daisy's cheek.

"Look, Pippen," Daisy said to the kid in the high chair beside her. "Isn't Tanya just a sweet little love muffin?"

"No!"

"Can I open my pez-ent from Uncle Jack?" Lacy asked in her tiny three-year-old voice.

"It's okay with me if it's okay with your Uncle Jack," Rhonda answered.

"Have at it kid," he said, although he would have preferred that Daisy wasn't sitting across the table when that stupid cat present was opened. Why he should give a shit, though, he didn't know that either.

Lacy tore off the bow and chucked it behind her shoulder. She ripped the paper and gasped as she tossed the shredded remains on the floor. "Kitty Magic! My fav-rut thing in the world!"

"Hey, that's what you said this morning when you got your Barbie Power Wheels," Billy reminded her.

Lily leaned across the table, and she and Rhonda chatted about what they'd been doing since high school. While Lacy and Amy Lynn took the cat and her kittens out of the box, the two women talked about kids and their lives; and when Lily said something about "Ronnie the Rat Bastard," Jack took it to mean she was getting a divorce. It also explained why she looked terminally pissed.

He took a long drink of his Dr. Pepper and sucked an ice cube into his mouth. He glanced across the table at Daisy and Tanya and Pippen. Tanya still stood in Daisy's lap, blowing raspberries. The little boy laughed and Daisy laughed, too. His gaze moved to her hands and her blood-red fingernails. A thin silver bracelet circled her slim wrist and a tiny heart rested against her pulse. The bracelet sparkled in the light, and as if she felt his gaze on her, she looked at him over the top of Tanya's dark head. Her smile fell and her brows drew together slightly. She stared at him through brown eyes that he used to think looked like melted chocolate. But that had been when he'd been ten years old and thought chocolate was the best thing in the world. Then he'd gotten older and discovered something better. Something darker and richer in those eyes. A knot twisted low in his belly. He wouldn't call it desire, but it wasn't disinterest either.

Billy plugged the mother cat with batteries and set it on the table. Lacy stood in her chair again, and Jack turned his attention to his niece. She stuck the kittens on the mother's side, and damn if it didn't make weird sucking sounds.

"It's a . . . well it's a nursing kitty." Daisy looked up from the pink Persian and laughter lit up her eyes. "Jack, why that's so sweet."

"Are those nipples on that thing?" Billy wanted to know.

"It looks like she has hearts instead of nipples," Jack told him.

"How come?" Amy Lynn wanted to know. They had a real mother cat at home, and she knew mommy cats didn't have hearts there.

Neither Billy nor Jack could think of an answer. Daisy looked at Amy Lynn and said, "Because hearts are cuter than nipples."

If they'd been alone, Jack might have told her exactly why she was wrong about that. Instead, he bit his ice cube in half and pushed it to one cheek.

"And they got some sunglasses, Lacy," Amy Lynn pointed out.

The center curtains on the stage parted and three big mechanical bears sprung to life, dancing and pretending to play instruments. A song about a happy frog filled the dining room, and Lacy clapped her hands.

Lily's kid let out a scream at the top of his lungs. Daisy handed Tanya back to Billy and she took the little boy from the high chair. She said something to Lily and walked from the room with the boy still screaming. Jack's gaze slid down the back of her tank top to her behind in those jean shorts.

"Did you see 'Monster Garage' the other night?" Billy asked over the music.

While Jack occasionally watched the show, Billy was a fanatic. "No, I missed that one."

"They turned a school bus into a pontoon boat?" he said, but the noise from the stage made it impossible for him to say any more.

Jack waited about five minutes before he followed Daisy and her nephew. He found the two of them in the play area. She'd cleaned Pippen's face, and he was playing in a pit of multicolored balls surrounded by mesh that went clear to the ceiling. She stood outside the mesh watching him wade through the balls as if he were walking upstream.

"How'd you manage to get yourself invited to Lacy's birthday party?" he asked as he came to stand beside her.

She glanced up into his face. "Lily and Pippen and I were already here when they walked in."

"And it was a complete surprise?"

She shook her head and her ponytail brushed her bare shoulders. "No. I knew you were going to be here, but I didn't expect Rhonda and Billy to invite us to sit with them."

"What's it going to take for you to leave me alone?"

She turned her attention back to her nephew. He picked up a plastic ball and threw it. It missed a little girl by about a foot. "You know what I want."

"To talk."

"Yes. There is something important we need to talk about."

"What?"

Sirens from a skeet-ball machine blared in the background. "Something too important to talk about in the middle of Showtime."

"Then why are you here, tonight? Stalking me and my family?"

"I'm not stalking you. I just wanted to remind you that I'm here, and I'm not going anywhere until you talk to me." She glanced down at her feet. "I have a letter Steven wrote to you. I don't have it on me, though."

"What does it say?"

She shook her head again, then stared straight ahead. "I don't know. I haven't read it."

"Send it to the shop."

"I can't do that. He asked me to give it to you in person."

"If it's so damn important, why didn't he give it to me himself? Instead of sending you?"

"Pippen, don't throw that," she told her nephew before she turned to face Jack. Red and blue lights from a video game to the right flashed on her bare shoulder, the side of her neck, and the corner of her mouth. "I think he meant to at first. For the first year of his illness, he believed he'd beat his cancer. We knew all along that no one had ever survived glioblastoma, but he was young and healthy and the early treatments seemed to be working. He fought so hard, Jack." She turned back to Pippen and grasped the mesh with her hands. "By the time he accepted that he was going to die, it was too late to talk to you in person." The little heart on her bracelet dangled from her wrist. He stared at it, not wanting to feel anything for Steven or for her. Not wanting to give a shit.

But he did have one question. "How long did he live after he accepted that he was going to die?"

"About eight or nine months."

That's what he thought. Steven had always wanted someone to "go first"—whether it was telling Daisy she had a big ugly hair bow, or jumping off a roof, or throwing rotten tomatoes at cars. Growing up, it had never bothered him, but that was a long time ago. "Then there was time to come and talk to me before he died. He didn't have to send you."

She laughed ruthlessly. "You've obviously never seen anyone who's gone through radical cancer treatments. If you had, you wouldn't say that." One of her hands dropped to her side, and tears shimmered along the bottoms of her eyelids as she gazed up at him. "You wouldn't have recognized him, Jack." One tear slid from her lashes and ran down her cheek. He clenched his hands to keep from reaching up and wiping it with his fingertips. "Toward the end," she continued, "he forgot how to tie his shoes, but he insisted on getting dressed every day like it mattered. So, I tied his shoes for him . . . every day. Like it mattered. And it did because it gave him a little dignity, I think. Some feeling like he was still an adult. A man."

A piece of his heart fell to his stomach and his breath with it. "Stop it, Daisy."

"Jack—"

"No." He knew she would not stop until she carved him up. Just like before. He wasn't about to let that happen. Not again. Not for anything. "I don't want to hear any more." He was sorry for Steven. Sorrier than he would have thought possible two minutes ago, but he would not let her tear him to shreds.

"I didn't mean to talk about this now." She wiped the tear from her cheek. "Meet with me later so you can hear me out."

"The only thing I want to hear from you, Daisy Monroe, is the word goodbye," he said, and then he walked away. He moved back into the dining room and told his brother and Rhonda he was leaving. For once he was grateful to the damn dancing bears and their loud annoying music that didn't allow for questions. He gave his nieces some money for game tokens and left. He didn't see Daisy when he walked back out, but he wasn't looking for her either.

He took a deep breath and kept right on moving. He didn't think he took a full breath again until he was home. Shut up in his house. Locked tight against the memory of Daisy and Steven and him. But the memories followed him inside, and he sat down hard on his mother's piano bench and put his hands on his knees.

He'd hated Steven for about as many years as he'd loved him like a brother. But even in his earliest rage, he'd never wanted Steven dead. Not really. Maybe there had been a time in the beginning when the thought of Steven wiped off the planet had held a certain appeal, but he had never wanted him to die the way Daisy had described it. Not like that. Not even back when his anger had burned the hottest.

When it came right down to it, he'd never wanted him to die at all. Because in the end, he understood Steven. He understood that he had betrayed Steven every bit as much as Steven had betrayed him.

It'd been Steven who'd told him about Daisy being stood up for that damn high school prom their senior year. It had been both their ideas that Jack take her since Steven already had a date. It had seemed so simple at the time. Take Daisy so she wouldn't spend the night crying her eyes out. No big deal, but that night had changed all their lives.

Jack didn't really remember the actual dance,

other than trying to touch as little of Daisy as possible. What he did remember, though, was standing on her front porch looking down at her, wanting her so much he ached, and telling himself to leave. To get into his car and drive away.

Then she kissed him.

Compared to kisses he'd experienced with other girls, it was nothing really. Just her closed lips pressed to his, but it had hit him square in the chest. He'd been stunned and angry and he'd pushed her away. Then she'd touched the side of his neck and looked up at him as if she wanted him every bit as much as he wanted her. As much as he'd always wanted her.

"Please, Jack," she'd whispered, and even as he'd lowered his mouth for more, he'd told himself it was a mistake. Even as he'd stood there, kissing her and tasting her mouth, he'd told himself to stop. Even as he'd kept his grasp on her shoulders, he'd pulled her into his chest and felt the weight of her breasts against him. Even as he told himself that it could not happen again, he'd known that it would. He'd wanted her for years, and one little bite had not been enough.

Not nearly.

He'd told himself to stay away, but even if he'd been able to control his eighteen-year-old lust, Daisy wouldn't let him. At Jimmy Calhoun's party the next night, she'd pulled him into a dark closet and put his hand on her breast.

"Touch me, Jack," she'd whispered into his mouth, and he'd about gone off in his boxer shorts.

A few days later he'd told Steven he couldn't hang

out because he was grounded. Then he'd jumped in his Camaro, picked Daisy up at her house, and they'd driven out to a deserted road. He'd parked and told her about Steven, about the two of them being attracted to her, and he explained why he and Daisy had to stop.

She said she understood. She agreed, then she'd kissed his ear and told him that Steven didn't have to find out.

"I love Steven. He's my friend," she'd said. "But I don't think of him the same way I think of you. I'm in love with you, Jack. I want more from you. I want you to show me how to make love."

That night he'd taken off her shirt and unhooked her bra. White with tiny blue dots on it. Her breasts were the most beautiful things he'd ever seen. Firm and white, her tight pink nipples fit perfectly into his mouth.

He hadn't made love to her that night. No, he'd tried to do the noble thing. He'd told her he didn't mess with virgins. He'd told himself it was okay as long as he didn't stick his hand in her panties and touch her there. He'd told himself to go slow with her, but that resolve quickly disappeared like a kid with candy. Then he'd had to tell himself it wasn't really wrong unless he took her hymen.

After two weeks of touching and kissing and rubbing against each other, he'd picked her up and driven with her to a hotel on the outskirts of Amarillo. They'd taken it all the way that night, and he'd learned the difference between sex and making love. He'd learned the difference between sex where just his genitals were involved, and sex that involved his soul. He'd learned that being inside of Daisy Lee burned him up and left his chest aching. And the whole time he'd known it was wrong. He'd known Steven loved her as much as he did, but he'd told himself that Daisy was right. It was okay as long as Steven didn't find out.

In public, he and Daisy behaved as they always had, as friends, but it hadn't been easy. Seeing but not touching had driven him insane. Watching her walk down the school halls or jump around in her little cheerleader skirt, had made him insanely jealous.

He hadn't been the only one driven crazy by their situation. Daisy had always wanted him just as much as he'd wanted her, and when he couldn't meet with her, which wasn't often, she'd accuse him of not loving her. Of being with other girls. She'd tell him she didn't love him anymore, then the next chance they got, they'd tear at each other's clothes and satisfy the lust that burned too hot.

Neither of them wanted to hurt Steven and they decided to wait until he left for college to be more open about their relationship. Steven had been accepted to the University of Washington, and after high school graduation, he planned to live with his sister and brother-in-law until he could afford his own apartment. Both Jack and Daisy planned to take classes at West Texas A&M, about seventy miles south. They'd planned to tell Steven that they were in love when he came home for Christmas that year.

Jack rose from the piano bench and moved into the dark kitchen. He flipped on the light and opened the refrigerator. He pushed aside a quart of milk and reached for a Lone Star instead.

Being with Daisy had been like having one long orgasm while on a roller coaster. Damn exciting, but not if you wanted some calm.

He popped the top off his beer and tossed it on the counter. Two weeks after he graduated from high school, his parents had been killed in a car wreck. They'd been out driving in their '59 Bonneville when a drunk driver hit them. That old Pontiac may have been built like a tank, but it hadn't been built with safety features. His father had been killed instantly. His mother died on the way to the hospital. And at the age of eighteen, he'd suddenly become responsible not only from himself but for Billy too.

Jack raised the bottle to his mouth and took a drink. Whenever he thought back on that time in his life, he had a hard time remembering details. He'd been torn up and confused and scared. And just plain raw. His whole life had changed in an instant, and it had seemed that the more he wanted space to think, the more clinging Daisy got. The more he pushed her away so he could breathe, the tighter she'd held on to him. He remembered the night he'd told her they needed time apart, that he needed time away from her to think. That he didn't want to see her for a while. She became hysterical. Then the next time he saw her, she was Steven's wife.

He recalled exactly what she'd been wearing that night. A blue sun dress with little white flowers. She and Steven had stood in his front yard and asked him to come outside. He remembered walking toward her and her looking so good to him that he'd wanted to grab her and hold her and tell her to stay with him forever.

Instead Steven told him that the two of them had married that afternoon. At first, he couldn't believe it. Daisy didn't love Steven. She loved him. But he'd taken one look at her guilty face and knew it was true. He grabbed her and told her she belonged to him, not Steven. He tried to kiss her and touch her and make her admit she loved him. Steven got between them, and Jack smashed his fist into Steven's face. They proceeded to beat the hell out of each other, but Steven Monroe had never been a fighter. He'd ended up taking the bad end of the beating.

Jack raised the beer to his mouth again and swallowed hard. The night he'd lost Daisy, he'd lost Steven too. He'd lost the girl he'd loved and craved and wanted to live with forever.

He'd lost his best friend. The boy who'd been by his side during every hair-brained adventure. Steven might have been a "you go first" kind of guy, but Jack had always known that Steven was right there behind him. Backing him up. Ready to go next. Then in the course of one night, they were both gone and Jack was alone.

He'd learned a valuable lesson that night that he'd lost everything. He'd learned that no one could take from you what you didn't give them. No one could slice your insides up if you didn't hand them the knife. He didn't think that made him bitter, just a man who learned from mistakes. And it didn't make him one of those commitment-phobic guys Rhonda was always accusing him of being.

Hell, he might get married one day. Marriage wasn't something he'd ever rule out, but it wasn't something he was looking for either. If it happened, it happened. He had a family. Billy and Rhonda and the girls were enough for him, but there was room in his life for someone else. He was only thirty-three. There was time.

Except Daisy. There would never be room for Daisy Monroe. Not only had she sliced up his insides, she'd stomped them into the ground. He would never allow Daisy into his life again.

No, he'd learned his lesson the first time.

Chapter 7

Daisy shoved her tortoise-shell Vuarnet sunglasses onto the bridge of her nose and looked over at Lily, who concealed her eyes behind lavender Adrienne Vittadinis.

Like a cop on a stakeout, Lily backed her Ford Taurus in between a truck and a minivan and shoved the car into park. The last strain of "Earl Had to Die" wound to a close, and the dying notes of an electric keyboard filled the space between the two sisters. Normally, Daisy had nothing against the Dixie Chicks, in fact she had two of their CDs, but if Lily hit the back arrow on the car's stereo one more time, Daisy wasn't responsible for what she might do next.

"Do you see him anywhere?" Lily asked as she scanned the parking lot to a stucco apartment complex off Eldorado Street. Her hand lowered from the steering wheel, hovered, then she hit the back button.

"Damn it!" Daisy swore, driven to near madness. "That's the fifth time in a row you've played that song."

Lily looked across the seat at Daisy. Her brows lowered, and frown lines creased her forehead. "You're counting? That's warped."

"Me! I'm not the one wearing out 'Earl Had to Die' while parked outside my soon to be ex-husband's apartment."

"It's not his apartment. He's renting a house over on Locust Grove near the hospital. It's *her* apartment. Kelly the skank," Lily said and returned her attention to the complex.

The Chicks started with the first verse *again*, and Daisy leaned over and hit the off button. The car was blessedly silent. After leaving Showtime last night, Lily had taken a detour, passing Kelly's apartment. She'd driven past three times like some crazed stalker before dropping Daisy off at their mother's house.

This morning she showed up bright and early to drop Pippen off so she could "find a job." Daisy took one look at her sister's flat hair and wrinkled running sweats, and she knew something was up. She told Lily she was coming along. She pulled on a pair of jean shorts, a black T-shirt, and shoved her feet into flip-flops as she twisted her hair up onto the back of her head and secured it with a claw.

"How long have you been doing this?" she asked.

Lily's hands tightened on the gray steering wheel. "Awhile."

"Why?"

"I have to see them together."

"Why?" she asked again. "That's crazy."

Lily shrugged, but didn't take her gaze from the apartment complex.

"What are you going to do if you see them together? Run them down with your car?"

"Maybe."

She didn't think her sister would actually mow Ronnie down, but the fact that she was sitting here thinking about it was a bit worrisome. "Lily, you can't kill them."

"Maybe I'll just clip them with the bumper. Or ram Ronnie's balls so he'll be useless to his girlfriend."

"You can't ram Ronnie Darlington's balls. You'll go to jail."

"Maybe I won't get caught."

"You'll get caught. The ex-wife always gets caught." She reached over and rubbed Lily's shoulder though her red jogging suit. "You have to stop doing this."

Lily shook her head as a tear slipped beneath her glasses and ran down her cheek. "Why does he get to be happy? Why does he just get to move on with his girlfriend and be happy while I feel like I have acid eating a hole in my heart? He should have to feel what he's done to us, Daisy. He should suffer like Pippen and me."

"I know."

"No, you don't. No one has ever broken your heart. Steven died, he didn't run off with a woman and break your heart."

Daisy dropped her hand to the seat. "You don't think watching Steven die broke my heart?"

Lily looked over at Daisy and brushed the tears streaming down her cheeks. "Yes, I guess. But it's different. Steven didn't leave you because he wanted to." She sucked in a deep breath and added, "You're lucky."

"What? That's a horrible thing to say."

"I don't mean that you're lucky Steven died, just that you don't have to think about Steven having sex with another woman. You don't have to wonder if he's kissing her and touching her and loving her."

"You're right. I have to think of him dead in the ground." She folded her arms beneath her breasts and stared at her sister. "I'm going to let that go because you're having a bad day." But she guessed she wasn't quite ready to let it go because she couldn't keep from adding, "I know you don't mean to be an insensitive brat. That's just the way you are."

"And I'm sure you don't mean to be so selfish. That's just the way *you* are."

Daisy's mouth fell open. She was sitting in her sister's car to keep Lily from doing something stupid, and *she* was selfish. "Yeah right, and I want to sit here watching Ronnie's apartment because I have nothing better to do."

"Do you think I wanted to sit in Showtime last night while you stalked Jack Parrish?"

"It's not the same thing. It's important that I speak with Jack. You know that." She turned her head and looked out the passenger-side window at an old lady in a pink housecoat walking her beagle down the sidewalk. "And I'm not stalking him."

"I don't think he sees it that way."

No, he didn't. And after last night, she supposed he had reason to think that. Going to Showtime and crashing his niece's birthday party might not have been one of her brightest ideas, but she was running out of time. She only had a few more days, and if Jack hadn't lied to her about being out of town, she wouldn't have wasted four of those days already. She was under the gun and felt the pressure mounting.

"Did you see how he was with Billy's little girls?" she asked. Watching him walk toward her with those two girls clinging to him, she'd felt a surprising little pinch in her heart. "He was really good with them, and you could see that they really love him. You can't fake something like that with kids."

"Did it make you think you should have stuck around and not married Steven?"

Daisy sank down in her seat and looked out the front. "No, but it made me realize that when I tell him about Nathan, he's probably going to be a lot angrier with me than I'd figured. Not that I thought he wouldn't be, but there's always been a part of me that hoped he'd understand." She took the claw out of her hair and leaned her head back against the seat. "Jack wasn't ready for a family. He'd just lost his mother and father, he wouldn't have been able to handle the news that I was pregnant. I did the right thing."

"But . . . ?" Lily prompted.

"But I've never let myself wonder what kind of father he would have made." She tossed the claw onto the center console. "I've never let myself think about that."

"And now you're thinking about it?"

"Yeah." Although it was probably best not to, she couldn't help *but* think about it.

The door to an upstairs apartment opened and

Ronnie stepped out with one of his arms around a dark-haired woman. Daisy had only met Ronnie twice, when he and Lily visited Seattle, but Daisy recognized him. He was good-looking with strategically disarrayed blond hair and a gee-shucks smile that fooled some women. Unlike Lily, Daisy had never been impressed, much less fooled.

"Turn off the car," Daisy told her sister. This morning, Ronnie's Stetson shaded his face and cast a shadow on the shoulders of his red cowboy shirt. He wore a belt buckle the size of a dessert plate and his wranglers were so tight they looked painted on.

"I'm not going to run him down."

"Turn it off Lily." They were too far away for Daisy to get a good look at Kelly's face, but even at this distance, she could see that her hair was pulled up on top of her head in a ponytail and that she had a big behind covered in black spandex shorts.

The engine shut off and Daisy reached over and took the keys from the ignition. She grabbed Lily's arm to keep her from opening the door.

"He's not worth it, Lily."

The two moved to a white monster truck with metallic red flames blazing down the sides. Ronnie helped "Kelly the skank" up into the truck, then he fired up the Ford and the two of them took off. Anger for her sister burned in Daisy's stomach as she watched them drive out of the parking lot. Lily covered her mouth but a high-pitch keening leaked through her fingers. Daisy reached across the center console and pulled her sister into her arms the best that she could.

"Lily, he's not worth your tears," she said as she smoothed her hair.

"I still love him so-ho much. Why can-can't he love me-me?" Lily cried. Daisy held her and felt her heart breaking too. What kind of worthless man abandoned his wife and child? What kind of A-moral A-hole ran around with another woman and emptied the family's bank account so he wouldn't have to pay for his child? The more Daisy thought about it, the angrier she got. Somehow, Ronnie would have to pay for hurting her sister.

"Honey, have you thought of maybe getting some counseling?" she asked her sister.

"I don't want to ta-talk about it with a stranger. It's too-too humiliating." After that her sentences became incoherent, and she mostly sounded like a distressed dolphin.

"Let me drive us home," Daisy said. Lily nodded and while Daisy ran around to the other side of the car, Lily crawled to the passenger seat. "Do you want a Dr. Pepper?" Daisy asked as they drove out of the parking lot. "It might help your raw throat."

Lily wiped her nose on her sleeve and nodded. "Eee-hee," she managed.

She drove to the Minute Mart and pulled into a slot in front of the store. She pocketed the keys in case Lily got ideas, grabbed a five from her purse, and put her sunglasses on the dashboard. "I'll be right back," she told Lily and opened the door. Once inside the store, she filled up a twenty-four-ounce cup with Dr. Pepper, sealed the top with a lid and grabbed a straw. When Lily calmed down, she'd talk to her about her lawyer and see what he was doing to help her.

"Good morning," the clerk said, his green uniform hung on his bony shoulders. His name tag said he was Chuck and that she should have a nice day. She doubted that was possible now.

"Morning." As Daisy handed over the five-dollar bill, a white Ford truck with red flames down the sides pulled into a parking slot a few cars away from Lily's Taurus. She watched with a sense of impending doom as Ronnie and Kelly stepped out of the truck. "Oh no."

The passenger door of the Taurus flew open and Lily shot out of the car like a bullet. She confronted the two right there on the sidewalk in front of the Minute Mart. Daisy could hear Lily's hysterical screaming through the glass, and she was sure the people at the gas pumps were getting a good show.

She set the straw on the counter and held up one hand, palm out. "I'll be right back." As Daisy yanked open the store's door, Lily called Kelly a whore and a fat-ass, and Kelly swung and slapped Lily across the face. Lily's sunglasses sailed off, and she raised her hand to retaliate. Ronnie grabbed her arm and shoved.

Lily fell and everything within Daisy narrowed, like looking in the wrong end of a telescope. Rage flowed through her like a toxic chemical, and she ran full steam, launching herself at her soon to be ex-brother-in-law. Years ago, Steven and Jack had taught her how to defend herself. She'd never used those lessons before, but she hadn't forgotten. Like riding a bike. She got a shoulder into his sternum.

He grunted and grabbed her hair. He shook her but she hardly felt it as she tucked her thumb and punched him in the eye.

"Ow, you crazy bitch!"

Without thinking about it, she kneed him just below his belt buckle. She didn't think she'd hit him square between the legs like she'd been aiming, but enough that the air left his lungs in a big whoosh. His fingers loosened and she stepped back. Ronnie doubled over and several long strands of Daisy's hair got tangled in his fist.

"You ever touch my sister again," she told him between breaths, "and I'll kill you, Ronnie Darlington."

He groaned and stared at her through squinty eyes. "You can try, you stupid bitch."

Daisy didn't mind being called a crazy bitch, because sometimes it was true. But she hated being called a stupid bitch. She launched herself forward again, but someone grabbed her around the middle and pulled her back. "You've won, buttercup."

She pushed at the arm around her stomach, but he pulled her onto her toes. "Let go. I'm going to kick his butt!"

"I think it's more likely that he'd kick yours. Then I'd have to step in and knock the shit out of him for laying a hand on you. And I really don't want to do that. Buddy and I came here for a fill-up and a cup of coffee, is all. We weren't planning on a brawl."

Daisy blinked and her peripheral vision came into focus again. She was aware of her heart pounding in her throat as she looked over her shoulder. "Jack?"

The shadow from his beige cowboy hat cut across his face, and she watched his mouth form the words,

"Good mornin'," but he didn't sound like there was anything good about it.

She turned her attention to Lily standing with her back against the front of the store. She had a cut on the bridge of her nose and a red palm print on her cheek. A man in a blue T-shirt stood next to her, talking to her as she shook her head. Kelly sat on her butt on the ground, and her ponytail was pulled to one side of her head. Ronnie straightened with a grunt and felt his crotch as if to make sure everything was still there.

"I hope you can't use it for a month." Daisy spat at him, and Jack pulled her tighter against the solid wall of his chest.

Then Jack spoke to Ronnie from beside Daisy's temple. "Take your girlfriend and get out of here while the two of you can still walk."

Ronnie opened his mouth, shut it again, then grabbed Kelly, who'd started screaming at the top of her lungs. He shoved her inside his truck, fired the engine, and the two of them took off, monster truck tires squealing out of the parking lot.

"Are you okay, Lily?" she called out to her sister.

Lily nodded and took her sunglasses from the man talking to her.

"What was that about?" Jack asked. "The two of you out here spreadin' sunshine for the hell of it?" He didn't let go, and she looked up at him again. The breeze picked up several strands of her blond hair and carried them across the front of his dress shirt. She raised her gaze past his mouth and looked deeper into the shadow created by the brim of his hat. His light green eyes stared back at her. Waiting.

"That's Lily's husband and his girlfriend."

He tilted his head back and the shadow slid from the middle of his nose to the deep bow of his top lip. "Ah."

The adrenaline in her veins made her feel suddenly shaky, and she was glad Jack held her so tight. "He's a rat bastard."

"So, I've heard."

Daisy wasn't surprised that Ronnie's reputation proceeded him. Lovett was a small town. "He emptied their bank account and won't give her any money for Pippen."

Jack slid his palm across her stomach as he dropped his arm. He took a step back, and the solid wall of his chest was replaced with cool morning air. Her hand throbbed, her head hurt, her shoulder ached, and her knees felt wobbly. It had been a long time since she'd felt a man's strength surrounding her, supporting her, and she would have liked nothing better than to melt right back into his chest and arms again. Of course, that was impossible. "I hurt my hand."

"Let me see." He turned her to face him and cradled her hand in his warm palm. The sleeves of his blue broadcloth shirt were rolled up his forearms, and over his breast pocket, was embroidered PAR-RISH AMERICAN CLASSICS, in black. "Wiggle your fingers for me," he said.

With his head bent over her hand, the brim of his hat almost touched her mouth. He smelled of soap and clean skin and his starched shirt. His thumb brushed the heel of her hand and little tingles radiated outward from her palm over her wrist and traveled up the inside of her arm. Her adrenaline was doing funny things to her. Either that or she'd pinched a nerve.

He lifted his gaze and his eyes stared into hers. For several long seconds he just looked at her. She'd forgotten that when you looked real close into Jack's eyes, you could see darker green flecks. She remembered now.

"I don't think it's broke, but you probably should get an X-ray." He dropped her hand.

She made a slow fist and winched. "How do you know it's not broken?"

"When I broke my hand, it swelled up almost immediately."

"How did you break your hand?"

"Fighting."

"With Steven?"

"No. At a roadhouse bar in Macon."

Macon? What had he been doing in Macon? In the last fifteen years, he'd had a whole life she knew nothing about. She was curious about it, but she doubted he'd tell her much if she were to ask.

The clerk from inside the store moved toward Daisy and she turned to him as he handed her her sunglasses. "Thanks, Chuck," she said and slid them on her face. He gave her the change and she took the Dr. Pepper with her good hand.

"Should I call the police?" he wanted to know. "I saw them hit the other blond woman first."

A police report might help in Lily's divorce, but Lily wasn't completely innocent. There was the little matter of Lily's stalking. She didn't know if Ronnie knew about that, but he might. "No. That's okay."

"If you change your mind, let me know," Chuck offered and headed back inside.

Daisy turned her attention to Lily and the man talking to her. "Is he with you?" she asked Jack.

"Yeah. That's Buddy Calhoun."

"Older or younger than Jimmy?"

"A year younger."

Daisy didn't remember much about Buddy beyond having the bad teeth and flaming red hair of all the Calhouns. She glanced around at the people in the parking lot and at the gas pumps at the far end. The ramifications of what she'd done that morning began to sink in. "I can't believe I fought in public." She raised the cool Dr. Pepper to her cheek. "I never even swear in public."

"If it's any consolation, I don't think you swore." No, it wasn't much comfort, especially when he added, "But your sister has a mouth like a trucker. We heard her clear over at the gas pumps."

Daisy didn't live in Lovett anymore, but her mother did. Her mother would be mortified. Daisy and Lily would probably be the latest topic at her single's dance. "Do you think very many people noticed us?"

"Daisy, you're standing at the intersection of Canyon and Vine. In case you've forgotten, it's about the busiest intersection in the city."

"So people are going to know that I socked Ronnie Darlington in the eye." She removed the cool cup from her cheek. Good lord, could things be any worse?

Evidently. "Yep, and that you kneed his balls."

"You saw that?"

"Yeah. Remind me not to piss you off." He glanced over her head. "Ready, Buddy?"

Buddy Calhoun turned and flashed Jack a straight white smile. So much for Buddy having the Calhoun bad teeth. His hair was a dark red too, not carrot like the others. He was better-looking too. "Be right there, J. P.," he drawled.

J. P.?

"Try to stay out of trouble," Jack said to her as he turned to go. "Next time someone might not be around to save you from doing something stupid, like going after a man who weighs twice what you do."

She put her bad hand on his arm to stop him. He was right. "Thanks, Jack. If you hadn't stepped in, something really bad could have happened." She shook her head. Maybe he didn't hate her as much as he wanted her to think. "When I saw him shove my sister . . . I don't even remember how it happened, but I just lost my mind and went after him."

"Don't make too much of it, Daisy." So much for feeling special. "You could have been anyone." His gaze dropped to her hand on his arm.

"Since I'm not just anyone, you should let me thank you properly," she offered in the hopes that perhaps they could now relate to each other on friendlier terms, and she could talk to him about Nathan.

One corner of his mouth slid up as his gaze moved to her breasts, up her chin, to her mouth. He wasn't fooled by her offer and was purposely trying to annoy her. "What did you have in mind?"

"Not what you have in mind."

From within the shadow of his hat, he finally looked into her eyes. "What then?"

"Lunch."

"Not interested."

"Dinner."

"No, ma'am." He stepped off the curb and said over his shoulder, "Come on, Buddy."

Daisy watched him move across the parking lot to a classic black Mustang parked at one of the gas pumps. Two razor-sharp creases ran down the back of his shirt and were tucked into the waistband of his Levi's. He wasn't wearing a belt, and his wallet made a bulge in his back pocket. Buddy followed and Daisy turned to her sister. The red welt on Lily's cheek had started to fade.

"Are you okay?" Daisy asked as Lily moved toward her.

"I'm okay." She reached for the Dr. Pepper and took a long drink. "I think I'm going crazy."

Really? "Maybe a little."

The two of them moved to Lily's Taurus and got inside. Lily spoke as she buckled her seat belt. "I'm sorry about what I said about Steven. You're right. I was being an insensitive bitch."

"I think I said you were a brat."

"I know you did. Let's go home."

Daisy started the car. "How long do you think it will take for Mom to find out?"

"Not long," Lily sighed. "She'll probably try to ground us."

Through the rearview mirror, she watched Jack's Mustang pull out of the parking lot.

"Daisy?"

"Yeah?"

"Thanks. You were really something going after Ronnie like that."

"Don't thank me, just promise you'll stop stalking him and Kelly the skank."

"Okay." She took a drink of her cup. "Did you see her butt, though?"

"It was huge."

"And flabby."

"Yeah, and you're a lot cuter and have better hair."

Lily smiled. "And breath."

Daisy chuckled. "Yeah."

When they got back to their mother's house, Lily grabbed Pippen and lay down on the couch with him. She turned on a Blue's Clues video and nestled her nose in his little mullet. "Love you, Pippy," she said. Without taking his eyes from the television, he raised his face and kissed his mother's chin.

"Did you get the job?" Louella asked from the kitchen, where she was baking cookies and filling the house with the smell of peanut butter.

"They said they'd call," Lily answered, hiding her smile behind her son's head.

"Chicken," Daisy whispered.

Lily was a mess, no doubt about it. Daisy had three days before she needed to return to her life in Seattle. Nathan's last day of school was today, and she needed to call him and ask how it went.

She had a lot to do. She had three days to help straighten out her sister's life, give Steven's letter to Jack and tell him he had a son. Then she could return home and get on with *her* life. She and Nathan could lie around on a beach somewhere, soaking up rays. She'd drink piña coladas while he watched girls in bikinis. Heaven for both of them.

But right now, all she wanted was to take a shower, put ice on her hand, and take a nap. Her adrenaline spent, she was tired and achy, but if not for Jack, she was positive she would be feeling a lot more achy right about now. Going after Ronnie like that hadn't been real smart, but she hadn't thought at all. She'd just reacted to him pushing Lily to the ground.

I think it's more likely that he'd kick yours. Then I'd have to step in and knock the shit out of him for laying a hand on you, Jack had said. He'd also said he would have come to the rescue of any woman. He'd told her not to make too much out of it.

But now as she thought back with a clearer head, she doubted he would have held just any woman a little bit longer than was absolutely necessary. Not like he'd held her, tight against his hard chest. And she really doubted he would have brushed just any woman's hand with his thumb. She also doubted he'd even known he was doing it.

She'd been so focused on everything else around her, she hadn't realized that Jack's touch had been a little more personal, lingered a second longer than just a Good Samaritan helping out any ol' woman.

She realized it now, and just the memory of his touch made her catch her breath. Her mother called out to her as she moved up the stairs to her bedroom. "Okay," she called back, then shut the door behind her. She leaned against it as a hot little tug pulled at her abdomen and between her thighs. The warmth of it spread across her flesh and her breasts grew heavy with it. She hadn't felt anything like this in a long time, but she knew what it was. Lust. Pent up sexual desire. Years of it pulling at her.

She closed her eyes. Maybe she'd imagined Jack's touch. Maybe it was all in her head, but she hadn't imagined how good it was to feel a solid healthy man again. So good to feel protected. So good to feel his chest against her back and his arm around her waist. God help her, she missed that feeling. Missed it so much that she'd wanted to melt into Jack. She wondered what he'd have done if she'd turned and kissed the side of his neck. Run her tongue up his throat and her hands all over the muscles of his chest. Naked, like he'd been in his kitchen that first night. Half naked with his jeans hanging low on his hips so she could slide her palms over his flat abdomen and sink to her knees as she pressed her face into his button fly.

Daisy's lids flew open. Jack was the last man on the planet she should be fantasizing about licking and touching. The last man on the plant who should make her think of sex.

It's been a long time, is all, she told herself as she pushed away from the door. She opened a drawer and pulled out a pair of bikini panties and her bra. She was thirty-three, and before Steven's illness, they'd had a very active sex life. Daisy liked sex and she missed it. She supposed it had only been a matter of time before her desire for intimacy returned. It was just too bad it had returned right now. Today. And it was really too bad Jack had been the trigger.

For so many obvious reasons, sex between her and Jack was out of the question.

Daisy walked from her room to the bathroom down the hall. But sex between her and someone other than Jack might be a possibility. She'd only been with two different men her whole life, maybe it was time to experiment. She had two and a half days now before she returned to Seattle. Maybe it was time to live it up before she returned home and was a mom again. Maybe she should add "get laid" to her to-do list.

A little stab of guilt poked her conscience. Steven was dead, so why did it feel like she was contemplating cheating on her husband? She didn't know, but there it was. Right in front of her, and she knew that her guilt would probably keep her from actually doing it with anyone.

Too bad, because she probably would have liked some no-strings-attached sex. The kind where you just grab someone, do it, and never see them again.

She turned on the bathtub and held her hand under the running water. But maybe if she just did it, she wouldn't feel guilty anymore. Maybe it was like losing her virginity all over again. The first time was the most difficult. After that, it got a whole lot easier. A whole lot funner, too.

Of course she didn't have a candidate. Maybe she should pick up some guy at a bar. Someone who looked like Hugh Jackman or that one guy in the Diet Coke commercial. No, those men reminded her too much of Jack. She should pick someone totally different. Someone like Viggo Mortensen or Brad Pitt. No, Matthew McConaughey.

Oh yeah.

But it would never be Jack. Never. That would be really really bad.

Or, a little voice inside her head whispered, *it would be really, really good.* As she dropped her shorts and pulled her T-shirt over her head, she was afraid that if she wasn't careful, the little voice in her head was going to get her into big, big trouble.

Chapter 8

*M*ost weekend nights, Slim Clem's packed 'em in from as far away as Amarillo and Dalhart. The live band played country, loud country, with an occasional southern-rock oldy thrown in. The big dance floors were always crowded, and the mechanical bulls were always running, taking on all comers with a pocket full of cash. Three different bars poured a continuous stream of icy beer, straight shots, or fruity drinks with paper umbrellas.

All manner of stuffed mammals and reptiles peered through glass eyes from built-in platforms high on the walls. If the Road Kill Bar was a taxidermist's dream, Slim Clem's was his wet dream. Although why anyone would proudly display a hog-nosed skunk was anyone's guess.

Within the dim bar, Wranglers, Rockies and Lees ruled. Worn tight and in every imaginable color by women stuffed into fringed cowgirl blouses with horses appliquéd on the back. T-shirts with conches and feathers, the bottoms shredded to look like fringe, were also a big favorite as well as prairie skirts with big ruffles or jacard dresses with sweetheart collars. Hair ranged from Texas big, teased and sprayed within an inch of its life—hat head—or hair so long and straight it hung to the waist or the backs of the knees.

The men preferred Wranglers or Levi's in blue or black, some so tight a person had to wonder where they'd packed their goods. While there were men who wore starched cowboy shirts with racing flames or American flags on them, T-shirts were the hands-down favorite. Most advertised beer and John Deere tractors, while others had a different message. The ubiquitous "Don't mess with Texas" was out in full force, while "Yeah, I'm drunk, but you're still ugly," competed with the ever hopeful "Let's get Nekid."

Cowboy boots kept time with the band, and belt buckles big enough to be considered lethal weapons flashed beneath the dance floor's multicolored lights.

Daisy had never been inside Slim Clem's. When she'd lived in Lovett before, she'd been too young. But she'd heard about it. Everybody had heard about it, and she figured it was about time she experienced it for herself.

That Friday afternoon, Lily got a job at the deli counter in Albertsons, and the two of them decided to celebrate at Slim's. Daisy hadn't really brought anything to wear to a honky-tonk, but in the back of her closet, she dug out her old cowboy boots. She shoved her feet into them, and while a little tight, they still fit. Her junior year in high school, she'd saved for several months to buy the red boots with the white heart inserts. Lucky for her, cowboy boots were never out of style in Texas.

In the box with her yearbooks, she pulled out her daddy's belt with the big silver buckle he'd won at the Top 'O Texas rodeo a few short months before a bull had stomped and killed him.

She put on her white cotton tank dress that closed down her breasts with eight little snaps, and she wrapped her daddy's rodeo belt around her hips. The name *Rowdy* was tooled into the brown leather in back. The buckle was heavy and hung down a little, but she thought she looked ready for a cowboy bar.

She rolled her hair on big curlers and stuck big hoops in her ears. She outlined her eyes with black liner, put on her shiniest red lipstick, and decided that she looked cowgirl chic.

Lily dressed for the bar in tight jeans and a pink blouse she tied just below her breasts so that her navel ring showed. Her makeup was heavier than Daisy's; and when she kissed Pippen goodbye on her mother's porch, she left big pink lip prints on his cheek.

On the way to Slim Clem's, Lily laughed and joked and seemed ready to get on with her life. Daisy was ready too. Tomorrow she was going to tell Jack about Nathan, and this time nothing would stop her. Not her own fear, not a kid's birthday party, and not even a half-naked woman in his house. She was leaving Sunday afternoon, and she had to tell him tomorrow. There was no other choice.

It was after nine when they walked into the bar. The band was singing Brooks and Dunn's "My Maria" as they paid their five-dollar cover charge. While the band hit the high notes of the song, Daisy and Lily made their way through the crowd to the closest bar and ordered two Lone Stars from the tap. Daisy paid for the first round, and the two of them lucked out and found a table near the dance floor. They sat in chairs next to each other and their conversation turned to a critique of the people around them.

"Get a load of that guy over there in the beige cowboy shirt and hat," Lily said next to Daisy's ear. Since that described quite a few of the men in the bar, she had to point with her glass. "He's got on jeans so tight, he must have been poured in 'em wet."

The cowboy in question was tall and lean and looked tough and hard enough to wrestle steers. " 'Wrangler butts drive us nuts,' " Daisy recited through a smile and raised her beer to her lips.

"Yes, they do," Lily agreed. Daisy couldn't recall the last time she'd been out with the girls; she'd forgotten how much she missed it. How much she needed to relax and laugh. Most of all, she was pleasantly surprised at how much she enjoyed being with her sister. The two of them laughed and scored the parade of male butts two-stepping and boot-scooting across the floor in front of them. Lily pointed to a guy in a pair of Roper's, and Daisy bent her head to one side. She had to admit, it took a very nice butt to look good in Roper's. Daisy gave him an eight, Lily a ten, they compromised on a nine.

"Did you see Ralph Fiennes's naked ass in *Red Dragon*?" Lily asked.

Daisy shook her head. "I don't really like to watch scary movies now that I live alone."

"Well, fast forward over the scary parts. You have to rent the video just to see Ralph's ass. He is definitely *fine*."

Daisy took a drink from her beer. "I saw him in *Maid in Manhattan*. The movie sucked, but he looked good."

"There's a minus six," Lily said as she pointed her glass at a man in a pair of denim bib overalls and a tank top. "The movie sucked because of J.Lo. They should have cast someone else." Lily smiled. "Like me."

Daisy felt a hand on her shoulder and turned to look up past a T-shirt that said HOLD MY BEER WHILE I KISS YOUR GIRLFRIEND and into the face of Tucker Gooch. She'd graduated high school with Tucker. His mother, Luda Mae, had taught Home Ec at Lovett high. Tucker had often been sent to her room to sit out his punishment for some misdeed, like getting caught making out in the girls' bathroom.

Daisy stood, and from what she could see of him now, his dark hair was quite thin on top, but his eyes still shined with mischief and his mouth was curved into an irresistible smile.

"Hello, Tucker. How are you?"

He gave her a big hug. "I'm good." He held her a little tight, but his hands didn't roam down her back to her behind like they used to. "Come dance with me," he said.

She looked at Lily. "Do you mind?"

Lily shook her head, and Daisy followed Tucker out onto the dance floor. The band struck up Toby Keith's, "Who's Your Daddy?" and Tucker lead her in the two-step. Before his illness, she and Steven had danced in a few clubs around Seattle. For several beats of the drum and slides of the steel guitar, she was afraid she'd forgotten how to dance. But dancing to country was in her blood, and she took to it again quicker than a chicken on a Cheeto. As Tucker spun her and moved with her across the floor, she felt another part of herself slide into place. The part of her that could relax and laugh and have fun.

At least for tonight.

Jack grabbed his beer from the bar, then raised the bottle of Pearl to his lips. Over the bottom of the bottle, his gaze came to rest on the dance floor across the bar and the flash of white. He'd noticed Daisy the second she and Lily walked in the door. Not that he'd been looking, but those two women were hard to miss. They didn't quite fit in at Slim Clem's. Like two eclairs in a meat-and-potatoes crowd, and Jack was certain there were more than a few men in the bar thinking about eating dessert before dinner.

He lowered the bottle and shoved his free hand up to his knuckles in the front pocket of his Levi's. He returned his gaze to Gina Brown, who stood in front of him talking about the mechanical bulls in back. Apparently, since she was here so much, Slim's had offered her a job giving riding lessons on the weekends.

"The gal I taught this afternoon was about sixty-five," she said. "I put her up on Thunder and . . ."

Jack didn't give a rat's about Thunder. What he wanted to know was if his "worst nightmare" had known he would be here. He wouldn't put it past her, but if she thought he was going to get all chatty with her, she was doomed to disappointment. Usually, Jack preferred bars that were a little less crowded than Slim's, but it was Buddy Calhoun's last night in town, and Buddy had talked him into coming to the bar. At the moment Buddy was taking his chances with one of the bulls in the back room. Personally, Jack didn't understand the appeal of getting thrown from a machine into a bunch of thick pads on the floor. He'd always figured that if you wanted to ride a bull, you should climb up onto a real one and take your chances.

". . . I swear, I about died. You would have laughed your behind off, if you'd been there," Gina said.

Jack, having missed the joke, smiled. "You're probably right."

"What's Buddy doing in town?" Gina asked.

"He's here on business." He settled his weight on one foot, one hip slightly higher than the other, and his gaze returned to Daisy and Tucker Gooch on the dance floor. The smooth glide of their steps kept perfect time to Toby's song about a sugar daddy and his young thing. Jack had always disliked Tucker. Tucker was the kind of guy who bragged about how often he had sex and who he was getting it from. As far as Jack was concerned, a guy who was getting plenty didn't have to talk about it.

"Working for you?"

"Yep." From Jack's position across the bar, all he

could really see of Daisy was a flash of her shiny hair and a glimpse of that white dress of hers. He didn't need to have a front-row seat to know what she was wearing, the picture of her walking through the door of Slim's in that dress was imbedded in his brain.

A cowboy in a ten-gallon hat moved in his line of vision, and he couldn't see anything at all.

"Damn," Buddy said as he came to stand beside Jack, "I almost lasted two minutes that last time, but I came down on my left nut and couldn't get upright for a few."

"Were you up on Twister?" Gina wanted to know. "Twister set on high is a real wild ride."

"It was the one closest to the door." Buddy took a drink of his beer then said, "You should give it a go, Jack."

Buddy was a real nice guy, but sometimes Jack wondered if he wasn't a couple sandwiches shy of a picnic. "As a general rule, I avoid anything that's gonna smash my left nut."

"Yeah." He shook his head and looked out over the crowd.

Gina laughed. "I'm going in the back. Are you going to be here for a while?" she asked Jack.

"I'm not sure."

She placed a hand on the front of his denim shirt and raised up onto her toes. "Well, don't leave without saying goodbye," she said against his mouth. She kissed him, her lips lingering just long enough to let him know she was interested in leaving with him. "Don't forget."

"Are you and Gina seeing each other?" Buddy asked as she walked away.

"Sometimes." Jack didn't know if he was all that interested in having her leave with him. Two weekends in a row tended to give her ideas.

"Look who's sitting at that table over there all by her lonesome, Lily Brooks. I thought about giving her a call yesterday, but I don't know her married name."

Jack glanced at Daisy's sister sitting by herself. "Why would you give Lily a call?"

"To see how she was doing, after that fight at the Minute Mart, and all. I figure, since she's going through a divorce, she might need someone to talk to."

Jack raised the Pearl to his lips, "You want to talk to Lily Brooks about her divorce?" *Right.*

Buddy grinned. "Those Brooks girls are nice-looking and built too."

Jack took a long drink then sucked a drop of beer from his top lip. Buddy would get no argument from him. If he hadn't already seen for himself that Daisy was as hot as ever, that outfit she was wearing tonight would have settled the issue. Even from across the bar, he could see that her dress was so tight, it looked like she'd taken a spray gun and painted herself.

Buddy set his beer on the bar. "I'm going to ask Lily to dance before someone beats me to it."

Jack watched him weave his way through the crowd and wondered if life wouldn't be easier if he could be more like Buddy Calhoun. Nothing seemed to bother him much, not even racking himself on a mechanical bull. Maybe there'd been a time when Jack had been like that, more laid-back, but it had been so long ago, he'd forgotten.

He took his hand from his pocket, and his gaze slid to the dance floor and the flash of white. A smile lifted the corners of his mouth, and he wondered how Lily and Daisy felt today about their public brawl in front of the Minute Mart. Jack had seen women fight each other, but he'd never seen a woman take on a man. Especially a man that had to outweight her by a good hundred or so pounds.

Jack turned and placed his forearms on the bar. The morning of the fight, he'd just been standing there at the Minute Mart, minding his own business, leaning against his Mustang while it filled with fuel, when he heard yelling. He'd glanced across the parking lot and recognized Lily. She was swearing like a truck driver, and when the man she was yelling at shoved her, Jack headed in her direction. About halfway there, the store's door flew open and Daisy charged Ronnie like a defensive linebacker, ramming him with her shoulder. She was a streak of black T-shirt and blond hair, and as Jack picked up his pace toward her, she curled up her fist, socked Ronnie in the eye, then kneed him.

Jack grabbed her from behind to keep her from getting hurt, but he hadn't expected the confusing mix of anger and protectiveness that had slammed into his chest. Growing up, Daisy had been a walking contradiction, both afraid and fierce at the same time. And just as he had while growing up, he'd wanted to shake her and hold her, to yell at her even as he wanted to smooth her hair.

But he *had* held her, he reminded himself. He'd held her with her back pressed to him, her butt smashed against the front of his fly. He'd touched her and he'd smelled her hair and the scent of her skin.

He raised his gaze past the beer spigots to the animated Budweiser sign. Red neon tubes outlined Dale Earnhardt Jr.'s NASCAR. The tires spun on the legendary number eight, as if Junior was doing one-eighty on the straightaways at the Texas Motor Speedway.

Daisy had been gone fifteen years, but one thing had not changed over all that time. No matter how much he hated to admit it, he wanted her. Still. Now. After all this time. After everything she'd done.

It didn't make sense, but he couldn't deny the proof. Just a glimpse of her in that dress tightened his scrotum and gave him a semi, right there in Slim Clem's. He wanted her with the same mindless craving he'd had when he'd been eighteen. A hot ache that remembered the taste of her mouth and wanted to get reacquainted with the soft curves of her body. But he was no longer eighteen. He had more control, and getting hard didn't mean he had to do a damn thing about it.

Nope, he was going to stand right there and watch the Bud sign behind the bar. That was all. He was going to finish his beer then go home. If Buddy didn't want to leave, he could catch a ride with someone else.

As the band struck up Kenny Chesney's "No Problem," Buddy and Lily joined Jack at the bar. Just as he turned to tell Buddy he was leaving in a few, his gaze landed on Daisy and Tucker walking toward him. The closer she got, the more he wished she'd just stayed the hell across the room. She wore some sort of dark smudged stuff around her eyes, her lips were a dark red, and her hair was big and curled and wild, like she'd just got laid. She looked a little smutty, which normally was his favorite, but not tonight. Not on her.

"Hey there, Jack." Tucker offered his hand. "How's it goin'?"

Jack shook it, then raised his beer to his mouth. "I can't really complain," he said just before he took a drink. "How's your hand?" he asked Daisy.

She made a slow fist. "It's better than it was yesterday," she said.

"I heard about you and Lily getting into a fight with Ronnie Darlington and Kelly Newman," Tucker told her.

"Ronnie's a rat bastard and Kelly's a skank," Lily said.

"Where did you hear about it?" Daisy wanted to know.

"Fuzzy Wallace was driving by on Vine and saw you two."

Daisy closed her eyes and swore.

Jack's gaze slid from her face, and he got a good look at that white dress. He could see the outline of her bra, and she must have been tan all over, because he could see the straps and the smooth edges cupping her breasts and pushing them up. His gaze slid over the little row of snaps closing the dress over her breasts, down her flat abdomen to the belt around her waist and that big silver buckle suspended right above her goodie box. The bottom of her dress hit her just about mid thighs, and when he glanced at her feet, he about choked. She was wearing red boots with white hearts. He remembered those boots. She used to wear them all the time. There'd been several times when he'd made love to her while she'd been wearing those boots. Usually when she wore a skirt, or a dress like she was wearing tonight, he'd just slip her panties off and not bother with the boots.

"If you have any more trouble, give me a call," Tucker offered, and Jack looked up as Tucker slipped his arm around her shoulders.

"Okay, I'll remember that," she said. She stepped forward and grabbed Jack's hand. "Jack promised he'd dance with me." She looked up at him with pleading eyes. "Didn't you?"

"Did I?"

"Yes."

He figured he had two options. He could leave her to Tucker or dance with her. He set his beer on the bar and slid his hand up her wrist to her elbow. "I guess I have a bad memory," he said. He took her arm and led her across the room.

The band broke into a slow smoky rendition of the Georgia Satellite's "Keep Your Hands to Yourself." Jack stopped in the middle of the dance floor and placed Daisy's palm against his. He placed his other hand on her waist and moved with her to the beat of the music. Through her thin dress, he felt the warmth of her skin. "You going home with Gooch?"

"He asked me." She set her hand lightly on his shoulder. "But no."

Her answer pleased him more than it should have, and he didn't like that one bit.

"I don't know where he got the idea that I'd actually consider it."

They moved past the stage and pink light shined in her hair, slid over her smooth forehead and cheeks, and dipped between her softly parted lips. "Maybe because your dress is so tight."

"It's not that tight."

He spun her then pulled her closer without missing a step. An inch of empty space separated her breasts from his chest, and he told himself that he held her there so he could hear her better. He brushed his thumb across the soft material of her dress and said just above her ear, "It's so tight, I can see the outline of your bra."

"Why are you staring at my bra, Jack?"

"Bored I guess."

"Uh-huh." She pulled far enough back to look up into his face. "You're trying to imagine what I look like naked."

He smiled as the band sang true love and sin. "Buttercup, I know what you look like naked."

Within the dark shadows of the dance floor, she blushed. A pink flush that rose up her throat to her cheeks. "Funny, I don't remember what you look like naked." Her eyes stared into his for less than a second before her gaze slid away and she focused on something beyond his shoulder.

She'd always been a bad liar. He didn't remember it ever bothering him before. For some reason, it did now. "Did you know I was going to be here?" he asked her.

She returned her gaze to his. "No," she answered and he didn't know if he believed her. "Are you going to be home tomorrow?"

"Why?"

"Because I'm coming over."

He stared down into her face, with her sexy-as-hell eye makeup and full lips. "I don't remember inviting you."

"You just said you have a bad memory."

"Perhaps for some things. Other things I'm real clear about. Like I remember those boots."

She smiled and her hand slid to the back of his shoulder. "I know," she said. "I can't believe they still fit. Remember when I used to wear them with my purple Wranglers?"

Purple Wranglers? He spun her a few times and hoped she got dizzy. While he'd been thinking about her bra and couldn't get rid of the memory of those boots up around his ears, all she could think about was shit he didn't care about and didn't want to discuss.

He brought her back close to his chest and she said, "And remember the hot-pink prairie skirt? Lord what a fashion nightmare."

Prairie Skirt? What the hell? Just for that, he should spin her until she puked. She was talking about stupid shit on purpose, just to make him insane. As if she wasn't thinking of hot sweaty sex, too. As if the sexual desire between them was all in his own head, when he knew, he just knew she had to feel it too. "Ah yes, the hot-pink prairie skirt," he said even though he wasn't even sure what a prairie skirt was. He brought her so close, her breasts brushed his chest, then he said, "I remember how it looked shoved up around your waist."

Her steps faltered as she pulled back and looked up at him. She licked the corners of her mouth. "I don't want to talk about sex."

Usually, he didn't either. Usually he was more of a doer than a talker. "Too bad." He slid his hand from her waist to the small of her back. "You want to talk to me, I get to pick the subject."

"There are more important things in life than sex."

He supposed that was true, but at the moment he couldn't think of anything. "Name one."

"Friendship."

"Right," he scoffed. "Spoken just like a girl."

"No, spoken like an adult."

Now she was really pissing him off. Until she'd blown back into town, he'd moved on with his life. He'd taken on a big dose of adulthood at an early age. He'd finished raising his brother and had single-handedly rescued the business after his father's death. Now, here she was, in her red boots and white dress, digging it all up again. "Sex was a big part of our past, Daisy, but you don't seem to want to talk about that."

"It wasn't that big a part, Jack."

"Bullshit."

The song ended and she stepped back from him. "Maybe for you. But it wasn't that big a part for me," she said, then turned on the heels of those red boots and walked away.

♦ ♦ ♦

Daisy tucked her chin and headed for the lady's room. Once inside, she wet a paper towel and pressed it to her cheeks. Her heart pounded in her throat and she looked at herself in the long mirror above the sink. Her eyes shined a little too bright. Her face was a little too flushed. Her skin was ultra sensitive, every cell responding to Jack's touch. He'd pulled her hard against him, and it had felt so good to feel the wall of his chest pressed against her breasts. It was a dang good thing she was leaving soon, because Jack reminded her of things better left forgotten. Like just how long it had been since she'd been with a man, and what it was like to feel the raw ache of lust, hot and vital, tugging at her breasts and between her thighs. And it wasn't just his talking about sex, it was him. It was the touch of his hands, his thumb brushing her waist, the deep timbre of his voice in her ear, and the smell of his skin. She was afraid if the song hadn't ended when it did, she would have combusted right there in the middle of the dance floor.

A woman in a T-shirt with black fringe joined her at the sink and she scooted over to make room. "It's really hot out there," she said as a way to explain her flushed cheeks.

"A little."

Daisy tossed the paper towels in the trash and opened the door.

Jack stood with one shoulder against the opposite wall, and when he saw her he straightened. "When are you going home, Daisy?" he asked and stepped in front of her.

She looked beyond his left shoulder toward the crowded bar. "When Lily is ready to leave."

There was a hard edge to his voice when he clarified, "When are you going home to Seattle?"

His lids were lowered over his green eyes as he looked down at her. She took a few steps backward so she wouldn't have to strain her neck looking up. "Sunday."

He followed. "Day after tomorrow, then?"

"Yes."

"Good."

"That's why we have to talk tomorrow." She took another step back.

Again he followed. "Because you want to be friends and chat about the past."

"Among other things." Her shoulders hit the back door and he reached beside her right hip and turned the knob. The door opened and he forced her outside. The warm breeze touched her face and neck and picked up the ends of her hair. He let go of the door and it slammed shut behind them.

The light above the door shined through his hair and lit up his green eyes and his knowing smile. "You don't want to talk any more than I do."

"Yes, I do."

She moved away from him and somehow ended up pressed against the wood shingle siding of Slim's. They stood within the deep shadows of the building and a big blue Dumpster. Thank goodness the bar didn't serve food, and the only smell coming from the closed Dumpster was stale beer and dust.

Jack planted one hand on the building beside her head, trapping her between him and the Dumpster.

"You always were a bad liar." He lowered his mouth to hers and said just above a whisper, "You can deny it all night, but I know what you want, Daisy."

She put her hands on his chest to stop him and instantly knew it was a mistake. Through the soft denim of his shirt and the hard muscles of his chest, she could feel the strong beating of his heart. It warmed her palms and spiked her blood pressure at her wrists. She turned her face to the side so she could breathe, but she couldn't quite bring herself to lower her hands. Not just yet. "I don't think you do."

He placed his fingers on her jaw and gently turned her face back to him. "You want me to take you home, or take you to the backseat of my car, or take you right here against this wall." His lips touched hers, and her breath caught in her throat. "Just like old times."

Her finger curled into his shirt and she held on. Oh, yes. She wanted that very much, but she wanted chocolate cake every day too. "That would be bad, Jack."

"No, Daisy. That would be good."

For one brief second, it occurred to her that she'd had the same thought not long ago. Then his lips brushed hers and she shuddered. She couldn't help it. Neither could she seem to help what followed. Her palms slid up his chest, over his shoulder, then back down to his flat stomach and the waistband of his jeans. His face was so close, his nose touched hers. She couldn't see his eyes clearly, but she could feel his hot gaze on her. Then he kissed her. A gentle press of his lips that she felt in the backs of her knees and the soles of her feet. She opened her mouth beneath his and his tongue touched hers, warm and wet and that's all it took to trip her senses into overload. Heat and need and greed rushed through her, too much, too fast, and she couldn't stop it. All she could do was hold on.

His pectoral muscles bunched as she slid her hands back up his chest to his shoulders. He fed her passionate open-mouthed kisses, and she devoured them, kissing him back. Undiluted lust twisted her stomach into knots and burned her up inside, urging her to touch as much of him as possible. To eat him up and worry about it later. He tasted so good. Like a warm healthy man. The kiss turned wild as she moved her hands over his shoulders and back, ran her fingers through his cool hair, and unfastened the pearl buttons on the front of his shirt.

He pulled back and looked into her face, his breathing hard and fast as if he'd just jogged five miles. "Daisy," he whispered and buried his face in the side of her neck. A deep moan vibrated his chest, and he slid his open mouth to the side of her throat. His hand slipped to her waist then over her belt around her hips. His fingers pulled up the bottom of her dress. His bare hand touched the top of her thigh, and slid to her behind, cupping her through the thin layer of her silk panties.

"Someone might see us," she warned, her voice a thin, lame protest.

He pulled her to her toes and his voice was a husky rasp when he asked, "Would you care?"

She guessed not because she pulled the front of his shirt wide and placed her palms on his flat stomach. His skin was hot to the touch and slightly damp, a toxic sheen of desire and testosterone that seeped through her fingertips, traveled up her arms and went straight to her head. His warm wet mouth sucked the hollow of her throat and her eyes drifted shut. It had been so long since she'd felt the push and pull of sex. The feverish rush and carnal ache. She felt it now, tugging her under until everything else was a blur.

He coaxed her leg around his waist, and the hard ridge of his erection pressed into her crotch, through the layers of his clothes and her thin panties. He grabbed her other thigh and lifted her up the wall until both her legs wrapped around his waist. Until his heated gaze met hers, then he shoved his pelvis against her.

"It's been so long," she moaned.

With his free hand, he popped the snaps down the front of her dress. His gaze held hers as he asked, "How long?" The backs of his fingers touched the swells of her breasts, the satin of her bra, and her cleavage. The bodice of her dress fell open and he lowered his gaze to her demi bra. Without looking up, he asked again, "How long has it been for you, Daisy?"

Every sensation in her body seemed to radiate outward from where their bodies touched. She ran her hands across his naked chest and combed her fingers through the short dark hair. "What?"

"How long has it been since you've had sex?"

She hadn't meant to make that particular confession out loud. "Awhile."

He pushed his palm flat against her breast. "How long's awhile?"

It was too late to take it back now. "Two years."

His fingers pressed into her flesh that rose above her bra. "We can't take this any further right here."

She moaned low in her throat and squeezed her thighs tighter. His knees buckled and he planted his hands on the side of the building by her head to keep them from falling. He moved his feet farther apart and brought his erection hard against her.

"I don't have a condom on me or in my car." He kissed her forehead. "Come home with me, Daisy."

It had been so long since she'd had to worry about condoms. Not since before she and Steven had tried to have another child and discovered that he couldn't. A long time since she'd had to worry about pregnancy or anything else. Over fifteen years since she'd been with anyone but Steven. With the last rational part of her brain, she knew she couldn't do this. Not with Jack. Not here. Not at his house. Not anywhere. "I can't do this with you," she said before she made the second biggest mistake of her life.

He kissed the side of her neck. "Sure you can."

"No, Jack." She lowered her feet to the ground and dropped her hands to her sides. "I'm not going to have sex with you."

He took a step back into the gold pool of light from the building and ran his fingers through the sides of his hair. He closed his eyes and pulled air deep into his lungs. "God damn you, Daisy," he said, his voice a rasp of lust and anger. "You're still as big a tease as you ever were."

"I didn't come here to tease you or have sex with you." His naked chest was too close, and the light from the building shined across his moist skin. She pressed her palms against the building behind her and fought the urge to reach out and touch him. To push her face to his chest and lick him like a Dreamsicle. She raised her gaze to his face. "I told you why I'm here."

He looked at her, his green eyes glittered with frustration. "You still think we can talk?"

"No, not tonight."

"That's what I thought," he said as he wiped her red lipstick from the corner of his mouth.

"Tomorrow."

He laughed without humor. "Daisy, if you show up at my house tomorrow, I'm going to give you what you really want," he said evenly as he buttoned his shirt. "Guaran-Goddamn-teed."

She frowned and didn't have to ask what he was talking about.

He told her anyway. "I'm going to fuck you till you faint," he said, then he turned and walked away.

She watched him leave, his broad shoulders disappearing as he moved down the side of the building toward the front. Within seconds, darkness swallowed him up and all she could hear was the thud of his boots and the hum of insects. She knew she should be outraged. Disgusted. Horrified. Relieved that she'd come to her senses before they'd had sex. Yes, she knew she should feel all those things, and maybe she would tomorrow. But tonight . . . tonight she felt none of those things. Beyond frustration, with lust pounding though her veins, she was more curious than anything. Was it possible to have sex until you fainted?

And if so, did Jack know from experience?

Chapter 9

*T*hat night, Daisy dreamed she flew around Lovett in nothing but her shorty pajamas, over the tops of the trees and power poles. Mount Rainier suddenly rose up out of the flat Texas panhandle, and she flew over that too. Her toes touched the snowy peak as higher and higher she soared. Out of control like a helium balloon, up and up she went, and she was terrified because she knew there was only one outcome. She was going to fall. It was inevitable, and it was going to hurt like hell.

Then just as she was about to break through the Earth's atmosphere, gravity sucked at her feet and yanked her back down. Down past Mount Rainier and the tops of the trees, and she knew she was going to die.

Before she hit, her eyes popped open and she realized two things at once. One, she wasn't going to go smack, and two, she was holding her breath. Morning light filtered across her bed and she let out a sigh of relief. But her relief was short-lived as the events of the prior evening came back to her all at once.

Smack.

The humiliation she hadn't felt last night brought her fully awake like a bucket of cold water. Now in the light of day, she recalled every excruciating detail. Jack's slick warm mouth, the feel of his bare chest and the touch of his hands on her.

She groaned and covered her face with a pillow. The memory of her legs wrapped around his waist was especially painful. She hadn't behaved like that since . . . since . . . since she'd pulled Jack into a closet their senior year in high school. Back then she'd been young and naive. She was neither of those things now.

Now she was an idiot.

Last night she'd wanted to lick Jack. Today she had to tell him about Nathan. How could she look him in the eyes after she'd kissed him and touched him. "Oh God," she said as she recalled in detail her confession that she hadn't had sex in two years. How could she face him after that?

She didn't have a choice, that's how.

She tossed the pillow off her head and got out of bed. Dressed in the same shorty pajamas as in her dream, she made her way downstairs. After Jack had left her against the wall at Slim Clem's, she'd gone back into the bar, pleaded food poisoning, and made Lily take her home. She hadn't seen Jack and, for that at least, was thankful.

Her mother sat at the breakfast nook in the

kitchen wearing a pink nylon nightgown. One side of her blond cotton-candy hair looked a little flat.

Last night, Pippen had been sound asleep when Lily dropped her off, so he'd spent the night. He was in his high chair next to his grandmother, eating cereal and drinking juice from his Tommy cup. He wore his coonskin cap, his Blue's Clues jammies, and a Cheerio was stuck to his cheek. "Good morning, Mom," she greeted as she poured herself a cup of coffee. "How's it going, Pip?"

"Watch 'toons," Pippen answered.

"You can watch cartoons after breakfast," Louella told him, then she glanced over at Daisy and used the tone of voice that let Daisy know she was very disappointed. "I heard what happened. Thelma Morgan called this morning and told me everything."

Daisy felt her cheek catch fire. "Thelma Morgan saw me?" Where had she been hiding? Behind the Dumpster? It was only eight in the morning, and the day was already shaping up to be pure hell.

"She pulled into the Minute Mart for a cup of coffee and a bear claw, and she saw the whole thing."

What? "Oh." Daisy let out a huge sigh of relief and laughed. "That."

"Yes that. What where you and Lily thinking? Making a fuss in public?" Louella took a bite of her toast. "For cryin' all night loud in a bucket."

"We were getting a Dr. Pepper at the Minute Mart," Daisy explained and purposely left out the part about Lily's stalking her soon to be ex. She walked across the kitchen and sat at the nook with her mother. "You-know-who," she paused and glanced at Pippen, "and Kelly pulled into the parking lot, and one thing led to another. Then you-know-who shoved Lily."

Louella pursed her lips and set her toast back on her plate. "You should have called the police."

Probably. "I didn't think. I just saw him push her and I lost my mind. Without giving it a thought, I slugged him in the eye and kneed him between the legs." She still couldn't believe she'd behaved like that.

One corner of her mother's pursed lips turned up. "Did you damage him?"

Daisy shook her head and blew into her cup. "I don't think so."

"That seems a shame." She pushed her plate aside. "Have you seen Jack?"

Yeah, she'd seen him. His naked chest and slick abdomen. His eyes at half mast and his lips moist from kissing her, but that wasn't what her mother wanted to know. "I haven't told him about Nathan yet," she answered and took a drink of her coffee. "I'm going over there this morning to talk to him."

One brow rose up Louella's forehead. "You've certainly put it off until the last moment."

"I know." She looked down at the bright yellow tabletop. "I used to be so sure I'd done the right thing. I used to believe that not telling Jack about Nathan and moving to Washington had been best for everyone."

"It was."

"I'm not so sure now." She brushed her hair behind her ears and took a deep breath. "Before I came back to town, I was sure. I was sure moving away with Nathan was the best choice, even for Jack." She looked back up. "We always meant to tell him, Mom. We wanted to give Jack a few years to get his life together, and then we planned to tell him."

Pippen dropped his empty cup on the floor and Louella bent to pick it up. "I know you did." She set it on the table.

"But the longer we put it off, the harder it got. Months and years passed and there was always an excuse why we couldn't tell him right then. I was trying to get pregnant with Steven's baby or Nathan was happy and we didn't want to disrupt his life. It was always something. Always an excuse, because how do you tell a man he has a child he doesn't know about?" She leaned forward and crossed her forearms on the table. "Now I'm not so sure I did the right thing all those years ago. I'm beginning to think I never should have left without telling him."

"I think you're afraid and now you're questioning everything."

"Maybe."

"Daisy, you were young and scared and you made the right decision at the time."

She'd always thought that too. She didn't know anymore. The only thing she knew for certain was that she'd been wrong to wait so long. How was she ever to make it right?

"Jack wasn't ready to be a father," her mother insisted. "Steven was."

"You always liked Steven more than Jack."

Her mother was quiet a moment than said, "That's not really true. I just always thought Steven was the stabler of the two. Jack was more wild. You can't blame a person for what's in his nature, but you can't rely on him either. Your daddy was reckless like that, and look what happened to him. To us."

"Daddy didn't die and leave us on purpose."

"No, but he did. He left me with two children, a busted-up Winnebego and three hundred dollars." Louella shook her head. "When it came to taking care of you and a baby, Steven was better prepared."

"Because his family had money."

"Money is important." She held up her hand as if Daisy were going to argue. "I know love is too. I loved your daddy. He loved me and he loved you girls, but love doesn't put food in your children's mouths. Love doesn't buy a winter coat or school shoes." Her mother reached across the table and grabbed Daisy's hand. "But even if you made the wrong decision all those years ago, it can't be changed now. Nathan has a good life. Steven was a wonderful father. You did the best thing for your child."

Listening to her mother, made it all sound so logical. Daisy wasn't so sure anymore that the choice should have been left up to logic. Being young and scared explained why she hadn't told him fifteen years ago. It didn't explain why she hadn't told him until now.

"Look at Lily," her mother said just above a whisper. "Her life was chaotic long before you-know-who finally moved out. He was always running around on her. Always doing crazy things. She never should have married that wild boy, and Pippen is paying the highest price. He doesn't talk as well as he should, and he is no where near ready for potty training. He's actually been back sliding in his behavior."

Daisy thought Lily could have done a lot more to protect and nurture Pippen, but she didn't say so. She hadn't been the perfect mother and wasn't about to cast aspersions on anyone else's parenting. "I'm going to call Nathan and remind him what time I'll be home tomorrow." She stood. "Then I'm going to Jack's," she said, and if she'd had any other option, she would have used it. He'd told her not to come to his house, and he'd given her that warning about fainting. Now, when she showed up, would he think she came there looking for sex?

Probably.

She took her coffee to her bedroom and called Nathan.

"I can't wait for you to get home," he said as soon as he picked up. "I can't wait to get away from Michael Ann."

"Come on now, she's not that bad."

"Mom, she still plays with Barbies. Last night, she tried to get me to be Ken."

"Isn't she a little old for Barbies?"

"Yeah, and Ollie tried to make me play dolls with her," he said, his voice cracking with pubescent indignation. "I hate it here."

"Well, this is your last night." She set her mug on the bedside table and pulled Steven's letter from the drawer. "Tomorrow they'll take you home, and I'll be there around three or three-thirty."

"Thank God. And Mom?"

"Yeah, sugar lump?"

"Promise you won't ever make me stay here again."

Daisy laughed. "I promise if you promise to get a hair cut."

There was a long pause and then he said, "Deal."

After she hung up the telephone, she took a shower and thought about the night before. Jack was probably over his anger by now. More than likely he'd found some willing woman to take home. While she'd been dreaming about flying, he'd probably been having wild sex and was no doubt relieved this morning that she'd stopped things between them before they'd gone too far. Now that the fever of the night before had passed, he probably wouldn't even remember that he'd threatened her.

Funny, though, the thought of him with another woman bothered her more than it should and more than she wanted to admit. The thought of him touching someone else made a lump in her stomach that hadn't been there that first night when she'd seen him and Gina together in his kitchen.

Daisy dressed in her black bra and panties and tried to understand how her feelings had changed so much in such a short time. She pulled a plain black T-shirt over her head and figured that the more she was around Jack, the more she relived the past. It was inevitable, really. She'd always loved Jack as a friend, then she'd fallen in love with him. She'd fallen so hard and so deep, and despite what she'd said the night before, sex had been a big part of their past. Being close to Jack brought up all the old feelings. All the old lust and obsession and jealousy.

She'd thought she could breeze back into town, tell Jack about Nathan and not have to deal with the rest of it. She'd thought it was buried and long gone.

She'd been wrong. It hadn't gone anywhere. No, it had been waiting for her right where she'd left it.

She pulled a pair of shorts out of a drawer. If there was a consolation to this whole confusing mess, it was that once she was back home, it would all be over. No more secrets. No more confusion. No more kissing Jack Parrish.

"Daisy, if you show up at my house tomorrow, I'm going to give you what you really want," Jack had warned. *"I'm going to fuck you till you faint."*

His warning had intrigued her last night, this morning it gave her pause. She definitely didn't want him to think she was showing up at his house to "faint." No, that was the last thing she wanted him to think.

She shoved the shorts back in a drawer and walked to her mother's bedroom. She riffled through the closet until she found a sleeveless dress made of heavy denim. It was so loose it didn't have buttons or a zipper. Tigger and Winnie the Pooh were sown on the bodice and around the hem. It was the antithesis of sexy: like a kindergarten teacher, and it could in no way be confused for a dress that inspired "fainting."

She pulled her hair into a ponytail and wore her black flip-flops. She couldn't bring herself to go out of the house without makeup, and applied a coat of mascara, blush, and pink lip gloss. She looked herself over one last time in the mirror and determined that she looked very drab and would not inspire interest, let alone lust, in any man. Especially a man like Jack.

She shoved Steven's letter in the side pocket of the

dress and grabbed her mom's car keys. All the way to Jack's, she had to fight the urge to turn around. She didn't have to guess or wonder how he would feel about Nathan now. She'd seen him with his nieces, and she knew.

She turned onto Jack's street and her fingers turned white on the steering wheel. Her mother was probably right, she'd done what she'd thought best at the time. What everyone else had thought best, too. Everyone except Jack. Jack would have a different view, and by the time she pulled her mom's Caddie behind Parrish American Classics, her stomach was in knots and she felt physically ill.

Jack's Mustang sat in front of the house, and she parked beside it. Her black flip-flops slapped her heels as she made her way across the yard and up the sidewalk. The house was still the same white color she remembered from her childhood. The same green shutters. The same yellow roses, although they weren't as well attended as they'd once been. Now they grew more wild, except for where someone had hacked at them next to the front porch.

Daisy knocked on the screen door as she had a week ago and hoped Jack was alone this time. That if he had picked up a woman, she'd left by now.

No one answered and she stuck her head inside and called out. The hum of the air-conditioner was the only sound filling the dark interior. She looked over her shoulder at Jack's Mustang and noticed that a light from inside the garage was on. Old elm trees towering overhead cast lacy shadows on the asphalt, and a slight breeze blew her ponytail as she moved to the back of the business. As quiet as possi-

ble, she opened the door and slipped inside. Sun
light from the windows high above her head threw
rectangular patches of light on five classic cars in
different stages of restoration. Some had their engines suspended on racks, other looked to be torn
down to their frames. Along the walls, and hidden
in the deeper shadows of the garage, were huge
pieces of equipment, work benches, a tool chest
taller than she was, and shelving that looked to hold
car parts. She moved between a gutted Corvette and
a shiny red-and-white land yacht that seemed to
stretch out forever. The four taillights of the classic
car stuck out like silver tubes of red lipstick.

She half expected to see buckets of oil and grease
and metal shavings on the floor. She didn't; the
garage was very clean and smelled like pine. It was a
lot cleaner than it had been when Jack's father had
been alive.

Despite the odds, Jack had made something of
himself. Something better than what he'd been
given. Certainly something more than anyone ever
expected of him, and in spite of her apprehension at
seeing him today, she was proud of Jack.

She looked up at the doorway to the offices and
stopped in her tracks beside the rear end of the red
and white car. Jack stood with his arms folded
across his chest, one shoulder shoved into the door
jam, watching her.

"Surprise," she said, her voice a little shaky as
he'd just about given her heart failure.

Flourescent lighting shone from the room behind
him and made his T-shirt appear incredibly white. A
scowl turned the corners of his mouth downward

and a lock of dark hair fell across his forehead. "Not really. Those shoes you're wearing make a lot of noise."

She looked down at her red toenails then back up at him. "Are you hiding from me in here?"

He slowly shook his head. "Not hardly." He looked completely at ease, but the tension that lay between them was anything but easy. His gaze on her was hot and intense, almost tangible as it lowered from her face to the front of her dress. One corner of his mouth lifted.

"The garage sure is different," she said into the silence. "You should be proud of yourself, Jack."

He looked back up into her face and his arms fell to his sides. "You didn't come here to tell me that."

"No."

He pushed away from the doorframe and moved toward her, the thud of his boot heels a menacing echo as he stepped into a long patch of light. She grasped one red fin on the rear of the car to keep from backing away from him.

"I told you what would happen if you came over here today," he said.

She didn't have to ask what he was talking about. She knew, and her failing heart pounded in her throat. "I came here just to talk."

"Then you shouldn't have worn that outfit."

She looked down at her mother's dress. "This?" She laughed despite the clog in her throat. "Jack, it's ugly."

"Exactly. It needs to be taken off and burned." He stood so close that Tigger and Winnie the Pooh were almost touching the front of his T-shirt.

She looked over his shoulder at a poster of a half-naked woman sprawled out on the hood of a beefed-up Nova. "We should talk right now."

His fingertips touched her chin and brought her gaze back to his. "Not now." His thumb swept her jaw, and he lowered his face until his nose touched hers. "Even in that stupid dress, you turn me on." Her stomach clinched and she could hardly breathe. "You're even more beautiful than you were growing up. And you were so beautiful back then you made me ache." His lips brushed hers, and he kissed the corner of her mouth. "All morning, I've been half hoping, half dreading seeing you walk through that door." His lips touched her cheek. "You shouldn't have come back, Daisy Lee. You should have stayed gone, but you didn't. You're here and I can't think of anything but getting inside of you. Deep inside where you're hot and wet and want me too." The tip of his tongue touched her earlobe and her purse fell to the floor. "The first night I saw you again, I told myself this wasn't going to happen. But it is, Daisy."

The warmth of his breath swept the side of her neck and across her flesh. Desire tightened her nipples and pooled between her legs, and she had to stop him now, or she was a goner. "Jack listen—"

"This was inevitable the second you stepped foot in town. I'm tired of fighting it," he interrupted, as his hand moved to the side of her head, his thumb stroking her temple as if he were trying to soothe her. "Tell me you feel it too. Tell me you want it as much as I do."

"Yes, but—"

"We can talk later. After we have sex."

She placed her palm on the front of his T-shirt. His muscles turned hard and everything in him seemed to still—except for his heart, which beat as fast as hers. Making love would make it more difficult to tell him about Nathan, but it was already going to be difficult. She didn't make a conscious decision to give in to her desire. It was just too big for her to deny any longer. It had been over two years now since she'd been with a man who desired her, and she had no willpower to resist Jack. She didn't want to resist him. He was right, this was inevitable. "You promise we'll talk later?"

"God, yes," he said on a rush of breath. His hands grabbed the front of her dress. "Anything, Daisy."

For days her body had responded to his, seeking an outlet for the passion he'd stirred back to life within her. And here it was. Here he was. Right in front of her. She pulled back and looked up into his face. "After you left last night, were you with someone else?"

"Almost, but I wanted you." He yanked her dress over her head and tossed it on the Corvette. She didn't even try to stop him and her T-shirt joined her dress. Within the natural light pouring in through the windows, she stood in front of him in her black bra and panties and flip-flops. He didn't give her time to think before he pulled her onto her toes and into his chest. She wrapped her arms around his neck, smashing her breasts into his chest as his mouth swooped down and covered hers in a rough kiss.

Unable to stop herself, she fell headfirst into a haze of lust and longing. And it felt good. Maybe too good. The carnal thrust of his tongue elicited an equally carnal response in her. The feel of his cotton T-shirt and Levi's against her bare skin sent a shiver down her spine. She ran her fingers through his hair as he fed her kisses from his hot, wet mouth. She moved against him, trying to get closer, trying to feel more of him. Wanting it so much her skin tingled with a powerful yearning. Wanting it all. All at once.

It had been so long. Too long to go so slow. A frustrated moan came from her throat and she dropped to her heels. She felt his long hard erection against her belly as her open mouth tasted the side of his neck. "Jack," she said between kisses to his throat. "You taste good. I want to eat you up."

"Jesus, Daisy," he groaned as his hands roamed her bare back. He pulled the covered elastic from her ponytail and her hair came free and brushed her bare shoulders. He grabbed two fistfuls of her hair and brought her mouth back to his. She kissed him as one of his hands slid down her spine and he unhooked her bra. He pulled the bra from her and tossed it on the trunk of the red and white car. His mouth came down on hers as his hands came up to cup her breasts. Her nipples puckered in his hot palms, and she shoved her hands beneath his shirt and ran them all over him, his stomach, chest and back.

He moved his hands to her behind, and he grabbed the backs of her thighs. He lifted her onto the trunk of the car and her bare feet rested on the wide chrome bumper. The cool metal brought her out of her haze just enough that she was aware of sitting in a shaft of sunlight, naked except for her panties. She covered her breasts with her hands. "What kind of car is this?" she asked as to cover her sudden embarrassment.

"What you have here is a Custom Lancer," he answered as he pulled his T-shirt over his head and tossed it next to her dress. "It seems appropriate for what I have in mind for you."

She licked her swollen lips. "What do you have in mind?"

"We're going to test the Level-Flight suspension." He pushed her knees apart and stepped between her thighs. "Drop your hands, buttercup."

When she'd had Nathan, her breasts had grown larger and she'd never lost the weight there. "I'm bigger than I used to be."

"I noticed." He grasped her wrists. "I want to see if you still have the little mark that looks like a love bite."

"I do."

He didn't force her to drop her hands, just said, "Show me."

"I have stretch marks." The thin pale lines were hardly visible now, but they were still there.

"I want to see all of you, Daisy."

"I'm older, Jack."

"So am I."

She leaned forward and placed her open mouth on his bare shoulder. "No, you're even better than you were." She kissed the hollow of his throat and he took her hands from her breasts and placed them on the waistband of his jeans.

"Unzip me," he said, his voice all smoky with passion. He reached into his back pocket, then tossed a condom on the trunk next to her.

Daisy pulled the metal top button until it came free. He wasn't wearing underwear, and she slid the metal tab downward, exposing the line of hair that grew from his navel to his groin. He was tucked to the left and she looked up into his face as she shoved her hand into his pants. She pressed her palm against the hard length of his penis, and he gazed at her through eyes totally gone with passion.

"Take it out," he said in a rough voice.

She pushed at the waistband of jeans and shoved them down his thighs. His erection jutted toward her, huge and smooth like hot marble, and she took him in her hand. His hard flesh burned her palm and she stroked his long shaft. She scooted down to sit on the car's bumper and pressed a kiss on the voluptuous head. She hadn't planned to kiss him there, but it had been a long time and she wanted it all. A bead of clear moisture rested in the cleft and she licked it clean. He smelled good. Tasted better, and was bigger than she remembered too. Or perhaps she'd forgotten.

He groaned his pleasure deep, deep within his chest and pushed her hair out of her face. She looked up at him and watched his eyes as she took him more fully into her mouth. His nostrils flared slightly and he pulled in a deep breath.

"Ah, Daisy," he whispered, then tilted his head back. Long ago, he'd taught her how to please him this way. She hadn't forgotten. She ran one hand up the back of his thigh and grasped his tight behind. In her free hand, she lightly cupped his testicles in her palm. With her tongue, she found his pulse just below the head of his penis.

It seemed she'd just started when he pushed her away. "I don't want to get off that way," he said and gently he lifted her onto the trunk once more. He forced her onto her back and pulled off her panties. Then he stepped between her legs. His gaze traveled from her face, down her throat to her breasts. He leaned over her and cupped between her thighs. "You make me feel eighteen again," he said as he rested his weight on his forearm next to her shoulder. "Like I can't control myself." He kissed the tip of her breast as he stroked her slick, sensitive flesh. "Like I'm going to go off before we get to the really good stuff."

She arched her back and moaned. "Then get to the good stuff."

"Daisy."

"Mmm?"

He kissed her birthmark then brushed the seam of his lips across the tip of her breast. "Your breasts are as beautiful as ever."

She might have laughed or argued or something if he hadn't opened his hot mouth and sucked her nipple inside his wet mouth. Instead she ran her fingers through his hair. She shut her eyes and let the waves of sensation roll through her until she feared that *she* was going to go off before they got to good stuff.

"Daisy open your eyes and look at me."

She did. He gazed down at her, his own eyes intense and feverish. He grabbed the condom and tore open the package. "I want to see your face when I'm inside of you." He rolled the lubricated latex over the head of his penis and down the shaft to his dark pubic hair. He put his hands beneath her bare bottom and pulled her to the edge of the car's trunk, positioning her. "I want you to see me."

She looked into his green eyes that were so familiar to her. "I see you," she said as he grasped her thighs. He plunged inside of her in one smooth stroke that buried him to her cervix. His grasp tightened on her thighs and her back arched. She cried out in pain and in pleasure, she wasn't sure which was more acute.

"Damn," he said between clenched teeth, then he cupped her face in his hands. "Sorry, Daisy." He placed a soft kiss on her cheek and nose and whispered against her mouth, "I'm sorry. Sorry. I'll make it feel good now. I promise." He withdrew, then thrust himself inside with more care, reminding her how good he was at keeping his promises. Slowly, he gave her incredible pleasure with smooth, measured strokes.

He stared into her eyes as he moved within her. "Is that better?"

"Mmm, yes."

"Tell me."

"So good, Jack." She felt weightless and she grabbed his shoulders and held on to him. "Don't stop. Whatever you do, just don't stop."

"Not a chance." He tilted her pelvis up without missing a beat of his pumping hips.

Heat flushed her skin, radiating outward from where they were joined, and she dug her fingers into him. His slow pace was driving her mad. "More. Give me more, Jack."

He kissed her forehead and his breathing rasped against her temple. He plunged faster. Harder. In and out. Building. Thrusting her toward climax.

"Daisy Lee." Her name on his lips sounded almost like a question, as if he pushed them both closer and closer. She was mindless to anything but the building pleasure, until she opened her mouth to scream. The sound died in her throat as wave after luscious wave rolled through her. Her muscles pulsed and contracted, gripping him hard.

On and on it went as he plunged into her. His breath hot against her temple until finally he shoved into her so hard he pushed her farther up the trunk of the car. He cursed her and God in the same incoherent sentence. He crushed her to his chest as if he wanted to absorb her and gave one final thrust. He made a sound deep in his throat, a sound somewhere between a guttural groan and a long drawn-out *ahhh*.

Daisy saw spots behind her closed eyelids, and her ears began to ring. She was going to faint. Right there on the Custom Lancer. It was going to happen. Just like he'd said she would, and she didn't care.

She didn't faint, though. Not really. She was just so light-headed she was afraid to move. She hadn't had sex in a long time, but she didn't recall it being so good. It had been. Of course it had been. But where his skin was stuck to hers, still tingled. She'd forgotten that part. Or maybe that had never happened before.

He remained embedded deep in her body, his chest smashed into hers and his forehead resting on

the car next to her right ear. She could feel his heart-
beat against her breast.

She open her eyes and looked up at the ventilation
overhead. Jack Parrish had just taken her some place
she'd never been before. He'd just given her a devas-
tating orgasm that had curled her toes and about
made her faint. She didn't know what to think about
that. In fact, she could hardly think at all. She was
too stunned.

He raised onto his forearms and looked down into
her face. A slow satisfied smile lifted the corners of
his mouth. "Wow. You're even better than you were
at eighteen."

Daisy looked into his sexy green eyes and felt alive
again. Like she'd been dead inside for a very long
time and hadn't even realized it until that moment.
Like coming into the sunlight after being trapped in
the dark. Raw emotion swept through her, and she
did the worst possible thing she could do.

She burst into tears.

Chapter 10

No one had ever cried on Jack before. Not after sex, anyway. Hell, Daisy hadn't even cried the night he'd taken her virginity.

He tossed his T-shirt on the kitchen counter and glanced over at Daisy who stood across the room from him, her arms folded beneath her breasts, staring at her toes. He was reminded of the first night he'd seen her since she'd been back. She'd been wearing a yellow rain slicker then. Now she had on that stupid Winnie the Pooh dress, the one he'd helped her get back into a few moments ago.

She'd thrown him a curve that was for sure. One second she'd been having a good time, moaning and scratching, and telling him she wanted more. In the next she'd burst into tears. What the hell had happened?

He'd excused himself to get rid of the condom in the employee's bathroom, and when he'd returned she'd been fighting to get her dress over her head. He was halfway convinced that if she'd been able to get her clothes on faster, she would have been long gone by now. Which might have been for the best.

She'd been so agitated he had to help her with her dress when what he'd really wanted was to toss it in the garbage. He'd put her purse on her shoulder, and instead of sending her on her way, like he would have any other hysterical woman who'd burst into tears on him, he'd brought her into his house. Why, he did not know. Except maybe because he'd told her he'd let her talk after they'd had sex.

Yeah, that was it, but now that his head was clear, he was pretty sure he didn't want to hear anything she had to say. Unless it had something to do with her getting naked and climbing on top of him.

He'd thought once they'd had sex, his desire for her would be sated. He'd be over it. He'd been wrong, and that bothered him because he didn't want to think about what that might mean. He didn't want to feel anything for her now. Not even lust.

He reached inside the refrigerator and pulled out a carton of milk. Before his mind traveled any further in the direction of the bedroom, he stopped and reminded himself that she was upset and crying and that she was Daisy Monroe. Three very good reasons why he had to stand across the room from her and keep his hands to himself.

"Before I apologize," he said as he shut the door with his foot, "I need to know what I'm apologizing for."

She looked up at him. She had black smudges beneath her red eyes and her face was all splotchy. "You didn't do anything, Jack."

He didn't think he had either, but with women, you just never knew. If there wasn't a problem, they'd invent one. "Do you want something to drink?" She shook her head and he raised the milk to his mouth and watched her over the bottom of the quart container. He lowered the milk and licked his top lip. Maybe he'd been too rough with her. He'd forgotten that she hadn't had sex in awhile. "Did I hurt you?"

She wiped her cheeks with her fingers. "No."

He set the milk on the counter and opened a cabinet. He filled a glass with ice and water then moved across the kitchen and handed it to her. His fingers brushed hers and he asked, "Why are you crying, Daisy?"

"I don't know."

"I think you do." She looked like crap. Kind of scary, but for some reason, the only thing that scared him was how much he still wanted her. "Tell me, Daisy."

She took a long drink of her water then pressed the cool glass against her cheek. "It's embarrassing." As if to prove her point, her face turned red and kind of connected the splotchy parts.

"Why don't you just tell me anyway?" Instead of putting distance between her body and his like he should, he leaned a hip into the counter next to her and folded his arms over his bare chest.

She glanced up at him out of the corners of her eyes then cut her gaze to the Elmo cookie jar on the counter. "Elmo?"

"Billy's girls gave it to me last Christmas, along with a bag of Oreos. Don't change the subject."

Her gaze remained on the bright orange cookie jar and she took a deep breath. "I just forgot about sex for a while." She shrugged. "And you reminded me."

"That's it?" There had to be more.

"Well, it was good sex."

"Daisy, it was better than good." They'd gone at it like two starving people at an all-you-can-eat. All hands and mouths and insatiable hunger. Racing for satisfaction. She'd come harder than anyone he'd ever been with, squeezing an orgasm from him that he felt clear to the soles of his feet.

It was a good thing she was leaving tomorrow. Because he could tell himself that he wouldn't go after her again, but he'd probably be lying about that. "Saying it was good is like saying the Rio Grande is just a river. It's a hell of an understatement." He put his fingers to her jaw and lightly brought her gaze back to his. Her eyelashes were stuck together over her shiny brown eyes. He brushed his fingertips across her soft skin then dropped his hand. "Why has it been so long since you've had sex?"

If it was possible, she turned even redder. "That's really not your business."

"You haven't had sex in two years, but you have it with me. I think that makes it my business."

She frowned and set her glass on the counter. Just when he thought she wasn't going to answer, she said, "For about the last year and a half of his life, Steven couldn't."

That surprised him. "And you didn't go elsewhere?"

"Of course not. What a horrible question."

He didn't think he was out of line. Fifteen years ago, she'd been having sex with him but had married Steven. "Some women might have."

"Not me. I was always faithful to Steven."

"He's been gone seven months."

"Almost eight now."

"Eight months is a long time to go without getting laid."

Her gaze slid from his to his mouth, down his throat and stopped on his chest. "Maybe for some people."

"No, most people."

She looked away. "You know that old saying, 'If you don't use it, you lose it.' It's true."

"You obviously haven't lost it."

She grabbed her glass and he watched her move to the kitchen sink. She looked out the window into the backyard and took a long drink. She set the water back down and her hands grasped the counter. "I did for a while. When you live with someone who is dying, sex is not a high priority. Believe me. Your life becomes consumed with doctor's appointments and trying new therapies. Figuring out the right medication to combat strokes and seizures and pain management."

He turned to gaze at her profile. He didn't want to know any of this. He didn't want to feel sorry for Steven, but he couldn't seem to help but ask, "Was Steven in a lot of pain?"

She shrugged. "He never liked to admit it, but I know that he was. I'd ask him and he'd just grab my hand and tell me not to worry about him." She laughed without humor. "I pretended not to worry, and he pretended everything was okay. He was better at his part than I was."

"Steven was always better at pretending than either you or me." For years he and Steven had pretended that Daisy was just a friend. A girl who was a buddy. Steven had been so much better at it than Jack.

She nodded. "He pretended right up until the last day. The night he died, he slipped into a coma, at home." She looked across her shoulder and her eyes met his across the distance. "Nathan and I watched him take his last breath. If you've ever seen something like that, it changes you. You get real clear about what's important." She swallowed hard and added, "About things you have to make right."

He stood very still as his stomach twisted into a knot. Daisy's words affected him more than he would have thought. He hadn't watched either of his parents die, and for that he was grateful. He had dark enough memories.

"Did you know that coffins have springs in them?"

"Yeah." He and Billy had had to pick out two. At that time, he hadn't had enough money to afford much of anything. His parents had been buried without springs and fancy satin pillows. "I knew that."

"Oh. That's right." She looked back out the window. "I remember your parents' funeral. You were so young to have such a horrible thing happen to you. I didn't appreciate how horrible then. Not really. I do now."

Jack moved to stand behind her and he raised his hands to grasp her arms. But before he touched her, he thought better of it and dropped them to his sides.

She took an envelope from a pocket in her ugly dress and set it next to the sink. "This is the letter from Steven. The one I told you about."

He really didn't want to read it, and knew that made him all kinds of a bastard. But he really didn't want to be reminded of the black hole of his past.

"Steven and I never meant to hurt you, Jack. We were all such good friends, and it never should have ended between us the way it did. We were so young and stupid. The night we came to you was one of the worst nights of my life." She paused a moment and said just above a whisper, "You were wearing a white T-shirt that night too."

Yes, they'd been standing in the moonlight. He'd been pleading with her not to leave him. He'd beaten the hell out of his best buddy, and now his best buddy was dead. Something in Jack had died that night too. For some reason, hearing about it this morning, made it more real then it had been in years. Brought it all back to life. Made the places in his soul burn. "Stop it, Daisy." He grabbed her arms below the sleeves of her T-shirt. "Don't say any more."

"I have to, Jack." She looked up over her shoulder into his face. "When you told me that we needed time away from each other, I was so scared. I didn't know what to do. You have to understand how scared and—" He lifted her chin as his mouth swooped down on hers, silencing her with a hard kiss. He pulled her back against his bare chest and wrapped his arm around her stomach. He did not want to hear anything; he just wanted to feel. Feel her pressed against the length of him. Naked. He wanted more mind-numbing sex again and again until he finally got her out of his system. Out of his head.

At first she stood stiff in his arms, her lips pressed together but when he softened the kiss, her lips parted. A silent invitation to take what he wanted.

The telephone rang and he let it. It rang as his tongue entered her mouth, and she tasted as she had before, on the trunk of the Custom Lancer. Warm and sweet like Daisy. She tasted of things long forgotten. Of soft skin and need and lust and a love that had ripped his heart out.

He pushed the memories from his head as he slid one hand to her right breast. The phone continued to ring as he cupped between her legs through the heavy denim. "Daisy," he spoke to the side of her head and breathed deep the scent of her hair. "Come to my bed and let me remind you about sex again."

The ringing stopped but instantly started again. Daisy slid out of his grasp and moved across the kitchen. "That might be important," she said.

He had a pretty good idea who it was. Buddy Calhoun was supposed to come by and pick up a Corvair Monza sitting in the shop and take it to his garage in Lubbock. Buddy was the best body man in the state, and one of the few restorers Jack trusted to take a vehicle out of his shop. But his timing sucked. Instead of pursuing Daisy, he walked to the telephone, his boot heels an angry thud against the old linoleum floor. "This better be good," he said into the receiver.

"Hello," a female voice spoke, "this is Louella Brooks. Is Daisy there?"

He glanced back at Daisy. "Oh, hello Mrs. Brooks. Yeah, she's right here."

Daisy walked across the kitchen and took the phone from him. "Hello?" She looked up at him and frowned. "What? What happened? Is she okay?" Her brows lifted almost to her hairline. "Good. Where's Pippen?" Daisy covered the side of her face with her hand. "Thank God." There was a pause and then she said, "Okay. I'm on my way." She hung up the telephone and turned to Jack.

"What's the matter?"

"My sister has officially lost her mind. That's what's the matter," she said as she moved to the counter and picked up her purse.

He ignored the ache between his legs as he reached for his T-shirt and pulled it over his head. "Is Lily okay?"

"No, she's a nut. What did she and mother do before I came to visit?" she asked, distracted as she shoved her hand inside her purse and pulled out a set of keys. "Run around acting weird and delusional? What are they going to do once I go back home?" She walked from the kitchen and through the living room. "Good gravy, I have my act together more than either of those women. Now, how darn scary is that?"

He didn't answer because he pretty much figured it was a rhetorical question and he didn't want to upset her more.

Through the screen door, he watched her jump in her mother's car and drive away. A glimpse of the Caddy's taillights and whine of the steering linkage as she pulled around to the street, was the last he expected to see or hear of Daisy Monroe.

Jack walked back through the empty house to the kitchen. He returned the milk to the refrigerator, and his gaze fell on the white envelope she'd left behind. Steven's letter. He picked it up and turned it over in his hands. His name was written in all capital letters in blue ink on the front.

He opened a cupboard door and stuck the envelope between two coffee mugs. He'd read it someday. But not now. Not when the memory of Daisy, naked on the back of the Custom Lancer was still so fresh in his head. Not when the taste of Steven's wife was still in his mouth.

Since she'd been back, he'd wondered if being with Daisy would be as good as he remembered. The answer was that it was better. Better in some way he didn't even try to define. He just knew that being with her was different. It was more than just sex. More than the pleasure he usually found being with a woman. More than a quickie on the trunk of a car.

It wasn't love. He knew for a fact that he wasn't in love with Daisy Lee. He might talk slow, but he wasn't stupid. And loving Daisy was just plain stupid. He didn't know why being with her felt different, but he didn't want to know either. He wasn't the kind of guy who dissected his life and looked for hidden meaning. No, he was the kind of guy who pushed it down deep until it went away. All he

knew for certain was that sex with her was better
than any he'd had in a long time, and it was a good
thing that she was leaving so he could return to his
life. His life before she'd blown into town and reminded him of things that were better left forgotten.

She was gone now, and there was no reason why
he should think of her again.

No reason at all.

A black-and-white tow truck pulled up to Ronnie's
house as Daisy and Louella drove past on their way
to the hospital. It was only a few blocks out of their
way on Locust Grove, and they had to see the de-
struction for themselves.

Ronnie's little house was beige stucco and someone had nailed a longhorn skull over the front door.
His yard consisted of stubby brown weeds, and it
would have been a drab scene if not for Lily's Red
Ford Taurus sticking half out the front room.

"Was Ronnie home?" Daisy asked as she floored
the Caddy and sped on. She figured all the cops
standing around were too busy gawking at Lily's
Taurus to take notice of a speeder.

"I don't think so, but we won't know for sure until we get to the hospital."

Daisy hated hospitals. No matter the city or state,
they all smelled and felt the same. Sterile and cold.
She'd spent enough time in them with Steven to
know that they dispensed a lot of medication and
advice, but rarely good news.

She and her mother walked through the small
hospital's emergency room doors and, after a few
moments, were taken to Lily. Pippen was at home

with Louella's next-door neighbor, and it was a good thing he wasn't with them. The second the nurse pushed back the green-and-blue striped curtain separating the beds, Louella burst into tears.

"It's okay, Mom," Daisy said, suddenly feeling like the only sane person in a family that had lost its collective mind. She took her mother's hand and held tight. "Lily's going to be okay."

But Lily didn't look okay. The left side of her face was swelling and there was a gash on her forehead. Blood caked her blond hair and the corners of her closed eyes. Some sort of bandaging immobilized her left arm, thick and very white, except where bright red blood seeped through. There was an IV in her right forearm, which wasn't bandaged, and her clothes had been cut off. A young male doctor in green scrubs lifted the sheet to listen to her heart and lungs. He looked up at them through wire-framed glasses.

Louella moved to the head of the bed and Daisy went with her. "Lily Belle. Momma's here. Daisy too."

Lily didn't respond and Daisy reached out to touch the side of her face that wasn't swollen. Her sister looked deadly pale, and if it weren't for the steady rise and fall of her chest, Daisy would have thought she really was dead. It was too much in an already emotionally charged day, and like the flip of a switch, Daisy's autopilot kicked in, and she felt herself go numb inside.

"What's the matter with her?" Louella asked.

"All we know so far," the young doctor answered, "is she has lacerations to her left arm and forehead and her ankle looks to be fractured. We won't know anything more until we get her CT scans."

"Why isn't she awake?"

"She took a pretty nasty hit to her forehead. I don't believe her skull is fractured and her pupils are responsive. We'll know more after we get a look at her X-rays."

"Was there anyone else hurt in the accident?" Daisy asked, praying Lily hadn't mowed down Ronnie and Kelly.

"She was the only one transported from the scene."

Which told Daisy nothing. Ronnie and Kelly could have been treated at the scene or, God forbid, dead. She hadn't seen Ronnie, but she hadn't been looking.

They were only permitted a few moments with Lily before she was wheeled away. They were told a doctor would talk to them shortly, but Daisy knew "shortly" could take hours.

She and her mother were shown to a small waiting room, and it looked and felt like every other waiting room she'd ever been in. She figured that all hospitals must choose colors from the same palate. Blues, greens, and a dash of maroon.

They sat together on a small blue sofa, and on the table next to Daisy sat a fake fern, a copy of *Reader's Digest*, *Newsweek*, and the Gideon Bible. She'd read a lot of *Reader's Digest* over of the last two and a half years, and she didn't even have a subscription.

A man and a woman stood near the door talking in hushed tones as if they raised their voice they'd scream. Daisy knew how they felt. She'd been here before, so many times. Finding distractions so she wouldn't scream and fall apart, concentrating on nice, even breaths so she could pretend her husband hadn't been dying. And now that her sister wasn't lying on a hospital gurney with blood crusted in her beautiful blond hair.

She picked up the *Reader's Digest* and flipped to "Humor in Uniform."

"She looked so white," Louella said, a tremble in her voice. "And there was so much blood."

"Scalps bleed a lot, Mom." She sounded so cool. As if she wasn't trembling inside, in the place where she shoved it all away. Down deep where she could control it. She'd gotten really good at sucking up her emotions and going numb inside. Never letting things get too close to the surface, because if she let that happen, she'd lose it for sure. Like with Jack today.

"How do you know?"

"Steven," she answered, and concentrated even harder on her magazine. She didn't want to think about Jack right now. She'd have to deal with him, and the repercussions of what she'd done, but not today. For now she pushed that problem down to the number two spot on her to-do list. Lily and the potential of murder charges moved to number one. She wondered how much a really good psychiatrist cost these days.

"Why wouldn't they tell us anything?"

"They don't know anything right now."

A police officer walked into the room and asked if they were related to Lily. He had a crewcut and wore a blue uniform and looked as if he could bench three hundred. He identified himself as Officer Neal Flegel. "I graduated high school with Lily and Ronnie," he said.

"You're Matt's little brother." Daisy shook his hand. "I went to a high school dance with Matt our sophomore year. Does he still live in Lovett?" she asked, because after all, this was Texas and manners came before emergencies.

"He just moved back from San Antone. I'll tell him you asked about him." He pulled out his notebook and got down to business. "I surely hated to see Lily in that car." He told them that the Taurus had come to a stop five feet inside Ronnie's living room. And as Daisy tried to figure out a subtle way of inquiring if Lily had killed Ronnie, Neal Flegel asked, "Do either of you have any reason to think she might have done this on purpose?"

That had actually been Daisy's first and only thought. "No." She shook her head and tried to look perplexed. "It must have been an accident."

"Her foot must have slipped," Louella said, and Daisy wondered if her mother actually believed it any more than she did. "And," Louella continued as if just struck by a thought, "she's been getting those blinding migraines lately."

"We spoke to Ronnie and he told us they'd been fighting a lot lately."

"You spoke to Ronnie today?" Daisy almost laughed with relief. "After the accident?"

"We contacted him at his girlfriend's."

"So he wasn't even home?"

"No one was in the home at the time."

"Thank God," Daisy sighed. Her sister wasn't going to fry for murder. This was Texas. If you were going to commit murder, Texas wasn't a good state to do it in. On the other hand, juries filled with Texas women did tend to sympathize with the wife of a cheating dog.

"Has she been suicidal?" Neal asked.

That gave both Daisy and her mother pause. Lily was depressed and pissed off, but Daisy didn't think she wanted to kill herself. Just Ronnie.

"No," Louella answered. "She just got a job working at Albertsons's deli. Things are looking up for her now."

"I was with her last night, and she was fine," Daisy told the officer. And it was the truth. Lily had been fine the night before. Daisy had only had to listen to "Earl Had to Die" twice. Once on the way to Slim Clim's and once on the way home.

Neal asked a few more questions and when he left, Daisy asked her mother, "Do you think she tried to kill herself?"

"Of course not," Louella said through a frown.

"Do you think she tried to kill Ronnie?"

"Daisy Lee, your sister's foot slipped, is all." And that was the end of the discussion.

Except that wasn't all. Not for Daisy. With Lily in the hospital and potentially homicidal, she couldn't possibly go home tomorrow. Nathan was not going to be happy.

She excused herself and found a bank of phones next to the Coke and candy machines. She used her calling card, and when Nathan got on the phone she tried to sound cheerful. Why, she really didn't know—other than that's what she was supposed to do.

"Hey there, Nathan."

"Hi, Mom."

She hesitated for a heartbeat, then cut right to the chase. "I have some news you're not going to like."

There was a long pause. "What?"

"Your aunt Lily was in a bad car accident this morning. She's in the hospital. I won't be coming home tomorrow."

He didn't ask about Lily. He was fifteen and concerned with his own problems. "You can't do this to me."

"Nathan, Lily is really hurt."

"I'm sorry about that, but you promised!"

"Nathan, I didn't know Lily was going to drive her car into Ronnie's living room."

"I got my hair cut! No way. No way, Mom. I am not staying here. They tried to make me eat Swedish meatballs last night."

They probably hadn't tried to make him do anything, but Nathan detested Swedish meatballs and chose to see it as a conspiracy. One more reason why he didn't like staying with them. Daisy sighed and wedged herself between the pay phone and the deep blue soda machine. "I don't know what to do, Nate. I really can't leave your grandmother and Lily right now. It isn't like I'm down here partying it up while you're consigned to hell."

"I want to come down there, then."

"What?"

"Mom, I hate it here. I'd rather be there with you."

She thought of Jack.

"You can't do this to me." Over the phone line, she could hear Nathan's voice crack with emotion he tried to hold back. "Please, Mom."

What were the chances he'd run into Jack before she spoke to him? Next to none. He'd probably just hang out and watch TV at his grandmother's house. And even if the two did accidently meet, so what? They didn't look anything alike. They wouldn't know who the other was. Nathan never asked about Jack, and she doubted he even remembered Jack's last name. "If that's what you really want, I'll call around and get you a flight down here."

His sigh of relief carried over the line. "I love you, Mom."

"Funny how you only remember to mention it when you're getting your way." She smiled. "Get your aunt Junie on the phone."

After she hung up from talking to Steven's sister, she called around and got a flight out of Seattle for the next day. It departed at six in the morning, had a three hour and forty minute layover in Dallas, and didn't arrive in Amarillo until almost five P.M. She thought about maybe driving to Dallas and picking Nathan up there. It was a six-hour drive, one way. Maybe they could spend the night in the big D. Go to Fort Worth and Cow Town and have barbeque. The more she thought of it, the more it appealed to her. She needed a vacation from her vacation, but when she called Nathan back, he told her that he'd rather sit for three hours in the Dallas-Fort Worth airport than eat barbeque and drive for six hours the next day. So much for getting away from the chaos.

But she supposed that no matter how tempting, she couldn't leave her mother and Lily right now.

She booked his ticket, and as she walked back to the waiting room, she wondered if her family had always been this insane, or if they were diving head-first into crazy creek on her behalf.

By the time she made it back to her mother, the doctor was sitting beside her on the short sofa. Daisy moved to stand by Louella.

"Is she awake?" her mother asked.

"She woke up about fifteen minutes ago. Her CT scans are clear. There isn't any brain trauma or injury to her internal organs. It's a good thing she was wearing her seat belt and that the car had air bags." He glanced up at Daisy. "Her ankle is broken and she's going to need surgery to pin the bones back together. An orthopedic surgeon is on his way from Amarillo."

After the doctor left, Louella stayed with Lily at the hospital and Daisy left to take care of Pippen. She put him down for a nap and finally changed out of her mother's Winnie the Pooh dress. With nothing else to occupy her mind, she thought of Jack. *Even in that stupid dress, you turn me on*, he'd said, which was just absurd.

She changed into a khaki skirt and white blouse and scrounged around in the kitchen for something to eat. She made a toasted cheese sandwich, some tomato soup, and a glass of iced tea. She took it to the breakfast nook, where the sun lit up the yellow table.

Having sex with Jack on the trunk of a car had been a mistake. No, having sex with him at all had been a mistake. But at the time, she hadn't possessed the will power to do much more than put up a half-hearted objection. She'd known she would regret it, but that hadn't stopped her.

She dunked her sandwich into her soup and took a bite. She'd had sex with Jack. It had been bad. No, it had been *wrong*. The sex had been good. Fabulous. So fabulous she'd burst into tears and embarrassed herself. Her face got hot just thinking about that—about that *and* the desire in Jack's green eyes when he'd looked at her, hot and alive touching her all over. Just the thought of it warmed her up.

She blew into her soup. She hated to admit it, but if her mother hadn't called, it was likely that she would have ended up in his bed. She'd probably still be there.

She took a drink of her tea. But what now? She didn't know, and with everything else going on in her life, she didn't have to think about it until everything settled a bit.

After Pippen got up from his nap, she took photographs of him out in her mother's garden. She shot him picking forbidden flowers while standing amongst the pink flamingos. For that short time, while she gazed at the world from behind her camera, her problems receded to the background.

Later when Louella came home, she noticed her mother looked about ten years older than she had that morning. The creases around her eyes seemed deeper, her cheeks paler. Daisy made her and Pippen some soup and sandwiches then left to go visit with Lily.

Her sister was asleep when she walked into her

hospital room. The cut on her forehead had been closed and bandaged. One side of her face was still swollen, her eyes were turning varying shades of black and blue, but the blood had been cleaned away.

Daisy wanted to ask her sister what had happened that morning, but Lily was heavily drugged and drifted in and out of consciousness. And each time she woke up, she started to cry and asked where she was. Daisy didn't even attempt to ask her about the accident.

She did the next day, though.

"Have the police talked to you yet?" she asked as she flipped through a *People* magazine she'd brought with her.

Lily licked her swollen lip. Her voice was a scratchy whisper when she said, "About what?"

Daisy stood and filled a plastic glass with cool water. She held the straw to Lily's mouth and answered, "About the car accident?"

Lily swallowed. "No. Mom said I wrecked my Taurus."

"You don't remember?"

She shook her head and winced. "I hated that car anyway."

"Did mom tell you how you wrecked it?"

"No. Did I run a stop sign?"

"Lily, you ran your Taurus through Ronnie's front room."

She stared at Daisy and blinked her black-and-blue eyes. But she didn't look as surprised as Daisy expected. "Seriously?"

"The police asked Mom and me if you're suicidal."

"I would never kill myself over Ronnie Darling-ton," she said without hesitation.

"Did you try to kill Ronnie?"

"No."

"Then what were you thinking? Did something happen?"

This time she did hesitate and she looked away when she answered, "I don't know."

Daisy had a feeling that she did know and that her memory loss was convenient. Something had happened, but Lily didn't want to talk about it today. Fine. There was always tomorrow.

When Daisy left the hospital, she drove into town and bought a car seat for Pippen. His other seat was still in the Taurus at the wrecking yard.

As she stopped for a traffic light at the intersection of Third and Main, she heard a deep throaty rumble just before Jack's Mustang blew through the intersection. She was two cars back, and she doubted he saw her. But just the split-second sight of him caused a disturbing tumble in her stomach as if they were in high school all over again and she was waiting for him at his locker. Her feelings for him were definitely a confused jumble of old emotions and new desires and all of it was better left alone.

At three-thirty that afternoon, Daisy strapped Pippen into her mother's Cadillac and they headed for Amarillo and Nathan.

Pippen wore little jean shorts, cowboy boots, and his DON'T MESS WITH TYRANNOSAURUS TEX T-shirt. Daisy held him in her arms while they waited in the baggage claim area. The half hour they stood there seemed to take forever, but when she saw Nathan's familiar face, it was like the sun had suddenly decided to shine after a week of gloomy weather.

His green Mohawk was gone and the tips of his short dark hair had been bleached white. He looked like a tall skinny porcupine carrying a big backpack with his skateboard attached to the back. She didn't care. She was so happy to see him she forgot about the No Public Displays of Affection rule. She stood on her tip toes and wrapped her free arm around his neck. She kissed his cheek and held on tight. He must have forgotten the rule too, because he dropped his backpack and hugged her—her and Pippen, right there in the Amarillo airport.

"Man, Mom. Don't ever leave me like that again."

She laughed and pulled back to look into his blue eyes. "I won't leave you. I promise," she said and turned her attention to Pippen. "This is your cousin. Isn't he cute?"

Nathan studied him for a moment. "Mom, the kid has a mullet."

She pretty much figured that a guy with porcupine hair shouldn't cast stones at a guy with a mullet. "It's not his fault," she said and looked into Pippen's face. "His mother won't cut off his baby curls."

Pippen stared up at her through his big blue eyes so much like Lily's, then returned his gaze to his older cousin. Daisy didn't know if Pippen's attention was drawn to him because he was another male or if he was attracted to the lip ring and dog chains.

"Hey there, little dude. Nice hair."

"Don't make fun," Daisy warned.

"I'm not." Nathan slicked his palms over the side

of his hair. "He's got business in the front, party in the back. Heh-heh-heh," he laughed as he tipped his head back.

"Watch 'toons!" Pippen said, then started to laugh too as if he'd just cracked a joke like Nathan.

"He wants you to watch cartoons with him. His favorite is 'Blues Clues.'"

"'Blue's Clues' suck." He picked up his backpack. "You gotta watch 'Sponge Bob Square Pants.'"

Nathan hadn't brought a suitcase, and as they headed for the car, it struck her that if everything had gone according to her original plan, she would have been back home now. In Seattle. Getting on with her life. Free of the past. Making a new start. Her and Nathan.

Since she'd arrived in Lovett, nothing had gone according to her plan, and she'd had to put her life on hold for just a little while longer. Her mother and sister needed her, and perhaps she could do something to help. Maybe just being here and taking care of Pippen was enough for now.

Her life hadn't completely gone to hell, she reminded herself. She'd been in hell. Lived it for over two years, and this wasn't even close. Not yet, anyway. Nathan was here and at some point, things had to get better.

Chapter 11

*T*he whine of a bench grinder filled the garage and filtered into Jack's office as he glanced over the master-parts list for the fifty-four Corvette; he simultaneously thumbed through Polaroids snapped of each part taken off the car so far. Everything from the chrome to the screws holding the taillight buckets had been cataloged and carefully stored away. The Blue Flame Six engine had been plucked from the cavity and would be torn down and steam-cleaned later. All rubber parts would have to be completely replaced as well as the leather interior. The fifty-four was supposedly a bitch to drive, but that was beside the point. The late and great Harley Earl had designed the sports car in his typical flamboyant style. The car had been designed for show rather than go.

Jack tossed the photographs aside and stood. That morning they'd removed the windshield and discovered more rust damage than he'd anticipated. The damage would have to be cut away and the brace rebuilt. He grabbed the Dodge Viper coffee mug that Lacy Dawn had given him for his birthday and walked from his office into the reception area.

Penny Cribs didn't come in until ten-thirty on Monday mornings, and a stack of mail sat on her empty desk. He refilled his coffee, and as he moved from the outer office into the garage, the noise from the bench grinder stopped. Jack blew into his mug and looked up at Billy who stood at the workbench. His safety glasses were pushed up his forehead, and he held a brake rotor in one hand. A skinny teenager stood talking to him, and they both turned as Billy pointed in Jack's direction.

Jack stopped in his tracks. The boy looked to be in his mid-teens and had a dog chain around his neck and one hanging down the side of his pants. He said something to Billy, then began walking toward Jack. Jack caught a glimpse of Billy's bemused smile before he turned his attention to the boy. He took a drink of his coffee and lowered the mug.

He'd always hired boys over the summer to sweep up or run for parts. But if this kid wanted a job, he was out of luck. Not so much because of the way he looked, but because he didn't have the sense to dress better and leave the chains on his dog when he went job hunting.

He had hair like a hedgehog, dark with white spikes on the ends. His bottom lip was pierced near one corner and his black T-shirt said anarchy in bloody red letters. He held a skateboard beneath one arm, and his jeans fit so loose, if he stood up straight, they'd fall down around his ankles.

"Can I help you?" Jack asked as the kid came to stand in front of him.

"Yeah. My mom told me you knew my dad?"

Jack knew a lot of dads. "Who's your mother?" he asked and took another drink of his coffee.

"Daisy Monroe."

The coffee scalded the back of his throat and he lowered it. Daisy hadn't left town.

"I don't know if she ever mentioned me. I'm . . ." his voice cracked and he swallowed hard. "I'm Nathan."

Whatever he'd expected Daisy and Steven's kid to look like, this was not it. First off, he'd thought their child was much younger. "She mentioned she had a son, but I thought you were about five."

A frown pulled his dark brows, and he stared at Jack through clear blue eyes. He looked a little confused like he didn't know how someone could mistake him with a five-year-old. "No. I'm fifteen."

The kid must have been conceived shortly after Steven and Daisy got married. The thought of Steven and Daisy together conjured up a long-buried animosity and bothered him more than it should have. More than it had a few days ago, before he'd made love to her on the trunk of the car just a few feet from where her son stood. Before he knew how good it was to be with her again. "I take it your mom is still in town?"

"Yeah." He stared at Jack as if he expected him to say something more. When he didn't, the boy added, "We're staying with my grandma until my aunt Lily gets better. My mom thinks that might take a week or so."

He'd wondered what had taken place to make Daisy run from his kitchen Saturday. "What happened to your aunt?"

"She drove her car into Ronnie's living room."

Damn, he guessed fighting in front of the Minute Mart hadn't been enough revenge for Lily. "Is she going to be okay?"

"I guess."

The grinder started once more and Jack showed Nathan into his office and shut the door against the noise. Even if Nathan had come dressed properly for a job interview, having Daisy's kid work in his shop would be a nightmare. Seeing him would remind Jack of Daisy. And no matter how sweet that particular memory, it was over and best forgotten.

"Your dad and I were good friends at one time. I was sorry to hear about his death."

Nathan set the tip of his skateboard by his black sneaker and leaned it against his leg. On closer inspection the underside of the board had a scantily dressed nurse painted on it. "Yeah. He was a good dad. I miss him a lot."

Jack had lost his father when he hadn't been much older than Nathan. He knew what it was like. Giving the kid an application to take with him wouldn't hurt. "Did he ever tell you about all the trouble he and I used to get into?"

Nathan nodded and the fluorescent lighting shined on his lip ring. "He told me about you guys stealing rotten tomatoes and throwing them at cars."

Steven had been blond, like a California surfer. Maybe it was the hair, but this kid didn't look like Steven had growing up. Not even a little bit. Didn't look a whole lot like his mother either. Maybe around the mouth. Well, except for the lip ring. "We made a tree fort in his backyard. Did he tell you about that?"

Nathan shook his head.

"It took us one whole summer. We made it out of wood we scrounged and old cardboard boxes." He smiled at the memory of them dragging home junk from miles away. "Your mom helped us, too. Then just when we finished, an F2 twister blew it all to hell."

Nathan laughed and motioned toward the door with his head. "Is that a 'Cuda 440-6 out there?"

"Yeah, it's got the original 426 Hemi."

"Sweet. When I get a job, I'm gonna buy a Dodge Charger Daytona with a 426 Hemi."

Now it was Jack's turn to laugh. He sat on the edge of his desk next to his Buick Riviera clock. He didn't want to rain on the kid's parade, but only about seventy Daytonas with a 426 Hemi had ever been produced. If he did manage to find one, it was going to run him about sixty grand. "Four-speed, right?"

"Yeah."

He took a drink. Naturally. The kid had just narrowed his odds even further considering Dodge had only put out about twenty four-speeds.

"I saw one once at a car show in Seattle." Nathan swallowed and his voice cracked with excitement. "The Daytona held the closed-course-track speed record for thirteen years. Ford and Chevy couldn't touch it."

Lord, he was just like Billy—and like Jack's father, Ray, had been. Blinded by speed. Jack loved fast cars too, but not like those two. How had Steven and Daisy managed to produce a gear head?

"Do you watch 'Monster Garage'?"

"Occasionally." Billy was the "Monster Garage" fanatic.

"Did you see the episode where they turned a NASCAR into a street sweeper?"

"No, I missed that one." But he'd heard all about it from Billy.

"It was tight."

Tight? Jack supposed that meant good.

Billy stuck his head in the door as Jack crossed his feet. "We've got a problem with the right-front rotor on that Plymouth."

There was always a problem with something, and Jack had learned not to sweat it long ago. "Billy come on in here and meet Steven and Daisy Monroe's boy, Nathan."

Billy came farther into the office wearing his dark blue shirt that buttoned up the front and had a Parrish American Classic's patch on the left breast pocket. Jack introduced them and they shook hands. Billy spoke first, "I was real sorry to hear about your dad. He was a good guy."

Nathan looked down at his shoes. "Yeah."

"Billy here loves 'Monster Garage,'" Jack said and

the two of them jumped into a discussion about which episodes were the best and which ones weren't.

"Turning that PT Cruiser into a wood chipper was lame," Nathan said.

"Jesse James wasn't into that one until they started feedin' stuffed animals through the chipper."

"Yeah, heh-heh-heh," Nathan laughed, tilting his head back a bit. "They blew stuffing all over the place."

"Did you see the Barbie get stuck in there?" Billy's eyes shined with humor and he laughed too, a rapid heh-heh-heh.

Christ, Jack thought, Billy had finally found someone who loved to watch "Monster Garage" as much as he did.

"Did you catch the episode with the Grim Reaper?" his brother asked.

"Yeah, that would have been tight if it'd worked."

Billy shook his head. "They smoked the first belt and the pump got too hot before they even got any of the cylinders to move those hydraulic arms."

"I heard a theory that the hearse was haunted and that's why the mission failed."

"The mission failed because the hydraulics failed."

"Did you see Jesse when the ambulance caught on fire?" Nathan asked, so excited his eyes shined with it. "That was cool."

"That's my favorite episode."

"Did you see his wife screaming at him?"

They both started to laugh at the same time. Billy's voice was lower, but Jack couldn't help but notice that their laughter was real similar. The same heh-heh-heh sound, and they both tipped their heads back at the same angle. The longer he looked at the two of them standing side by side swapping "Monster Garage" moments, the clearer he saw beyond Nathan's bizarre hair and the lip ring.

Then within the span of a second, the world around Jack shifted and changed. The hair on the back of his neck rose and his scalp got tight. Time ground to a halt, cracked down the middle, and fell in halves.

A half-second ago, everything had been okay in Jack's life, and in the next it wasn't. One half he'd been noticing his brother and Nathan laughing and sounding alike, and in the next he was looking at a fifteen-year-old version of his father, Ray Parrish. For half a second he'd been sitting on the edge of his desk and in the next he was standing with coffee down the front of his shirt, scalding his chest. "Christ!"

"What's the matter?" Billy asked.

He didn't take his gaze from Nathan. He looked at the shape of his face and nose, and there was no turning back the clock to a few seconds ago. He was definitely looking at a young version of his father. It was so obvious, he didn't know why it had taken him so long to see it. "You didn't come here for a job, did you?"

Nathan's smile fell and he picked up his skateboard. "No."

Suddenly, it all made perfect sense. Daisy's insistence that they talk. That she had something to tell him. Something she couldn't talk about on the phone or in a letter or at Showtime Pizza. Something important like a son. He felt like someone had kicked him in the stomach. "When is your birthday?"

"I've got to go now."

He reached out and grabbed Nathan's arm. "Tell me."

Nathan's eyes got wide and he dropped his skateboard. He tried to back up, but Jack didn't let go. He couldn't.

"December," he finally answered.

Jack pulled him even closer. "And you're fifteen aren't you?"

He could see Nathan's throat work as he tried to swallow. "Yes," he said just above a whisper.

On some level Jack knew he frightened Nathan and that he should let go. He should calm down, but he couldn't. Thoughts raced through his head until it felt like something was squeezing his brain. "Son of a bitch."

Billy grabbed a hold of Jack's shoulder and stepped between him and Nathan. "What's the matter with you? Have you lost your mind?"

Yes. He'd lost his mind. He let go and Nathan took off so fast, it was like he'd never been there. Except that his skateboard was still on the floor. Nurse-side up.

Jack stared after him. "Didn't you see it, Billy?"

"All I see is you acting crazy."

He shook his head and turned to his brother. "He looks like dad."

"Who?"

"Nathan. Daisy's son."

"Daisy and *Steven's* son."

Jack pointed to the empty doorway. "Did he look like Steven to you?"

"I don't really remember what Steven looked like, to tell you the truth."

"Not like our dad." He set the mug on his desk. He had a son. No. Impossible. He'd always used contraceptives. But not always with Daisy. They'd been young and stupid and still believed nothing bad would ever affect them. "She was pregnant when she left and she didn't tell me."

Billy put his hands up. "Wait, I never even knew the two of you were involved back then. And even if you were, how do you know he's your kid?"

"You're not listening to me." He scrubbed his face with his hands. "There's a picture. A picture of dad when he graduated high school. He looks just like that kid." He dropped his hand to his sides. "That's why she's here," he spoke his thoughts out loud as if they made better sense that way, when in reality, they made no sense at all. "To tell me about him."

"This is crazy. He's fifteen."

Yes. It was crazy. Crazy as hell to think he had a fifteen-year-old son. A son he'd never known about because he'd never been told. "I'm right, Billy."

Billy stepped in front of him and looked him in the eye. "You better make damn sure you're right before you go grabbing that kid and scaring him again. You don't know for sure he's yours, but even if he is, he might not know it."

Billy was right. "I didn't mean to scare him."

Movement beyond Billy caught Jack's attention and he looked through the open doorway at Penny.

He pushed by his brother and said on his way past the secretary, "I'm going out for a while."

He walked out the back of the garage, across the driveway, to his house. He went straight to a spare room that used to belong to Billy and he opened the closet crammed with boxes. He pulled out one after the other and dumped them on the floor. Old trophies and magazines, keepsakes from his and Billy's childhood that their mother had carefully packed away, fell everywhere.

"What are we looking for?" Billy asked as he picked up a box.

Jack hadn't even realized Billy had followed. "Mom and Dad's old wedding album. The picture is in their wedding album."

They found the album in the fifth box they opened. The outside was covered in lace and silk flowers, the girly stuff his mother had favored. The lace had yellowed, the flowers flattened; Jack flipped it open. Inside, the pages had lost their stickiness and the photographs behind the loose cellophane slid together. The picture Jack searched for fell at his feet, and he knelt to pick up the black-and-white photo of his father at the age of seventeen. In one corner of the picture, his father had written in faded black ink, *To my favorite girl Carolee, Love Ray.*

Jack stood and stared at the photo. He hadn't imagined it. Give his father hedgehog hair and a lip ring, and he'd look a hell of a lot like Nathan Monroe. Only he wasn't Nathan Monroe. He was a Parrish.

Billy came to stand behind Jack and he looked over his shoulder. His low whistle sounded louder than usual in the empty room. "Do you think Steven knew?"

Jack shrugged. She'd been three months pregnant; at some point Steven had to have known. He walked out of the bedroom and down the hall into the kitchen. He opened a cabinet and pulled Steven's letter from where he'd place it Saturday. With the photograph of his father still in one hand, he tore open the envelope and read:

Jack,

Please excuse my handwriting and misspellings. As my illness progresses it gets more difficult for me to concentrate. It is my hope that you never see this letter. That I will beat this disease and tell you these things in person once I am well again. If not, I want to write down my thoughts before I am unable.

Let me begin by saying simply that I have missed you, Jack. I don't know if you have missed me or forgiven me, but I have missed my buddy. There have been many times in the past fifteen years when I have wanted to call and talk to you. Many times I have laughed by myself thinking of the things we used to do. The other day I saw two boys riding their bikes in the rain and I remembered the many times we used to ride our bikes in real toad-stranglers. Riding around Lovett, finding the deepest puddles to ride through. Or the times sitting on my mother's sofa, watching the old Andy Griffith shows, and laughing our asses off when Barney locked himself in jail. I think that is when I miss you the most, when I laugh alone. And I know it is my fault. There have been many times I have felt the loneliness of losing you, my friend.

I have never forgotten the last time we saw each other and the horrible things we said. I married Daisy, and you loved her. But I loved her too, Jack. I still do. After all these years I love her as much as the day I married her. I know she loves me. I know she has always loved me, and yet some times she gets a very far away look in her eyes, and I wonder if she is thinking about you. I wonder if she is thinking that she is sorry she chose to come with me to Seattle. I wonder if she thinks what her life might have been like with you, and I wonder if she still loves you like she did. If it is any consolation, then know that I have suffered a bit of hell, because I know how much she loved you once and perhaps still does.

The night we left Lovett, Daisy was three months pregnant with your child. She's no doubt told you all of this by now. When she came to me and told me she was carrying your baby, she was very afraid and believed that you didn't love her any longer. I let her believe it even though I knew it probably wasn't true. She believed not telling you about the baby was for the best. She didn't think you could handle the pressure of having a child at that time in your life. I let her believe that too. I told her she was right, that you couldn't, but I knew it wasn't true. I knew you could do anything you set your mind to doing. So I married her and took her away from you. I know that I should regret what I did, but I can't. I don't regret one day that I have spent with her and Nathan. But I do regret the way in which things were done and not telling you about Nathan sooner.

Nathan is a good boy. He is a lot like you. Fearless and impatient and buries everything deep. I know that Daisy will do her absolute best to raise him, but I believe he needs you. It has been my pleasure to raise him, and of all my regrets in this life, and there are many, I regret that I will not get to see him grow into a man. I would have liked to have seen that.

In closing, I ask that you forgive me, Jack. I know that is perhaps asking too much of you, but I'm asking anyway. I am asking so you can let go of the bitterness and go on with your life. On a purely selfish level, I am asking with the hope that you will forgive me so that I can die with a clearer conscience. And so that when I see you on the other side, we can em-

*brace as friends once more. If you can't forgive me, I
understand. I don't know that I could ever forgive
you if I were in your place. I took a lot from you, Jack.
But maybe you can occasionally look back and laugh
at the good times we had together.*

Steven

The letter and photograph of his father fell to the
counter as Jack struggled to catch his breath. His insides felt sliced up, just like they had fifteen years ago.

"Is he yours?"

Jack nodded.

"That's goddamn evil," Billy said. "She's a damn
evil bitch."

For years he'd felt betrayal because his best buddy
had married his girlfriend. He hadn't even known
the half of it. It had never even occurred to him that
when they'd left, they'd taken his child. It had not
occurred to him that their betrayal ran so deep.

"What are you going to do?"

He unbuttoned his shirt and pulled it from the
waistband of his pants. "Talk to Daisy."

"Well, don't start yelling at her first thing."

"I thought you just said she was an evil bitch."

"She is. I'm not even going to ask you if you want
to be a part of Nathan's life, because I know you. I
know how you are. I know that you're hurt and angry, and you have every damn right to feel that way.
But she's his mama and she could just pack him up
and take him away."

For years he'd pushed it back and locked it away. He'd walled up all the pain and anger. Since Daisy had been back, it had seeped out a little. But nothing like this morning. This morning the walls he'd built were blown all to hell.

"Jack, promise you won't go medieval?"

He wasn't promising a damn thing.

Chapter 12

$\mathcal{D}$aisy laid Pippen on her mother's bed and partially closed the door behind her. His little world was chaotic and he'd been so tired and cranky for the past few days. Daisy had taken him to the hospital to see Lily this morning, and he hadn't wanted to leave. He was scared and upset and had cried all the way home, finally falling asleep as they pulled into the driveway. Her mother was still at the hospital with Lily, waiting for news from the doctors as to when Lily might come home.

Daisy changed into her dark green tank top and khaki shorts. She swept her hair up off the back of her neck and secured it with a big black claw. She was exhausted and in serious need of caffeine. She might have curled up beside Pippen, but Nathan wasn't home and she didn't want to be asleep when he returned.

She moved down the stairs to the kitchen and grabbed a Coke out of the refrigerator. Nathan had stuck a note to the refrigerator door with a little magnet in the shape of Texas. He wrote that he was out riding his skateboard. The note didn't say when he'd be back, though. She had wanted to remind him that he needed to estimate when he'd be back, so she wouldn't worry so much.

This was Lovett, she reminded herself. There really wasn't that much to worry about. There weren't that many places he could get into trouble, but if there was one thing she'd learned from having a boy, it was that if there wasn't trouble, they'd invent it. If there was a puddle, they'd jump in the middle of it. A rock, they'd throw it. A Coke can, they'd smash it. A bird, they'd pretend to shoot it. A handrail on a set of five or more cement steps, they'd ride it on a skateboard, fall and need stitches.

The doorbell rang as Daisy popped the top to her Coke. She took a long drink as she moved through the living room. A bowl of glass fruit sat on a wooden end table and she placed the can next to it. She opened the door and half expected to see Nathan playing a silly joke by making her answer the door. He was like that sometimes. Wanting to be treated as an adult, yet at times acting like her little boy. But it wasn't her son.

Jack stood on her mother's porch, sunlight overhead. The shadow of his straw cowboy hat concealed the top half of his face. A little flutter tickled her chest and before she could think better of it, the corners of her lips turned up. "Hey there."

"Are you alone?" he asked, and her smile fell at the flat tone in his voice and grim line of his mouth.

He knows, was her first thought, but just as quickly she dismissed the thought. He couldn't know. "Pippen's here but he's asleep."

"Where is Nathan?"

Oh, God. The fluttering in her chest picked up a notch or two. "He's riding his skateboard."

He didn't wait for her to invite him in. "No. He's not," he said as he walked into the house, bringing with him the scent of a warm Texas morning on his skin. He handed her Nathan's board as he passed.

She took it from him and held it against her breasts. A ribbed T-shirt hugged the muscles of Jack's arms and chest and made him appear bigger and badder than usual. "Where is he?"

He turned and looked at her for several nerve-racking moments before he said, "I don't know."

"How did you get this?"

"He came to see me this morning."

"He did?" Nathan's going to the garage wasn't a coincidence. It was a surprise, but not a real shock. Nathan was the kind of kid who jumped into things first and thought later. A lot like Jack had been.

"He left the board on his way out."

She didn't think that he'd said anything to Jack about being his biological child. Of course, it hadn't occurred to her that he'd ever show up at the garage on his own either. "What did he say?"

"He talked about Steven and about 'Monster Garage.'"

Maybe he doesn't know. Maybe he was being a hard-ass for a totally different reason. This was Jack, after all. The king of hard-asses. "That's it?"

"I think he really came by to get a good look at me." He pushed up the brim of his straw hat and she got a good look at *him*. If the glittering rage in his green eyes hadn't removed all doubt about what he knew or suspected, the next words out of his mouth did. "I read Steven's letter."

Now she was shocked. "How did you get Steven's letter?"

"You left it Saturday."

Had she? She didn't remember. A lot had happened Saturday. "You just read it today?"

"I didn't want to read it at all." His voice was deadly calm when he said, "Tell me, Daisy. I want to hear you say it. After all these years."

His veneer of calm did not fool her for a second. His anger rolled off him like heat waves rolling across asphalt. Her speeding heart fell right to the pit of her stomach. She'd waited fifteen years for this moment. Knew it had to happen at some point, and there was no other way to say it but, "He's your son, Jack."

His expression didn't change. "Does he know?"

"Yes. He's known most of his life."

"So, I'm the only one who wasn't told."

"Yes."

"Do you have any idea," he said in that same *awful* calm tone, "what I'd like to do to you?"

Yes, she had a pretty good idea. She didn't think Jack would hurt her, but she took a step back. "I was going to tell you."

"Is that so?" One brow lifted up his forehead. "When?"

"The first night I saw you. I came to your house to tell you, but Gina was there. I told you I needed to speak with you about something important. I told you that night and the night of Shay's wedding, and at the pizza place, and at Slims." Her face felt hot, and she took another step back and tossed the skateboard on her mother's blue floral couch. "I came to the garage to tell you Saturday, but then . . . Lily ran her car into Ronnie's living room. Which is why I guess I forgot all about leaving Steven's letter." She pulled the claw from the back of her hair and took a deep breath. He had a right to his anger. She should have told him years ago. She was a coward. "That's why I'm in town. I'm here to tell you that you have a son."

His gaze locked with her. "He's fifteen."

She swept her hair back up, twisted it, and secured it once more. "Yes, he is."

"You're telling me fifteen years too goddamn late. You should have told me when you missed your first period." He thought a moment then added, "Unless you didn't know whose it was back then."

"I knew." Now he was just being mean. "You were the first person I was ever with. How could you think such a horrible thing?"

"Maybe because up until a few days before you married my best friend, you were having sex with me. How do I know that you weren't doing us both at the same time?"

"You know I wasn't. You're just being ugly now."

"You don't know ugly," he said and his temper finally rose to the surface. He took a step toward her and stared down into her face. His eyes narrowed and the line of his jaw hardened. "You did the lowest thing a woman can do to a man. You had my child and kept him from me. I should have been there when he was born. I should have been there to see him. To see him take his first steps and ride his first bike. I should have been there to hear his first words, but I wasn't. Steven was, though. Steven got to hear him say Daddy, not me." He was dead serious when he added, "It's a good thing you're not a man, because I'd beat the hell out of you. I'd enjoy it, too."

One of the hardest things she'd ever done was stand there toe-to-toe with Jack and not take another step back or look away from his angry eyes. "You have to understand that we never meant to hurt you. We both loved you."

"Bullshit."

"It's the truth."

"If that's what you do to people you love, I can't imagine what you have in store for people you hate."

Her head began to pound and she put a hand to her brow, but she didn't remove her gaze from his. "You have to remember what it was like between you and me back then. We were fighting and making up all the time. That first month, I was so scared, and I told myself I was just late. Then the second month I told myself not to think about it, but by the third month, I had to face it." She dropped her hand. "Your parents had just died and you were going through such a bad time. The night I came to tell you I was pregnant, you said you needed a break from me. I didn't think you loved me anymore. I didn't know what to do." The backs of her eyes stung but she refused to give in to tears. "I didn't have anyone to talk to about it but Steven. I went to him and he asked me to marry him. He said he'd take care of me and my baby."

"You keep forgetting that the baby was mine. That I should have been told about it before the two of you ran off to Seattle."

"We talked about telling you, but we thought that if you knew, you'd want to marry me out of obligation, but Jack, you were in no position to take care of me and a baby. You were only eighteen and already dealing with so much. It seemed like the only solution."

"No, it was the easy way out for you. Steven had money and I had nothing."

"That's not why I married him. You know that I always loved Steven. If you weren't so angry, you'd remember that you loved him too." She placed her hands on his bare arms. Jack might never forgive her, but she had to make him understand. "I married him because I was scared. You didn't love me anymore, and I didn't know what to do."

"How did it feel, Daisy?" His voice lowered, got rough and smooth at the same time. "How did it feel to get back at me for not loving you? Did taking my child make you feel good? Did it satisfy your revenge?"

"It wasn't about revenge."

He grabbed her wrists and removed her hands from his arms. "Did lying with Steven Monroe get me out of your head. Your heart? When you were with him, were you thinking of me?"

"No!"

"Remembering how it used to be between us?" His voice lowered even further and he pinned her wrists behind her back. "How good it was." He pulled her up against his body and said against her temple, "How good it still is."

The brim of his hat touched the top of her head. "Stop it, Jack."

"All those years, were the two of you laughing it up over what you'd done to me?"

"No, Jack. It wasn't like that. No one was laughing." Her heart knocked in her chest and she swallowed hard. "Believe me. I know I should have told you sooner."

His voice got real quiet next to her ear when he asked, "Who's listed as daddy on that boy's birth certificate?"

"Steven."

He pulled back far enough to look into her face. "Goddamn you, Daisy."

"We thought it would be easier for him in school. I'm sorry."

"I don't give a flying fuck how sorry you are. Because it's not half as sorry as you're going to be."

"What do you mean?"

He set her back on her heels and slid his hands to her shoulders. "All those years ago when you chose Steven over me because I was just a poor kid with grease on my hands, working in my daddy's garage—that's not how things are now. I'm not poor anymore, Daisy. I can afford a real good lawyer, and if I have to, I'll fight you."

"There won't be a fight."

"I want to know my son."

"You can get to know him. I want you to. And when we leave—"

"When *you* leave," he interrupted. "He stays."

"That's ridiculous. He's not staying here with you. His home is with me. In Seattle."

"We'll see about that."

"I know you're angry. I don't blame you."

"Nice to know you don't blame *me*." He released her and turned to the door.

"I should have told you about Nathan years ago, but don't punish him because you're mad at me." She followed close behind him to the front porch. "He's been through so much. He lost his dad and now this."

Jack turned around so fast she almost ran into his chest. "He didn't lose his dad. Steven Monroe wasn't his father."

Daisy wisely didn't point out that Nathan thought of Steven as his dad and had loved him. "Nathan's been through a lot in the past few years. He needs a little peace. Some calm in his life." She didn't add that she needed it too. "I'll talk to him. See what he wants to do, and I'll call you."

"I'm not going to wait around for you to call me, Daisy Lee." He moved down the steps toward his Mustang parked at the curb. "After I talk to Nathan,

I'll tell you how it's going to be," he said as he walked away, the morning sun shining down on his straw hat and his wide shoulders.

"Wait." She ran down the steps after him. "You can't talk to him alone. I'm his mother. He doesn't know you."

He walked around the front of the car then stuck his key in the driver's side door. "Whose fault is that?"

She looked at him from across the top of the car. "I should be there."

He looked back at her and laughed. "Like I should have been there for the past fifteen years?"

She grabbed the door handle to jump in his car but the door was locked. Then she remembered Pippen and realized she couldn't go even if she forced her way into his car. "Nathan is my son. You can't exclude me."

"Get used to it."

"We can work this out. I know we can." She didn't know anything of the sort, but she was determined to keep things from getting too ugly. "I should have told you. I know that, and except for handing over my son, I'll try and make it up to you."

"How? On the trunk of a car?" He unlocked the Mustang's door. "Not interested."

So much for keeping things from getting too ugly.

Nathan sat with his back against the basketball pole at Lovett High. The backboard and hoop cast an oblong shadow on the court to the free-throw line.

He gazed across the football field to the tennis courts. He didn't like it here. He didn't know what he expected Texas to look like, maybe like Montana. He and his dad had been to Montana once, but Texas wasn't like that. Texas was flat. And hot. And brown.

Texas was nothing at all like Seattle.

He pushed with his feet and slid up the pole until he stood. He adjusted the chain around his neck and glanced at the high school behind him. "High school," he scoffed. It wasn't even as big as the grade school he'd gone too. They probably all wore cowboy boots and rode horses to school. Probably all listened to crappy country and western music and chewed tobacco. Probably nobody rode skateboards or listened to Korn or Weezer or played Sniper Fantasy for XBOX.

Nathan pulled up his pants and hardly noticed when they slipped back down his hips. Problems bigger than his baggy pants occupied his thoughts. He'd dropped his skateboard at Jack Parrish's garage, and then he'd run away like a big scared baby.

He *really* wished he hadn't done that, but the way Jack had grabbed his arm had freaked him out. And the way he'd looked and swore at him, too. One second they'd all been laughing, and in the next, Jack had grabbed him and stared at him so intensely, he'd about capped his pants. Nathan didn't know if Jack had figured it out in that moment, but by the look on his face, he thought maybe he had. Then before Nathan had even realized what he was doing, he ran away like a little kid.

Jack probably thought he was a dork.

With a shrug of his shoulders he told himself he

didn't care. His dad had told him lots of stories about Jack. He made him sound real cool, like someone Nathan would really like. But he didn't think he liked Jack. He liked Billy, though. Billy watched "Monster Garage." Billy was cool.

He picked up a rock and threw it hard against the backboard. It made a satisfying thwack, rebounded and almost hit him in the head. Obviously, his mom hadn't told Jack yet. Nathan had just assumed that she'd told him already or he never would have walked into that garage today. After all, that's why she was here. To tell Jack about him. At least, that's why she'd *said* she was coming here.

He moved back across the field toward the opening in the chain link fence. He was pretty mad at his mom, and feeling really stupid. Plus, he had to figure out a way to get his board back. Maybe he'd just let Jack keep it because he really didn't want to walk back into the garage and ask for it back. Not now.

The grass beneath his black skater shoes squished and he figured the sprinklers had been on that morning. Water droplets collected on the leather toes of his shoes and he watched them roll off. His mom should be back from the hospital by now. He had to tell her where he'd been. She'd probably get mad at him, but he didn't really care. The more he thought about it, the madder he got at *her*. If his mother had told Jack, or at least told Nathan that she hadn't, he wouldn't have gone to the garage and made such a dick weed out of himself.

When he looked up, he noticed a girl walking toward him a few feet away on the other side of the fence. Through the links he could see that she had shiny dark hair and smooth tan skin like she spent time sunbathing. They met at the opening at the same time, and he stepped aside to let her go through first. Instead, she stopped and stared at him.

"You're not from around here. I know most everyone, but I've never seen you," she said with a definite Texas twang, drawing out her words. She had big brown eyes, and beneath one arm she held poster board and construction paper.

"I live in Washington," he told her.

"Washington, D.C.?" She said it like his mother and grandmother did. Like there was an *r* in the word "wash." She wore a blue T-shirt with the words Ambercrombie and Fitch in silver glittery letters. She was a prep, and he didn't like preppie girls. Girls who shopped at Ambercrombie and Fitch and The Gap. Goodie-two-shoe girls.

"No. State."

"Are you here visitin' someone?"

No, he had no use for preppie girls . . . but she had the kind of lips that made him think of kissing. Which he'd been thinking about a lot lately. "Yeah, my grandma, Louella Brooks, and my aunt Lily." He'd kissed one girl in the sixth grade, but he didn't think that counted.

A frown pulled at her brows. "Lily Darlington?"

"Yep."

"Ronnie's cousin Bull is married to my aunt Jessica." She laughed. "We're practically related."

He doubted that made them related at all. And what the heck kind of name was Bull? "What's your name?"

"Brandy Jo. What's yours?"

Despite being a prep and having a drawl, Brandy Jo was hot. The kind of hot that made his stomach feel fuzzy and his chest feel heavy and made him think about how complicated girls were. And it was at these times, when he was thinking about girls, that he missed his dad the most. "Nathan," he answered. A guy just couldn't ask his mother about certain stuff.

She studied him a moment and her gaze lowered to his lip. "Did that hurt?"

He didn't have to ask her what she was talking about. "No," he answered and hoped his voice didn't crack. He *hated* when that happened. "I'm getting a tattoo next."

Her big brown eyes rounded and he could tell she was impressed. "Your parents will let you?"

No. He'd have to get it without his mother knowing somehow. A few months ago they'd made a deal, he could keep his lip ring if he promised to never get a tattoo as long as he lived. He'd promised, but he figured he only had to keep his word until he was eighteen and old enough to get one himself. Tattoos were cool. "Sure."

"Where?"

He pointed to his shoulder. "Right there. I don't know what I want yet, but when I do, I'm definitely getting a tat."

"If I could get one, I think I'd get a little red heart on my hip."

Which Nathan thought was pretty lame and really girly. "That'd be cool." He dropped his gaze to the poster boards beneath her arm. "What are you doing with that stuff?"

"I'm gonna teach city-rec art classes to little kids this summer. It's gonna be a lot of fun, and I'll get paid five-seventy-five an hour."

Teaching art to little kids didn't sound like a lot of fun to Nathan, but getting paid five-seventy-five an hour was sweet. He quickly did the math in his head and figured that if a kid worked five hours a day, five days a week, he could make around five hundred and seventy dollars in one month. He could buy a lot of CDs or new board trucks with that kind of money.

A black Mustang pulled alongside the curb on the other side of the fence, and Nathan watched Jack Parrish get out. He pushed his cowboy hat up his forehead and gazed at Nathan over the top of the car. "You forgot your board at the garage."

Jack didn't look so scary this time, but the fuzzy feeling in Nathan's stomach got worse. Like when he rode the Zipper too many times at the Puyallup fair. "Yeah."

Brandy Jo looked from Nathan to Jack then back again. "See ya around."

Nathan glanced at her. "Okay, see ya." As she walked away, he returned his attention to the man both his mom and dad said was his biological father. As far as Nathan could see, he didn't look much like Jack.

"I took your skateboard to your grandmother's."

Nathan stepped through the opening in the fence and stood next to the passenger door. If the feeling didn't go away, he was afraid he'd get sick. And he *really* didn't want to do that. "Was my mom home?"

"Yes. She and I talked." He rested a forearm on the top of the car. "She said you've always known that I'm your father."

"Yeah." He swallowed past the lump forming in his throat. He didn't know why he felt so weird. It wasn't like he cared what Jack thought. He'd gone to the garage earlier out of mild curiosity. That was it. He didn't care what anyone thought. "I've known."

"Well, I'm glad that at least she didn't lie to you." Jack looked at the watch strapped around his wrist and tapped his fingers three times on the top of the car. "Do you want a ride home?"

"Okay." Nathan waited for Jack to unlock the door, then he climbed inside. He sat in the soft beige leather seat and his stomach churned a little bit more. He didn't know what this car was worth, but a lot more than his mom's stupid minivan back in Seattle. That's for sure. "Is this a Shelby?"

"Yep. It's a nineteen-sixty-seven GT 500."

Nathan didn't know that much about Mustangs except that if you were going to have one, this was the one. "What's the engine?" he asked as he shut the door.

"The original 428 Police Interceptor."

"Tight."

"I like it." Jack shifted, glanced behind him, then pulled back out onto the street.

"How fast will it go?"

"A hundred and thirty-two. Of course that's nothing compared to the Daytona. How fast did you say it was clocked on the closed course?"

"Two hundred on the closed course. One-eighty right out of the showroom in nineteen sixty-nine."

Jack laughed and moved his hand from the steering wheel to shift again. "You know, Billy could use some help with that Barracuda that's in the shop. Since you're here for a while and going to own a Daytona someday, you might want to give him a hand with that Hemi."

Was he kidding? Nathan would crap all over himself just to *touch* a Hemi. "That could be cool, I guess. But I don't know how long I'm gonna be in town."

Jack looked over at him, the shadow of his hat fell across his nose. "We'll talk to your mom and see how long you're going to be here." He turned his attention back to the road and shifted the big engine into third. "Of course, just 'cause you're family doesn't mean we can pay you more than the other guys."

Pay? As in earn money working on a Hemi? He'd crap all over himself *twice.* Nathan looked down at the chain hanging from one loop of his pants. He cleared his throat and bobbed his head a few times. "Sweet."

"We'll start you out at seven-fifty an hour."

He tried to do the math in his head, but something that usually came pretty easy to him was impossible at the moment. "Okay."

"Nathan?"

He looked back across the car at Jack. "Yeah?"

"I should have known about you before today," he said, but he kept his gaze on the road.

Nathan agreed, but he didn't say so.

"If I had known, I would have been in your life. No one could have kept me out."

He didn't know what to say to that, so he kept quiet.

"Maybe while you're here, we could get to know each other."

"Cool."

"And if we don't get on each other's nerves too much, you could think about staying the summer."

The whole summer? In Loserville? No way.

"When the 'Cuda's done, I'm going to need someone to test-drive it for me. You think you could do that?"

He bit the inside of his lip ring to keep from smiling. *Oh man!* "I could do that."

"You got your driver's license, right?"

His excitement plummeted. "No, I'm only fifteen. You gotta be sixteen."

"Not in Texas. You can get it when you're fifteen."

"Really?"

"Yep. You have to have your license to test-drive the 'Cuda for me. It's company policy for insurance purposes. That means you'd have to sign up for driver's education. That might take half the summer."

Since before Nathan could remember, he'd dreamed of the day he'd get his driver's license.

"You don't have to give me your answer today. Think it over and let me know."

If he stayed in Texas for the summer, he could get

it early. Plus work on a Hemi and make serious bank. He adjusted the chain around his neck. "I'll have to ask my mom." And she wasn't going to like it one bit. She was always telling him no. She didn't want him to have fun or grow up. She wanted him to be bored and stay a little kid forever.

"I'll talk to her for you."

"You would?"

"Oh yeah." His smile showed his white teeth. "It will be my pleasure."

Chapter 13

"*Y*ou remember Azelea Lingo, don't you?"

"No," Daisy answered absentmindedly as she stared out her mother's front-room window.

"Sure you do, she's the one who bought Lily half a vacuum when she got married," Louella continued as if Daisy had been at Lily's wedding, which she hadn't.

"How does a person buy half a vacuum for a wedding present?" Daisy asked, although she really didn't give a damn at the moment. It had been over an hour since Jack had come and gone. Over an hour and she hadn't seen hide nor hair of him or Nathan.

"She put it on layaway and Lily had to pay to get it off. Cost her fifty bucks for a ninety-dollar vacuum. And you know, Azelea isn't poor. She's so big she has to sit down in shifts, so it isn't like she can't afford a whole vacuum."

Daisy had started to leave a dozen times only to decide that staying put was the best course.

"Anyway, Azelea's husband, Bud, left her a few years back and married a gal from Amarillo. Only the gal in Amarillo doesn't know that Bud's been sneaking back to Lovett the whole time for a little lovin' on the side with Azelea."

Daisy massaged the deep crease that had formed between her brows. Her head was going to explode.

"What is it, darlin'?" Louella paused in her story to ask Pippen. "Oh, you want your hat? Daisy, honey, where's Pip's hat?"

Daisy was so tense it felt like she had to unlock her jaw to speak. "Probably in your bedroom."

"Go check grandma's bed."

"You go," Pippen demanded in his tiny voice.

"We'll go together."

Daisy kept her gaze out the window as they left the room. She grabbed a handful of her mother's dark blue velvet drapes and pressed her forehead to the glass. Since Nathan hadn't returned, she figured Jack had found him, and all sorts of scenarios ran through her head. Ranging from the two of them sitting somewhere talking to Jack kidnapping Nathan and heading some place where she'd never find them. The last scenario she didn't really think was likely, but with Jack she never knew.

She opened the front door, and stuck her head out to look up and down the street. There was no sign of either of them.

"You're letting all the bought air out. Shut that," her mother said as she entered the room. Daisy glanced behind her, at her mother dressed in a pink blouse with fake pearls sown on it and a denim prairie skirt. Pippen stood beside her, wearing his coonskin cap and a pair of Big Bird pull-ups.

"This afternoon as I was leaving the hospital, they brought in Bud Lingo," her mother continued where she'd left off. "Appears he had heart failure while he was with Azelea. I couldn't stay at the hospital, but I am powerful curious to know what's gonna happen when Bud's wife gets her tail up here from Amarillo." Louella walked to the cabinet where she kept her VHS tapes and opened it up. "And their youngest girl, Bonnie, was there too. She's the one who had that real ugly baby last Valentine's Day. Lord, when I picked the blanket off the baby's face in church, I 'bout had heart failure myself. It was all bald and pink and skinny like a newborn rat, bless her heart. Of course, I lied and told her it was precious. You remember Bonnie, don't you. Short. Dark hair . . ."

Her mother was determined to make Daisy's head explode. Daisy stepped out onto the porch and shut the door behind her. She sat on the first step and rested her temple against the white post that supported the roof. Her nerves were frazzled. Her head pounded, and her patience had deserted her awhile ago. It was barely one o'clock in the afternoon, and she knew the day was bound to get worse. Jack hated her now, and he was going to make her life a misery, just as he'd promised the first night she'd seen him. While she understood his anger at her, she couldn't let things get ugly. If they did, the one person who was totally innocent would be the one to suffer the most. Nathan.

She glanced downward at her bare feet and red toenails. For the first time, she noticed the perfect fingertip bruises on her thighs. She didn't have to wonder how they'd gotten there. Jack. He'd left his mark on her long after he'd made love to her.

It was apropos, she supposed. Jack had left his mark on her years ago too, and she didn't mean Nathan. He'd marked her where no one could see. He'd left an indelible mark on her heart and her soul. One that no matter how far away she traveled, how long she stayed away, or how long she hid from it, had not faded nearly as much as she'd thought.

Despite his feeling toward her, she was very much afraid that she was falling in love with Jack again. She knew the signs just as surely as she knew better than to let it happen.

The sooner she grabbed Nathan and got out of town, the better. Jack knew he had a son now. He could call or write or visit Seattle sometime in the future. Lily was recovering and would be home soon, but she was still a basket case. Yet, Daisy had problems of her own, and she had to get away before her life fell completely apart.

From half a block away, she heard the unmistakable rumble of Jack's Mustang. She looked up and turned her attention to the black car moving toward her. As she stood, the car rolled to a stop at the curb in front of her mother's house. Jack shut the car off then turned to look at her. From across the distance, their gazes met: His angry; hers resigned to his anger. Daisy leaned her head to one side and looked beyond Jack to Nathan. Her son sat in the passenger seat and kept his attention pinned to his lap. He said something, then the two of them exited the Mustang. Both doors shut at the same time, and Jack waited for Nathan at the front of the car. The hot Texas sun baked Daisy's shoulders, and it took every ounce of her self-control to keep her feet planted at the bottom of the steps and not running toward her son.

The two moved up the walk, their strides keeping perfect time with the other. Nathan's hands swung at his sides; his walk, an I'm-fifteen-and-trying-so-desperately-to-be-cool amble. Yet his blue eyes were guarded; he was wondering if he was in trouble or not.

Jack had one hand buried to his knuckles in the front pocket of his Levi's, the other hung loose at his side. As always, he moved as if he were in no hurry to get anywhere in particular.

"Where have you been, Nathan?" she asked when he stopped in front of her. She had to fight the urge to throw her arms around him and tell him everything would be okay. "I've been very worried about you. You know I hate it when you leave and don't tell me when you'll be back."

"We went for a little drive," Jack told her.

A furrow appeared between Nathan's brows and she asked him, "Are you okay?"

"Yeah."

But he didn't look okay. He looked tired and upset, and his cheeks were pink from the heat. "Are you hungry?"

"A little."

"Why don't you go inside and have your grandma fix you something to eat."

He turned to Jack. "I guess I'll see you later."

"Count on it," he said. "I'll call you after I talk to Billy."

"Cool." With his pants riding low on his hips, and his dog chains jingling, Nathan moved up the steps.

"Where did you find him?" Daisy wanted to know as she watched her son shut the door.

"At the high school. He was talking to some girl."

"Where did you take him after that?" She turned to face him. The blazing sun penetrated the thick weave of his hat and shot pinholes of light across his nose and mouth.

"Around."

"Around where?"

He smiled. "Just around."

She placed her hand across her brows and shielded her eyes from the sun. He was really enjoying this. "What did you talk about?"

"Cars."

"And?"

"Him working for me this summer."

"Impossible," she said and waved the notion away with her hand. "We have plans."

"Change them. Nathan says he wants to work for me this summer."

She looked up into his green eyes, surrounded by those long dark lashes of his. "Are you going to tell me that he came up with that all on his own?"

He shook his head and white pinholes of light slid along his top lip. "Doesn't matter who came up with it. It's what we both want."

"We can't stay here all summer." She felt a bead of perspiration slip between her breasts. "I've already been here longer than I intended."

"There's no reason for you stay. In fact, it might be better if you left."

"I'm not leaving my son here with you. You've known him an hour and you've already manipulated him into staying."

"I simply offered Nathan a job helping Billy tear down a Hemi 426. He jumped at it."

She lifted her hands upward. "Of course he did. The child has slept on NASCAR sheets most of his life and had his first car picked out at the age of three. A Porsche 911."

"Jesus!" he swore. "You let my son pick a European piece of shit?"

Under any other circumstance, she might have laughed. "What the heck does it matter?"

"He's a Parrish." He grabbed his hat from his head and rubbed his forehead against his short sleeve. "It matters to us." He ran his fingers through one side of his hair then jammed the hat back on. "If he'd been raised right, he'd know better," he said in a low grumble.

How dare he criticize the way she'd raised Nathan. She may not have always been the best mother, but she'd always tried her best. She'd kill anyone who tried to hurt him.

"If he'd been raised right," Jack continued, "he wouldn't have a ring through his lip and dog chains hanging off him."

Her nerves snapped, and in an instant she forgot all about trying to get along with Jack for Nathan's sake. She no longer cared whether Jack had a right to his anger, he'd just crossed the line and insulted her son. "He's a great kid," she said and poked her finger in Jack's chest. "What's on the outside isn't as important as what's on the inside."

Jack glanced down at her finger then back up into her eyes. "He looks like a hedgehog."

"A lot of boys where we live look like that." She poked him twice more. "Goat-roper!"

His eyes widened then narrowed. He wrapped his hand around hers and removed her finger. "You've turned into a Yankee woman with no manners and a bad accent."

Daisy gasped, and this time she went for the kill. She stood on the balls of her feet and said, "I'll take that as a compliment coming from a second-rate grease monkey."

"You conceited bitch." He grabbed hold of her shoulders like when they were ten years old and fighting over who had the best bike. They cut into each other with words, going at it tooth and nail, and all the while never raising their voices above a low rumble.

"You always did think the sun rose and set on your scrawny butt," he said.

"And you always thought you were God's gift to a pair of jeans." She put her hands on his chest and shoved, but he didn't move at all. "But I'm here to tell you on behalf of all women, what you've got in your jeans isn't that extraordinary."

"You thought so Saturday on the trunk of the Custom Lancer. In fact, you burst into tears because you enjoyed what I've got in my jeans."

"Don't flatter yourself. It'd been a long time. It could have happened with anyone." She smiled, too angry to be embarrassed. "You could have been Tucker Gooch," she added, knowing full well that Jack had always disliked Tucker.

He laughed. "Tucker doesn't have what it takes to make you bawl like you just had a religious conversion."

The front door opened and Louella stuck her head out. "You're putting on quite a show for the neighbors."

Jack let go of Daisy's shoulders and had the grace to look embarrassed. "Good afternoon, Miz Brooks."

"Hello, Jackson. Hot enough for ya?"

"Hotter than a stolen tamale," he said, taking off his hat and exchanging pleasantries as if to show *he'd* been raised right.

"I haven't seen you in a long time."

"No, ma'am."

"How's your brother?"

"He's fine. Thanks for askin'."

"Well, tell him I said hello."

"I'll do that. How've you been, Miz Brooks?"

Daisy sat on the second to the last concrete step. She rested her forehead in her hand and waited for her mother to break into a long-winded story about her near heart failure at having seen Bonnie Lingo's ugly baby. And for once, Daisy was grateful because it would give her time to compose herself.

Instead Louella said, "Well aren't you kind to ask. I'm feeling just fine."

"Glad to hear it, ma'am."

Daisy could almost feel her mother staring a hole in the back of her head. Since she already felt like an idiot for fighting with Jack on the front lawn, she refused to turn around and receive her mother's meaningful glare. "Did Nathan hear us?" she asked.

"No. We couldn't hear you inside, but we did see you two going at it."

"Great," Daisy whispered.

She heard the front door shut behind her mother, and she dropped her hand and looked up at Jack. "We have to get along."

He shook his head. Even with bad-hat hair, he managed to look good. "Not going to happen."

"Then we're going to have to fake it. For Nathan's sake."

"Well, I'll tell you something, buttercup," he said as he stuck his hat back on his head. "I just don't think I'm that good at lying."

His recent lie about a trip to Tallahassee came to mind. "Right."

A frown wrinkled his brows. "Not as good as you, anyway."

She stood on the bottom step and looked into his face. "Do you think Nathan will want to stay here with you knowing that you hate me?" She didn't wait for him to answer. "He likes to act all grown up. He likes to think that I baby him, but the fact is, he still needs me."

The furrow in his forehead smoothed. "Are you saying you're going to let him stay for the summer?"

She didn't think she had a choice. She'd talk to Nathan, and if he really wanted to work in Jack's garage and get to know him, Daisy wouldn't stand in his way. "If that's what he wants—but I won't leave him here alone with you. I left him with relatives in Seattle for less than two weeks, and he couldn't handle it."

She let out a deep breath and thought out loud. "He only brought a backpack full of clothes. I have the one suitcase. Neither one of us would last the summer on what we brought." She was going to have to make a trip home to Seattle to get some of their things.

Jack folded his arms over his wide chest and smiled. He'd won this round and he knew it.

"You have to promise, no more fighting."

"Agreed."

"We have to get along."

"In front of Nathan."

But Daisy wasn't through with him. "You have to pretend to like me."

He tilted his head back and the shadow from his hat slid from his nose, over his lips, to his chin. "Don't push your luck."

Daisy added water to the vase of fresh-cut lilies and returned it to the spot on the stand next to her sister's hospital bed. Daisy disliked the cloying scent of lilies. They reminded her of death. "I'm not going to be here when you go home tomorrow," she said and reached for the vase filled with peach tulips and white roses.

"Are you and Nathan going home?" Lily asked as she reached for the lime Jell-O on her dinner tray.

"Just me, and just for a few days." Daisy moved to the sink and added water to the vase. "It seems we're going to stay the summer." Lily didn't say anything and Daisy looked over her shoulder at her sister. She had a white bandage covering the stitches on her forehead. One eye was black and blue, the other green and yellow. Her top lip was still a little swollen, her left forearm was bandaged and her right ankle and foot were in some sort of traction cast.

"What happened?" Lily finally asked. "Did you tell Jack about Nathan?"

"Not exactly." She set the vase next to the other and sat in a chair beside Lily's bed. "Nathan kind of told him," she answered, then filled her sister in on the rest. "I tried to tell Jack how sorry I am, but he isn't ready to hear it."

Lily turned her head on the pillow and her blue eyes gazed out from all the color on her face. "I'm sorry is just two words, Daisy. They don't mean anything unless you really mean them. Ronnie used to tell me he was sorry every time he cheated, but what he really meant was that he was sorry he got caught again. Sometimes sorry isn't enough."

From outside the room, Dr. Williams was paged to star-line four; inside, Daisy got a real good glimpse into suffering on the other side, from the person feeling the most pain.

"Yes, I know." She wrapped her hands around the wooden arms of the chair. "That's mostly why I've agreed to stay for the summer. I owe Jack. I may have done things for what I thought were the right reasons, but I shouldn't have waited fifteen years to tell Jack about Nathan. I have a lot of guilt about that."

"Don't let guilt make you crazy." Lily set her Jell-O back on the tray. "Remember the night we went to Slim Clem's?"

"Of course."

"I slept with Buddy Calhoun that night."

Daisy was too stunned to speak.

"He came over after I got home and we hooked up. He was real sweet and the sex was great. But after he left, I started to feel guilty, like I was cheating on my marriage. Ronnie had cheated on me for years, left Pippen and me for another woman, and *I* was feeling guilty." She scratched her forehead next to the bandage. "It was crazy, and I got so mad I drove over to his house. He wasn't home, but I drove up and down his street waiting for him, getting madder and madder. I don't remember much after that, but I guess I got so mad, I drove my car into his front room."

"Lily." She stood and walked to the bed. "What are you saying? Not to let guilt make me that insane, or I should probably expect Jack's Mustang to plow through mother's front room?"

"Neither. I don't know. I just know that I want to feel normal again." She pushed the tray away. "Can you scratch my big toe?"

Daisy moved to the end of the bed scratched her sister's toe. Lily's ankle was huge.

"What did you tell the police about the accident?"

"That I was going to see Ronnie about child support and I must have gotten one of my bad migraines and accidently hit the gas instead of the brake."

"They bought it?"

She shrugged. "I went to school with Neal Flegel. He never did like Ronnie very much. He gave me a ticket for failure to control speed. My insurance is paying for the damage to the house, but I'm sure the premiums will go so high I won't be able to drive for a while."

Which Daisy figured was probably a blessing. "Have you given any more thought about counseling?"

"Yeah, I've thought about it. Might not be a bad thing." Lily reached for the controls and lowered the bed. "But I think running my car into Ronnie's put things into perspective for me."

That sounded healthy.

"No man is worth making me feel so bad about myself. When I'm not being crazy, I'm a pretty nice person."

Daisy smiled. "Darn right."

"Ronnie isn't worth spit, let alone worth me."

"Nope."

"I'm going to concentrate on getting better and raising Pippen. I'm over feeling bad about Ronnie. I don't need a man in my life to make me feel important."

"That's true." Lily really did sound as if she were on the road to complete mental health.

"Why should I base my self-worth on a man who counts his hard-ons as personal growth?"

Daisy laughed. "You shouldn't."

Lily pulled off a piece of tape holding a cotton ball to the inside of her elbow. "Men are the scum of the earth and should be killed."

Well, maybe not *complete* mental health.

Chapter 14

Jack watched his son as Billy showed him how to remove the crankshaft from the Hemi 426. Since he'd picked Nathan up at the high school that first day, he'd been trying not to stare. He didn't want to scare the kid again, but after three days of him working in the garage, he was finding it more difficult not to study him. Even with his hedgehog hair and lip ring, Nathan resembled the Parrish side of the family even more than Jack did himself.

Jack rolled up his sleeves, grabbed a socket, and removed the few remaining bolts. He didn't work on actual restoration as much as he used to. Mostly he spent his time making deals or chasing parts all over the country. Running the business side while Billy was in charge of the labor side, but for the last three days, he'd been spending a lot more time in the garage with the mechanics.

"The lobes are retarded," Billy said as he inspected the camshaft. "Just like we thought."

"What does that mean?" Nathan asked.

"It means they're warped," he answered.

"And it means that the valves stay open too long or not long enough and the engine loses power," Jack added.

Nathan looked up at him from across the big V8, and there was a hesitance in his eyes that Jack hated to see there. He kept his gaze on his son as he spoke, "The replacement should be here by the time you and Billy are ready to rebuild."

My son.

Billy handed the shaft to Nathan, and he held it up to study the lobes. "What do we do with this old one?"

"Toss it in the scrap-metal Dumpster I showed you outside," Billy told him.

As Jack watched Nathan move from the garage, his blue coveralls baggy in the butt, he thought he should feel more than he did for the boy. Something more than a lump in his throat and an avid curiosity. He should feel a connection to Nathan. A connection like he'd had with his own father, but he didn't.

Nathan was connecting with Billy, though. He'd watched them work side by side all week. Nathan seemed to feel comfortable with the other mechanics who worked in the garage, too. But around Jack, he was more quiet and reserved.

That night over a bottle of Lone Star in Billy's backyard, he talked to Billy about it.

"I don't think Nathan likes me much," he said as he watched Lacy and Amy Lynn play on the big jungle gym Billy had built for them last summer. It was around seven o'clock and shade from two oaks crept halfway across the lawn to the patio where he and Billy sat. "He seems to like you a lot more than me."

"I think he's just more nervous around you."

The two brothers sat on Adirondack chairs, legs stretched out in front of them, their cowboy boots crossed at the ankles. Jack wore a jean shirt with the arms cut off while Billy had on a wife-beater. Rhonda had taken the baby with her to some sort of makeup party and had left Billy in charge of the older girls.

"I don't know what I can do to make him more comfortable," Jack said as he raised the bottle to his lips and took a drink.

"For starters, you can stop staring daggers at his mother when she comes and picks him up, like you did today."

That afternoon was the first time he'd seen Daisy since they'd had it out in her momma's front yard. She'd been in Seattle for a few days and he hadn't known she was back until she showed up. Just as he hadn't known he looked at her any certain way.

"And when he brings up his dad," Billy continued, "you can quit getting so pissed off."

"Steven isn't his dad." Jack looked at his brother and said, "I never say anything bad about him."

"You don't have to. Whenever Nathan brings him up and you're around, your eyes get hard and you make that sound through your teeth like you're an air hose." Billy sat forward and yelled across the yard. "Lacy, don't walk in front of your sister like that when she's swingin'. She's likely to kick you in the head again."

Jack set his bottle on the arm of the chair. "Does Nathan talk about Steven when I'm not around?"

"Yeah." Billy sat back. "It sounds like before Steven got sick, they used to do a lot together."

Jack caught himself making that air-hose noise Billy was talking about. He was jealous. Jealous of a dead man and jealous of his own brother. He didn't like the feeling one bit.

"I know you're angry, and you have every right, but you need to remember that Nathan loved Steven. Right or wrong, sounds like Steven was a good daddy to him."

"Steven didn't have the right to be good, bad or indifferent. He and Daisy took off together. They got married and kept my son from me for fifteen years."

"Which are you more pissed off about? That Daisy didn't tell you about Nathan, or that she chose Steven and not you all those years ago?"

"That she took Nathan." Of course that was worse, but the two were so connected, he couldn't separate them.

"You look at her like you hate her now, but I saw the way you were looking at her at Lacy's birthday party. You were eye-eatin' her the second you sat down."

Had he? Probably. "I used to have a real thing for her, growing up," he confessed as he watched Amy Lynn jump from the swing and land on her feet.

"I read Steven's letter, and it sounds to me like you *both* had a 'thing' for Daisy Brooks. Sounds like you both loved her."

There was no use denying it. "Since about the eighth grade, I guess. Maybe even before that." As he watched Amy Lynn get back in her swing, he thought back to before the night Steven and Daisy had married. "Being with her was like . . . racing down the old highway pushing a hundred and fifty. You know that feeling you get when you're balls-to-the-wall? Your heart's up in your throat and adrenaline is crawling across your skin and making your hair stand up?"

"Yeah, I know."

"It was like that." Jack shook his head, then reached for his beer. He'd never talked to anyone about Daisy before. "I was crazy about her, but we used to fight a lot. She was so jealous, and I would throw a fit if any other boy even looked at her."

Billy leaned forward in his chair again. "Amy Lynn, don't swing so high." He sat back and said, "Well, you must have made up a time or two or else she wouldn't have ended up pregnant."

Jack recalled with perfect clarity the many times he'd made love to her in the backseat of his car, standing up somewhere with her legs around his waist, or in her bedroom while her mom worked late. "I think we used to fight just so we could make up in the backseat of my Camaro."

"Sounds like teenage hormones," Billy said, looking over at Jack though his clear blue eyes as if things had been that simple.

"It was more than just hormones." He'd been with girls before Daisy, but with her, it had been more than just getting off. Last Saturday on the back of the Custom Lancer proved that she could still make him feel that way. After all these years. Of course, that had been before he'd found out about Nathan. Now all he felt for her was a biting anger. He took a drink, and rested the bottle on the top of his right thigh. "I thought she was it for me. She's all I used to think about."

"If you were in love with her, why did you break up with her?"

"How do you know that I broke up with her?"

"It was in Steven's letter."

"It was?" He recalled little about the letter other than the mention of Nathan. "Mom and dad had just died and I was dealing, or trying to deal, with all of that." He lifted a finger off the bottle and pointed at his brother. "You remember what pure hell that was."

"Sure."

"About that same time Daisy got even more possessive and emotional than usual. It seemed like she was always hanging on my neck, and the more I tried to get her to loosen her grasp, the more she choked me. I just couldn't handle it, so I told her we needed time apart. The next thing I knew, she'd married my best friend."

"Pregnant women get really weird. Believe me, I've been through it three times now."

"I didn't know she was pregnant."

"True. She told Steven and not you because you'd dumped her."

"I didn't dump her." Christ, Billy was starting to piss him off. "I just needed some time to think. If I'd known, I would have done the right thing."

"I know you would have."

Finally, a little support from his family.

"But she felt dumped all the same, and she went to Steven and he helped her out instead of you."

"What the hell? You're my brother. You're supposed to be on my side."

"I am. Always. But you're so angry, I just don't think you can see things clearly, is all. I understand how you feel, but someone needs to point out to you that you had a hand in Daisy marrying Steven."

"Maybe," he conceded for the sake of argument, but he wasn't sure he believed it. "But that doesn't excuse either of them from not telling me about my son. I'll never forgive Daisy for that."

"Well, you know what Tim McGraw says about never?"

He didn't give a shit what Tim McGraw had to say about anything. Tim was married to Faith Hill, and Faith hadn't run off with his babies and kept them a secret for fifteen years.

Billy took a long pull off his beer and told him anyway. "Old Tim says something about the trouble with never is never never works. I think there's some wisdom in that."

And Jack thought Billy needed to slow down on the Lone Star. "I was thinking that maybe I'd grab the boat and take Nathan to Lake Meredith fishing," he said purposely directing the conversation away from Daisy. "Maybe camp out for a night."

"Rhonda and I took the girls and camped out at the lake last summer. We stayed at that Stanford-Yake campsite right there by the marina. It had a real nice comfort station for the girls."

"I don't care how nice the toilets are." Billy cared

because he had to live with four females who'd bitch about it.

"I thought you might want to ask Nathan's momma to come along."

Jack stood and walked across the patio. "What's gotten into you?" He wanted to get to know his son without anyone else around. Now that he knew about his reaction whenever Nathan brought up Daisy or Steven, he could control it. "Are you being contrary just to piss me off?"

Billy laughed and stood also. "No, I just thought Nathan might be more comfortable with her there. He might open up more."

Maybe, but sleeping with Daisy in the same tent was not going to happen. It wasn't even an option. And it had nothing to do with sex and everything to do with him maybe putting a pillow over her head while she slept. He moved to the Rubbermaid garbage can by the side of the house, opened the lid, and tossed the bottle inside. "We'll be okay alone." He secured the lid down tight. "We'll catch some walleye and maybe a few largemouth bass."

"Sounds good."

"Hey, you two," Jack called across the yard. "Get over here and give me some sugar so I can leave."

Lacy slid down the yellow plastic slide, and a few seconds later Amy Lynn jumped off the swing. They both ran across the lawn. Lacy with her head down as usual—Jack knelt on one knee, safely removing his nuts from head-butting level.

Billy moved across the patio and threw away his bottle. "Maybe next week sometime, we should have Nathan over so he can meet his cousins."

"To meet your two yard babies?" Jack asked as he grabbed Lacy and set her on his knee.

"I'm not a yard baby," Amy Lynn protested, but she wrapped her arms around his neck and kissed his cheek.

"What are you, then? A yard bird?"

"What's that?"

"A chicken"

"Nuh-uh."

"Swear to God. That's what your grandma Parrish called chickens. 'Course, she was raised on a farm in Tennessee and they really did have chickens in their yard." He gave Lacy a kiss, then set her back on her feet. He stood with Amy Lynn's arms still around his neck.

"Don't go," she protested.

"Got to." He tickled her armpits and she giggled and dropped to her feet. "I have to make some big fishin' plans."

"You'll have fun," Billy predicted as he scooped up Lacy and followed Jack to the gate at the side of the house. "Nathan's a good kid. You can tell he's being raised right."

Jack glanced over his shoulder at Billy. "You saw the way he looks. That ring though his lip and that hair. Those dog chains and his pants down around the crack of his ass."

"That's the way some kids look today. Doesn't mean he wasn't raised right."

True, but Jack wasn't in the mood to give Daisy credit for anything, especially since Billy seemed determined to play devil's advocate. "When he was three, he wanted a Porsche 911."

Billy stopped dead in his tracks. "He's a Parrish."
Finally, he'd made his point.

Jack raised his hand and knocked twice on Louella Brooks's front door. The sun was beginning to set, washing the porch in dull gray light.

The door swung open and he came face-to-face with Daisy. Her hair was down around her shoulders, kind of messy as if she'd just got out of bed. She wore a pink dress that tied behind her neck and laced up between her breasts. Her feet were bare and she was sexy as hell. A contrary mix of anger and desire pulled low in his abdomen.

"Hi, Jack."

"Hey. Is Nathan around?"

"Nathan left with my mother, but . . ." Her brows lowered and she licked her lips. "What time is it?"

He looked at his watch. "A little after eight."

"Oh. Well, Mom and Nathan went over to Lily's to help her with dinner."

"How's your sister?"

She brushed her fingertips beneath her eyes. "Better. She went home from the hospital two days ago."

"Did I wake you up?"

"I guess I nodded off during 'Frasier' reruns." She gave him a warm, sleepy smile. "Nathan should be back anytime."

"Do you mind if I wait for him?"

"Are you going to be nice?" She drew out the word *niiiiiice*. Daisy Lee had found her accent.

"Reasonably."

She thought about if for a moment, then stepped back. "Come on in."

He followed her through the darkened living room. The technicolor light from the televison flashed white and blue patches across her bare shoulders and back. She led him into the kitchen and flipped the switch.

It had been a long time since he'd been in Louella Brooks's kitchen.

"Would you like something to drink? Tea, Coke, water?" She smiled back over her shoulder at him. "Bourbon?"

"No thanks."

She raked her finger through the top of her hair as she opened the refrigerator and pulled out a blue bottle of water with her free hand. Her fingers combed through her hair to the ends, then she twisted the top off the bottle and knocked the door shut with her hip.

"How was your trip?" he asked.

"It was real sad." The silk strands of her hair slid back in place, and she leaned a shoulder into the refrigerator and looked up at him. "I finally packed up most of Steven's things. Junie came over and got what she wanted. Good Will came and got the rest."

Jack saw the sadness in her brown eyes and told himself he didn't care. She lifted the bottle to her lips and took a long drink. When she lowered it again, a clear drop of water rested on her top lip. "I have some photos for you." The droplet rested there for several long moments before it slid down and disappeared into the seam.

"What photos?" If they were pictures of her and Steven and Nathan living it up in Seattle, then she could keep them.

"The photo taken in the nursery when Nathan was born, of him riding his trike, blowing out birthday candles, playing football. Stuff like that." She held up a finger. "I'll be right back."

He didn't want her to be reasonable. Giving him photos went beyond pretending to be nice in public. He didn't want her to be nice at all. He didn't want to watch crystal drops of water slide between her pink lips. He didn't want to watch her leave, his gaze slipping down her back to her behind and the bottom of the dress where it touched the backs of her thighs.

When she returned, she had a shoe box under one arm. "I have tons of pictures of Nathan; these are just a few that I thought you might like." She carried them to the breakfast nook and took a seat. Jack slid into the seat across from her as she took off the lid to the shoe box. She pulled out a few photos and handed them to him. "This is his hospital picture. He was kind of bruised up because they had to use forceps on him."

Jack gazed down at the photo in his hand of a tiny baby with a bruise on his cheek. His eyes were kind of puffy and his mouth was pursed as if he where about to kiss someone. The next picture was of Daisy as he remembered her looking in high school. Like the day she'd left him. Her hair was big, and she sat in a hospital bed holding a baby wrapped up tight in a striped blanket. His baby boy. His girl. Only by then she hadn't been his anymore.

"I didn't know if you'd want that one because I'm in it," she said, "but I'm in all the pictures taken in the hospital." She dug out a few more. "Any of these you don't want, just leave them with me." This time when she handed the photos over, she leaned across the table. "This was taken on Nathan's first birthday." She pointed to a baby standing on a kitchen chair. He had chocolate cake smeared on his face, clear up into his hair, and he wore a huge grin. The remains of a smashed cake sat on the table in front of him.

"I'd just made his cake and turned my back to wash the dishes," Daisy explained. "When I turned back, he was standing on that chair and had grabbed big hunks of cake. By the time I got my camera, he'd stuffed a bunch in his mouth and rubbed it on the top of his head." Jack laughed and she looked up from the photo and smiled. "He was such a pistol," she said and returned her attention to the picture. His gaze slid to the side of her neck. Her breasts were pressed against the table, pushing her cleavage over the top of her dress. If he leaned forward, he could smell her hair. "That was about the time we had to start locking him in our bedroom," she said.

Jack leaned way back. "Why?"

She straightened. "Because that boy started crawling out of his crib when he was seven months old. We had to get him a little bed that was really low to the ground because we were afraid he'd hurt himself. Then one day, a little after his first birthday, I was making his bed, and under his satin baby pillow, I found three screw drivers." She shook her head. "The only thing I could figure out was that he was roaming around the house after Steven and I fell asleep. So that's when we had to lock him in our bedroom with us."

The three of them all in bed together. One big happy family. It should have been him. It should have been him with her and with Nathan. But she'd chosen Steven.

She should have chosen him. It should have been him in that bed, but the harsh truth was that he couldn't blame her for her choice.

Not anymore. Not when she'd chosen Steven because she'd been eighteen and scared. But being eighteen and scared didn't excuse her from keeping his son from him. He didn't think he'd ever forgive her for that.

She spread some more photos out on the table. "I have a lot of photographs of Nathan through the years. He's my favorite subject. I have some really nice black-and-whites of him that I took a few years ago when we went climbing around the rocks at the bottom of Snoqualmie Falls. Black and white just balanced everything around him beautifully." Her lips turned up at the corners. "Color would have been too overwhelming, and he would have been lost in the shot."

"You sound like you know a lot about taking pictures." He had one of those auto-everything cameras, and still forgot to bring it to the girls' parties.

"I'm a photographer. It's what I used to do for a living."

He hadn't known that about her. Didn't know very much about her life in Seattle, as a matter of fact.

"It's what I plan to do again. I'm going to open my own studio. I've been checking into small business loans, and I talked to a realtor about leasing a space in Belltown, which is in the downtown area." She dug through the box and handed him more photos. "It's going to be a little scary at first, but with the money I get from selling our house, and the money I received from Steven's life insurance policies, we'll be okay."

She was moving on with her life. Moving forward while he felt as if he were firmly stuck in the past. Unable to move.

Louella walked into the kitchen with Nathan trailing behind, wearing even more chains than usual and a black T-shirt with a skateboarder on the front.

Daisy slid from behind the table and moved to meet them. "Nathan, Jack came over to talk to you."

Nathan's gaze met his over the top of Daisy's head. Jack set the photo on the table and stood. He turned his attention to Daisy's mother. She had blue smudges beneath her eyes and her hair listed left. "Good evening, Miz Brooks."

"Evening, Jackson."

"How are you?"

"I've felt better," she said. "Lily insists that she stay at her own home when it would be better if she stayed here." She set her big black purse on the counter and moved to stand a few feet in front of him. "Last year Tiny Barnett's youngest girl, Tammy, had woman trouble and had to have surgery. Did you hear what happened to her?"

Jack wasn't sure Louella was speaking to him. She was looking at him, but he didn't know anyone named Tiny Barnett or her daughter Tammy.

Evidently a reply wasn't necessary, though. "She died because she went home from the hospital early."

"Mom," Daisy said on a sigh, "Lily isn't going to die."

"That's what Tammy thought too. Left behind a little boy about Pippen's age. Left a husband too. He was a Yankee fella from one of those eastern states, and when Tammy made her heavenly journey, he packed up that baby and left. Tiny hasn't seen hide nor hair of him since. And Tiny is a good woman. She's stuck with Horace Barnett all these years. And everyone knows that man was born tired and raised lazy. I don't think he ever did work a job for more than a month straight."

She paused and it all came back to Jack in a flash. The reason he and Steven usually waited on the porch for Daisy. Fifteen years, and she hadn't changed. Louella Brooks could still talk water up hill.

"And he had that mentally retarded sister, bless her heart. She used to come by the diner and order gizzards, every now and again. I used to think that . . ."

Jack felt a pressure in the back of his skull and looked behind Louella to Daisy and Nathan. They stood in profile, Nathan a few inches taller than his mother. He stared down at Daisy, his narrowed gaze communicating something. Daisy shrugged as if to say, "What do you want me to do?" While Louella rambled on about gizzards and chicken fried steak, Daisy and Nathan carried on a whole conversation without saying a word. Mother and son.

Nathan rocked back on his heels and slashed his finger across his throat. Daisy covered her mouth with her hand and started shaking her head. They were a family. Just the two of them. Comfortable with each other. Relaxed. He wasn't a part of it.

As if she felt his gaze on her, Daisy looked at Jack, then she burst into laughter.

"Goodness, Daisy. What's gotten into you?" Louella asked as she turned to look at her daughter.

"Just thought of something that happened today." She brushed her hair behind her ears and said, "Jack came over to talk to Nathan, so maybe we should leave them to it."

"Actually, I was hoping that you and Nathan could walk me out to my car."

"Cool."

"Sure."

He turned his attention to Louella. "Good evening, ma'am. Give Lily my best the next time you see her."

"I will."

The three of them walked through the living room and out the front door, with Jack bringing up the rear.

"Why didn't you stop her?" Nathan asked as soon as the door was shut behind them.

They moved from the porch and down the sidewalk. The setting sun filled the night sky with blazing reds and oranges, fading in the distance to pink and purple. It seemed to catch in strands of Daisy's hair, turning it gold.

"No one can stop your grandmother once she gets started," Daisy answered.

"All the way home from Lily's she would *not* stop talking about someone named Cyrus."

"Cyrus is your great uncle who died when he was fourteen, bless his heart."

"And I give a crap because why?"

"Nathan!"

Jack chuckled.

"Don't encourage his bad behavior, Jack," she said as they came to the end of the sidewalk.

"Wouldn't dream of it." He turned to his son. "How do you feel about fishing?"

He shrugged. "My dad and I used to fish all the time."

Jack forced a smile. "I'm going bass fishing this weekend, and I wanted you to come along. I thought we'd leave Saturday morning and come back sometime Sunday."

Nathan looked at Jack then turned to his mother.

"We don't have plans this weekend. Go ahead. You'll have fun."

Nathan didn't say anything and Jack spoke to cover the silence. He opened his mouth and heard himself say, "Daisy why don't you come along too?" And he couldn't believe it. The pressure in the back of his skull moved up and squeezed his brain. He'd just done the one thing that he'd gotten mad at Billy for even suggesting.

All he could do now was hope like hell she refused.

Chapter 15

A slight breeze rippled across the surface of Lake Meredith while sunlight reflected off the water like bits of tinfoil. Birds circled overhead, fish jumped, and the heavy bass guitar and hard drum beats of Godsmack pounded the air like a fist.

Daisy sat cross-legged in the front of Jack's boat and gazed at Nathan through the lens of the Fuji digital camera she'd brought with her when she'd returned from Seattle. She wore her white one-piece swimsuit beneath a red tank top and jean shorts. A big straw hat shielded her face from the sun.

Nathan brought his pole back to cast and she snapped his picture. He wore a ball cap, the bill curved low on his forehead and just above his silver and black Oakley sunglasses. His khaki shorts rode low on his behind and showed his red and white striped boxers. He wore skater shoes without socks.

His cheeks were very pink, and he'd taken off his T-shirt although she'd warned him against it.

"You treat me like a baby," he'd complained like a baby. But he gave in and allowed her to rub him down with sun screen.

She turned her camera on Jack, who stood across the stern from Nathan fishing from the opposite side of the boat. He'd pushed his straw cowboy hat low on his forehead and wore a pair of sunglasses with mirrored blue lenses. His old green T-shirt was worn around the neck and the short sleeves fit loose around the hard mounds of his biceps. Earlier he'd caught her staring at the little hole in the shoulder, and he'd told her it was his lucky fishing shirt. A pair of faded Levi's hugged his hips and thighs. The edge of the waistband was slightly frayed, and the five-button fly cupped his package in soft faded denim. She wondered how much luck those pants brought him. Probably a lot. On his feet he wore cowboy boots. What else?

He glanced across his shoulder at her and she snapped his picture. Irritation wrinkled his brow before he turned his attention back to his line. She didn't know if he was irritated because she was taking his picture or because Godsmack had just said the F-word again. Although, she'd certainly heard him throw that word around. *I'm going to fuck you till you faint* came to mind.

He'd picked her and Nathan up that morning driving a white Dodge Ram truck. To her surprise, it wasn't "vintage." It was fairly new and pulling a twenty-one-foot bass boat. When he'd asked her and Nathan the other day if they wanted to go fishing, she'd envisioned an aluminum boat with a little putt-putt motor. She should have known better. Jack wasn't the kind of guy to have a putt-putt anything.

The gray-and-red boat had dual consoles with seats that looked better suited for a race car. A third fishing chair was perched in the back by the huge outboard engine. Below the clock on the wood-grain console was the CD player. Earlier as they'd set up camp, Nathan and Jack made a deal. They would alternate music. Jack went first and then Nathan. The problem was that Jack had a human-sized CD case, while Nathan had a case about the size of the New York phone book. They were in for a ground-thumping few days.

Nathan caught the first fish. A twelve-inch Walleye that brought the first real joy she'd seen on his face in a long time. Jack netted it for him and helped him remove the hook. With their head bent over the fish, Daisy snapped a few pictures. She was too far away and the music was too loud for her to hear what they said to each other, but when Nathan tipped back his head and laughed, Daisy felt it in her chest. The pang in her heart wasn't solely due to the pleasure of her son's laughter, though. It was Jack too. He was reaching out to Nathan. Trying to make a connection with his son, and for some reason that Daisy didn't understand, she felt herself fall a little more in love with him. Not the fast wham-bam love of adolescence. Not the flash of heat and fire like a lightning bolt, which she'd once tried and failed to grasp in the palm of her hand. This was easier. A gentle beat against her heart, a soothing *ahh* in her chest, which scared her more than the first time

she'd fallen for him. This love was more mature. She
was more mature, and she knew exactly what to do
about it.

Absolutely nothing.

Matt Flegel had called her the other night and
asked her to dinner. It had been so long since a man
had asked her out; she'd been shocked. She'd sput-
tered something about contacting him once she returned from her camping trip. At the time, she
hadn't really wanted to go. Now she wondered if it
wasn't a good idea. Something to take her mind off
Jack and her feelings for him.

She snapped another picture and watched Jack
through her lens as he returned to his fishing pole
and picked it up. The sun glinted off the silver reel as
the spool spun around and around. The movement
of his hands and arms was smooth and precise, and
his boots were planted a shoulder's width apart.
The CD player shut off and she could hear the soft
tick-tick-tick of his reel. Her heart picked up its soothing pace and she clicked his photo.

White sunlight poured over one side of him while
the shade of his hat slashed across his nose and
mouth. He brought in the line and reached up to
pull a weed from the hook. Then in one fluid motion, he flipped the bale with his thumb, flung the
tip of the pole straight out to his side, then whipped
it forward again. His lure sailed across the water as a
breeze bowed the line, catching it on a current like a
spider web, suspending it in air for a few short moments before the lure hit the water with a *kerplunk*
and pulled the line down with it.

She lowered her camera and looked away. She

couldn't hide behind her lens from either her feelings or his. Jack hated her, and he'd never forgive her. He'd made that perfectly clear. Around her, he was very guarded, and she didn't even know why he'd asked her to come along on this fishing trip. He acted like she was a necessary evil, like bug spray. She was leaving at the end of the summer, and she probably wouldn't see him again until next year. There was no future for her and Jack, except that at some point she hoped it would be possible for them to be friends again.

She wasn't going to hold her breath, though.

She was making a future for herself and Nathan a thousand or so miles away in Washington. She'd talked to Nathan about selling their house, and he was okay with it. He'd been sad, like she was. The house held as many good memories as bad, but he liked the idea of moving into a loft in Belltown even if it meant a change in schools. She'd already called a realtor, a friend of Junie's, and put the house on the market. Junie had always had an extra key, so she arranged to give a copy to the realtor.

Daisy was definitely getting on with her life now. She'd never been on her own before. Never solely responsible for all decisions. She was scared. And if she thought about it too much, she got little anxiety attacks, but she knew things would be okay.

It was well past noon and everyone was hungry by the time they made it back to camp. While the boys cleaned the fish they'd caught, Daisy set the picnic table with a red-and-white checkered cloth and red plastic plates and utensils.

When she spoke with Jack the night before, she insisted that they split the meals. He was in charge of dinner. She wondered if he'd pull out a package of hotdogs and a bag of chips and call it good.

She set a roasted chicken, salad, and a loaf of rye bread on the table. By the time she'd sliced the chicken and added dried pieces of fruit and raspberry dressing to the salad, Nathan and Jack were walking from the shore toward her. Nathan had put on his shirt and he carried his ball cap. His hair was sweaty and smashed to his head. She couldn't help but notice that when Nathan forgot to act cool, he moved a lot like Jack did. More easy and relaxed. Jack took off his sunglasses and brushed the side of his face against the shoulder of his lucky T-shirt— which had proved to be lucky once again, since he'd caught two smallmouth bass and a crappie.

"I'm going to change and be right back," he said as he tossed his hat and glasses on the table. He moved toward the four-man tent they'd pitched beneath a cottonwood tree. "Watch out for faaar ants," he warned, drawing out the vowels. "I saw a nest of 'em over by the toilets." He grabbed a fistful of his shirt and pulled it over his head as he threw the tent flap back.

"Mom," Nathan called to her.

Daisy pulled her gaze from the tent and the fleeting glimpse of Jack's bare back, the smooth planes and indent of his spine, the sliver of the white elastic just above the bluer waistband of his jeans . . . "Hmm?"

"What's a faaar ant?" he asked just above a whisper.

"Fire." She chuckled and shook her head. "Fire ant. They have a nasty bite that burns."

Nathan smiled. "Well, why didn't he just say fire?"

"He thinks he did." She placed some chicken and salad on a plate and handed it to Nathan. She'd brought a Thermos of ice tea, and she put ice in three red Dixie Cups and poured. "Are you having a good time?" she asked her son.

Nathan sat and shrugged in that way of his that could have meant anything. "I guess." Then he grinned and drawled like a Texan, "I'm gonna catch my limit if it harelips the governor."

"Just don't get bit by faaar ants," she warned him.

Nathan tipped back his head and laughed a steady *heh-heh-heh.*

"What are y'all laughing about?" Jack asked as he walked toward them, closing the snaps on his shirt. It was beige, cowboy cut, with the arms hacked off.

"Nathan says he's going to catch his limit if it harelips the governor."

Jack looked up and his green gaze touched Daisy's face from across the table. "Damn straight." He grabbed a plate and placed a few pieces of chicken on it. "What is that?" he asked as he looked into the salad bowl.

"Salad."

He scowled. "It looks like chick food. Like flower petals, weeds, and leathery fruit chunks."

Nathan laughed and Daisy frowned at him. "It's very good."

"I'm going to take your word on that." He put three pieces of bread on his plate and then looked across the table at her. "Butter?"

"You still eat butter?" She hadn't used butter in so long, it hadn't occurred to her to pack any. "I have cream cheese."

He shook his head and walked away. He moved to the back of his truck, lowered the tailgate and rummaged around in his cooler. When he returned, he had a stick of butter. He unwrapped the stick then set it on the table. "You've been living up North too long, Daisy Lee." He pulled a pocket knife out of his front pocket and made wafer-thin pats. "Do you want some of this?" he asked Nathan.

Nathan nodded and Jack stabbed a few thin pats with the knife, then handed it over to him. Nathan laid them out on his rye bread and paused a moment to eye the knife before he handed it back.

"How about you, Daisy?"

"When was the last time you cleaned that knife?"

"Hmm." He finally sat down and pretended to think a moment. "Last . . . no, the year before last. It was right after I used it to gut an armadillo."

Nathan laughed as he took a big bite of his bread.

She was sure he was lying. Well, almost sure. "No thanks," Daisy answered.

"Pansy-ass," he said right before he sank his teeth into his bread covered in little squares of yellow butter.

She took a big bite of her salad. "Scardy-cat. Afraid of a little arugula and raspberry dressing."

"Hell, yeah," he said as thin creases appeared in the corners of his green eyes. "If a man eats stuff like that, the next thing he knows, he's wearing pink and tying a sweater around his neck."

Nathan held up his hand and Jack gave him five.

"I thought you liked my raspberry salad."

"No," Nathan said. "I'm hungry."

Daisy didn't believe him. Jack was turning him into a traitor. A guy just like him.

"So what did you bring for dinner?" she asked.

Jack used his armadillo-gutting knife to cut his chicken. "Wild rice."

"That's it?"

"No, I brought some real lettuce and some bleu cheese dressing."

"We're having wild rice and salad?"

He stared across the table at her as if she couldn't possibly be so dense. "And the fish."

"You were that sure you'd catch our dinner, that you didn't bring anything else?"

"Hell, yeah. I wore my lucky shirt."

Daisy turned her attention to Nathan, who was highly amused.

Jack took a long drink of tea then set the glass on the table. "I coat the fish in flour, then fry 'em up."

"Sounds good," Nathan said.

Jack lifted a finger off his red plastic glass and pointed at his son. "It's the kind of meal that'll put hair on a guy's tea bag."

Her confusion must have shown on her face because Nathan cleared things up for her. "Gonads."

Gee, she probably could have gone all weekend without knowing that. "But," Daisy said weakly, "I'm not a guy."

"And you don't have a tea bag," her son pointed out needlessly.

She shook her head and placed a hand on her chest. "And I sincerely don't want a tea bag. Ever."

"That's what they all say before they try it," Jack said through a grin, then he and Nathan busted up laughing as if they got some secret joke that she didn't.

As she looked across the table at her son laughing, she felt left out. Left out of the guy club, but this was what she wanted, wasn't it? Since she'd flown down here weeks ago? Jack and Nathan to get to know each other? For Nathan to know his real father? Tea bag and gutting knife and all?

Yes, but not at her expense. She didn't want to be excluded. She wanted to be a part of the tea bag club, too. It wasn't fair to be excluded because she didn't have the right equipment. Growing up, Jack had used the same tactic to exclude her from a lot of things.

"I know what you're doing, Jack," she said.

He looked at her.

"You're trying to exclude me like you and Steven used to when you didn't want me around."

His brows lowered but his smile stayed in place. "What are you talking about, buttercup?"

"Remember when you excluded me from your television club. You made a rule that in order to be a member, I had to pee on a tree while standing."

"I remember that, but I don't remember anything about a television."

She thought a moment. "It was the CBS club or something like that."

He thought a moment, then said, "Ahh. You mean the NBBC. I forgot about that." He grinned. "You thought that was a televison club?"

"Of course."

He shook his head and chuckled. "Honey, that was the Nekkid Boobs and Butts Club. It's where we got together and looked at porn."

"Sweet."

"You guys had porn? You were in the sixth grade, for cryin' out loud." She was appalled. "You were little pervs and I didn't even know it."

His grin told her that she didn't even know *the half* of it.

Chapter 16

*A*fter lunch, Daisy dragged a chaise longue to the shore and dropped her shorts. She wore sunglasses and her white one-piece swimming suit, cut high on the hips. It had a built-in bra top and thin straps. The boys had gone fishing again, and she'd opted to stay behind. She pulled out the latest issue of *Studio Photography & Design* and stretched out on the chaise. She read an article on the Hasselblad V-System and dreamed about the spectacular photographs she could take with it. Then she must have fallen asleep for real, because she dreamed she'd won first place in a Kodak photography contest and she hadn't even entered. She dreamed she was up on stage, bluffing her way through a speech about a photograph she didn't remember taking, and Steven was in the front row watching.

She dreamed about him often, and in her dreams, he always appeared as he had before his illness.

Healthy and happy and she was always glad to see him. He never spoke, he just gave her a smile that let her know that he was okay, and that she was okay too.

The sound of an outboard engine woke her up and she opened her eyes. Her sunglasses where still on her face, but the trade magazine had slipped to the ground. She sat up and wondered how long she'd been asleep. She swung her feet to the side and took off her sunglasses. The sun was definitely lower, although it would be a long time before it set. Her tan skin had a twinge of red; she would pay for falling asleep in the Texas sunlight.

She tossed her glasses and the magazine on the chair then stood. She moved toward the shore as Jack's boat came toward her, parting the water with its pointed nose. Daisy raised a hand to her forehead and shielded her eyes from the sun. Jack stood at the bow; his cowboy shirt unsnapped, the edges fluttering against his bare chest and stomach. Nathan sat in the driver's seat, his intent gaze on Jack.

"Turn it off and raise the motor," Jack called out.

Nathan looked down and the sound of the engine got louder as it rose out of the water, then it stopped. The boat drifted closer and gently bumped into the shoreline.

Jack looked over his shoulder as he spoke to Nathan, telling him what a great job he'd done. He turned back and went down on one knee to grab a rope tied to the front of the boat.

"You got sunburned while we were gone," Jack said as he slowly raised his gaze to hers.

Daisy looked down at herself. She pressed her fingers to her chest above her suit. Her fingertips left white prints on her pink skin. "I fell asleep."

He dropped the anchor over the side of the boat into shallow water, then he jumped down from the bow and stood in front of her, blocking the sun. "You burned your love bite."

Again she glanced down at herself. Visible just above the top of her swimsuit, her birthmark was a little darker than the rest of her skin. "What are you doing staring at my birthmark?"

The corners of his mouth slid upward into a slow, sexy grin. "Just making casual conversation, buttercup," he drawled.

Asking about her love bite wasn't casual. The last time he'd commented on it, they'd both been naked. The heated look in his eyes told her he was remembering that time too.

Daisy swallowed passed the sudden lump in her throat. She lowered her gaze from his mouth, past the thin line of hair that ran down his chest and flat stomach to his navel. She recalled perfectly what his skin felt like beneath her palms.

"Mom, guess what?"

Daisy returned her gaze to Jack's, to the desire he tried but failed to hide. "What?"

"I caught a bigmouth bass." Nathan jumped from the boat and landed next to Jack.

"It's a beauty," Jack confirmed and his gazed dropped to her mouth.

She turned her attention to her son. Whatever was between her and Jack was best left alone. "Show me."

Nathan jumped back up on the bow of the boat,

then moved to the stern. Daisy walked passed Jack and waded into the water up to her hips. She held on to the outside of the boat as Nathan opened the live well and pulled out a stringer.

Jack watched his son as he held up the bass for his mother. It swung close to Daisy's face and she jumped back.

"You're such a girl," Nathan said through a teasing laugh.

Jack turned and moved up the shore toward camp. He and Nathan had had a good time fishing. He felt closer to his son than he had before they'd come to the lake. While they fished, Nathan had talked about his life, and Steven had been a big part of that life.

"Before I quit, I was quarterback on my Optimist football team," he'd told Jack. "My dad told me you guys played football growing up."

His dad. Jack had been very careful not to show the slightest emotion. "We did," he'd said past the bitter taste in his mouth. "I played quarterback until I quit my junior year."

Nathan had nodded. "That's what dad said. He said you had to quit to work for your dad, and that's how he got to be quarterback his last two years of school and get all the good lookin' girls."

"Your dad was a pretty smooth guy. He never had any problems with the girls." The longer they talked about Steven, the easier it got. The easier it was to swallow the bitterness. Jack remembered what it was like to lose a father—the confusion and the loneliness. For a few hours, he was able to forget about anger and betrayal and talk to Nathan about what it had been like to grow up with Steven Monroe.

In the end, he was surprised to discover the more he talked about Steven, the more he got to know Nathan. And the more he got to know his son, the more he wanted to know. He still didn't feel like a father, although he wasn't even sure what a father was supposed to feel like.

Jack poured some water into a basin and washed his fishy hands with liquid soap. He glanced up as Nathan tore off his shoes and shirt and jumped into the lake next to Daisy. She hollered his name as he splashed her.

It was very clear to Jack how Nathan felt about his mother. He might bitch that she babied him, but he loved her. He might have hedgehog hair and a ring through his lip, but Billy was right. Daisy and Steven had done a good job raising Nathan. He was a good kid.

And Jack had nothing to do with it. He grabbed a towel and dried his hands. He tried not to let the bitterness he'd hidden from Nathan rise up and eat a hole in him. He succeeded in keeping it tapped down, right next to the burning ache in his gut that wanted Daisy Lee so bad it was driving him half crazy.

How could he still want her? Want to touch her as he sealed his mouth to hers? To feel the golden strands of her hair tangled around his fingers and the warmth of her skin against his palms? To smell her neck and to look into her brown eyes as he made love to her? How could he want that and at the same time want to shake her and hurt her as much as she'd hurt him? It didn't make a bit of sense to him.

Jack hung the towel on one shoulder and watched Nathan dive at Daisy. She screamed and he pulled her under. Jack smiled despite himself. Daisy had a way of making him laugh when he didn't want to. Of making him remember things that brought a smile to his lips before he even realized what she was doing. Of reminding him that they'd had a lot of good times together in the past, before things had gotten so fucked up.

If he closed his eyes, he could remember back to what she felt like in his arms. The weight of her body as she leaned into him. The texture of her hair as he rested his chin on the top of her head. The sound of her voice saying his name in anger or in ecstasy. The tastes and textures of Daisy Lee. He remembered it all and wished like hell he didn't.

Jack started charcoal burning in the fire pit and got out a cookstove. He put some Jimmy Buffet on the portable CD player and mixed flour, salt and pepper for the fish. While Jimmy sang about fins circling around, Jack couldn't seem to keep his eyes off a certain white swimsuit jumping around and diving into the lake. Coming back up and looking almost transparent, but not quite.

When he and Nathan had returned this last time, Jack had stood on the bow of the boat and watched her walk toward the water. Toward him, looking like she was an underwear model wearing one of those one-piece teddies that was cut up real high on her hips. Sexy as hell. Like a living, breathing wet dream. And for a few seconds he'd wondered what it would be like if this was really his life. To return from a day out with his son and have Daisy waiting for them. To grab her up and hold her against him. To touch her all he wanted. Anytime he wanted. Anywhere he wanted. For a few brief seconds, the thought of that life nearly sent him to his knees.

But that was not his life. Not reality, and he had no business even thinking about it.

Jack rolled the fish in the flour, then started the rice on the cookstove. Daisy and Nathan returned from the lake and took turns changing in the tent. When Daisy emerged, she wore a soft blue pullover sweat shirt with GAP on the front, matching sweat pants, and white Nikes with a blue swoosh. Her hair was pulled back in one of those claw things. She set the picnic table while Jack cooked the fish in a skillet over the coals. They ate dinner together like a family. Talking and laughing. Jack had to remind himself that it wasn't real.

After dinner they played poker with wooden matchsticks. When it got dark, Jack got out the lanterns and they played until Nathan yawned and announced that he was going to bed.

"It's early," Jack pointed out and tossed in his cards.

"I'm a tired camper," he said as he headed toward the tent.

"He does this sometimes. A few days ago, he went to bed right after dinner and slept clear through till breakfast," Daisy informed Jack as she gathered the cards and stuck them in the box. "I think he's growing so fast, he just gets worn from the inside out."

Jack rose and moved out of the pool of light to his truck. He grabbed his jean jacket out of the cab, then walked to the fire pit. Stars crammed the big Texas sky as he stirred the coals. He threw a few logs in the pit and took a seat in one of the folding chairs he'd placed around the pit. He stretched his legs out in front of him and watched the wood catch fire. He thought about their sleeping arrangements and wondered if he should have borrowed another tent from Billy. Sleeping in the same tent wasn't going to be easy. Jack had never slept in such close proximity to a woman when they both weren't naked. This would be a first, and thank God Nathan would be between him and Daisy. Because lately his thoughts were definitely carnal where she was concerned, and he'd hate to fall asleep and wake up face-first in her cleavage.

"It's been a long time since Nathan and I got to get away and just relax," Daisy said and sat in a chair next to him. "Thanks, Jack."

"You're welcome." He threaded his fingers together over his stomach, crossed his booted ankles, and pushed all thoughts of Daisy's cleavage from his brain. The fire cracked and popped. In between comfortable silences, Daisy told him more about her plans to sell the house she'd shared with Steven, and more about opening her own photography studio. She was ready to get on with her life and eager to start.

They talked about Billy and his family, and she filled him in on the latest with Lily. Lily's divorce was to be final in a few days. According to Daisy,

Lily was finally getting herself together. Jack had his doubts, but he didn't mention them.

"Being back here in Texas brings back a lot of memories for me," Daisy said. "Most of them good." He could feel her gaze on him and he looked across his shoulder at her. Firelight danced in her hair and across her face. It touched her mouth and drew his gaze to her lips. "Remember when you and I and Steven made that time capsule out of a coffee can and buried it in your backyard?" she asked.

Yeah, he remembered that, but he shook his head and glanced up at the sky crammed with stars in the inky black night. He hoped she'd let it drop. He should have known better.

"We put our most valuable treasures in a coffee can, and we were supposed to dig it up in fifty years."

She laughed and Jack returned his gaze to her profile.

"I can't remember what I put in there." She thought a moment then snapped her fingers. "Oh, yeah. A fake diamond ring you'd won for me at the fair. A pink fuzzy barrette Steven had found someplace and given me. You put some Matchbox cars in there, and Steven put some of those green army men." She looked over at him and a frown creased her brow. "There had to be more."

"Your diary," he said.

"That's right." She started to laugh, but it died on her lips. "How did you remember that?"

He just shrugged and rose to stir the logs on the fire. "Good memory, I guess."

"Did you dig it up?" He didn't answer and she moved to stand next to him. "Jack?"

He pushed a log with the toe of his boot. It snapped and shot red embers up into the darkness. "Me and Steve."

"When?" she asked.

"About a week after we buried it. We had to know what was in your diary. It was killing us."

She gasped. "You guys invaded my privacy. Abused my trust. You were horrible!"

"Yep, and as I recall, your diary was boring as hell. Steven and I thought we were going to read all kinds of juicy stuff. Like who you had a crush on or if you'd kissed a boy. Or what really goes on at those girly slumber parties you were always going to." He shoved his hands in the front pockets of his Levi's and shifted his weight to one foot. "As I recall, it was mostly filled with stuff about your damn cat."

"Mr. Skittles?" Her mouth fell open and she grasped his arm through his jacket and turned him to face her. "You read my private thoughts about Mr. Skittles?"

"I hated that cat. Every time I walked into your house, he hissed at me."

"That's because he could tell you were up to no good."

Jack laughed and looked down into her face as the firelight danced across her cheeks and nose. Where Daisy Lee was concerned, he'd always been up to no good. He grabbed her hand to remove it from his jacket, but he held it instead. "You don't even know the half of it."

"Sylvia told me she showed you her bottom in the fifth grade."

He had seen quite a few bottoms by the fifth grade. "It wasn't as good as yours." He brought her hand to his mouth and pressed a kiss to her knuckles. He looked into her eyes. "Your bottom was always the best."

She blinked once and her lids lowered to half-mast. Her lips parted. She wanted him every bit as much as he wanted her. It would have been so easy to slide his other hand behind her head and bring her mouth to his. Desire twisted in his groin and urged him to grab her up and hold her against him. He dropped her hand.

"I've missed you, Jack," she said. "I didn't even realize how much until I came back." She took a step forward and raised onto the balls of her feet. She ran her palms up his jacket to the sides of his neck. "Did you ever miss me?" She placed her soft lips against his, then asked, "Even a little?"

He stood completely still, staring into her dark eyes. His chest burned as he breathed in her exhaled breath.

"Even when you didn't want to miss me?"

The dull throb of desire settled heavy in his groin, and he grabbed her shoulders and pushed her away. "Don't do this, Daisy."

She looked up at him. "Matt Flegel asked me out."

Shit. "Bug?"

"He never liked when you called him that."

"Are you going to go out with him?"

"Do you care?"

He looked right into her eyes and answered as if he didn't want to punch Flea in the face. "No. I don't care what you do."

"Then I'll probably go out with him." She turned on her heels and bid him goodnight over her shoulder as if she hadn't just tried to kiss him and get something going. He watched her disappear into the tent and he turned back to the fire.

She could do whatever she wanted, he told himself as he took a seat. So could he. He hadn't had sex since he'd had it with her on the back of the Lancer. Maybe that was his problem. Maybe he needed to get laid to get her out of his head.

He waited until the coals burned to ash before he entered the tent. When his eyes adjusted to the darkness, he discovered that Nathan had taken the sleeping bag on the far side, which left Daisy asleep in the middle. What she thought of sleeping so close to Jack, he didn't know. She seemed okay with it because she was out.

Jack took off his boots and jacket and crawled into his sleeping bag. He put his hands behind his head and stared up at the ceiling of the tent. He could almost hear her breathing. Almost hear a soft hush of breath pass her lips.

He turned his head and looked at her through the darkness. Her back was to him and her blond hair spilled across her pillow. He'd made love to her. He'd made a child with her, but he'd never spent the night with her. Never seen her sleep.

His last thoughts as he fell asleep were of her, wondering what she'd do if he hooked his arm around her waist and pulled her into his chest.

When he woke, the ceiling of the tent was awash in predawn light. He figured he'd gotten about five hours as he grabbed his jean jacket, shoved his feet in his boots, and headed out of the tent. Early morning shadows clung to the campground and the buttes surrounding the lake. He built a fire and put coffee on to percolate. The sun rose over the water as he poured his first cup. Nathan was the first to join him. His son's hair stuck straight up in back, and he wore a big blue sweat shirt, jeans and his sneakers. Nathan grabbed a bottle of juice and a bag of Chips Ahoy and the two of them walked to the shore.

"Today before we leave," Jack said as he blew into his coffee, "we'll go after some channel cats."

"My dad and I went deep-sea fishing once." Nathan ripped open the bag and held it toward Jack, offering him a cookie. "Have you ever done that?"

"Thanks." Jack took one chocolate-chip cookie and bit into it. "I try to fish in the Gulf at least once a year. Next time I go, maybe you can come along."

"Tight." Nathan stuck the bag under one arm and polished off two cookies before he spoke again. "My dad and I used talk about stuff."

Jack took a drink and looked out over the lake, at the morning sun lighting up the surface like glass. He wondered if Daisy had told him that she had a hot date with Flea. It wasn't his place to ask. "What kind of stuff?"

"Stuff a guy can't talk to his mom about."

"Like?" he asked and ate his cookie.

"Girls."

Ah. "Do you have something on your mind?"

Nathan nodded and took a drink of his juice.

"Maybe I can help you out. I've known a girl or two."

He looked at his toes and his cheeks turned pink. "Girls are complicated. Boys aren't that complicated."

"That's true. Girls are contrary as hell. They tell you one thing and expect you to get the meaning to something else."

He turned and looked up at Jack. "You said you and dad used to look at porn. So, what I want to know is . . ." He blinked a few times then asked, "Where do you touch girls? I saw a diagram in health class, but it was confusing. Boys aren't confusing. Everything we have is just hanging out there."

Whoa. "We're not talking about a girl's emotions are we?"

He shook his head. "My friend stole his mom's book about sex. It sounds like you have to touch a girl everywhere at once."

Nathan looked so serious. And he'd come to Jack. Not Daisy. "Any girl in particular you're thinking about touching?"

"No. I'd just like to have it all figured out before my first time."

"You want to be an expert right out of the chute?" Jack thought Nathan was a little young to be worrying about sex. Then he thought back to the NBBC and he realized Nathan wasn't too young at all.

"Well, yeah. It's going to be scary enough the first time without worrying about sucking at it."

Jack rocked back on his heels and weighed his words. He really didn't want to screw this up. Warmth spread through him and tightened his chest like a fist around his heart. Suddenly, for the first time in his life, he felt like a dad. His son had come to him with questions about sex, just like countless other sons had gone to their fathers. Just like he had. "The first thing you have to know is that any fool can have sex, but it takes a real man to make love. If you don't feel something for a girl, then you have no business unzipping your pants."

"Yeah."

"You have to wear a condom. Always. If you're not mature enough to protect yourself and the female, then you're not mature enough to have sex." As he spoke, he wondered if Nathan got the irony of this conversation. He waited for him to point out that Jack hadn't always practiced what he was preaching, and he took a drink of his coffee as he figured out a good response. He'd obviously have to admit that he hadn't always been responsible, but that—

"I know about safe sex," Nathan said, interrupting Jack's thoughts.

Jack swallowed. "That's good." He smiled at his son, vastly relieved that there would be no hard questions about his own sex life.

"What I want to know is . . ." Nathan stole a look back at the tent. "Where is the clitoris exactly?"

Jack's smile fell and he opened his mouth. No words came out so he closed it.

Nathan had no problem forming his words, though. "And what the heck is a G-spot?"

Chapter 17

Driving wasn't as easy as Nathan thought it would be. On his second day of driver's education, he got to drive a Saturn. Not exactly his idea of a hot car, but the other class had to drive a station wagon. By the third week, he'd mastered the Saturn and figured he was ready to take his new dream car for a spin. Jack's Shelby Mustang. Jack didn't know it yet, but Nathan wanted to drive that car. *Bad*.

After the first week, he'd made a few friends with some of the other boys in his class. They didn't ride horses or listen to crap-ola music. Some of them did chew tobacco, though, which was cool with Nathan.

On the day of classes, his mom dropped him off in front of the high school. He usually walked to Jack's afterward because it was only a few blocks away. He'd been in Lovett for a month now, and he guessed it wasn't as bad as he thought it was the first few days he'd been here. He liked working in Jack's garage. He liked shooting the bull with the other mechanics, he thought as he walked to the back of the school.

Jack had shown him the business side of running Parrish American Classics, and it looked pretty cool. Maybe he could come here and work next summer too; and when he graduated from high school, he could work with Jack and Billy full-time.

That'd be tight, but his mom would have a fit. She wanted him to go to college like his dad. She talked about it as if he had no say in it at all. She was trying to run his life like he was a little kid.

Nathan picked up a rock from the blacktop and threw it at the basketball backboard like he had that day he'd first met Jack. The rock fell to the ground and he kicked it.

He didn't know what to call Jack anymore. Calling him Jack felt weird, but he couldn't call him dad. His dad was Steven Monroe, but Jack was starting to feel like his dad too. They got along pretty good now. Sometimes after work, they just hung out and talked about cars and stuff. He'd gone over to Billy's and met the rest of the family, too. Billy's little girls screamed and giggled a lot, and the middle one ran with her head down and you had to watch out for her.

Jack usually invited his mom to come along, and it was kind of like they were a family, but not. Sometimes Nathan caught Jack looking at his mom like he loved her. Then he'd blink or look away or say something and Nathan would think he was imagining things. If Jack was in love with his mom, Nathan really didn't know how he felt about that. Maybe it was okay since Jack was his dad. Sort of.

Jack had only made him mad one time. Nathan had gotten angry at his mom on the Fourth of July, and he'd yelled at her because she wanted to know where he was going and what he was doing. Jack had given him a really hard look and said, "You don't talk to your mother like that. Now apologize."

He would have apologized anyway. His mom bugged him sometimes, but he loved her. He hated to see how sad it made her when he yelled. It made him feel like his chest was caving in, but he never realized he was doing it until it was too late.

Nathan started across the field to the opening in the fence. It was Saturday and he didn't have work. Maybe he'd go take a nap for a while or play the XBOX that his mom had brought back with her when she'd gone to Seattle.

His footsteps slowed as he watched Brandy Jo move through the opening and walk toward him. She wore a red dress with tiny straps and big chunky flip-flops on her feet.

"Hi, Nathan. I haven't seen you in awhile. What are you up too?"

"Taking driver's ed." He stood up a little straighter, then slouched to put his hands in his pockets. Brandy Jo was about the prettiest girl he'd ever seen. Even wearing those big shoes, the top of her head barely reached his chin. He got that caving-chest feeling, only this time it had nothing to do with his mom. "What are you doing here on Saturday?"

"I forgot my sweater in the school."

The sun shone in her dark hair, and when she licked her pink lips, his stomach twisted. "Need help?" he asked and almost groaned out loud. *Of course she didn't need help.*

"No, but I'd like your company."

He swallowed and tried not to smile. He nodded and said, "Cool."

"When are you going to get your driver's license?" she asked as they walked around the side of the school.

"I have to take the test pretty soon." Her bare arm bumped him right beneath the sleeve of his T-shirt and his shoulder kind of tingled.

"I got my license last month," she said.

"Do you have a car?"

She shook her head and her hair brushed the tops of her shoulders. "Do you?"

"Jack is going to let me drive his." He bumped his arm into hers to see what would happen, and the tingle traveled across his chest.

"Who's Jack?"

"He's . . . like my dad."

She looked up at him through her big brown eyes. "What do you mean? 'Like your dad'? Is he your step-dad?"

"No. He's my real dad, but I just met him about a month ago."

She stopped on her big flip-flops. "You just met him?" she asked, in the drawl of hers that he was starting to think was real cute.

"Yeah. I've always known about him, but when my dad died . . . When my first dad . . . other dad . . ." He sighed. "It's confusing."

"My mom's been married three times," Brandy Jo told him as they started toward the front again. "My daddy died, but my baby brother's daddy lives in Fort Worth. I have another step-daddy right now, but it's not looking too good. Everybody's family is confusing for one reason or another."

They walked side by side into the building, bumping arms and pretending it was an accident. Brandy Jo found her sweater in the art room and somehow by the time they walked back outside, Nathan held her hand in his. His throat kinda closed, and then she smiled up at him and he thought his heart stopped. It squeezed tight and he was afraid he'd pass out right there next to the stupid boulder with the words "Lovett Stallions" chiseled in it. Right there beneath the hot Texas sun. Right in front of the prettiest girl he'd ever seen. He *really* didn't want to do that.

Nathan looked down at Brandy Jo as she talked about her family. He squeezed her hand, and she moved closer until their arms touched. His heart swelled like a balloon in his chest and it felt good and horrible and overwhelming. He'd never been in love before. Well, except with Nicole Kidman, but that didn't count. But on that day, beneath the endless blue sky over his head, Nathan Monroe fell in love for the first time in his life.

Daisy stuck her thumb in the end of the garden hose and sprayed down the hood of her mother's Cadillac with water. Then she plunged a soft sponge into a bucket of soapy water and washed dirt from the car. The hot afternoon sun beat down on her, and she could feel it toast her shoulders, chest and her back above the scoop of her red tank top.

She'd spent most of her day over at Lily's, cleaning house and doing laundry while Lily sat on the couch with her cast resting on pillows. Lily's divorce was final now, and her lawyer had come through for her. He'd showed the judge bank statements prior to Ronnie draining the account, and the judge had ordered Ronnie to pay Lily ten thousand dollars, monthly child support, and he had to pay Pippen's medical insurance, too.

Her mother was still over at Lily's fetching and toting. Daisy knew that her sister was having a hard time doing simple tasks since she'd come home from the hospital. She didn't mind helping out, but Lily's messed up life had put Daisy in a bad mood.

Actually, it was more than just a bad mood. She felt unsettled, but Lily had very little part in that. Lately, Daisy's mood had more to do with the sum total of her life rather than just one piece. She was anxious to get on with her life, yet scared and uncertain. Her house in Washington hadn't sold yet, but it had only been on the market for about a month. She was moving forward with her plans to open a photography studio, yet she felt a stitch of anxiety when she thought of leaving Texas. It seemed to her that one moment she was crystal clear about what she wanted, and in the next she was confused as hell.

She'd gone out twice with Matt and she'd had a good time. But when he'd kissed her, she'd known there wouldn't be a third time. She was in love with someone else, and it wasn't fair to Matt.

Daisy leaned as far as possible over the Caddy's

hood and washed a spot she'd missed. She glanced up as one of the biggest reasons for her confusion pulled his Mustang beside the curb in front of her mother's house.

Jack got out of his car and walked across the yard toward her. A lock of dark hair hung over his forehead, and for once he wasn't wearing a hat. Sunlight refracted little blue pinwheels off the lenses of his sunglasses. His green shirt buttoned up the front and he wore faded Levi's. It was Saturday and he hadn't shaved. Dark stubble shadowed his face and drew attention to the sensual lines of his mouth. Every time she saw him, her heart squeezed a little while her head told her to run screaming in the opposite direction.

"Hey there," she said as she straightened and rinsed soap from the hood. "What are you up to, besides no good?"

"I'm looking for Nathan. I thought he might stop by my house after his driver's ed class, but he didn't."

"He's not here yet," she said and could feel his gaze on her from behind his glasses. "I'm sure he'll be here soon if you want to wait."

"I'll wait a few," he said as he glanced down the street. He'd been doing that a lot since they'd returned from the lake about a month ago. Undressing her with his eyes then turning away. Of course it was entirely possible that he wasn't even looking at her with any more interest than a bug. It was very possible that she was imagining it all. Kind of like wishful thinking. Which made her not only sad and pathetic and extremely delusional, but as crazy as the rest of her family. Scary thought.

She picked up the bucket and hose and moved to the opposite side of the car from Jack.

"Tomorrow night, Billy and some of the guys are getting together to play football over at Horizon View Park." He rested his weight on one foot and returned his gaze to her. "I talked to Nathan about it the other day, and he was going to get back to me about whether he could make it."

"We don't have anything planned, so I don't have a problem with him going." Daisy set the bucket on the ground and raised the hose to the roof of the car. "Tackle or flag?"

"Flag football is for sissy men," he scoffed as he moved to stand directly across from her. "And girls."

She decided to let that one pass. "I don't want Nathan to play without a helmet and pads."

"We'll make sure he has all the right equipment." He tilted his head to the side as if he where sizing her up too. "Why don't you come on down in one of your old cheerleader outfits? You can do cartwheels and backflips like you used to." The corners of his mouth slid upward into a purely carnal smile. "Or those toe-touch jumps. You used to give a beauty of a crotch-shot."

Daisy's thumb found the end of the hose again and water sprayed across the roof of the car, hit Jack's chest and shoulders, and splattered his sunglasses.

"Oops," she said and removed her thumb.

His brows lowered and disappeared behind the lenses. "You did that on purpose."

She gasped. Scandalized. "No. I didn't."

"Yes," he said very slowly, "you did."

"Wrooong." She shook her head, stuck her thumb in the end of the hose again and hit him dead center in his chest between his shoulders. Water sprayed up to his chin and down to the front of his shirt. "Now that," she said when she pulled her thumb out, "was on purpose."

"Do you have any idea," he spoke as he removed his sunglasses and stuffed them in the pocket of his soggy shirt, "what I'm going to do to you?"

"Nothing."

His green gaze promised retribution as he walked around the hood of the car. "Wrooong," he mimicked her.

She took a step back. "Stay where you are."

"Scared?"

"No." She took another step back.

"You should be, baby girl."

"What are you going to do?"

"Quit movin' and you'll find out."

She stood her ground, raised the hose and shot him in the head with a stream of water. He ducked, and before she could even think to run he was on her, pinning her against the back passenger door and wresting the hose from her hands.

"Jack, no!" She started to laugh. "I'll never do it again. I swear."

He looked down into her face and water ran from a lock of hair hanging above his forehead and dripped on his cheek. His long eyelashes were wet and tangled on the ends. "I know you won't," he said as he pulled out the front of her tank top and shoved the hose inside.

"That's cold—*auggg*!" She grabbed his hand and attempted to wrestle the hose from her shirt.

"Laugh it up, funny girl." He pinned her with his body and was getting just as wet as she was.

"Stop!" Water shot between her cleavage and ran down her stomach. Her nipples puckered from the cold. "That's freezing."

With his face just above hers he said, "Tell me how sorry you are."

She was laughing so hard she could barely talk. "Sooooo sorry," she managed as she tried to squirm her way out from beneath him. His hips held her exactly where he wanted her.

"That's not good enough." He pulled the hose from her shirt and dropped it on the ground. "Show me," he said, his voice rough.

Daisy's laughter died on her lips and she looked into his face. Really looked at the desire shining through his green eyes. He stood with his feet on the outsides of hers. His thighs, hips and lower abdomen pressed into her, and she was suddenly aware that at least eight inches of him was very happy to see her. A ribbon of warm sensation uncurled in her stomach. Her heart told her to stay while her head screamed at her to run. "How?"

"You know how." He lowered his gaze to her mouth. "And make it good."

She ran her cold hands up his wet chest and shoulders and through the side of his hair. She lifted her face and slid one hand to the back of his head. She touched her mouth to his and she felt her heart expand. It filled her chest and made breathing difficult and there was no denying it for exactly what it was. She'd felt it before. Only this time it was stronger. Less confused. Like turning the camera's focus ring until it was very clear.

She was in love with Jack Parrish. Again. Her heart had won this round.

The thinnest slice of sunlight separated their mouths. They both held their breaths; their gazes locked. Waiting for the other to make the first move.

Daisy gave him a sweet little peck. "Is that good?"

His lips brushed across hers as he shook his head. "Try again."

"How about this?" Her lips parted and she touched the seam of his mouth with the tip of her tongue.

He sucked in a breath and his voice was rough when he asked, "Is that the best you can do?"

She raised a hand to the side of his face and brushed her fingers against the stubble of his jaw. "No, but I don't think you can handle the best I can do."

"Try me."

Daisy's eyes drifted shut and she melted into him just a little. The tips of her breasts brushed the front of his shirt and her nipples puckered from more than the cold. Warmth spread across her flesh and settled between her legs. She pressed her open mouth to his and kissed him. At first she gave him soft teasing kisses that had Jack chasing her tongue for more. A frustrated groan rose from his chest, and he tilted his head to one side and turned up the heat. He forced her mouth open wider and took over.

With their lips locked together, he wrapped his arms around her and took a step back. He grabbed her behind in his big hands and pulled her onto the tips of her toes.

He drew back and looked into her face. "You feel good." Very slowly he let her body slide down his, then he pulled her back up. "No one has ever felt as good as you." His mouth covered hers again. Cold water from the hose ran across her toes as the kiss turned hot.

Behind her, Daisy heard someone clear his throat, a split second before Nathan's voice penetrated her lust-filled haze. "Ah, Mom?"

Jack raised his face, and she dropped onto her heels and spun around. "Nathan!" It took a few dazed moments for her to realize that he wasn't alone. A teenaged girl stood next to him. Nathan looked from her face to Jack's and his cheeks turned deep red.

"How long have you been standing there?" Jack asked, his voice calm and collected for a man who'd just had his hands on Daisy's behind, sliding her up and down his body.

"We saw you from down the street." Nathan returned his gaze to Daisy. He didn't say anything more and she couldn't tell what he was thinking.

Daisy forced a smile on her face and said, "Are you going to introduce your friend?"

"This is Brandy Jo." He pointed toward Daisy. "That's my mom and Jack."

"It's a pleasure to meet y'all."

Daisy moved to take a step forward but Jack's hand on the waistband of her shorts kept her in front of him. She looked up over her shoulder at him, he raised a brow, and the light dawned. Jack was using her for cover. She felt heat creep up her neck to her cheek. Just like Nathan. The only person who didn't seem embarrassed was Jack.

She turned her attention to Nathan and Brandy Jo. "Do you live close by?" she asked, to cover the awkward silence.

"Over on Taft." Brandy Jo glanced up at Nathan. "The first day Nathan and I met, I told him that we're kind of related. My aunt Jessica is married to Ronnie Darlington's cousin Bull."

Well, at least she wasn't a blood relative to Ronnie. "Lily and Ronnie's divorce was final a few weeks ago."

"Oh. I didn't know that." She smiled and said just above a whisper, "Ronnie's a dog and no one could figure out what Lily ever saw in him."

Brandy Jo was obviously a smart girl.

"I came by to talk to you about that football game tomorrow night," Jack said.

"And you couldn't find anything to do until I got here, so you decided to make out with my mom in the front yard?"

Daisy's mouth fell open.

Jack laughed. "It seemed like a good way to pass the time."

Daisy turned around and looked at him.

"*What?*" he said through an evil grin. "You thought so too."

Chapter 18

$\mathcal{D}$aisy had lived in the Northwest for fifteen years, but she'd never forgotten how seriously Texans took their football. Be it the Texas Stadium in Dallas, a high school field in Houston, or a small park in Lovett, football was considered a second religion and was worshiped accordingly.

Amen.

What Daisy hadn't known was that this particular game was an annual event. A yearly meeting where grown men gathered to sweat, ram into each other, and compare battle wounds. There were no yardline markers. No referees. No goalposts. Just two side-lines and end zones marked off with DayGlo orange spray paint, and someone with a stopwatch. Jack's team wore red practice jerseys, the other team wore blue.

Each team brought grit and spit and a desire to tear each other's heads off all in the name of fun.

This was football in its rawest, purest form, and Nathan Monroe was going to be the only player who wore pads and a helmet. A fact that angered him to no end.

Daisy tried to talk him out of his anger by pointing out that he was fifteen and he was playing against men who were all a lot older and bigger. He didn't seem to care that he'd get hurt, only that he'd looked like a wuss.

"Nathan, I paid over five thousand dollars for your straight teeth," she'd told him. "You're not going to get them knocked out."

It wasn't until some time later, when Brandy Jo showed up at the park and told him she liked the way he looked in pads and helmet, that his mood seemed to brighten a bit.

She and Nathan caught a ride with Jack to the park, and as the three of them moved closer to the playing field, Jack took a closer look at her dress. "That doesn't look like your cheerleader outfit," he said when Nathan walked over to Billy to get his red-mesh jersey.

Daisy had ignored Jack's suggestion that she wear her cheerleader skirt and sweater, and had chosen instead a peach apron dress that crisscrossed down the back. She looked down at the hem of the dress just above her knees. "Too long?"

"And it doesn't have a back."

"I guess I won't be doing any of those toe-touch jumps that you were apparently so fond of in high school."

His gaze scanned the members of his team assembled in the center of the field. "In the dress you got

on, you'd probably hurt your pom-poms. And that
would be a true shame."

"You don't need to worry about my pom-poms."
She stopped at the red sideline. "They're fine."

"They certainly are," he said over his shoulder as
he continued toward his team.

Daisy stared after him and smiled. He wasn't
wearing anything beneath his mesh jersey, and his
tan skin showed through the tiny holes. Her gaze
slid down his back to his tight, butt-hugging football
pants. Jack Parrish was mighty fine himself. His
pants encased his legs to just below his knees, and
he wore black football socks and cleats. He moved
as if he hadn't a care in the world. As if he wasn't
about to spend the next hour or so getting run over
and the stuffing knocked out of him.

Tucker Gooch called her name and waved to her
from the middle of the blue team. She waved back to
him and noticed a lot of faces she'd gone to school
with. Cal Turner and Marvin Ferrell. Lester Crandall
and Leon Kribs. Eddy Dean Jones and several of the
Calhoun boys, Jimmy and Buddy included. She
wondered if Buddy knew that after he'd had sex
with Lily, she'd gone crazy and driven her car into
Ronnie's front room.

Probably not.

She recognized a lot of other faces too. The people
she'd grown up with in Lovett. Penny Kribs and little Shay Calhoun. Marvin's wife, Mary Alice, and
Gina Brown.

Jealousy knotted Daisy's stomach. She wondered
if Gina and Jack had been together in the past
month. They probably had. Jealousy moved up from

her stomach to twist her heart. She knew the feeling and was familiar with it. She'd felt it fifteen years ago when just the thought of Jack with someone else used to torment her, sending her emotions bubbling up over the top.

But Jack wasn't hers and she wasn't a kid anymore. She knew what to do with jealousy now. She didn't fight it or pretend it didn't exist. She felt every prickly thorn of it. Then she let it go as best she could.

Her head won this round over her heart, and she sat in a folding chair next to Rhonda and the girls on the sidelines. All three little girls wore red cheerleader outfits and jumped about like their legs were made of springs.

"Last year Billy tore a groin muscle," Rhonda told her as she pulled off Tanya's socks so the baby could wiggle her toes. "He whined about it for three weeks."

"Marvin broke his thumb last year," Mary Alice added as she leaned forward in her chair.

Groins and thumbs weren't covered by padding and helmets. Daisy stood, ready to drag Nathan away from the team huddle, then she sat back down. He would never forgive her if she did that. So she crossed her fingers instead.

The game kicked off at seven-thirty. It was ninety degrees in the shade and sweat poured off the players. Jack was the quarterback for the red team, and Daisy had forgotten how much she liked to watch him play. Every time he drew his arm back to drill that ball down the field, his jersey pulled up and Daisy was treated to a view of his flat stomach and navel just above the waistband of his pants. When he got knocked flat, she got a glimpse of his chest.

Horizon View Park was soon filled with the shouts of men calling out to each other, cleats pounding down the field and muscle hitting muscle. Of bodies hitting the ground with an audible thud followed by a whoosh, and the cheers and jeers of spectators on the sides.

In the first quarter, Jack threw a short pass to Nathan, who caught it and ran with it for about ten yards before he got tackled. Daisy held her breath until her son got back up and brushed a chunk of grass from his helmet. In the second quarter, Jimmy Calhoun made a touchdown for the red team. Unfortunately he was tackled in the end zone and went down hard. When he was finally able to get back up, he limped to the car and Shay took him to the hospital. Everyone predicted a knee injury. Buddy hoped it wasn't something more permanent.

"Shay's got her heart set on a big family," he said as he watched his brother being whisked away. "Hope he didn't rupture any *thang* vital."

During half-time, Daisy helped Rhonda and Gina pass bottles of water out to both teams. Each man looked somewhat worse for the wear, and they had half the game left. On the blue team, Leon Krib's left eye was swelling, and Marvin Ferrell had a busted lip. While Tucker Gooch wrapped his ankle, he asked for her phone number.

She didn't give it to him.

She excused herself and talked to Nathan to make sure he was all right. Billy grabbed him around the neck and rubbed his knuckles in Nathan's hair. Instead of getting angry like Daisy half expected, Nathan laughed and socked Billy in the gut.

"Billy really wants a little boy," Rhonda told her. "But he's going to have to settle for playing with Nathan."

Billy only had about three weeks before she and Nathan were returning to Seattle. Daisy wondered how Nathan felt about leaving. If he was still excited to get back home.

Was she? Her little tug of anxiety turned into a hard yank at the thought, and she was very much afraid the answer was no. Just yesterday she and Nathan had been driving through the small downtown area of Lovett and she'd noticed a vacant space right next to Donna's Gifts on Fifth. Before she even realized what she was doing, she'd visualized herself there. A sign hanging beneath the striped awning. DAISY MONROE PHOTOGRAPHY painted on it. Or maybe she'd name her business Buttercup or . . .

Her heart and head were at war, and she'd better figure things out quick before she signed a lease in Seattle.

She handed water to Eddy Dean who had bloody knuckles and to Cal Turner who was already limping. But the limp didn't keep Cal from asking her to meet him at Slim's later that night. She glanced at Jack, standing a few feet away, deep in conversation with Gina. He stood with his hands on his hips, a white towel hanging off one shoulder. Gina gestured to the left, but Jack's gaze was on Daisy as she approached him.

"I'll talk to you later," Gina said and moved to the sidelines.

"Okay, thanks." Jack grabbed two bottles of water and twisted the cap off one. He had a bloody raspberry on his left elbow and his white pants were covered in green. He drank half of one bottle and poured the rest over his head.

"Are you going to go out tonight with Cal?" he asked as he wiped his face with the towel.

She'd wondered if he'd heard Cal. "Would that bother you?"

He looked at her over the top of the white cotton, then hung the towel around his neck. "Would it matter to you if it does?"

She turned her attention to the sidelines and Gina. "Yes."

Jack placed his fingers on her cheek and brought her gaze back to his. "Yes, it would bother me. Don't go out with Cal or Flea or anyone else."

"I'm not going out with Cal or anyone else." She looked down at her feet then raised her gaze back up the lacing of his football pants, his red jersey, then into his green eyes. "Are you still going out with Gina?"

He moved to stand so close they almost touched, and he tucked her hair behind one ear. "I haven't been with anyone," he said just above a whisper. "Not since I put you on the Custom Lancer."

She wondered if he was talking about the car. Knowing Jack, she doubted it. "Really?"

"Yeah." His fingertips slipped to the side of her neck. "How about you?"

She smiled because she couldn't help it. "Of course not."

He smiled too. "That's good." He pressed a quick

kiss to her mouth then walked around her toward the rest of his team. As kisses went, it shouldn't have counted. It was hardly a kiss at all, but it had been just wet enough to leave the taste of him on her lips. Just warm enough to slide inside and light a fire next to her heart.

During the third quarter, the blue team scored a touchdown, but Daisy wasn't paying close attention to the game. She had bigger worries on her mind. She was in love with Jack. She could no longer ignore it. She'd come to Lovett to tell Jack about Nathan. She hadn't meant to fall in love with him again, but it had happened, and now she had to decide what she was going to do about it. Fifteen years ago, she'd run away from the pain of Jack not loving her in return. She wasn't going to run this time. When and if she left, she would know how Jack felt about her.

Three minutes into the fourth quarter, Jack got creamed by Marvin Ferrell, who had to outweigh Jack by a good hundred pounds. He went down with a *umph*, and Daisy's heart dropped a few inches. He lay on his back for several long moments until Marvin helped him to his feet. Jack moved his head from side to side as if getting out the kinks, then he slowly walked back to the huddle. His next pass was a fifty-foot bomb to Nathan, who ran it all the way for a touchdown. Nathan tore off his helmet and spiked it into the ground. He jumped around, giving high-fives, and smashing knuckles with his teammates. Jack hooked his arm around Nathan's shoulders. Father and son, their heads close as they talked and walked to the sidelines, both of them smiling as if they'd just won the million-dollar lotto.

After the game, Nathan was still so excited he forgot himself and gave Daisy a hug that picked her up off her feet.

"Did you see that touchdown?" he asked and released her.

"Of course. It was a beauty."

Nathan pulled the shoulder pads over his head as Brandy Jo and a group of teenagers approached. They all seemed quite impressed that a fifteen-year-old had been invited to play football with the men.

"I got to play because Jack and Billy play on the red team," he said.

A boy wearing a Weezer T-shirt asked, "Who're Jack and Billy?"

"Billy's my uncle." Nathan paused and looked over the top of Daisy's head. "And Jack's my dad."

She felt Jack behind her a split second before he squeezed her shoulders. She looked up into his unfathomable eyes and his pleased smile, she then turned her attention back to Nathan. The two men in her life stared at each other and seemed to reach an unspoken understanding. No weeping or crying or falling on each other's necks. Just an acknowledgment like the slapping of hands and smashing of knuckles.

Instead of coming home and celebrating his touchdown with her and Jack, Nathan asked if he could go hang out with his new friends. By the way her son looked at Brandy Jo, Daisy knew she'd just been usurped in her son's life by a fifteen-year-old girl with long brown hair and a Texas twang. She felt an unexpected pang of jealousy. Nathan was growing up much too quickly, and she missed the little boy who used to hold her hand and look up at her as if she were the most important thing in his world.

"Are you ready to go now?" Jack lowered his face to the top of her head. "I want to get you out of here before Cal comes over and hits on you again."

He wasn't really fooling her. She could hear the pain in his voice. "What hurts?"

"My shoulder," he answered as they moved toward the parking lot, "like a son of a bitch."

"I don't understand why you guys don't wear pads." She held up a hand. "Don't say it. I know. Pads are for sissies."

Jack opened the passenger-side door for her. She moved to get inside but looked back across the field one last time at Nathan. "He's growing up too fast," she said as she watched him walk in the other direction with Brandy Jo on his arm. "He was always so rowdy and independent. I couldn't take him anywhere cause he'd just run off. So I got one of those leashes you put on little kids so you don't lose 'em. I always felt so much better knowing he was on the other end of the leash. I'd give a hard tug, and he'd come rolling out from wherever he was hiding from me." She grasped the top of the car door that separated her body from Jack's. "I wish I could just give him a tug now and make sure he stays out of trouble."

Jack put his hands on the outside of hers. "He's a good boy, Daisy. He'll be fine."

She looked up into his eyes and he leaned forward

and gently pressed his mouth to hers, easing into a kiss so slow and sweet, it just seemed to melt her heart. He smelled of sweat and grass and Jack. His thumbs brushed over the backs of her hands as the tip of his slick tongue touched hers. Jack took his time, and the kiss turned more deeply intimate. It touched places deep in her soul that recognized him. This was more than a mating of mouths. More than the hot rush of sex that demanded to be satisfied.

When he pulled back, he looked at her the way he used to all those years ago. His guard down. His wants and needs and desires unmistakably clear in his green eyes.

"Come home with me," he said as his hands moved to cover hers in his warm palms.

She swallowed and the corners of her mouth turned up. She didn't have to ask what he had planned. "I thought your shoulder hurt?"

"Not that bad."

"I could massage it for you."

He shook his head. "You need to save your energy to massage other things."

Chapter 19

Daisy ran her hands across Jack's smooth shoulders and pushed her fingers into his knotted muscles. She massaged his back and ran her thumbs up and down the indent of his spine. A bead of water dropped from his wet hair, slid down his back and was absorbed in the thick blue towel hung low on his hips.

The drive from the park to Jack's had taken less than ten minutes. Usually it took fifteen, but Jack had run several stop signs and blown through a traffic light.

At present, he sat on a ladder-back kitchen chair next to the dining room table. His legs straddled the seat while his arms rested across the top rung. He'd insisted on taking a quick shower to get rid of the grime before he'd let her touch him, and when he'd come out wearing nothing but a towel, she'd about jumped him then and there.

"How's this feel?" she asked as her palms slid down his hard muscles, then up again.

"Like something I could get used to." The heat from his skin warmed her hands, and she felt the contours and textures as she learned the definition of him all over again.

"Daisy?"

She looked down at the back of his head. The dining room light shone through his dark hair, picking out strands the color of coffee. "Hmm?"

"When we were at Lake Meredith, you said you've missed me." He reached up and grasped her by the wrist. "Is that true?" He looked over his shoulder at her. His intense gaze told her the answer was very important to him.

"Yes, Jack. It's true."

He pulled her arm down around his chest and said, next to her right cheek, "I missed you too, Daisy Lee. All these years I've missed you more than I knew." His placed his free hand on the left side of her face. "More than I ever wanted you to know."

Her chest got tight and achy, and she lowered her mouth and said against his lips. "I love you, Jack."

He closed his eyes and let out his breath. He was quiet for several long moments then he said, "I have always loved you. Even when I didn't want to."

"Turn around," she whispered.

His eyes opened. "What?"

"Stand up."

As soon as he stood and turned toward her, she put her hand on his shoulders and pushed him back down again. "I don't know what happens next for us," she said as she pulled up her dress and sat in his lap facing him. He spread his thighs and her bottom hit the seat of the chair. Her bare feet hung over the sides. "Whatever it is, I will always love you. I can't help it."

His hands slid up and down her thighs as his green eyes looked at her through his lashes. "I'll show you what happens next." His palms moved to her waist and his fingers searched the tie on the side of her dress.

She settled more firmly between his legs and asked, "Is that a tent pole or are you happy to see me?"

A blatantly sexual smile pushed the corners of his mouth upward. "Both. Wanna see?"

"Oh yeah." She moved her hands from his shoulders and down his chest. Her palms covered his nipples and she leaned forward and kissed the side of his throat. The thick towel and the thin layer of her panties separated them.

Jack tugged and the top of her dress loosened. "Raise your arms," he told Daisy. She did as he asked, and he slid the dress above her waist and pulled it over her head. Her hair fell free about her bare shoulders, and Jack looked into her brown eyes, at the passion staring back at him. He tossed the dress on the floor, then covered her naked breasts with his hands. Her puckered nipples poked the centers of his palms and he brushed them with his thumbs. Her lids lowered a fraction and she licked her lips. He knew her. He knew the weight of her against him and the beat of her heart in his palms. He knew the sigh of pleasure on her lips and the scent of her skin.

This was Daisy. His Daisy.

"Are you sure your shoulder doesn't hurt?"

Shoulder? He didn't give a shit about his shoulder. The only pain he felt was in his groin. "Nothing hurts as bad as wanting you." Every fantasy he'd ever had had begun and ended with Daisy Lee. Now here she was. Except for a strap of silk panties, naked in his lap. If he had his way, she would never leave.

Her soft hand slid down his belly and she pulled at the towel around his waist. She unwrapped him like a Christmas present, then reached inside and closed her fist around his erection. He was so hard he throbbed. He sucked in his breath. He looked at Daisy, past the rose-colored tips of her breasts, down her tan abdomen and belly button to her tiny white panties. Within her small hand, she held his thick shaft. She brushed her thumb over the head. Lust pulled his gut into a hard knot and he had a difficult time drawing air into his lungs. He wrapped his hand over hers and moved it up and down, sliding within the soft velvet of her palm. She leaned forward and kissed his throat. Her warm moist tongue leaving a trail of fire.

He raised her face to his, and his hungry mouth slanted across her lips. He gave her hot, feeding kisses; there was nothing tender or soft in what he gave this time. The moment his mouth touched hers, it was greedy, a maddening chase and follow. A slick advance and retreat of hot tongues and mouths. She arched into him, crushing her hard nipples into his chest and shoving her crotch against his erection.

He wanted this. He wanted it every damn day of his life. He wanted the drive of her tongue in his mouth, the weight of her in his arms, the catch in his chest when he looked into her eyes or buried his nose in her neck.

He wanted her. All of her. Forever. He loved her. He'd always loved her.

Jack stood and the towel fell to the floor. He set Daisy on the kitchen table in front of him and looked down into her dazed eyes.

"Lie down, buttercup." She rested back on her elbows and watched as he kissed her breasts and sucked her puckered nipple into his mouth. He worked her over until her breath was choppy, then he worked his way south. He sucked a patch of skin next to her belly button and reached for the chair behind him. He pulled off her panties then sat between her thighs.

"Jack," she said, her voice a dry whisper. "What are you doing?"

He put her bare feet on his shoulders and kissed each ankle—"I'm going down." He bit the inside of her thigh as he brushed his thumb across her slick clitoris and pushed a finger deep inside where she was very hot and very wet. He parted her slick flesh and placed a hand beneath her bottom. He raised her as he brought his mouth down on her.

She tasted like Daisy. Good. Like sex and desire and everything he'd ever wanted.

She moaned his name as her head fell back. He kissed her between her legs. In the same spot he'd kissed her fifteen years ago—only he was better at it now. Better at knowing how to use his tongue and how hard to draw her into his mouth. He teased and sucked until she used her feet to push him back.

She rose from the table and stood in front of him, a little unsteady on her feet as she looked down at him. "I want you, Jack."

He picked up the towel from the floor and wiped his mouth. "I need to get a condom."

She stared at him as if she didn't know what he was talking about. Then she said, her voice heavy with passion, "How long has it been since you've had sex without a condom?"

So long he couldn't remember. "Probably the last time I was with you fifteen years ago."

She smiled as she grabbed the towel from him and tossed it aside. She grasped his shoulders, then she put her feet on the low rung at the bottom of the chair and stood. He wrapped his arms around her and kissed her stomach. "I had my period last week," she said as she lowered herself over his lap. "I won't get pregnant this time."

He might have protested. He might have questioned her more, but the head of his penis touched her slick crotch, and he slid inside her hot wet body. There was no thought of protesting anything after that.

A groan tore into Jack's chest. Her hot flesh surrounded him and a shudder worked its way up his spine. Her lips were parted. Her breathing shallow, and her cheeks were flushed pink. The hunger in her brown eyes was focused on him as if he were the only man who could give her exactly what she needed.

She squeezed her muscles around him and he felt every ripple of her tight passage. He had to fight to keep from coming right then and there. Every cell in his body was focused on her. On the way she felt in side. On the warmth of her contracting muscles. On the sharp pain and dull ache twisting his groin.

"Goddamn," he swore and he moved his hands to her hips. "You feel so good." He lifted her and brought her back down. It was like white-hot liquid enveloped him, and he didn't think he'd felt any- thing as good as the inside of Daisy.

She raised her hands to the sides of his head and brought his mouth to hers. "I love you, Jack," she said as they moved together, building a slow and steady rhythm that turned into a fever. He grabbed her behind and brought her down hard, again and again. Driving up as she pushed down, and every- thing got a whole lot hotter and wilder. Their breath- ing became ragged with the punctuating thrust of his hips. She grasped his bare shoulders and clung to him as the walls of her body pulsed around him. It went on and on faster, harder, pumping into her again and again until the air whooshed from his lungs.

Daisy moaned and squeezed him tight, pulsing and constricting around him. The strong contrac- tions of her orgasm wrung a release from him that he felt up into his chest. He came deep inside where she was hot and slick, and even as he pumped into her one last time, he knew he wanted more.

He wanted it forever.

Daisy didn't burst into tears this time. She almost did the next time, though. Jack took her hand and led her to his bed where he made love to her again. He was so sweet and loving and drew out the torture until she'd had a multiple orgasm. The first of her life, and that had her feeling kind of weepy.

She lay on her stomach on blue sheets. The rest of the bedding was in a tangled heap by her feet. Jack lay half on top of her; his arm around her waist, one leg between hers. His groin pressed into her behind and hip. A lamp flooded the bed with warm yellow light, and the only sound in the room was of heavy, spent breathing. Their skin was glued together and a warm fluttery afterglow settled on her flesh. She hadn't felt this happy and content in a very long time. Jack loved her. She loved him. Things were going to work out for them this time.

She thought Jack had fallen asleep until he moaned. "My God, it just keeps getting better. I didn't think anything could top the chair."

Daisy smiled.

"Damn, did you just come twice?"

"Yes. Thank you."

"You're welcome."

His hand stirred at her waist, as if he tried to lift it but didn't have the energy. Carefully, she turned onto her back and looked at him. His hair was stuck to his forehead and his eyes were closed.

"What time is it?" she asked.

His lids fluttered open and he lifted his arm from across her stomach. He looked at his watch and said, "Early."

She grabbed his wrist and looked at the digital face. "I have to get going before Nathan gets home."

Jack rolled on his side and spread his fingers wide on her stomach just below her breasts. "Don't leave," he murmured as he kissed her shoulder.

"I have to." She sat up and pushed the hair from her face. "But I'll come back for breakfast."

"Don't leave Lovett." He lay on his side and raised onto his elbow. "You and Nathan should move here."

She'd been thinking along those lines too. She just hadn't known he had also. "When did you decide this?" she asked and looked down into his green eyes.

"Probably when we were fishing, but I got serious about it yesterday when we were swapping spit in your momma's front yard and I didn't care who was watching." He sat up and took her hand in his. "I wanted people to watch. I wanted people to see us together. I wanted people to see us kissing today. I want everyone to know that you're mine." He kissed her fingertips. "I want a life with you and our son."

It was exactly what she wanted too. Hearing him say it made it less scary.

"I love you, Daisy Lee. I've loved you all of my life."

She looked into the pain and passion in his gaze. "I love you too, Jack." *But,* a little voice in her head wondered, *was it enough this time?* It hadn't been last time.

She excused herself to go to the bathroom, and when she returned, Jack had pulled on a pair of jeans. While she'd been in the bathroom, he retrieved her dress and panties and they lay on his rumpled bed. She stepped into her panties and he helped her with her dress.

"So, what are you going to feed me for breakfast?" he asked as he adjusted a strap on her back.

"I'll think of something good."

"Something with whipped cream?"

She tied the strap at her side. "And a cherry."

He placed his arms around her and pulled her back against his chest. "I love cherries," he said against the side of her neck.

His bare chest warmed her skin and she had to fight the urge not to turn and kiss his neck. If she did that, she wouldn't make it home before Nathan. "Jack, I want this to work between us this time."

He squeezed her tight. "It will."

He sounded so confident she almost believed him. "Let's talk to Nathan about it together."

"Whatever you want."

"I don't know how he'll feel about moving to Lovett, and I don't want him to think we're moving too fast." She stepped out of his embrace and smoothed her hands over the wrinkles on her dress. "It hasn't been a year since Steven's death, and I don't want him to be uncomfortable with you and me together." She looked about the floor to see if he'd remembered her shoes. "I don't care what other people think, but I don't want Nathan to think we're together just to replace his dad." Her shoes must still be in the kitchen, and she returned her attention to Jack.

The loving man who'd just held her and assured her everything would work out this time turned to stone right before her eyes. His shoulders straightened. His jaws clenched and his gaze hardened.

"What's wrong?"

He walked across the room, passed the yellow

light that spilled into the gray shadows. "How long do we have to call Steven 'Nathan's dad'?"

Daisy watched his bare back and said, "I thought you might be getting over that."

"I thought so too." He yanked open a dresser drawer and pulled out a T-shirt. "But I don't think I'll ever get over what that bastard took from me."

She closed her eyes for several painful heartbeats. "Don't talk about Steven like that."

He laughed without humor. "That's rich." He shoved his arms through the short sleeves. "You defending Steven Monroe to me."

"I'm not defending Steven."

He pulled the shirt over his head and down his stomach. "Then what are you doing?"

"I loved Steven for most of my life. He was not only my husband; he was my best friend. We laughed and cried together. I could talk to him about anything."

"Could you talk to him about how you felt about me?"

She'd almost had it this time. Almost, but it was slipping through her fingers like sand.

"Deep down the pit of your stomach where it gets tight at just the thought of being with me." He stalked back across the room and stopped just inches from her. "Did you tell him that?"

"No, but he knew." She looked up into his face, at the passion and bitterness in his green eyes. At the same passion and bitterness she'd seen the first night she'd seen him. "Being with Steven wasn't *at all* like being with you. It was different. It was . . ."

"What?"

"Calm. It wasn't scary. It didn't hurt. I could breathe around him. I didn't feel like if I didn't touch him, I would die. Like a part of something inside of me belonged to someone else."

"Isn't that the way it's supposed to feel? Isn't it supposed to feel like I want to smash you against my chest so hard I can still feel you after you leave?" He grabbed her shoulders and slid his hands to the sides of her face. "Breathe the same breath. Feel the same heartbeat as you melt inside of me?"

Tears stung her eyes and she didn't even try to stop them. Her heart was breaking and her dreams had just slipped through her fingers. Again. "It's not enough. It wasn't enough last time. And it isn't enough this time either."

"What does it take, then? I love you. I've never loved any woman the way I love you."

She believed him. "Forgiveness," she said as the first tears spilled from her eyes. "You have to forgive me, Jack. You have to forgive me and you have to forgive Steven, too."

He dropped his hands from her and took a step back. "That's asking a lot, Daisy."

"Too much?"

"Where Steven is concerned, yes."

"And me?"

He looked at her and his silence was her answer.

"How can we be together if you can't forgive me of the past?"

"We won't think about it." He grabbed his boots and shoved his feet inside.

"For how long? For how long won't we think about it before it comes up again? Tomorrow? A week from now? Next year? Do you really think we can live with that between us?"

"I love you, Daisy," he said without looking at her. "It's enough."

"You also hate me."

"No." He shook his head and his gaze met hers. "No, I hate what you did. How could I not hate that you kept my son from me?"

"What I did was wrong." She wiped her tears from her face. "I admit that. I should have told you about Nathan. I was scared and a coward. One day turned into one year. One year into two, and the longer I put it off, the harder it got. There is no excuse." She held out her hand to him, then dropped it to her side. "You have to understand. Steven—"

"Oh, I understand Steven," he interrupted. "I understood him the night y'all stood in my front yard and told me you were married. I understood that he loved you as much as I did and when he saw an opportunity to take you from me, he took it. He took my son too. And what you have to understand is, I can't just forget something like that."

"I'm not asking you to forget, but if you and I are to have a future, you have to get past it."

"You say it like it's easy."

"It's the only way."

"I don't know if I can. Especially where Steven is concerned."

"Then we can't be together. It would never work."

"Just like that? You get to decide?" He pointed a

finger at her and slashed his hand through the air. "You get to say 'get over it' or get out of my life? You get to tell me how to feel?"

She shook her head and gazed at him through the blur of her tears. She breathed past the searing pain in her chest. She knew Jack felt it too. It was there in his raw gaze, and just like the last time, there was no way to stop it. "No. I'm telling you that you have a right to your anger. You have a right to it for the rest of your life. But it seems to me very lonely company when you can have so much more if you could somehow let it go."

Chapter 20

*O*n the drive to Daisy's, neither of them spoke. The deep purr of the Shelby's engine was the only sound within the dark interior of the Mustang. Jack pulled the car next to the curb, and Daisy looked at him through the inky darkness one last time. Giving him one last chance to change things that he could not change. To say the words that he could not say.

How could she ask him to forget and forgive? As if it were that easy. As if it hadn't eaten a permanent hole in his gut. As if it wasn't always there, right below the surface.

So he watched her walk away. Into her mother's house, and he slid the Shelby in gear and drove home. He hadn't tried to stop her this time. There would be no fight. No one to hit.

But the pain was just as bad as it had been fifteen years ago. No, he thought as he walked back into his house. It was worse now. Now that he knew what could have been. Now that he'd had a taste of that life.

The chair he'd sat in while he'd made love to Daisy was still pushed away from the table. The table where she'd lain while he'd taken her into his mouth. He stared at it as the hole in his gut burned hotter. Burned up into his chest and throat—he about choked on it.

He picked up the chair, carried it out the back door and tossed it into the pitch-black yard. Then he turned and stared at the heavy wooden table that had belonged to his mother. Where they'd eaten family meals.

Where he'd eaten Daisy.

In his present mood, he probably could have picked up the whole damn table and chucked it outside with the chair, but it wouldn't fit out the door. He went to the shed and grabbed his power tools. When he returned, he flipped the table with one hand. It hit the floor with a loud satisfying crash. He popped a beer, fired up his Black & Decker, and got busy.

By the time he was finished, the table was in pieces and lying about the yard along with the chair. He'd gone through a six pack and started on a bottle of Johnny Walker. Jack had never been a big drinker. Never thought it solved a damn thing. Tonight he just wanted to dull the pain.

With glass in hand, he moved from the dining room, passed his open bedroom door. Passed the lamplight shining on his messed up sheets that he was sure still held the scent of her skin. He walked into the living room and drained his glass. He didn't bother turning on the light. He sat on his black leather sofa. In the dark. Alone.

Light from the kitchen spilled out into the hall and almost reached the toe of his boot. He was tired and beat up from the football game and from Daisy, but he knew he wouldn't sleep. He'd told her he loved her and she'd said it wasn't enough. She wanted more.

He closed his eyes and the room spun. He felt the pitch and roll of his stomach. He'd fucked up. He'd let her into his life. He'd known better. He'd known she'd carve him up again like he had a big X on his chest. He'd held his arms wide and given her a good shot, too.

I'm telling you that you have a right to your anger. You have a right to it for the rest of your life. She'd told him. *But it seems to me very lonely company when you can have so much more if you could somehow let it go.*

Jack was a man who was used to fixing things. Of working until it was as close to perfect as possible. But he knew his limitations. He knew the impossible when it faced him.

What Daisy asked of him was impossible.

Jack didn't even realize he'd fallen asleep on the couch until Billy's voice woke him up.

"What the hell?"

Jack's eyes opened and he squinted against the light. Billy stood before him wearing his work overalls. "What—" His mouth felt like it was stuffed with cotton and he swallowed. "What are you doing here?"

"It's almost ten. The shop's been open for an hour."

Jack was sprawled out with his feet on the coffee table, and he'd slept with his boots on. He picked his head up from the back of the couch and felt like he'd been hit with a brick. "Ah, Christ."

"Have you been drinkin'?"

"Yeah."

"By yourself?"

Jack stood and his stomach rolled. "Sounded like a good idea at the time." He moved into the kitchen and grabbed a bottle of orange juice. He raised it to his mouth and drank until his throat wasn't so dry.

"Why are there only five chairs where the table used to be?" Billy asked as he looked across the hall into the dining room.

"I'm redecorating."

Billy glanced at Jack, then returned his gaze to the five remaining chairs. "Where's the table?"

"In the backyard with the missing chair."

"Why?"

"I like it this way."

He moved to the back door and looked out. He let out a low whistle and said, "Having woman trouble?"

Jack reached into a cupboard and pulled out a bottle of aspirin. Woman trouble sounded as if it were fixable. Like a little fight or squabble.

"Daisy Lee?"

"Yep. She comes back into my life. Fucks it up and leaves it that way."

"Are you sure it's fucked up?"

"Yeah. I'm sure." He swallowed four aspirins and asked, "Has Nathan shown up yet?"

"Yep. Right on time."

"Give me a few minutes to shower and shave and get my shit together, and I'll be there."

"Maybe you should take a day off."

"Can't. Nathan will be leaving in a few weeks, and I want to spend as much time with him as possible."

It took Jack a good forty-five minutes to pull himself together enough to show up at the garage. His body ached and head pounded.

Nathan looked at him and his brows lowered. "Are you okay?"

"Yes." Jack carefully nodded and sank into the chair behind his desk.

"Did you take too many bad hits in the game yesterday?"

"A few." He'd taken the worst hit after the game. "What are you doing tonight?"

"I'm going bowling with Brandy Jo." He shifted his weight to one foot and pulled his lip ring into his mouth. "I was thinking about kissing her. I think she wants me to, but I don't want to suck at it." His gaze stared into Jack's and he asked, "How did you learn to kiss a girl?"

Jack smiled and his headache subsided at bit. "Lots of practice. And don't worry about not being good at it right out of the chute. If Brandy Jo really likes you, she'll want to practice with you."

Nathan nodded as if that made sense. "Did you practice with my mom?"

He pretended to give it some thought, but the truth was the memory of the first time he'd kissed Daisy on her porch was imbedded in his mind, eating at his brain like acid. "No, I'd turned pro before I dated your mom."

Nathan sat and they talked about girls and what girls liked to do besides put on makeup and shop. He was pleased to hear that Nathan was thinking about more than just how to make out with Brandy Jo. He wanted to buy her something nice and do nice things for her.

They talked about cars and Jack was surprised to hear that Nathan was over his obsession with the Dodge Daytona. He now wanted to buy a Mustang, like Jack's Shelby. Nathan was to get his driver's license next week. Jack saw the snow job a mile away. He'd let Nathan drive the Shelby. Not a problem, as long as Jack was in the car.

Jack spent the rest of the day at his desk trying to tune out the irritating whine of sanders and power tools. Around two o'clock, his head quit pounding, but the pain and anger in his chest remained. A constant reminder of what he'd almost had, and what he'd lost.

When Nathan came to work that Thursday, it got a whole lot worse. He mentioned that Daisy was leaving Monday for Seattle. They'd sold their house.

That night as Jack finally dealt with the mess in his backyard, he couldn't help but think of Daisy and how she was getting on with her life. Moving forward, while he seemed forever stuck in the past.

He put all the pieces to his mother's table in a shed on the side of the house and he stuck the chair in there too. Maybe he should move. He'd thought of it a time or two. He'd thought of converting the house into more office space. That in turn would open up more space in the garage.

Jack sat on the back porch and looked out over the

yard. He couldn't see tearing it down. The house held too many memories for him and Billy. It's where he and Steven had dug up the time capsule and read Daisy's diary. Right in the corner of the yard under the maple tree. It's where they'd reburied it too.

He stood, and before he could give himself time to think better of it, he walked to the shed and grabbed a shovel. The earth was packed solid. Sweat ran down the side of his face as he dug for over an hour. It was somewhere around seven-thirty and the sun was still blazing when the end of the shovel finally hit the old red can. He exhumed it from its twenty-one-year-old hiding place. The paint was faded and it showed signs of rust. The plastic lid had turned a dull yellow but was still intact.

Jack took the can to the back porch. He sat on the top step and dumped it out. Green army men, Hans Solo and Princess Lea Star Wars figures, and a switch comb fell out first. Next, Jack's "Dukes of Hazzard" Matchbox car, a whistle and a pack of trick gum. Daisy's diary, a fuzzy pink barrette, and a cheap ring with about a three-carat hunk of glass fell on top of the pile. She'd said he'd given her the ring. He didn't remember it, though.

He picked up the ring and put it in his breast pocket. He reached for the little white book with a yellow rose on it, the lock busted from the last time he'd held it in his hands. The pages had yellowed and the ink had dulled. He leaned forward, rested his forearms on the tops of his knees, and read:

Mr. Skittles bit Lily on the nose today. I think she was trying to kiss him, Daisy had written when they'd all been in about the sixth grade. *My mom put a stupid Snow White in our front yard. It's sooooo embarrassing.* Jack smiled and flipped passed references of her cat and yard decoration. He stopped when he saw his name.

> *Jack got in big trouble for climbing on the roof at school. He had to stay after and I think he got a whooping. He said he didn't care, but he looked sad. It made me sad too. Steven and I walked home without him. Steven said Jack would be okay.*

Jack remembered that. He hadn't gotten whooped, but he'd had to wash all the windows in the school. His gaze skimmed past more entries about her cat, what they'd all had for dinner, and about the weather.

> *Jack yelled at me today. He called me a stupid girl and told me to go home. I cried and Steven told me Jack didn't really mean it.*

Jack didn't remember that one, but if he'd yelled at her it was probably because he had a little crush on her and didn't know what to do about it.

> *Steven gave me a sticker for my bike. It's a rainbow. He says it's too girly for his bike. Jack said it looked weird. Sometimes he hurts my feelings. Steven says he doesn't mean to. He doesn't have sisters.*

He'd never known she was so sensitive. Well, yeah, he guessed he'd known that. But he'd never known she'd gotten upset over stuff like saying a sticker was weird.

Yesterday was Halloween. My mom made me be Annie Oakley again 'cause I haven't outgrown the stupid costume from last year. Jack was Darth Vader and Steven dressed up as Princess Lea. Steven had big cinnamon buns over his ears to look like her. I laughed so hard I about wet myself.

Jack chuckled. He remembered that costume, but he'd forgotten most of the other things Daisy had written about. He'd also forgotten that Steven loved to tell jokes. A lot of them Daisy had jotted down in her diary. He'd forgotten that Steven was a pretty funny kid and that they'd spent hours together laughing about Mrs. Jansen walking her old dog, or their favorite episode of "The Andy Griffith Show."

I don't know why they talk about that show so much, Daisy had written. *It's stupid. "The Love Boat" is sooooooo much better.*

Yeah, and Jack remembered he and Steven laughing about "The Love Boat" behind Daisy's back.

The more Jack read, the more he laughed out loud at some of the things they all used to do. The more he laughed, the more he felt some of his anger subside— which surprised the hell out of him.

The more he read, the more he saw a pattern of Daisy turning to Steven when she was upset about something, or when Jack had unknowingly hurt her feelings. Last Sunday night, she'd told him that Steven was not only her husband, but her best friend. She'd said she could talk to him about anything. That she and Steven had laughed and cried together.

Jack wasn't the type of guy who cried. Instead he stuffed everything deep until it disappeared. Only it didn't. Daisy had been right. They couldn't be together if he couldn't get past his anger. Yes, he had a right to it, but being right *was* very lonely.

Jack shut the diary and looked out over his backyard. He had two choices. He could live the rest of his life with a chest full of anger and bitterness. Alone. Or he could move on. Like Daisy had said. At the time she'd said it, it hadn't seemed possible. Now he felt the glimmer of something in the pit of his soul.

Yeah, Daisy and Steven had kept his child a secret. Yeah, that sucked, but he couldn't let it eat at him any longer. He had to let it go or he was afraid he'd die a bitter and lonely old man. He hadn't known Nathan for the first fifteen years of his life, but Jack figured he had a good fifty or so ahead of him. And he had to decide how he wanted to spend those years.

He stood and shoved everything back into the old coffee can. He walked back into his house and took the letter Steven had written him from the drawer he'd tossed it in. This time when he read it, he read something he'd missed the first time. Steven wrote about the two of them and how much he'd missed Jack over the years. He talked about loving Daisy and Nathan. He ended by asking Jack's forgiveness. He asked Jack to let go of his bitterness and to get on with his life. And for the first time in fifteen years, Jack was going to try to do just that.

He didn't have a plan. He just thought of his life,

and he didn't try to stop the memories. Good or bad. He didn't tap them down or shut them out.

He felt every damn one of them.

Friday after work, he asked Nathan to follow him into his office. They stood next to each other as he pulled out the coffee can and handed Nathan the switch comb. "This was your dad's when he was in sixth grade," he said without a trace of anger. "I thought you might like to have it."

Nathan pushed the button on the handle, and surprisingly it sprang open. He combed the side of his hair. "Sweet." Nathan took the *Star Wars* figures but decided against the green army men.

"You're getting your license Monday, right?"

"Yeah. Mom says I can drive her Caravan sometimes." He frowned. "I told her, no way."

"It's hard to be cool in a Caravan." Jack tried and failed not to smile. "Hard to burn 'em off."

Nathan shook his head. "She just doesn't get it."

Jack grabbed the coffee can and wrapped an arm around Nathan's shoulders. Together they walked from the office. "And she won't either."

" 'Cause she's a girl."

"No, son. Because she's not a Parrish." At least not yet.

"Mom! Guess what?" Nathan said the second he walked into the back of the house. "Jack let me drive the Shelby. Sweet!"

Daisy was up to her elbows in cake frosting. She was throwing a party for Pippen, who'd gone three days without peeing in his pull-ups. "What? You'll kill yourself."

"He was very safe," Jack said from the doorway. "He even reminded *me* to put on my seat belt."

At the sight of him standing there in a pair of khaki pants and a white dress shirt with the sleeves rolled up, her heart seemed to squeeze and swell all at the same time.

His gaze met hers and something hot and vital simmered in his eyes. When he spoke, it was low and sexy. "Good evenin', Daisy Lee," he said, and the velvet in his voice seemed to reach across the distance and touch her.

There was definitely something different about him tonight, but before she could respond, Lily hobbled into the kitchen on crutches. "Hey, Jack. How's it goin'?"

He turned to Lily and whatever had been between Daisy and Jack evaporated like a heat mirage. "Hey, Lily. Hot enough for ya?"

"Shoot. It's hotter than a honeymoon hotel." She moved to the counter and looked in the mixing bowl. "Did you drop by for Pippen's potty party?" Lily stuck her finger into the cake frosting, then licked it clean.

"Yes, Jackson, you have to stay," Louella insisted as she walked from her bedroom into the kitchen. "We bought coonskin hats for everyone, and we'll eat off Thomas the Tank Engine plates."

Nathan moaned as if in severe pain and Jack looked at his son as if he sympathized. But he said, "I'd love to stay, Miz Brooks. Thank you." He moved to the counter next to Daisy, and the sleeve of his shirt brushed her arm as he tasted her frosting. He licked it off and looked down into her gaze.

"Mmm, that's good, buttercup." Then he bent down and whispered into her ear, "I wanna lick this off your thighs."

"Jack!"

He chuckled and grabbed her hand. "If y'all will excuse us for a few minutes, I need to talk to Daisy." He pulled her behind him out the back door. As soon as the door shut behind them, he drew her against him and lowered his mouth to hers. The kiss was sweet and gentle and so heartbreaking she pulled away.

"I've missed you, Daisy," he said.

"Jack, don't. This has been so difficult for me."

He pressed his finger to her lips. "Let me finish." He dropped his hand to the side of her neck and looked into her eyes. "I'm in love with you. It feels like I've been in love with you my whole life. You're it for me, Daisy. You always have been." His thumb lightly brushed her jaw. "Over the years, I've held on to a whole stomachful of anger and bitterness. I blamed you and Steven for everything, when the truth is, I had a hand in what happened to us. I still don't like that I wasn't around when Nathan was growing up, but I just have to believe things happened the way they did for a reason. I can't fight it or argue with it or hold on to it. I'm just letting it go. Like you said."

"Are you sure you can do that?"

"I'm tired of being mad at you," he said as if he meant it. "And I'm tired of being mad at Steven too. I loved Steven when we were kids. We were buddies. In the letter he wrote to me, he asked if I ever missed him." Jack took a deep breath, then cleared his throat.

"I've missed the Steven I grew up with every day. He's gone, and I can't hate a dead man." His paused and his gaze skimmed her face. "Remember the first night you came to my house and I told you I'd make your life a misery?"

She smiled. He'd broken her heart, and now he was fixing it. "Yes."

"I want you to forget I ever said that, because I want to spend the rest of your life trying to make you happy." He fished around in his breast pocket and pulled out a cheap little ring. The gold was chipped off the band and the glass "diamond" had dulled. He reached for her hand and placed it in her palm. "I gave you this ring when we were in the sixth grade. If you'll have me, Daisy, I'll buy you a real one."

Her mouth fell open. "This is the ring I put in the time capsule."

"Yeah. I dug it back up the other day. I have your diary too." His fingers brushed the side of her throat. "Marry me, Daisy Lee."

She nodded. "I love you with all my heart, Jack Parrish. I have always loved you, and I believe it is my fate to love you forever."

He let out a pent-up breath like there had been a doubt. He pulled her into a hug that lifted her off her feet. "Thank you," he said and pressed his smile to her lips.

The back door opened and Nathan stepped out. "Mom, you have to come inside. Grandma—" He stopped when he realized what was going on.

Jack set Daisy on her feet and she turned to face her son. Jack wrapped his arms around her middle and pulled her back against his chest. Nathan looked from one to the other until his gaze stopped on Daisy.

"Your grandma is what?" Daisy asked.

"She's rambling on about people I don't know and don't give a crap about again," he answered, distracted by the sight of the two of them. He raised his gaze to Jack. "What's going on?"

"I asked your mother to marry me."

Nathan stood perfectly still as he absorbed what that meant.

"I've loved your mother since the second grade when I looked across the playground and saw her standing there with a stupid red hair bow." Jack's fingers brushed her stomach as he spoke. "I let her get away once. I'm not going to make that mistake again." He pulled her tighter against his chest. "I want the two of you to move here and live with me."

"To Lovett?"

"Yeah. What do you think?"

Daisy didn't remember him asking her what she thought.

Nathan looked at both of them as he mulled over his options. "Do I get the Shelby?"

For several long moments Daisy feared Jack would say yes. "No, but you can have your mom's Caravan."

"That's not funny."

"Maybe we can work something out."

Nathan smiled and nodded as he walked back into the house. "Sweet," he said.

Jack leaned down and whispered into her ear, "Can we skip the potty party?"

"No." She turned and wrapped her arms around him. Breathing in the smell of his shirt and of him. "But we don't have to stay long."

She felt him press a smile on the top of her head. "Sweet."

Welcome to
Avon Romance Superleader

CONFIDENTIAL!

He has secrets . . . deep, dark
and mysterious . . . but he can't keep
passions hidden for too long . . .

Each month, learn every intimate detail
in the lives of these men . . .
the heroes of the Avon Romance Superleaders.
What makes them tick? What are the things
they don't want anyone to know?

Following is a preview of four upcoming
Avon Romance Superleaders
written by three of Avon's brightest stars:
Elizabeth Bevarly in January,
Rachel Gibson in February,
and, in March and April,
a *super special event*—
back-to-back books by *Eloisa James.*

So read ahead . . . and discover the innermost secrets
of four outstanding heroes!

Ramsey Sage
CONFIDENTIAL!

in *The Thing About Men*
by Elizabeth Bevarly
Coming January 2004

Name: Ramsey Sage
Nickname: Too nasty to mention here
Hometown: Prefers to forget
Car: No car; rides a Harley
First kiss: Can't remember . . .
Super secret: Undercover cop

*A*nd they were going to have a lot more to chat about than Claire had initially thought, too. Like how his arrival had made this temporary arrangement with Anabel suddenly seem much less temporary.

"Is Anabel here?" Mr. Sage asked before making a move to enter.

"Not yet," Claire told him. "It's taken nearly a week to get everything worked out with the authorities in North Carolina. But I spoke with the social worker assigned to the case yesterday, and he said he'd be here with her this afternoon. I'm actually expecting them anytime now. It was rather fortuitous that you were located as quickly as you were."

And also rather amazing, especially since no one seemed to know *why* Ramsey Sage had been drunk in a seedy bar in an obscure village in Central America when they found him. Nor did anyone seem to know how he had gotten there. Even Chandler's private detective still had a lot of pieces missing from the puzzle that was Ramsey Sage, because Ramsey Sage himself had evidently been no help at all providing any answers. It was something Claire decided not to think about, mostly because it didn't bode well for his being named Anabel's permanent guardian.

"Please come in," she invited Ramsey Sage again, stepping aside to offer a physical punctuation mark to the invitation.

But he hesitated for a moment, as if he were reluctant to enter. He surveyed what he could see of the big house from his place on the front porch, and when his gaze returned to hers, Claire could see from his expression that he didn't approve. Why he wouldn't approve, she couldn't imagine. It was certainly a vast improvement over the crowded, spartan institution where she'd grown up, and the tiny, spartan apartment she and Olive had shared in college. She'd made the place as warm and inviting as she could, especially on the inside, and she couldn't imagine why anyone—especially a harsh, raggedy, beat-up man like Ramsey Sage—would disapprove.

Although he smiled at her again as he took a step forward, the naturally breezy grin he had displayed a moment ago was gone, and the one he wore now was decidedly more manufactured. Claire tried not to notice how the air around her seemed to come alive as he passed. She couldn't help noticing, though, how he smelled of heavy machinery and raucous man and endless summer nights, a combination she found strangely appealing since she'd never been drawn to any of those things before. Oh, certainly she enjoyed a summer evening as much as the next person, but she couldn't imagine anything that might make one seem endless.

Then Ramsey Sage looked at her again with his smoldering green gaze, and she suddenly had a very good idea indeed what might make a summer night seem to go on forever, an especially graphic, surprisingly explicit idea, in fact, one that had her squirming on her flowered chintz sofa beneath Ramsey Sage, her blouse gaping open, her skirt hiked up over her hips, her brassiere pushed high, her pearl necklace clenched in his teeth as he tore it from her neck and sent the perfect little beads scattering across the Oriental rug and hardwood floors before dragging his hot mouth across her collarbone and down between her breasts, moving over to close his lips over one nipple, tugging her inside, laving her, licking her, tasting her deeply, and then . . . and then . . . and then . . .

And, good *heavens*, where had such a thought come from? Claire wondered as she shook the image out of her brain. Heat flooded her cheeks, and her lips parted in shock, and she hoped like hell that Ramsey Sage couldn't tell what she was thinking about. Because not only did Claire normally not think about such things in such detail, she didn't think about them in mixed company. And she certainly didn't think about them with men like Ramsey Sage cast in the role of seducer.

Seducer nothing, she thought as she closed the door behind him, wishing she could close the door on her rampant thoughts as easily. Ramsey Sage looked like the kind of man who would take whatever he wanted, whoever he wanted, whenever he wanted, the rest of the world be damned. And the wantee, Claire was certain, would go along quite willingly, and when it was over, be left feeling as if she had just experienced the highest summit of joy.

She followed Mr. Sage into the living room, but following him left her gazing, however involuntarily, at his backside—all right, so maybe it wasn't all *that* involuntary—and she couldn't help nothing, dammit, that his backside was every bit as noteworthy as his front side had been. Because his faded jeans hugged his taut hindquarters and strong thighs with much affection, and his denim work shirt strained against the muscles of his broad back. His arms were nicely bulked with sinew without being overblown, his biceps and forearms curving appreciably with muscle, his skin bronzed and powerful beneath that oddly erotic, barbed-wire tattoo.

And, strangely, Claire found herself wanting to trace the circumference of that tattoo with her fingertips, and oh, my, but that endless-summer-night thing was starting up again, growing more and more graphic and explicit in her mind—and on her body, too, she had to admit—with every passing moment.

Clink, clink, clink went the chains on his boots as he walked.

And *zing* went the strings of her heart.

"Won't you sit down, Mr. Sage?" she said as he continued across the living room to where Chandler stood to greet him upon his arrival. And also as she continued to ogle his backside. "This is Handler, ah, I mean *Chandler*. Chandler Edison. He's my, um . . . my attorney."

Boy, she was really going to have to be careful. Because in addition to misintroducing Chandler by a moniker that had been what Claire was thinking about doing to Mr. Sage's backside, she had almost called Chandler her "buttorney." That would have really been embarrassing.

"Mr. Edison, good to finally meet you," Ramsey Sage said as he approached Chandler, politely extending his hand again, and surprising Claire once more with his manners.

"Mr. Sage," Chandler replied as he shook the proffered hand, though with none of the easiness Ramsey Sage exhibited, and with all of the reluctance one might expect of Chandler, seeing as how he had a nasty aversion to denim.

"Call me Ramsey," Ramsey told Chandler. Then he turned to Claire and added, "You, too, Miss Willoughby."

Claire told herself to extend the same courtesy to him, but something prohibited her. She wasn't sure she could be responsible for her actions if she heard her given name spoken in that dark, velvety baritone of his. So she only nodded her acknowledgment of his comment and decided to skirt the issue as best she could by calling him nothing at all. The last thing she needed to do anyway was slip up and address him as Mr. Hunka Hunka Burnin' Love.

And just what had gotten into her anyway? she demanded of herself. This was getting silly. Ramsey Sage was a walking, talking warning label for decent women everywhere. He was unkempt, unclean, and uncompromising. Not to mention potentially dangerous. She was probably crazy to even invite him into her home, whether he approved of it or not. And she was even crazier to think there was any chance he would be able to care for Anabel. She bit back the panic that began to rise in her throat and wondered what she was supposed to do. If Ramsey Sage couldn't take on the care and feeding of his niece, then who could? Claire certainly didn't want to be responsible for the little girl any longer than she had to be. She didn't know the first thing about children.

How had she gotten into this mess? And more to the point, what was she going to do to get out of it?

Jack Parrish
CONFIDENTIAL!

in *Daisy's Back in Town*
by Rachel Gibson
Coming February 2004

Name: Jackson Lamott Parrish
Nickname: Jack
Hometown: Lovett, Texas
Car: Red '63 T-Bird with red interior
First Kiss: Daisy Lee Brooks . . . in her cute little
cheerleader uniform
Super Secret: Has been known to hang out at The
Road Kill bar

"*M*y my," his voice drawled in the darkness, "if it isn't
Daisy Lee Brooks."

It had been fifteen years, and his voice had changed. It
was deeper than the boy she'd known, but she would have
recognized that nasty tone anywhere. No one could pack as
much derision into his voice as Jack. She'd understood it
once. Known what lay behind it. She didn't kid herself that
she figured him out anymore.

"Hello, Jack."

"What do you want, Daisy?"

She stared at him through the screen and shadows, at the
outline of the man she'd once known so well. The knot in
her stomach pulled tighter. "I wanted to . . . I need to talk to
you. And I thought . . ." She took a deep breath and forced
herself to stop stammering. She was thirty-three. So was he.
"I wanted to tell you that I was in town before you heard it
from someone else."

"Too late." The rain pounded the rooftop and the silence

that stretched between them. She could feel his gaze on her. It touched her face and the front of her yellow rain slicker, and just when she thought he wasn't going to speak again, he said, "If that's what you came to tell me, you can go now."

There was more. A lot more. She'd promised Steven that she'd give Jack a letter he'd written a few months before his death. The letter was in her purse; now she had to tell Jack the truth about what had happened fifteen years ago, then hand over the letter. "It's important that I talk to you. Please."

He looked at her for several long moments, then he turned and disappeared into the depths of his house. He didn't open the screen for her, but he hadn't slammed the wood door in her face, either. He'd made it clear that he was going to be as difficult as possible. But then, when had he ever made things easy?

Just as it always had, the screen door squeaked when she opened it. She followed him through the living room toward the kitchen. His tall outline disappeared around the corner, but she knew the way.

The inside of the house smelled of new paint. She got an impression of dark furniture and a big-screen television. The outline of Mrs. Parrish's piano pushed against one wall, and she wondered briefly how much had changed since she'd last walked through the house. The light flipped on as she moved into the kitchen, and it was like stepping into a time warp. She half expected to see Mrs. Parrish standing in front by the almond-colored stove, baking bread or Daisy's favorite snicker doodle cookies. The green linoleum had the same worn patch in front of the sink and the countertops were the same speckled blue and turquoise.

Jack stood in front of the refrigerator, his top half hidden behind the open door. His tan fingers curled around the chrome handle, and all she could really see was the curve of his behind and his long legs. One pocket of his snug Levi's had a three-corner tear, and the seams looked like they were almost worn through. Adrenaline rushed through her veins, and she balled her hands into fists to keep them from shaking.

Then he rose to his full height, and everything seemed to slow, as if someone flipped a switch on a movie projector. When he turned and shut the refrigerator door, holding a quart of milk in one hand by his thigh, her attention momentarily centered on the thin line of dark hair rising from the waistband of his jeans and circling his navel. She lifted her gaze past the hair on his flat belly and the defined muscles of his chest. If she'd had any lingering doubts, seeing him like this removed them. This was not the boy she'd once known. This was definitely a man.

She forced herself to look up past his strong chin, the etched bow of his tan lips, and into his eyes. She felt the back of her throat go dry. Jack Parrish had always been a good-looking boy, now he was a lethal man. One lock of his thick hair hung over his forehead and touched his brow. Those light-green eyes and long black lashes that she remembered, that had once looked at her so full of passion and possession, watched her as if he were no more interested in seeing her than a stray dog.

"Did you come here to stare?"

She moved farther into the kitchen and shoved her hands into the pockets of her raincoat. "No, I came to tell you that I'm in town visiting my mother and sister."

He raised the milk and drank from the carton, waiting for her to elaborate.

"I thought you should know."

His gaze met hers over the carton, then he lowered it. Some things hadn't changed after all. Jack Parrish, bad boy and all around hell-raiser, had always been a milk drinker. "What makes you think I give a shit?" he asked and wiped the back of his hand across his mouth.

"I didn't know if you would. I mean, I did wonder what you'd think, but I wasn't sure." This was so much harder than she'd envisioned. And what she'd envisioned had been pretty dang hard.

"Now you don't have to wonder." He pointed with his milk carton toward the other room. "If that's all, there's the door."

"No, that's not all." She looked down at the toes of her boots, the black leather spotted by the rain. "Steven wanted me to tell you something. He wanted me to tell you that he's sorry about . . . everything." She shook her head and corrected herself. "No, . . . was sorry, I mean. He's been gone seven months and it's still hard for me to remember him in the past tense. It seems wrong somehow. Like if I do, he never existed." She looked back at Jack. His expression hadn't changed. "The flowers you sent were really nice."

He shrugged and set the milk on the counter. "Penny sent them."

"Penny?"

"Penny Colten. Married Leon Cribs; she works for me now."

Well, Penny hadn't sent them and signed his name without his knowledge. "Thank Penny for me."

"Don't make it a big deal."

She knew how much Steven had once meant to him. "Don't pretend you don't care that he's gone."

He raised a dark brow. "You forget I tried to kill him."

"You wouldn't have killed him, Jack."

"No, you're right. I guess you just weren't worth it."

The conversation was headed in the wrong direction, and she had to turn it around. "Don't be ugly."

"You call this ugly?" He laughed, but not with pleasure. "This is nothing, buttercup. Stick around and I'll show you how ugly I can get."

She already knew how ugly Jack could get, but while she

might be a coward, she was also as stubborn as ragweed. Just as Jack was not the same boy she'd once known, she was not the same girl he'd once known, either. She'd come to tell him the truth. Finally. Before she could get on with the rest of her life, she had to tell him about Nathan. It had taken her fifteen years to get to this point, and he could get ugly all he wanted, but he was going to listen to her.

A flash of white caught the corner of Daisy's eye a second before a woman entered the kitchen wearing a man's white dress shirt.

"Hey y'all," the woman said as she moved to stand by Jack.

He looked down at her. "I told you to stay in bed."

"I got bored without you."

Heat crept up Daisy's neck to her cheeks, but she seemed to be the only embarrassed person in the room. Jack had a girlfriend. Of course he did. He'd always had a girlfriend or two. There had been a time when that would have hurt.

"Hello, Daisy. I don't know if you remember me. I'm Gina Brown."

It didn't hurt any longer, and Daisy was a bit ashamed to admit to herself that what she mostly felt was an overwhelming relief. She'd come all the way from Seattle to tell him about Nathan, and now all she felt was relief. Like an axe had been lifted from her throat. She guessed she was more of a coward than she thought. Daisy smiled and moved across the kitchen to offer Gina her hand. "Of course I remember you. We were in American Government together our senior year."

"Mr. Simmons."

"That's right."

"Remember when he tripped over an eraser on the floor?" Gina asked, as if she weren't standing there wearing Jack's shirt and, Daisy would bet, nothing else.

"That was so funny. I just about—"

"What the hell is this?" Jack interrupted. "A damn high school reunion?"

Both women looked up at him and Gina said, "I was just being polite to your guest."

"She isn't my guest and she's leaving." He pinned his gaze on Daisy, just as cold and unyielding as when she'd first walked in the door.

"It was nice to see you, Gina," she said.

"Same."

"Good night, Jack."

He shoved his hip into the counter and crossed his arms over his chest.

"See you two around." She walked back through the dark house and out the door. The rain had stopped and she dodged puddles on her way to her mother's Caddie parked on the side of the garage. Next time, she would definitely call first.

Just as she reached for the door, she felt a hand on her arm, whipping her around. She looked up into Jack's face. Security lights shined down on him and the angry set of his jaw. His eyes stared into hers, no longer cold but filled with a burning rage.

"I don't know what you came here looking for, absolution or forgiveness," he said, his drawl more pronounced than before, "but you won't find it." He dropped her arm as if he couldn't stand the touch of her.

"Yes, I know."

"Good. You stay away from me, Daisy Lee," he said. "You stay away or I'll make your life a misery."

She looked up into his dark face, at the passion and anger that had not abated in fifteen years.

"Just stay away," he said one last time, before turning on his bare heels and disappearing into the shadows.

She knew she would be wise to heed his warning. Too bad she didn't have that option.

Although he didn't know it yet, neither did he.

Stephen Fairfax-Lacy
CONFIDENTIAL!

in *A Wild Pursuit*
by Eloisa James
Coming March 2004

Name: Stephen Fairfax-Lacy
Nickname: The Puritan
Hometown: London
Car: A sleek carriage with fine horses (it is the
Regency, after all!)
First kiss: A gentleman does not tell such things
Super secret: Would like to begin a scandalous
affair . . .

---

*T*he Puritan had arms like steel. He didn't pay a bit of attention to her wiggling, just picked her up and turned her around and then when she looked up at his face, she suddenly stopped protesting.

He didn't kiss like a Puritan. Or an old man either.

He kissed like a hungry man. Bea's first sensation was triumph. So the Puritan had pretended that he didn't notice her charms. Ha! That was all an act. He was just—he was just like—but then somehow, insidiously, she lost her train of thought.

He was kissing her so sweetly, as if she were the merest babe in arms. He didn't even seem to wish to push his tongue into her mouth. Instead he rubbed his lips against hers, danced on her mouth, his hands cupping her head so sweetly that she almost shivered. She quite liked this.

Oh, she felt his tongue. It sung on her lips, patient and tasting like raspberries. Without thinking her own tongue tangled with his for a second. Then she realized what she was doing and clamped her mouth shut. There was nothing she hated more than a man pushing his great tongue where it didn't belong.

But he didn't. He just nibbled her lips and his mouth drifted across her face and pressed her eyes shut, and then closed back on hers with a ravenous hunger that made her soften, ache deep inside.

He probably thinks I'm a virgin, Bea thought in a foggy sort of way.

His mouth was leaving little trails of fire. He was nibbling her ear and she was tingling all over. In fact, she wanted— she wanted him to try again. Come back, she coaxed silently, turning her face toward his lips. Try to kiss *me*, really kiss *me*. But he didn't. Instead his tongue curled around the delicate whorls of her ear, and Bea made a hoarse sound in her throat. He answered it by nipping her earlobe, which sent another twinge deep between her legs.

He tugged her hair and she obediently tipped her face back, eyes closed, and allowed him to taste her throat, all the time begging silently that he return, return, kiss her again . . . But he seemed to be feasting on her throat and he hadn't even tried to touch her breasts. Men *always* . . .

But that was the thought that woke Bea. She hadn't been thinking of grappling in the field when she dressed in the morning. These particular breasts aren't meant to withstand a man's hand. There was more cotton than flesh.

She opened her mouth to say something but at that moment he apparently decided he had tormented her enough and his mouth closed over hers.

She could no more fight that masculine strength than she could rise to her feet. He didn't coax this time; he took, and she gave. And it wasn't like all the other times, when she tolerated a moment or two of this kind of kissing. The Puritan's kiss was dark and sweet and savage all at once. It sent quivers through her legs and made her strain to be closer. His hands moved down her back, assured, possessive. In a moment he would bring them around to her front, and her breasts were aching for . . .

Except those breasts were covered by wads of cotton.

She tore her mouth away, gasping and stared at him. She didn't even think about giving him a seductive glance. She was too stunned.

"I like you when you're like this," he said, and there was that sweetness to his eyes again. He reached out and rubbed some rain from her cheeks. "You look rain-washed and very young. Also rather startled. It seemed to me that you've been inviting kisses. Was I wrong?"

"No," she said, trying hard to think what to say next. All her practiced seductive lines seems to have fled from her head.

"Alas," he said, even more gently, tucking her hair behind her ear. "I can hardly offer marriage to a woman half my age. So I'm afraid that I shall have to leave your kisses, sweet though they are, to some younger man."

Bea's mouth almost fell open. Marriage? Didn't he know who she was? "I don't want—" she began, but her voice was hoarse. She stopped. "As it happens, I am not interested in marriage either," she said quite sedately. "I find that I am, however, be very interested in *you*." She twisted forward and kissed his lips, a promise of pleasure. And she was absolutely honest about that. With him, there would be no boundaries.

But it was he who pulled back. She had been so sure he would lunge at her that she smiled—but the smile faded.

He *was* a Puritan. His eyes had gone cold, dark, condemning. "I thought you played the lusty trollop for fun."

She raised her chin. Her chest had gone icy cold. "Actually, no," she said, and she was very pleased to find her tone utterly calm and with just a hint of sarcasm. "I play myself."

"Yourself? Do you even known who you are, under all that facepaint?"

"I assure you that I do."

"You play a part you needn't," he said, eyes fixed on hers. "You are young and beautiful, Beatrix. You should marry and have children."

"I think not."

"Why?"

"You simply want to make me like everyone else," she said sharply. "I like wearing *macquillage*. I would rather not look like *myself*, as you put it. And I find it incalculably difficult to imagine myself sitting by the fire wearing a lace cap and chattering about my brood of children."

"I think *yourself* is beautiful. All your paints have washed away at the moment. You never needed them."

"I didn't say I needed them. I enjoy them," she retorted, and then added, deliberately, "Just as I occasionally enjoy the company of a man in my bedchamber."

For a moment they just looked at each other, Puritan to trollop. "Am I to take it that you are not interested in taking a mistress?" she asked steadily, meeting his eyes. She was no child to be whipped by his condemnation.

"Actually, I am," he said deliberately. "But I have little interest in one so . . . practiced."

Bea got to her feet, shaking out her skirts. Then she bent over and picked up her mangled spencer, shaking it out and folding it over her arm, taking a moment to make absolutely certain that her face wouldn't reveal even for a second what she felt.

Then she looked him straight in the face. "That was cruel, and quite shabby, Mr. Fairfax-Lacy. I would not have expected it of you."

"I'm sorry."

She nodded and began to turn toward the gate. After all, she'd had much worse things said to her, mostly by women, but then there was her dear father. So when he caught her arm, she turned toward him with a little smile that was almost genuine.

"Don't you think we should take our bedraggled selves home?"

It was rather amusing to see how badly he felt. There was real anguish in his eyes. "I feel like the worst sort of bastard. Kissing you in a field and then insulting you."

At that, she grinned. "I gather you wish I were an innocent, Mr. Fairfax-Lacy. But I am not. I truly enjoyed that kiss." The smile she gave him was as wicked and lazy as any she'd ever bestowed on a man. "And I would very much have enjoyed your company in my bedchamber as well. But I have never forced myself on a man. I fully understand that you are looking for a far more respectable mistress. Perhaps even a possible marriage partner, given your wish for inexperience?"

Men were such dolts! He stared at her as if she were as alien as that hairy goat.

"It was a lovely kiss," she said. Then she turned and made her way across the field, and when the goat rolled his wicked eyes and snapped his lips over a Pomona green satin ribbon, all that remained of her bonnet, she just smiled at him.

Which startled the animal so much that he galloped off to the other end of the field, leaving her hat behind.

Rees, Lord Godwin
CONFIDENTIAL!

in *Your Wicked Ways*
by Eloisa James
Coming April 2004

Name: Rees, Lord Godwin
Nickname: The Sinner
Hometown: London
Conveyance: Anything that he can ride fast
First Kiss: He'd rather think about his *best* kiss
Super secret: He's developed a passion for his own
wife . . .

"*I* had no idea that this part of Hyde Park existed," Helene
said with fascination, a short time later. The grasses to either
side of the little winding path had grown so tall that they
touched the slouching limbs of the huge oaks. Daisies poked
their heads above the seas of grasses like intrepid soldiers,
fighting off nettles and thistles growing breast high.

"I've never met another soul here," Rees said. "All the polite sort prefer raked gravel paths."

Sometimes the oak trees bent down as if they'd been hum-
bled, brushing their branches to the ground, and then suddenly they would fall back, leaving a patch of emerald green
grass, or a cascade of daisies. Within twenty minutes, she
could no longer hear any din from the city at all, no sound of
carriages, bells, or whistles. "It's like being in the country,"
she said, awed.

They rounded the bend and the trees trailed off again,
forming another clearing. "Just look, Rees! Aren't they
beautiful?" she cried, running into the middle of a lake of
frothy white flowers shaped like stars.

Rees stood on the path, his face unreadable. The sun fell relentlessly on his harsh face, on the lines around his eyes, the scowling eyebrows, the generous lower lip, those two dimples . . .

And Helene realized with a great thump of her heart that she'd never gotten over that first infatuation with him, that first blinding passion that had driven her out her bed chamber window, and into his carriage, the better to make their way to Gretna Green.

She almost dropped the flowers she held, the realization was so blinding.

When Rees appeared at her side, hamper in hand and sat next to her on the grass. Helene couldn't even bring herself to speak. She'd spent nine years telling herself that the brief infatuation that led to their elopement was a dream, a fribble, a moment's blindness.

But it wasn't. Oh, it wasn't.

Numbly she helped Rees pull a tablecloth from the basket and load it with pieces of chicken, pie, fruit, and a bottle of wine.

She refused a glass of wine. "Hair of the dog," Rees said, "and very nice hair it is." He grinned at her. He had a chicken leg in his hand and was eating it like a savage. And he had that wicked look about him again, the one that made her think about the muscles hidden by his white shirt.

To her surprise, Helene found that she was hungry. She put a plate of chicken on her knee and began struggling to cut it properly.

"Don't bother," Rees said lazily. He was lying on his side, looking twice as comfortable in a bed of flowers as he did in a drawing room. "Just eat it, Helene."

She looked at him with disdain. "I don't eat with my fingers. I discarded that habit in the nursery."

"Who's to see? There's only you and I, and we're nothing more than an old married couple."

Old married couple implied comfort and ease, and she didn't feel any of that with Rees, particularly with the secret prickling awareness she had of his body. He had removed his jacket and rolled up his sleeve and his bronzed arm lay all too close to her. "It seems to me that you are always removing your clothing," she told him, eyeing him with distinct hostility. How dare he be so comfortable, while she was both over-heated and hungry? Her beautiful little blue jacket felt altogether winterish with the sun shining on her back.

In answer, he sat up. Helene edged back. Rees was overpowering at close quarters. "Here," he said simply, holding the chicken leg to her lips.

"I couldn't!" But she hadn't eaten all day. Her stomach gave a little gurgle.

Rees laughed. "Go ahead. There's no one to see."

"You're here," she said mulishly.

"I don't count," he said, giving her an oddly intent look. "That's one of the nicer things about being married, I always thought."

She took a bite. The chicken was delicious, faintly reminiscent of lemon. "It's exquisite," she admitted, taking another bite.

"I pay my cook one hundred guineas a year," Rees said, ripping off a little strip of chicken and bringing it to her lips.

When she didn't open her mouth immediately, he rubbed the chicken on her lip. "Oh my, your lips are greasy," he said, leaning closer.

"Oh!" Helene said, licking her lips.

"Very nice," Rees said, and there was a dark, velvety something in his voice that made the little coil in Helene's stomach grow tighter.

"Give me a real kiss, Rees," she said.

His hand was stroking her neck. It froze for a moment.

"Do you remember how you used to kiss me before we were married?" she asked.

"Aye," he said, "I must have been a beast, always pulling you into a corner. . . ."

"I loved it," Helene admitted.

"You never—"

"Ladies don't."

But Rees had clear memories of his wife refusing to kiss him with an open mouth, telling him he was disgusting to want such a thing. He hesitated. Their newfound friendship was so fragile and (although he didn't really want to think such a thing) important to him. He didn't . . .

So she came to him. The wife who hated kissing opened her mouth and timidly, sweetly, begged for entrance.

Rees had always known he was no gentleman. And he'd known for years that he had no control around his wife either. Nothing seemed to have changed. He plunged into her mouth so violently that she toppled backwards into a bed of flowers and he came with her, his limbs tangling with hers, devouring her mouth.

All the while, some part of him was waiting for her to tear her mouth away, to push him away, to scream that he was depraved, disgusting . . .

But the only thing that happened was that slender arms wound around his neck and a slender body tucked itself into the hard curves of his body with such melting softness that he could barely stop himself from groaning with the pure delight of it.